UNDERSTANDING PREJUDICE
AND DISCRIMINATION

Edited by Scott Plous
Wesleyan University

Boston   Burr Ridge, IL   Dubuque, IA   Madison, WI   New York
San Francisco   St. Louis   Bangkok   Bogotá   Caracas   Kuala Lumpur
Lisbon   London   Madrid   Mexico City   Milan   Montreal   New Delhi
Santiago   Seoul   Singapore   Sydney   Taipei   Toronto

McGraw-Hill Higher Education

A Division of The McGraw-Hill Companies

UNDERSTANDING PREJUDICE AND DISCRIMINATION

Published by McGraw-Hill, a business unit of The McGraw-Hill Companies, Inc., 1221 Avenue of the Americas, New York, NY 10020. Copyright © 2003 by The McGraw-Hill Companies, Inc.

Some ancillaries, including electronic and print components, may not be available to customers outside the United States.

This book is printed on acid-free paper.

5 6 7 8 9 0 QPF/QPF 0 9 8 7 6

ISBN 978-0-07-255443-4
MHID 0-07-255443-6

Vice president and editor-in-chief: *Thalia Dorwick*
Publisher: *Stephen D. Rutter*
Senior sponsoring editor: *Rebecca H. Hope*
Developmental editor: *Sienne Patch*
Senior marketing manager: *Chris Hall*
Project manager: *Christine Walker*
Production supervisor: *Enboge Chong*
Media technology producer: *Ginger Warner*
Interior designer: *Laurie Jean Entringer*
Cover designer: *Ryan Brown*
Cover art: Copyright © 2002, *Allison Plous*
Senior supplement producer: *David A. Welsh*
Compositor: *Carlisle Communications, Ltd.*
Typeface: *10/12 Book Antiqua*
Printer: *Quebecor World Fairfield, PA*

The credits section for this book begins on page 587 and is considered an extension of the copyright page.

Library of Congress Cataloging-in-Publication Data

Understanding prejudice and discrimination / [compiled and edited by] Scott Plous.—1st ed.
    p. cm.
    A compilation of readings from a broad range of scholarly disciplines, most edited, adapted, or revised for this anthology and several never published before.
    The text is supported by a variety of instructional materials, including a web site offering interactive exercises and demonstrations, streaming video clips, and other resources.
    Includes index.
    ISBN 0-07-255443-6
    1. Prejudices. 2. Racism. 3. Discrimination. 4. Stereotype (Psychology) 5. Toleration—Study and teaching. I. Plous, Scott.

HM1091 .U53 2003
303.3'85—dc21

2002071946

www.mhhe.com

To Fijare's generation

Contents

Preface

This book has been a twelve-year labor of love. Its contents, chosen from more than 100,000 pages of source material, have been shaped and reshaped over the years as the core of a college seminar on the psychology of prejudice. After the first section of the book (designed to lay a foundation for later readings), you should be able to thumb through any section listed in the Contents and find stand-alone pages with intriguing—or, in some cases, even shocking—boxed material relevant to the topic. This boxed material serves to spice up the longer readings and set each section's context more fully than would a simple collection of readings.

Some background: When I first taught a seminar on prejudice, my approach was to focus heavily on the stock-in-trade of social science: theories, studies, statistics, and conclusions. As time went on, however, I realized that any comprehensive look at prejudice must include other ways of understanding. After all, if human diversity cannot, by its very nature, be understood narrowly, the same must be true of human prejudices toward that diversity.

Accordingly, the surveys, experiments, and other studies in this anthology are set in a cultural and historic context that includes personal narratives, news stories, legal decisions, poetry, social commentary, and assorted other material. Several readings come from people on the receiving end of prejudice (often referred to as "targets" of prejudice), whereas other readings focus on perpetrators, bystanders, and social institutions. All source documents are listed in a "Source Notes" section in the back of the book, and they draw from a range of scholarly disciplines, including psychology, sociology, anthropology, ethnic studies, women's studies, philosophy, and history.

The result is an unusual combination of readings in which laboratory studies and national opinion polls appear side by side with U.S. Supreme Court decisions and *New York Times* articles. Most readings have been edited, adapted, or revised specifically for this anthology, and several have never been published before.

The authors, too, reflect a high degree of diversity. In these pages, you will find articles and essays by contemporary scholars such as Claude Steele, Peggy McIntosh, Sam Gaertner, Jack Dovidio, Sandra Graham, and Stephen Jay Gould; classic studies from pioneers such as Gordon Allport and Milton Rokeach; and words of wisdom from Martin Luther King, Jr., the Dalai Lama, Gloria Steinem, Thich Nhat Hanh, Audre Lord, César Chávez, and other leading lights.

Organization

The anthology is organized like an hourglass. The first two sections, "Homo Stereotypus" and "Stigmatization," cover broad topics that relate to all forms

ix

of prejudice—stereotyping, categorical thinking, stigmatization, and so forth. The next six sections each focus on a specific type of prejudice: old-style racism, modern racism, sexism, anti-Semitism, prejudice against Native Americans, and heterosexism. The last two sections, "Making Connections" and "Reducing Prejudice," return to broader issues.

Why devote separate sections to different types of prejudice? Quite simply, because each type of prejudice is unique enough to warrant it. For example, sexism is unique in that the people who are prejudiced often love the people whom they are prejudiced against. Heterosexism is unique in that lesbian, gay, bisexual, and transgendered people are frequently victimized by members of their own family. Prejudice toward disabled people (covered mainly in the section on stigmatization) is unique in that it involves a minority group anyone can join within the span of a single day, and the only minority group to which all of us will belong if we live long enough.

Each form of prejudice has its own history, its own distinct context. Consequently, the readings on racism include issues specific to African Americans, Mexican Americans, Native Americans, and other groups, rather than lumping all minority groups together and treating racism as a generic process. Yet at the same time, it would be a mistake to examine individual forms of prejudice without ultimately considering the way they relate to each other and to other social issues. For that reason, the last two sections of the anthology link prejudice reduction with social and environmental justice. As Martin Luther King, Jr., said so eloquently when explaining his opposition to the Vietnam War: "I have fought too hard and long to end segregated public accommodations to segregate my own moral concerns. It is my deep conviction that justice is indivisible, that injustice anywhere is a threat to justice everywhere."[1]

UnderstandingPrejudice.org

In addition to publishing this anthology, McGraw-Hill has generously supported the creation of a web site entitled *UnderstandingPrejudice.org*. On the web site, you will find interactive exercises and demonstrations, streaming video clips, and several other prejudice-related resources. For instance, the site offers:

- A slide tour of advertisements in which visitors are challenged to detect how prejudice is used to sell products and services
- A visual demonstration of how friendship preferences at the individual level can lead to surprising patterns of segregation at the group level
- An interactive exercise that probes implicit attitudes to see whether people have hidden biases toward certain groups

For each section of the anthology, *UnderstandingPrejudice.org* also has links to other web sites and a bibliography for further reading. All information,

---

[1]King, M. L., Jr. (1968). The role of the behavioral scientist in the civil rights movement. *American Psychologist, 23*, p. 182.

links, and activities on the web site are freely available to anyone with Internet access.

Baseline Survey

Perhaps the most important feature of the web site is a Baseline Survey that you should take before reading this book. The purpose of the Baseline Survey is to record a "snapshot" of your thinking before being exposed to the material ahead. *If you have not yet completed the Baseline Survey, please do so before reading the anthology.* That way, you will have an unbiased record of your thoughts.

Please trust me: you will get more from the anthology by taking the Baseline Survey early on. The survey takes only 15–20 minutes to complete, you are not asked for any identifying information, and the survey will store your answers in a secure, password-protected area so that you can view them at a later time. Then, once you have finished reading the anthology, you'll be able to go back and compare your initial survey answers with your current thinking. Most readers find the results illuminating.

Note to Instructors

Another feature of *UnderstandingPrejudice.org* is a "Teacher's Corner" that includes a sample course syllabus, class assignments, and ideas for how to enrich each section of the anthology. One decision instructors will need to make is how to treat the material contained in the anthology's appendix: "Animals as an Outgroup." In my experience, this material works best when assigned before the section entitled "Making Connections" (the web site's sample syllabus lists the readings in this order). Other instructors may choose to exclude these readings, to assign only some of them, or to make them optional (e.g., as an extra-credit assignment). The reason this material appears in an appendix rather than a regular section is that scholars differ in opinion as to whether "speciesism" represents a bona fide case of prejudice and discrimination. Of course, regardless of one's own views, these readings can be fruitfully assigned and discussed in class, if for no other reason than to explore what it means to be prejudiced.

As the foregoing comments suggest, the anthology is designed to allow instructors flexibility in arranging the material. Most sections can be omitted in part or whole, reordered, or augmented without compromising the educational value or understandability of their contents. Likewise, the anthology can be used as either a primary or supplemental text. The only piece of advice I would offer instructors is to leave the first three sections in their original order, so as to create a foundation for later material.

Three Warnings

Before concluding this preface, let me issue three small warnings. First, the topics covered in this anthology are necessarily selective. Rather than attempting to provide exhaustive coverage, I have chosen to focus on a small number of prejudices, often leaning toward little known or underreported information that is especially intriguing or noteworthy. The price paid for this unorthodox choice is that relatively little coverage is given to other important topics such as ageism, classism, and cross-cultural studies of prejudice. Each of these topics could rightly have claimed a section of the anthology, and their omission here is in no way intended to indicate their lack of importance.

The second warning is that some of the readings are quite critical of certain institutions. For example, the U.S. government is taken to task for its internment of Japanese citizens during World War II, for failing to admit more refugees during the Holocaust, for its support of slavery, and for other discriminatory actions and omissions over the years. Similarly, several organized religions are criticized for their role in perpetuating racism, sexism, and heterosexism. These criticisms are not intended to be disrespectful, anti-American, or antireligious; they are simply part of the story, and censoring them would yield a less than full account. Indeed, the very impulse to defend or discount the failings of cherished institutions has played a central role in the history of prejudice.

One last warning is that the anthology includes a number of bigoted statements and images—everything from homophobic hate speech to Nazi-era caricatures of Jewish people to an early South Carolina statute calling for the branding and disfigurement of slaves who steal. Again, the reason for including this material is to render a full and truthful account that avoids sanitizing the topic. Prejudice is *ugly,* and even though surveys and laboratory experiments yield invaluable insights, they tell only part of the story (consider, for example, how ethical guidelines and practical considerations limit the experimental study of hate crimes). If prejudice is likened to a toxic chemical spill, laboratory studies are best viewed as a careful analysis of the compound in question; such analyses are critically important, but they represent only one approach to understanding.

Acknowledgments

Many students, colleagues, and friends made valuable contributions to this anthology. For superb student research assistance, I am grateful to Joel Bartlett, Heather Cohen, Jenny Fields, Julius Onah, Amy Sanchez, Alexandra Sedlovskaya, Sabelo Sibanyoni, Rachel Torrance, Sonia Vesely, Rebecca Weisgrau, and Curtis Yee. For unparalleled library reference assistance: Steve Bischof, Joe Cavanagh, Kendall Hobbs, Erhard Konerding, EunJoo Lee, Heather MacFarlane, Alan Nathanson, and Ed Rubacha. For remarkable patience in the face of relentless interlibrary loan and circulation requests: Dianne Kelly, Kathy Stefanowicz, Kate Wolfe, and Randy Wilson. For additional library assistance kindly offered: Helen Aiello, Rachel Cheng, Elizabeth Mainella, and Roberta Raczka.

For photographic research, materials, and assistance, I am indebted to Randy Bytwerk, Olga Katz, Jim Mason, John Wareham, and the California

History Section of the California State Library. For assistance compiling information on U.S. presidential slave holdings: Paul Bergeron, Michael Birkner, Doug Clanin, Bryan Craig, Wayne Cutler, Eric Foner, Larry Gara, Sara Huyser, Rob Lopresti, John Pearce, Paulette Schwarting, Richard Sewell, Cinder Stanton, and Lois Zur. For text translations: Ruth Striegel-Moore and Elke Weber. For miscellaneous other acts of generosity: Mahzarin Banaji, Jack Dovidio, John Dower, Gail Eisnitz, Dick Etulain, Robert Fikes, Charles Greenberg, Betita Martínez, Doug Massey, James Plous, Christina Reyes, Ben Roussel, and Ervin Staub.

For editorial, design, and production assistance through all phases of the project, I wish to thank Rebecca Hope, Laurie Entringer, Mary Kazak, Laurie McGee, Sienne Patch, Kate Russillo, Steve Rutter, and Christine Walker. For administrative and budgetary assistance: Cathy Race and JoAnn Brazinskas. For gathering a veritable mountain of reprint permissions, Sherry Hoesly of the Permissions Group.

I am profoundly grateful to dozens of authors and publishers for contributing material to this collection, often without fee and in many cases graciously consenting to the abridgment and adaptation of original work (for a list, see page 587). A large number of Wesleyan students also contributed to the anthology by providing critical feedback and suggestions over the years. To these students, I express my respect, appreciation, and affection.

And finally, to Allison and Lotus, I give my deepest thanks and love. Our book, written alongside this one in an ancient unpaved language, remains my greatest source of joy and wonder.

In Conclusion

Although this anthology has benefited from the wise counsel of many colleagues, students, and friends, it is sure to contain errors of commission and omission that are wholly mine. I would therefore welcome feedback with any corrections, ideas for improvement, or suggestions for material to add in future editions. Feedback may be sent to:

Professor Scott Plous
Department of Psychology
Wesleyan University
Middletown, CT 06459
Email: feedback@understandingprejudice.org

In conclusion, I have done my best to assemble a multifaceted set of readings that are educational, thought-provoking, and socially useful. As the terrorist attacks of September 11, 2001, made painfully clear, the world community needs greater understanding and a deeper respect for cultural, ethnic, and religious differences. My goal in publishing this anthology is to offer a humble contribution toward this much-needed end.

I

Homo Stereotypus: Wired for Trouble

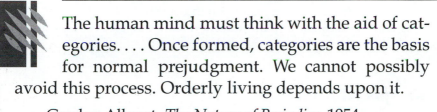 The human mind must think with the aid of categories. . . . Once formed, categories are the basis for normal prejudgment. We cannot possibly avoid this process. Orderly living depends upon it.

—Gordon Allport, *The Nature of Prejudice*, 1954

I

SECTION OVERVIEW

Most sections of this anthology contain a wide variety of articles drawn from different sources and disciplines. This introductory section, however, includes only two primary readings.

The first article is a general overview of social-psychological research on prejudice, discrimination, and stereotyping. This reading sets the stage for much of the material in later sections. The second article explores the social construction of race, focusing mainly on the question *"Who is Black?"* As the reading shows, the answer to this question has changed over time and says as much about the line drawers as about race itself.

Take Special Notice

Because the psychology overview is dense with research findings, theories, and terminology, it may take longer to complete than most other readings in the anthology. One way to reduce your reading time and increase comprehension is to first look through two glossaries in the back of the book: "Social Science and Research Terms" and "Prejudice-Related Terms" (the third glossary, "Statistical Terms," is best used on an "as-needed" basis). Because the overview contains terminology and theories that are used throughout the book, it is especially important to read this article carefully.

Questions Worth Pondering

- This section is entitled *"Home Stereotypus:* Wired for Trouble" because humans are cognitively predisposed to harbor prejudice and stereotypes. What are these cognitive predispositions, and how can they be overcome?
- What is the value of "minimal group" research? Does it uncover some of the mechanisms involved in prejudice, or is it a misleading oversimplification?
- In defining who is Black, what psychological purpose does the "one-drop rule" serve? Why don't contemporary Americans object to the one-drop rule?
- Would you like to see society abandon racial classifications altogether? (*Note:* If so, it would have to eliminate race-based affirmative action programs.)
- If, as the readings suggest, oppression is like a birdcage, what are the strongest wires in your own life? Do certain products and advertisements act as wires? Certain images and ideas?

THE PSYCHOLOGY OF PREJUDICE, STEREOTYPING, AND DISCRIMINATION: AN OVERVIEW

SCOTT PLOUS

The killing of Americans and their civilian and military allies is a religious duty for each and every Muslim. . . . We—with God's help—call on every Muslim who believes in God and wishes to be rewarded to comply with God's order to kill Americans and plunder their money whenever and wherever they find it.

[The September 11th attack] gave a harsh lesson to these arrogant peoples, for whom freedom is but for the white race . . . God willing, America's end is near.

—OSAMA BIN LADEN, in a February, 1998, appeal to Muslims, and a videotaped statement in the fall of 2001[1]

To Begin, a Few Definitions

It is hard to imagine more classic examples of prejudice than the statements of Osama Bin Laden. Although social scientists often differ in the precise way they define "prejudice," most agree that it involves a prejudgment, usually negative, about a group or its members (Fiske, 1998; Jones, 1997; Nelson, 2002). As commonly used in psychology, prejudice is not merely a statement of opinion or belief, but an attitude that includes feelings such as contempt, dislike, or loathing. For Osama Bin Laden, non-Muslim Americans are the main target of prejudice, and his hatred is so great that he would like to see them die.

Where prejudices lurk, stereotypes are seldom far behind. The term "stereotype," coined in 1798 by the French printer Didot, originally referred to a printing process used to create reproductions (Ashmore & Del Boca, 1981). Journalist Walter Lippmann (1922) later likened stereotypes to "pictures in the head," or mental reproductions of reality, and from there, the term gradually came to mean generalizations—or, quite often, overgeneralizations—about the members of a group. As with prejudice, these generalizations can at times be positive (e.g., women are nurturing, Asians excel at math), but for the most part, they tend to be negative and resistant to change. For example, before the U.S. civil rights movement reached its peak, the *Encyclopædia Britannica* entry for "Races of Mankind" relied on centuries-old pseudoscientific stereotypes of

---

[1]The first quote comes from "Britain's bill" (2001, p. B4), and the second from "God willing" (2001). The September 11, 2001, terrorist attack involved the hijacking of four U.S. commercial airplanes and resulted in the death of more than three thousand people.

Black people as unevolved and childlike. In its 1964 edition, the encyclopedia described "woolly-haired groups" as having:

> dark skin sometimes almost black, broad noses, usually a rather small brain in relation to their size, especially among the taller members of the group, with forearms and shins proportionately long. In the skeleton there is a smoothness of contour which even in adults often recalls the bony form of a child, and among some members of the group the forehead has that prominent and smooth form which is so characteristic of the infant of our own race. (Buxton, 1964, p. 864A)

Today it would be shocking for a respected encyclopedia to print a stereotype such as this, yet other stereotypes concerning race, gender, religion, and sexual orientation remain widespread. For instance, as recently as 1999, Merriam-Webster (the largest dictionary publisher in the United States) listed thesaurus terms for *homosexual* such as "fruit" and "pederast" (Carvajal, 1999).

Stereotypes are not only harmful in their own right; they do damage by fostering prejudice and discrimination. After all, if encyclopedia readers are led to believe that Black people have intellectual limitations, why spend time and money educating Black children? As used here, "discrimination" involves putting group members at a disadvantage or treating them unfairly as a result of their group membership. More specifically, "personal discrimination" refers to acts of discrimination committed by individuals (e.g., a manager who refuses to hire Jewish employees), whereas "institutional discrimination" refers to discriminatory policies or practices carried out by organizations and other institutions (e.g., an anti-Semitic immigration policy).

Prejudice, stereotyping, and discrimination often go hand in hand, but it is also possible to have one without the others. When an ethnic group is stereotyped with a neutral or positive attribute such as "family-oriented," prejudice and discrimination may not be involved. Similarly, a generalized prejudice against "foreigners" or "amputees" may not include specific stereotypes or acts of discrimination. There are even times when discrimination takes place without prejudice or stereotyping, either intentionally or unintentionally. For an illustration of how this can occur, consider the following hypothetical problem:

> Suppose your school or organization is accused of sex discrimination because the overall percentage of female job candidates offered a position in the last five years is less than the overall percentage for male candidates. To get to the bottom of this problem, you launch an investigation to see which departments are discriminating against women. Surprisingly, however, the investigation finds that within each department, the percentage of female job applicants who are offered a position is identical to the percentage of male applicants who are offered a position. Is this possible? Can each department practice nondiscrimination, while the organization as a whole hires more men than women?

TABLE 1   A Hypothetical Example of Sex Discrimination

	Number of Applicants	Number of Job Offers	Percentage Offered Jobs
Department A			
Women	500	50	10%
Men	1000	100	10%
Department B			
Women	1000	50	5%
Men	500	25	5%
Combined Total			
Women	1500	100	6.67%
Men	1500	125	8.33%

This problem is a variant of Simpson's Paradox (a well-known paradox in statistics), and the answer to it is *yes*—nondiscriminatory conditions at the departmental level can result in hiring differences at the organizational level. To see how this might happen, imagine a simplified organization with two equally important departments, Department A and Department B, each of which receive the same number of job applications. As shown in Table 1, if Department A were to offer a position to 10 percent of its job applicants (female as well as male), and Department B were to offer a position to 5 percent of its job applicants (female as well as male), neither department would be discriminating on the basis of sex. At the level of the organization, however, more positions would be going to men than to women, because of the higher number of jobs offered by Department A than Department B. Unless there is a good reason for this difference in hiring, the pattern may represent a form of institutionalized sex discrimination.

As these examples show, prejudice, stereotyping, and discrimination are distinct from one another, even though in daily life they often occur together. Consequently, this overview discusses each one separately, beginning with research on prejudice.

Prejudice

Throughout the past century, research on prejudice has closely reflected the ideological leanings of society, telling us as much about the personal biases of the scientific community as about prejudice itself. According to John Duckitt (1992), psychological research on prejudice first emerged in the 1920s and was based on American and European race theories that attempted to prove White superiority. For instance, after reviewing 73 studies on race and intelligence, an influential 1925 *Psychological Bulletin* article concluded that the "studies taken all together seem to indicate the mental superiority of the white race" (Garth, 1925, p. 359). In light of medical, anthropological, and psychological studies purporting to demonstrate the superiority of White people, many social scientists viewed prejudice as a natural response to "backward" races.

This perspective changed in the 1930s and 1940s with progress in civil rights, successful challenges to colonialism, and the rise of anti-Semitism. Following the Holocaust, several influential theorists came to regard prejudice as pathological, and they searched for personality syndromes associated with racism, anti-Semitism, and other forms of prejudice. The most prominent of these theorists was Theodor Adorno, who had fled Nazi Germany and concluded that the key to prejudice lay in what he called an "authoritarian personality." In their book *The Authoritarian Personality*, Adorno and his coauthors (1950) described authoritarians as rigid thinkers who obeyed authority, saw the world as black and white, and enforced strict adherence to social rules and hierarchies. Authoritarian people, they argued, were more likely than others to harbor prejudices against low-status groups.

Later researchers criticized Adorno's work, contending that authoritarianism had not been measured properly, that it did not account for cultural and regional differences in prejudice, and that the theory's psychoanalytic assumptions lacked research support (Altemeyer, 1981; Martin, 2001; Pettigrew, 1958). Yet Adorno and his colleagues were right in at least three respects. First, a politically conservative form of authoritarianism, known as "right-wing authoritarianism," does correlate with prejudice. Well-designed studies in the United States, Canada, South Africa, Russia, and elsewhere have found that right-wing authoritarianism is associated with a variety of prejudices (Altemeyer, 1996; Duckitt & Farre, 1994; McFarland, Ageyev, & Abalakina, 1993). Second, people who view the social world hierarchically are more likely than others to hold prejudices toward low-status groups. This is especially true of people who want their own group to dominate and be superior to other groups—a characteristic known as "social dominance orientation" (Pratto, Sidanius, Stallworth, & Malle, 1994). Social dominance orientation tends to correlate with prejudice even more strongly than does right-wing authoritarianism, and studies have linked it to anti-Black and anti-Arab prejudice, sexism, nationalism, opposition to gay rights, and other attitudes concerning social hierarchies (Altemeyer, 1998; Sidanius, Levin, Liu, & Pratto, 2000; Sidanius & Pratto, 1999). Finally, Adorno and his coauthors were correct in pointing out that rigid categorical thinking is a central ingredient in prejudice.

Categorical Thinking

The relationship between prejudice and categorical thinking was first systematically explored by Gordon Allport (1954) in his classic book *The Nature of Prejudice*. Although Allport recognized the emotional, social, economic, and historic dimensions of prejudice, he also proposed that prejudice is partly an outgrowth of normal human functioning. In a much-quoted passage of the book, Allport wrote:

The human mind must think with the aid of categories. . . . Once formed, categories are the basis for normal prejudgment. We cannot possibly avoid this process. Orderly living depends upon it. (p. 20)

The natural tendency to categorize is easy to see in Figure 1. The shape on the far left is a square, and the shape on the far right is a diamond. The intermediate shapes, however, do not fit into a recognized category, and as a result, they are simply assimilated to one of the preexisting categories (e.g., as a "rotated square" or an "off-centered diamond"). In the realm of social perception, the same thing happens with biracial people, bisexual people, and others who are not easily categorized.

Social categories form an indispensable part of human thought, but because attributes such as race, sex, and age lie along a continuum, social labels are never more than approximations. In fact, it is surprisingly difficult to think of two categories that do not overlap with each other (that is, two categories with a fixed boundary that cleanly separates each side). At first, you might think of well-known opposites such as night and day, earth and sea, or alive and dead. Upon reflection, though, it becomes apparent that there is no fixed point separating these categories. Night and day form a continuum rather than two discrete categories. The boundary between earth and sea changes with the tides and is impossible to mark. Even the line between life and death is a fuzzy one. Does life cease with the last breath? With the last heart beat? When the brain stops all activity?

You might think of categories such as women and men, or people and the environment, but these divisions are also blurrier than they might seem. For example, many people cannot be easily categorized as female or male; they are, instead, "intersexuals" born with ambiguous genitalia (Angier, 1996). And what about the boundary between ourselves and the outside world? Most directly, of course, each of us breathes the immediate environment into our lungs and releases molecules back into the environment. But in a global economy, our connection with the environment reaches further than that; our blood may have elements from Brazilian rainwater that nourished orange trees only a month ago, and our tissues may hold minerals from the soil of a dozen or more countries. Thus, the idea that people constitute a category

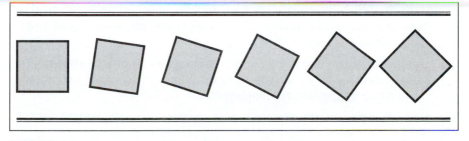

FIGURE 1
A continuum of shapes ranging from a square to a diamond.

separate from the environment is really not accurate—categories such as "people" and "oranges" represent useful linguistic conventions, nothing more.

Despite the usefulness of categories in everyday life, they can be devastating when people falsely isolate themselves from the environment, from animals and nature, or from each other. For a vivid illustration of this point, we need only look at the social construction of race in America. According to the best scientific estimates, at least 75 percent of African Americans have White ancestry, and 1–5 percent of the genes carried by American Whites are from African ancestors (Davis, 1991). From a biological point of view, then, Blacks and Whites comprise a continuum rather than a dichotomy (for an authoritative statement on this point, see Figure 2). Nonetheless, a false belief in the purity of racial categories has enabled Whites to mistreat Blacks for centuries without realizing that in many cases, they are harming the descendant of a White person.

Assimilation and Contrast

An intriguing and important consequence of categorical thinking is its tendency to distort perceptions. Typically, these distortions take the form of minimizing differences within categories ("assimilation") and exaggerating differences between categories ("contrast"). For example, when Joachim Krueger and Russell Clement (1994) asked people to estimate several daily temperatures for Providence, Rhode Island, they found a smaller gap between temperature estimates for November 15 and November 23 (dates within the category "November") than between November 30 and December 8 (dates

---

American Anthropological Association Statement on Race

In the U.S. both scholars and the general public have been conditioned to viewing human races as natural and separate divisions within the human species based on visible physical differences. With the vast expansion of scientific knowledge in this century, however, it has become clear that human populations are not unambiguous, clearly demarcated, biologically distinct groups. . . . Given what we know about the capacity of normal humans to achieve and function within any culture, we conclude that present-day inequalities between so-called racial groups are not consequences of their biological inheritance but products of historical and contemporary social, economic, educational and political circumstances.

—Adopted by the AAA Executive Board as an official statement representing "the contemporary thinking and scholarly positions of a majority of anthropologists," May 17, 1998

FIGURE 2
Excerpts from an American Anthropological Association statement affirming that people do not fall into biologically distinct racial groups (American Anthropological Association, 1999).

from two different months). Both time intervals spanned eight days, and in reality the temperature change in Providence was not greater in the latter case than the former—it simply *seemed* greater because December is, on average, colder than November.

In this connection, Myron Rothbart and his colleagues (1997) tell an old Yiddish story of a peasant whose farm was located near the border of Poland and Russia, where boundary markers shifted with every international dispute:

> The peasant did not know from one year to the next whether his farm was in Russia or Poland, and eventually hired a surveyor to resolve the uncertainty. After weeks of painstaking assessment, the surveyor finally announced that the farm was just inside the Polish border. "Thank God," the peasant cried with relief, "now I won't have to endure any more Russian winters!" (Rothbart, Davis-Stitt, & Hill, 1997, p. 123)

Humor aside, assimilation and contrast effects have been observed in a wide variety of domains, including estimates of line length, judgments of speech sounds, impressions of faces, and evaluations of attitudes (Brown, 1995; Tajfel & Wilkes, 1963). Robert Goldstone (1995) even found an assimilation effect in color perception. In this study, students were shown a random series of letters and numbers that ranged in color from very red to very violet. Results showed that even when a letter and number had exactly the same hue, students rated the letter as being similar in color to other letters, and the number as being similar in color to other numbers (e.g., in the diagram in Figure 3, they saw the "L" as redder than the identically colored "8").

With respect to prejudice, the implication of this research is that differences within groups will tend to be minimized and differences between groups will tend to be exaggerated. Moreover, if these differences are consistent with well-known stereotypes, the distortion in perception may be highly resistant to change. In one study, for example, participants were unable to break free of gender stereotypes even when encouraged to do so (Nelson, Biernat, & Manis, 1990). In this experiment, people were asked to judge the

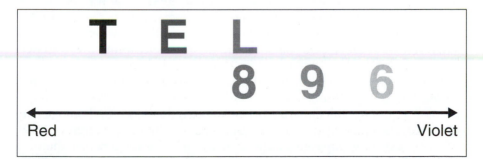

FIGURE 3
In a study on color perception, Robert Goldstone (1995) found that the "L" above was perceived as more red than the "8," even though the "L" and "8" were actually identical in hue. Figure reprinted with permission of the American Psychological Society.

height of various men and women from a series of photographs. Each photograph showed only one person, and participants were told:

> In this booklet, the men and women are actually of equal height. We have taken care to match the heights of the men and women pictured. That is, for every woman of a particular height, somewhere in the booklet there is also a man of that same height. Therefore, in order to make as accurate a height judgment as possible, try to judge each photograph as an individual case; do not rely on the person's sex. (p. 669)

Despite these instructions and a $50 cash prize for the person who made the most accurate judgments, people perceived the males to be, on average, a few inches taller than the females. In other words, they were either unable or unwilling to disregard the categories "male" and "female," and the perception of men as taller than women prevailed.

Outgroup Homogeneity

A close cousin of assimilation is the "outgroup homogeneity effect." In the language of social psychology, an "ingroup" is a group to which someone belongs, and an "outgroup" is a group to which the person does not belong (hence, one person's ingroup may be another person's outgroup, and vice versa). Research on the outgroup homogeneity effect has found that when it comes to attitudes, values, personality traits, and other characteristics, people tend to see outgroup members as more alike than ingroup members. As a result, outgroup members are at risk of being seen as interchangeable or expendable, and they are more likely to be stereotyped (see Figure 4). This perception of sameness holds true regardless of whether the outgroup is another race, religion, nationality, college major, or other naturally occurring group (Linville, 1998).

In one of the first studies to document the outgroup homogeneity effect, Princeton University researchers asked students in four different "eating clubs" to rate members of their own group and members of three other groups on personality dimensions such as "introverted-extroverted" and "arrogant-humble" (Jones, Wood, & Quattrone, 1981). The results showed that students tended to rate members of their own group as more varied in personality than members of the outgroup—regardless of which group students were in. Later research on outgroup homogeneity found that the effect is strongest when the ingroup and outgroup are enduring, real-life groups (rather than groups created artificially in laboratory experiments), and when the ingroup is large (Mullen & Hu, 1989). If the ingroup is small and the attributes in question are important to its identity, the outgroup homogeneity effect may disappear or even reverse (Simon, 1992; Simon & Pettigrew, 1990).

Why are outgroups generally seen as more homogeneous than ingroups? One answer is that people usually have less contact with outgroup members than ingroup members, and indeed, there is good evidence for this explanation (Islam & Hewstone, 1993; Linville & Fischer, 1993). But contact alone cannot explain the outgroup homogeneity effect, because some studies have found that the effect is unrelated to the number of ingroup or out-

FIGURE 4
This illustration comes from Sir Edward Burnett Tylor's 1881 book *Anthropology: An Introduction to the Study of Man and Civilization*. On the page opposite this drawing, Tylor wrote: "The people whom it is easiest to represent by single portraits are uncivilized tribes, in whose food and way of life there is little to cause difference between one man and another" (Tylor, 1881, p. 78).

group members a person knows (e.g., Jones, Wood, & Quattrone, 1981). Furthermore, perceptions of outgroup homogeneity are sometimes found among groups that have extensive contact with each other, such as females and males (Park & Rothbart, 1982; Park & Judd, 1990). When men complain that "women are all alike" and women complain that "men are all alike," their charges rarely stem from a lack of contact.

The best explanation is that a variety of factors produce the outgroup homogeneity effect. In addition to the fact that people usually have more contact with ingroup members, they tend to organize and recall information about ingroups in terms of persons rather than abstract characteristics (Ostrom, Carpenter, Sedikides, & Li, 1993; Park & Judd, 1990). In many cases, people are also more motivated to make distinctions among ingroup members with whom they will have future contact (Linville, 1998). When these factors operate together, the end result is often an ingroup that appears to have a diverse assortment of individuals, and an outgroup that appears relatively homogeneous and undifferentiated.

Ingroup Bias

When most people think of racism and other forms of bias, they picture one group having negative feelings toward another group. Although this dynamic certainly takes place, research since the 1970s has found that many group biases are more a function of favoritism toward one's own group than negative feelings toward other groups. As Marilyn Brewer (1999, p. 438) put it in her summary of the evidence, "Ultimately, many forms of discrimination and bias may develop not because outgroups are hated, but because positive emotions such as admiration, sympathy, and trust are reserved for the ingroup." The tendency of people to favor their own group, known as "ingroup bias," has been found in cultures around the world (Aberson, Healy, & Romero, 2000; Brewer, 1979, 1999).

Interestingly, ingroup bias is so pervasive that its absence among Black children was partly responsible for the 1954 U.S. Supreme Court decision outlawing school segregation. In its landmark *Brown v. Board of Education* decision, the Court cited research by social psychologists Kenneth and Mamie Clark showing that Black children preferred to play with White dolls—a reversal of the ingroup bias that children would normally be expected to display (Clark, 1950; & Clark, 1947). Noting that school segregation instilled a sense of inferiority among Black children, the Court concluded that "Separate educational facilities are inherently unequal."

At the time of this decision, Clark and Clark's findings were highly controversial and were not embraced by the American Psychological Association (Ludy & Crouse, 2002). In fact, Henry E. Garrett—a former president of the American Psychological Association who served as thesis adviser to Mamie Clark and statistics instructor to Kenneth Clark—testified against the Clarks' research and referred to Kenneth Clark as "none too bright . . . he was about a C student, but he'd rank pretty high for a Negro" (Kluger, 1976, p. 502). Garrett later went on to publish a pro-segregation pamphlet entitled *Heredity: The Cause of Racial Differences in Intelligence,* in which he claimed that:

> Black and White children do *not* have the same potential, they do *not* learn at the same rate, and environment is not the sole cause of non-achievement. . . . evidence shows the average Negro to be biologically *immature,* vis-a-vis the White; his brain is less well developed. . . . Despite glowing accounts of ancient African achievements, over the past 5,000 years the history of Black Africa is a cultural blank. (Garrett, 1971, pp. 3, 5, 13, emphasis in original)

Ironically, in 1970 Kenneth Clark proved Garrett wrong about Black potential by becoming president of the American Psychological Association (24 years after Garrett held the same position). And in 1994, the American Psychological Association honored Clark with its prestigious Award for Outstanding Lifetime Contribution to Psychology. In making this award, the Association referred to Clark's contributions as "blazing the trail" for others and being "instrumental in having the Court find that racial segregation in the schools is psychologically damaging to children" (Ludy & Crouse, 2002, p. 48).

Minimal Groups, Social Identity, and the Role of Self-Esteem

One of the most startling aspects of ingroup bias is how easily it is triggered. This finding was documented in a series of experiments by Henri Tajfel (1970, 1981). Tajfel and his colleagues invented what is now known as the "minimal group procedure"—an experimental technique in which people who have never met before are divided into groups on the basis of minimal information (e.g., a preference for one type of painting versus another, or even just the toss of a coin). What Tajfel discovered is that groups formed on the basis of almost any distinction are prone to ingroup bias. Within minutes of being divided into groups, people tend to see their own group as superior to other groups, and they will frequently seek to maintain an advantage over other groups. One study even found that when participants were given the reward matrix in Table 2, they preferred an ingroup/outgroup award distribution of 7/1 points rather than 12/11 points, denying members of their own group 5 points (7 instead of 12) in order to maintain a high relative advantage over the outgroup (Allen & Wilder, 1975; Wilder, 1981).

In another minimal group experiment, students were divided into two groups after a lottery drawing and were asked to allocate up to 100 chips to each group member (Locksley, Ortiz, & Hepburn, 1980). Although in this particular study awarding chips to the other group would have cost no chips in return, students awarded an average of 20 fewer chips to members of the outgroup than to members of their own group. Other investigations have found that a coin toss can elicit ingroup biases even when the experimenters explicitly state that group membership is "just a matter of chance" (Billig & Tajfel, 1978; Rabbie & Horwitz, 1969). Summarizing the results of one such study, Michael Billig and Henri Tajfel (1978, p. 48) observed that "the very mention of 'groups' by the experimenters was sufficient to produce strong intergroup discrimination."

Although it may seem odd that group favoritism develops so easily, these findings are consistent with research showing that social bonds and attraction can readily form on the basis of seemingly minor characteristics. For instance, one study found that people are more likely to cooperate with another person when they learn that the person shares their birthday (Miller, Downs, & Prentice, 1998). Even major life decisions—such as whom to love, where to live, and what occupation to pursue—can be influenced by relatively minor

TABLE 2   Sample Reward Matrix Used in Minimal Group Research

Member no. _____ of _____ group	7	8	9	10	11	12	13	14	15	16	17	18	19
Member no. _____ of _____ group	1	3	5	7	9	11	13	15	17	19	21	23	25

Note: Participants in a study by Allen and Wilder (1975) were given a matrix with points that corresponded to money. Their task was to allocate points to someone in their group (top row) and someone in the outgroup (bottom row) by choosing one of the 13 options above (e.g., 7 points for the ingroup member and 1 point for the outgroup member).

similarities. In a well-crafted set of studies, Brett Pelham and his colleagues (Pelham, Jones, Mirenberg, & Carvallo, 2002; Pelham, Mirenberg, & Jones, 2002) found that when compared with the percentage expected by chance:

- Women are more likely to marry men who share the first letter of their last (maiden) name.
- People are more likely to live in cities that include their birthday number (e.g., people born on March 3 are more likely than others to live in Three Rivers, Michigan).
- People named Louis are more likely to live in St. Louis, people named Paul to live in St. Paul, people named Helen to live in St. Helen, and people named Mary to live in St. Mary.
- At some point after receiving their social security card, women named Florence are more likely to move to Florida, women named Georgia to move to Georgia, women named Louise to move to Louisiana, and women named Virginia to move to Virginia.
- People whose names begin with Geo (e.g., George, Geoffrey) are over-represented among geoscientists, and people named Dennis, Denis, Denise, and Dena are overrepresented among dentists.

Pelham and his colleagues explain these results in terms of "implicit egotism," or an unconscious preference for things associated with the self. According to Pelham, even though letter and number preferences may seem trivial, such preferences are psychologically meaningful because of their connection to people's self-concept and identity. In keeping with this account, laboratory research on implicit egotism has found that when people high in self-esteem are dealt a blow to their self-concept, they display an increased preference for the letters in their name and the numbers in their birthdate, as if to restore their sense of worth (Jones, Pelham, Mirenberg, & Hetts, 2002).

Returning to the topic of prejudice, Tajfel hypothesized that ingroup biases arise from similar dynamics concerning the need for self-esteem. In the view of Tajfel and his colleagues, people maintain their self-esteem in part by identifying with groups and believing that the groups they belong to are better than other groups (Tajfel, 1981; Tajfel & Turner, 1986). Consequently, even experimentally created minimal groups give people a chance to bolster their self-esteem through ingroup biases. Tajfel's theory, known as "social identity theory," is supported by both laboratory and field studies. For example, research shows that after university football teams win a game, students are more likely to (1) wear clothes that identify the school, and (2) use the word "we" when describing the game's outcome, especially if their self-esteem has recently been challenged by a personal failure (Cialdini, Borden, Thorne, Walker, Freeman, & Sloan, 1976). In addition, a meta-analysis[2] of 34 separate studies found that people who are high in self-esteem—and who therefore

---

[2]"Meta-analysis" is a statistical technique that analyzes the combined results from multiple studies.

have the most to lose if their self-esteem is undercut—exhibit more ingroup bias than do people low in self-esteem (Aberson et al., 2000).

Research also indicates that when people experience a drop in self-esteem, they become more likely to express prejudice. This tendency was poignantly demonstrated in an experiment that altered students' self-esteem by giving them bogus feedback after an intelligence test (Fein & Spencer, 1997). On a random basis, half the students were told they scored in the top 10 percent for their university, and half were told that they scored below average. Then, in what appeared to be an unrelated study, students were asked to evaluate a job candidate who was presented as either Jewish or Italian. The results showed that students who suffered a blow to their self-esteem later evaluated the candidate more negatively when she seemed Jewish than when she seemed Italian, whereas no difference was found among students who were given positive feedback about their intelligence. Moreover, students who received negative feedback about their intelligence showed a rebound in self-esteem after devaluing the Jewish candidate; that is, by putting down the Jewish candidate, they increased their self-esteem.

An unfortunate implication of this research is that for some people, prejudice represents a way of maintaining their self-esteem. At the same time, the link between prejudice and self-esteem suggests a hopeful message: It may be possible to reduce prejudice with something as simple as a boost in self-esteem. Fein and Spencer (1997) found this to be the case in a follow-up experiment similar to the preceding one. In the second experiment, anti-Jewish prejudice was eliminated after students increased their self-esteem by writing a few paragraphs about something they valued. Thus, at least one effective means of decreasing prejudice may be to address the sources of insecurity that underlie it.

Causal Attributions

Prejudice is also closely connected to the way that ingroup and outgroup members explain each other's behavior. These explanations, known in psychology as "causal attributions," are both a symptom and source of prejudice. If, for example, a single mother's homelessness is attributed to dispositional factors such as personal laziness, poor character, or lack of ability, prejudice toward single mothers is likely to persist. In contrast, if her homelessness is attributed to situational factors such as corporate job layoffs or domestic partner violence, prejudice toward single mothers may not come into play or may even be reduced. The problem, when it comes to prejudice, is that people often make uncharitable attributions for the behavior of outgroup members. They do this in at least three ways:

1. *Just-world attributions in an unjust world.* In many situations, causal attributions implicitly follow a "just-world" ideology that assumes people get what they deserve and deserve what they get (Lerner, 1980; Montada & Lerner, 1998). For example, people who hold just-world beliefs are more likely than others to blame poor people for being impoverished and, to some extent, are more likely to blame women for being battered or raped (Cowan

& Curtis, 1994; Cozzarelli, Wilkinson, & Tagler, 2001; Schuller, Smith, & Olson, 1994). The difficulty with such attributions is that the world is not always just; people often find themselves in unfair circumstances, whether by birth, happenstance, or other factors beyond their control. In such cases, a just-world ideology downplays the role of situational factors and says, in essence, that the problem of social injustice lies not in society but in the victims of prejudice.

2. *The fundamental attribution error.* In addition to just-world beliefs, people have a more general tendency to attribute behavior to dispositional causes. Even when behaviors are undeniably caused by situational factors, people will sometimes favor dispositional explanations—a misjudgment known as the "fundamental attribution error" (Ross, 1977). For example, in one of the earliest studies published on this topic, participants were presented with an essay written by someone who was either explicitly forced to take a particular position or someone who had free choice in selecting a position (Jones & Harris, 1967). Even when participants were expressly told that the essay's author was forced to take a certain position, they tended to believe that the author truly held that position. In the realm of prejudice, Elliot Aronson, Timothy Wilson, and Robin Akert (2002, p. 481) offer a textbook illustration of the fundamental attribution error in action:

> When the Jews were first forced to flee their homeland during the third Diaspora, some 2,500 years ago, they were not allowed to own land or become artisans in the new regions in which they settled. Needing a livelihood, some took to lending money—one of the few professions to which they were allowed easy access. Although this choice of occupation was an accidental byproduct of restrictive laws, it led to a dispositional attribution about Jews: that they were interested only in dealing with money and not in honest labor, like farming. . . . This dispositional stereotype contributed greatly to the barbarous consequences of anti-Semitism in Europe during the 1930s and 1940s and has persisted even in the face of clear, disconfirming evidence such as that produced by the birth of the state of Israel, where Jews tilled the soil and made the desert bloom.

3. *The ultimate attribution error.* Taking the fundamental attribution error one step further, Thomas Pettigrew (1979) suggested that an "ultimate attribution error" occurs when ingroup members (1) attribute negative outgroup behavior to dispositional causes (more than they would for identical ingroup behavior), and (2) attribute positive outgroup behavior to one or more of the following causes: (a) a fluke or exceptional case, (b) luck or special advantage, (c) high motivation and effort, and (d) situational factors. This attributional double standard makes it virtually impossible for outgroup members to break free of prejudice against them, because their positive actions are explained away while their failures and shortcomings are used against them. Although the research record is somewhat mixed, studies generally support Pettigrew's analysis (Hewstone, 1990). One study found, for example, that White students were more likely to interpret a shove as violent—and more likely to explain it

dispositionally—when the shove came from a Black person than a White person (Duncan, 1976). Another study found that Hindu participants were more likely to make dispositional attributions for negative behaviors than positive behaviors when the actor was Muslim, but they showed the opposite pattern when the actor was Hindu (Taylor & Jaggi, 1974). And a meta-analysis of 58 different experiments found that on traditionally masculine tasks, male successes were more likely than female successes to be attributed to ability, whereas male failures were more likely than female failures to be attributed to bad luck or lack of effort (Swim & Sanna, 1996).

Subtle Forms of Prejudice

As this brief review shows, the roots of prejudice are many and varied. Some of the deepest and most intensively studied roots include personality factors such as right-wing authoritarianism and social dominance orientation, cognitive factors such as the human tendency to think categorically, motivational factors such as the need for self-esteem, and social factors such as uncharitable ingroup attributions for outgroup behavior. Research on these factors suggests that prejudiced attitudes are not limited to a few pathological or misguided individuals; instead, prejudice is an outgrowth of normal human functioning, and all people are susceptible to one extent or another.

Yet there is also reason for optimism: When viewed historically, there is no doubt that many virulent strains of prejudice and discrimination are on the decline. Gone are the days of Nazi Germany and the Holocaust, of legalized slavery, of Jim Crow segregation and lynchings by the Ku Klux Klan. Gone are the days when most women worldwide could not vote or hold political office, when Chinese immigrants were barred from entering the United States, when thousands of Japanese-American citizens were incarcerated without having committed a crime. Since the late 1950s the percentage of White Americans supporting Black-White intermarriage has risen steadily from 4 percent to 61 percent, and the percentage who say they would vote for a well-qualified Black presidential candidate has climbed from 35 percent to a whopping 96 percent (see Figure 5). In the United States, multiculturalism and diversity are more widely embraced than ever before, as evident from the soaring popularity of Latin and Caribbean music and cuisine; holidays such as Kwanzaa and Martin Luther King, Jr., Day; observance of Black History Month and American Indian Heritage Month; commemorative coins and stamps honoring Susan B. Anthony, Sacagawea, and Black Heritage; and celebrations of gay, lesbian, bisexual, and transgender pride.

In response to these societal changes, psychological researchers have increasingly turned their attention from blatant forms of prejudice to more subtle manifestations (Crosby, Bromley, & Saxe, 1980; Page, 1997). This shift in focus does not imply that traditional displays of prejudice have disappeared, but rather, that contemporary forms of prejudice are often difficult to detect and may even be unknown to the prejudice holders. For example, in a study that examined whether HIV-positive bisexuals are blamed for contracting

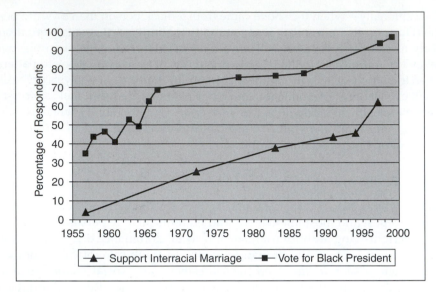

FIGURE 5

Over the past 50 years, public opinion research has documented a steady rise in the number of White Americans who support interracial marriage between Blacks and Whites, and who say they would vote for a well-qualified presidential candidate who happened to be Black. (*Note:* All data from the Gallup Organization).

their disease, the results did not indicate a uniform pattern of prejudice (McBride, 1998). Bisexuals who got HIV from unsafe sex or intravenous drug use were not blamed significantly more than HIV-positive heterosexuals under the same conditions. When HIV was described as coming from a blood transfusion, however, bisexuals were far more likely than heterosexuals to be blamed for their disease. Why should sexual orientation make a difference with blood transfusions but not with unsafe sex or drug use? According to the report, people saw no reason to consider sexual orientation when there was a clear behavioral cause for HIV (e.g., unsafe sex or drug use). Somewhat paradoxically, it was only in the absence of blameworthy behavior that judgments of responsibility became vulnerable to prejudice.

Subtle Racism   Since the 1970s researchers have studied several interrelated forms of subtle racism (see Table 3 for an overview). The central focus of this research has been on White prejudice toward Black people, and even though each form of subtle racism has distinct features, the results have consistently pointed in the same direction: White people are most likely to express anti-Black prejudice when it can plausibly be denied (both to themselves and to others). Studies have found, for example, that Black job candidates and Black college applicants are likely to face prejudice when their qualifications are ambiguous but not when their qualifications are clearly strong or weak (Dovidio & Gaertner, 2000; Hodson, Dovidio, & Gaertner, 2002). Similarly, a study on obedience to authority found that White participants discriminated when selecting job applicants for an interview, but only when instructed to do so by someone in authority—a situation that allowed them to deny personal responsibility and prejudice (Brief, Dietz, Cohen, Pugh, & Vaslow, 2000). In this rather disturbing study, roughly half the participants received a fictitious letter from the company's president saying:

> Our organization attempts to match the characteristics of our representatives with the characteristics of the population to which they will be assigned. The particular territory to which your selected representative will be assigned contains relatively few minority group members. Therefore, in this particular situation, I feel that it is important that you do not hire anyone that is a member of a minority group. (p. 80)

Participants who received this statement selected fewer than half as many Black applicants for an interview as did participants who received no such statement. The bottom line: Under conditions of attributional ambiguity that allow people to appear unprejudiced, even "subtle" forms of racism can exact an enormous toll on racial minorities.

Subtle Sexism   Just as there is subtle racism, research shows there is subtle sexism. For example, Janet Swim and her colleagues (1995) have documented the presence of "modern sexism," a form of prejudice analogous to the "modern racism" listed in Table 3. In contrast to old-fashioned sexism—which portrays women as unintelligent and incompetent—modern sexism is characterized by a denial that sex discrimination continues to be a problem, antagonism toward women's groups, and a belief that the government and

TABLE 3   Forms of Subtle Racism

Name	Primary Citations	Description of Main Features
Symbolic racism	Kinder & Sears (1981); McConahay & Hough (1976); Sears (1988)	Symbolic racists reject old-style racism but still express prejudice indirectly (e.g., as opposition to policies that help racial minorities)
Ambivalent racism	Katz (1981)	Ambivalent racists experience an emotional conflict between positive and negative feelings toward stigmatized racial groups
Modern racism	McConahay (1986)	Modern racists see racism as wrong but view racial minorities as making unfair demands or receiving too many resources
Aversive racism	Gaertner & Dovidio (1986)	Aversive racists believe in egalitarian principles such as racial equality but have a personal aversion toward racial minorities

news media show too much concern about the treatment of women. Studies also suggest that sexism is marked by an ambivalence similar to what Irwin Katz (1981) described in his theory of "ambivalent racism." According to Peter Glick and Susan Fiske (1996, 2001), "ambivalent sexism" includes two separate but interrelated components: (1) *hostile sexism,* which involves negative feelings toward women, and (2) *benevolent sexism,* a chivalrous ideology that offers protection and affection to women who adopt conventional gender roles. Because benevolent sexism may superficially seem like positive regard rather than prejudice, it can go unnoticed or even be embraced by women themselves (Glick et al., 2000). As in the case of positive stereotypes, however, benevolent sexism is far from benign. Not only does it restrict women's freedom and encourage dependence upon men, but the presence of benevolent sexism among females means that women often act as prisoner and guard at the same time.

Stereotyping

Consistent with research on prejudice, psychological studies have found that stereotyping is a natural and common process in cultures around the world. To see how this process works, consider a 1956 *American Anthropologist* report that described the Nacirema people in stereotypic terms:

> They are a North American group living in the territory between the Canadian Cree, the Yaqui and Tarahumare of Mexico, and the Carib and Arawak of the Antilles. . . . Nacirema culture is characterized by a highly developed market economy which has evolved in a rich natural habitat. While much of the people's time is devoted to economic pursuits, a large part of the fruits of these labors and a considerable portion of the day are spent in ritual activity. The focus of this activity is the human body, the appearance and health of which loom as a dominant concern in the ethos of the people. (Miner, 1956, p. 503)

When you form an image of the Nacirema people, what comes to mind? Do they seem like an advanced civilization or a primitive culture? What kind of clothing do you think the Nacirema people wear, what do their rituals look like, and what type of dwellings do you think they inhabit? Take a moment to reread the 1956 description and answer these questions before continuing.

Since the 1970s social scientists have documented that people quickly form judgments of social groups, and that these judgments are often stereotypic when little is known about outgroup members. In the preceding description, for instance, the Nacirema people may seem undeveloped or backward. In truth, however, the Nacirema people are quite developed— only the spelling of their name, "Nacirema," is backward!

As this spoof from the *American Anthropologist* shows, it is easy to form stereotypic images of others even when the outgroup is not all that different from ourselves. Stereotypes, like other generalizations, frequently serve as mental shortcuts and are especially likely to be applied when people are busy or distracted (Gilbert & Hixon, 1991). One study found, for example, that when college students were distracted for 25 seconds with a request to remember an eight-digit number, they were later more likely to remember stereotypic attributes about another person (Pendry & Macrae, 1994). As discussed next, stereotypes can even be activated outside conscious awareness by a fleeting image or word related to the stereotyped group, and once activated, can influence attitudes and behavior (Greenwald & Banaji, 1995).

Explicit and Implicit Biases

The origins of stereotype research date back to a study by Daniel Katz and Kenneth Braly (1933) in which 100 Princeton University students were asked to indicate the traits most characteristic of 10 different social groups. Students displayed a high level of agreement about the traits of certain racial and ethnic groups, such as Negroes (described as superstitious by 84 percent of the students, and as lazy by 75 percent), and Jews (described as shrewd by 79 percent). Since the time of Katz and Braly's study, researchers have developed a wide range of techniques to measure stereotypes, yet with the rise of subtle racism, it is hard to say whether racial stereotypes have decreased over the years or whether they have simply become less likely to be expressed (Devine & Elliot, 1995; Lee, Jussim, & McCauley, 1995; Macrae, Stangor, & Hewstone, 1996). Public opinion polls have generally shown a decline in racial stereotyping, but one study found that when survey questions were worded to avoid implying a politically correct answer, many people expressed agreement with racial stereotypes (Plous & Williams, 1995). In this study, a majority of respondents endorsed at least one stereotypic Black-White difference in inborn ability (e.g., Blacks have greater rhythmic ability than Whites), and nearly half endorsed at least one stereotypic difference in anatomy (e.g., Blacks have thicker skulls than Whites).

In part because of the difficulty in assessing people's endorsement of stereotypes, researchers have increasingly relied on indirect methods of assessment. Borrowing heavily from cognitive psychology, these indirect methods have allowed researchers to "get under the hood" and find out what people think under conditions that prevent the management of outward impressions. Results from this research suggest that in addition to the explicit stereotypes that Katz and Braly measured, people harbor "implicit" biases outside of their awareness—that is, they hold prejudiced attitudes and stereotypic associations about certain groups even without realizing it (Banaji, Hardin, & Rothman, 1993; Fazio, Jackson, Dunton, & Williams, 1995; Gaertner & McLaughlin, 1983). Although implicit biases are often correlated with explicit biases—meaning that they tend to go together—the two are not the same. For instance, when White students in one study were observed during interracial interactions, their explicit attitudes predicted later racial biases in verbal behavior, whereas their implicit attitudes predicted biases in nonverbal behavior (Dovidio, Kawakami, & Gaertner, 2002).

How is it possible to measure implicit attitudes and beliefs when people may not even know that they have them? One of the most common ways is with an experimental technique known as "priming" (Wheeler & Petty, 2001; Wittenbrink, Judd, & Park, 1997). Typically, participants in these studies are exposed to a word or image that brings to mind thematically related ideas or associations concerning a target of prejudice (e.g., an ethnic minority group). Then, once an implicit prejudice or stereotype has been activated, researchers can assess its strength, content, and effect on other attitudes, beliefs, and behavior.

In an early experiment using this technique, Patricia Devine (1989) had White college students watch a screen capable of displaying words so rapidly as to be undetected. In one experimental condition, participants were shown a subliminal series in which 80 percent of the words were stereotypically associated with African Americans (e.g., *jazz, rhythm, athletic, basketball, slavery*). In another condition, only 20 percent of the words were associated with African Americans. Next, people were asked to read a brief scenario and judge the actions of a person it described. Devine found that people in the 80 percent condition—who, unbeknownst to them, had been heavily primed with stereotypic words—later judged the person as relatively more hostile (in keeping with the general activation of a stereotype concerning African Americans). Furthermore, this activation occurred regardless of how high or low participants had scored on explicit measures of racism, suggesting that even when people do not believe in racial stereotypes, merely *knowing* about the stereotypes may be enough to trigger discrimination.

One of the most popular techniques for probing implicit biases is the Implicit Association Test, or IAT (Greenwald et al., 2002; Greenwald, McGhee, & Schwartz, 1998). The IAT is a computer-based test that measures how rapidly people are able to categorize various words and images, and it capitalizes on the fact that most of us identify words and images more rapidly when they come from closely related categories than when they come from unrelated categories. For instance, if you associate librarians with intelligence and boxers with violence, you can probably tell in a split second that synonyms for intelligence like *smart* and *brainy* relate to the dual category "librarians or intelligence," and synonyms for violence like *aggression* and *hostility* relate to the dual category "boxers or violence." But what if we switch the elements around, and you are asked whether *smart* and *brainy* relate to the dual category "librarians or violence" or to the dual category "boxers or intelligence"? In this case it will probably take you longer to match *smart* and *brainy* with the category containing "intelligence," because these dual categories contain elements that are not stereotypically related to each other. Thus, by comparing the speed with which people categorize words or images, the IAT indirectly assesses how closely people associate certain elements with each other. To examine racial stereotypes, for example, the test might replace librarians and boxers with Whites and Blacks. With this version of the IAT, faster responses to "Whites or intelligence" and "Blacks or violence" (compared with "Whites or violence" and "Blacks or intelligence") could indicate the presence of an implicit stereotype.

The IAT has been used to measure a variety of hidden associations, such as implicit racial and gender stereotypes, attitudes toward elderly people, and preferences for particular political candidates (Greenwald et al., 1998; Nosek, Banaji, & Greenwald, 2002). Implicit associations have even been detected in minimal group research, when people have no prior group experience yet display positive associations with ingroup member names and negative associations with outgroup member names (Ashburn-Nardo, Voils, & Monteith, 2001). As with other measures of implicit stereotyping, IAT scores have also been linked to behavioral measures of discrimination. For instance, one study found that White students with pro-White IAT scores later treated a White conversation partner better than a Black conversation partner, as judged by independent raters who watched videotapes of the conversations (McConnell & Leibold, 2001).

Consequences of Stereotyping

Once activated, stereotypes can powerfully affect social perceptions and behavior. This point was brought home in an experiment that used rap music to prime racial stereotypes (Johnson, Trawalter, & Dovidio, 2000). As shown in Figure 6 on page 24, Black and White students who heard a four-minute segment of violent rap music later rated a Black male's violent behavior as being more character-based than did control-group students who were not exposed to rap music. Students exposed to rap music also rated a Black male's intelligence-related job qualifications lower than did control students. The effect of violent rap music did not differ significantly between Black or White students, or between females and males. Nor did violent rap music influence judgments about a White male. According to the study's authors, violent rap music activates a stereotype among Blacks and Whites alike that Black males are violent and unintelligent.

The activation of stereotypes can also lead people to behave in ways consistent with the stereotype. For instance, studies have found that when college students are exposed to stereotypic words and images relating to old age, they later walk more slowly and perform more slowly on a word recognition task (Bargh, Chen, & Burrows, 1996; Kawakami, Young, & Dovidio, 2002). Likewise, students primed with "soccer hooligan" stereotypes answer fewer general knowledge questions correctly, whereas students primed with professor stereotypes show improved performance (Dijksterhuis & van Knippenberg, 1998). One study even found that when students were asked to write an essay about someone named Tyrone Walker (a Black-sounding name), they subsequently performed more poorly on a math test than did students who were asked to write an essay about Erik Walker (Wheeler, Jarvis, & Petty, 2001). Although the reason for these effects is not entirely clear, it appears that when stereotypic representations of behavior are activated, relevant behavior also becomes activated (Wheeler & Petty, 2001).

In addition to the effects of priming, people who are stereotyped face a second burden: the threat that their behavior will confirm a negative stereotype. Claude Steele and his colleagues have shown that this burden, known as

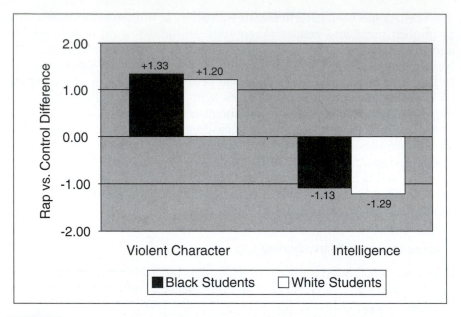

FIGURE 6
In an experiment by Johnson, Trawalter, and Dovidio (2000), Black and White students exposed to violent rap music later: (1) rated a Black male's violent behavior as being more character-based than did control-group students, and (2) rated a Black male's intelligence-related job qualifications lower than did control students.

stereotype threat, can create anxiety and hamper performance on a variety of tasks (Steele, 1997). For example, telling African-American students that a test is diagnostic of their verbal ability, or preceding the test with an information form that asks for their race, leads to a significant drop in test scores (Steele & Aronson, 1995). African-American students also miss more golf shots when they are told that a golfing test measures "sports intelligence," whereas White students miss more shots when they are told the test measures "natural athletic ability" (Stone, Lynch, Sjomeling, & Darley, 1999). With respect to gender stereotypes, female math students taking a difficult test show a drop in performance when told that the test reveals gender differences in math ability (Spencer, Steele, & Quinn, 1999). An especially interesting study along these lines found that when Asian women are made aware of their ethnicity, their math performance improves (in keeping with the stereotype of Asians as good at math), but when they are made aware of their gender, their math performance declines (Shih, Pittinsky, & Ambady, 1999). And the same pattern occurs with young children: When Asian girls are made aware of their ethnicity (by coloring a picture of Asian children eating with chopsticks), their math performance improves, but when they are made aware of their gender (by coloring a picture of a girl with a doll), their math performance declines (Ambady, Shih, Kim, & Pittinsky, 2001).

Stereotyping Among Children

The vulnerability of children to stereotype threat implies that stereotypes are learned early in life. How early is early? Several studies have observed ingroup biases by age 3 or 4 and the development of racial and gender stereotyping soon after (Aboud, 1988; Cameron, Alvarez, Ruble, & Fuligni, 2001; Martin, Wood, & Little, 1990). One Israeli investigation even documented anti-Arab prejudice in children as young as 2½ years of age (Bar-Tal, 1996). Although it may seem hard to believe that children can distinguish among social groups at such an early age, research on gender recognition has found that children typically begin to form social categories within the first year of life. Infants are often able to discriminate between female and male faces by the age of 9 months, and sometimes as early as 5 months (Leinbach & Fagot, 1993).

There are also direct parallels in the content of stereotypes held by children and adults. Barbara Morrongiello and her colleagues convincingly illustrated this point with a pair of studies on gender stereotyping (one study with adult participants and the other with children). In the first study, mothers watched videotapes of a child engaged in risk-taking behaviors and were asked to (1) stop the videotape when they would normally intervene, and (2) say whatever they would normally say to their own child in such a situation (Morrongiello & Dawber, 2000). In keeping with traditional gender stereotypes, the results indicated that mothers of daughters stopped the tape sooner and more frequently than did mothers of sons. Moreover, mothers of daughters were more likely to verbalize warnings about the risk of injury, whereas mothers of sons were more likely to encourage risk-taking behavior. This gender bias is similar to the finding that mothers underestimate the crawling ability of female infants and overestimate the crawling ability of male infants, even when no actual differences exist (Mondschein, Adolph, & Tamis-LeMonda, 2000).

As disconcerting as these results are for mothers, there is no reason to suppose that fathers would fare differently; decades of research have documented gender stereotypes among both men and women (Swann, Langlois, & Gilbert, 1999; Tavris, 1992). But what about children? In a second study, Morrongiello and her colleagues found that children 6 to 10 years of age mirror adults by displaying the same stereotype of girls as vulnerable to injury (Morrongiello, Midgett, & Stanton, 2000). In this experiment, children were presented with drawings of a girl or boy engaged in one of four play activities (riding a bicycle, swinging on a swing, climbing on monkey bars, or sliding down a slide). Half of the drawings depicted a child smiling confidently, and half showed the child looking wary. In addition, each activity was presented in one of four ways: as having no risk, low risk, moderate risk, or high risk (see Figure 7). For example, in the swing series a child was pictured sitting safely on a swing (no risk), sitting on a swing while holding a can of soda (low risk), crouching with feet on the swing (moderate risk), or standing on the swing with shoes untied (high risk). In all, each participant in the study was shown a set of 64 drawings (4 activities × 4 levels of risk × 2 facial expressions × 2 genders of the child depicted = 64 drawings) and asked to sort

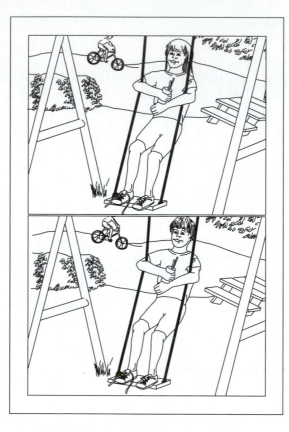

FIGURE 7
Sample "high-risk" drawings used by Morrongiello, Midgett, and Stanton (2000) in their study of children's risk perception. Reprinted with permission of Barbara Morrongiello.

the drawings by how much risk of injury there was. The results: Girls and boys both tended to rate the risk of injury as greater for girls than boys, even though in reality boys routinely experience more injuries than do girls.

Stereotypes in the Media

One of the main places that children and adults learn stereotypes is the mass media. Content analyses have found that advertisements, television programs, movies, and other media are saturated with racial and gender stereotypes (Entman & Rojecki, 2000; Furnham & Mak, 1999; Plous & Neptune, 1997). Although the cumulative effect of these stereotypes is hard to assess, the sheer volume of advertising suggests that most Americans are exposed to stereotypes on a daily basis. Advertisements occupy almost 60 percent of newspaper space, 52 percent of magazine pages, 18 percent of radio time, and

17 percent of television prime time (Collins & Skover, 1993). On an individual level, American teenagers watch an average of more than 350,000 television commercials by the time they are 18 years old (Kern-Foxworth, 1994)— roughly equivalent to watching advertisements nonstop from 9:00 A.M. to 5:00 P.M. every day for a year.

Studies indicate that these advertisements profoundly influence how people perceive and relate to one another. For example, one experiment found that, compared with members of a control group, male interviewers who had watched sexist television commercials later judged a female job applicant as less competent, remembered less biographical information about her, and remembered more about her physical appearance (Rudman & Borgida, 1995). Another study found that children who were raised in a community without television had less sex-typed perceptions than did children who were raised in comparable communities with television, and that sex-typed attitudes increased once television was introduced (Kimball, 1986). In still another investigation, women who were exposed to sex-role-reversed advertisements later became more self-confident and independent in their judgments (Jennings, Geis, & Brown, 1980). These studies and many more document the influence of advertisements on social perception and behavior.

Beyond advertising, other media-based stereotypes wield considerable influence. For instance, research has shown that:

- White television viewers who watch a stereotyped comic portrayal of African Americans are later more likely to judge a Black defendant guilty of an assault (Ford, 1997).
- Males who view movie scenes objectifying women are later more likely to believe that a date rape victim experienced pleasure and "got what she wanted" (Milburn, Mather, & Conrad, 2000).
- College students who watch a music video objectifying women later rate a woman as more sexual and submissive when she reciprocates a man's advances (Hansen & Hansen, 1988).
- Heterosexual men who look at attractive women in magazine erotica later rate their romantic partners as less attractive (Kenrick, Gutierres, & Goldberg, 1989).

In many cases the immediate effects of stereotype activation fade after a few minutes, but regardless of their duration, each activation reinforces stereotypic thinking in the long run. Additionally, evidence suggests that once a stereotype is activated, it can be reactivated by something as simple as a disagreement with someone in the stereotyped group, and if brought to mind frequently enough, can become chronically accessible (Ford, 1997; Kunda, Davies, Adams, & Spencer, 2002). Thus, even though media-based stereotypes may seem harmless when considered individually, their cumulative effect over time can be substantial.

Stereotypes from Direct Experience

Stereotypes are learned not only from the mass media, but from direct experience as well. Although some stereotypes are grounded in truth (e.g., it is true that men are, on average, more aggressive than women), many are distortions that arise from otherwise adaptive modes of thought. To illustrate, try the following exercise: Look around you for 5 or 10 seconds and make a note of what is in your environment. Then, after you have carefully observed your surroundings, close your eyes and recall everything that you noticed. As with the *American Anthropologist* passage on the Nacirema, do not read further until you have taken a few moments to give this exercise a try.

What did you recall seeing? If you are like most people, the items you noticed were the most salient things in the environment—objects that were prominent, large, colorful, or attention-getting in some way. When we observe the environment, we do not give equal weight to every element; instead, we are highly selective. Without even being aware of it, we automatically filter what we see in a way that gives greatest weight to whatever is most salient.

Normally, this kind of automatic filtering is highly beneficial. After all, which is more important to notice—an oncoming car or a pebble along the side of the road? Just as with categorical thinking, our focus on salient stimuli allows us to process a large amount of information efficiently. Yet also like categorical thinking, our focus on salient stimuli can lead to systematic distortions in perception, and, at times, to prejudice and stereotyping.

An experiment by Loren Chapman (1967) shows how salience can distort the judgments people make. Chapman projected a series of word pairs, such as *bacon-tiger*, onto a screen in front of the participants in his study. For example, in a typical series, the word on the left side of the screen was *bacon, lion, blossoms,* or *boat,* and the word on the right side was *eggs, tiger,* or *notebook.* Chapman balanced the word pairs so that each left-side word appeared an equal number of times with each right-side word, yet he found that when participants were asked to estimate the frequency of various word pairs, they reported seeing illusory correlations. For instance, people estimated that when *bacon* appeared on the left, *eggs* was paired with it an average of 47 percent of the time. Similarly, participants thought that when *lion* was on the left, *tiger* was the word that appeared with it most often.

Although illusory correlations can occur for a variety of reasons, one key element is that distinctive pairings are better remembered than other pairings (Hamilton, Dugan, & Trolier, 1985; Mullen & Johnson, 1990). In the case of Chapman's research, certain word pairs stood out because the two words were thematically related. Yet distinctiveness also increases when rare events or attributes are paired with one another—a result that can sometimes lead to stereotyping.

This connection was illustrated in an experiment that presented people with brief statements describing the behavior of individuals from one of two groups: "Group A" or "Group B" (Hamilton & Gifford, 1976). Group A had twice as many members as Group B, but the proportion of desirable and undesirable behaviors represented in the statements was the same within each group. Roughly 70 percent of the time the statements described a desirable behavior (e.g., "visited a sick friend in the hospital"), and roughly 30 percent of the time the statements described an undesirable behavior (e.g., "always talks about himself and his problems"). In other words, the most infrequent—and hence, most distinctive—statements described undesirable behaviors on the part of the minority group (Group B).

Under these conditions, people significantly overestimated the frequency of undesirable minority behaviors. As shown by the bolded entries in Table 4, participants recalled 52 percent of undesirable behaviors as coming from Group B, even though the actual percentage was only 33 percent. Furthermore, subsequent research has shown that this kind of illusory correlation is especially pronounced when the distinctive pairings involve negative behavior and are consistent with preexisting stereotypes (Hamilton & Rose, 1980; Mullen & Johnson, 1990). In such instances, the salience of unusual pairings can strongly reinforce minority stereotypes.

Self-Perpetuating Stereotypes

Once stereotypes are learned—whether from the media, family members, direct experience, or elsewhere—they sometimes take on a life of their own and become "self-perpetuating stereotypes" (Skrypnek & Snyder, 1980). As discussed earlier, one way this can happen is by people experiencing a stereotype threat that lowers their performance. Stereotypes can also become self-perpetuating when stereotyped individuals are made to feel self-conscious or inadequate. For example, research on self-objectification has found that when women take a difficult math test while wearing a swimsuit, they perform more poorly than do women wearing regular clothes, whereas men show no such decline in performance (Fredrickson, Roberts, Noll, Quinn, & Twenge, 1998). Even subliminal priming can lead to self-perpetuating stereotypes. For instance, when people over 60 years old are subliminally exposed to words such as _senile, incompetent,_ and _Alzheimer's,_ they show signs of memory loss (Levy, 1996).

TABLE 4   An Example of Illusory Correlation

Statement Content	Group A	Group B	Total
	Actual Distribution of Statements		
Desirable Behaviors	18 (67%)	9 (33%)	27 (100%)
Undesirable Behaviors	8 (67%)	**4 (33%)**	12 (100%)
	Perceived Distribution of Statements		
Desirable Behaviors	17.5 (65%)	9.5 (35%)	27 (100%)
Undesirable Behaviors	5.8 (48%)	**6.2 (52%)**	12 (100%)

Note: This table is based on data from a study by Hamilton and Gifford (1976). Even though only 4 out of 12 undesirable behavior statements involved Group B (the minority group), participants later recalled more of the undesirable behaviors coming from Group B (average = 6.2) than Group A (average = 5.8).

In a dramatic demonstration of how priming can lead to self-perpetuating stereotypes, Mark Chen and John Bargh (1997) subliminally exposed White students to either White or Black male faces taken from popular magazines. Then, once racial stereotypes were implicitly activated, students were paired with another White student who had not been exposed to any faces, and the pair was asked to play a game together. The results showed that (1) compared with students primed with White faces, students primed with Black faces later displayed more hostility during the game (consistent with racial stereotypes concerning Black hostility), and (2) this hostility in turn led the unexposed partner to respond with an increase in hostility. The unsettling conclusion: Simply by looking at Black faces, White people may be primed to behave in ways that elicit hostility from Black people.

Self-perpetuating dynamics have also been documented in interactions between women and men. Perhaps the best-known experiment on this point was published by Mark Snyder, Elizabeth Tanke, and Ellen Berscheid (1977). In this study, male-female pairs were audiotaped for ten minutes while they got acquainted with each other via the telephone (the male and female soundtracks were recorded separately for later analysis). Unbeknownst to the women, though, the men were first given one of eight randomly assigned snapshots of a woman—ostensibly their partner—so they could have "a mental picture of the person they're talking to." In reality, four snapshots were of women previously rated as highly attractive, and four were of women rated as unattractive. Thus, some of the men were led to believe that their conversation partner was physically attractive, and others were led to believe that their partner was unattractive.

Not surprisingly, when independent raters later listened to the male soundtrack of these conversations, men who thought they were talking with an attractive woman were judged as more sociable, sexually warm and permissive, outgoing, and humorous than men who thought they were talking with an unattractive woman. Of greater interest were ratings of the female soundtrack. Presumably in response to differences in male behavior, women who were initially perceived as attractive actually *sounded* more stereotypically attractive than did women who were originally thought to be unattractive, even though their male partner's preconceptions were induced at random and had nothing to do with how physically attractive the women actually were. What makes these results remarkable is that male beliefs affected female behavior so strongly that outside listeners—who knew nothing of the experimental hypotheses or attractiveness of the women—could hear the difference.

Reducing Stereotypes

As the foregoing review suggests, stereotypes are learned at an early age and can be stubbornly resistant to change. Even when people encounter a stereotyped group member who violates the group stereotype, they often continue to maintain the stereotype by splitting it into subtypes (Judd, Park, & Wolsko, 2001; Kunda & Oleson, 1995; Richards & Hewstone, 2001; Weber & Crocker,

1983). For example, when encountering a Jewish philanthropist, people with anti-Semitic stereotypes may distinguish philanthropic Jews from "money-hungry Jews" by creating a subtype for "good Jews." As a result of subtyping, stereotypes become impervious to disconfirming evidence.

Yet all is not lost. Studies indicate that stereotypes can be successfully reduced and social perceptions made more accurate when people are motivated to do so (Fiske, 2000; Neuberg, 1989; Sinclair & Kunda, 1999). One of the most effective ways this can be done is with empathy. Simply by taking the perspective of outgroup members and "looking at the world through their eyes," ingroup bias and stereotype accessibility can be significantly reduced (Galinsky & Moskowitz, 2000). Research also suggests that stereotype threat can be lessened with a change in orientation. For instance, one promising experiment found that when African-American college students were encouraged to think of intelligence as malleable rather than fixed, their grades increased and they reported greater enjoyment of the educational process (Aronson, Fried, & Good, 2002).

Even implicit stereotypes can be modified (Blair, 2002). In a study on the effects of counterstereotypic imagery, for example, Irene Blair and her colleagues found that implicit gender stereotypes declined after people spent a few minutes imagining a strong woman (Blair, Ma, & Lenton, 2001). Likewise, Nilanjana Dasgupta and Anthony Greenwald (2001) found that pro-White biases on the IAT declined after people were exposed to pictures of admired Black Americans and disliked White Americans (e.g., Bill Cosby and Timothy McVeigh). Still another study found that implicit and explicit anti-Black biases were reduced after students took a semester-long course on prejudice and conflict (Rudman, Ashmore, & Gary, 2001). As these findings show, stereotypes may be widespread and persistent, but they are also amenable to change when people make an effort to reduce them.

Discrimination

In a 1993 Gallup poll, 77 percent of White Americans said they felt Black people overestimated the amount of discrimination there is against Blacks (Wheeler, 1993). According to Gallup's most recent figures, 74 percent of White Americans believe that Blacks in their community are treated as well as Whites, and 79 percent believe that Blacks have as good a chance as Whites to get any job for which they're qualified (Ludwig, 2000). Yet Black Americans have a very different view. According to Gallup, only 36 percent of Black Americans feel they are treated as well as Whites, and only 40 percent feel they have equal job opportunities.

Where lies the truth? Are Black Americans treated as well as Whites, or do they face racial discrimination? As seen in Table 5, discrimination is a more serious problem than most White Americans (and some Black Americans) believe. For example, in a review of more than 100 studies, the Institute of Medicine concluded that discrimination contributes to racial disparities in

TABLE 5 Sample *New York Times* Articles on Racial Discrimination (Dates in Parentheses)

Topic and Article Title

Medical Care
 Doctor Bias May Affect Heart Care, Study Finds (2/25/99)
 In Treating Patients for Pain, a Racial Gap (12/28/99)
 Discrimination Is Painful. It Can Also Be Agonizing (4/9/00)
 Medical Students' Biases Can Begin Early (6/20/00)
 Hidden in the World of Medicine, Discrimination and Stereotypes (6/19/01)
 Minorities Get Inferior Care, Even If Insured, Study Finds (3/21/02)

Criminal Justice
 Task Force Reports Race Bias in Courts (4/24/96)
 Study of U.S. Courts Finds Race and Sex Bias Common (6/11/97)
 New Study Adds to Evidence of Bias in Death Sentences (6/7/98)
 Whitman Says Troopers Used Racial Profiling (4/21/99)
 In Turnpike Arrests, 80% Were Minority (5/1/99)
 Racial Bias Shown in Police Searches, State Report Asserts (12/1/99)
 Discrepancy by Race Found in the Trying of Youths (2/3/00)
 Racial Bias Found in Six More Capital Cases (6/11/00)
 Victims' Race Affects Decisions on Killers' Sentence, Study Finds (4/30/01)

Lending
 Ohio Mortgage Bank Settles Discrimination Complaint (10/19/95)
 Fleet Agrees to Settle Accusation of Loan Discrimination (5/8/96)
 Mortgage Lender Settles Bias Complaints (4/4/98)
 Home Loans Discriminate, Study Shows (5/13/98)
 Agriculture Dept. to Settle Lawsuit by Black Farmers (1/5/99)
 Study Discerns Disadvantage for Blacks in Home Mortgages (11/14/99)
 Analysis Shows Racial Bias in Lending, Schumer Says (4/9/00)

Employment
 Texaco to Make Record Payout in Bias Lawsuit (11/16/96)
 Avis to Pay $3.3 Million to Settle Racial Bias Suit (12/23/97)
 Brokerage Settles Lawsuit on Racial and Sexual Bias (4/9/98)
 Agency Finds Racial Bias in Baltimore's Police Force (12/24/98)
 U.P.S. Says It Settled Bias Suit for $12 Million (1/19/99)
 Boeing to Settle a Bias Suit for $15 Million (1/23/99)
 Coca-Cola Reaches a Settlement with Some Workers in Bias Suit (6/15/00)
 $10.1 Million Settlement Offered in Race Bias Suit (12/31/00)
 Alabama: Settlement in Bias Suit (9/29/01)
 Social Security Agency Settles Workers' Bias Case (1/16/02)

Housing
 Settlement in a Bias Case Sets a Record (9/24/96)
 A Co-op Must Pay $640,000 for Denying Sublet to Black (5/14/97)
 Landlord and Real-Estate Broker Settle Racial Bias Suits (8/1/99)

Education
 Programs for Gifted Favor Whites, Study Says (6/18/98)
 Study Finds Racial Bias in Public Schools (3/1/00)
 Studies Point Up Racial Discrimination in Special Education (3/3/01)

Miscellaneous
 Denny's Bias Case to Yield Payments (12/12/95)
 Apology Made in Race Bias Case (11/22/98)
 Settlement Expected in Insurance Bias Case (6/21/00)

health care and higher death rates among minorities from cancer, heart disease, diabetes, and HIV infection (Smedley, Stith, & Nelson, 2002). Here are findings from just a few studies discussed in the review:

- Among elderly cancer patients with daily pain, Blacks were 63 percent more likely than Whites to receive no pain medication (Bernabei et al., 1998).
- Among patients with diabetes and other conditions, Blacks were 3.3 times more likely than Whites of the same sex, age, and income to have a lower limb amputated (Gornick et al., 1996).
- Following a heart attack, Black women were 63 percent less likely and Black men were 37 percent less likely than White men to undergo coronary artery bypass surgery, after adjusting for age, insurance status, and other factors (Giles, Anda, Casper, Escobedo, & Taylor, 1995).

And minorities suffer from discrimination in many other ways. For instance, Hispanics and Blacks spend an average of over $3,000 more than Whites to locate and buy the same house (Yinger, 1995), frequently receive harsher criminal sentences than Whites for the same offense (Mauer, 1999), and are generally less likely to be hired than comparable White job applicants, despite the existence of affirmative action (Turner, Fix, & Struyk, 1991). One study even found that the size of a state's prison population is better predicted by the state's Black population than by its rate of violent crime (Mauer, 1999).

In addition to Blacks, Hispanics, and other racial and ethnic minorities, several other groups experience continuing discrimination. Women not only earn an average of $.76 for every male dollar (Bowler, 1999), but they represent only 3–5 percent of senior managers at Fortune 1500 companies (Federal Glass Ceiling Commission, 1995), and they face employment discrimination of such magnitude that recent settlements have run into the hundreds of millions of dollars (Molotsky, 2000; Truell, 1997). People with disabilities, too, face substantial employment and housing discrimination. To take but one example, a U.S. Justice Department study found that the Fair Housing Act's handicap-access provision was violated in 98 percent of the housing developments investigated (Belluck, 1997). People with stigmatizing attributes perceived to be controllable, such as obesity or a minority sexual orientation, are also vulnerable to severe discrimination (Crandall, 1994; Crocker, Cornwall, & Major, 1993; Human Rights Campaign, 2001). For instance, overweight people encounter discrimination at virtually every stage of employment, including selection, placement, compensation, promotion, discipline, and discharge (Roehling, 1999).

Although this brief overview and list of target groups is far from exhaustive—and does not take into account the combined effects of multiple group memberships, such as being an overweight woman of color—it shows that discrimination remains a critical problem. Yet despite the prevalence of discrimination, one of the greatest barriers to its removal is, strangely enough, the difficulty people have detecting it at the individual level. Why should this be? First, individuals cannot serve as their own control group and test whether they would have received better treatment as a member of more privileged groups (Fiske, 1998). Second, discrimination is easier to detect with aggregated evidence than single cases, because single cases are easy to explain away (Crosby, 1984). Third, individuals may deny discrimination to avoid feeling that they are being mistreated by others or that they do not have control over their situation (Ruggerio & Taylor, 1997; Taylor, Wright, Moghaddam, & Lalonde, 1990). As a result of these and other reasons, women and minorities are more likely to perceive discrimination against their group than against themselves personally (Crosby, 1984; Taylor, Wright, & Porter, 1994).

Prejudice and Discrimination from the Target's Perspective

Traditionally, psychological research on prejudice and discrimination has focused on the attitudes and behavior of majority group members. When women, minority members, or other targets of discrimination have been involved, their role has often been peripheral—either as the object of prejudice (e.g., an experimental assistant who elicits prejudiced responses), or as someone who reacts to other people's prejudices (Shelton, 2000). Beginning in the 1990s, however, researchers began paying greater attention to women and minorities as active agents who choose and influence the situations they are in (Crocker, Major, & Steele, 1998; Feagin, 1994; Swim & Stangor, 1998). Results from this research have already enriched and broadened the field in a number of ways.

One obvious benefit of including the target's perspective is that it offers a more complete understanding of the interpersonal and intergroup aspects of prejudice, stereotyping, and discrimination. For instance, when Joachim Krueger (1996) studied the personal beliefs of Blacks as well as Whites, he uncovered a mutually held misperception: Members of both groups underestimated how favorably they were viewed by the other side. In effect, Krueger found that Blacks and Whites each thought, "We like them, but they don't like us," a belief that set the stage for misunderstanding, suspicion, and conflict. Similarly, when Charles Judd and his colleagues studied the racial attitudes of Black and White students, they found a key difference that could lead to intergroup conflict. Whereas Black participants tended to regard race as an important and positive part of their identity, White participants tended to respond in a more race-neutral way (Judd, Park, Ryan, Brauer, & Kraus, 1995). The problem, as Judd and his coauthors put it, is as follows:

> If members of ethnic minority groups are eager to have their group identity recognized, and yet the dominant White majority strives to maintain the belief that there are no differences between various ethnic groups, this is bound to create a state of tension and conflict between the two groups. . . . Thus, when White Americans are heard to make such statements as, "Why do we need an African American student union?" or "Why do we need to have special courses on ethnic minorities? Doesn't this simply promote intergroup conflict and constitute differential treatment of minorities versus Whites?"—a view that White Americans may consider truly egalitarian—

the reaction of an African American may in all likelihood be that this is the newest form of prejudice and racism. (pp. 470, 479)

To bridge this divide, each side must recognize these differences in perspective when balancing the goals of multiculturalism and color-blindness.

Another benefit of studying the target's perspective is that it yields information about the psychological and health consequences of exposure to prejudice and discrimination (Clark, Anderson, Clark, & Williams, 1999). Research suggests, for example, that the discrimination African Americans experience is associated with self-reported ill health, lower psychological well-being, and the number of bed-days away from work during the previous month (Williams, Yu, Jackson, & Anderson, 1997). Studies have also found that the blood pressure of African Americans rises when they are under stereotype threat (Blascovich, Spencer, Quinn, & Steele, 2001) or are exposed to racist incidents or attitudes (Armstead, Lawler, Gorden, Cross, & Gibbons, 1989; McNeilly et al., 1995), and that elevations in blood pressure are especially high among working-class Black people who report accepting unfair treatment rather than challenging it (Krieger & Sidney, 1996). In the latter study, blood pressure differences were in some cases equal to or larger than those associated with lack of exercise, smoking, and an unhealthy diet.

One additional benefit of considering the target's perspective is that it can suggest effective ways to reduce prejudice, stereotyping, and discrimination. Although researchers have been reluctant to explore this topic for fear of shifting the burden of prejudice reduction from perpetrators to targets, there is a growing appreciation of the ability targets have to shape interactions with majority group members (Major, Quinton, McCoy, & Schmader, 2000). For instance, Jennifer Eberhardt and Susan Fiske (1996) recommend the following tactics for employees who want to reduce the amount of discrimination they encounter at work:

- Given the human tendency to think categorically, try to prime other people to categorize you in desirable ways (e.g., by increasing the salience of positive categories such as "educated" or "manager").
- Emphasize joint goals, common fate, and other areas of similarity with majority group members so that they identify with you and see you as an individual rather than simply as a stereotypic outgroup member.
- In conversations, meetings, and policy statements, remind majority group members of the values you share, such as a sense of fairness, so that people are encouraged to act in accord with these values.
- Praise majority group members when they behave in a fair-minded and egalitarian way, both to reinforce their behavior and to establish positive standards of conduct.
- If possible, try to avoid interacting with majority group members who are at high risk of prejudice and stereotyping: people who are stressed or distracted, who have recently suffered a blow to their self-esteem,

who feel threatened or insecure, or who show signs of rigid thinking or high social dominance orientation.

As Janet Swim and Charles Stangor (1998, p. 6) wrote in their book *Prejudice: The Target's Perspective,* a consideration of target experiences improves the quality of research on prejudice and "gives a voice to target groups, validates their experiences, helps pinpoint their unique strengths and weaknesses, and can potentially increase empathy for the targets of prejudice in today's society."

Reducing Prejudice and Discrimination

On September 24, 1973, an Ojibwe Indian chief from California, dressed in full regalia, landed in Rome and claimed possession of Italy "by right of discovery," just as Christopher Columbus had claimed America nearly 500 years earlier. "I proclaim this day the day of the discovery of Italy," he said.

"What right," asked the chief, "did Columbus have to discover America when it had already been inhabited for thousands of years? The same right that I have to come now to Italy and proclaim the discovery of your country."

Although the *New York Times* referred to this claim as "bizarre" (Krebs, 1973), the newspaper's criticism only helped illustrate the chief's point: It is bizarre to claim possession of a country "by right of discovery" when the country has long been occupied by other people. What the chief did in making his claim was to reverse people's perspective and invite them to see the world from an American Indian point of view.

Research on empathy and role playing suggests that this type of reversal in perspective can reduce prejudice, stereotyping, and discrimination (Batson et al., 1997; Galinsky & Moskowitz, 2000; McGregor, 1993; Stephan & Finlay, 1999). Indeed, empathy training programs appear to reduce prejudice regardless of the age, sex, and race of participants (Aboud & Levy, 2000). In addition, empathy has the practical advantage of being relatively easy to apply in a wide range of situations. To become more empathic toward the targets of prejudice, all one needs to do is to consider questions such as *How would I feel in that situation?*, *How are they feeling right now?*, or *Why are they behaving that way?* Role-playing exercises have also been used to practice responding effectively to prejudiced comments (Plous, 2000).

Another powerful method of reducing prejudice and discrimination is to establish laws, regulations, and social norms mandating fair treatment (Oskamp, 2000). In psychology, "norms" are expectations or rules for acceptable behavior in a given situation, and research suggests that even one person's public support for antiprejudice norms is enough to move other people in that direction (Blanchard, Lilly, & Vaughn, 1991). Moreover, experiments on antigay and anti-Black prejudice have found that an individual's support for antiprejudice norms can sway the opinions of highly prejudiced people as well as those medium or low in prejudice (Monteith, Deneen, & Tooman, 1996). Normative information is especially potent and enduring when it concerns ingroup members. For example, when White students in one study were told that their fellow students held less racist views than they had thought, this normative information continued to exert a prejudice-lowering effect one week later (Stangor, Sechrist, & Jost, 2001).

Even longer-lasting reductions in prejudice are possible when people are made aware of inconsistencies in their values, attitudes, and behaviors. Milton Rokeach (1971) demonstrated, for instance, that when students spent roughly half an hour considering how their values, attitudes, and behaviors were inconsistent with the ideal of social equality, they showed significantly greater support for civil rights more than a year later. These results are consistent with cognitive dissonance theory, which postulates that (1) the act of holding psychologically incompatible thoughts creates a sense of internal discomfort, or *dissonance,* and (2) people try to avoid or reduce these feelings of dissonance whenever possible (Festinger, 1957). According to this analysis, students in Rokeach's study held incompatible thoughts such as "I support social equality" and "I've never contributed time or money to a civil rights group" and sought to reduce feelings of dissonance by increasing their support for civil rights. Other researchers have used dissonance-related techniques to reduce antigay, anti-Asian, and anti-Black prejudice (Hing, Li, & Zanna, 2002; Leippe & Eisenstadt, 1994; Monteith, 1993).

One of the most heavily studied techniques for prejudice reduction is intergroup contact (Hewstone & Brown, 1986). In *The Nature of Prejudice,* Gordon Allport (1954, p. 281) hypothesized the following:

> Prejudice (unless deeply rooted in the character structure of the individual) may be reduced by equal status contact between majority and minority groups in the pursuit of common goals. The effect is greatly enhanced if this contact is sanctioned by institutional supports (i.e., by law, custom or local atmosphere), and provided it is of a sort that leads to the perception of common interests and common humanity between members of the two groups.

This contention, now widely known as the "contact hypothesis," has received broad research support. In a meta-analysis of 203 studies from 25 countries—involving 90,000 participants—Thomas Pettigrew and Linda Tropp (2000) found that 94 percent of studies supported the contact hypothesis (that is, 94 percent of the time, prejudice diminished as intergroup contact increased).

With this level of support, why hasn't intergroup contact eliminated prejudice from society? The problem with using contact to reduce prejudice is not that the contact hypothesis is wrong, but that it is so difficult to meet the conditions Allport outlined. In many real-world environments the fires of prejudice are stoked by conflict and competition between groups that are unequal in status, such as Israelis and Palestinians, Whites and Blacks, or longtime citizens and recent immigrants (Esses, Jackson, & Armstrong, 1998; Levine & Campbell, 1972). Under conditions of competition and unequal status, contact can even increase prejudice rather than decrease it. For example, in a review of studies conducted during and after school desegregation in the United States, Walter Stephan (1986) found that 46 percent of studies reported an increase in prejudice among White students, 17 percent reported a decline in prejudice, and the remainder reported no change.

The key is to craft situations that will lead to cooperative and interdependent interactions in pursuit of common goals, shifting people to recategorize from "us and them" to "we" (Desforges et al., 1991; Dovidio & Gaertner, 1999; Sherif, Harvey, White, Hood, & Sherif, 1988). Classroom research has found that cooperative learning techniques increase the self-esteem, morale, and empathy of students across racial and ethnic divisions and also improve the academic performance of minority students without compromising the performance of majority group students (Aronson & Bridgeman, 1979). One of the earliest of these techniques to be studied, the "jigsaw classroom," divides students into small, racially diverse work groups in which each student is given a vital piece of information about the assigned topic (thereby making each group member indispensable to the others). The jigsaw technique was originally developed specifically to reduce racial prejudice, and decades of research suggest that it is highly effective at promoting positive interracial contact (Aronson & Patnoe, 1997).

A Concluding Note

This review began with unambiguously prejudiced statements made by Osama bin Laden. As discouraging as it is to read these statements, it is worth noting that they do not represent the most common forms of prejudice in daily life. Abundant evidence suggests that fewer and fewer people embrace overt forms of bigotry, and that public expressions of prejudice are more likely than ever to be condemned. Thus, although terrorism, hate crimes, and other forms of fanaticism constitute serious social problems, most forms of contemporary prejudice are manifested more subtly.

At the same time, subtle prejudices present considerable challenges of their own. At a societal level, it may be even more difficult to reduce subtle forms of prejudice than extreme forms of prejudice, not only because they are more widespread, but because they arise from normal thought processes, tend to be more ambiguous, and frequently take place outside of awareness. As the research in this review makes clear, our species might aptly be described as *Homo Stereotypus*—an animal predisposed to prejudice, stereotyping, and discrimination, but one that also possesses the capacity to overcome these biases if motivated to do so (Blair, 2002; Fiske, 2000; Monteith & Voils, 2001). Indeed, perhaps the most important conclusions to emerge from prejudice research are these: (1) no one capable of human thought and speech is immune from harboring prejudice, (2) it often takes deliberate effort and awareness to reduce prejudice, and (3) with sufficient motivation, it can be done.

REFERENCES

Aberson, C. L., Healy, M., & Romero, V. (2000). Ingroup bias and self-esteem: A meta-analysis. *Personality and Social Psychology Review, 4,* 157–173.

Aboud, F. (1988). *Children and prejudice.* Oxford, England: Basil Blackwell.

Aboud, F. E., & Levy, S. R. (2000). Interventions to reduce prejudice and discrimination in children and adolescents. In S. Oskamp (Ed.), *Reducing prejudice and discrimination* (pp. 269–293). Mahwah, NJ: Erlbaum.

Adorno, T. W., Frenkel-Brunswik, E., Levinson, D. J., & Sanford, R. N. (1950). *The authoritarian personality*. New York: Harper & Brothers.

Allen, V. L., & Wilder, D. A. (1975). Categorization, belief similarity, and intergroup discrimination. *Journal of Personality and Social Psychology, 32*, 971–977.

Allport, G. W. (1954). *The nature of prejudice*. Reading, MA: Addison-Wesley.

Altemeyer, B. (1981). *Right-wing authoritarianism*. Winnipeg, CA: University of Manitoba Press.

Altemeyer, B. (1996). *The authoritarian specter*. Cambridge, MA: Harvard University Press.

Altemeyer, B. (1998). The other "authoritarian personality." In M. P. Zanna (Ed.), *Advances in Experimental Social Psychology* (vol. 30, pp. 47–92). New York: Academic Press.

Ambady, N., Shih, M., Kim, A., & Pittinsky, T. L. (2001). Stereotype susceptibility in children: Effects of identity activation on quantitative performance. *Psychological Science, 12*, 385–390.

American Anthropological Association. (1999). AAA statement on race. *American Anthropologist, 100*, 712–713.

Angier, N. (1996, February 4). Intersexual healing: An anomaly finds a group. *New York Times*, p. E14.

Armstead, C. A., Lawler, K. A., Gorden, G., Cross, J., & Gibbons, J. (1989). Relationship of racial stressors to blood pressure responses and anger expression in Black college students. *Health Psychology, 8*, 541–556.

Aronson, E., & Bridgeman, D. (1979). Jigsaw groups and the desegregated classroom: In pursuit of common goals. *Personality and Social Psychology Bulletin, 5*, 438–446.

Aronson, E., & Patnoe, S. (1997). *The jigsaw classroom: Building cooperation in the classroom* (2nd ed.). New York: Addison Wesley Longman.

Aronson, J., Fried, C. B., & Good, C. (2002). Reducing the effects of stereotype threat on African American college students by shaping theories of intelligence. *Journal of Experimental Social Psychology, 38*, 113–125.

Aronson, E., Wilson, T. D., & Akert, R. (2002). *Social psychology* (4th ed.). Upper Saddle River, NJ: Prentice Hall.

Ashburn-Nardo, L., Voils, C. I., & Monteith, M. J. (2001). Implicit associations as the seeds of intergroup bias: How easily do they take root? *Journal of Personality and Social Psychology, 81*, 789–799.

Ashmore, R. D., & Del Boca, F. K. (1981). Conceptual approaches to stereotypes and stereotyping. In D. L. Hamilton (Ed.), *Cognitive processes in stereotyping and intergroup behavior* (pp. 1–35). Hillsdale, NJ: Erlbaum.

Banaji, M. R., & Hardin, C. D., & Rothman, A. (1993). Implicit stereotyping in person judgment. *Journal of Personality and Social Psychology, 65*, 272–281.

Bargh, J. A., Chen, M., & Burrows, L. (1996). Automaticity of social behavior: Direct effects of trait construct and stereotype activation on action. *Journal of Personality and Social Psychology, 71*, 230–244.

Bar-Tal, D. (1996). Development of social categories and stereotypes in early childhood: The case of "the Arab" concept formation, stereotype and attitudes by Jewish children in Israel. *International Journal of Intercultural Relations, 20*, 341–370.

Batson, C. D., Polcarpou, M. P., Harmon-Jones, E., Imhoff, H. J., Mitchener, E. C., & Bednar, L. L. (1997). Empathy and attitudes: Can feeling for a member of a stigmatized group improve feelings toward the group? *Journal of Personality and Social Psychology, 72*, 105–118.

Belluck, P. (1997, November 25). Housing laws broken, says U.S. in suits. *New York Times*, p. A14.

Bernabei, R., Gambassi, G., Lapane, K., Landi, F., Gatsonis, C., & Dunlop, R. (1998). Management of pain in elderly patients with cancer. *Journal of the American Medical Association, 279*, 1877–1882.

Billig, M., & Tajfel, H. (1978). Social categorization and similarity in intergroup behaviour. *European Journal of Social Psychology, 3,* 27–52.

Blair, I. V. (2002). The malleability of automatic stereotypes and prejudice. *Personality and Social Psychology Review, 6,* 242–261.

Blair, I. V., Ma, J. E., & Lenton, A. P. (2001). Imagining stereotypes away: The moderation of implicit stereotypes through mental imagery. *Journal of Personality and Social Psychology, 81,* 828–841.

Blanchard, F. A., Lilly, T., & Vaughn, L. A. (1991). Reducing the expression of racial prejudice. *Psychological Science, 2,* 101–105.

Blascovich, J., Spencer, S. J., Quinn, D., & Steele, C. (2001). African Americans and high blood pressure: The role of stereotype threat. *Psychological Science, 12,* 225–229.

Bowler, M. (1999, December). Women's earnings: An overview. *Monthly Labor Review,* pp. 13–21.

Brewer, M. B. (1979). In-group bias in the minimal intergroup situation: A cognitive-motivational analysis. *Psychological Bulletin, 86,* 307–324.

Brewer, M.B. (1999). The psychology of prejudice: Ingroup love or outgroup hate? *Journal of Social Issues, 55,* 429–444.

Brief, A. P., Dietz, J., Cohen, R. R., Pugh, S. D., & Vaslow, J. B. (2000). Just doing business: Modern racism and obedience to authority as explanations for employment discrimination. *Organizational Behavior and Human Decision Processes, 81,* 72–97.

Britain's bill of particulars: "Planned and carried out the atrocities." (2001, October 5). *New York Times,* pp. B4–B5.

Brown, R. (1995). *Prejudice: Its social psychology.* Oxford: Blackwell.

Buxton, L. H. D. (1964). Races of mankind. *Encyclopædia Britannica* (vol. 18, pp. 864–865). Chicago: William Benton.

Cameron, J. A., Alvarez, J. M., Ruble, D. N., & Fuligni, A. J. (2001). Children's lay theories about ingroups and outgroups: Reconceptualizing research on prejudice. *Personality and Social Psychology Review, 5,* 118–128.

Carvajal, D. (1999, January 20). Thesaurus takes action to remove gay slurs. *New York Times,* p. A29.

Chapman, L. J. (1967). Illusory correlation in observational report. *Journal of Verbal Learning and Verbal Behavior, 6,* 151–155.

Chen, M., & Bargh, J. A. (1997). Nonconscious behavioral confirmation processes: The self-fulfilling consequences of automatic stereotype activation. *Journal of Experimental Social Psychology, 33,* 541–560.

Cialdini, R. B., Borden, R. J., Thorne, A., Walker, M. R., Freeman, S., & Sloane, L. R. (1976). Basking in reflected glory: Three (football) field studies. *Journal of Personality and Social Psychology, 34,* 366–375.

Clark, K. B. (1950). *The effects of prejudice and discrimination on personality development (Midcentury White House Conference on Children and Youth).* Washington, DC: Federal Security Agency, Children's Bureau.

Clark, K. B., & Clark, M. P. (1947). Racial identification and preference in Negro children. In T. M. Newcomb and E. L. Hartley (Eds.), *Readings in social psychology* (pp. 169–178). New York: Holt.

Clark, R., Anderson, N. B., Clark, V. R., & Williams, D. R. (1999). Racism as a stressor for African Americans: A biosocial model. *American Psychologist, 54,* 805–816.

Collins, R. K. L., & Skover, D. M. (1993). Commerce & communication. *Texas Law Review, 71,* 697–746.

Cowan, G., & Curtis, S. R. (1994). Predictors of rape occurrence and victim blame in the William Kennedy Smith case. *Journal of Applied Social Psychology, 24,* 12–20.

Cozzarelli, C., Wilkinson, A. V., & Tagler, M. J. (2001). Attitudes toward the poor and attributions for poverty. *Journal of Social Issues, 57,* 207–227.

Crandall, C. S. (1994). Prejudice against fat people: Ideology and self-interest. *Journal of Personality and Social Psychology, 66,* 882–894.

Crocker, J., Major, B., & Steele, C. (1998). Social stigma. In D. Gilbert, S. T. Fiske, & G. Lindzey (Eds.), *Handbook of social psychology* (4th ed., vol. 2, pp. 504–553). Boston, MA: McGraw-Hill.

Crocker, J., Cornwell, B., & Major, B. (1993). The stigma of overweight: Affective consequences of attributional ambiguity. *Journal of Personality and Social Psychology, 64,* 60–70.

Crosby, F. (1984). The denial of personal discrimination. *American Behavioral Scientist, 27,* 371–386.

Crosby, F., Bromley, S., & Saxe, L. (1980). Recent unobtrusive studies of Black and White discrimination and prejudice: A literature review. *Psychological Bulletin, 87,* 546–563.

Dasgupta, N., & Greenwald, A. G. (2001). On the malleability of automatic attitudes: Combating automatic prejudice with images of admired and disliked individuals. *Journal of Personality and Social Psychology, 81,* 800–814.

Davis, F. J. (1991). *Who is Black? One nation's definition.* University Park, PA: Pennsylvania State University Press.

Desforges, D. M., Lord, C. G., Ramsey, S. L., Mason, J. A., Van Leeuwen, M D., & West, S. C. (1991). Effects of structured cooperative contact on changing negative attitudes toward stigmatized social groups. *Journal of Personality and Social Psychology, 60,* 531–544.

Devine, P. G. (1989). Stereotypes and prejudice: Their automatic and controlled components. *Journal of Personality and Social Psychology, 56,* 5–18.

Devine, P. G., & Elliot, A. J. (1995). Are racial stereotypes *really* fading? The Princeton trilogy revisited. *Personality and Social Psychology Bulletin, 21,* 1139–1150.

Dijksterhuis, A., & van Knippenberg, A. (1998). The relation between perception and behavior, or how to win a game of Trivial Pursuit. *Journal of Personality and Social Psychology, 74,* 865–877.

Dovidio, J. F., & Gaertner, S. (1999). Reducing prejudice: Combating intergroup biases. *Current Directions in Psychological Science, 8,* 101–105.

Dovidio, J. F., & Gaertner, S. (2000). Aversive racism and selection decisions: 1989 and 1999. *Psychological Science, 11,* 315–319.

Dovidio, J. F., Kawakami, K., & Gaertner, S. L. (2002). Implicit and explicit prejudice and interracial interaction. *Journal of Personality and Social Psychology, 82,* 62–68.

Duckitt, J. H. (1992). Psychology and prejudice: A historical analysis and integrative framework. *American Psychologist, 47,* 1182–1193.

Duckitt, J., & Farre, B. (1994). Right-wing authoritarianism and political intolerance among whites in the future majority-rule South Africa. *Journal of Social Psychology, 134,* 735–741.

Duncan, B. L. (1976). Differential social perception and attribution of intergroup violence: Testing the lower limits of stereotyping of blacks. *Journal of Personality and Social Psychology, 34,* 590–598.

Eberhardt, J. L., & Fiske, S. T. (1996). Motivating individuals to change: What is a target to do? In C. N. Macrae, C. Stangor, & M. Hewstone (Eds.), *Stereotypes and stereotyping* (pp. 369–415). New York: Guilford Press.

Entman, R. M., & Rojecki, A. (2000). *The Black image in the White mind: Media and race in America.* Chicago, IL: University of Chicago Press.

Esses, V. M., Jackson, L. M., & Armstrong, T. L. (1998). Intergroup competition and attitudes toward immigrants and immigration: An instrumental model of group conflict. *Journal of Social Issues, 54,* 699–724.

Fazio, R. H., Jackson, J. R., Dunton, B. C., & Williams, C. J. (1995). Variability in automatic activation as an unobtrusive measure of racial attitudes: A bona fide pipeline? *Journal of Personality and Social Psychology, 69,* 1013–1027.

Feagin, J. R. (1994). *Living with racism: The black middle-class experience.* Boston, MA: Beacon Press.

Federal Glass Ceiling Commission. (1995, March). *Good for business: Making full use of the nation's human capital.* Washington, DC: U.S. Government Printing Office.

Festinger, L. (1957). *A theory of cognitive dissonance.* Evanston, IL: Row, Peterson and Company.

Fein, S., & Spencer, S. J. (1997). Prejudice as self-image maintenance: Affirming the self through derogating others. *Journal of Personality and Social Psychology, 73,* 31–44.

Fiske, S. T. (2000). Interdependence reduces prejudice and stereotyping. In S. Oskamp (Ed.), *Reducing prejudice and discrimination* (pp. 115–135). Mahwah, NJ: Erlbaum.

Fiske, S. T. (1998). Prejudice, stereotyping, and discrimination. In D. T. Gilbert, S. T. Fiske, & G. Lindzey (Eds.), *The handbook of social psychology* (4th ed., pp. 357–411). New York: McGraw-Hill.

Ford, T. E. (1997). Effects of stereotypical television portrayals of African-Americans on person perception. *Social Psychology Quarterly, 60,* 266–278.

Fredrickson, B. L., Roberts, T., Noll, S. M., Quinn, D. M., & Twenge, J. M. (1998). That swimsuit becomes you: Sex differences in self-objectification, restrained eating, and math performance. *Journal of Personality and Social Psychology, 75,* 269–284.

Furnham, A., & Mak, T. (1999). Sex-role stereotyping in television commercials: A review and comparison of fourteen studies done on five continents over 25 years. *Sex Roles, 41,* 413–437.

Gaertner, S. L., & Dovidio, J. F. (1986). The aversive form of racism. In J. F. Dovidio and S. L. Gaertner (Eds.), *Prejudice, discrimination, and racism* (pp. 61–89). Orlando, FL: Academic Press.

Gaertner, S. L., & McLaughlin, J. P. (1983). Racial stereotypes: Associations and ascriptions of positive and negative characteristics. *Social Psychology Quarterly, 46,* 23–30.

Galinsky, A. D., & Moskowitz, G. B. (2000). Perspective-taking: Decreasing stereotype expression, stereotype accessibility, and in-group favoritism. *Journal of Personality and Social Psychology, 78,* 708–724.

Garrett, H. E. (1971). *Heredity: The cause of racial differences in intelligence.* Kilmarnock, VA: Patrick Henry Press.

Garth, T. R. (1925). A review of racial psychology. *Psychological Bulletin, 22,* 343–364.

Gilbert, D. T., & Hixon, J. (1991). The trouble of thinking: Activation and application of stereotypic beliefs. *Journal of Personality and Social Psychology, 60,* 509–517.

Giles, W. H., Anda, R. F., Casper, M. L., Escobedo, L. G., & Taylor, H. A. (1995). Race and sex differences in rates of invasive cardiac procedures in US hospitals. *Archives of Internal Medicine, 155,* 318–324.

Glick, P., & Fiske, S. T. (1996). The Ambivalent Sexism Inventory: Differentiating hostile and benevolent sexism. *Journal of Personality and Social Psychology, 70,* 491–512.

Glick, P., & Fiske, S. T. (2001). An ambivalent alliance: Hostile and benevolent sexism as complementary justifications for gender inequality. *American Psychologist, 56,* 109–118.

Glick, P., Fiske, S. T., Mladinic, A., Saiz, J. L., Abrams, D., & Masser, B. (2000). Beyond prejudice as simple antipathy: Hostile and benevolent sexism across cultures. *Journal of Personality and Social Psychology, 79,* 763–775.

"God willing, America's end is near." (2001, December 28). *New York Times,* p. B2.

Goldstone, R. L. (1995). Effects of categorization on color perception. *Psychological Science, 6,* 298–304.

Gornick, M. E., Eggers, P. W., Reilly, T. W., Mentnech, R. M., Fitterman, L. K., & Kucken, L. E. (1996). Effects of race and income on mortality and use of services among Medicare beneficiaries. *New England Journal of Medicine, 335,* 791–799.

Greenwald, A. G., & Banaji, M. R. (1995). Implicit social cognition: Attitudes, self-esteem, and stereotypes. *Psychological Review, 102,* 4–27.

Greenwald, A. G., Banaji, M. R., Rudman, L. A., Farnham, S. D., Nosek, B. A., & Mellott, D. S. (2002). A unified theory of implicit attitudes, stereotypes, self-esteem, and self-concept. *Psychological Review, 109,* 3–25.

Greenwald, A. G., McGhee, D. E., & Schwartz, J. L. K. (1998). Measuring individual differences in implicit cognition: The implicit association test. *Journal of Personality and Social Psychology, 74,* 1464–1480.

Hamilton, D. L., Dugan, P. M., & Trolier, T. K. (1985). The formation of stereotypic beliefs: Further evidence for distinctiveness-based illusory correlations. *Journal of Personality and Social Psychology, 48,* 5–17.

Hamilton, D. L., & Gifford, R. K. (1976). Illusory correlation in interpersonal perception: A cognitive basis of stereotypic judgments. *Journal of Experimental Social Psychology, 12,* 392–407.

Hamilton, D. L., & Rose, T. L. (1980). Illusory correlation and the maintenance of stereotypic beliefs. *Journal of Personality and Social Psychology, 39,* 832–845.

Hansen, C. H., & Hansen, R. D. (1988). How rock music videos can change what is seen when boy meets girl: Priming stereotypic appraisal of social interactions. *Sex Roles, 19,* 287–316.

Hewstone, M. (1990). The "ultimate attribution error"? A review of the literature on intergroup causal attribution. *European Journal of Social Psychology, 20,* 311–335.

Hewstone, M., & Brown, R. (Eds.). (1986). *Contact and conflict in intergroup encounters.* Oxford, UK: Basil Blackwell.

Hing, L. S. S., Li, W., & Zanna, M. P. (2002). Inducing hypocrisy to reduce prejudicial responses among aversive racists. *Journal of Experimental Social Psychology, 38,* 71–78.

Hodson, G., Dovidio, J. F., & Gaertner, S. L. (2002). Processes in racial discrimination: Differential weighting of conflicting information. *Personality and Social Psychology Bulletin, 28,* 460–471.

Human Rights Campaign. (2001). *Documenting discrimination.* Washington, DC: Author.

Islam, M. R., & Hewstone, M. (1993). Dimensions of contact as predictors of intergroup anxiety, perceived out-group variability, and out-group attitude: An integrative model. *Personality and Social Psychology Bulletin, 19,* 700–710.

Jennings, J., Geis, F. L., & Brown, V. (1980). Influence of television commercials on women's self-confidence and independent judgment. *Journal of Personality and Social Psychology, 38,* 203–210.

Johnson, J. D., Trawalter, S., & Dovidio, J. F. (2000). Converging interracial consequences of exposure to violent rap music on stereotypical attributions of blacks. *Journal of Experimental Social Psychology, 36,* 233–251.

Jones, J. M. (1997). *Prejudice and racism* (2nd ed.). New York: McGraw-Hill.

Jones, J. T., Pelham, B. W., Mirenberg, M. C., & Hetts, J. J. (2002). Name letter preferences are not merely mere exposure: Implicit egotism as self-regulation. *Journal of Experimental Social Psychology, 38,* 170–177.

Jones, E. E., & Harris, V. A. (1967). The attribution of attitudes. *Journal of Experimental Social Psychology, 3,* 1–24.

Jones, E. E., Wood, G. C., & Quattrone, G. A. (1981). Perceived variability of personal characteristics in in-groups and out-groups: The role of knowledge and evaluation. *Personality and Social Psychology Bulletin, 7,* 523–528.

Judd, C. M., Park, B., Ryan, C. S., Brauer, M., & Kraus, S. (1995). Stereotypes and ethnocentrism: Diverging interethnic perceptions of African American and White American youth. *Journal of Personality and Social Psychology, 69,* 460–481.

Judd, C. M., Park, B., & Wolsko, C. (2001). Measurement of subtyping in stereotype change. *Journal of Experimental Social Psychology, 37,* 325–332.

Katz, D., & Braly, K. (1933). Racial stereotypes of one hundred college students. *Journal of Abnormal and Social Psychology, 28,* 280–290.

Katz, I. (1981). *Stigma: A social psychological analysis.* Hillsdale, NJ: Erlbaum.

Kawakami, K., Young, H., & Dovidio, J. F. (2002). Automatic stereotyping: Category, trait, and behavioral activations. *Personality and Social Psychology Bulletin, 28,* 3–15.

Kenrick, D. T., Gutierres, S. E., & Goldberg, L. L. (1989). Influence of popular erotica on judgments of strangers and mates. *Journal of Experimental Social Psychology, 25,* 159–167.

Kern-Foxworth, M. (1994). *Aunt Jemima, Uncle Ben, and Rastus: Blacks in advertising yesterday, today, and tomorrow.* Westport, CT: Greenwood Press.

Kimball, M. M. (1986). Television and sex-role attitudes. In T. M. Williams (Ed.)., *The impact of television: A natural experiment in three communities.* Orlando, FL: Academic Press.

Kinder, D., & Sears, D. O. (1981). Prejudice and politics: Symbolic racism versus racial threats to the good life. *Journal of Personality and Social Psychology, 40,* 414–431.

Kluger, R. (1976). *Simple justice: The history of* Brown v. Board of Education *and Black America's struggle for equality*. New York: Alfred A. Knopf.

Krebs, A. (1973, September 25). Florida cleric moves. *New York Times*, p. 36.

Krieger, N., & Sidney, S. (1996). Racial discrimination and blood pressure: The CARDIA study of young Black and White adults. *American Journal of Public Health, 86*, 1370–1378.

Krueger, J. (1996). Personal beliefs and cultural stereotypes about racial characteristics. *Journal of Personality and Social Psychology, 71*, 536–548.

Krueger, J., & Clement, R. W. (1994). Memory-based judgments about multiple categories: A revision and extension of Tajfel's accentuation theory. *Journal of Personality and Social Psychology, 67*, 35–47.

Kunda, Z., Davies, P. G., Adams, B. D., & Spencer, S. J. (2002). The dynamic time course of stereotype activation: Activation, dissipation, and resurrection. *Journal of Personality and Social Psychology, 82*, 283–299.

Kunda, Z., & Oleson, K. (1995). Maintaining stereotypes in the face of disconfirmation: Constructing grounds for subtyping deviants. *Journal of Personality and Social Psychology, 68*, 565–579.

Lee, Y.-T., Jussim, L. J., & McCauley, C. R. (Eds.). (1995). *Stereotype accuracy: Toward appreciating group differences*. Washington, DC: American Psychological Association.

Leinbach, M. D., & Fagot, B. I. (1993). Categorical habituation to male and female faces: Gender schematic processing in infancy. *Infant Behavior and Development,16*, 317–332.

Leippe, M. R., & Eisenstadt, D. (1994). Generalization of dissonance reduction: Decreasing prejudice through induced compliance. *Journal of Personality and Social Psychology, 67*, 395–413.

Lerner, M. J. (1980). *The belief in a just world: A fundamental delusion*. New York: Plenum Press.

Levine, R. A., & Campbell, D. T. (1972). *Ethnocentrism: Theories of conflict, ethnic attitudes, and group behavior*. New York: Wiley.

Levy, B. (1996). Improving memory in old age through implicit self-stereotyping. *Journal of Personality and Social Psychology, 71*, 1092–1107.

Linville, P. W. (1998). The heterogeneity of homogeneity. In J. M. Darley & J. Cooper (Eds), *Attribution and social interaction: The legacy of Edward E. Jones* (pp. 423–462). Washington, DC: American Psychological Association.

Linville, P. W., & Fischer, G. W. (1993). Exemplar and abstraction models of perceived group variability and stereotypicality. *Social Cognition, 11*, 92–125.

Lippmann, W. (1922). *Public opinion*. New York: Harcourt, Brace and Company.

Locksley, A., Ortiz, V., & Hepburn, C. (1980). Social categorization and discriminatory behavior: Extinguishing the minimal intergroup effect. *Journal of Personality and Social Psychology, 39*, 773–783.

Ludwig, J. (2000, February 28). Perceptions of Black and White Americans continue to diverge widely on issues of race relations in the U.S. (Poll Release retrieved January 4, 2001, from the web site http://www.gallup.com/poll/releases/pr000228.asp).

Ludy, B. T., Jr., & Crouse, E. M. (2002). The American Psychological Association's response to *Brown v. Board of Education:* The case of Kenneth B. Clark. *American Psychologist, 57*, 38–50.

Macrae, N. C., Stangor, C., & Hewstone, M. (1996). *Stereotypes and stereotyping*. New York: Guilford.

Major, B., Quinton, W. J., McCoy, S. K., & Schmader, T. (2000). Reducing prejudice: The target's perspective. In S. Oskamp (Ed.), *Reducing prejudice and discrimination* (pp. 211–237). Mahwah, NJ: Erlbaum.

Martin, J. L. (2001). *The Authoritarian Personality*, 50 years later: What lessons are there for political psychology? *Political Psychology, 22*, 1–26.

Martin, C. L., Wood, C. H., & Little, J. K. (1990). The development of gender stereotype components. *Child Development, 61*, 1891–1904.

Mauer, M. (1999). *Race to incarcerate*. New York: The New Press.

McBride, C. A. (1998). The discounting principle and attitudes toward victims of HIV infection. *Journal of Applied Social Psychology, 28*, 595–608.

McConahay, J. B. (1986). Modern racism, ambivalence, and the Modern Racism Scale. In J. F. Dovidio and S. L. Gaertner (Eds.), *Prejudice, discrimination, and racism* (pp. 91–125). Orlando, FL: Academic Press.

McConahay, J. B., & Hough, J. C., Jr. (1976). Symbolic racism. *Journal of Social Issues, 32,* 23–45.

McConnell, A. R., & Leibold, J. M. (2001). Relations among the Implicit Association Test, discriminatory behavior, and explicit measures of racial attitudes. *Journal of Experimental Social Psychology, 37,* 435–442.

McFarland, S., Ageyev, V., & Abalakina, M. (1993). The authoritarian personality in the United States and the former Soviet Union: Comparative studies. In W. F. Stone, G. Lederer, & R. Christie (Eds.), *Strength and weakness: The authoritarian personality today* (pp. 199–225). New York: Springer-Verlag.

McGregor, J. (1993). Effectiveness of role playing and antiracist teaching in reducing student prejudice. *Journal of Educational Research, 86,* 215–226.

McNeilly, M. D., Robinson, E. L., Anderson, N. B., Pieper, C. F., Shah, A., & Toth, P. S. (1995). Effects of racist provocation and social support on cardiovascular reactivity in African American women. *International Journal of Behavioral Medicine, 2,* 321–338.

Milburn, M. A., Mather, R., & Conrad, S. D. (2000). The effects of viewing R-rated movie scenes that objectify women on perceptions of date rape. *Sex Roles, 43,* 645–664.

Miller, D. T., Downs, J. S., & Prentice, D. A. (1998). Minimal conditions for the creation of a unit relationship: The social bond between birthdaymates. *European Journal of Social Psychology, 28,* 475–481.

Miner, H. (1956). Body ritual among the Nacirema. *American Anthropologist, 58,* 503–507.

Molotsky, I. (2000, March 23). U.S. is offering record amount in sex-bias suit. *New York Times,* pp. A1, A22.

Mondschein, E. R., Adolph, K. E., & Tamis-LeMonda, C. S. (2000). Gender bias in mothers' expectations about infant crawling. *Journal of Experimental Child Psychology, 77,* 304–316.

Montada, L., & Lerner, M. J. (Eds.). (1998). *Responses to victimizations and belief in a just world.* New York: Plenum Press.

Monteith, M. J. (1993). Self-regulation of prejudiced responses: Implications for progress in prejudice-reduction efforts. *Journal of Personality and Social Psychology, 65,* 469–485.

Monteith, M. J., Deneen, N. E., & Tooman, G. D. (1996). The effect of social norm activation on the expression of opinions concerning gay men and Blacks. *Basic and Applied Social Psychology, 18,* 267–288.

Monteith, M. J., & Voils, C. I. (2001). Exerting control over prejudiced responses. In G. B. Moskowitz (Ed.), *Cognitive social psychology: The Princeton symposium on the legacy and future of social cognition* (pp. 375–388). Mahwah, NJ: Erlbaum.

Morrongiello, B. A., & Dawber, T. (2000). Mothers' responses to sons and daughters engaging in injury-risk behaviors on a playground: Implications for sex differences in injury rates. *Journal of Experimental Child Psychology, 76,* 89–103.

Morrongiello, B. A., Midgett, C., & Stanton, K. (2000). Gender biases in children's appraisals of injury risk and other children's risk-taking behaviors. *Journal of Experimental Child Psychology, 77,* 317–336.

Mullen, B., & Hu, L. (1989). Perceptions of ingroup and outgroup variability: A meta-analytic integration. *Basic and Applied Social Psychology, 10,* 233–252.

Mullen, B., & Johnson, C. (1990). Distinctiveness-based illusory correlations and stereotyping: A meta-analytic integration. *British Journal of Social Psychology, 29,* 11–28.

Nelson, T. D. (2002). *The psychology of prejudice.* Boston, MA: Allyn and Bacon.

Nelson, T. E., Biernat, M. R., & Manis, M. (1990). Everyday base rates (sex stereotypes): Potent and resilient. *Journal of Personality and Social Psychology, 59,* 664–675.

Neuberg, S. L. (1989). The goal of forming accurate impressions during social interactions: Attenuating the impact of negative expectancies. *Journal of Personality and Social Psychology, 56,* 374–386.

Nosek, B. A., Banaji, M., & Greenwald, A. G. (2002). Harvesting implicit group attitudes and beliefs from a demonstration web site. *Group Dynamics: Theory, Research, and Practice, 6,* 101–115.

Oskamp, S. (2000). Multiple paths to reducing prejudice and discrimination. In S. Oskamp (Ed.), *Reducing prejudice and discrimination* (pp. 1–19). Mahwah, NJ: Erlbaum.

Ostrom, T. M., Carpenter, S. L., Sedikides, C., & Li, F. (1993). Differential processing of in-group and out-group information. *Journal of Personality and Social Psychology, 64,* 21–34.

Page, S. (1997). An unobtrusive measure of racial behavior in a university cafeteria. *Journal of Applied Social Psychology, 27,* 2172–2176.

Park, B., & Judd, C. M. (1990). Measures and models of perceived group variability. *Journal of Personality and Social Psychology, 59,* 173–191.

Park, B., & Rothbart, M. (1982). Perception of out-group homogeneity and levels of social categorization: Memory for the subordinate attributes of in-group and out-group members. *Journal of Personality and Social Psychology, 42,* 1051–1068.

Pelham, B. W., Mirenberg, M. C., & Jones, J. T. (2002). Why Susie sells seashells by the seashore: Implicit egotism and major life decisions. *Journal of Personality and Social Psychology, 82,* 469–487.

Pelham, B.W., Jones, J. T., Mirenberg, M. C., & Carvallo, M. (2002). *Implicit egotism: Implications for interpersonal attraction.* Manuscript submitted for publication.

Pendry, L. F., & Macrae, C. N. (1994). Stereotypes and mental life: The case of the motivated but thwarted tactician. *Journal of Experimental Social Psychology, 30,* 303–325.

Pettigrew, T. F. (1958). Personality and sociocultural factors in intergroup attitudes: A cross-national comparison. *Journal of Conflict Resolution, 2,* 29–42.

Pettigrew, T. F. (1979). The ultimate attribution error: Extending Allport's cognitive analysis of prejudice. *Personality and Social Psychology Bulletin, 5,* 461–476.

Pettigrew, T. F., & Tropp, L. R. (2000). Does intergroup contact reduce prejudice? Recent meta-analytic findings. In S. Oskamp (Ed.), *Reducing prejudice and discrimination* (pp. 93–114). Mahwah, NJ: Erlbaum.

Plous, S. (2000). Responding to overt displays of prejudice: A role-playing exercise. *Teaching of Psychology, 27,* 198–200.

Plous, S., & Neptune, D. (1997). Racial and gender biases in magazine advertising: A content-analytic study. *Psychology of Women Quarterly, 21,* 627–644.

Plous, S., & Williams, T. (1995). Racial stereotypes from the days of American slavery: A continuing legacy. *Journal of Applied Social Psychology, 25,* 795–817.

Pratto, F., Sidanius, J., Stallworth, L. M., & Malle, B. F. (1994). Social dominance orientation: A personality variable predicting social and political attitudes. *Journal of Personality and Social Psychology, 67,* 741–763.

Rabbie, J. M., & Horwitz, M. (1969). Arousal of ingroup-outgroup bias by a chance win or loss. *Journal of Personality and Social Psychology, 13,* 269–277.

Richards, Z., & Hewstone, M. (2001). Subtyping and subgrouping: Processes for the prevention and promotion of stereotype change. *Personality and Social Psychology Review, 5,* 52–73.

Roehling, M. V. (1999). Weight-based discrimination in employment: Psychological and legal aspects. *Personnel Psychology, 52,* 969–1016.

Rokeach, M. (1971). Long-range experimental modification of values, attitudes, and behavior. *American Psychologist, 26,* 453–459.

Ross, L. (1977). The intuitive psychologist and his shortcomings: Distortions in the attribution process. In L. Berkowitz (Ed.), *Advances in experimental social psychology* (vol. 10, pp. 173–220). New York: Academic Press.

Rothbart, M., Davis-Stitt, C., & Hill, J. (1997). Effects of arbitrarily placed category boundaries on similarity judgments. *Journal of Experimental Social Psychology, 33,* 122–145.

Rudman, L. A., Ashmore, R. D., & Gary, M. L. (2001). "Unlearning" automatic biases: The malleability of implicit prejudice and stereotypes. *Journal of Personality and Social Psychology, 81,* 856–868.

Rudman, L. A., & Borgida, E. (1995). The afterglow of construct accessibility: The behavioral consequences of priming men to view women as sexual objects. *Journal of Experimental Social Psychology, 31,* 493–517.

Ruggiero, K. M., & Taylor, D. M. (1997). Why minority group members perceive or do not perceive the discrimination that confronts them: The role of self-esteem and perceived control. *Journal of Personality and Social Psychology, 72,* 373–389.

Schuller, R. A., Smith, V. L., & Olson, J. M. (1994). Jurors' decisions in trials of battered women who kill: The role of prior beliefs and expert testimony. *Journal of Applied Social Psychology, 24,* 316–337.

Sears, D. O. (1988). Symbolic racism. In P. A. Katz and D. A. Taylor (Eds.), *Eliminating racism: Profiles in controversy* (pp. 53–84). New York: Plenum.

Shelton, J. N. (2000). A reconceptualization of how we study issues of racial prejudice. *Personality and Social Psychology Review, 4,* 374–390.

Sherif, M., Harvey, O. J., White, B. J., Hood, W. R., & Sherif, C. W. (1988). *The Robbers Cave experiment: Intergroup conflict and cooperation.* Middletown, CT: Wesleyan University Press.

Shih, M., Pittinsky, T. L., & Ambady, N. (1999). Stereotype susceptibility: Identity salience and shifts in quantitative performance. *Psychological Science, 10,* 80–83.

Sidanius, J., Levin, S., Liu, J., & Pratto, F. (2000). Social dominance orientation, anti-egalitarianism and the political psychology of gender: An extension and cross-cultural replication. *European Journal of Social Psychology, 30,* 41–67.

Sidanius, J., & Pratto, F. (1999). *Social dominance: An intergroup theory of social hierarchy and oppression.* Cambridge, England: Cambridge University Press.

Simon, B. (1992). The perception of ingroup and outgroup homogeneity: Reintroducing the intergroup context. In W. Stroebe and M. Hewstone (Eds.), *European review of social psychology* (vol. 3, pp. 1–30). New York: John Wiley & Sons.

Simon, B., & Pettigrew, T. F. (1990). Social identity and perceived group homogeneity: Evidence for the ingroup homogeneity effect. *European Journal of Social Psychology, 20,* 269–286.

Sinclair, L., & Kunda, Z. (1999). Reactions to a Black professional: Motivated inhibition and activation of conflicting stereotypes. *Journal of Personality and Social Psychology, 77,* 885–904.

Skrypnek, B. J., & Snyder, M. (1980). On the self-perpetuating nature of stereotypes about women and men. *Journal of Experimental Social Psychology, 18,* 277–291.

Smedley, B. D., Stith, A. Y., & Nelson, A. R. (Eds.). (2002). *Unequal treatment: Confronting racial and ethnic disparities in health care.* Washington, DC: National Academy Press.

Snyder, M., Tanke, E. D., & Berscheid, E. (1977). Social perception and interpersonal behavior: On the self-fulfilling nature of social stereotypes. *Journal of Personality and Social Psychology, 35,* 656–666.

Spencer, S. J., Steele, C. M., & Quinn, D. M. (1999). Stereotype threat and women's math performance. *Journal of Experimental Social Psychology, 35,* 4–28.

Stangor, C., Segrist, G. B., & Jost, J. T. (2001). Changing racial beliefs by providing consensus information. *Personality and Social Psychology Bulletin, 27,* 486–496.

Steele, C. (1997). A threat in the air: How stereotypes shape intellectual identity and performance. *American Psychologist, 52,* 613–629.

Steele, C., & Aronson, J. (1995). Stereotype threat and the intellectual test performance of African Americans. *Journal of Personality and Social Psychology, 69,* 797–811.

Stephan, W. G. (1986). The effects of school desegregation: An evaluation 30 years after *Brown.* In M. J. Saks & L. Saxe (Eds.), *Advances in applied social psychology* (vol. 3, pp. 181–206). Hillsdale, NJ: Erlbaum.

Stephan, W. G., & Finlay, K. (1999). The role of empathy in improving intergroup relations. *Journal of Social Issues, 55,* 729–743.

Stone, J., Lynch, C. I., Sjomeling, M., & Darley, J. M. (1999). Stereotype threat effects on Black and White athletic performance. *Journal of Personality and Social Psychology, 77,* 1213–1227.

Swann, W. B., Jr., Langlois, J. H., & Gilbert, L. A. (Eds.). (1999). *Sexism and stereotypes in modern society: The gender science of Janet Taylor Spence.* Washington, DC: American Psychological Association.

Swim, J. K., Aikin, K. J., Hall, W. S., & Hunter, B. A. (1995). Sexism and racism: Old-fashioned and modern prejudices. *Journal of Personality and Social Psychology, 68,* 199–214.

Swim, J. K., & Sanna, L. J. (1996). He's skilled, she's lucky: A meta-analysis of observers' attributions for women's and men's successes and failures. *Personality and Social Psychology Bulletin, 22,* 507–519.

Swim, J. K., & Stangor, C. (Eds.). (1998). *Prejudice: The target's perspective.* San Diego, CA: Academic Press.

Tajfel, H. (1970, November). Experiments in intergroup discrimination. *Scientific American,* pp. 96–102.

Tajfel, H. (1981). *Human groups and social categories.* Cambridge: Cambridge University Press.

Tajfel, H., & Turner, J. C. (1986). The social identity theory of intergroup behavior. In S. Worchel and W. G. Austin (Eds.), *Psychology of intergroup relations* (2nd ed., pp. 7–24). Chicago, IL: Nelson-Hall.

Tajfel, H., & Wilkes, A. L. (1963). Classification and quantitative judgement. *British Journal of Psychology, 54,* 101–114.

Tavris, C. (1992). *The mismeasure of woman.* New York: Simon & Schuster.

Taylor, D. M., & Jaggi, V. (1974). Ethnocentrism and causal attribution in a south Indian context. *Journal of Cross-Cultural Psychology, 5,* 162–171.

Taylor, D. M., Wright, S. C., Moghaddam, F. M., & Lalonde, R. N. (1990). The personal/group discrimination discrepancy: Perceiving my group, but not myself, to be a target for discrimination. *Personality and Social Psychology Bulletin, 16,* 254–262.

Taylor, D. M., Wright, S. C., & Porter, L. E. (1994). Dimensions of perceived discrimination: The personal/group discrimination discrepancy. In M. P. Zanna & J. M. Olson (Eds.), *The psychology of prejudice: The Ontario Symposium, Volume 7* (pp. 233–255). Hillsdale, NJ: Erlbaum.

Truell, P. (1997, November 18). Smith Barney accord seen in bias case. *New York Times,* pp. D1, D13.

Turner, M. A., Fix, M., & Struyk, R. J. (1991). *Opportunities denied, opportunities diminished: Racial discrimination in hiring.* Washington, DC: Urban Institute Press.

Tylor, E. B. (1881). *Anthropology: An introduction to the study of man and civilization.* New York: D. Appleton and Company.

Weber, R., & Crocker, J. (1983). Cognitive processes in the revision of stereotypic beliefs. *Journal of Personality and Social Psychology, 45,* 961–977.

Wheeler, C. G. (1993, October). 30 years beyond "I have a dream." *Gallup Poll Monthly,* pp. 2–10.

Wheeler, S. C., Jarvis, W. B. G., & Petty, R. E. (2001). Think unto others: The self-destructive impact of negative racial stereotypes. *Journal of Experimental Social Psychology, 37,* 173–180.

Wheeler, S. C., & Petty, R. E. (2001). The effects of stereotype activation on behavior: A review of possible mechanisms. *Psychological Bulletin, 127,* 797–826.

Wilder, D. A. (1981). Perceiving persons as a group: Categorization and intergroup relations. In D. L. Hamilton (Ed.), *Cognitive processes in stereotyping and intergroup behavior* (pp. 213–257). Hillsdale, NJ: Erlbaum.

Williams, D. R., Yu, Y., Jackson, J. S., & Anderson, N. B. (1997). Racial differences in physical and mental health. *Journal of Health Psychology, 2,* 335–351.

Wittenbrink, B., Judd, C. M., & Park, B. (1997). Evidence for racial prejudice at the implicit level and its relationship with questionnaire measures. *Journal of Personality and Social Psychology, 72,* 262–274.

Yinger, J. (1995). *Closed doors, opportunities lost: The continuing costs of housing discrimination.* New York: Russell Sage Foundation.

WHO IS BLACK? ONE NATION'S DEFINITION

F. JAMES DAVIS

In a taped interview conducted by a blind, black anthropologist, a black man nearly ninety years old said: "Now you must understand that this is just a name we have. I am not black and you are not black either, if you go by the evidence of your eyes. . . . Many of the people I see who are thought of as black could just as well be white in their appearance. Many of the white people I see are black as far as I can tell by the way they look. Now, that's it for looks. Looks don't mean much. The thing that makes us different is how we think. What we believe is important, the ways we look at life" (Gwaltney, 1980:96).

How does a person get defined as a black, both socially and legally, in the United States? What is the nation's rule for who is black, and how did it come to be? And so what? Don't we all know who is black, and isn't the most important issue what opportunities the group has? Let us start with some experiences of three well-known American blacks—actress and beauty pageant winner Vanessa Williams, U.S. Representative Adam Clayton Powell, Jr., and entertainer Lena Horne.

For three decades after the first Miss America Pageant in 1921, black women were barred from competing. The first black winner was Vanessa Williams of Millwood, New York, crowned Miss America 1984. In the same year the first runner-up—Suzette Charles of Mays Landing, New Jersey—was also black. The viewing public was charmed by the television images and magazine pictures of the beautiful and musically talented Williams, but many people were also puzzled. Why was she being called black when she appeared to be white? Suzette Charles, whose ancestry appeared to be more European than African, at least looked like many of the "lighter blacks." Notoriety followed when Vanessa Williams resigned because of the impending publication of some nude photographs of her taken before the pageant, and Suzette Charles became Miss America for the balance of 1984. Beyond the troubling question of whether these young women could have won if they had looked "more black," the publicity dramatized the nation's definition of a black person.

Some blacks complained that the Rev. Adam Clayton Powell, Jr., was so light that he was a stranger in their midst. In the words of Roi Ottley, "He was white to all appearances, having blue eyes, an aquiline nose, and light, almost blond, hair" (1943:220), yet he became a bold, effective black leader—first as minister of the Abyssinian Baptist Church of Harlem, then as a New York city councilman, and finally as a U.S. congressman from the state of New York. Early in his activist career he led 6,000 blacks in a march on New York City Hall. He used his power in Congress to fight for civil rights legislation and other black causes.

In his autobiography, Powell recounts some experiences with racial classification in his youth that left a lasting impression on him. During Powell's freshman year at Colgate University, his roommate did not know that he was a black until his father, Adam Clayton Powell, Sr., was invited to give a chapel talk on Negro rights and problems, after which the roommate announced that because Adam was a Negro they could no longer be roommates or friends.

Another experience that affected Powell deeply occurred one summer during his Colgate years. He was working as a bellhop at a summer resort in Manchester, Vermont, when Abraham Lincoln's aging son Robert was a guest there. Robert Lincoln disliked blacks so much that he refused to let them wait on him or touch his luggage, car, or any of his possessions. Blacks who did got their knuckles whacked with his cane. To the great amusement of the other bellhops, Lincoln took young Powell for a white man and accepted his services (Powell, 1971:31–33).

Lena Horne's parents were both very light in color and came from black upper-middle-class families in Brooklyn (Horne and Schickel, 1965; Buckley, 1986). Lena lived with her father's parents until she was about seven years old. Her grandfather was very light and blue-eyed. Her fair-skinned grandmother was the daughter of a slave woman and her white owner, from the family of John C. Calhoun, well-known defender of slavery. One of her father's great-grandmothers was a Blackfoot Indian, to whom Lena Horne has attributed her somewhat coppery skin color. One of her mother's grandmothers was a French-speaking black woman from Senegal and never a slave. Her mother's father was a "Portuguese Negro," and two women in his family had passed as white and become entertainers.

Lena Horne's parents had separated, and when she was seven her entertainer mother began placing her in a succession of homes in different states. Her favorite place was in the home of her Uncle Frank, her father's brother, a red-haired, blue-eyed teacher in a black school in Georgia. The black children in that community asked her why she was so light and called her a "yellow bastard." She learned that when satisfactory evidence of respectable black parents is lacking, being light-skinned implies having an underclass white parent and is thus a disgrace in the black community. When her mother married a white Cuban, Lena also learned that blacks can be very hostile to the white spouse, especially when the "black" mate is very light. At this time she began to blame the confused color line for her childhood troubles. She later endured hostility from blacks and whites alike when her own second marriage, to white composer-arranger Lennie Hayton, was finally made public in 1950 after three years of keeping it secret.

The One–Drop Rule Defined

As the above cases illustrate, to be considered black in the United States not even half of one's ancestry must be African black. But will one-fourth do, or one-eighth, or less? The nation's answer to the question "Who is black?" has long been that a black is any person with *any* known African black ancestry (Myrdal, 1944:113–18; Berry and Tischler, 1978:97–98; Williamson, 1980:1–2). This definition reflects the long experience with slavery and later with Jim Crow segregation. In the South it became known as the "one-drop rule," meaning that a single drop of "black blood" makes a person a black. It is also known as the "one black ancestor rule," some courts have called it the "traceable amount rule," and anthropologists call it the "hypo-descent rule," meaning that racially mixed persons are assigned the status of the subordinate group (Harris, 1964:56). This definition emerged from the American South to become the nation's definition, generally accepted by whites and blacks alike (Bahr, Chadwick, and Stauss, 1979:27–28). As we shall see, this American cultural definition of blacks is taken for granted as readily by judges, affirmative action officers, and black protesters as it is by Ku Klux Klansmen.

Let us not be confused by terminology. At present the usual statement of the one-drop rule is in terms of "black blood" or black ancestry, while not so long ago it referred to "Negro blood" or ancestry. The term "black" rapidly replaced "Negro" in general usage in the United States as the black power movement peaked at the end of the 1960s, but the black and Negro populations are the same. Terms such as "African black," "unmixed Negro," and "all black" are used here to refer to unmixed blacks descended from African populations.

We must also pay attention to the terms "mulatto" and "colored." The term "mulatto" was originally used to mean the offspring of a "pure African Negro" and a "pure white." Although the root meaning of mulatto, in Spanish, is "hybrid," "mulatto" came to include the children of unions between whites and so-called "mixed Negroes." For example, Booker T. Washington and Frederick Douglass, with slave mothers and white fathers, were referred to as mulattoes (Bennett, 1962:255). To whatever extent their mothers were part white, these men were more than half white. Douglass was evidently part Indian as well, and he looked it (Preston, 1980:9–10). Washington had reddish hair and gray eyes. At the time of the American Revolution, many of the founding fathers had some very light slaves, including some who appeared to be white. The term "colored" seemed for a time to refer only to mulattoes, especially lighter ones, but later it became a euphemism for darker Negroes, even including unmixed blacks.

A quadroon is one-fourth African black and thus easily classed as black in the United States, yet three of this person's four grandparents are white. An octoroon has seven white great-grandparents out of eight and usually looks white or almost so. Most parents of black American children in recent decades have themselves been racially mixed, but often the fractions get complicated because the earlier details of the mixing were obscured generations ago. Like so many white Americans, black people are forced to speculate about some of the fractions—one-eighth this, three-sixteenths that, and so on.

Black Leaders, But Predominantly White

Many of the nation's black leaders have been of predominantly white ancestry. During slave times, Robert Purvis was the son of a wealthy white Charleston merchant and a free mulatto woman. His father sent him north to be educated at Amherst College and then to live a life of leisure near Philadelphia. He could have passed as white, but instead helped form the American Anti-Slavery Society and became an effective abolitionist leader (Bennett, 1962:252). During the Reconstruction period after the Civil War, all but three of the twenty black congressmen and two black senators in Washington, D.C., were mulattoes, and some were very light. W. E. B. Du Bois—sociology professor, critic of Booker T. Washington's view that change toward racial equality had to be gradual, and founder in 1910 of the National Association for the Advancement of Colored People (NAACP)—had French, Dutch, and African ancestors (Bennett, 1962:279).

Walter White, president of the NAACP from 1931 to 1955, was estimated by anthropologists to be no more than one sixty-fourth African black. Both his parents could have passed as white (White, 1948:13; Cannon, 1956:13). When he told whites he was black, they would often say "Are you sure?" They could not understand why a white man wanted to be black (White, 1948:3–4). He had fair skin, fair hair, and blue eyes, yet he chose not to pass as white. He had been raised as a segregated Negro in the Deep South and had experienced white discrimination and violence.

In a biography of Walter White, his second wife, a brunette white, reveals their experiences as an "interracial couple" (Cannon, 1956:14). When they toured the world with an American goodwill mission and were referred to as an interracial couple, puzzled people often asked White how he happened to marry a "colored" woman. The black press was outraged by this marriage (Cannon, 1956:12–13), as it had been decades earlier by the marriage of Frederick Douglass to a white and by the second marriage of Lena Horne. Although the genetic crossing in White's marriage was minute at most, he had married across the social group barrier, outside the black community.

Another major black leader of the twentieth century, A. Philip Randolph, was predominantly white. His mother and his mother's father both could pass as white (Anderson, 1972:31). As a boy, Randolph shared his minister father's outrage when the Jim Crow laws were passed in Jacksonville, Florida, depriving blacks of political participation and segregating the library, streetcars, and other public facilities. In New York, Randolph became a leading black editor. He was chiefly responsible for pressuring President Franklin Roosevelt into signing the World War II order against racial segregation in war industries and for getting President Harry Truman to sign the order in 1948 to desegregate the U.S. armed forces. He also organized marches on Washington, D.C., including the gigantic rally in 1963 at which the Rev. Dr. Martin Luther King, Jr., gave his "I have a dream" speech. We may note also that King had an Irish grandmother on his father's side and apparently some American Indian ancestry (Bennett, 1965:18).

Plessy, Phipps, and Other Challenges in the Courts

Homer Plessy was the plaintiff in the 1896 precedent-setting "separate-but-equal" case of *Plessy v. Ferguson* (163 U.S. 537). This case challenged the Jim

Crow statute that required racially segregated seating on trains in interstate commerce in the state of Louisiana. The U.S. Supreme Court quickly dispensed with Plessy's contention that because he was only one-eighth Negro and could pass as white he was entitled to ride in the seats reserved for whites. Without ruling directly on the definition of a Negro, the Supreme Court briefly took what is called "judicial notice" of what it assumed to be common knowledge: that a Negro or black is any person with any black ancestry. (Judges often take explicit "judicial notice" not only of scientific or scholarly conclusions, or of opinion surveys or other systematic investigations, but also of something they just assume to be so, including customary practices or common knowledge.) This has consistently been the ruling in the federal courts, and often when the black ancestry was even less than one-eighth. The separate-but-equal doctrine established in the Plessy case is no longer the law, as a result of the judicial and legislative successes of the civil rights movement, but the nation's legal definition of who is black remains unchanged.

State courts have generally upheld the one-drop rule. For instance, in a 1948 Mississippi case a young man, Davis Knight, was sentenced to five years in jail for violating the antimiscegenation statute. Less than one-sixteenth black, Knight said he was not aware that he had any black lineage, but the state proved his great-grandmother was a slave girl. In some states the operating definition of black has been limited by statute to particular fractions, yet the social definition—the one-drop rule—has generally prevailed in case of doubt. Mississippi, Missouri, and five other states have had the criterion of one-eighth. Virginia changed from one-fourth to one-eighth in 1910, then in 1930 forbade white intermarriage with a person with any black ancestry. Persons in Virginia who are one-fourth or more Indian and less than one-sixteenth African black are defined as Indians while on the reservation but as blacks when they leave (Berry, 1965:26). While some states have had general race classification statutes, at least for a time, others have legislated a definition of black only for particular purposes, such as marriage or education. In a few states there have even been varying definitions for different situations (Mangum, 1940:38–48). All states require a designation of race on birth certificates, but there are no clear guidelines to help physicians and midwives do the classifying.

Louisiana's latest race classification statute became highly controversial and was finally repealed in 1983 (Trillin, 1986:77). Until 1970, a Louisiana statute had embraced the one-drop rule, defining a Negro as anyone with a "trace of black ancestry." This law was challenged in court a number of times from the 1920s on, including an unsuccessful attempt in 1957 by boxer Ralph Dupas, who asked to be declared white so that a law banning "interracial sports" (since repealed) would not prevent him from boxing in the state. In 1970 a lawsuit was brought on behalf of a child whose ancestry was allegedly only one two-hundred-fifty-sixth black, and the legislature revised its law. The 1970 Louisiana statute defined a black as someone whose ancestry is more than one thirty-second black (La. Rev. Stat. 42:267). Adverse publicity about this law was widely disseminated during the Phipps trial in 1983 (discussed below), filed as *Jane Doe v. State of Louisiana*. This case was decided in a district court in May 1983, and in June the legislature abolished its one thirty-second statute and gave parents the right to designate the race of newborns, and even to change classifications on birth certificates if they can prove the child is white by a "preponderance of the evidence." However, the new statute in 1983 did not abolish the "traceable amount rule" (the one-drop rule), as demonstrated by the outcomes when the Phipps decision was appealed to higher courts in 1985 and 1986.

The history in the Phipps (Jane Doe) case goes as far back as 1770, when a French planter named Jean Gregoire Guillory took his wife's slave, Margarita, as his mistress (Model, 1983:3–4). More than two centuries and two decades later, their great-great-great-great-granddaughter, Susie Guillory Phipps, asked the Louisiana courts to change the classification on her deceased parents' birth certificates to "white" so she and her brothers and sisters could be designated white. They all looked white, and some were blue-eyed blonds. Mrs. Susie Phipps had been denied a passport because she had checked "white" on her application although her birth certificate designated her race as "colored." This designation was based on information supplied by a midwife, who presumably relied on the parents or on the family's status in the community. Mrs. Phipps claimed that this classification came as a shock, since she had always thought she was white, had lived as white, and had twice married as white. Some of her relatives, however, gave depositions saying they considered themselves "colored," and the lawyers for the state claimed to have proof that Mrs. Phipps was three-thirty-seconds black (Trillin, 1986:62–63, 71–74). That was more than enough "blackness" for the district court in 1983 to declare her parents, and thus Mrs. Phipps and her siblings, to be legally black.

In October and again in December 1985, the state's Fourth Circuit Court of Appeals upheld the district court's decision, saying that no one can change the racial designation of his or her parents or anyone else's (479 So. 2d 369). Said the majority of the court in its opinion: "That appellants might today describe themselves as white does not prove error in a document which designates their parents as colored" (479 So. 2d 371). Of course, if the parents' designation as "colored" cannot be disturbed, their descendants must be defined as black by the "traceable amount rule." The court also concluded that the preponderance of the evidence clearly showed that the Guillory parents were "colored." Although noting expert testimony to the effect that the race of an individual cannot be determined with scientific accuracy, the court said the law of racial designation is not based on science, that "individual race designations are purely social and cultural perceptions and the evidence conclusively proves those subjective perspectives were correctly recorded at the time the appellants' birth certificates were recorded" (479 So. 2d 372). At the rehearing in December 1985, the appellate court also affirmed the necessity of designating race on birth certificates for public health, affirmative action, and other important public programs and held that equal protection of the law has not been denied so long as the designation is treated as confidential.

When this case was appealed to the Louisiana Supreme Court in 1986, that court declined to review the decision, saying only that the court "concurs in the denial for the reasons assigned by the court of appeals on rehearing" (485 So. 2d 60). In December 1986 the U.S. Supreme Court was equally brief in stating its reason for refusing to review the decision: "The appeal is dismissed for want of a substantial federal question" (107 Sup. Ct. Reporter, interim ed. 638). Thus, both the final court of appeals in Louisiana and the highest court of the United States saw no reason to disturb the application of the one-drop rule in the lawsuit brought by Susie Guillory Phipps and her siblings.

Census Enumeration of Blacks

When the U.S. Bureau of the Census enumerates blacks (always counted as Negroes until 1980), it does not use a scientific definition, but rather the one accepted by the general public and by the courts. The Census Bureau counts what the nation wants counted. Although various operational instructions have been tried, the definition of black used by the Census Bureau has been the nation's cultural and legal definition: all persons with any known black ancestry. Other nations define and count blacks differently, so international comparisons of census data on blacks can be extremely misleading. For example, Latin American countries generally count as black only unmixed African blacks, those only slightly mixed, and the very poorest mulattoes. If they used the U.S. definition, they would count far more blacks than they do, and if Americans used their definition, millions in the black community in the United States would be counted either as white or as "coloreds" of different descriptions, not as black.

Instructions to our census enumerators in 1840, 1850, and 1860 provided "mulatto" as a category but did not define the term. In 1870 and 1880, mulattoes were officially defined to include "quadroons, octoroons, and all persons having any perceptible trace of African blood." In 1890 enumerators were told to record the *exact* proportion of the "African blood," again relying on visibility. In 1900 the Census Bureau specified that "pure Negroes" be counted separately from mulattoes, the latter to mean "all persons with some trace of black blood." In 1920 the mulatto category was dropped, and black was defined to mean any person with any black ancestry, as it has been ever since.

In 1960 the practice of self-definition began, with the head of household indicating the race of its members. This did not seem to introduce any noticeable fluctuation in the number of blacks, thus indicating that black Americans generally apply the one-drop rule to themselves. One exception is that Spanish-speaking Americans who have black ancestry but were considered white, or some designation other than black, in their place of origin generally reject the one-drop rule if they can. American Indians with some black ancestry also generally try to avoid the rule, but those who leave the reservation are often treated as black.

No other ethnic population in the nation, including those with visibly non-caucasoid features, is defined and counted according to a one-drop rule. For example, persons whose ancestry is one-fourth or less American Indian are not generally defined as Indian unless they want to be. The same implicit rule appears to apply to Japanese Americans, Filipinos, or other peoples from East Asian nations and also to Mexican Americans who have Central American Indian ancestry, as a large majority do. For instance, a person whose ancestry is one-eighth Chinese is not defined as just Chinese, or East Asian, or a member of the mongoloid race. The United States certainly does not apply a one-drop rule to its white ethnic populations either, which include both national and religious groups. Americans do not insist that an American with a small fraction of Polish ancestry be classified as a Pole, or that someone with a single remote Greek ancestor be designated Greek, or that someone with any trace of Jewish lineage is a Jew and nothing else.

Uniqueness of the One–Drop Rule

Not only does the one-drop rule apply to no other group than American blacks, but apparently the rule is unique in that it is found only in the United States and not in any other nation in the world. In fact, definitions of who is black vary quite sharply from country to country, and for this reason people in other countries often express consternation about our definition. James Baldwin relates a revealing incident that occurred in 1956 at the Conference of Negro-African Writers and Artists held in Paris. The head of the delegation of writers and artists from the United States was John Davis. The French chairperson introduced Davis and then asked him why he considered himself Negro, since he certainly did not look like one. Baldwin wrote, "He *is* a Negro, of course, from the remarkable legal point of view which obtains in the United States, but more importantly, as he tried to make clear to his interlocutor, he was a Negro by choice and by depth of involvement—by experience, in fact" (1962:19).

The phenomenon known as "passing as white" is difficult to explain in other countries or to foreign students. Typical questions are: "Shouldn't Americans say that a person who is passing as white *is* white, or nearly all white, and has previously been passing as black?" or "To be consistent, shouldn't you say that someone who is one-eighth white is passing as black?" Those who ask such questions need to realize that "passing" is much more a social phenomenon than a biological one, reflecting the nation's unique definition of what makes a person black. The concept of "passing" rests on the one-drop rule and on folk beliefs about race and miscegenation, not on biological or historical fact.

The definition of a black person as one with any trace at all of black African ancestry is inextricably woven into the history of the United States. It incorporates beliefs once used to justify slavery and later used to buttress the castelike Jim Crow system of segregation. Developed in the South, the definition of "Negro" spread and became the nation's social and legal definition. Because blacks are defined according to the one-drop rule, they are a socially constructed category in which there is wide variation in racial traits.

The one-drop rule has long been taken for granted throughout the United States by whites and blacks alike. Most Americans seem unaware that this definition of blacks is extremely unusual in other countries, perhaps even unique to the United States, and that Americans define no other minority group in a similar way. The personnel officer, the census taker, the judge, and the black political caucus leader all readily classify a predominantly white mulatto as a black person. Arbitrary and contradictory as our one-drop rule is, it is deeply embedded in the social structures and cultures of both the black and the white communities in the United States and strongly resistant to change.

Miscegenation and Beliefs

Much of the rhetoric advanced in the 1950s and 1960s against desegregating the public schools and other public facilities in the American South featured the assertion that racial integration would destroy the purity of the races. In a speech in 1954, U.S. Representative John Bell Williams of Mississippi referred to the day the U.S. Supreme Court announced its decision in the case of *Brown v. Board of Education of Topeka, Kansas* (347 U.S. 483) as Black Monday. Then, in a book called *Black Monday,* Yale-educated Circuit Court Judge Thomas Brady of Mississippi contended that the *Brown* decision would lead to "the tragedy of miscegenation." He wrote fiercely that he and the South would fight and die for the principles of racial purity and white womanhood rather than follow the Supreme Court's decision. He maintained that God opposes racial mixing and that Southern whites had a God-given right to keep their "blood" white and pure (Blaustein and Ferguson, 1957:7–8). It was, of course, centuries too late to keep the races pure in the South.

The vast majority of Americans defined as blacks are not pure descendants of the slaves from Africa, but racially mixed (Bennett, 1962: chap. 10). Thus, members of the black community, as defined by the one-drop rule, vary all the way from a diminishing number of unmixed African blacks to those who appear to be of purely European origin. At the same time, only traces of the many different tribal cultures of the people captured in sub-Saharan Africa remain. The slaves came from an extensive area of West and West Central Africa from Senegal to Angola, from coastal and inland regions, from many different tribes, from different religions, and speaking a variety of languages. Today's black culture and sense of identity are largely the products of the centuries of experience in the United States, along with a few African survivals.

As Gunnar Myrdal (1944) pointed out, it is the social and legal definition of the black population in the United States that has counted, not its scientific accuracy. However, this socially constructed category has meaning only in relation to the realities of race and miscegenation. In order to understand the emergence of the one-drop rule and its implications, then, it is necessary to explore some of the complexities of the process of miscegenation. This requires at least a brief and nontechnical consideration of the scientific criteria used in the physical anthropology of race.

We must first distinguish racial traits from cultural traits, since they are so often confused with each other. As defined in physical anthropology and biology, *races* are categories of human beings based on average differences in physical traits that are transmitted by the genes not by blood. *Culture* is a shared pattern of behavior and beliefs that are learned and transmitted through social communication. An *ethnic* group is a group with a sense of cultural identity, such as Czech or Jewish Americans, but it may also be a racially distinctive group. A group that is racially distinctive in a society may be an ethnic group as well, but not necessarily. Although racially mixed, most blacks in the United States are physically distinguishable from whites, but they are also an ethnic group because of the distinctive culture they have developed within the general American framework.

Racial Classification and Miscegenation

The system of racial classification noted for discussion here is based on the measurement of visible traits of human anatomy, an approach that has been supplanted by research on the frequency of certain gene markers. Earlier physical anthropologists found hair form, nose shape, and head shape to be the most dependable criteria for establishing reasonably discrete racial categories, although some other traits were found to be valuable for classifying subraces. If a cross-section of a strand of hair is round, the hair will be straight; if it is flat, the hair will be extremely curly; if it is oval-shaped the hair will be wavy. The nasal index (the ratio of the length of the nose to its width) provides the narrow, wide, and intermediate types. The cephalic index (the ratio of the length of the head to its width) yields round-headed, long-headed, and intermediate types. Lip eversion and the color of hair, eyes, and skin have proven to be only somewhat reliable for racial classification, and still other traits, such as body type, even less reliable.

Using mainly hair form, nose shape, and head shape, A. L. Kroeber (1948:140) arrived at three major races: caucasoid, mongoloid, and negroid, commonly referred to as white, yellow, and black. On the average, he found caucasoids to have the longest heads and mongoloids the roundest; mongoloids the straightest hair and negroids the most tightly curled; caucasoids the narrowest noses and negroids the broadest. Comparing just negroids and caucasoids, he found that the former usually have rounder heads, frizzier hair, and broader noses. Other anatomical classifiers have found four or five races, and some have refined the subgroups and ended up with many races (Hooton, 1948; Coon, 1962; Garn, 1965). More recent researchers prefer to focus on the frequency of traits in different human populations and to reject the assumption that there are pure races.

Although negroids are very dark, skin color is poorly correlated with Kroeber's more dependable racial criteria, largely because of the dark-skinned peoples of India, Pakistan, Bangladesh, and some contiguous areas. Physical anthropologists believe the dark skin color is explained by variation and selective adaptation of that trait to climate, not by genetic influence from African populations. Thus, there is wide variation in skin color among Kroeber's subgroups of the caucasoid race, which are Nordic, Alpine,

Mediterranean, Hindu (the "dark whites"), and the Ainu of the Japanese island of Hokkaido.

Efforts to improve on racial classification by using blood types have not proved very successful. The major blood types have been found to have different frequencies among Kroeber's caucasoid, mongoloid, and negroid groups. However, all the blood types are found in all of Kroeber's three races, and the differences are not great. Put another way, the correlation between blood type and external anatomical traits is small. Sickle-cell anemia is a genetic, blood-connected factor that illustrates the dubious relationship between blood type and race. This disease is frequent among American blacks and the West African peoples from which slaves came, but it is also frequent among non-negroid populations in Greece, Southern India, and some other areas of the world. In fact, in the past the sickle-cell trait was found in regions that had high rates of malaria, and it appears to have been an adaptive response to that disease (Newman, 1973:266–67).

What are the overall results of centuries of miscegenation in the United States? At least three-fourths of all people defined as American blacks have some white ancestry, and some estimates run well above 90 percent. The blacks with no white lineage are mainly in the more isolated, rural areas of the Deep South, notably in South Carolina. As many as one-fourth of all American blacks have some American Indian ancestry, and a great many people classed as Indians have some black background (Pettigrew, 1975:xiii). Thus, the color spectrum among the black population ranges from ebony to lighter than most whites, and the other racial traits show a similar range of variation.

In terms of gene frequencies, apparently somewhere between one-fifth and one-fourth of the genes of the American black population are from white ancestors. The national estimates by physical anthropologists have ranged from about 20 percent to 31 percent, with recent opinion apparently inclining toward the lower figure. The estimates vary considerably for different regions, with Northern blacks having the larger percentages of "white genes." Keep in mind that most American blacks throughout the nation have some "white genes," but that there are regional and local variations in the estimated amount. For example, it has been estimated that in Detroit 25 percent of the genes in the black population are "white genes"; in Oakland, California, 22 percent; in New York City, 19 percent; in two counties of Georgia, 11 percent; and in Charleston, South Carolina, 4 percent (Reed, 1969:765).

It has been estimated that about 1 percent of the genes of the white population of the United States are from African ancestors. Estimates ranging up to 5 percent, and suggestions that up to one-fifth of the white population have some genes from black ancestors, are probably far too high. If these last figures were correct, the majority of Americans with some black ancestry would be known and counted as whites! The peak years for passing as white were probably from 1880 to 1925, with perhaps from 10,000 to 25,000 crossing the color line each year, although such estimates are most likely inflated. By 1940 the annual number had apparently declined to no more than 2,500 to 2,750 a year (Burma, 1946:1822; Williamson, 1980:103). At least since the

1920s, apparently, most mulattoes who could pass have remained in the black population.

A further genetic point is very important and has a bearing especially on the question of passing as white. Genes are randomly distributed in individuals, so, although it is extremely improbable, a mulatto who is half white and half unmixed black might not have inherited any genes from African ancestors (Trillin, 1986:75). The smaller the proportion of any ancestry, the more probable it is that there are no genes from that lineage. In other words, having one or more black ancestors does not prove that an individual has some negroid traits or can transmit genes from African forebears. The widely held belief is that an individual's racial traits and genetic carriers are necessarily in direct proportion to the person's fraction of African black ancestry. Some persons with three-eighths or even one-half African lineage have been known to pass as white, presumably in cases in which the number of "negroid genes" was much less than the proportion of African ancestry. In instances where someone has received no "negroid genes" at all from the known African ancestors, that person not only appears white but is in biological fact white.

It is important to note that miscegenation is a biological process that requires sexual contact but not intermarriage. Many estimates of the extent and effects of miscegenation are based solely on intermarriage data, because good data of other kinds are not easy to find. It is also important to note that the mixing of genes is continuous within a group defined by the one-drop rule, even if sexual contact with the out-group declines or ceases. That is, miscegenation occurs when there is sexual contact between unmixed African blacks and mulattoes, and between mulattoes and other mulattoes, not just when there is mixing between whites and African blacks or whites and mulattoes. In all four of these instances, genes from populations derived from Europe and sub-Saharan Africa are being mixed. In mulatto-mulatto unions, genes are mixed whether the ancestry of one individual is mainly white and the other mainly black, or the ratios are more nearly even. This genetic mixing is not publicly defined as such, and the marriages concerned are certainly not thought of as intermarriages. Yet very often these unions involve much more miscegenation than occurs between whites and near-white "blacks."

WORKS CITED

Anderson, Jervis. 1972. *A. Philip Randolph: A Biographical Portrait.* New York: Harcourt Brace Jovanovich.

Bahr, Howard M., Bruce A. Chadwick, and Joseph H. Stauss. 1979. *American Ethnicity.* Lexington, Mass.: D. C. Heath & Co.

Baldwin, James. 1962. *Nobody Knows My Name.* New York: Dell Publishing Co.

Bennett, Lerone, Jr. 1962. *Before the Mayflower: A History of the Negro in America, 1619–1962.* Chicago: Johnson Publishing Co.

Bennett, Lerone, Jr. 1965. *What Manner of Man: A Biography of Martin Luther King, Jr.* Abridged ed. New York: Pocket Books.

Berry, Brewton. 1965. *Race and Ethnic Relations.* 3rd ed. Boston: Houghton Mifflin Co.

Berry, Brewton, and Henry L. Tischler. 1978. *Race and Ethnic Relations.* 4th ed. Boston: Houghton Mifflin Co.

Blaustein, Albert P., and Clarence Clyde Ferguson, Jr. 1957. *Desegregation and the Law.* New Brunswick, N. J.: Rutgers University Press.

Buckley, Gail Lumet. 1986. *The Hornes: An American Family.* New York: Alfred A. Knopf.

Burma, John G. 1946. "The Measurement of 'Passing.' " *American Journal of Sociology* 52 (July), 18–22.

Cannon, Poppy. 1956. A Gentle Knight: My Husband, Walter White. New York: Rinehart & Co.

Coon, Carleton. 1962. *The Origin of Races.* New York: Alfred A. Knopf.

Garn, Stanley M. 1965. *Human Races.* 2nd ed. Springfield, Ill.: Charles C. Thomas.

Gwaltney, John Langston. 1980. *Drylongso: A Self-Portrait of Black America.* New York: Vintage Books.

Harris, Melvin. 1964. *Patterns of Race in the Americas.* New York: W.W. Norton.

Hooton, E. A. 1948. *Up From the Ape.* New York: Macmillan Co.

Horne, Lena, and Richard Schickel. 1965. *Lena.* Garden City, N.Y.: Doubleday & Co.

Kroeber, Alfred L. 1948. *Anthropology.* New York: Harcourt, Brace & Co.

Mangum, Charles Staples, Jr. 1940. *The Legal Status of the Negro in the United States.* Chapel Hill: University of North Carolina Press.

Model, F. Peter, ed. 1983. "Apartheid in the Bayou." *Perspectives: The Civil Rights Quarterly* 15 (Winter-Spring), 3–4.

Myrdal, Gunnar, assisted by Richard Sterner and Arnold M. Rose. 1944. *An American Dilemma.* New York: Harper & Bros.

Newman, William M. 1973. *American Pluralism: A Study of Minority Groups and Sociological Theory.* New York: Harper & Row.

Ottley, Roi. 1943. *New World A-Coming.* Cleveland: World Publishing Co.

Pettigrew, Thomas F. 1975. *Racial Discrimination in the United States.* New York: Harper & Row.

Powell, Adam Clayton, Jr. 1971. *Adam by Adam: The Autobiography of Adam Clayton Powell, Jr.* New York: Dial Press.

Preston, Dickson J. 1980. *Young Frederick Douglass: The Maryland Years.* Baltimore: Johns Hopkins University Press.

Reed, T. Edward. 1969. "Caucasian Genes in American Negroes." *Science* 165 (August 22), 762–68.

Trillin, Calvin. 1986. "American Chronicles: Black or White." *New Yorker,* April 14, 1986, pp. 62–78.

White, Walter. 1948. *A Man Called White: The Autobiography of Walter White.* New York: Viking Press.

Williamson, Joel. 1980. *New People: Miscegenation and Mulattoes in the United States.* New York: The Free Press.

Why Oppression Is Hard to See

Consider a birdcage. If you look very closely at just one wire in the cage, you cannot see the other wires. If your conception of what is before you is determined by this myopic focus, you could look at that one wire, up and down the length of it, and be unable to see why a bird would not just fly around the wire anytime it wanted to go somewhere. Furthermore, even if, one day at a time, you myopically inspected each wire, you still could not see why a bird would have trouble going past the wires to get anywhere. There is no physical property of any one wire, nothing that the closest scrutiny could discover, that will reveal how a bird could be inhibited or harmed by it except in the most accidental way.

It is only when you step back, stop looking at the wires one by one, microscopically, and take a macroscopic view of the whole cage, that you can see why the bird does not go anywhere; and then you will see it in a moment. It will require no great subtlety of mental powers. It is perfectly obvious that the bird is surrounded by a network of systematically related barriers, no one of which would be the least hindrance to its flight, but which, by their relations to each other, are as confining as the solid walls of a dungeon.

It is now possible to grasp one of the reasons why oppression can be hard to see and recognize: one can study the elements of an oppressive structure with great care and some good will without seeing the structure as a whole, and hence without seeing or being able to understand that one is looking at a cage and that there are people there who are caged, whose motion and mobility are restricted, whose lives are shaped and reduced.

—Marilyn Frye, *The Politics of Reality: Essays in Feminist Theory,* 1983

II

Stigmatization

The following classes of aliens shall be excluded from admission into the United States, in accordance with the existing acts regulating immigration, other than those concerning Chinese laborers: All idiots, insane persons, paupers or persons likely to become a public charge.

—*United States Statutes at Large,* Chapter 551, Section 1, passed by the United States Congress on March 3, 1891

II

SECTION OVERVIEW

In previous centuries the term "stigma" was used to describe a distinguishing mark burned or cut into the flesh (as was often used with slaves and criminals). Nowadays, a stigma is any mark of disgrace or inferiority.

As the readings in this section show, many groups are stigmatized in American society, including people with physical disabilities, dwarfs, fat people, and racial minorities. In some cases, these groups have been stigmatized for millennia. For example, *Leviticus* (from the Old Testament) explicitly forbids anyone who is blind, lame, too short, too tall, or physically deformed from approaching an altar. In other cases, the stigma is a product of contemporary culture. For instance, overweight people suffer from severe stigmatization as a result of current societal norms favoring thinness (a change from the plumpness that was considered ideal a few generations ago).

Take Special Notice

As you read this section's articles, ask yourself whether you stigmatize any groups. If, after thinking about it, you realize that you would not date certain people because of their height, weight, or other physical characteristics over which they have no control, consider whether this is different from excluding people on the basis of their race.

Questions Worth Pondering

- What makes a group susceptible to being stigmatized? (*Note:* It is not simply the result of being unusual, because supermodels are not stigmatized.)
- How is antifat prejudice psychologically similar to other forms of prejudice, such as racism and homophobia? How is it different?
- If you are not attracted to fat people or to individuals with disabilities, does this mean that you are prejudiced?
- How can "attributional ambiguity" lead to racial segregation?
- Has attributional ambiguity ever led you to discriminate against others without knowing it?
- Do you agree with Claude Steele that stigmatization has played an important role in creating Black-White differences in educational outcomes?

The Stigma of Physical Disabilities

From Biblical Times

No man among your descendants for all time who has any physical defect shall come [near the altar]. No man with a defect shall come, whether a blind man, a lame man, a man stunted or overgrown, a man deformed in foot or hand, or with mis-shapen brows or a film over his eye.

  —Leviticus 21:17–20

Centuries Later

No person who is diseased, maimed, mutilated or in any way deformed so as to be an unsightly or disgusting object or improper person to be allowed in or on the public ways or other places in this city, shall therein or thereon expose himself to public view.

  —Chicago Municipal Code, §36–34, 1966 [*Note:* This law was repealed in 1974, but Columbus, Ohio; Omaha, Nebraska; and other U.S. cities maintained similar ordinances until the mid-1970s or later.]

Disabled Children in Ancient Greece

Let there be a law that no deformed child shall live.
—Aristotle, *The Politics*, Book VII

A Defective Race of Human Beings

Those who believe as I do, that the production of a defective race of human beings would be a great calamity to the world, will examine carefully the causes that lead to the intermarriage of the deaf with the object of applying a remedy. . . . A law forbidding congenitally deaf persons from intermarrying would go a long way towards checking the evil.

—Alexander Graham Bell, inventor of the telephone, *Memoir Upon the Formation of a Deaf Variety of the Human Race*, 1884

Eliminating the Unfit

There are two leading factors in producing a man and making him what he is—one the endowment given at birth, the other the environment into which he comes. . . . If we can improve stock by eliminating the unfit or by favoring the endowed—if we give to those who have and take away from those who have not even that which they have—we can greatly accelerate and direct the course of evolution.

—James McKeen Cattell, fourth president of the American Psychological Association, *Popular Science Monthly,* 1902

It is better for all the world, if instead of waiting to execute degenerate offspring for crime, or to let them starve for their imbecility, society can prevent those who are manifestly unfit from continuing their kind. . . . Three generations of imbeciles are enough.

—U.S. Supreme Court, *Buck v. Bell,* affirming the right of Virginia to employ forced sterilization, May 2, 1927

NO PITY: PEOPLE WITH DISABILITIES FORGING A NEW CIVIL RIGHTS MOVEMENT

JOSEPH P. SHAPIRO

Nondisabled Americans do not understand disabled ones.

That was clear at the memorial service for Timothy Cook, when longtime friends got up to pay him heartfelt tribute. "He never seemed disabled to me," said one. "He was the least disabled person I ever met," pronounced another. It was the highest praise these nondisabled friends could think to give a disabled attorney who, at thirty-eight years old, had won landmark disability rights cases, including one to force public transit systems to equip their buses with wheelchair lifts. But more than a few heads in the crowded chapel bowed with an uneasy embarrassment at the supposed compliment. It was as if someone had tried to compliment a black man by saying, "You're the least black person I ever met," as false as telling a Jew, "I never think of you as Jewish," as clumsy as seeking to flatter a woman with "You don't act like a woman."

Here in this memorial chapel was a small clash between the reality of disabled people and the understanding of their lives by others. It was the type of collision that disabled people experience daily. Yet any discordancy went unnoticed even to the well-meaning friends of a disability rights fighter like Cook. To be fair to the praise givers, their sincere words were among the highest accolade that Americans routinely give those with disabilities. In fairness, too, most disabled people gladly would have accepted the compliment some fifteen years before, the time when the speakers' friendships with Cook had begun. But most people with disabilities now think differently. As a result of an ongoing revolution in self-perception, they no longer see their physical or mental limitations as a source of shame or as something to overcome in order to inspire others. Today they proclaim that it is okay, even good, to be disabled. Cook's childhood polio forced him to wear heavy corrective shoes, and he walked with difficulty. But taking pride in his disability was for Cook a celebration of the differences among people and gave him a respectful understanding that all share the same basic desires to be full participants in society.

Never has the world of disabled people changed so fast. Rapid advances in technology, new civil rights protections, a generation of better-educated disabled students out of "mainstreamed" classrooms, and political activism mean more disabled people are seeking jobs and greater daily participation in American life. But prejudice, society's low expectations, and an antiquated welfare and social service system frustrate these burgeoning attempts at independence. As a result, the new aspirations of people with disabilities have gone unnoticed and misunderstood by mainstream America.

There are hundreds of different disabilities. Some are congenital; most come later in life. Some are progressive, like muscular dystrophy, cystic fibrosis, and some forms of vision and hearing loss. Others are static, like the loss of a limb. Disability law also applies to people with perceived disabilities such as obesity or stuttering, which are not disabling but create prejudice and discrimination. Each disability comes in differing degrees of severity. Hearing aids can amplify sounds for most deaf and hard-of-hearing people but do nothing for others. Some people with autism spend their lives in institutions; others graduate from Ivy League schools or reach the top of their professions.

Medicine once promised to wipe out disability by finding cures. Instead, doctors spurred a disability population explosion by keeping people alive longer. In World War I, only four hundred men survived with wounds that paralyzed them from the waist down, and 90 percent of them died before they reached home. But in World War II, two thousand paraplegic soldiers survived, and over 85 percent of them were still alive in the late 1960s.[1] The development of antibiotic drugs and new medical procedures improved the odds. As recently as the 1950s, death remained likely in the very early stages of a spinal cord injury as a result of respiratory, bladder, and other health complications. Now doctors neutralize those problems, and paraplegics and quadriplegics can live long, healthy lives.

There are some 35 million to 43 million disabled Americans, depending on who does the counting and what disabilities are included. In 1991 the Institute of Medicine, using federal health survey data, came up with a total of 35 million—one of every seven Americans—who have a disability that interferes with daily activities like work or keeping a household. "Disability ranks as the nation's largest public health problem, affecting not only individuals with disabling conditions and their immediate families, but also society at large,"[2] the report concludes.

There are some 30 million African Americans. So, even at the lowest estimate, disabled people could be considered the nation's largest minority. Not all disabled people, however, see themselves as part of a minority group. Many even deny they are disabled, to avoid the taint accompanying that label.

Disability is the one minority that anyone can join at any time, as a result of a sudden automobile accident, a fall down a flight of stairs, or disease. Fewer than 15 percent of disabled Americans were born with their disabilities. "Disability knows no socioeconomic boundaries," notes Patrisha Wright, the Washington lobbyist for the Disability Rights Education and Defense Fund. "You can become disabled from your mother's poor nutrition or from falling off your polo pony." And since disability catches up with most of us in old age, it is a minority that we all, if we live long enough, join. "It doesn't matter if your name is Kennedy or Rockefeller, or Smith or Jones, your family's been touched," says Wright.

Disabling Images

Like any other minority group, disabled people have become sensitized to depictions in popular culture, religion, and history. There they find constant descriptions of a disabled person's role as either an object of pity or a source of inspiration. These images are internalized by disabled and nondisabled people alike and build social stereotypes, create artificial limitations, and contribute to the discrimination and minority status hated by most disabled people.

In the Old Testament, being blind, lame, deaf, crippled, sick, or diseased is a sign of having done something to incur God's disfavor.[3] Disability is brought on by sin. In the New Testament, people with disabilities are cursed or possessed by evil. Today, many of these traditional views remain in the church. There are evangelical preachers who claim the power to heal those with the proper faith, and the more commonplace Sunday school stories cast the disabled as pitiable. Many churches now make an effort to reach out to people with disabilities, such as the United Methodist General Conference, which revised its hymnal to delete "dumb," "lame," and other references offensive to people with disabilities.[4] Other churches and synagogues welcome disabled worshipers by installing wheelchair ramps, buying large-print hymnals, or providing sign-language interpreters.

Portrayals in literature and popular culture, too, shape our images of disability. Often a disabled character is depicted as helpless and childish, like Tiny Tim in Charles Dickens's "A Christmas Carol." But it was more common in classical literature (as it often is today) for an author to exaggerate a disability as an emblem of a character's "sinister, evil or morally flawed" nature, according to Kean College special education professor Arthur Shapiro. William Shakespeare, Shapiro notes, gave Richard III a hunchback, even though the real king had no such disability, to make more ominous and obvious his ability to murder ruthlessly. Shakespeare's king speaks of being "deform'd, unfinished, sent before my time," of dogs barking at him because they were frightened by his looks, and feeling "determined to prove a villain" because of his anger over his disability.[5] Another such villain is Herman Melville's Captain Ahab, who lost a leg to Moby Dick and his mind in a madly obsessive pursuit of revenge.

These images undergird some of society's deepest fears and prejudices about people with disabilities, says Shapiro in an article co-written with Howard Margolis. "Lenny, the mentally retarded character in Steinbeck's *Of Mice and Men* who killed living things—including a young woman—because he was unaware of his own strength, is an image that may very well be involved in the minds of those who oppose group homes for the developmentally disabled," they write.[6] And journalist Paul Glastris speaks of the blow to his own self-image at finding himself, at fourteen, living in a Shriners Hospital for Crippled Children, being fitted for a prosthetic arm and discovering a mural of the limbless and evil Captain Hook menacing the pretty and good Wendy and Peter Pan.[7]

The modern successor to these diabolical characters is a staple of horror movies. Freddy Krueger, the villain of the *Nightmare on Elm Street* films, was turned into a hateful, sadistic killer because of his disfigurement, caused by a fire that left him more monster than human being. Every movie season has its examples of such fiendish disabled people, from the coldhearted banker in a wheelchair in the 1946 film *It's a Wonderful Life* to Jack Nicholson's demented joker, disfigured by a fall into a vat of acid, in 1989's hit *Batman,* and Danny De-Vito's embittered Penguin, abandoned by his parents when he was born with flippers instead of arms in the 1992 sequel *Batman Returns.*

The precursor of the modern horror movie was the freak show. Scholars of disability history debate whether the carnival sideshows amounted to a crass exploitation of people with disabilities or their glorification. Between the 1860s and early 1900s, disabled people were seen as marvels of nature, not as frightening freaks, argues Robert Bogdan, a Syracuse University professor of special education.[8] Doctors in the new twentieth century decreed that these freaks were no longer "benign curiosities" but "pathological" and "diseased," Bogdan argues. They became, he says, " 'sick' and to be pitied." Other scholars, including historian David Gerber, claim that the willingness of dwarfs and others to be put on display only shows the extreme extent of their victimization and that other forces, like movies, brought about the end of the freak show.[9] One of the first horror films was the 1932 movie *Freaks,* in which the circus sideshow attractions extract a bitter and bloody revenge on a beautiful aerial artist and her lover, the strongman.

Just as disabled people have begun protesting the power of pictures on a charity telethon, they are objecting, too, to the way they are portrayed in popular culture and the media. Language has been one of the first battlegrounds. Disabled people resent words that suggest they are pitiful, childlike, dependent, or objects of admiration—words that, in effect, convey the imagery of poster children and supercrips. "Invalid" is out, as is "afflicted with" and "patient," unless the person is really in a sickbed, or common adjectives such as "brave" and "courageous," since most disabled people are not seeking to be models of inspiration.

"Disabled" has become the usage of choice, replacing "handicapped" in recent years and becoming the first word to emerge by consensus from within the disability community itself. More acceptable still is "person with a disability," since it emphasizes the individual before the condition. One of the most common attacks on the disability movement is to mock the politically correct terms often used to describe disability. Yet it is almost always nondisabled people who use prettifying euphemisms. Virtually no disabled person uses these cute phrases. Concoctions like "the vertically challenged" are silly and scoffed at. The "differently abled," the "handicapable," or the "physically and mentally challenged" are almost universally dismissed as too gimmicky and too inclusive. "Physically challenged doesn't distinguish me from a woman climbing Mt. Everest, something certainly I'll never do," says Nancy Mairs, an essayist and poet with multiple sclerosis. Only by using direct terminology, she argues, will people think about what it means to be disabled and the accommodations she needs, such as wheelchair-accessible buildings or grab bars in bathrooms.

Dianne Piastro, who writes the syndicated column "Living with a Disability," complains that such terms suggest that disability is shameful and needs to be concealed in a vague generality. "It's denying our reality instead of saying that our reality, of being disabled, is okay," says Piastro. Mary Johnson, editor of *The Disability Rag,* complains that such euphemistic terms come from nondisabled "do-gooders" who "wouldn't understand disability culture if we ran over their toes with a wheelchair." These words have "no soul" and "no power," says Johnson. "They're like vanilla custard."

Is there a word with the requisite soul power? There was a surprise when Johnson's magazine surveyed its readers. Newly in vogue among some physically disabled people is the very word that is the ultimate in offensiveness to others: "cripple." "It's like a raised gnarled fist," says Cheryl Wade, a Berkeley, California, performance artist, who likes "crippled" because it is a blunt and accurate description of her body, which has been twisted by rheumatoid arthritis. "Crips," "gimps," and "blinks" have long been for the exclusive, internal use by people of those disabilities. (Terms for nondisabled people include "walkies" and "TABs" for the "temporarily able-bodied," a you'll-get-yours-yet reminder that disability hits most of us in old age if not before.)

No Less Worthy a Life

In Nazi Germany, doctors marked children and adults with mental retardation, mental illness, epilepsy, chronic illness, and severe disabilities for mass murder. Disabled children, and later disabled adults, were put to death by lethal injection of Luminal, a sedative, or, if that did not work, morphine-scopolamine. Others died in the regime's first experiments with lethal carbon monoxide gas.[10] Some 200,000 disabled men, women, and children would die, according to historian Hugh Gregory Gallagher.[11] "Lebensunwertes Leben"—life unworthy of life—was the concept the Nazi doctors used to justify their practice of direct medical euthanasia.[12] Later the Nazi regime would extend its grim biomedical vision to other undesirables—6 million Jews and other victims of the Holocaust.

The Nazi biomedical campaign came out of the worldwide eugenics movement of the 1920s. As historian and psychiatrist Robert Jay Lifton notes in *The Nazi Doctors,* the early German practitioners of eugenics looked with envy at their American colleagues, who with ease could enforce coercive sterilization, using a simple form of vasectomy first developed at a U.S. penal institution around the turn of the century.[13] By 1920, twenty-five states had laws requiring compulsory sterilization of the "criminally insane" and others considered genetically inferior. German physician Fritz Lenz, a leading advocate of sterilization, complained in 1923 that his country was far behind the

United States in experiments with sterilization. Lenz praised America for having laws that prohibited marriage by people with epilepsy and mental retardation and banned interracial marriage. And he bemoaned Germany's lack of eugenics research institutions to compare with those in the United States, where, Lifton notes, work carried on by Charles B. Davenport at Cold Spring Harbor, New York, was funded by the Carnegie Institution.[14]

Unlike in Germany, flirting with the eugenics movement in the United States never resulted in mass extermination, but a few American doctors and scientists did argue for the extermination of people with mental retardation, epilepsy, mental illness, blindness, and "deformations," so that they would not have a chance to perpetuate future generations with their "deficiencies."[15] One of these was Dr. Foster Kennedy, a man with impeccable credentials as professor of neurology at Cornell Medical College and director of the Department of Neurology of Bellevue Hospital.[16] He was also the president of the Euthanasia Society of America, which was created in 1938.[17] Writing in the *American Journal of Psychiatry* in 1942, Kennedy outlined a proposal for killing "defective" children—he referred to them as "defective products" and "Nature's mistakes"—which he proposed was a humane alternative to letting them live.[18] When a "defective" child turned five, Kennedy suggested, the parents or guardians should be allowed to ask a panel of doctors that the child "be relieved of the burden of living." Kennedy compared this to the "solace" given a "stricken horse."[19] If the panel found the child to have "no future nor hope of one," Kennedy wrote, "then I believe it is a merciful and kindly thing to relieve that defective—often tortured and convulsed, grotesque and absurd, useless and foolish, and entirely undesirable—of the agony of living."[20]

Kennedy's support of involuntary euthanasia was scorned, particularly as World War II ended and understanding of the roots of the Holocaust spread. But the idea that it was somehow right or humane to end the lives of disabled people never went away. In 1972, when a Florida state representative, who was also a doctor, introduced a "death with dignity" bill, he suggested that some 1,500 people in state institutions, 90 percent of the total, "might qualify for elimination."[21] The House passed the bill in principle, but it did not become law.

Throughout U.S. history, doctors have routinely ended the lives of infants born with Down syndrome or various birth defects, although those children were in no danger of dying. The practice was given national exposure in 1983, when the Reagan Administration opposed the parents of "Baby Jane Doe," a Long Island infant born with spina bifida. The baby's mother and father chose to withhold medical treatment, agreeing with their doctors that it was more humane for the severely disabled child to die. Surgeon General C. Everett Koop argued that this amounted to involuntary euthanasia. He knew it occurred often. In 1973, two doctors, writing in the *New England Journal of Medicine*, revealed that forty-three infants with various disabilities had been allowed to die in the special care nursery of the Yale-New Haven Hospital "rather than face lives devoid of meaningful humanhood."[22] A California state court in 1979 ruled in favor of the parents of Philip Becker, a thirteen-year-old with Down syndrome, who wanted to withhold life-saving heart surgery, arguing that his life was not worth living. He was spared death only because another couple adopted him.[23]

Disability groups, torn among themselves and wary of compromising their effectiveness on other issues by taking sides on abortion, have side-stepped the volatile abortion debate. They will not be able to keep doing so. New research is allowing more and more conditions to be identified through genetic counseling, making more parents face the choice of selective abortion. New experiments with gene therapy and the Human Genome Project, a bio-logical moonshot to map all the genes in the human body, may bring break-throughs to cures but also usher in the day that parents can choose to endow children with genes for good looks, height, or superior intelligence—or choose to avoid even mildly disabling conditions.

NOTES

1. Irving Kenneth Zola, "The Oration: Ageing and Disability: Toward a Unifying Agenda," *Australian Disability Review* I, no. 3 (1988).

2. Andrew M. Pope and Alvin R. Tarlov, eds., *Disability in America: Toward a National Agenda for Prevention* (Washington: National Academy Press, 1991), p. I–I.

3. Charles J. Kokaska et al., "Disabled People in the Bible," *Rehabilitation Literature* 45, no. 1–2 (January–February 1984).

4. Marjorie Hyer, "Methodists Approve Revised Hymnal," *Washington Post,* May 4, 1988.

5. William Shakespeare, *Richard III,* act I, sc. i.

6. Howard Margolis and Arthur Shapiro, "Countering Negative Images of Disability in Classical Literature," *English Journal,* March 1987; see also Robert Bogdan and Douglas Biklen, "Handicapism," *Social Policy* 8 (March/April 1977) and Robert Bogdan et al., "The Disabled: Media's Monster," *Social Policy* 13 (Fall 1982).

7. Paul Glastris, "The Case for Denial: What the Handicapped Movement Can Learn from a Totally Normal Guy," *The Washington Monthly,* December 1988.

8. Robert Bogdan, *Freak Show: Presenting Human Oddities for Amusement and Profit* (Chicago and London: The University of Chicago Press, 1988), pp. 11–12.

9. David Gerber, "Volition and Valorization in the Analysis of the 'Careers' of People Exhibited in Freak Shows," *Disability, Handicap & Society* 7, no. 1 (1992).

10. Robert J. Lifton, *The Nazi Doctors: Medical Killing and the Psychology of Genocide* (New York: Basic Books, 1986), p. 55.

11. Hugh Gregory Gallagher, *By Trust Betrayed: Patients, Physicians, and the License to Kill in the Third Reich* (New York: Henry Holt and Company, 1990), p. xx.

12. Lifton, p. 21.

13. Ibid., p. 22.

14. Ibid., p. 23.

15. Ibid.

16. Rita L. Marker et al., "Euthanasia: A Historical Overview," *Maryland Journal of Contemporary Legal Issues,* Summer 1991, pp. 275–76.

17. The Euthanasia Society of America later became the Society for the Right to Die, which in 1992 merged with another prominent right-to-die group, Concern for Dying, and was renamed Choice in Dying.

18. Foster Kennedy, "The Problem of Social Control of the Congenital Defective," *American Journal of Psychiatry* 99 (1942).

19. Ibid.

20. Ibid.

21. Evelyn W. Lusthaus, "Involuntary Euthanasia and Current Attempts to Define Persons with Mental Retardation As Less Than Human," *Mental Retardation* 23, no. 3 (June 1985).

22. Duff and A. Campbell, "Moral and Ethical Dilemmas in the Special Care Nursery," *New England Journal of Medicine* 289 (1973), pp. 890–94.

23. Lusthaus.

Exhibiting the Insane

A most shocking custom, one continuing at least to the end of the eighteenth century, was that of exhibiting the insane patients to the gaze of curious sightseers for a set admission fee. . . . It was customary, particularly on Sundays and holidays, for idlers and thrill-seekers to gather about the cell windows of the insane which stood at ground level and to take turns at "teasing the crazy people," with the aim of rousing them into raving fury.

Gradually the insane department of Pennsylvania Hospital [the first general hospital in America, cofounded by Benjamin Franklin] became known as one of the show places of Philadelphia, as contemporary Bedlam was of London. . . . At Bedlam, where, until the year 1770, visitors paid a fee at the famous "penny gates" to gain entrance to what was considered London's most amusing "raree-show," the practice seems to have been introduced mainly as a means of replenishing the institutional income. It is said that more than £400 were netted in admission fees at Bedlam in one year.

—Albert Deutsch, *The Mentally Ill in America,* 1949

Dwarfs as Pets and Presents

Dwarfs in Roman times, who became the pets of emperors and great ladies, commonly went naked. . . .

Later, in the Middle Ages, they were to be found attached to nearly every Court and the lively dwarf, with his quips and cranks, frequently played the part of jester.

They were given unlimited license of speech, and often became the pets and favorites of their Royal masters or the Court ladies of the time. . . .

Charles IX and his mother had a great partiality for them and sent emissaries to fetch them from various countries. In 1572, Charles received three dwarfs as a present from the Emperor of Germany, and in the same year added others to his suite who were brought from Poland.

—C. J. S. Thompson, *The Mystery and Lore of Monsters,* 1968

IN EUROPE, OUTCRY IS LOUD OVER A SPORT CALLED DWARF-TOSSING

PAUL HEMP

EDENBRIDGE, England—When Vera Squarcialupi first heard that some people in Britain were practicing a sport called dwarf-throwing, she thought it must be a joke. "I just rejected it," says the member of the European Parliament.

Once she was convinced it was true, Ms. Squarcialupi, an Italian Communist, introduced a proposal that condemns competitions where "particularly robust men" prove their strength by "throwing a person of restricted growth, i.e. a dwarf, as far as possible." And she isn't alone in objecting: Members of Britain's Parliament and groups for the handicapped have also protested.

Dwarf-throwing contests are said to have originated in Australia as part of a competition between nightclub bouncers. In Europe, dwarf-throwing has taken place only in England and involves just one willing dwarf. But even if the practice isn't widespread, it is creating considerable controversy. "It's appalling that such a practice would be considered entertainment in this day and age," says John Hannam, a British M.P. Ms. Squarcialupi adds, "This is a new form of exploitation, using a human being as an object."

Dwarf-rights groups say the sport is dangerous and demeaning. "If this were black-people-throwing or paraplegic-throwing, people would be horrified," says Pam Rutt, the acting chairman of the Association for Research into Restricted Growth and herself a dwarf. "It's nothing less than freak-show entertainment."

Comedy Act

But to Danny Bamford, the promoter who organizes dwarf-throwing contests in England, it is just good fun. "People say it's degrading," says Mr. Bamford, a wisecracking former welterweight boxer with bleached-blond shoulder-length hair. "But it allows the little fellow to show he can go out and be someone."

The little fellow is Lenny the Giant, a 4-foot-4-inch, 98-pound dwarf. (Lenny, after checking with Mr. Bamford, declines to give his family name. "Just call him Lenny Bamford," says his manager.) Lenny and Mr. Bamford are part of a four-man comedy act called the Oddballs, whose specialty is a striptease dance done with balloons.

On a recent evening, Lenny is performing with the Oddballs at a cabaret show in a community center in a run-down section of Edenbridge, a town south of London. His attire is a jogging suit and a motorcycle crash helmet. As Mr. Bamford attaches leather belts around Lenny's hips and shoulders, the manager keeps up a lively patter.

"Lenny, have you ever been hurt?"

"No."

"Is it fun?"

"Yes."

The Contest Begins

Mr. Bamford peers out through the smoke toward the audience. "There's been some controversy about dwarf-throwing," he shouts at the crowd. "But twist Lenny's ear and he'll tell you it's been a lot of fun and he's met a lot of people. All right, who wants to throw the dwarf?"

Each contestant picks Lenny up by his harness and—while the laughing, hard-drinking crowd screams, "one, two, THREE"—swings him underhanded onto a pile of mattresses. Lenny lies motionless while the toss is measured, then bounces up and acknowledges the cheers and laughter with a grin, ready for the next throw.

The Edenbridge contest is won by Jim Clark, a postal clerk from nearby Bexley Heath, with a toss that is well shy of the English record of 12 feet 5 inches. "A lot of people say it's easy," Mr. Bamford says by way of explanation for the mediocre performance, "but when you've got [98-pounds] of dead weight. . . ."

Ms. Rutt says that this is dangerous, regardless of how far Lenny is thrown. Dwarfism, a hormonal imbalance restricting growth that can be caused by a number of medical conditions, also involves a spinal disorder. Dwarfs like Lenny risk serious injury from jarring or twisting, she says, adding, "He could end up in a wheelchair."

But Lenny doesn't seem worried. Talking after the show in a makeshift dressing room crowded with drunken, middle-aged women seeking autographs, he says his training in karate and judo has prepared him for the sport.

Lenny seems out of place in this seedy milieu. Well-dressed and eager to please, he time and again offers to get drinks for a visitor and graciously gives a seat to one of the teetering autograph seekers. The 29-year-old emigrated with his family from India 20 years ago and still lives with his mother. Before joining the Oddballs, he worked in a factory making circuit boards for personal computers.

He professes to enjoy being thrown and says that those who criticize the sport do so out of ignorance. "I don't know how they can say they think it's wrong when they haven't even seen the show," he says. Mr. Bamford pipes in, "It was Lenny's idea, and as soon as he says he doesn't want to do it anymore, we won't do it."

Mr. Clark, who had the winning toss at Edenbridge, wonders what all the fuss is about. "It's just a bit of fun that's not detrimental to anyone," he says. "The little chap is a professional entertainer and if he's happy with the arrangement and is getting paid for it, then it's okay with me. He's not drugged or anything." (Lenny makes an average of about $72 a night for the Oddballs act.)

Another dwarf, a retired acrobat, wrote to a British show-business publication recently saying he saw nothing degrading about being thrown, although he was past the age where he would consider it himself.

Ms. Rutt sees it differently. Even if Lenny is happy with his job, dwarf-tossing "perpetuates the image of dwarfs as non-people, as freaks, as something weird," she says. Besides, "if people get the idea that dwarf-throwing is all the rage and just for fun," she says, "thugs and drunks on the street at night will say, 'Let's throw the dwarf!' "

Dwarfs have a long history as entertainers and as objects of ridicule. Household dwarfs were common in ancient Egypt and Rome and also in Renaissance Europe. In the 18th and 19th centuries, Russian noblemen kept innumerable dwarfs, and elaborate dwarf weddings were celebrated at court; in 1710, a dwarf couple spent their wedding night in the czar's bedchamber.

Like Lenny, many dwarfs today still make their living in the entertainment business as circus performers, comedians or actors. But while dwarf entertainers capitalize on their unusual condition, critics point out that they at least use skills—something not necessary for being a human projectile.

Notwithstanding the criticism, the practice could be spreading. A bar in Chicago plans to start holding contests this month. And if Mr. Bamford has his way, dwarf-tossing will spread still further. He wants to stage a world championship next year, after holding national contests in Finland, Italy, Germany and the U.S. He also plans to take four dwarfs and the English winner down under to challenge the "Australian champion."

His plans may come to naught, however. For one thing, the manager of the Australian bar where dwarf-tossing is said to have begun says the bar won't hold any more contests, partly because the novelty has worn off. For another, the outcry might be great enough to get the practice stopped in Britain.

Lenny, however, says he hopes to continue being thrown "if the protestors don't stop it. It's fun. And"—he casts a questioning glance at Mr. Bamford as if seeking approval—"It's your job."

As Much Fun as Playing Grumpy or Sleepy

Maybe I'm insensitive, but I don't see what the fuss [about dwarf-tossing is] all about. As long as the dwarf who is tossed is a consenting, adult dwarf, why should anyone else object? In fact, the [dwarf who was tossed in Australia] said he enjoyed it as much as his usual work, which is playing Grumpy or Sleepy in a stage production of "Snow White."

—Excerpted from Mike Royko's syndicated column in the *Chicago Tribune,* March 5, 1985

An Offshoot: Dwarf Bowling

ALBANY, N.Y.—Gov. Mario M. Cuomo signed legislation Tuesday banning dwarf tossing and dwarf bowling in New York bars. . . . Dwarf tossing is a competition in which people pick up dwarfs, who are wearing harnesses, and heave them as far as possible at a padded target. It produced an offshoot, dwarf bowling, in which a helmuted dwarf is strapped to a skateboard and rolled into bowling pins.

—Associated Press, July 25, 1990

AVOIDANCE OF THE HANDICAPPED: AN ATTRIBUTIONAL AMBIGUITY ANALYSIS

MELVIN L. SNYDER, ROBERT E. KLECK, ANGELO
STRENTA, AND STEVEN J. MENTZER

This paper illustrates a general strategy for detecting motives that people wish to conceal. The strategy involves asking people to choose between two alternatives, one of which accidentally happens to satisfy the motive that we suspect is present but hidden. For instance, we think that most people wish to avoid contact with the physically handicapped but do not want to admit it. If we give a person a choice between sitting next to a handicapped person or sitting beside a normal[1] one, he may choose the handicapped so as to conceal his desire to avoid. However, if we ask a person to choose between two movies, one of which apparently by accident happens to entail sitting next to a handicapped person, the other next to a normal, he can avoid the handicapped while appearing to exercise a preference for a movie. By having enough people make such decisions and by varying which movie is associated with the handicapped person, or more generally, by varying which of two alternatives happens to satisfy the suspected motive, we can see whether people consistently make choices that satisfy it. Thus, we would look for more frequent avoidance of the handicapped when there is a choice between the two movies than when there is not.

To demonstrate the utility of the general strategy that we have outlined, we decided to test whether people are motivated to avoid the handicapped but are unwilling to acknowledge that motive. Being around the handicapped seems to make people feel uncomfortable (Kleck, 1966, 1968). There are a variety of reasons why this might be so, for example, fear of the unknown, uncertainty about how to respond, or perhaps the reminder that the handicap provides of our own mortal physicality (Becker, 1973). At the same time, few handicapped people do anything to deserve their fate, and we may believe that we should treat the handicapped with kindness (Kleck, Ono, & Hastorf, 1966). The motive to avoid is not socially acceptable and may not be personally acceptable either.

To test for the presence of this unacceptable motive, our general strategy calls for giving people a choice between two alternatives, one of which accidentally happens to satisfy the motive. The alternatives we used were the same as in our example above—movies.

---

[1] *Editor's note:* The term *normal* was in common usage when this article was first published, as was the convention of using masculine pronouns such as *he* and *his* when referring to both sexes. Today, American Psychological Association guidelines discourage the use of *normal* (to avoid stigmatizing others as being *abnormal*), and they require that gendered pronouns be used accurately.

Experiment 1

Method

Subjects.   Subjects were 21 males and 4 females enrolled in Dartmouth College. They were recruited through a newspaper ad and through posters offering $2.00 to participate for half an hour in an experiment on film evaluation. One subject was deleted from the different movie condition because he knew a confederate. After the deletion there were 12 subjects in each condition.

Confederates.   Confederates were three college-age males. Each session re-quired the services of two of them, one to play the role of a handicapped person, the other to play the normal. None of the confederates were handicapped. The confederate assigned to the handicapped condition for a particular session wore a metal leg brace.

The Setting.   A partition divided the wall at the far end of a large room. The furniture arrangement on one side of the partition was the mirror image of the other side. On each side was a television monitor on a table. The monitor faced out from the corner made by the partition and the wall, at about a 45° orientation from each. A few feet away, there were two chairs facing the mon-itor. The one closer to the partition was empty. On one side of the partition sat the normal confederate. On the other side sat the confederate with the metal brace. In addition, Canadian crutches, which are made of metal, were leaning against the table that held the monitor.

Procedure.   The subject came into the room at the opposite end from the mon-itors and confederates, and he or she sat parallel to the far wall and in line with the partition.

Cover Story.   The experimenter said that he was interested in people's reac-tions to some comedy films from the days of silent movies. They would be watching a film and then evaluating it. To make sure the subject had a chance to notice both confederates, the experimenter left the room for approximately 60 seconds, saying he had to get the film description(s).

Same Movie Condition.   In the same movie condition, the experimenter told sub-jects that usually he gave people a choice between two movies but that one of the videotape machines was broken and therefore he could show only one movie. He then told the name of the movie and gave the subject a brief descrip-tion of it, which he said the subject should read while he went into the next room to rewind the videotape. The experimenter returned after 2 minutes. When the subject finished reading, his attention was directed to a table located at the end of the partition. It was a small triangular table with the apex pointing toward the subject in line with the partition edge. The table was equidistant from the two confederates and from the two empty chairs. The subject was told to pick up a background questionnaire from the table, take a seat in front of either monitor, and fill out the questionnaire; the movie would begin shortly. After the movie, the real subject and the normal confederate were taken from the room, and the real subject was put in another room by himself and was asked to fill out a movie evaluation form. Then the experimenter came in, probed for suspicion, and gave a debriefing.

Different Movie Condition.   The only difference from the same movie condition is that there was no mention of a broken videotape machine. Subjects were told that they had a choice of two movies and were given a description of each. They were told which movie was to be shown on which side of the partition. Signs taped to the edge of the table below each monitor repeated this information. They were told to sit by the monitor showing the film they would like to see. The two movies were described as follows:

> *Slapstick.* This film covers the great era of visual comedy and the clowns who made it great. Included in the film are some of the top comics of the 1920s. Charlie Chase, Monty Banks, Fatty Arbuckle, Larry Semon, Andy Clyde, and others appear.

> *Sad Clowns.* Charlie Chaplin, Buster Keaton, and Harry Langdon, Hollywood's comedy greats, all had widely differing styles and techniques, but a common ability to mix laughter and tears.

The following were counterbalanced: which movie was associated with the handicapped person, which side of the partition the handicapped person was on, which confederate was handicapped. The experimenter was blind as to which side of the partition the handicapped person was on. The confederates' behavior prior to the subject's choice of which side to sit on was standardized. Neither confederate looked up. Each appeared preoccupied with the background questionnaire.

Results

The first two columns of Table 1 present the choice data for the first experiment. In the same movie condition, 58% of the subjects sat with the handicapped confederate. In the different movie condition, however, in which subjects have an excuse for avoidance, only 17% sat with the handicapped. Thus, as predicted, there is greater avoidance of the handicapped in the different movie condition than in the same movie condition. This difference between conditions is significant, $\chi^2(1) = 4.44$, $p < .05$.

TABLE 1   Seating Choices

Choice	Experiment 1		Experiment 2		
	Same movie	*Different movie*	*Same movie*	*Different movie*	*Social comparison*
Handicapped	7	2	11	6	5
Normal	5	10	1	6	7

For purposes of assessing alternative explanations, it is useful to ask for each condition whether results differ from the 50-50 split one would expect by chance. In the same movie condition, the slight preference for the handicapped person (58%) does not differ from the null hypothesis of 50%, $\chi^2(1) = 0.33$, *ns*. In the different movie condition, however, the 83% who chose the normal person and avoided the handicapped person is significantly greater than chance, $\chi^2(1) = 5.33$, $p < .05$. This pattern permits an alternative interpretation of the results in terms of social comparison (Festinger, 1954). The argument is as follows: In the same movie condition the subjects choose seats at random; in the different movie condition subjects believe that the two confederates have exercised a choice between the two movies. Because social comparison tendencies are stronger with a similar, that is, normal, other than with a dissimilar other, subjects are more influenced by the normal's choice. Thus, rather than avoiding the handicapped person, the subject is choosing a movie he believes to be superior on the basis of its selection by the normal. To test this explanation, we ran a second experiment, repeating the two original conditions, adding a third condition, and making a few other changes.

Experiment 2

Method

The physical setting was maintained for the two old conditions, but the new condition involved some modifications. Two partitions were used to divide the far wall into three sections, each with a television monitor. The two outer sections were occupied, one by the handicapped confederate, the other by the normal. Signs were tacked to the partitions to indicate which movie each was going to see; they were never going to see the same movie. The middle section was always left for the subject. There were two additional signs on the table in front of the subject, and he was told to take the sign with the title of the movie he wished to see and place it on top of the middle TV monitor and sit down. In this condition, there is never any possibility of sitting next to the handicapped person, and there is no choice of seat, only a choice of movie. Avoidance of the handicapped, therefore, cannot be a motive for movie choice. Although it makes no sense to look for avoidance in this condition, it does make sense to look for social comparison processes; that is, if the social comparison explanation for the results of the first experiment is correct, we would expect subjects to prefer the movie chosen by the normal. Because the new condition required a different physical setup in the same room, to run the study efficiently and orderly without doing great violence to assumptions of random assignment, we alternated running first four subjects in the original arrangement (the same and different movie conditions) and then two in the new social comparison condition. Within each physical setup, the various counterbalanced conditions were run in truly random fashion. And of course, within the original setup, assignment to the same or different conditions was also random.

Besides the new condition, there were some additional changes. Subjects were again Dartmouth undergraduates, 25 males and 14 females, but this time they were recruited from introductory psychology and were given extra credit for participation instead of money. Three subjects were eliminated: a female in the same movie condition who was a friend of the experimenter of the first study and had discussed it with him; a male in the different movie condition who was suspicious of the confederates; and a female in the different movie condition who was so preoccupied with a book that she read it whenever she could—even during the movie—and consequently never noticed the handicap. The confederates were two female students enrolled in a local high school. When the subject appeared, each confederate briefly looked up and then returned to working on the questionnaire. This time the questionnaire contained the Nowlis (1965) Mood Adjective Checklist (MACL). The MACL was given again after the movie, along with an evaluation form. The rationale for giving the MACL was that mood may be related to how people react to comedy.

Results

The third and fourth columns of Table 1 present the choice results for the second experiment. As in the first experiment, a comparison of the two original conditions shows fewer people choosing to sit next to the handicapped person in the different movie condition (50%) than in the same movie condition (92%), $\chi^2(1) = 5.04$, $p < .05$. Again, there is greater avoidance of the handicapped when there is an excuse for doing so. In the second study, for some reason, across these two conditions people more often chose the handicapped person than they did in the first study, $\chi^2(1) = 5.37$, $p < .05$. This could be the result of a variety of factors, such as different subjects, female confederates, younger confederates.

An interesting possibility is that the confederates' looking up briefly when the subject arrived resulted in a more frequent choice of the handicapped. An explanation is available in terms of self-awareness theory (Wicklund, 1975). Self-awareness is enhanced by directing attention to self using mirrors, videotapes, audiences, and so forth. It seems plausible that eye contact enhances self-awareness. One of the consequences of self-awareness is greater conformity to salient standards. In this case the standard is probably being kind to the handicapped (Kleck et al., 1966), which is accomplished by sitting next to him or her. In this way eye contact may have led to greater affiliation with the handicapped. Snyder, Grether, and Keller (1974) report data consistent with this line of reasoning, which they interpret in a similar way. They found that hitchhikers could improve their chances of getting a ride by staring at approaching drivers.

Whatever the explanation may be, the difference between experiments is useful. The second experiment shows a significant preference for the handicapped person in the same movie condition, $\chi^2(1) = 8.33$, $p < .01$. And together, the two experiments show that the movie choice variation has the same effect at different places on the scale of net tendencies to approach or avoid the handicapped.

Now let us turn to the new condition, in which avoidance is irrelevant because the subject has no choice of seats but in which social comparison effects are possible. If in the different movie condition people sit with the normal not in order to avoid the handicapped but rather to see the movie that they believe the normal selected, they should prefer the movie the normal selected in this new condition. There is only a slight preference for the normal's movie. Seven subjects rather than the six expected by chance choose the normal's movie and this result is, of course, well within the range of chance expectation, $\chi^2(1) = 0.33$, *ns*. There does not seem to be a social comparison effect. This is not too surprising if we keep in mind that the normal confederate was a high school student discriminably younger and therefore different from the subject. Further evidence against a social comparison explanation of the main results is the significant preference for the handicapped person in the same movie condition. Every subject but one did so. Social comparison theory would suggest that a more similar other, that is, the normal, would be preferred to inform the subject as to the appropriate response to the movie. Finally, social comparison theory suggests that the results should be stronger for subjects who are the same sex as the confederates (Zanna, Goethals, & Hill, 1975). If anything, the results tended slightly in the other direction: a little stronger for females in the first study when the confederates were male and a little stronger for males in the second study when the confederates were female. In short, there were no obvious consistent sex differences, and certainly none that would suggest a social comparison explanation.

Discussion

Our goal was to illustrate a general strategy for detecting motives that people wish to conceal. We suspected that people desire to avoid the handicapped but do not wish to admit it. In a kind of bootstrap operation, we have demonstrated the general strategy by using it to reveal this motive. The strategy is to ask people to choose between two alternatives, one of which accidentally happens to satisfy the suspected motive.

Concretely, we had subjects choose between sitting with a handicapped person or a normal, or choose between two movies, one of which entailed sitting next to a handicapped person, the other of which entailed sitting next to a normal. In the latter case, we predicted greater avoidance of the handicapped because, objectively, motivation is ambiguous and avoidance of the handicapped can masquerade as a motive preference. In both experiments we found, as predicted, greater avoidance when the choice between people was also a choice between movies.

These results still leave open the following question. When the subject does avoid the handicapped, who is the subject trying to fool: the handicapped person, the experimenter, or himself? If the phenomenon of rationalized avoidance occurs in the absence of the experimenter, imagine what the experience of the handicapped person may be like in a world so complex that it is much more like our different movie condition than like our same movie condition. The data suggest that the handicapped person may be repeatedly rebuffed in social encounters by people who give what may seem to them to be reasonable excuses. The handicapped person can then distill the attitudes of others toward him in the same way that we can in the current study. This casts doubt on whether people really fool the handicapped when they give an excuse for avoiding.

The handicapped are probably not the only group of people to receive such treatment. For one, Gaertner and Dovidio (1977) present data suggesting that blacks are comparably treated. Subjects were led to believe that a confederate was either black or white. Then it was made to appear that the confederate was in need of help because a stack of chairs had fallen on him. In addition to varying race of victim, the experimenters also varied the number of bystanders present. Either the subject was the only potential helper, or she was led to believe that she was one of three potential helpers. When the subject was alone, the black was helped slightly and nonsignificantly more than the white was. When there were three potential helpers, however, the black victim was helped only half as often as the white one. The interpretation the authors offered for these results is that people do not want to help the black victim but will only act on that desire when they have an excuse such as the assumption that others had already helped or the thought that somebody else would be a better helper. We concur with this interpretation. We would argue that the three-helper condition is much like our different movie condition. It permits the person to act on an unacceptable motive because it provides other plausible causes for doing so. Once again, ambiguity about the motive behind behavior permits the person to fulfill an objectionable desire.

We believe that the layperson often uses informal versions of this strategy to get information without creating offense. Two women inspect the menu posted outside a French restaurant, trying to decide whether to enter. The wealthier one, suspecting that the other thinks it is too expensive but is too shy to say so, asks whether the other is more in the mood for Italian cuisine than for French. When the other replies that yes, she is more in the mood for Italian food, the first will conclude that the French restaurant was too expensive for her friend, but her friend is saved the embarrassment of admitting it. And there are times when the person with the hidden motive will make the excuse herself. For example, without prompting she may state that she is not in the mood for French cuisine. In short, the creation of causal ambiguity can smooth social interaction and permit participants to save face by providing socially acceptable rationalizations for behavior.

REFERENCES

Becker, E. (1973). *The denial of death*. New York: Free Press.

Festinger, L. (1954). A theory of social comparison processes. *Human Relations, 7*, 117–140.

Gaertner, S. L., & Dovidio, J. F. (1977). The subtlety of white racism, arousal, and helping behavior. *Journal of Personality and Social Psychology, 35*, 691–707.

Kleck, R. E. (1966). Emotional arousal in interactions with stigmatized persons. *Psychological Reports, 19,* 12–26.

Kleck, R. E. (1968). Physical stigma and nonverbal cues emitted in face-to-face interaction. *Human Relations, 21,* 19–28.

Kleck, R. E., Ono, H., & Hastorf, A. H. (1966). The effect of physical deviance upon face-to-face interaction. *Human Relations, 19,* 425–436.

Nowlis, V. (1965). Research with the Mood Adjective Checklist. In S. S. Tomkins & C. E. Izard (Eds.), *Affect, cognition, and personality.* New York: Springer.

Snyder, M., Grether, J., & Keller, K. (1974). Staring and compliance: A field experiment on hitch-hiking. *Journal of Applied Social Psychology, 4,* 165–170.

Wicklund, R. A. (1975). Objective self-awareness. In L. Berkowitz (Ed.), *Advances in experimental social psychology* (Vol. 8). New York: Academic Press.

Zanna, M. P., Goethals, G. R., & Hill, J. F. (1975). Evaluating a sex-related ability: Social comparison with similar others and with standard setters. *Journal of Experimental Social Psychology, 11,* 86–93.

The Management of Stigma

Number of photographs, out of 35,000 at the Franklin Delano Roosevelt Presidential Library, that show the former president seated in a wheelchair: 2

—Source: Hugh Gregory Gallagher, *FDR's Splendid Deception,* 1985

CITING INTOLERANCE, OBESE PEOPLE TAKE STEPS TO PRESS CAUSE[1]

CAREY GOLDBERG

NORWOOD, Mass.—Walk in Deidra Everett's shoes a moment: You know that you dress nicely; that you are well-spoken; that you are clean and friendly and funny and smart. Yet when you go for a job interview, your potential employer's eyes tend to sweep your person and fill with horror.

You can joke about it—"the look"—but it has happened so many times that you have almost given up. The unemployment rate in Massachusetts is under 3 percent. Your office administration skills are in desperate demand. But you, as you are often reminded by stares and gibes from strangers, are fat. Fat.

"I'm an upbeat and confident person," said Ms. Everett, 33 years old, 5-foot-10 and about 440 pounds. "But you get kicked enough and even the strongest people say, 'You know, I just don't want to be kicked anymore. I'll be strong in my own little world.' "

Deidra Everett's personal trials fit into a picture that scholars and advocates have been building for years. Overall, their work increasingly suggests that weight may now draw more open and widespread discrimination than race or gender or age. And opposition to such discrimination is mounting.

There have been lawsuits, "size acceptance" talks, and a current campaign by a fat woman for bigger seat belts in cars, as well as the recent pushes in San Francisco and elsewhere to pass ordinances banning discrimination based on a person's size.

The prejudice turns up in almost all spheres of life, from the classroom to the office to the streets.

Being fat "seems to have a consistent strong effect, more consistent than any other form of discrimination I've seen, though part of that may be because people feel freer to talk about it," said Mark Roehling, an assistant professor of management at Western Michigan University, who last year published an analysis of the extensive research on weight discrimination.

But the efforts to fight the discrimination appear tiny in a country where more than half the population is now considered overweight, and nearly 18 percent obese. Unlike other groups that face discrimination, fat people have not organized extensively to demand their rights. Their most prominent advocacy group, the National Association to Advance Fat Acceptance, has only about 5,000 members.

And the task before such advocates is daunting. Studies indicate that opinions about fat people turn negative in childhood and stay negative: As early as nursery school, they have found, children prefer drawings of peers in wheelchairs, on crutches or with facial disfigurements to those of fat children.

"Fat hatred is being taught to our children," said Miriam Berg, president of the Council on Size and Weight Discrimination, a national nonprofit group. "I know from how children react to me: at age 1½, babies love me and smile at me; you come to 2½ and already they look at me with fear; it begins that young, unless they grow up in a household with people of different sizes."

It could be said that fat hatred begins even before birth: According to a national survey, 16 percent of the general adult population would abort a child if they knew it would be untreatably obese, said Dorothy C. Wertz, an ethicist and sociologist at the University of Massachusetts Medical School who specializes in genetics and who performed the study. By comparison, she said, 17 percent would abort if the child would be mildly retarded.

By elementary school, another study showed, children use words like "dirty," "lazy," "ugly," "stupid" and "sloppy" to describe the silhouette of a fat child.

A National Education Association position paper says that "for fat students, the school experience is one of ongoing prejudice, unnoticed discrimination, and almost constant harassment."

"From nursery school through college," the paper continued, "fat students experience ostracism, discouragement and sometimes violence."

Indeed, studies have shown that fat students are less likely to go to college and that their parents are less likely to pay for it; once there, they face still more hostile attitudes from their fellow students; a 1988 study found that students would prefer to marry an embezzler, a cocaine user, a shoplifter or a blind person rather than an obese person.

Trouble in the Workplace

The job market presents other challenges. Studies have found that fat white women tend to earn significantly less than their thinner counterparts. One study found that highly obese women earn 24 percent less while the moderately obese earn about 6 percent less. Another survey found that among 81 employers, about 16 percent considered obesity "an absolute bar to employment" and 44 percent considered it conditional medical grounds for passing over an applicant.

Dr. Roehling's review of 29 such studies found evidence for discrimination at every stage of the work process: hiring, placement, promotion, discipline and wages.

"I talk to managers here in Michigan, and they tell me flat out they wouldn't hire people because they're fat," he said.

The elements of such discrimination may be complex. Dr. Roehling said that employers described several concerns, from worries about the costs of their health insurance premiums to worries that their customers will respond negatively to a fat employee.

The interplay of cause and effect can also be complex: is a woman fat because she is poor, for example, or poor because she is fat? In general, it does seem that obesity causes poverty and other disadvantages rather than the disadvantages that cause obesity, said Esther Rothblum, a psychology professor at the University of Vermont who has done extensive research on the stigma associated with weight.

The evidence, she said, shows clearly that being fat makes people "downwardly mobile," because of obstacles they face to education, work and marriage. (Studies indicate that being fat does not seem to hinder developing friendships and good relations with colleagues, she noted.)

For the Deidra Everetts of the world, the outcome is simple: seeking to avoid "the look," she tells potential employers about her weight in preliminary phone interviews.

"They hear the word 'fat' and they're like, 'Gasp!' I can't believe you said that!' " she said. "Eventually, they say, 'You know the job I was calling you about? I'm really thinking it isn't something you'd be interested in.' "

It feels like discrimination, she said, but how can she prove it? Unless the employer curses her and says, " 'You're not going to get hired until you lose 300 pounds,' " Ms. Everett said, "unless someone says that—and even if they do, it's legal. They can look me right in the eye and say, 'You're too fat!' "

Indeed they can—anywhere except Michigan, Washington, D.C., Santa Cruz, Calif., and San Francisco, which are the only places to have passed laws against weight-based discrimination.

San Francisco, which passed its ordinance in May of 2000, did so at the instigation of some members of what Larry Brinkin, the member of the city's Human Rights Commission staff who handled the issue, calls the "fat liberation movement." Its advocates had been pressing for years for such a law, he said, but really gained traction after an incident in which a local health club put up a billboard depicting a space alien and declaring, "When they come, they'll eat the fat ones first."

Though the sign was clearly meant to be comical, advocates picketed the health club, giving momentum to the push for a law. City hearings at which dozens of fat people testified to the discrimination they had encountered, and the failure of all their attempts to lose weight, added impetus, as well.

Some in San Francisco disapproved, saying that the law was frivolous and that fat people could solve their problems simply by losing weight. The *San Francisco Chronicle* editorialized against the law, saying that fat people would be healthier if they lost weight, and that "it is true that genetics can be a factor in obesity, but that is not always the case."

The law passed the city's Board of Supervisors unanimously, however, and now, Mr. Brinkin said, the commission is working on implementing it, wrestling with such issues as whether theaters should be asked to have a row of free-standing seats without arms that can accommodate large people.

Though they lack such special laws to protect them in most places, fat people are increasingly taking discriminators to court, experts say. They have no solid estimates on the number of such cases but put them in the dozens each year nationwide. About 150 people call the Council on Size and Weight Discrimination with complaints each year, though not all will sue.

The case law on obesity discrimination has accumulated to the point that a book about it came out, *Tipping the Scales of Justice: Fighting Weight-Based*

Discrimination (Prometheus Books), by Sondra Solovay, a lawyer in Berkeley, Calif. It argues that "discrimination against fat people is the civil rights hurdle of the new millennium."

Thus far, Ms. Solovay says, the outcomes of weight discrimination cases vary from place to place, in large part because there is no federal law protecting fat people.

Perhaps the trickiest question is whether obesity should be considered a disability. Courts have ruled that the Americans With Disabilities Act provides protection in some cases, particularly those concerning highly obese people, but not in others, depending on the circumstances.

What is clear, Ms. Solovay said, is that using a disability claim has tended to provide the best legal success. But "there are huge ideological objections" to using such an argument, she added, because many fat people want to argue not that they are disabled, but that they are perfectly able to do the same work as thinner colleagues.

Little Help from the Law

Many of the daily battles some fat people face do not lend themselves to the courtroom, however—from plane seats that are too narrow to strangers who spout cruel taunts to doctors who refuse to believe that many diets only backfire. And then there are the insurers.

"The hardest thing to live with as a fat person is that you can't get health insurance," said Ms. Berg of the Council on Size and Weight Discrimination. "When people call me up and say, 'My H.M.O. kicked me out; what should I do?' I have nothing to tell them. Nothing."

A person's weight does influence many health insurers, and a significantly overweight applicant can be turned down, said Janet Trautwein, director of federal policy for the National Association of Health Underwriters. "It's not an appearance thing," she said. "It's just strictly a health status factor, and it's used in combination with other factors like, 'Do you smoke, have high blood pressure, high cholesterol or diabetes?' "

In some states, she said, insurers may charge higher premiums for overweight members.

Elizabeth Fisher, a programmer in Baton Rouge, Louisiana, decided not to let one such moment of daily difficulty go by. She was buying a new car, and found that the one she wanted, a Honda Odyssey minivan, did not make a seat belt big enough for her; nor would Honda offer an extender, as many other companies do.

This summer, Ms. Fisher petitioned the National Highway Traffic Safety Administration to require carmakers to offer the option of longer seat belts on new vehicles and seat-belt extenders on existing ones. Her fight had such resonance that it has gained national publicity.

"This issue is much larger than one fat woman who can't buckle her seat belt," said Ms. Fisher, who is expecting a decision soon from the agency. "There are millions of people in the United States who weigh more than 215 pounds, the current upper weight limit required for seat belts by N.H.T.S.A. And because fat is more prevalent in certain racial and ethnic populations, more common in women than in men, and more common in older people than young, denying fat people the protection of being included within the limits of federal seat-belt regulations disproportionately affects these disadvantaged groups."

Some people justify attacking fat people by saying it is their choice to be fat, Ms. Everett said, "but who in the name of God would choose to live a life like this?"

RACE AND THE SCHOOLING OF BLACK AMERICANS

CLAUDE STEELE

My former university offered minority students a faculty mentor to help shepherd them into college life. As soon as I learned of the program, I volunteered to be a mentor, but by then the school year was nearly over. Undaunted, the program's eager staff matched me with a student on their waiting list—an appealing nineteen-year-old black woman from Detroit, the same age as my daughter. We met finally in a campus lunch spot just about two weeks before the close of her freshman year. I realized quickly that I was too late. I have heard that the best way to diagnose someone's depression is to note how depressed you feel when you leave the person. When our lunch was over, I felt as gray as the snowbanks that often lined the path back to my office. My lunchtime companion was a statistic brought to life, a living example of one of the most disturbing facts of racial life in America today: the failure of so many black Americans to thrive in school. Before I could lift a hand to help this student, she had decided to do what 70 percent of all black Americans at four-year colleges do at some point in their academic careers—drop out.

I sense a certain caving-in of hope in America that problems of race can be solved. Since the sixties, when race relations held promise for the dawning of a new era, the issue has become one whose persistence causes "problem fatigue"—resignation to an unwanted condition of life.

This fatigue, I suspect, deadens us to the deepening crisis in the education of black Americans. One can enter any desegregated school in America, from grammar school to high school to graduate or professional school, and meet a persistent reality: blacks and whites in largely separate worlds. And if one asks a few questions or looks at a few records, another reality emerges: these worlds are not equal, either in the education taking place there or in the achievement of the students who occupy them.

As a social scientist, I know that the crisis has enough possible causes to give anyone problem fatigue. But at a personal level, perhaps because of my experience as a black in American schools, or perhaps just as the hunch of a myopic psychologist, I have long suspected a particular culprit—a culprit that can undermine black achievement as effectively as a lock on a schoolhouse door. The culprit I see is *stigma,* the endemic devaluation many blacks face in our society and schools. This status is its own condition of life, different from class, money, culture. It is capable, in the words of the late sociologist Erving Goffman, of "breaking the claim" that one's human attributes have on people. I believe that its connection to school achievement among black Americans has been vastly underappreciated.

This is a troublesome argument, touching as it does on a still unhealed part of American race relations. But it leads us to a heartening principle: if blacks are made less racially vulnerable in school, they can overcome even substantial obstacles. Before the good news, though, I must at least sketch in the bad: the worsening crisis in the education of black Americans.

Despite their socioeconomic disadvantages as a group, blacks begin school with test scores that are fairly close to the test scores of whites their age. The longer they stay in school, however, the more they fall behind; for example, by the sixth grade blacks in many school districts are two full grade levels behind whites in achievement. This pattern holds true in the middle class nearly as much as in the lower class.

Even for blacks who make it to college, the problem doesn't go away. As I noted, 70 percent of all black students who enroll in four-year colleges drop out at some point, as compared with 45 percent of whites. At any given time nearly as many black males are incarcerated as are in college in this country. And the grades of black college students average half a letter below those of their white classmates. At one prestigious university I recently studied, only 18 percent of the graduating black students had grade averages of B or above, as compared with 64 percent of the whites. This pattern is the rule, not the exception, in even the most elite American colleges. Tragically, low grades can render a degree essentially "terminal" in the sense that they preclude further schooling.

Standing ready is a familiar set of explanations. First is societal disadvantage. Black Americans have had, and continue to have, more than their share: a history of slavery, segregation, and job ceilings; continued lack of economic opportunity; poor schools; and the related problems of broken families, drug-infested communities, and social isolation. Any of these factors—alone, in combination, or through accumulated effects—can undermine school achievement. Some analysts point also to black American culture, suggesting that, hampered by disadvantage, it doesn't sustain the values and expectations critical to education, or that it fosters learning orientations ill suited to school achievement, or that it even "opposes" mainstream achievement. These are the chestnuts, and I had always thought them adequate. Then several facts emerged that just didn't seem to fit.

For one thing, the achievement deficits occur even when black students suffer no major financial disadvantage—among middle-class students on wealthy college campuses and in graduate school among black students receiving substantial financial aid. For another thing, survey after survey shows that even poor black Americans value education highly, often more than whites.

Neither is the problem fully explained, as one might assume, by deficits in skill or preparation which blacks might suffer because of background disadvantages. I first doubted that such a connection existed when I saw flunk-out rates for black and white students at a large, prestigious university. Two observations surprised me. First, for both blacks and whites the level of preparation, as measured by Scholastic Aptitude Test scores, didn't make much difference in who flunked out; low scorers (with combined verbal and quantitative SATs of 800) were no more likely to flunk out than high scorers (with combined SATs of 1,200 to 1,500). The second observation was racial: whereas only 2 percent to

11 percent of the whites flunked out, 18 percent to 33 percent of the blacks flunked out, even at the highest levels of preparation (combined SATs of 1,400).

From elementary school to graduate school, something depresses black achievement *at every level of preparation, even the highest.* Generally, of course, the better prepared achieve better than the less prepared, and this is about as true for blacks as for whites. But given any level of school preparation (as measured by tests and earlier grades), blacks somehow achieve less in subsequent schooling than whites (that is, have poorer grades, have lower graduation rates, and take longer to graduate), no matter how strong that preparation is. Put differently, the same achievement level requires better preparation for blacks than for whites—far better: among students with a C+ average at the university I just described, the mean American College Testing Program (ACT) score for blacks was at the 98th percentile, while for whites it was at only the 34th percentile. This pattern has been documented so broadly across so many regions of the country, and by so many investigations (literally hundreds), that it is virtually a social law in this society.

Clearly, something is missing from our understanding of black underachievement. Disadvantage contributes, yet blacks underachieve even when they have ample resources, strongly value education, and are prepared better than adequately in terms of knowledge and skills. Something else has to be involved. That something else could be of just modest importance—a barrier that simply adds its effect to that of other disadvantages—or it could be pivotal, such that were it corrected, other disadvantages would lose their effect.

🖎   🖎   🖎

That something else, I believe, has to do with the process of identifying with school. I offer a personal example:

I remember conducting experiments with my research adviser early in graduate school and awaiting the results with only modest interest. I struggled to meet deadlines. The research enterprise—the core of what one does as a social psychologist—just wasn't *me* yet. I was in school for other reasons—I wanted an advanced degree, I was vaguely ambitious for intellectual work, and being in graduate school made my parents proud of me. But as time passed, I began to like the work. I also began to grasp the value system that gave it meaning, and the faculty treated me as if they thought I might even be able to do it. Gradually I began to think of myself as a social psychologist. With this change in self-concept came a new accountability; my self-esteem was affected now by what I did as a social psychologist, something that hadn't been true before. This added a new motivation to my work; self-respect, not just parental respect, was on the line. I noticed changes in myself. I worked without deadlines. I bored friends with applications of arcane theory to their daily lives. I went to conventions. I lived and died over how experiments came out.

Before this transition one might have said that I was handicapped by my black working-class background and lack of motivation. After the transition the same observer might say that even though my background was working-class, I had special advantages: achievement-oriented parents, a small and attentive college. But these facts alone would miss the importance of the identification process I had experienced: the change in self-definition and in the activities on which I based my self-esteem. They would also miss a simple condition necessary for me to make this identification: treatment as a valued person with good prospects.

I believe that the "something else" at the root of black achievement problems is the failure of American schooling to meet this simple condition for many of its black students. Doing well in school requires a belief that school achievement can be a promising basis of self-esteem, and that belief needs constant reaffirmation even for advantaged students. Tragically, I believe, the lives of black Americans are still haunted by a specter that threatens this belief and the identification that derives from it at every level of schooling.

The Specter of Stigma and Racial Vulnerability

I have a good friend, the mother of three, who spends considerable time in the public school classrooms of Seattle, where she lives. In her son's third-grade room, managed by a teacher of unimpeachable good will and competence, she noticed over many visits that the extraordinary art work of a small black boy named Jerome was ignored—or, more accurately perhaps, its significance was ignored. As genuine art talent has a way of doing—even in the third grade—his stood out. Yet the teacher seemed hardly to notice. Moreover, Jerome's reputation, as it was passed along from one grade to the next, included only the slightest mention of his talent. Now, of course, being ignored like this could happen to anyone—such is the overload in our public schools. But my friend couldn't help wondering how the school would have responded to this talent had the artist been one of her own, middle-class white children.

Terms like "prejudice" and "racism" often miss the full scope of racial devaluation in our society, implying as they do that racial devaluation comes primarily from the strongly prejudiced, not from "good people" like Jerome's teacher. But the prevalence of racists—deplorable though racism is—misses the full extent of Jerome's burden, perhaps even the most profound part.

He faces a devaluation that grows out of our images of society and the way those images catalogue people. The catalogue need never be taught. It is implied by all we see around us: the kinds of people revered in advertising (consider the unrelenting racial advocacy of Ralph Lauren ads) and movies (black women are rarely seen as romantic partners, for example); media discussions of whether a black can be President; invitation lists to junior high school birthday parties; school curricula; literary and musical canons. These details create an image of society in which black Americans simply do not fare well. When I was a kid, we captured it with the saying "If you're white you're right, if you're yellow you're mellow, if you're brown stick around, but if you're black get back."

In ways that require no fueling from strong prejudice or stereotypes, these images expand the devaluation of black Americans. They set up a jeopardy of double devaluation for blacks, a jeopardy that does not apply to whites. Like anyone, blacks risk devaluation for a particular incompetence, such as a failed test or a flubbed pronunciation. But they further risk that such performances will confirm the broader, racial inferiority they are suspected of. Thus, from the first grade through graduate school, blacks have the extra fear that in the eyes of those around them their full humanity could fall with a poor answer or a mistaken stroke of the pen.

Moreover, because these images are conditioned in all of us, collectively held, they can spawn racial devaluation in all of us, not just in the strongly prejudiced. They can do this even in blacks themselves: a majority of black children recently tested said they like and prefer to play with white rather than black dolls—almost fifty years after Kenneth and Mamie Clark, conducting similar experiments, documented identical findings and so paved the way for *Brown v. Topeka Board of Education.* Thus Jerome's devaluation can come from a circle of people in his world far greater than the expressly prejudiced.

In ways often too subtle to be conscious but sometimes overt, I believe, blacks remain devalued in American schools, where, for example, a recent national survey shows that through high school they are still more than twice as likely as white children to receive corporal punishment, be suspended from school, or be labeled mentally retarded.

Tragically, such devaluation can seem inescapable. Sooner or later it forces on its victims two painful realizations. The first is that society is preconditioned to see the worst in them. Black students quickly learn that acceptance, if it is to be won at all, will be hard-won. The second is that even if a black student achieves exoneration in one setting—with the teacher and fellow students in one classroom, or at one level of schooling, for example—this approval will have to be rewon in the next classroom, at the next level of schooling. Few from any group could hope to sustain so daunting and everlasting a struggle. Thus, I am afraid, too many black students are left hopeless and deeply vulnerable in America's classrooms.

"Disidentifying" with School

I believe that in significant part the crisis in black Americans' education stems from the power of this vulnerability to undercut identification with schooling, either before it happens or after it has bloomed. Bruce Hare, an educational researcher, has documented this process among fifth-grade boys in several schools in Champaign, Illinois. He found that although the black boys had considerably lower achievement-test scores than their white classmates, their overall self-esteem was just as high. This stunning imperviousness to poor academic performance was accomplished, he found, by their de-emphasizing school achievement as a basis of self-esteem and giving preference to peer-group relations—a domain in which their esteem prospects were better. They went where they had to go to feel good about themselves.

But recall the young student whose mentor I was. She had already identified with school, and wanted to be a doctor. How can racial vulnerability break so developed an achievement identity? To see, let us follow her steps onto campus: Her recruitment and admission stress her minority status perhaps more strongly than it has been stressed at any other time in her life. She is offered academic and social support services, further implying that she is "at risk" (even though, contrary to common belief, the vast majority of black college students are admitted with qualifications well above the threshold for whites). Once on campus, she enters a socially circumscribed world in which blacks—still largely separate from whites—have lower status; this is reinforced by a sidelining of minority material and interests in the curriculum and in university life.

Quickly, I believe, a psychic defense takes over. She *disidentifies* with achievement; she changes her self-conception, her outlook and values, so that achievement is no longer so important to her self-esteem. She may continue to feel pressure to stay in school—from her parents, even from the potential advantages of a college degree. But now she is psychologically insulated from her academic life, like a disinterested visitor. Cool, unperturbed. But, like a painkilling drug, disidentification undoes her future as it relieves her vulnerability.

The prevalence of this syndrome among black college students has been documented extensively, especially on predominantly white campuses. Among a sample of blacks on one predominantly white campus, Richard Nisbett and Andrew Reaves, both psychologists, and I found that attitudes related to disidentification were more strongly predictive of grades than even academic preparation (that is, SATs and high school grades).

To make matters worse, once disidentification occurs in a school, it can spread like the common cold. Blacks who identify and try to achieve embarrass the strategy by valuing the very thing the strategy denies the value of. Thus pressure to make it a group norm can evolve quickly and become fierce. Defectors are called "oreos" or "incognegroes." One's identity as an authentic black is held hostage, made incompatible with school identification. For black students, then, pressure to disidentify with school can come from the already demoralized as well as from racial vulnerability in the setting.

Stigmatization of the sort suffered by black Americans is probably also a barrier to the school achievement of other groups in our society, such as lower-class whites, Hispanics, and women in male-dominated fields. For example, at a large midwestern university I studied, women match men's achievement in the liberal arts, where they suffer no marked stigma, but underachieve compared with men (get lower grades than men with the same ACT scores) in engineering and premedical programs, where they, like blacks across the board, are more vulnerable to suspicions of inferiority.

Wise Schooling

"When they approach me they see . . . everything and anything except me. . . . [this] invisibility . . . occurs because of a peculiar disposition of the eyes. . . ."
—RALPH ELLISON, *Invisible Man*

Erving Goffman, borrowing from gays of the 1950s, used the term "wise" to describe people who don't themselves bear the stigma of a given group but who are accepted by the group. These are people in whose eyes the full humanity of the stigmatized is visible, people in whose eyes they feel less vulnerable. If racial vulnerability undermines black school achievement, as I have argued, then this achievement should improve significantly if schooling is made "wise"—that is, made to see value and promise in black students and to act accordingly.

And yet, although racial vulnerability at school may undermine black achievement, so many other factors seem to contribute—from the debilitations of poverty to the alleged dysfunctions of black American culture—that one might expect "wiseness" in the classroom to be of little help. Fortunately, we have considerable evidence to the contrary. Wise schooling may indeed be the missing key to the schoolhouse door.

In the mid-seventies black students in Philip Uri Treisman's early calculus courses at the University of California at Berkeley consistently fell to the bottom of every class. To help, Treisman developed the Mathematics Workshop Program, which, in a surprisingly short time, reversed their fortunes, causing them to outperform their white and Asian counterparts. And although it is only a freshman program, black students who take it graduate at a rate comparable to the Berkeley average. Its central technique is group study of calculus concepts. But it is also wise; it does things that allay the racial vulnerabilities of these students. Stressing their potential to learn, it recruits them to a challenging "honors" workshop tied to their first calculus course. Building on their skills, the workshop gives difficult work, often beyond course content, to students with even modest preparation. Working together, students soon understand that everyone knows something and nobody knows everything, and learning is speeded through shared understanding.

The wisdom of these tactics is their subtext message: "You are valued in this program because of your academic potential—regardless of your current skill level. You have no more to fear than the next person, and since the work is difficult, success is a credit to your ability, and a setback is a reflection only of the challenge." The black students' double vulnerability around failure—the fear that they lack ability, and the dread that they will be devalued—is thus reduced. Explaining Xavier University's extraordinary success in producing black medical students, a spokesman said recently, "What doesn't work is saying, 'You need remedial work.' What does work is saying, 'You may be somewhat behind at this time but you're a talented person. We're going to help you advance at an accelerated rate.' "

The work of James Comer, a child psychiatrist at Yale, suggests that wiseness can minimize even the barriers of poverty. Over a fifteen-year period he transformed the two worst elementary schools in New Haven, Connecticut, into the third and fifth best in the city's thirty-three-school system without any change in the type of students—largely poor and black. His guiding belief is that learning requires a strongly accepting relationship between teacher and student. "After all," he notes, "what is the difference between scribble and a letter of the alphabet to a child? The only reason the letter is meaningful, and worth learning and remembering, is because a *meaningful* other wants him or her to learn and remember it." To build these relationships Comer focuses on the overall school climate, shaping it not so much to transmit specific skills, or to improve achievement, as to establish a valuing and optimistic atmosphere in which a child can—to use his term—"identify" with learning.

These are not isolated successes. Comparable results were observed, for example, in a Comer-type program in Maryland's Prince Georges County, in the Stanford economist Henry Levin's accelerated-schools program, and in Harlem's Central Park East Elementary School, under the principalship of Deborah Meier. And research involving hundreds of programs and schools points to the same conclusion: black achievement is consistently linked to conditions of schooling that reduce racial vulnerability.

What Makes Schooling Unwise

But if wise schooling is so attainable, why is racial vulnerability the rule, not the exception, in American schooling?

One factor is the basic assimilationist offer that schools make to blacks: You can be valued and rewarded in school (and society), the schools say to these students, but you must first master the culture and ways of the American mainstream, and since that mainstream (as it is represented) is essentially white, this means you must give up many particulars of being black—styles of speech and appearance, value priorities, preferences—at least in mainstream settings. This is asking a lot. But it has been the "color-blind" offer to every immigrant and minority group in our nation's history, the core of the melting-pot ideal, and so I think it strikes most of us as fair. Yet non-immigrant minorities like blacks and Native Americans have always been here, and thus are entitled, more than new immigrants, to participate in the defining images of the society projected in school. More important, their exclusion from these images denies their contributive history and presence in society. Thus, whereas immigrants can tilt toward assimilation in pursuit of the opportunities for which they came, American blacks may find it harder to assimilate. For them, the offer of acceptance in return for assimilation carries a primal insult: it asks them to join in something that has made them invisible.

Now, I must be clear. This is not a criticism of Western civilization. My concern is an omission of image-work. In his incisive essay "What America Would Be Like Without Blacks," Ralph Ellison showed black influence on American speech and language, the themes of our finest literature, and our most defining ideals of personal freedom and democracy. In *The World They Made Together,* Mechal Sobel described how African and European influences shaped the early American South in everything from housing design and land use to religious expression. The fact is that blacks are not outside the American mainstream but, in Ellison's words, have always been "one of its major tributaries." Yet if one relied on what is taught in America's schools, one would never know this. Thus it is not what is taught but what is *not* taught, what teachers and professors have never learned the value of, that reinforces a fundamental unwiseness in American schooling, and keeps black disidentification on full boil.

Deep in the psyche of American educators is a presumption that black students need academic remediation, or extra time with elemental curricula to overcome background deficits. This orientation guides many efforts to close the achievement gap—from grammar school tutoring to college academic-support programs—but I fear it can be unwise. Bruno Bettelheim and Karen Zelan's article "Why Children Don't Like to Read" comes to mind: apparently to satisfy the changing sensibilities of local school boards over this century, many books that children like were dropped from school reading lists; when children's reading scores also dropped, the approved texts were replaced by simpler books; and when reading scores dropped again, these were replaced by even simpler books, until eventually the children could hardly read at all, not because the material was too difficult but because they were bored stiff. So it goes, I suspect, with a great many of these remediation efforts. They can even undermine students' ability to gain confidence from their achievement, by sharing credit for their successes while implying that their failures stem from inadequacies beyond the reach of remediation.

The psychologist Lisa Brown and I recently uncovered evidence of just how damaging this orientation may be. At a large, prestigious university we found that whereas the grades of black graduates of the 1950s improved during the students' college years until they virtually matched the school average, those of blacks who graduated in the 1980s worsened, ending up considerably below the school average. The 1950s graduates faced outward discrimination in everything from housing to the classroom, whereas the 1980s graduates were supported by a phalanx of help programs. Black students on today's campuses may experience far less overt prejudice than their 1950s counterparts but, ironically, may be more racially vulnerable.

The Elements of Wiseness

For too many black students school is simply the place where, more concertedly, persistently, and authoritatively than anywhere else in society, they learn how little valued they are.

Clearly, no simple recipe can fix this, but I believe we now understand the basics of a corrective approach. Schooling must focus more on reducing the vulnerabilities that block identification with achievement. I believe that four conditions, like the legs of a stool, are fundamental.

- If what is meaningful and important to a teacher is to become meaningful and important to a student, the student must feel valued by the teacher for his or her potential and as a person.

- The challenge and the promise of personal fulfillment, not remediation (under whatever guise), should guide the education of these students.
- Racial integration is a generally useful element in this design, if not a necessity. Segregation, whatever its purpose, draws out group differences and makes people feel more vulnerable when they inevitably cross group lines to compete in the larger society.
- The particulars of black life and culture—art, literature, political and social perspective, music—must be presented in the mainstream curriculum of American schooling, not consigned to special days, weeks, or even months of the year, or to special-topic courses and programs aimed essentially at blacks. Such channeling carries the disturbing message that the material is not of general value.

Finally, if I might be allowed a word specifically to black parents, one issue is even more immediate: our children may drop out of school before the first committee meets to accelerate the curriculum. Thus, although we, along with all Americans, must strive constantly for wise schooling, I believe we cannot wait for it. We cannot yet forget our essentially heroic challenge: to foster in our children a sense of hope and entitlement to mainstream American life and schooling, even when it devalues them.

THE STEREOTYPE TRAP

SHARON BEGLEY

The students had no idea of the real purpose of the study they had volunteered for—it is, after all, standard operating procedure in psychology to keep subjects in the dark on that little point. (If volunteers know they're being studied for, say, whether they will help a blind child cross a busy street, it tends to skew their behavior.) So when 40 black and 40 white Princeton undergraduates volunteered to play mini-golf, the psychologists dissembled a bit. This is a test of "natural ability," Jeff Stone and his colleagues informed some of the kids. This is a test of "the ability to think strategically," they told others. Then the students—nongolfers all—played the course, one at a time. Among those told the test measured natural ability, black students scored, on average, more than four strokes better than whites. In the group told the test gauged strategic savvy. the white kids scored four strokes better, the researchers reported. "When people are reminded of a negative stereotype about themselves—'white men can't jump' or 'black men can't think'—it can adversely affect performance," says Stone, now at the University of Arizona.

Another group of students, 46 Asian-American female undergrads at Harvard, thought they were taking a tough, 12-question math test. Before one group attacked the advanced algebra, they answered written questions emphasizing ethnicity ("How many generations of your family have lived in America?"). Another group's questionnaire subtly reminded them of their gender ("Do you live on a co-ed or single-sex dorm floor?"). Women who took the math test after being reminded of their Asian heritage—and thus, it seems, the stereotype that Asians excel at math—scored highest, getting 54 percent right. The women whose questionnaire implicitly reminded them of the stereotype that, for girls, "math is hard," as Barbie infamously said, scored lowest, answering 43 percent correctly.

The power of stereotypes, scientists had long figured, lay in their ability to change the behavior of the person holding the stereotype. If you think women are ninnies ruled by hormonal swings, you don't name them CEO; if you think gays are pedophiles, you don't tap them to lead your Boy Scout troop. But five years ago Stanford University psychologist Claude Steele showed something else: it is the targets of a stereotype whose behavior is most powerfully affected by it. A stereotype that pervades the culture the way "ditzy blondes" and "forgetful seniors" do makes people painfully aware of how society views them—so painfully aware, in fact, that knowledge of the stereotype can affect how well they do on intellectual and other tasks. Now, with half a decade of additional research under their belts, psychologists are discovering the power of stereotypes not only over blacks, but over women, members of ethnic minorities and the elderly, too. And the research is shedding light on such enduring mysteries as why black kids, even those from middle-class families and good schools, often score lower than white kids on standardized tests.

In their seminal 1995 study, Steele and Joshua Aronson, now at New York University, focused on how the threat posed by stereotypes affects African-Americans. They reasoned that whenever black students take on an intellectual task, like an SAT, they face the prospect of confirming widely held suspicions about their brainpower. This threat, the psychologists suspected, might interfere with performance. To test this hunch, Steele and Aronson gave 44 Stanford undergrads questions from the verbal part of the tough Graduate Record Exam. One group was asked, right before the test, to indicate their year in school, age, major and other information. The other group answered all that, as well as one final question: what is your race? The results were sobering. "Just listing their race undermined the black students' performance," says Steele, making them score significantly worse than blacks who did not note their race, and significantly worse than all whites. But the performance of black Stanfordites who were not explicitly reminded of their race equaled that of whites, found the scientists.

You do not even have to believe a negative stereotype to be hurt by it, psychologists find. As long as you care about the ability you're being tested on, such as golfing or math, and are familiar with the stereotype ("girls can't do higher math"), it can sink you. What seems to happen is that as soon as you reach a tough par 3 or a difficult trig problem, the possibility of confirming, and being personally reduced to, a painful stereotype causes enough distress to impair performance. "If you are a white male and you find yourself having difficulty, you may begin to worry about failing the test," says psychologist Paul Davies of Stanford in an upcoming paper. But "if you are a black male . . . you begin to worry . . . about failing your race by confirming a negative stereotype." It's a sort of "oh God, they really are right about people like me" reaction.

You don't outgrow it, either. Becca Levy of Yale showed over-60 volunteers subliminal messages (through words flashed quickly on a monitor) and then tested them on memory. Seniors who saw words like "Alzheimer's," "senile" and "old" always scored worse than seniors who saw words like "wise" and "sage"—in some tests, 64 percent better. Does it matter? In a follow-up, Levy used the same subliminal priming. But this time she asked the volunteers whether they would accept life-prolonging medical intervention. Those seniors primed with positive stereotypes usually said yes; those reminded of senility and frailty said no. "What's so frightening," says Levy, "is that the stereotype, at least in the short run, overwhelms long-held beliefs."

Stereotypes seem to most affect the best and the brightest. Only if you're black and care about academics, or female and care about math, will you also care if society thinks you're bad at those things. A girl whose sense of self-worth is tied up in her poetry, for instance, is less likely to freeze up when her facility with calculus is belittled. To test the effect of the "bimbo" stereotype, scientists at the University of Waterloo in Ontario showed men and women undergrads TV commercials with and without gender stereotypes. (In one, a student says her primary goal in college is to meet "cute guys.") Then the students, who all said they were good at math and that it mattered to them, took a standardized test. Women who saw the commercials with female stereotypes not only did worse on the math problems than did women who saw gender-neutral commercials, as well as worse than men: they actively avoided math problems in favor of verbal ones. But the effect of stereotypes didn't end there. Women who saw stereotyped ads expressed less interest in math-based careers like financial analysis and physics afterward, and more interest in math-free fields like writing. "Exposure to stereotypic commercials persuades women to withdraw" from fields like math and science where they are the targets of stereotypes, Davies says. Of course, if the stereotype is positive, it can induce you to persist in something you're supposed to be good at even if you're not. Steele admits sheepishly that he keeps playing sports (even though he's no Tiger Woods) because, as a black man, he's told by society that he's a natural.

The power of stereotypes may explain the persistent gap between black and white kids on standardized tests even when the black kids come from middle and upper socioeconomic classes. Tellingly, that gap widens with age. Little kids have comparable scores on standardized tests, but by sixth grade, black kids lag by two full grade levels in many districts. It is around sixth grade, Steele points out, that "race becomes a big factor in the social organization of school"—and hence a more powerful reminder of which group you belong to.

Can the pernicious effects of stereotypes be vanquished? If no one reminds you of a negative stereotype, your performance doesn't suffer. It can actually improve if instead you think of a positive stereotype—Steele recommends bellowing something like "You are Stanford students!"

III

Racism Then

 While we are, as I may call it, *Scouring* our Planet, by clearing America of Woods, and so making this Side of our Globe reflect a brighter Light to the Eyes of Inhabitants in Mars or Venus, why should we in the Sight of Superior Beings, darken its People? why increase the Sons of Africa, by Planting them in America, where we have so fair an Opportunity, by excluding all Blacks and Tawneys, of increasing the lovely White and Red?

—Benjamin Franklin, *Observations Concerning the Increase of Mankind*, 1751

III

Section Overview

Previous sections have explored several psychological factors involved in prejudice, including categorical thinking, cognitive dissonance, stereotyping, and stigmatization. The next six sections examine specific forms of prejudice in detail, beginning with overt forms of racism that were once widespread in Europe and the United States.

Our journey commences in the nineteenth-century salons of England and France, with the public exhibition of an African woman known as the Hottentot Venus. It then arrives on American shores with an examination of slavery and its many psychological rationales, including rationales embraced by U.S. presidents and other leaders. As the readings show, a core tenet of early racism was the notion that Black people are unevolved and animal-like. Indeed, Black people were frequently used in Southern medical experiments, much as laboratory animals are used today.

The readings continue with a brief examination of racism during the years of Jim Crow. Finally, the section concludes with a look at anti-Japanese prejudice during World War II, as well as the way that language has been used to cover up the mass incarceration of Japanese Americans.

Take Special Notice

See if you can connect historical forms of prejudice with modern-day manifestations. As illustrated by the reading entitled "Sampler of Dissonance-Reducing Statements," prejudice and stereotypes are very resilient to external logic. Consequently, they can change forms rapidly and have a very long half-life.

Questions Worth Pondering

- Did you already know how many slaves were held by early U.S. presidents? Did you know about the treatment of Mexican Americans in "Operation Wetback"? Why isn't this information more widely known?
- Do you support the idea of U.S. government compensation (or "reparatons") for the enslavement of African Americans?
- During World War II, did the U.S. government put Japanese Americans into concentration camps?
- If you had been a classmate of Anne Moody's, would you have joined her sit-in?
- What role, if any, has society's behavior toward animals played in setting the psychological stage for its treatment of racial minorities?

THE HOTTENTOT VENUS

STEPHEN JAY GOULD

I had a little friend in nursery school. I don't even remember her name. But I do recall some secret advice that I offered her one day at the playground. I told her that the enormous surrounding creatures known as adults always looked up when they walked, and that we little folk would therefore find all manner of valuable things on the ground if only we kept our gazes down. Were my paleontological predispositions already in evidence?

Carl Sagan and I both grew up in New York, both interested in biology and astronomy. Since Carl is tall and chose astronomy, while I'm short and chose paleontology, I always figured that he'd be looking up (as he did with some regularity in hosting his TV series *Cosmos*), while I'd be sticking to my old but good advice and staring at the ground. But I one-upped him (literally) last month in Paris.

A few years back, Yves Coppens, professor at the Musée de l'Homme in Paris, took Carl on a tour of the museum's innards. There, on a shelf in storage, they found the brain of Paul Broca floating in Formalin in a bell jar. Carl wrote a fine essay about this visit, the title piece of his book *Broca's Brain*. A few months ago, Yves took me on a similar tour. I held the skull of Descartes and of our mutual ancestor, the old man of Cro-Magnon. I also found Broca's brain, resting on its shelf and surrounded by other bell jars holding the brains of his illustrious scientific contemporaries—all white and all male. Yet I found the most interesting items on the shelf just above. Perhaps Carl never looked up.

This area of the museum's "back wards" holds Broca's collection of anatomical parts, including his own generous and posthumous contribution. Broca, a great medical anatomist and anthropologist, embodied the great nineteenth-century faith in quantification as a key to objective science. If he could collect enough human parts from enough human races, the resultant measurements would surely define the great scale of human progress, from chimp to Caucasian. Broca was not more virulently racist than his scientific contemporaries (nearly all successful white males, of course); he was simply more assiduous in accumulating irrelevant data, selectively presented to support an a priori viewpoint.

These shelves contain a ghoulish potpourri: severed heads from New Caledonia; an illustration of foot binding as practiced upon Chinese women—yes, a bound foot and lower leg, severed between knee and ankle. And, on a shelf just above the brains, I saw a little exhibit that provided an immediate and chilling insight into nineteenth-century *mentalité* and the history of racism: in three smaller jars, I saw the dissected genitalia of three Third-World women. I found no brains of women, and neither Broca's penis nor any male genitalia grace the collection.

The three jars are labeled *une négresse, une péruvienne,* and *la Vénus Hottentotte,* or the Hottentot Venus. Georges Cuvier himself, France's greatest anatomist, had dissected the Hottentot Venus upon her death in Paris late in 1815. He went right to the genitalia for a particular and interesting reason, to which I will return after recounting the tale of this unfortunate woman.

In an age before television and movies made virtually nothing on earth exotic, and when anthropological theory assessed as subhuman both malformed Caucasians and the normal representatives of other races, the exhibition of unusual humans became a profitable business both in upper-class salons and in street-side stalls (see Richard D. Altick's *The Shows of London,* or the book, stage, and screen treatments of the "Elephant Man"). Supposed savages from faraway lands were a mainstay of these exhibitions, and the Hottentot Venus surpassed them all in renown. (The Hottentots and Bushmen are closely related, small-statured people of southern Africa. Traditional Bushmen, when first encountered by Europeans, were hunter-gatherers, while Hottentots were pastoralists who raised cattle. Anthropologists now tend to forgo these European, somewhat derogatory terms and to designate both groups collectively as the Khoi-San peoples, a composite word constructed from each group's own name for itself.) The Hottentot Venus was a servant of Dutch farmers near Capetown, and we do not know her actual group membership. She had a name, though her exploiters never used it. She was baptized Saartjie Baartman (Saartjie, or "little Sarah" in Afrikaans, is pronounced Sar-key).

Hendrick Cezar, brother of Saartjie's "employer," suggested a trip to England for exhibition and promised to make Saartjie a wealthy woman thereby. Lord Caledon, governor of the Cape, granted permission for the trip but later regretted his decision when he understood its purposes more fully. (Saartjie's exhibition aroused much debate and she always had supporters, disgusted with the display of humans as animals; the show went on, but not to universal approbation.) She arrived in London in 1810 and immediately went on exhibition in Piccadilly, where she caused a sensation, for reasons soon to be discussed. A member of the African Association, a benevolent society that petitioned for her "release," described the show. He first encountered Saartjie in a cage on a platform raised a few feet above the floor:

> On being ordered by her keeper, she came out. . . . The Hottentot was produced like a wild beast, and ordered to move backwards and forwards and come out and go into her cage, more like a bear in a chain than a human being.

Yet Saartjie, interrogated in Dutch before a court, insisted that she was not under restraint and understood perfectly well that she had been guaranteed half the profits. The show went on.

After a long tour of the English provinces, Saartjie went to Paris where an animal trainer exhibited her for fifteen months, causing as great a sensation as in England. Cuvier and all the great naturalists of France visited her and she posed in the nude for scientific paintings at the Jardin du Roi. But she died of an inflammatory ailment on December 29, 1815, and ended up on Cuvier's dissecting table, rather than wealthy in Capetown.

Why, in an age deluged with human exhibitions, was Saartjie such a sensation? We may offer two answers, each troubling and each associated with one of her official titles—Hottentot and Venus.

On the racist ladder of human progress, Bushmen and Hottentots vied with Australian aborigines for the lowest rung, just above chimps and orangs. (Some scholars have argued that the earliest designation applied by seventeenth-century Dutch settlers—*Bosmanneken,* or "Bushman"—was a literal translation of a Malay word well known to them—*Orang Outan,* or "man of the forest.") In this system, Saartjie exerted a grim fascination, not as a missing link in a later evolutionary sense, but as a creature who straddled that dreaded boundary between human and animal and thereby taught us something about a self still present, although submerged, in "higher" creatures.

Contemporary commentators emphasized both the simian appearance and the brutal habits of Bushmen and Hottentots. In 1839, the leading American anthropologist S. G. Morton labeled Hottentots as "the nearest approximation to the lower animals. . . . Their complexion is a yellowish brown, compared by travellers to the peculiar hue of Europeans in the last stage of jaundice. . . . The women are represented as even more repulsive in appearance than the men." Mathias Guenther cites an 1847 newspaper account of a Bushman family displayed at the Egyptian Hall in London:

> In appearance they are little above the monkey tribe. They are continually crouching, warming themselves by the fire, chatting or growling. . . . They are sullen, silent and savage—mere animals in propensity, and worse than animals in appearance.

And the jaundiced account of a failed missionary in 1804:

> The Bushmen will kill their children without remorse, on various occasions; as when they are ill shaped, or when they are in want of food, or when obliged to flee from the farmers or others; in which case they will strangle them, smother them, cast them away in the desert or bury them alive. There are instances of parents throwing their tender offspring to the hungry lion, who stands roaring before their cavern, refusing to depart before some peace offering be made to him.

Guenther reports that this equation of Bushman and animal became so ingrained that one party of Dutch settlers, out on a hunting expedition, shot and ate a Bushman, assuming that he was the African equivalent of the Malay orang.

Cuvier's monograph of Saartjie's dissection, published in *The Mémoires du Muséum d' Histoire Naturelle* for 1817, followed this traditional view. After discussing and dismissing various ill-founded legends, Cuvier promised to present only "positive facts"—including this description of a Bushman's life:

> Since they are unable to engage in agriculture, or even in a pastoral life, they subsist entirely on hunting and pilfering. They live in caves and cover themselves only with the skins of animals they have killed. Their

only industry involves the poisoning of their arrows and the manufacture of nets for fishing.

His description of Saartjie herself emphasizes all points of superficial similarity with any ape or monkey. (I need hardly mention that since people vary so much, each group must be closer than others to some feature of some other primate, without implying anything about genealogy or aptitude.) Cuvier, for example, discusses the flatness of Saartjie's nasal bones: "In this respect, I have never seen a human head more similar to that of monkeys." He emphasizes various proportions of the femur (upper leg bone) as embodying "characters of animality." He speaks of Saartjie's small skull (no surprise for a woman four and a half feet tall), and relegates her to stupidity according to "that cruel law, which seems to have condemned to an eternal inferiority those races with small and compressed skulls." He even abstracted a set of supposedly simian responses from her behavior: "Her movements had something brusque and capricious about them, which recall those of monkeys. She had, above all, a way of pouting her lips, in the same manner as we have observed in orang utans."

Yet a careful reading of the entire monograph belies these interpretations, since Cuvier states again and again (although he explicitly draws neither moral nor message) that Saartjie was an intelligent woman with general proportions that would not lead connoisseurs to frown. He mentions, in an offhand sort of way, that Saartjie possessed an excellent memory, spoke Dutch rather well, had some command of English, and was learning a bit of French when she died. (Not bad for a caged brute; I only wish that more Americans could do one-third so well in their command of languages.) He admitted that her shoulders, back, and chest "had grace"; and with the gentilesse of his own race, spoke of *sa main charmante* ("her charming hand").

Yet Saartjie's hold over well-bred Europe did not arise from her racial status alone. She was not simply the Hottentot or the Hottentot woman, but the Hottentot Venus. Under all official words lay the great and largely unsaid reason for her popularity. Khoi-San women do exaggerate two features of their sexual anatomy (or at least of body parts that excite sexual feelings in most men). The Hottentot Venus won her fame as a sexual object, and her combination of supposed bestiality and lascivious fascination focused the attention of men who could thus obtain both vicarious pleasure and a smug reassurance of superiority.

Primarily—for, as they say, you can't miss it—Saartjie was, in Altick's words, "steatopygous to a fault." Khoi-San women accumulate large amounts of fat in their buttocks, a condition called steatopygia. The buttocks protrude far back, often coming to a point at their upper extremity and sloping down toward the genitalia. Saartjie was especially well endowed, the probable cause of Cezar's decision to convert her from servant to siren. Saartjie covered her genitalia during exhibitions, but her rear end was the show, and she submitted to endless gaze and poke for five long years. Since European women did not wear bustles at the time, but indicated by their clothing only what nature had provided, Saartjie seemed all the more incredible.

Cuvier well understood the mixed bestial and sexual nature of Saartjie's fascination when he wrote that "everyone was able to see her during her eighteen-month stay in our capital, and to verify the enormous protrusion of her buttocks and the brutal appearance of her face." In his dissection, Cuvier focused on an unsolved mystery surrounding each of her unusual features. Europeans had long wondered whether the large buttocks were fatty, muscular, or perhaps even supported by a previously unknown bone. The problem had already been solved—in favor of fat—by external observation, the primary reason for her disrobing before scientists at the Jardin du Roi. Still, Cuvier dissected her buttocks and reported:

> We could verify that the protuberance of her buttocks had nothing muscular about it, but arose from a [fatty] mass of a trembling and elastic consistency, situated immediately under her skin. It vibrated with all movements that the woman made.

But Saartjie's second peculiarity provided even greater wonder and speculation among scientists; and Saartjie heightened the intrigue by keeping this feature scrupulously hidden, even refusing a display at the Jardin. Only after her death could the curiosity of science be slaked.

Reports had circulated for two centuries of a wondrous structure attached directly to the female genitalia of Khoi-San women and covering their private parts with a veil of skin, the so-called *sinus pudoris,* or "curtain of shame." (If I may be permitted a short excursion into the realm of scholarly minutiae—the footnotes of more conventional academic publication—I would like to correct a standard mistranslation of Linnaeus, one that I have made myself. In his original description of *Homo sapiens,* Linnaeus provided a most unflattering account of African blacks, including the line: *feminae sinus pudoris.* This phrase has usually been translated, "women are without shame"—a slur quite consistent with Linnaeus's general description. In Latin, "without shame" should be *sine pudore,* not *sinus pudoris.* But eighteenth-century scientific Latin was written so indifferently that misspellings and wrong cases are no bar to actual intent, and the reading "without shame" has held. But Linnaeus was only stating that African women have a genital flap, or *sinus pudoris.* He was also wrong, because only the Khoi-San and a few related peoples develop this feature.)

The nature of the *sinus pudoris* had generated a lively debate, with partisans on both sides claiming eyewitness support. One party held that the *sinus* was simply an enlarged part of the ordinary genitalia; others called it a novel structure found in no other race. Some even described the so-called "Hottentot apron" as a large fold of skin hanging down from the lower abdomen itself.

Cuvier was determined to resolve this old argument; the status of Saartjie's *sinus pudoris* would be the primary goal of his dissection. Cuvier began his monograph by noting: "There is nothing more famous in natural history than the *tablier* (the French rendering of *sinus pudoris*) of Hottentots of, and, at the same time, no feature has been the object of so many arguments." Cuvier resolved the debate with his usual elegance: the *labia minora,* or inner lips, of the ordinary female genitalia are greatly enlarged in Khoi-San women, and may hang down three or four inches below the vagina when women stand, thus giving the impression of a separate and enveloping curtain of skin. Cuvier preserved his skillful dissection of Saartjie's genitalia and wrote with a flourish: "I have the honor to present to the Academy the genital organs of this woman prepared in a manner that leaves no doubt about the nature of her *tablier.*" And Cuvier's gift still rests in its jar, forgotten on a shelf at the Musée de l'Homme—right above Broca's brain.

Yet while Cuvier correctly identified the nature of Saartjie's *tablier,* he fell into an interesting error, arising from the same false association that had inspired public fascination with Saartjie—sexuality with animality. Since Cuvier regarded Hottentots as the most bestial of people, and since they had a large *tablier,* he assumed that the *tablier* of other Africans must become progressively smaller as the darkness of southern Africa ceded to the light of Egypt. (In the last part of his monograph, Cuvier argues that the ancient Egyptians must have been fully Caucasian; who else could have built the pyramids?)

Cuvier knew that female circumcision was widely practiced in Ethiopia. He assumed that the *tablier* must be at least half-sized among these people of intermediate hue and geography; and he further conjectured that Ethiopians excised the *tablier* to improve sexual access, not that circumcision represented a custom sustained by power and imposed upon girls with genitalia not noticeably different from those of European women. "The negresses of Abyssinia," he wrote, "are inconvenienced to the point of being obliged to destroy these parts by knife and cauterization" (*par le fer et par le feu,* as he wrote in more euphonious French).

Cuvier also told an interesting tale, requiring no comment in repetition:

> The Portuguese Jesuits, who converted the King of Abyssinia and part of his people during the 16th century, felt that they were obliged to proscribe this practice [of female circumcision] since they thought that it was a holdover from the ancient Judaism of that nation. But it happened that Catholic girls could no longer find husbands, because the men could not reconcile themselves to such a disgusting deformity. The College of Propaganda sent a surgeon to verify the fact and, on his report, the reestablishment of the ancient custom was authorized by the Pope.

I needn't burden you with any detailed refutation of the general arguments that made the Hottentot Venus such a sensation. I do, however, find it amusing that she and her people are, by modern convictions, so singularly and especially unsuited for the role she was forced to play.

If earlier scientists cast the Khoi-San peoples as approximations to the lower primates, they now rank among the heroes of modern social movements. Their languages, with complex clicks, were once dismissed as a guttural farrago of beastly sounds. They are now widely admired for their complexity and subtle expression. Cuvier had stigmatized the hunter-

gatherer life styles of the traditional San (Bushmen) as the ultimate degradation of a people too stupid and indolent to farm or raise cattle. The same people have become models of righteousness to modern ecoactivists for their
understanding, nonexploitive, and balanced approach to natural resources.
Of course, as Guenther argues in his article on the Bushman's changing image, our modern accolades may also be unrealistic. Still, if people must be ex-
ploited rather than understood, attributions of kindness and heroism sure
beat accusations of animality.

Furthermore, while Cuvier's contemporaries sought physical signs of
bestiality in Khoi-San anatomy, anthropologists now identify these people as
perhaps the most paedomorphic of human groups. Humans have evolved by
a general retardation (or slowing down) of developmental rates, leaving our
adult bodies quite similar in many respects to the juvenile, but not to the
adult, form of our primate ancestors—an evolutionary result called paedo-
morphosis, or "child shaping." On this criterion, the greater the extent of pae-
domorphosis, the further away from a simian past (although minor
differences among human races do not translate into variations in mental or
moral worth). Although Cuvier searched hard to find signs of animality in
Saartjie's lip movements or in the form of her leg bone, her people are, in general, perhaps the least simian of all humans.

Finally, the major rationale for Saartjie's popularity rested on a false
premise. She fascinated Europeans because she had big buttocks and genitalia and because she supposedly belonged to the most backward of human groups. Everything fit together for Cuvier's contemporaries.
Advanced humans (read modern Europeans) are refined, modest, and sexually restrained (not to mention hypocritical for advancing such a claim).
Animals are overtly and actively sexual, and so betray their primitive character. Thus, Saartjie's exaggerated sexual organs record her animality. But
the argument is, as our English friends say (and quite literally in this case),
"arse about face." Humans are the most sexually active of primates, and
humans have the largest sexual organs of our order. If we must pursue this
dubious line of argument, a person with larger than average endowment
is, if anything, more human.

On all accounts—mode of life, physical appearance, and sexual
anatomy—London and Paris should have stood in a giant cage while
Saartjie watched. Still, Saartjie gained her posthumous triumph. Broca inherited not only Cuvier's preparation of Saartjie's *tablier,* but her skeleton
as well. In 1862, he thought he had found a criterion for arranging human
races by physical merit. He measured the ratio of radius (lower arm bone)
to humerus (upper arm bone), reasoning that higher ratios indicate longer
forearms—a traditional feature of apes. He began to hope that objective
measurement had confirmed his foregone conclusion when blacks averaged .794 and whites .739. But Saartjie's skeleton yielded .703 and Broca
promptly abandoned his criterion. Had not Cuvier praised the arm of the
Hottentot Venus?

Saartjie continues her mastery of Mr. Broca today. His brain decomposes in a leaky jar. Her *tablier* stands above, while her well-prepared skeleton gazes up from below. Death, as the good book says, is swallowed up in victory.[1]

Postscript

Saartjie Baartman herself continues to fascinate us across the ages; her exploitation has never really ended. In an antiquarian bookstore in Johannesberg, I found and bought the following remarkable print (I still cannot view it without a shudder despite its intended humor, and I reproduce it here as a comment upon history and current reality that we dare not ignore). The print is a satirical French commentary (published in Paris in 1812) on English fascination with Saartjie's display. It is titled: *Les curieux en extase, ou les cordons de souliers* (The curious in ecstasy, or the shoelaces). Spectators concentrate entirely upon sexual features of the Hottentot *Venus*. One military gentleman observes her steatopygia from behind and comments, *"Oh! godem quel rosbif."* The second

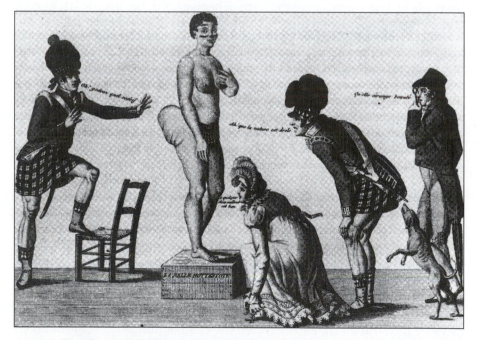

A satiric French print of 1812 commenting on English fascination with the Hottentot Venus. The soldier behind her examines her steatopygia, while the lady in front pretends to tie her shoelace in order to get a peek at Saartjie's tablier.

---

[1]*Editor's note:* In May of 2002, the Musée de l'Homme returned the remains of Saartjie Baartman to South Africa for a memorial service and burial.

man in uniform and the elegantly attired lady are both trying to sneak a peek at Saartjie's tablier. (This is the subtle point that an uninformed observer would miss. Saartjie displayed her buttocks but, following the customs of her people, would never uncover her tablier). The man exclaims "how odd nature is," while the woman, hoping to get a better look from below, crouches under pretense of tying her shoes (hence the title). Meanwhile, the dog reminds us that we are all the same biological object under our various attires.

To bring the exploitation up to date, W. B. Deatrick sent me the cover of the French magazine *Photo* for May, 1982. It shows, naked, a woman who calls herself "Carolina, la Vénus hottentote de Saint-Domingue." She holds an uncorked champagne bottle in front. The fizz flies up, over her head, through the letter O of the magazine's title, down behind her back and directly into the glass, which rests, as she crouches (to mimic Saartjie's endowment), upon her outstretched buttocks.

Molasses and Rum

Several early presidents owned slaves, and some were involved directly in the slave trade. For example, Thomas Jefferson sold some of his slaves to pay off debts, and he included "25 negroes little and big" as part of his daughter Martha's marriage dowry. Likewise, Andrew Jackson sold slaves to secure mortgages. And in 1766, George Washington wrote the letter below exchanging a slave for one hogshead of molasses, one of rum, and various other supplies:

> Sir:
>   With this letter comes a negro (Tom), which I beg the favor of you to sell in any of the Islands you may go to, for whatever he will fetch, and bring me in return from him
>   One hhd of best molasses
>   One ditto of best rum
>   One barrel of lymes, if good and cheap
>   One pot of tamarinds, containing about 10 lbs.
>   Two small ditto of mixed sweetmeats, about 5 lbs. each
>   And the residue, much or little, in good old spirits. That this fellow is both a rogue and a runaway . . . I shall not pretend to deny. But that he is exceeding healthy, strong, and good at the hoe, the whole neighborhood can testify . . . which gives me reason to hope he may with your good management sell well, if kept clean and trim'd up a little when offered for sale.
>   I shall very chearfully allow you the customary commissions on this affair, and must beg the favor of you (lest he should attempt his escape) to keep him handcuffed till you get to sea.

In 1781, when one of his slaves was executed for a crime, Washington appealed for and was granted a tax credit equal to the slave's market value plus three years of interest. With respect to slave children, he required fieldwork starting around age 11 (his instructions were: "so soon as [small boys and girls] are able to work out I expect to reap the benefit of their labour"). In the last year of his life, Washington owned more than 300 slaves, making him one of the nation's largest slaveholders at that time.

—Sources: *The Papers of Thomas Jefferson; Correspondence of Andrew Jackson; The Writings of George Washington; George Washington's Mount Vernon*

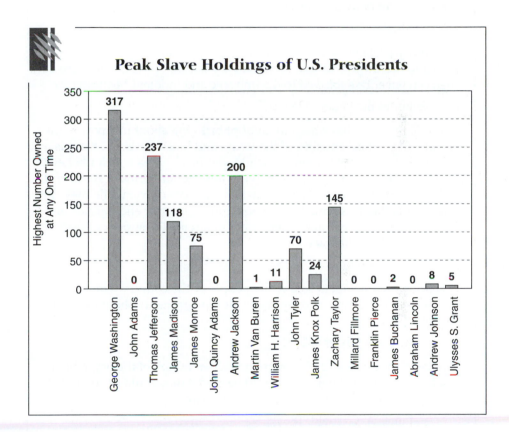

Peak Slave Holdings of U.S. Presidents

Some Presidential Statements on Race

Never yet could I find that a black had uttered a thought above the level of plain narration; never see even an elementary trait of painting or sculpture. . . . Blacks, whether originally a distinct race, or made distinct by time and circumstances, are inferior to the whites in the endowments both of body and mind.

> —Thomas Jefferson, 1787

It is, verily I believe, the true interest of Mexico that Texas should be annexed to the United States. . . . in the very nature of things, our race of men can never be subjected to the imbecile and indolent Mexican race.

> —James Buchanan, 1844

I am not, nor ever have been in favor of bringing about in any way the social and political equality of the white and black races. . . . there is a physical difference between the white and black races which I believe will for ever forbid the two races living together on terms of social and political equality. And inasmuch as they cannot so live, while they do remain together there must be the position of superior and inferior, and I as much as any other man am in favor of having the superior position assigned to the white race.

> —Abraham Lincoln, 1858

It is upon the intelligent free white people of the country that all Governments should rest, and by them all Governments should be controlled.

> —Andrew Johnson, 1861

[I have] a strong feeling of repugnance when I think of the negro being made our political equal and I would be glad if they could be colonized, sent to heaven, or got rid of in any decent way.

> —James A. Garfield, 1865

The present Chinese labor invasion . . . is pernicious and should be discouraged. Our experience in dealing with weaker races—the negroes and Indians, for example—is not encouraging. . . . I therefore would consider with favor suitable measures to discourage the Chinese from coming to our shores.

> —Rutherford Hayes, 1879

Presidential Statements on Race (*continued*)

The enfranchisement of the negro . . . explains everything in the political condition of the South that needs any explanation. . . . Under such circumstances the choice of the white voters was quickly and naturally made. The alternatives presented to them were, to be ruled by an ignorant and an inferior race, or to band themselves in a political union not to be broken until the danger passed.

   —Woodrow Wilson, 1881

The simply appalling and universal dishonesty of the [Chinese] working classes, the racial slowness, and much lower average of intelligence, gives them an efficiency far below the workmen of England and America.

   —Herbert C. Hoover, 1902

As a race and in the mass [the Negroes] are altogether inferior to the whites.

   —Theodore Roosevelt, 1906

I think one man is just as good as another so long as he's honest and decent and not a nigger or a Chinaman. . . . I am strongly of the opinion that negros ought to be in Africa, yellow men in Asia and white men in Europe and America.

   —Harry S. Truman, 1911

Biological laws tell us that certain divergent people will not mix or blend. The Nordics propagate themselves successfully. With other races, the outcome shows deterioration on both sides.

   —Calvin Coolidge, 1921

Men of both [Black and White] races may well stand uncompromisingly against every suggestion of social equality. Indeed, it would be helpful to have that word "equality" eliminated from this consideration; to have it accepted on both sides that this is not a question of social equality, but a question of recognizing a fundamental, eternal and inescapable difference. . . . Racial amalgamation there cannot be.

   —Warren G. Harding, 1921

[Social equality does not mean] that a Negro should court my daughter.

   —Dwight D. Eisenhower, 1956

Punishment for Stealing and Destroying Property

Be it further enacted by the authority aforesaid, That if any negro or other slave shall hereafter steal or destroy any goods, chattels, or other provisions whatsoever . . . such negro or slave so offending, excepting children, whose punishment is left wholly to the discretion of the said justice, shall be adjudged by such justice to be publicly and severely whipped, not exceeding forty lashes; and if such negro or other slave punished as aforesaid, be afterwards, by two justices of the peace, found guilty of the like crimes, he or they, for such his or their second offence, shall either have one of his ears cut off, or be branded in the forehead with a hot iron, that the mark thereof may remain; and if after such punishment, such negro or slave for his third offence, shall have his nose slit . . . and in case they shall be found guilty a fourth time, of any the offences before mentioned, then such negro or other slave shall be adjudged to suffer death, or other punishment, as the said justices shall think fitting.

—*An Act for the Better Ordering and Governing of Negroes and Slaves*, Article X, South Carolina Statutes at Large, 1712

Insurance for Slave Owners

In the 1840s and 1850s, American slave owners insured thousands of slaves, usually for two-thirds to three-fourths of their market value up to $800 per "head." An 1849 business prospectus for North Carolina Mutual explained: "The insurance on slaves in this State opens a new field of thought to our Planters, and other slave owners, and proposes to secure them in the possession of that kind of property, which constitutes half of the actual wealth of the State."

Insurance companies charged higher premiums for slaves engaged in coal mining, railroad operations, and other risky occupations, and slave life insurance policies commonly had stipulations such as "in case the said slave shall die for want of proper medical or personal attendance . . . this Policy shall be void." The Aetna Insurance Company of Hartford also included a policy rider that voided claims for slaves who were lynched, worked to death, or who committed suicide.

—Sources: *Journal of Southern History,* November, 1977; *New York Times,* July 24, 2000

A Sampler of Dissonance–Reducing Statements in Support of Slavery

The following statements served to reduce cognitive dissonance, or psychological discomfort, felt by slave-owners who simultaneously held two conflicting cognitions: (1) I am a good person, and (2) I am regarding other people as my personal property.

Blacks Benefit from Slavery

"Blacks are immeasurably better off here than in Africa, morally, socially & physically. The painful discipline they are undergoing, is necessary for their instruction as a race, & I hope will prepare & lead them to better things" (General Robert E. Lee, 1856, in Nolan, 1991, p. 12).

"The mere physical development of the negro is improved by his transport and enslavement. As an animal, in stature, in muscular energy, in activity, and strength, the negro has arrived at his greatest development while in slavery" (Cobb, 1858, p. 49).

"[Blacks] are elevated from the condition in which God first created them, by being made our slaves. None of that race on the whole face of the globe can be compared with the slaves of the South. They are happy, content, unaspiring, and utterly incapable, from intellectual weakness, ever to give us any trouble by their aspirations" (Hammond, 1866/1978, pp. 319–320).

"Among any savage people, the introduction and establishment of domestic slavery is necessarily an improvement of the condition and wealth and well-being of the community in general, and also of the comfort of the enslaved class" (Ruffin, 1853, pp. 3–4).

"Never before has the black race . . . attained a condition so civilized and so improved, not only physically, but morally and intellectually. It came among us in a low, degraded, and savage condition, and in the course of a few generations it has grown up under the fostering care of our institutions, reviled as they have been, to its present comparatively civilized condition" (Calhoun, 1853, p. 630).

Dissonance–Reducing Statements (continued)

Slaves Are Happy and Do Not Suffer

"[Slaves] form the happiest portion of our society. A merrier being does not exist on the face of the globe, than the negro slave of the United States" (Dew, 1832/1970, p. 111).

"Southern slavery has become a benign and protective institution, and our negroes are confessedly better off than any free laboring population in the world" (Fitzhugh, 1857/1960, p. 201).

"The average condition of the slave at the South is infinitely superior, morally and materially, in all respects, to that of the labouring class under any other circumstances in any other part of the world" (Holmes, 1852, p. 730).

Economics Prevent Cruelty

"Both interest and inclination, the desire of profit and the sense or sentiment of duty concur to render the slave-owner considerate and kind toward the slave" (Holmes, 1852, p. 729).

"Planters have a powerful motive in their interest to be kind and gentle to their slaves; and, if that motive hath not been found at all times sufficient to restrain the impulses of passion, it certainly does so very generally" (Collins, 1811/1971, p. 12).

"Coincidence of economic interests is coincidence of all interests" (Hughes, 1854, p. 264).

Slaves Are Machines/Property

"Our slaves are our machinery, and we have as good a right to profit by them as do the northern men who profit by the machinery they employ" (Clayton, 1833, in Hecht, 1972, p. 521).

"A negro is an instrument, which requires to be incessantly acted upon to the performance of its duty. . . . a mere machine, without either will or motion, other than you impress upon him" (Collins, 1811/1971, pp. 165, 172).

"[A slave] is a threefold product. He is produced bodily, motively, and locally. Breeding is bodily production; circulation, local production" (Hughes, 1854, p. 102).

Dissonance–Reducing Statements (continued)

Slaves Do Not Suffer As Whites Do

"What would be the cause of insupportable pain to a white man, a negro would almost disregard" (Carroll, 1900/1969, p. 61).

"Women of colour have easier parturitions, in general, than white Europeans; and . . . brutes have easier parturitions than the human species" (White, 1799, p. 73).

"[Black] griefs are transient. Those numberless afflictions, which render it doubtful whether heaven has given life to us in mercy or in wrath, are less felt, and sooner forgotten with them" (President Thomas Jefferson, 1794/1955, p. 139).

Slaves Lack Intelligence

"The prominent defect in the mental organization of the negro, is a want of judgement. He forms no definite idea of effects from causes. He cannot comprehend, so as to execute the simplest orders, unless they refresh his memory as to some previous knowledge. He is imitative, sometimes eminently so, but his mind is never inventive or suggestive" (Cobb, 1858, p. 35).

"In dealing with a negro we must remember that we are dealing with a being possessing the form and strength of a man, but the intellect only of a child" (Canning, in Dew, 1832/1970, p. 105).

Religious Support for Slavery

"Under the law of God the Negro, like every other animal, is the property of man" (Carroll, 1900/1969, p. 289).

"Slavery was established and sanctioned by Divine Authority, among even the elect of Heaven—the favoured children of Israel" (Dew, 1832/1970, p. 9).

"God not only *gave* slaves to Abraham, as evidence of his blessing, but he commanded the Jews to make slaves of the heathen round about them: 'of them shall ye buy bondmen and bondmaids. Moreover, of the children of the strangers that do sojourn among you, of them shall ye buy, and of their families that are with you, which they begat in your land, and they shall be your possessions; and ye shall take them as an inheritance for your children after you to inherit them for a possession. They shall be your bondmen forever' " (Cobb, 1858, p. 55).

Dissonance–Reducing Statements (continued)

Slavery Is Necessary

"Slave labor products have now become necessities of human life, to the extent of more than half the commercial articles supplied to the Christian world" (Christy, 1860, p. 215).

"Negro slavery has become the most necessary of all human institutions. . . . To emancipate all the negroes would be to starve Western Europe and our North" (Fitzhugh, 1857/1960, pp. 201–202).

"If an immediate emancipation of the negroes were to take place, the whole southern country would be visited with an immediate general famine, from which the productive resources of all the other states of the Union could not deliver them" (Dew, 1832/1970, 95).

Slavery Is Natural

"The negro is a slave by nature, and can never be happy, industrious, moral or religious, in any other condition than the one he was intended to fill" (Cartwright, 1851, p. 698).

"Man is a social and gregarious animal, and all such animals hold property in each other. Nature imposes upon them slavery as a law and necessity of their existence. . . . [Slavery] is, and ever must be, coeval and coextensive with human nature" (Fitzhugh, 1857/1960, p. 235).

"The natural relation between the White and the Negro is that of master and servant" (Carroll, 1900/1969, p. 101).

"Slavery existed throughout the whole of the ancient, and in a very large portion of the modern world. . . . [It is] a necessary and inevitable consequence of the principles of human nature" (Dew, 1832/1970, p. 28).

Slaves Prefer Slavery

"In America, if let alone, they [blacks] always prefer the same kind of government, which we call slavery, but which is actually an improvement on the government of their forefathers, as it gives them more tranquility and sensual enjoyment, expands the mind and improves the morals, by arousing them from that natural indolence so fatal to mental and moral progress" (Cartwright, 1851, p. 694).

Dissonance–Reducing Statements (continued)

"Slaves in the French colonies were for a time liberated, and even in Cayenne, where the experiment succeeded best in consequence of the paucity of slaves, it completely demonstrated the superiority of slave over free black labor; and generally the reestablishment of slavery was attended with the most happy consequences, and even courted by the negroes themselves, who became heartily tired of their short lived liberty" (Dew, 1832/1970, p. 90).

Abolition Would Hurt the Slaves

"We cannot get rid of slavery without producing a greater injury to both the masters and slaves" (Dew, 1832/1970, p. 106).

"Slaves never die of hunger, scarcely ever feel want. The bestowing upon men equality of rights, is but giving license to the strong to oppress the weak" (Fitzhugh, 1854, p. 233).

"The free laborer must work or starve. He is more of a slave than the negro, because he works longer and harder for less allowance than the slave, and has no holiday, because the cares of life with him begin when its labors end. He has no liberty, and not a single right" (Fitzhugh, 1857/1960, p. 18).

Slaveholders Are Caring

"The slaveholder is better than others—because he has greater occasion for the exercise of the affections. His whole life is spent in providing for the minutest wants of others, in taking care of them in sickness and in health. Hence he is the least selfish of men" (Fitzhugh, 1854, pp. 247–248).

"Look to the slave holding population of our country, and you every where find them characterized by noble and elevated sentiment, by humane and virtuous feelings. We do not find among them that cold, contracted, calculating selfishness, which whithers and repels every thing around it. . . . The most cruel masters are those who have been unaccustomed to slavery" (Dew, 1832/1970, p. 109).

"[The South] has kept pace with its brethren in other sections of the Union where slavery does not exist. It is odious to make the comparison; but I appeal to all sides whether the South is not equal in virtue, intelligence, patriotism, courage, disinterestedness, and all the high qualities which adorn our nature" (Calhoun, 1853, p. 630).

Dissonance–Reducing Statements (continued)

Abolitionism Is Fanaticism and Is Only the First Step

"Emancipation itself would not satisfy these fanatics: —that gained, the next step would be to raise the negroes to a social and political equality with the whites; and that being effected, we would soon find the present condition of the two races reversed. They and their northern allies would be the masters, and we the slaves" (Calhoun, 1853, p. 633).

"The history of abolitionism in the United States has been the history of fanaticism everywhere" (Cobb, 1858, p. ccx).

Abolitionists Hate Slaves

"Hatred to slavery is very generally little more than hatred of negroes" (Fitzhugh, 1857/1960, p. 201).

Slavery Is Not the Issue

"Everyone of the leading Abolitionists is agitating the negro slavery question merely as a means to attain ulterior ends, and those ends nearer home. They would not spend so much time and money for the mere sake of the negro or his master, about whom they care little. But they know that men once fairly committed to negro slavery agitation— once committed to the sweeping principle 'that man being a moral agent, accountable to God for his actions, should not have those actions controlled and directed by the will of another,' are, in effect, committed to Socialism and Communism" (Fitzhugh, 1857/1960, p. 253).

Abuses Are Part of the System

"That the system places the negro where his natural rights may be abused, is true; yet this is no reason why the system is in itself wrong" (Cobb, 1858, p. 52).

Slavery Is Inevitable

"Two races, differing in manners, customs, language, and civilization, can never harmonize upon a footing of equality. One must rule the other, or exterminating wars must be waged" (Dew, 1832/1970, p. 80).

[*Note:* Full citations are given in the Source Notes.]

THE USE OF BLACKS FOR MEDICAL EXPERIMENTATION AND DEMONSTRATION IN THE OLD SOUTH

TODD L. SAVITT

"An abundance of materials in the southern medical journals reveals that slaves had a fairly significant role in medical education and in experimental and radical medical and surgical practice of the antebellum South," remarked J. Walter Fisher in a 1968 article describing some of the medical uses to which slaves were put in the Old South.[1] Further investigation into this subject indicates that southern white medical educators and researchers relied greatly on the availability of Negro patients for various purposes. Black bodies often found their way to dissecting tables, operating amphitheaters, classroom or bedside demonstrations, and experimental facilities. This is not to deny that white bodies were similarly used.[2] In northern cities and in southern port towns such as New Orleans, Louisville, Memphis, Charleston, and Mobile, where poor, transient whites were abundant, seamen, European immigrants, and white indigents undoubtedly joined blacks in fulfilling the "clinical material" needs of the medical profession. But blacks were particularly easy targets, given their positions as voiceless slaves or "free persons of color" in a society sensitive to and separated by race. This open and deliberate use of blacks for medical research and demonstration well illustrates the racial attitudes of antebellum white southerners.

Interestingly, people generally assumed that information gained from observation of Negro bodies was applicable to Caucasians. Despite the political rhetoric then current in the Old South about a separate medicine for blacks and for whites,[3] the research and teaching reflected, in fact, the opposite. Negroes did not seem to differ enough from Caucasians to exclude them from extensive use in southern medical schools and in research activities.[4]

Use of blacks for medical experimentation and demonstration was not the result of a conscious organized plan on the part of white southerners to learn more about the differences between the races or even how better to care for their black charges. The examples related in this article reflect the actions of individual researchers and medical institutions. Taken together, however, a pattern emerges. Blacks were considered more available and more accessible in this white-dominated society: they were rendered physically visible by their skin color but were legally invisible because of their slave status.

Throughout history medicine has required bodies for teaching purposes. Students had to learn anatomy, recognize and diagnose diseases, and treat conditions requiring surgery; researchers had to try out their ideas and new techniques; and practitioners had to perform autopsies to confirm their diagnoses and to understand the effects of diseases on the human body. The need for human specimens became more recognized and more emphasized in

America during the first half of the nineteenth century as the ideas of the French school of hospital medicine reached this country. And medical schools throughout the United States, including those in the South, attempted to meet the new demands of students for a modern education. Clinics, infirmaries, and hospitals were opened in conjunction with those colleges; patients, however, were not always willing to enter. Medicine thus capitalized on the need of the indigent and the helpless for medical care. In the South white attitudes toward blacks ensured the selection of patients of this group as specimens, though some whites were also used.

Competition for students among southern medical schools was fierce during the thirty years preceding the Civil War, which led each institution to publicize the positive aspects of its program in newspapers, medical journals, circulars, and magazines. One of the major requisites of any school was an abundant supply of clinical material—living patients for medical and surgical demonstrations as well as cadavers for anatomical dissections and pathological examinations. Institutional reputations were made and broken on the basis of the availability of teaching specimens. The Transylvania University Medical Department in Lexington, Kentucky, serves as a case in point. One of the causes for its decline from eminence during the 1830s was its purported difficulty in procuring bodies for clinical teaching. Despite numerous attempts by both faculty and students to dispel rumors about the shortage of specimens and demonstration materials at the medical school, it was impossible to reverse the negative impressions of students. On the other hand, a medical school was established in nearby Louisville (Louisville Medical Institute) in 1837, owing in part to the presence of a large black (as well as transient white) population, well suited to the needs of teaching institutions.[5]

To train students in disease management, the better southern medical schools either established infirmaries or arranged with local authorities to treat patients in poor houses or city hospitals. In Georgia, Kentucky, Alabama, South Carolina, Virginia, and presumably in other southern states the patients used for the education of students were frequently black. Newspaper advertisements by the Atlanta Medical College, for example, encouraged owners to send their sick and injured slaves to the infirmary for treatment. There, "An intelligent nurse and faithful servant will be in constant attendance." No mention of the presence of medical students was necessary. The boarding fee was reasonable (fifteen cents per day), and the doctor's fee was waived if the case turned out to be incurable and the slave had to be sent home.[6]

South Carolina medical institutions were even more explicit in their public requests for black patients. The hospital of the Medical College of the State of South Carolina admitted slaves, poor whites, and free blacks. As an inducement to lure patients from the competing medical-school hospital, infirmary officials made owners of slaves liable for no professional charges, the only account rendered being that for food and nursing. This was so, they explained, because "The sole object of the Faculty . . . [is] to promote the interest of Medical education within their native State and City."[7] The surgery established by the faculty of the other school, the Medical College of South

Carolina, admitted slaves and free blacks only. An advertisement placed in the Charleston *Courier* requested planters with servants "laboring under Surgical diseases," local physicians with slave patients requiring surgical intervention, and "Such [free] persons of color as may not be able to pay for Medical advice . . . ," to call at the hospital. "The object of the Faculty . . . ," the announcement continued, "is to collect as many interesting cases, as possible, for the benefit and instruction of their pupils."[8]

By 1841 the Medical College of the State of South Carolina had established a permanent year-round hospital with large wards for black and white patients. College officials claimed that they had little trouble filling beds at this new infirmary, because "the slave population of the city, and neighboring plantations, is capable of furnishing ample materials for clinical instruction." Students at the school saw not only "all the common diseases of the climate" but also a variety of operative procedures, owing to the presence of a slave population "peculiarly liable to surgical diseases requiring operations for their relief."[9] The medical college continued to use black patients for surgical demonstrations throughout the antebellum years. During the late 1850s, for instance, surgical cases occurring among blacks while school was in session were admitted to the "Coloured Wards" of a newly constructed public hospital and were reserved for the exclusive use of student doctors.[10]

The use of black patients for medical-school training was not confined to the lower South. The Hampden-Sydney College Medical Department (called the Medical College of Virginia after 1854) located in Richmond employed many of the same techniques as the South Carolina and Georgia institutions to attract Negroes into its infirmary wards. Faculty physicians announced in an 1853 publication that "The number of negroes employed in our factories will furnish materials for the support of an extensive hospital, and afford to the student that great desideratum—clinical instruction." They placed ads in country editions of Richmond newspapers informing rural slaveholders of the infirmary's facilities, charged lower rates for blacks, and attempted (unsuccessfully) to establish first a slave hospital, then a free hospital for all indigents and for slaves.[11]

The attitudes of white southerners both toward the use of human bodies in medical education and toward blacks were silently but clearly revealed in the medical profession's heavy reliance on Negro cadavers. Human anatomical dissection was illegal in many states during the antebellum period,[12] although medical schools continued to teach anatomy. Southern blacks, because of their helpless legal and inconsequential social positions, thus became prime candidates for medical-school dissections. Physicians usually found it much more convenient to obtain black specimens than white. "In Baltimore," commented Harriet Martineau after an 1834 visit, "the bodies of coloured people exclusively are taken for dissection, 'because the whites do not like it, and the coloured people cannot resist.' "[13] Dr. Henry M. Dowling of Leesburg, Virginia, had little difficulty receiving permission for an autopsy on a twelve-year-old slave girl with a suspected case of worms because the victim's owner was "a gentleman of intelligence, and unaffected by the vulgar prejudices entertained on this subject . . ." by others.[14]

When it came to obtaining Caucasian bodies for postmortem examinations, however, even "gentlemen of intelligence" found ways to refuse physicians. For example, of twenty-four individual autopsies reported by white southern physicians in the *Transylvania Journal of Medicine and the Associate Sciences* (1828–1839) and the *Transylvania Medical Journal* (1849–1851) nineteen were performed on blacks and only five on whites, in a state where the white population far exceeded the black.

Occasionally, the prevailing attitude of whites—that dissection was acceptable when confined to the black population—was expressed in print. A correspondent to the Milledgeville, Georgia, *Statesman and Patriot* in 1828 agreed that it was necessary to dissect corpses to learn anatomy but opposed the use of whites for such a procedure. He endorsed a proposal then before the state legislature that permitted local authorities to release bodies of executed black felons to medical societies for the purpose of dissection, assuring the safety of white corpses. "The *bodies of colored* persons, whose execution is necessary to public security, may, we think, be with equity appropriated for the benefit of a science on which so many lives depend, while the measure would in a great degree secure the sepulchral repose of those who go down into the grave amidst the lamentations of friends and the reverence of society."[15]

The Kentucky House of Representatives seriously considered a similar proposal. It rejected by the narrow margin of seven votes a bill "to authorize and require the Judges of the different Circuit Courts of this state to adjudge and award the corpses of negroes, executed by sentences of said judges, to the Faculties of the different chartered Colleges in this state, for dissection and experiment."[16] In Virginia the vast majority of cadavers obtained for dissection at the five antebellum medical schools were those of Negroes.[17] The faculty of the Medical College of Georgia in Augusta hired, between 1834 and 1852, several slaves to act as intermediaries in the purchase of bodies from masters in the surrounding plantation country. In 1852 it purchased Grandison Harris in Charleston to obtain cadavers and to perform janitorial duties. He robbed graves and also bought black bodies for the next fifty years or so.[18] And the Medical College of South Carolina openly acknowledged in its circular of 1831 that it obtained "Subjects . . . for every purpose" from the black rather than the white population of Charleston so as to carry on "proper dissections . . . without offending any individuals."[19]

Some whites took advantage of southern blacks by testing new techniques or remedies in the name of medical progress. In several instances physicians purchased blacks for the sole purpose of experimentation; in others the doctors used free blacks and slaves owned by others. Though white subjects were included in one or two cases of experimentation, blacks always made up the overwhelming majority of patients. A few major medical breakthroughs did result from the research performed upon Negroes, for which the physicians involved received fame and glory. The slaves, identified, if at all, by first name only, are unknown now to their descendants and to the general public.

NOTES

1. Fisher, "Physicians and Slavery in the Antebellum Southern Medical Journal," *Journal of the History of Medicine and Allied Sciences*, XXIII (January 1968), 45. W. Montague Cobb discussed a similar theme in "Surgery and the Negro Physician: Some Parallels in Background," National Medical Association, *Journal*, XLIII (May 1951), 145–52, especially 147–48.

2. David C. Humphrey, "Dissection and Discrimination: The Social Origins of Cadavers in America, 1760–1915," New York Academy of Medicine, *Bulletin*, XLIX (September 1973), 819–27; John B. Blake, "Anatomy," in Ronald L. Numbers, ed., *The Education of American Physicians: Historical Essays* (Berkeley, Los Angeles, and London, 1980), 34–35, 37.

3. John Duffy, "A Note on Ante-Bellum Southern Nationalism and Medical Practice," *Journal of Southern History*, XXXIV (May 1968), 274–76; John S. Haller, Jr., "The Negro and the Southern Physician: A Study of Medical and Racial Attitudes, 1800–1860," *Medical History*, XVI (July 1972), 247–51; Todd L. Savitt, *Medicine and Slavery: The Diseases and Health Care of Blacks in Antebellum Virginia* (Urbana, Chicago, and London, 1978), 7–17.

4. Commenting on this irony, the anatomist W. Montague Cobb, himself black, wrote in 1951, ". . . our [white] colleagues recognized in the Negro [on the dissecting table] a perfection in human structure which they were unwilling to concede when that structure was animated by the vital spark." Cobb, "Surgery and the Negro Physician," 148.

5. Robert Peter, *The History of the Medical Department of Transylvania University* (Louisville, 1905), 61; catalogues of the Medical Department of Transylvania University, 1829–1855, in the library at Transylvania College, Lexington, Kentucky; "Preamble and Resolutions of the Dissecting Class [of Transylvania Medical College, 1837/38]," Appendix to Thomas D. Mitchell, "Transylvania Catalogue of Medical Graduates, with an Appendix, Containing a Concise History of the School from Its Commencement to the Present Time," *Transylvania Journal of Medicine and Associate Sciences*, XI (January–March 1838), 229–30. For a discussion of the history of anatomy in antebellum Kentucky see Wayne C. Williams, "The Teachers and Teaching of Anatomy in the Medical Department of Transylvania University, 1799–1857," (unpublished paper in author's and Savitt's possession), 7–16. Mr. Williams is Director of the Audiovisual Dept., East Carolina University School of Medicine. See also John H. Ellis, *Medicine in Kentucky* (Lexington, Ky., 1977), 13.

6. Quoted in Franklin M. Garrett, *Atlanta and Environs: A Chronicle of Its People and Events* (2 vols., Athens, Ga., 1954), I, 395–96 (quotation on p. 395), from Atlanta *Weekly Intelligencer*, October 12,1855. See also Gerald L. Cates, "Medical Schools in Ante-Bellum Georgia" (unpublished M.A. thesis, University of Georgia, 1968), 92–93.

7. Charleston *Courier*, November 14, 1837.

8. *Ibid.*, November 16, 1837.

9. *Annual Circular of the Trustees and Faculty of the Medical College of the State of South Carolina . . . Session of 1840-41* (Charleston, 1840), 5–6.

10. "A Plan of Organization for the Roper Hospital. Adopted by the Medical Society, Jan. 3, 1846," *Rules and Regulations for the Government of the Trustees and Officers of the Roper Hospital* (Charleston, 1861), 11–12; *Annual Circular of the Trustees and Faculty of the Medical College of the State of South Carolina . . . Session of 1857–58* (Charleston, 1858), 17. See also Joseph I. Waring, *A History of Medicine in South Carolina, 1825–1900* (Columbia, S.C., 1967), 75–76, 79n.

11. "An Address to the Public in Regard to the Affairs of the Medical Department of Hampden-Sydney College, by Several Physicians of the City of Richmond, 1853," quoted in Wyndham B. Blanton, *Medicine in Virginia in the Nineteenth Century* (Richmond, 1933), 38–39 (quotation); Richmond *Enquirer,* May 8, 1860; "Notes of the Hampden-Sydney Medical Department Minutes," in William T. Sanger, *Medical College of Virginia Before 1925, and University College of Medicine 1893–1913* (Richmond, 1973), 8; editorial, "A State General Hospital," *Virginia Medical and Surgical Journal,* I (April 1853), 173–74; editorial, "The Virginia Free Hospital," *ibid.*, III (June 1854), 273–75. For more descriptive details see Savitt, *Medicine and Slavery,* 282–86.

12. George B. Jenkins, "The Legal Status of Dissecting," *Anatomical Record,* VII (November 1913), 387–88; John B. Blake, "The Development of American Anatomy Acts," *Journal of Medical Education,* XXX (August 1955), 434.

13. Harriet Martineau, *Retrospect of Western Travel* (2 vols., London and New York, 1838), I, 140, quoted in Humphrey, "Dissection and Discrimination," 819.

14. Dowling, "Case of Verminose Disease," *Transylvania Journal of Medicine and the Associate Sciences,* II (May 1829), 250.

15. Milledgeville *Statesman and Patriot,* August 16, 1828. The author wishes to thank Professor Larry Morrison, History Department, Virginia Polytechnic Institute and State University, for bringing this newspaper article to his attention.

16. *Journal of the House of Representatives of the Commonwealth of Kentucky . . .* (Frankfort, Ky., 1833), 107 (quotation), 122–23, 177–78. See also John D. Wright, Jr., "Robert Peter and Early Science in Kentucky" (unpublished Ph.D. dissertation, Columbia University, 1955), 61, 70; F. Garvin Davenport, *Ante-Bellum Kentucky: A Social History, 1800–1860* (Oxford, Ohio, 1943), 23.

17. Savitt, *Medicine and Slavery,* 290–93; James O. Breeden, "Body Snatchers and Anatomy Professors: Medical Education in Nineteenth-Century Virginia," *Virginia Magazine of History and Biography,* LXXXIII (July 1975), 321–45.

18. Lane Allen, "Grandison Harris, Sr.; Slave, Resurrectionist and Judge," Georgia Academy of Science, *Bulletin,* XXXIV (April 1976), 192–99.

19. Fry, *Night Riders,* 173–74.

An Early Entry for "Negro"
from *The Encyclopaedia Britannica*

NEGRO (Spanish and Italian *Negro,* from Latin *Niger,* black) in anthropology designates the distinctly dark as opposed to the fair, yellow, and brown varieties of mankind. . . .

By the nearly unanimous consent of anthropologists this type occupies at the same time the lowest position in the evolutionary scale, thus affording the best material for the comparative study of the highest anthropoids and the human species. The chief points in which the Negro either approaches the *Quadrumana* or differs most from his own congeners are:—(1) the abnormal length of the arm, which in the erect position sometimes reaches the knee-pan, and which on an average exceeds that of the Caucasian by about 2 inches; (2) prognathism, or projection of the jaws (index number of facial angle about 70, as compared with the Caucasian 82); (3) weight of brain, as indicating cranial capacity, 35 ounces (highest gorilla 20, average European 45); (4) full black eye, with black iris and yellowish sclerotic coat, a very marked feature; (5) short flat snub nose, deeply depressed at the base or frontal suture, broad at extremity, with dilated nostrils and concave ridge; (6) thick protruding lips, plainly showing the inner red surface; (7) very large zygomatic arches—high and prominent cheekbones; (8) exceedingly thick cranium, enabling the Negro to butt with the head and resist blows which would inevitably break any ordinary European's skull; (9) correspondingly weak lower limbs, terminating in a broad flat foot with low instep, divergent and somewhat prehensile great toe, and heel projecting backwards ("lark heel"); (10) complexion deep brown or blackish . . .; (11) short, black hair, eccentrically elliptical or almost flat in section, and distinctly woolly . . .; (12) thick epidermis, cool, soft, and velvety to the touch, mostly hairless, and emitting a peculiar rancid odour . . .; (13) frame of medium height, thrown somewhat out of the perpendicular by the shape of the pelvis, the spine, the backward projection of the head, and the whole anatomical structure; (14) the cranial sutures, which close much earlier in the Negro than in other races. To this premature ossification of the skull, preventing all further development of the brain, many pathologists have attributed the inherent mental inferiority of the blacks, an inferiority which is even more marked than their physical differences.

—From the Ninth Edition, Volume XVII, 1884

Spoken on the Floor of the U.S. Congress

Ours, sir, is the Government of a white race . . . . In the whole history of man . . . there is no instance whatever of any civilized colored races being found equal to the establishment of free popular government.

—Senator John C. Calhoun, January 4, 1848

I believe that one such man as Washington, or Newton, or Franklin, or Lincoln glorifies the Creator of the world and benefits mankind more than all the Chinese who have lived, and struggled, and died on the banks of the Hoang Ho . . . . Let us keep pure the blood which circulates through our political system; dignify, enoble, and exalt our sovereign—the people; preserve our national life from the gangrene of oriental civilization.

—Senator John Franklin Miller, February 28, 1882

Many [negro voters are] almost too ignorant to eat, scarcely wise enough to breathe, mere existing human machines—is it any wonder that many of these people would spoil their ballots, and that the judges, in the discharge of their duty, would exclude them, as the law requires?

—Representative David A. De Armond, April 25, 1898

You could shipwreck 10,000 illiterate white Americans or Englishmen or Scotchman, of whom not one knew a letter in a book, on a desert island, and in three weeks they would have a fairly good government, conceived and administered upon fairly democratic lines . . . . You could shipwreck an equal number of American Indians . . . or 10,000 negroes, every one of whom was a graduate of Harvard University, and in less than three years they would have retrograded governmentally to the old tribal relations, half the men would have been killed and the other half would have two wives apiece.

—Representative John Sharp Williams, December 20, 1898

The colored race, even when it has been educated to a limited degree, is still unfit for suffrage, for the simple reason that the negroes do not possess that moral character and that moral fiber which are necessary to good citizenship . . . . [South Carolina] had a hundred and twenty-five thousand negroes of voting age and we had a hundred thousand whites. Now, can you lift yourselves over the fence with your boot straps and beat that by honest methods? . . . . We stuffed ballot boxes. We shot them. We are not ashamed of it.

—Senator Ben Tillman, February 26, 1900

An Early Aunt Jemima Advertisement

The story of Aunt Jemima, whom we know as Pancake Queen,
 Starts on an Old Plantation, in a charming Southern scene.

Here folks grow sweet magnolias and cotton in the sun,
 And life was filled with happiness and old-time Southern fun.

The owner, Colonel Higbee, a most kind and gracious host,
 Served his guests fine dishes, though they liked his pancakes most.

Of course, the cook who made them—or so the legend goes—
 Was good old Aunt Jemima, as our pretty picture shows.

Aunt Jemima's pancake fame
 soon spread throughout the South.

Folks loved that fluffy tenderness
 that melted in yo' mouth.

Girls crowded 'round Jemima,
 in their dainty crinolines,

And oh! Those Southern Colonels,
 you should have seen their grins!

> —Source: Marilyn Kern-Foxworth, *Aunt Jemima, Uncle Ben, and Rastus: Blacks in Advertising, Yesterday, Today, and Tomorrow,* 1994

Some Examples of Jim Crow

South Carolina, 1950s

It shall be unlawful for any person, firm, or corporation engaged in the business of cotton textile manufacturing in this state to allow or permit operatives, help and labor of the different races to labor and work together within the same room, or to use the same doors of entrance and exit at the same time . . . or to use the same stairway and windows at the same time, or to use at any time the same lavatories, toilets, drinking-water buckets, pails, cups, dippers, or glasses.

Montgomery, Alabama, 1958

It shall be unlawful for white and colored persons to play together . . . in any game of cards, dice, dominoes, checkers, pool, billiards, softball, basketball, football, golf, track, and at swimming pools or in any athletic contest.

> —Jim Carnes, *Us and Them: A History of Intolerance in America*, 1995 [*Note:* At one point, the penalty for whites and blacks who played "any game of cards or dice, dominoes, or checkers" together in Birmingham, Alabama, was six months in prison.]

COMING OF AGE IN MISSISSIPPI

ANNE MOODY

During my senior year at Tougaloo I had become very friendly with my social science professor, John Salter, who was in charge of NAACP activities on campus.[1] During the last week of school, he told me that sit-in demonstrations were about to start in Jackson and that he wanted me to be the spokesman for a team that would sit-in at Woolworth's lunch counter. The two other demonstrators would be classmates of mine, Memphis and Pearlena. Around ten o'clock the morning of the demonstrations, NAACP headquarters alerted the news services. As a result, the police department was also informed, but neither the policemen nor the newsmen knew exactly where or when the demonstrations would start. They stationed themselves along Capitol Street and waited.

To divert attention from the sit-in at Woolworth's, the picketing started at J.C. Penney's a good fifteen minutes before. The pickets were allowed to walk up and down in front of the store three or four times before they were arrested. At exactly 11 A.M., Pearlena, Memphis, and I entered Woolworth's from the rear entrance. We separated as soon as we stepped into the store, and made small purchases from various counters. Pearlena had given Memphis her watch. He was to let us know when it was 11:14. At 11:14 we were to join him near the lunch counter and at exactly 11:15 we were to take seats at it.

Seconds before 11:15 we were occupying three seats at the previously segregated Woolworth's lunch counter. In the beginning the waitresses seemed to ignore us, as if they really didn't know what was going on. Our waitress walked past us a couple of times before she noticed we had started to write our own orders down and realized we wanted service. She asked us what we wanted. We began to read to her from our order slips. She told us that we would be served at the back counter, which was for Negroes.

"We would like to be served here," I said.

The waitress started to repeat what she had said, then stopped in the middle of the sentence. She turned the lights out behind the counter, and she and the other waitresses almost ran to the back of the store, deserting all their white customers. I guess they thought that violence would start immediately after the whites at the counter realized what was going on. There were five or six other people at the counter. A couple of them just got up and walked away. A girl sitting next to me finished her banana split before leaving. A middle-aged white woman who had not yet been served rose from her seat and came over to us. "I'd like to stay here with you," she said, "but my husband is waiting."

---

[1] *Editor's note:* "Tougaloo" refers to Tougaloo College, a predominantly African-American liberal arts college in Mississippi. The NAACP, or National Association for the Advancement of Colored People, is a multiracial civil rights organization founded in 1909.

The newsmen came in just as she was leaving. They must have discovered what was going on shortly after some of the people began to leave the store. One of the newsmen ran behind the woman who spoke to us and asked her to identify herself. She refused to give her name, but said she was a native of Vicksburg and a former resident of California. When asked why she had said what she had said to us, she replied, "I am in sympathy with the Negro movement." By this time a crowd of cameramen and reporters had gathered around us taking pictures and asking questions, such as Where were we from? Why did we sit-in? What organization sponsored it? Were we students? From what school?

I told them that we were all students at Tougaloo College, that we were represented by no particular organization, and that we planned to stay there even after the store closed. "All we want is service," was my reply to one of them. After they had finished probing for about twenty minutes, they were almost ready to leave.

At noon, students from a nearby white high school started pouring in to Woolworth's. When they first saw us they were sort of surprised. They didn't know how to react. A few started to heckle and the newsmen became interested again. Then the white students started chanting all kinds of anti-Negro slogans. We were called a little bit of everything. The rest of the seats except the three we were occupying had been roped off to prevent others from sitting down. A couple of the boys took one end of the rope and made it into a hangman's noose. Several attempts were made to put it around our necks. The crowds grew as more students and adults came in for lunch.

We kept our eyes straight forward and did not look at the crowd except for occasional glances to see what was going on. All of a sudden I saw a face I remembered—the drunkard from the bus station sit-in. My eyes lingered on him just long enough for us to recognize each other. Today he was drunk too, so I don't think he remembered where he had seen me before. He took out a knife, opened it, put it in his pocket, and then began to pace the floor. At this point, I told Memphis and Pearlena what was going on. Memphis suggested that we pray. We bowed our heads, and all hell broke loose. A man rushed forward, threw Memphis from his seat, and slapped my face. Then another man who worked in the store threw me against an adjoining counter.

Down on my knees on the floor, I saw Memphis lying near the lunch counter with blood running out of the corners of his mouth. As he tried to protect his face, the man who'd thrown him down kept kicking him against the head. If he had worn hard-soled shoes instead of sneakers, the first kick probably would have killed Memphis. Finally a man dressed in plain clothes identified himself as a police officer and arrested Memphis and his attacker.

Pearlena had been thrown to the floor. She and I got back on our stools after Memphis was arrested. There were some white Tougaloo teachers in the crowd. They asked Pearlena and me if we wanted to leave. They said that things were getting too rough. We didn't know what to do. While we were trying to make up our minds, we were joined by Joan Trumpauer. Now there were three of us and we were integrated. The crowd began to chant, "Communists,

Communists, Communists." Some old man in the crowd ordered the students to take us off the stools.

"Which one should I get first?" a big husky boy said.

"That white nigger," the old man said.

The boy lifted Joan from the counter by her waist and carried her out of the store. Simultaneously, I was snatched from my stool by two high school students. I was dragged about thirty feet toward the door by my hair when someone made them turn me loose. As I was getting up off the floor, I saw Joan coming back inside. We started back to the center of the counter to join Pearlena. Lois Chaffee, a white Tougaloo faculty member, was now sitting next to her. So Joan and I just climbed across the rope at the front end of the counter and sat down.

There were now four of us, two whites and two Negroes, all women. The mob started smearing us with ketchup, mustard, sugar, pies, and everything on the counter. Soon Joan and I were joined by John Salter, but the moment he sat down he was hit on the jaw with what appeared to be brass knuckles. Blood gushed from his face and someone threw salt into the open wound. Ed King, Tougaloo's chaplain, rushed to him.

At the other end of the counter, Lois and Pearlena were joined by George Raymond, a student from Jackson State College. Then a Negro high school boy sat down next to me. The mob took spray paint from the counter and sprayed it on the new demonstrators. The high school student had on a white shirt; the word "nigger" was written on his back with red spray paint.

We sat there for three hours taking a beating when the manager decided to close the store because the mob had begun to go wild with stuff from other counters. He begged and begged everyone to leave. But even after fifteen minutes of begging, no one budged. They would not leave until we did. Then Dr. Beittel, the president of Tougaloo College, came running in. He said he had just heard what was happening.

About ninety policemen were standing outside the store; they had been watching the whole thing through the windows, but had not come in to stop the mob or do anything. President Beittel went outside and asked Captain Ray to come and escort us out. The captain refused, stating the manager had to invite him in before he could enter the premises, so Dr. Beittel himself brought us out. He had told the police that they had better protect us after we were outside the store. When we got outside, the policemen formed a single line that blocked the mob from us. However, they were allowed to throw at us everything they had collected. Within ten minutes, we were picked up by Reverend King in his station wagon and taken to the NAACP headquarters on Lynch Street.

After the sit-in, all I could think of was how sick Mississippi whites were. They believed so much in the segregated Southern way of life, they would kill to preserve it. I sat there in the NAACP office and thought of how many times they had killed when this way of life was threatened. I knew that the killing had just begun. "Many more will die before it is over with," I thought. Before the sit-in, I had always hated the whites in Mississippi. Now I knew it was impossible for me to hate sickness. The whites had a disease, an incurable disease in its final stage. What were our chances against such a disease? I thought of the students, the young Negroes who had begun to protest, as young interns. When these young interns got older, I thought, they would be the best doctors in the world for social problems.

"Operation Wetback"

In the 1950s many Americans were alarmed by the number of immigrants from Mexico. As a result, then United States Attorney General Herbert Brownell, Jr., launched "Operation Wetback," to expel Mexicans from this country. Among those caught up in the expulsion campaign were American citizens of Mexican descent who were forced to leave the country of their birth. To ensure the effectiveness of the expulsion process, many of those apprehended were denied a hearing to assert their constitutional rights and to present evidence that would have prevented their deportation. More than 1 million persons of Mexican descent were expelled from this country in 1954 at the height of "Operation Wetback."

> —United States Commission on Civil Rights, *The Tarnished Golden Door: Civil Rights Issues in Immigration,* 1980 [*Note:* "Wetback" is a derogatory term for a Mexican, especially a laborer who crosses the U.S. border; "wet" refers to the Rio Grande, a common entry point.]

THE AMERICAN CONCENTRATION CAMPS: A COVER–UP THROUGH EUPHEMISTIC TERMINOLOGY

*RAYMOND Y. OKAMURA

A large body of literature now exists on the subject of the mass incarceration of Japanese Americans during World War II. Much of it is flawed by the persistent use of euphemistic terminology. Instead of calling the event an imprisonment, authors have used the terms "evacuation" and "relocation." Since Japanese Americans were in fact confined against their will, the "evacuation-relocation" nomenclature is a distortion. Those writing seem unable to accept the fact that over 120,000 men, women, children, and babies were expelled from their homes and locked up in American concentration camps.

In this paper,[1] I will examine the use of official language as a cover for either embarrassing or horrible truths. In a sense the government (including the executive, legislative, and judicial branches) circumvented the obvious unconstitutionality of detaining American citizens without evidence, charge, or trial through euphemisms. Thus, although Japanese Americans were herded into barbed wire compounds surrounded by guard towers and armed sentries, the government insisted that only an "evacuation" or "relocation" was involved. The linguistic deception fostered by the United States government, and institutionalized by numerous scholars thereafter, bears a striking resemblance to the propaganda techniques of the Third Reich.

The government of the Third Reich (Nazi Germany) utilized an elaborate system of euphemisms to cover up what was actually happening to millions of European Jews, Gypsies, and other groups deemed undesirable. "Emigration," "evacuation," "final solution," "relocation," "resettlement," and "special treatment" were used as code words for the Nazi program of methodical mass murder. The extermination camps in occupied Poland were referred to simply as "the east"; and the various concentration camps where victims were gathered and confined to await "resettlement in the east" were called "assembly centers," "protective custody camps," "reception centers," "relocation centers," and "transit camps." Even more sardonically the prison city of Terezin, which served as a way station to the gas chambers at Auschwitz, was described in official literature as a "health resort," "model ghetto," "paradise ghetto," and "retirement home."[2]

Nazi officials were very careful about what they put in writing and masked their intentions with euphemistic language. The actual order, presented here in translation, to annihilate the Jewish people, was cryptically phrased:

*Raymond Y. Okamura lives in Berkeley, California. He spent three years at the Gila River Concentration Camp in Arizona.

Complementing the task which was conferred upon you already on 24 January 1939, to solve the Jewish problem by means of emigration and evacuation in the best possible way according to present conditions, I charge you herewith to make all necessary preparations . . . for a total solution of the Jewish question within the area of German influence in Europe.[3]

Later, the Nazi defendants at the Nuremberg War Crimes Trials claimed that they knew nothing more than what the written documents stated.[4] Until the truth emerged, the Nazi terminology deceived not only the general populace, but the victims as well. Many Jews were tricked into turning themselves in for "evacuation" and "resettlement." The euphemistic language made it easier for the vast number of government workers involved in the machinery of death to carry out their tasks.[5]

Nazi Germany was not unique in the use of deceptive terminology for propaganda purposes.[6] Governments generally do not readily admit wrongdoing nor think badly of themselves; any government in power can be expected to hide, misrepresent, or rationalize its unsavory activities. But once the government changes hands, and facts emerge, the liberated people usually do not perpetuate the distortions of the former government. For example, it would be unthinkable today for anyone to suggest that the events which took place in Nazi-occupied Europe should be called an "evacuation" and "relocation" simply because those were the terms used at the time. Such euphemisms have been relegated to their proper place as historical footnotes, and the main body of literature on the Holocaust uses terms more reflective of the facts.

The United States was no exception to the tendency of governments to characterize their own actions in propagandistic terms. An array of euphemisms—some chillingly identical to the Nazi euphemisms—was developed by the U.S. government for the mass incarceration of Japanese Americans.[7] That the government promoted euphemistic language at that time is understandable; what puzzles is the continuing and uncritical adherence to the government-coined expressions—even to this date—by nearly everyone concerned. If this practice persists no one will be able to testify to the magnitude of the occurrence, and the United States will have utilized propaganda to maintain an historical image.

In early 1942, federal officials were faced with a perplexing problem: how to satisfy the growing demands from the West Coast that every single person of Japanese ancestry be locked up. There was no problem with respect to adult Japanese nationals against whom there was even the flimsiest bit of evidence. Non-citizens could be classified as "alien enemies deemed dangerous" and summarily interned under individual warrants by the Justice Department.[8] The question was how to imprison a large number of innocent people—especially American citizens—under the aegis of law. Since there was no evidence whatsoever against the vast majority of Japanese Americans, and since most of the target population consisted of babies, children, and invalids who could not possibly be dangerous, some method had to be found to permit the incarceration of an entire group of people based solely on their ancestry. The solution which emerged after numerous consultations between government and military officials was the extensive use of euphemistic, vague, or misleading terms which could cover the massive violation of constitutional and human rights.[9]

"Evacuation" and "relocation" are the two most commonly used terms to describe the World War II experience of Japanese Americans. A close examination of the definitions of these words, however, reveals the underlying propagandistic intent. "Evacuation" is the process of temporarily moving people away from an immediate and real danger, such as a fire, flood, or bomb threat. Similarly, "relocation" is the process of more permanently moving people away from a long-term hazard, such as an unsafe building, earthquake fault, or contaminated environment. Both terms strongly suggest that the movement is for the protection or safety of the affected people. It was precisely for this reason that the government selected such words. There is no hint in either term that people are to be confined, detained, imprisoned, or restrained in any way. Thus, if these terms are accepted at face value, complaints and lawsuits about false imprisonment or unlawful detention are effectively precluded.

The cryptic language used in Executive Order 9066 is reminiscent of that used in Nazi orders. Franklin D. Roosevelt's order never mentioned detention or imprisonment. Instead, the true intent of the order was disguised as follows:

> I hereby authorize and direct the Secretary of War, and the Military Commanders whom he may from time to time designate . . . to prescribe military areas . . . from which any or all persons may be excluded, and with respect to which, the right of any person to enter, remain in, or leave shall be subject to whatever restriction the Secretary of War or the appropriate Military Commander may impose in his discretion. The Secretary of War is hereby authorized to provide for residents of any such area who are excluded therefrom, such transportation, food, shelter, and other accommodations as may be necessary.[10]

The United States government and military officials knew exactly what those seemingly innocuous phrases meant, and they promptly set about building concentration camps. "Any or all persons" meant only persons of Japanese ancestry; "may be excluded" meant being evicted from one's home and locked up; "the right to leave shall be subject to whatever restriction" meant being shot if one tried to escape; and "shelter and other accommodations" meant tar paper barracks surrounded by barbed wire fences and guard towers.

A follow-up directive from Secretary of War Henry L. Stimson to the designated Military Commander General John L. DeWitt was even more Hitlerian in tone:

> In order to permit the War Department to make plans for the proper disposition of individuals whom you contemplate moving outside your jurisdiction, it is desired that you make known to me your detailed plans for evacuation. Individuals will not be entrained until such plans are furnished and you are informed that accommodations have been prepared at the point of detraining.[11]

The subsequent public proclamation by General DeWitt puts the Nazi propagandists to shame:

> Whereas, it is necessary, in order to provide for the welfare and to ensure the orderly evacuation and resettlement of Japanese voluntarily migrating from Military Area No. 1, to restrict and regulate such migration . . . all alien Japanese and persons of Japanese ancestry . . . are hereby prohibited from leaving that area for any purpose until and to the extent that a future proclamation or order of this headquarters shall so permit or direct.[12]

The "future proclamation or order" turned out to be a proscription condemning Japanese Americans to imprisonment. The entire process of incarceration was couched in euphemistic terminology. The detention orders were called "civilian exclusion orders." The temporary detention camps where they were initially confined were named "assembly centers" or "reception centers." All written orders contained the curious phrase "non-alien," which turns out to be a code word for a citizen of the United States of America.[13]

Government and military officials took great pains to assure that everyone within their control used this language. For example, General DeWitt gave this instruction to his subordinate military commanders:

> The Evacuation Center has been established for the purpose of caring for Japanese who have been moved from certain military areas. They have been moved from their homes and placed in camps under guard as a matter of military necessity. The camps are not "concentration camps" and the use of this term is considered objectionable. Evacuation Centers are not internment camps. Internment camps are established for another purpose and are not related to the evacuation program.[14]

Dillon S. Myer, director of the so-called "War Relocation Authority," issued similar instructions to the civilian staff:

> The term "camp" when used to refer to a relocation center is likewise objectionable. It leads people to confuse the relocation centers administered by the War Relocation Authority with the detention camps and internment camps administered by other agencies. The evacuees are not "internees."[15]

No matter what the government called them, the facilities were in reality concentration camps and the inmates were prisoners. General DeWitt left no doubt that the Japanese Americans were to be confined:

> It is hereby ordered that all persons of Japanese ancestry, both alien and non-alien, who now or shall hereafter reside, pursuant to Exclusion Orders and Instructions from this Headquarters, within the bounds of established Assembly Centers, Reception Centers or Relocation Centers . . . are required to remain within the bounds of Assembly Centers, Reception Centers or Relocation Centers at all times unless specifically authorized to leave.[16]

For the concentration camps located outside of the Western Defense Command jurisdiction, Secretary of War Stimson issued similar orders.

> All persons of Japanese ancestry, and all members of their families, both alien and non-alien, who now or shall hereafter be or reside, pursuant to orders and instructions of the Secretary of War, or pursuant to the orders and instructions of the Commanding General, Western Defense Command and Fourth Army, or otherwise, within the bounds of any of said War Relocation Project Areas are required to remain within the bounds of said War Relocation Project Areas at all times unless specifically authorized to leave.[17]

The written orders were enforced with barbed wire fences, guard towers, search lights, and machine guns. It was clearly understood by both guards and prisoners that the restrictions would be maintained with physical violence, if necessary. General DeWitt set forth the following policy:

> The military police on duty at relocation centers and areas shall perform the following functions: . . . They will maintain periodic motor patrols around the boundaries of the center or area in order to guard against attempts by evacuees to leave the center without permission. . . . They shall apprehend and arrest evacuees who do leave the center or area without authority, using such force as is necessary to make the arrest.[18]

The euphemistic language accomplished a number of important objectives for the government: (1) it sidetracked legal and constitutional challenges; (2) it allowed the government to maintain a decent public image; (3) it helped lead the victims into willing cooperation; (4) it permitted the White civilian employees to work without self-reproach; and (5) it kept the historical record in the government's favor.

Appeals to the judicial system failed miserably. The government had laid the legal foundation well, and the courts became part of the semantic conspiracy. The majority of the U.S. Supreme Court accepted the euphemistic terminology without examination, refused to consider the real facts of the case, and rendered decisions upholding the government's actions. The language of the court majority in the Fred T. Korematsu case is a classic example:

> Korematsu was under compulsion to leave the area not as he would choose, but via an Assembly Center. The Assembly Center was conceived as a part of the machinery for group evacuation. The power to exclude includes the power to do it by force if necessary. And any forcible measure must necessarily entail some degree of detention or restraint. . . . Regardless of the true nature of the assembly and relocation centers— and we deem it unjustifiable to call them concentration camps with all the ugly connotation that term implies—we are dealing specifically with nothing but an exclusion order.[19]

Justice Owen J. Roberts, however, did not subscribe to such escapist nonsense, and stated in dissent:

> An Assembly Center was a euphemism for a prison. No person within such a center was permitted to leave except by Military Order. . . . We further know that . . . so-called Relocation Centers, a euphemism for concentration camps, were established. . . . But the facts above recited . . . show that the exclusion was but part of an over-all plan for forcible detention.[20]

The general American public knew little about the concentration camps in its midst. Most White Americans wanted Japanese Americans out of the way; they were not particular about how it was to be accomplished; once it was done, they did not care to know what the camps were like.[21] The newspapers, then the main source of information for the public, worked closely with military authorities. Most newspapers printed army press releases verbatim, and many city rooms became an extension of the army public relations office. In prose that only a government press agent could have authored, the lead paragraph in a Central California newspaper article announced:

> Free to come and go as they wish within the limits of their new abodes provided for them by a considerate nation, more than 500 evacuated Japanese were in assembly centers near Pinedale and at the Fresno District Fairground today.[22]

Not only did the newspapers adopt the government euphemisms, they added distortions of their own. The press consistently ignored the fact that American citizens were involved in the lockup. The detainees were invariably identified as "Japs," "Nips," "aliens," "enemy aliens," "dangerous aliens," or, if the editor was charitable, as "Japanese" or "Nipponese." Whenever it became necessary to refer to American citizens, code terms like "non-aliens" or "other persons of Japanese ancestry" were substituted. The barbed wire enclosures were variously labeled "alien assembly center," "alien reception center," "enemy alien camp," "Japanese alien camp," "Japanese relocation center," or just "Jap Camp."[23] Unless one took a great deal of trouble to find out, a general newspaper reader would not have known that native-born Americans were being held prisoner in these camps.

A few noteworthy exceptions to the press whitewash, however, deserve mention. A *Tacoma News-Tribune* editorial stated:

> In this war we are seeing more euphemistic terms than in previous conflicts. Consequently, the concentration camp which the government is starting to build at Puyallup is termed an "assembly center." But it is a concentration camp, even though temporary.[24]

The *Washington Post* editorialized:

> The government of the United States—sometimes referred to as a symbol of democracy—now holds some 70,000 American citizens in places eu-

phemistically called "relocation centers". . . . No violation of law has been charged against them. No court of law has sentenced them. They have been found guilty of nothing save the peculiar pigmentation of their skins.[25]

There was almost total cooperation by Japanese Americans in their own incarceration. Attempts to evade the round-up were rare, and nearly everyone appeared at the designated time to the declared place. Certainly the fear of consequences was an important factor; but a large number of Japanese Americans accepted—or wanted to believe—the government's assurances that they were only to be "evacuated" to a "resettlement center." Those who had faith in the government were in for a rude shock when they arrived at the detention camp site. One anonymous detainee wrote to a friend on the outside:

> This evacuation did not seem too unfair until we got right to the camp and were met by soldiers with guns and bayonets. Then I almost started screaming.[26]

Estelle Ishigo observed as she entered the Pomona Detention Camp:

> The first sight of the barbed wire enclosure with armed soldiers standing guard as our bus slowly turned in through the gate stunned us with the reality of this ordered evacuation.[27]

The Puyallup Detention Camp was described in the following way by Ted Nakashima:

> The resettlement center is actually a penitentiary—armed guards in towers with spotlights and deadly tommy guns, fifteen feet of barbed-wire fences, everyone confined to quarters at nine, lights out at ten o'clock. The guards are ordered to shoot anyone who approaches within twenty feet of the fences.[28]

Given the grim daily existence, the inmates adopted much of the government euphemisms as a psychological shield against the stark reality of the barbed wire and guard towers. Life perhaps seemed more bearable if they pretended that they were "evacuees" instead of prisoners, and that they were living in a "relocation center" and not a concentration camp. One indication of the emotional scars left by the incarceration is the continued use of the government euphemisms by the former prisoners. The terms "evacuation" and "relocation" are still used within the Japanese American community (usually with a capital "E" and "R") as a kind of ingroup code and safety-valve to prevent the outpouring of emotion.

For the civilian employees who ran the concentration camps, the euphemisms made their jobs more agreeable. The White staff members could think of themselves, not as concentration camp wardens, but more as friends, teachers, and social workers who were there to care for the "evacuees." It would have been devastating to staff morale if they ever admitted to themselves that they were, in fact, part of the oppressive machinery to keep the Japanese Americans behind barbed wire. They diligently created a mountain of red-tape, replete with endless questionnaires, reports, regulations, and procedures, all of which made it extremely difficult for anyone to be released on parole. Perhaps the White employees deluded themselves; but a recent study shows that many of the staff members were engaged in repression and thought control.[29]

The historic record of the incarceration has been distorted by the pervasive influence of official terminology. All of the primary documents were controlled by the government; and nearly all of the contemporaneous publications were written from the point of view of the government. Inmate newspapers, circulars, and letters were subjected to censorship; all camp records and reports were written by government employees and scholars; outside reporters and scholars had to submit to strict government regulations in order to gain access to the camps. Books published during, or shortly after the episode, invariably used the government euphemisms without qualification or explanation. Since most of these early books were written by camp administrators and government employed or affiliated scholars, it is no wonder that the "evacuation-relocation" nomenclature saturates these works. A survey of books published before the mid-1960s reveals the consistent use of euphemistic terms in the titles, such as "Evacuation of Japanese Americans," "Japanese American Evacuation and Resettlement," "Japanese Americans in the Relocation Centers," "Japanese American Relocation Center," "Japanese Evacuation," and "Japanese Relocation Camp."[30]

Beginning with the ethnic awareness movements in the late 1960s, the terms concentration camp and internment have frequently appeared in book titles. Although many authors have used titles like "America's Concentration Camps," "Concentration Camps USA," and "The Internment Years," none has systematically replaced euphemistic terminology in their text. An incongruous situation presently exists wherein authors provocatively use internment or concentration camp in their titles, but revert to the old "evacuation-relocation" nomenclature in their text, tables, and illustrations.[31] The record needs rewriting.

The words used to depict an event are crucial to one's perception and understanding of the occurrence. Henry Stuart Hughes, in commenting about Ludwig Wittgenstein's philosophy, once wrote.

> (Earlier) he had maintained that language proceeded from reality—that the structure of the real world determined the structure of speech. Now he had come to believe that the reverse was the case: language, as the vehicle for understanding reality, determined the way in which people saw it.[32]

NOTES

1. This paper is a modified version of a written statement submitted to the "Commission on Wartime Relocation and Internment of Civilians" at the public hearing in Seattle, Washington on September 11, 1981. The commission was established by Public Law 96-317 (94 Stat 964) on July 31, 1980 to "review the facts and circumstances surrounding Executive Order Numbered 9066, issued on February 19, 1942, and the impact of such Executive order on American citizens and permanent resident aliens . . . (and to) recommend appropriate remedies." Hearings were also held in Anchorage, Chicago, Los Angeles, New York, St. Paul (Pribilof Islands), San Francisco, Unalaska (Aleutian Islands), and Washington, D.C. during the latter half of 1981.

2. Walter and Michi Weglyn provided valuable research assistance for this section. For a discussion on the Nazi euphemisms, see Lucy S. Dawidowicz, *The War Against the Jews 1933–1945* (Holt, Rinehart and Winston, 1975), pp. xiii, 130, 134, 136, 139; Gerald Green, *The Artists of Terezin* (Schocken Books, 1978), pp. 20–21; Walter Laqueur, *The Terrible Secret* (Little, Brown, 1980), pp. 17–18; John Toland, *Adolf Hitler* (Doubleday, 1976), Vol. II, pp. 861–862.

3. Document 710-PS, Exhibit USA-509, Reichmarshall Hermann Goring to SS Gruppenfuhrer Reinhard Heydrich, July 1941; *Trial of the Major War Criminals before the International Military Tribunal* (Nuremberg: International Military Tribunal, 1947–1948), IX: 518-519, XXVI: 266–267.

4. See, for example, the testimony of Arthur Seyss-Inquart, *Trial of the Major War Criminals,* XVI: 19. Also, according to Gordon K. Hirabayashi, Robert H. Jackson (Supreme Court justice and chief U.S. prosecutor) complained to Frank L. Walters (a member of the prosecution staff who coincidentally was Hirabayashi's lawyer) that the Nazi defendants cited the U.S. Supreme Court decisions on the Japanese American cases as a defense. Unfortunately, such a citation could not be found in the official text of proceedings. But in all likelihood, if such a claim was made, it would have been erased from the transcript. *Tu quo que* arguments were prohibited under the rules of the Tribunal, and any mention of similar misdeeds by the victorious nations was stricken from the record. See Bradley F. Smith, *Reaching Judgement at Nuremberg* (Basic Books, 1977), pp. 81, 102.

5. George M. Kren and Leon Rappoport, *The Holocaust and the Crisis of Human Behavior* (Holmes and Meier, 1980), pp. 7, 87, 138.

6. Canada also used euphemistic terms to describe the incarceration of Japanese Canadians in prison camps. See Ken Adachi, *The Enemy That Never Was* (McClelland and Stewart, 1976), pp. 218, 251–252.

7. Although the United States did not engage in wholesale murder, there is an analogue in the group incarceration of a nation's own citizens and residents based solely on ancestry.

8. Presidential Proclamation 2525, December 7, 1941 (6 Fed Reg 6321); based on 50 USC 21-23 (1940), 1 Stat 577 (1798). The Justice Department was more comfortable about its actions, and used straight-forward terms like internment, internee, and internment camp. Internees held by the Justice Department were entitled to individual hearings, were granted protections of the Geneva Prisoners of War Convention of 1929, and were given the right to appeal to a neutral consul (Spain). American citizens held in the regular concentration camps had far fewer rights in comparison.

9. The individual who devised this semantic solution has not been positively identified, but Colonel Karl R. Bendetsen is the most likely candidate. Bendetsen was a lawyer by profession, a representative of the Provost Marshall General during the crucial discussion phase, and eventually head of the "Wartime Civil Control Administration," the military-civilian agency responsible for implementing the

detention orders. See Roger Daniels, *Concentration Camps USA* (Holt, Rinehart and Winston, 1972), pp. 44–70; Michi Weglyn, *Years of Infamy* (William Morrow, 1976), pp. 69, 94.

10. Executive Order 9066, February 19, 1942 (7 Fed Reg 1407).

11. U.S. War Department, *Final Report: Japanese Evacuation from the West Coast 1942* (U.S. Government Printing Office, 1943), p. 26.

12. Public Proclamation No. 4, Western Defense Command and Fourth Army, March 27, 1942 (7 Fed Reg 2601).

13. Final Report: Japanese Evacuation, pp. 45, 96–100, 513–515.

14. Ibid., p. 216.

15. Memorandum to all staff members, War Relocation Authority, Tule Lake Project, Newell, California, October 2, 1942.

16. Civilian Restrictive Order No. 1, Western Defense Command and Fourth Army, May 19, 1942 (8 Fed Reg 982).

17. Public Proclamation No. WD-1, War Department, August 13, 1942 (7 Fed Reg 6593).

18. Circular No. 19, Western Defense Command and Fourth Army, September 17, 1942, *Final Report: Japanese Evacuation,* p. 527.

19. *Korematsu v. U.S.,* December 18, 1944 (323 US 214, at 221–223).

20. Ibid., at 230–232.

21. For example, the White residents of Owens Valley, California were appallingly ignorant about the massive Manzanar Concentration Camp right in their backyards. See Isami Arifuku Waugh and Raymond Okamura, "Book Review/Camp and Community," *Amerasia Journal,* Vol. 5, No. 1 (1978), 133–136.

22. "First Japanese Enter Fresno Assembly Centers," *The Fresno Bee,* May 11, 1942.

23. See newspaper articles listed in Raymond Okamura, "Pilgrimage Guide to the Temporary Detention Camps," *Pacific Citizen,* Holiday Issue, December 19–26, 1980, pp. 56–59. Also check other newspapers in the area printed on the same dates: competing newspapers frequently published near-identical articles, obviously taken from army press releases.

24. "Camp at Puyallup," *The Tacoma News-Tribune,* March 31, 1942.

25. "General DeWitt's Statement," *The Washington Post,* April 15, 1943.

26. Audrie Girdner and Anne Loftis, *The Great Betrayal* (Macmillan, 1969), p. 147.

27. Estelle Ishigo, *Lone Heart Mountain* (Anderson, Ritchie and Simon, 1972), p. 9.

28. Ted Nakashima, "Concentration Camp: U.S. Style," *The New Republic,* Vol. 106, No. 24 (June 15, 1942), 822.

29. "Prof. Says WRA 'Spied' on JAs in WW2," *Pacific Citizen,* April 24, 1981. See article by Peter T. Suzuki, "Anthropologists in Wartime Camps for Japanese Americans: A Documentary Study." *Dialectical Anthropology* Vol. 6, No. 1 (1981), 23–60.

30. Raymond Okamura, "The Concentration Camp Experience from a Japanese American Perspective," *Counterpoint: Perspectives on Asian America* (Los Angeles: University of California Asian American Studies Center, 1976), pp. 27–30.

31. Ibid., p. 29. Also see pamphlet by Edison Uno, "Concentration Camps, American-style" (reprint from *Pacific Citizen,* Special Holiday Edition, December 1974), wherein the author strongly argues for the use of the term concentration camp, yet captions his charts as "relocation camps" and "assembly centers."

32. *Holocaust and Crisis of Human Behavior,* p. 137. Quotation from H. Stuart Hughes, *The Sea Change: Migration of Social Thought, 1930–1965* (Harper and Row, 1975), p. 53.

WESTERN DEFENSE COMMAND AND FOURTH ARMY
WARTIME CIVIL CONTROL ADMINISTRATION

Presidio of San Francisco, California
April 24, 1942

INSTRUCTIONS
TO ALL PERSONS OF
JAPANESE
ANCESTRY

Living in the Following Area:

All of that portion of the City and County of San Francisco, State of California, bounded on the north by California Street, bounded on the east by Van Ness Avenue, bounded on the south by Sutter Street, and bounded on the west by Presidio Avenue.

Pursuant to the provisions of Civilian Exclusion Order No. 20, this Headquarters, dated April 24, 1942, all persons of Japanese ancestry, both alien and non-alien, will be evacuated from the above area by 12 o'clock noon, P. W. T., Friday, May 1, 1942.

No Japanese person living in the above area will be permitted to change residence after 12 o'clock noon, P. W. T., Friday, April 24, 1942, without obtaining special permission from the representative of the Commanding General, Northern California Sector, at the Civil Control Station located at:

> Japanese American Citizens' League Auditorium,
> 2031 Bush Street,
> San Francisco, California.

Such permits will only be granted for the purpose of uniting members of a family, or in cases of grave emergency.

The Civil Control Station is equipped to assist the Japanese population affected by this evacuation in the following ways:

1. Give advice and instructions on the evacuation.
2. Provide services with respect to the management, leasing, sale, storage or other disposition of most kinds of property, such as real estate, business and professional equipment, household goods, boats, automobiles and livestock.
3. Provide temporary residence elsewhere for all Japanese in family groups.
4. Transport persons and a limited amount of clothing and equipment to their new residence.

The Following Instructions Must Be Observed:

1. A responsible member of each family, preferably the head of the family, or the person in whose name most of the property is held, and each individual living alone, will report to the Civil Control Station to receive further instructions. This must be done between 8:00 A. M. and 5:00 P. M. on Saturday, April 25, 1942, or between 8:00 A. M. and 5:00 P. M. on Sunday, April 26, 1942.
2. Evacuees must carry with them on departure for the Assembly Center, the following property:
    (a) Bedding and linens (no mattress) for each member of the family;
    (b) Toilet articles for each member of the family;
    (c) Extra clothing for each member of the family;
    (d) Sufficient knives, forks, spoons, plates, bowls and cups for each member of the family;
    (e) Essential personal effects for each member of the family.

All items carried will be securely packaged, tied and plainly marked with the name of the owner and numbered in accordance with instructions obtained at the Civil Control Station.

The size and number of packages is limited to that which can be carried by the individual or family group.

3. No pets of any kind will be permitted.
4. The United States Government through its agencies will provide for the storage at the sole risk of the owner of the more substantial household items, such as iceboxes, washing machines, pianos and other heavy furniture. Cooking utensils and other small items will be accepted for storage if crated, packed and plainly marked with the name and address of the owner. Only one name and address will be used by a given family.
5. Each family, and individual living alone, will be furnished transportation to the Assembly Center or will be authorized to travel by private automobile in a supervised group. All instructions pertaining to the movement will be obtained at the Civil Control Station.

**Go to the Civil Control Station between the hours of 8:00 A. M. and 5:00 P. M.,
Saturday, April 25, 1942, or between the hours of 8:00 A. M. and 5:00 P. M.,
Sunday, April 26, 1942, to receive further instructions.**

J. L. DeWITT
Lieutenant General, U. S. Army
Commanding

SEE CIVILIAN EXCLUSION ORDER NO. 20.

Source: California State Library, California History Section

How to Tell Japanese from Chinese People

- Most Chinese avoid horn-rimmed spectacles.
- Although both have the typical epicanthic fold of the upper eyelid (which makes them look almond-eyed), Japanese eyes are usually set closer together.
- Those who know them best often rely on facial expression to tell them apart: the Chinese expression is likely to be more placid, kindly, open; the Japanese more positive, dogmatic, arrogant.
- Japanese are nervous in conversation, laugh loudly at the wrong time.
- Japanese walk stiffly erect, hard-heeled. Chinese, more relaxed, have an easy gait, sometimes shuffle.

—From "How to Tell Your Friends from the Japs," *Time,* December 22, 1941. © 1941 Time Inc. Reprinted by permission.

Not Normal Human Beings

Fighting Japs is not like fighting normal human beings. . . . We are not dealing with humans as we know them. We are dealing with something primitive. Our troops have the right view of the Japs. They regard them as vermin.

—Sir Thomas A. Blamey, World War II commander of the Allied land forces in New Guinea, *New York Times*, January 9, 1943

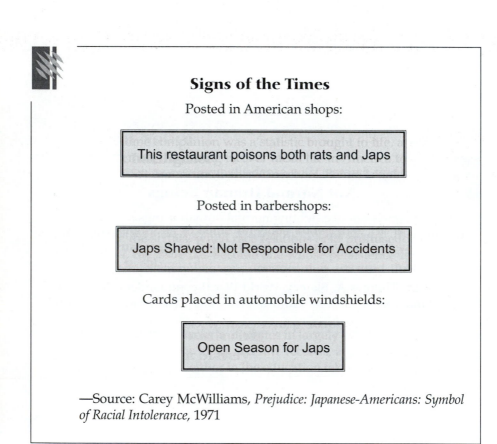

Signs of the Times

Posted in American shops:

> This restaurant poisons both rats and Japs

Posted in barbershops:

> Japs Shaved: Not Responsible for Accidents

Cards placed in automobile windshields:

> Open Season for Japs

—Source: Carey McWilliams, *Prejudice: Japanese-Americans: Symbol of Racial Intolerance*, 1971

Scalping in World War II

As reported by Edgar L. Jones, an American war correspondent during World War II, U.S. soldiers in the Pacific were known to have "boiled the flesh off enemy skulls to make table ornaments or carved their bones into letter openers." Some of these activities were well publicized while the war was going on—for example, the practice of collecting grisly battlefield trophies from the Japanese dead or near dead in the form of scalps, gold teeth, ears, bones, and skulls. In May of 1944, *Life* magazine published a full-page photograph of a young woman posing with a Japanese skull she had been sent by her boyfriend in the Pacific. Another well-known *Life* photograph revealed the practice of using Japanese skulls as ornaments on U.S. military vehicles.

On the West Coast of the United States, Japanese-Americans were also treated as less than human. They were not merely driven from their homes and rounded up like cattle, but actually forced to live in facilities meant for animals for weeks or months before being moved to their final "relocation camps." In the state of Washington, 2,000 Japanese-Americans were crowded into the Portland stockyard, where they slept on gunny-sacks filled with straw. In California, evacuees were squeezed into stables at racetracks such as Santa Anita and Tanforan. At Santa Anita, which eventually housed 8,500 Japanese-Americans, only four days elapsed between the removal of horses and arrival of the first Japanese-Americans, and the only bathing facilities were horse showers. Other evacuees were initially housed in horse or cattle stalls at various fairgrounds. At the Puyallup center in Washington (which was called "Camp Harmony"), some people were even lodged in converted pigpens.

—Adapted from John W. Dower, *War Without Mercy: Race and Power in the Pacific War*, 1986

The Japanese Internment: An Epilogue

They were concentration camps. They called it relocation, but they put them in concentration camps, and I was against it. We were in a period of emergency, but it was still the wrong thing to do.

—President Harry Truman, in a 1961 interview published in *Plain Speaking: An Oral Biography of Harry S. Truman,* 1974

I have made a lot of mistakes in my life. . . . One is my part in the evacuation of the Japanese from California in 1942. . . . We picked up these people—they were, of course, of foreign extraction, but they were our citizens—our fellow citizens. We picked them up and put them in concentration camps. That's the truth of the matter. And as I look back on it—although at the time I argued the case—I am amazed that the Supreme Court ever approved it.

—U.S. Supreme Court Justice Tom Clark, *San Diego Union,* July 10, 1966

A grave injustice was done to both citizens and permanent resident aliens of Japanese ancestry by the evacuation, relocation, and internment of civilians during World War II. . . . These actions were carried out without adequate security reasons and without any acts of espionage or sabotage . . . and were motivated largely by racial prejudice, wartime hysteria, and a failure of political leadership. . . . For these fundamental violations of the basic civil liberties and constitutional rights of these individuals of Japanese ancestry, the Congress apologizes on behalf of the Nation.

—Civil Liberties Act of 1988, passed by the U.S. Congress on August 10, 1988

IV

Racism Now

 The most important thing to appreciate about the thinking of whites on race, we now believe, is that many of them do not very often think about it at all. . . . They neither suffer directly from the problem of racial inequality, nor see themselves as directly responsible for it. The problem of race is, like many other problems of public policy, a secondary concern in the daily lives of whites and of only occasional interest to them.

—Paul M. Sniderman and Thomas Piazza, *The Scar of Race,* 1993

IV

SECTION OVERVIEW

Before the civil rights movement, racism in the United States was often expressed overtly and unapologetically. In contrast, modern forms of racism tend to be far more subtle, and the psychological underpinnings of modern racism are quite different from the underpinnings of older styles of racism.

This section examines some of the hot-button racial issues of the day, including immigration, residential segregation, interracial marriage, racial profiling, and the debate over affirmative action (i.e., policies designed to level the playing field in higher education and the workplace). The readings are intended to explore racism in a wide variety of contemporary social contexts, deepening the analysis and making it more applicable to daily life.

Take Special Notice

As you read this section, see if you can locate yourself in the material. For example, as you read David Cole's article on myths about immigration, ask yourself whether you have ever believed any of the myths. When you review the results of public opinion polls on racial profiling, compare your own views with those of the general public. As you look at Peggy McIntosh's list of White privileges and weigh arguments for and against affirmative action, consider some of the ways that these issues have affected you at a personal level.

Questions Worth Pondering

- Do any of David Cole's immigration myths describe beliefs you have had?
- If you were to take the Implicit Association Test, do you think your score would show a hidden bias toward Whites, Blacks, or neither?
- Who is responsible for the anti-Black discrimination described in the article "Service with a Sneer"? Do you agree with the business executive who said that society is to blame?
- What is the difference between an equal opportunity policy and an affirmative action policy? Do the two policies contradict each other?
- James Amirkhan and his colleagues discuss four possible goals of affirmative action. Which of these goals do you see as most important?

FIVE MYTHS ABOUT IMMIGRATION:
THE NEW KNOW–NOTHINGISM

DAVID COLE

For a brief period in the mid–nineteenth century, a new political movement captured the passions of the American public. Fittingly labeled the "Know-Nothings," their unifying theme was nativism. They liked to call themselves "Native Americans," although they had no sympathy for people we call Native Americans today. And they pinned every problem in American society on immigrants. As one Know-Nothing wrote in 1856: "Four-fifths of the beggary and three-fifths of the crime spring from our foreign population; more than half the public charities, more than half the prisons and almshouses, more than half the police and the cost of administering criminal justice are for foreigners."

At the time, the greatest influx of immigrants was from Ireland, where the potato famine had struck, and Germany, which was in political and economic turmoil. Anti-alien and anti-Catholic sentiments were the order of the day, especially in New York and Massachusetts, which received the brunt of the wave of immigrants, many of whom were dirt-poor and uneducated. Politicians were quick to exploit the sentiment: There's nothing like a scapegoat to forge an alliance.

I am especially sensitive to this history: My forebears were among those dirt-poor Irish Catholics who arrived in the 1860s. Fortunately for them, and me, the Know-Nothing movement fizzled within fifteen years. But its pilot light kept burning, and is turned up whenever the American public begins to feel vulnerable and in need of an enemy.

Although they go by different names today, the Know-Nothings have returned. As in the 1850s, the movement is strongest where immigrants are most concentrated: California and Florida. The objects of prejudice are of course no longer Irish Catholics and Germans; 140 years later, "they" have become "us." The new "they"—because it seems "we" must always have a "they"—are Latin Americans (most recently, Cubans), Haitians and Arab-Americans, among others.

But just as in the 1850s, passion, misinformation and short-sighted fear often substitute for reason, fairness and human dignity in today's immigration debates. In the interest of advancing beyond know-nothingism, let's look at five current myths that distort public debate and government policy relating to immigrants.

- *America is being overrun with immigrants.* In one sense, of course, this is true, but in that sense it has been true since Christopher Columbus arrived. Except for the real Native Americans, we are a nation of immigrants.

    It is not true, however, that the first-generation immigrant share of our population is growing. As of 1990, foreign-born people made up only 8 percent of the population, as compared with a figure of about 15 percent from 1870 to 1920. Between 70 and 80 percent of those who immigrate every year are refugees or immediate relatives of U.S. citizens.

Much of the anti-immigrant fervor is directed against the undocumented, but they make up only 13 percent of all immigrants residing in the United States, and only 1 percent of the American population. Contrary to popular belief, most such aliens do not cross the border illegally but enter legally and remain after their student or visitor visa expires. Thus, building a wall at the border, no matter how high, will not solve the problem.

- *Immigrants take jobs from U.S. citizens.* There is virtually no evidence to support this view, probably the most wide-spread misunderstanding about immigrants. As documented by a 1994 A.C.L.U. Immigrants' Rights Project report, numerous studies have found that immigrants actually create more jobs than they fill. The jobs immigrants take are of course easier to see, but immigrants are often highly productive, run their own businesses and employ both immigrants and citizens. One study found that Mexican immigration to Los Angeles County between 1970 and 1980 was responsible for 78,000 new jobs. Immigrants own more than 40,000 companies in New York, which provide thousands of jobs and $3.5 billion to the state's economy every year.

- *Immigrants are a drain on society's resources.* This claim fuels many of the recent efforts to cut off government benefits to immigrants. However, most studies have found that immigrants are a net benefit to the economy because, as a 1994 Urban Institute report concludes, "immigrants generate significantly more in taxes paid than they cost in services received." The Council of Economic Advisers similarly found in 1986 that "immigrants have a favorable effect on the overall standard of living."

Anti-immigrant advocates often cite studies purportedly showing the contrary, but these generally focus only on taxes and services at the local or state level. What they fail to explain is that because most taxes go to the federal government, such studies would also show a net loss when applied to U.S. citizens. At most, such figures suggest that some redistribution of federal and state monies may be appropriate; they say nothing unique about the costs of immigrants.

Some subgroups of immigrants plainly impose a net cost in the short run, principally those who have most recently arrived and have not yet "made it." California, for example, bears substantial costs for its disproportionately large undocumented population, largely because it has on average the poorest and least educated immigrants. But that has been true of every wave of immigrants that has ever reached our shores; it was as true of the Irish in the 1850s, for example, as it is of Salvadorans today. From a long-term perspective, the economic advantages of immigration are undeniable.

Some have suggested that we might save money and diminish incentives to immigrate illegally if we denied undocumented aliens public services. In fact, undocumented immigrants are already ineligible for most social programs, with the exception of education for schoolchildren, which is constitutionally required, and benefits directly related to health and safety, such as emergency medical care and nutritional assistance to poor women, infants and children. To deny such basic care to people in need, apart from being inhumanly callous, would probably cost us more in the long run by exacerbating health problems that we would eventually have to address.

- *Aliens refuse to assimilate, and are depriving us of our cultural and political unity.* This claim has been made about every new group of immigrants to arrive on U.S. shores. Supreme Court Justice Stephen Field wrote in 1884 that the Chinese "have remained among us a separate people, retaining their original peculiarities of dress, manners, habits, and modes of living, which are as marked as their complexion and language." Five years later, he upheld the racially based exclusion of Chinese immigrants. Similar claims have been made over different periods of our history about Catholics, Jews, Italians, Eastern Europeans and Latin Americans.

  In most instances, such claims are simply not true; "American culture" has been created, defined and revised by persons who for the most part are descended from immigrants once seen as anti-assimilationist. Descendants of the Irish Catholics, for example, a group once decried as separatist and alien, have become Presidents, senators and representatives (and all of these in one family, in the case of the Kennedys). Our society exerts tremendous pressure to conform, and cultural separatism rarely survives a generation. But more important, even if this claim were true, is this a legitimate rationale for limiting immigration in a society built on the values of pluralism and tolerance?

- *Noncitizen immigrants are not entitled to constitutional rights.* Our government has long declined to treat immigrants as full human beings, and nowhere is that more clear than in the realm of constitutional rights. Although the Constitution literally extends the fundamental protections in the Bill of Rights to all people, limiting to citizens only the right to vote and run for federal office, the federal government acts as if this were not the case.

  In 1893 the executive branch successfully defended a statute that required Chinese laborers to establish their prior residence here by the testimony of "at least one credible white witness." The Supreme Court ruled that this law was constitutional because it was reasonable for Congress to presume that nonwhite witnesses could not be trusted.

  Growing up, I was always taught that we will be judged by how we treat others. If we are collectively judged by how we have treated immigrants—those who appear today to be "other" but will in a generation be "us"—we are not in very good shape.

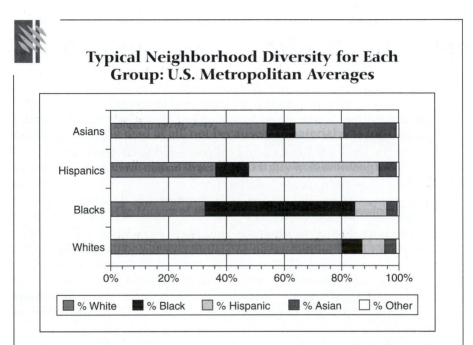

Typical Neighborhood Diversity for Each Group: U.S. Metropolitan Averages

This graph, based on U.S. Census data from the year 2000, shows that residential segregation is highest among Whites (Native Americans, who are not shown above, were once highly segregated on reservations, but a majority of Native Americans now live off reservations). [Data source: Lewis Mumford Center, University of Albany]

Mixing That Which God Separated

In 1998 South Carolina repealed its law banning interracial marriage. Yet that same year, the Community Relations Coordinator of Bob Jones University (a Christian evangelical school in South Carolina) informed a prospective applicant that "God has made people different from one another and intends those differences to remain. Bob Jones University is opposed to intermarriage of the races because it breaks down the barriers God has established."

The letter continued: "When Jesus Christ returns to the earth, He will establish world unity, but until then, a divided earth seems to be His plan."

Racial separation has long been justified as God's will. More than 100 years earlier, Brigham Young, leader of the Mormon Church, said to his followers: "Shall I tell you the law of God in regard to the African race? If the white man who belongs to the chosen seed mixes his blood with the seed of Cain, the penalty, under the law of God, is death on the spot. This will always be so."

In the case of Bob Jones University, national protests led the school to publicly revoke its ban on March 3, 2000. Three days later, however, students were told they would need a note from their parents approving any interracial dating.

—Sources: Cox News Service, February 3, 2000; Brigham Young, *Journal of Discourses*, 1865; *USA Today*, November 5, 1998; *New York Times*, March 8, 2000 [Note: Repeal of the South Carolina law was largely symbolic, because the U.S. Supreme Court ruled in 1967 that such bans are unconstitutional.]

Another Ban Repealed

On November 7, 2000, voters in Alabama repealed a 99–year-old law that banned white people and "Negroes" from marrying one another. Section 102 of the Constitution had barred the Legislature from passing any law that would "authorize or legalize any marriage between any white person and a Negro or descendant of a Negro."

While that's good news, Alabamians can't exactly jump up and down with glee. Only 59.5 percent of Alabama voters wanted to abolish the state's ban on love across racial lines. That means that a substantial portion of the state's voting population still believes that black and white people should not be able to marry.

There were 25 counties across the state that rejected the measure. Sixty-six percent of voters in Lamar County, located in the western central part of the state, wanted to keep the ban in place. It took the votes from the state's big cities and majority-black counties to erase the ban.

—*"Prejudice Takes a Hit," The Times-Picayune*, November 11, 2000. Permission granted by The Times-Picayune Publishing Corporation. All rights reserved. Reprinted with permission.

An Inside Look at Multiracial Identities Within a Mexican–American Family

Finding and becoming comfortable with one's racial identity is probably one of the most difficult things a member of a racial minority will ever face. Denial of one's background exacts a psychological toll that may outweigh the benefits of the higher status and prestige accorded to whiteness. But it is not difficult to understand why many mixed and fair-skinned Latinos choose a white identity. Those who embrace their Latino identity face many costs and few concrete benefits.

Besides the emotional turmoil involved in coming to grips with one's background, identity selection exposes a person to the judgment of others. Rarely a day goes by that my identity is not called into question. Many people assume that I am white because of my surname and appearance and openly wonder how it is possible that a Latino could be named Johnson.

I exercised a good deal of choice in embracing a Mexican American identity. Born with light skin and an Anglo surname, I could have passed as white. Still, to say that I had free choice would be an overstatement. I grew up with a Mexican American mother and grandmother and until the seventh grade lived in a mixed working-class white and Mexican American community. To deny that part of my background and life history would have been painful, if not impossible.

My blond-haired, blue-eyed brother made a different choice. He recognizes our family history and treats it as just that—as historical fact with little relevance to his daily life. My half-brother, who looks a bit like me, followed my brother's example in fashioning his racial identity. They neither deny their Mexican American heritage, as our mother did, nor openly embrace it as I have done. The point is that both choices come with costs—costs from which whites are generally immune.

—Adapted from Kevin Johnson, *How Did You Get to Be Mexican? A White/Brown Man's Search for Identity,* 1999

ONCE APPALLED BY RACE PROFILING, MANY FIND THEMSELVES DOING IT[1]

SAM HOWE VERHOVEK

Ron Arnold understands racial profiling. "I'm a black American, and I've been racially profiled all my life," said Mr. Arnold, a 43–year-old security officer here, "and it's wrong."

But Mr. Arnold admits that he is engaging in some racial profiling himself these days, casting a wary eye on men who look to be of Middle Eastern descent. If he saw a small knot of such men boarding a plane, he said: "I'd be nervous. It sickens me that I feel that way, but it's the real world."

Adrian Estala, 27, a risk-management consultant in Houston who is Hispanic, is struggling with the same emotions. Mr. Estala is "absolutely against" racial profiling, he said, because it is a fundamental violation of liberty. But asked about sharing an airplane flight with Arab-looking men, he said he would be anxious.

"Absolutely I have to be honest," Mr. Estala said. "Yes, it would make me second-guess."

On the other side of the divide, Arab-Americans find such views offensive. "Think what it really means," said Nadeem Salem, a second-generation American who leads the Association of Arab-Americans in Toledo, Ohio. "People's civil liberties are being tarnished, compromised. That's not what this country is all about."

For many Americans who say they have deeply believed that it was wrong for law enforcement officers to single out members of minorities for special interrogation or searches, the terrorist attacks on September 11 have prompted a painful confrontation with the sudden anxieties they acknowledge feeling in the presence of one minority in particular.[2] With all of the hijackers involved believed to have Arab backgrounds, these Americans say, officials have ample reason to zero in on that group. "It's not right," said Virginia Hawthorne, a retired accountant from Bremerton, Washington, "but it's justified."

Such sentiments seem to have been in play on Thursday in Minneapolis when three Middle Eastern-looking men were denied permission to board a Northwest Airlines flight after several passengers complained of their presence, an airline spokesman said. The men were later permitted to take a Delta flight.

---

[1]From "Americans Give in to Race Profiling" by Sam Howe Verhovek, *The New York Times*, September 23, 2001. Copyright © 2001 The New York Times Co. Reprinted by permission.

[2]*Editor's note:* On September 11, 2001, four U.S. commercial airplanes were hijacked by terrorists. Two airplanes were flown into New York's World Trade Center, one was flown into the Pentagon, and one crash-landed in Pennsylvania. All told, more than three thousand people were killed.

While expressing regret at what they portrayed as the need for more detailed interrogations of people of Arab background, many people said the subjects should understand and accept it.

"They shouldn't be offended," said Leslie Brenaman, a retired Boeing graphics designer, who is white. "They shouldn't take it personally after what's happened."

Ashraf Khan, 32, a mobile phone salesman from New Braunfels, Texas, who was ordered off a Delta Airlines flight from San Antonio on Monday while bound for his brother's wedding in Pakistan, said he was distressed by the pilot's action, which the airline said it was investigating. Delta offered a later flight, but by that time Mr. Khan had missed his connecting flight and the wedding.

"I am really depressed about the whole situation," he said, "the way they've treated me, like I'm some sort of criminal."

In interviews around the country, many people expressed revulsion at the spate of attacks on Muslims, as well as on Hindus and Sikhs, and the vandalism at mosques. Those interviewed spoke of national ideals of colorblindness—but in nearly the same breath they said that for the sake of national safety, the police should single out Arab-looking men for questioning.

Kathy Komlance, 43, who was wearing an American flag T-shirt as she worked at a taffy stand at the Mid-South Fair in Memphis, said she favored checking their credentials. "I think a person who is Arab should be questioned if they get on a bus or plane or go in a government building," Ms. Komlance said. "You don't want to be afraid of Arabs, Iranians or other foreign people. But how do you differentiate and figure out which one is the bad one from those who love freedom and our country?"

A CNN/*USA Today*/Gallup poll taken a few days after the attacks showed that Americans were supporting special measures intended for those of Arab descent. In the survey, 58 percent backed more intensive security checks for Arabs, including those who are United States citizens, compared with other travelers; 49 percent favored special identification cards for such people, and 32 percent backed "special surveillance" for them.

In the interviews, many people said they hoped the need for the sort of racial profiling they favored would be temporary, while others were firmly against racial profiling and said there was no justification for it.

"They should interrogate everybody the same way," said LaVonne James, a Seattle parks department worker. "I mean, at airports, they should stop everybody the same way, search luggage, ask all the questions."

And some said they were going out of their way to be friendlier than ever to Arab-Americans. Sasha Nyary, who works for a community development organization in Brooklyn and is the mother of a daughter, Lily, 2, said she was seeking out a mosque and Arab-owned businesses.

"There are a couple of ways I can walk to get to Lily's school at Third Avenue and Atlantic," Ms. Nyary said, "and this week I've deliberately chosen to go down the south side of Atlantic so I can maximize the number of Arab shopkeepers I see."

Many people who belong to minorities said they felt especially torn by their newfound acceptance of at least one form of racial profiling.

"I've seen prejudice all my life, with me growing up as an African-American male," said Jermaine Johnson, 19, a business management student at Southwest Tennessee Community College in Memphis. "I try not to judge."

But Mr. Johnson added: "I would not feel comfortable at all if an Arab-looking person sat next to me on a plane. I would be nervous, I mean right now it could be anyone and that's not good if they sit next to you on a plane. I don't feel comfortable with the ones I don't know. It's hard to know who to trust."

American Opinion in the Month After the Terrorist Attacks of September 11, 2001

Question	*Source*	*Response*
Please tell me if you would favor or oppose each of the following as a means of preventing terrorist attacks in the United States. How about . . . requiring Arabs, including those who are U.S. citizens, to undergo special, more intensive security checks before boarding airplanes in the U.S.?	CNN/*USA Today*	Favor: 58% Oppose: 41% No opinion: 1%
What about . . . closely monitoring the whereabouts of legal immigrants to the United States from Arab and Muslim countries? Would you strongly favor this, accept this if necessary, or think this would go too far?	*Newsweek*	Favor: 53% Accept: 29% Too far: 17% Don't know: 1%
There are many factors that could go into the profile of a suspected terrorist, such as having contacts with terrorist groups. Do you think . . . being Arab or Muslim . . . should be part of the profile of a suspected terrorist, or not?	ABC News	Should be: 51% Should not: 45% No opinion: 4%
Based on the recent events (the terrorist attacks on the World Trade Center and the Pentagon, September 11, 2001), do you think U.S. immigration laws should be tightened to restrict the number of immigrants from Arab or Muslim countries into the United States?	Wirthlin Quorum Poll	Yes: 83% No: 16% Don't know: 1%
Thinking of the situation here in the United States, please tell me if you support or oppose giving the police powers to stop and search . . . any one who appears to be Arab or Muslim, at random?	ABC News	Support: 42% Oppose: 55% No opinion: 3%
Please tell me if you would favor or oppose the government doing each of the following as a way to prevent terrorist attacks in the United States. . . . Allow the federal government to hold Arabs who are U.S. (United States) citizens in camps until it can be determined whether they have links to terrorist organizations.	*Time*/CNN	Favor: 31% Oppose: 65% Not sure: 4%

—Source: Roper Center for Public Opinion Research, January, 2002

RACE TO INCARCERATE

MARC MAUER

Two hundred years ago, Quakers and other reformers in Pennsylvania developed the institution of the penitentiary. Derived from the concept of "penitence," the new institution emphasized having sinners engage in hard labor and reflect upon the errors of their ways. Prior to this, the jails that existed in Europe and the U.S. served primarily to detain defendants who were awaiting trial and debtors who had not fulfilled their obligations. They were not places of punishment for felons.

After a defendant was convicted of an offense, various measures were employed with the goal of deterring the individual from engaging in anti-social behavior in the future. Deviant behavior was viewed not as reflecting a flaw in society but, rather, as sinful and pervasive in society. Those who had offended were generally subjected to relatively swift and severe sanctions, which often varied depending on one's status in the community. For persons of some means who had committed relatively minor offenses, fines were frequently imposed as punishment. Lower-status persons convicted of offenses—servants, apprentices, slaves, and laborers—were usually subjected to the stocks or public whippings.

After the Revolution, though, new ways of thinking about crime and punishment began to emerge. In 1787, influential Quakers and other leaders in Pennsylvania, led by Dr. Benjamin Rush, organized the Philadelphia Society for Alleviating the Miseries of Public Prisons.[1] The initial experiment in confining convicted offenders took place in 1790: it involved converting sixteen cells at Philadelphia's Walnut Street Jail into housing for felons. This was later replaced and expanded upon at the Eastern State Penitentiary in 1829. Tellingly, the first inmate admitted to the Eastern State Penitentiary was a "light skinned Negro in excellent health."[2]

Two centuries later, issues of race and class with the prison system have become a fundamental feature of the national landscape. What is particularly remarkable is how little the institutional model has changed since the nineteenth century. While the philosophical orientation and stated goals of the prison have fluctuated, the basic concept of imprisoning people in cages remains the central feature of the system.

It is a bit jarring, of course, to speak of "caging" human beings, since we normally prefer to use this term for animals and to conjure up fond feelings for our favorite zoo (although our common feelings about the constraints placed on animals in cages have also changed markedly in recent years). But whether call them "cells," or "housing units," or any other new name, it is difficult to deny that the basic reality of the system is that of the cage.

African Americans and the Criminal Justice System

If we started to put white America in jail at the same rate that we're putting black America in jail, I wonder whether our collective feelings would be the same, or would we be putting pressure on the president and our elected officials not to lock up America, but to save America?

—FORMER ATLANTA POLICE CHIEF ELDRIN BELL[3]

Half of all prison inmates are now African American, and another 17 percent are Hispanic—percentages *far* out of proportion to their numbers in the general population. Of the 455 persons executed for rape in the first half of the twentieth century, 405, or almost 90 percent, were black men. Looking at the race of rape victims, it has been reported that "no cases are known in which any white man was executed for the rape of a black woman."[4]

By the mid-1990s, one in fourteen adult black males was locked up in a prison or jail on any given day. For young black men, the situation was far worse. A study by The Sentencing Project found that in 1989 nearly one in four black males in the age group 20–29 was under some form of criminal justice supervision on any given day—either in prison or jail, or on probation or parole. A follow-up study in 1995 then found that this figure had increased to almost one in three, a remarkable rise over a short period of time. Further, a black boy born in 1991 stood a 29 percent chance of being imprisoned at some point in his life, compared to a 16 percent chance for a Hispanic boy and a 4 percent chance for a white boy.

For black women, the absolute numbers were not quite as overwhelming, but the trends were at least as disturbing. From 1985 to 1995, there was a 204 percent growth in the number of black women in federal and state prisons, considerably greater even than the 143 percent increase for black males or the 126 percent increase in the overall inmate population.

As if this weren't enough, leading academics, political pundits, and members of Congress began to refer to this new generation of criminals as containing a group of "superpredators." The animal imagery is inescapable here. To many Americans, some combination of bad family, bad culture, or bad genes created this young thug whose behavior is presumably beyond the capacity of modern law or social science to improve.

The Hidden Impact of Incarceration

The negative consequences of high incarceration rates in some communities may actually lead to increases in crime in those communities. For example, for children whose parents are imprisoned, feelings of shame, humiliation, and a loss of social status may result.[5] Children begin to act out in school or distrust authority figures, who represent the people who removed the parent from the home. Lowered economic circumstances in families experiencing imprisonment also lead to greater housing relocation, resulting in less cohesive neighborhoods. In far too many cases, these children come to represent the next generation of offenders.

The impact of rising incarceration on the next generation of children has been exacerbated in recent years by the growing number of women who are sentenced to prison. From 1980 to 1995, the number of women in prison increased by 417 percent, compared to a 235 percent increase for men. Three fourths of the women in prison in 1991 were mothers, and two thirds had children under the age of 18. Altogether, an estimated 1.5 million children have parents in prison.

The impact of the criminal justice system on communities goes beyond issues of economic well-being and family stabilization. It also includes issues of democratic participation and political influence. One of the most dramatic ways in which this emerges is voting rights. Almost all states have laws restricting the right to vote for convicted felons. Forty-six states deny the right to vote to anyone who is imprisoned, thirty-two restrict voting privileges of offenders on probation and/or parole, and in fourteen states anyone ever convicted of a felony can lose the right to vote for life. For example, an 18-year-old first offender convicted of writing a bad check in Florida or Virginia who successfully completes a sentence to probation loses the right to vote for life. The only means by which voting rights can be regained in such instances is through gubernatorial action, a cumbersome and bureaucratic process few offenders are able to negotiate.

A study conducted by The Sentencing Project and Human Rights Watch in 1998 concluded that an estimated 3.9 million Americans, or one in fifty adults, was either currently or permanently disenfranchised as a result of a felony conviction.[6] Of these, 1.4 million were African American males, representing 13 percent of all black men. In those states that impose disenfranchisement on ex-felons, the figures are truly enormous; one in four black men are permanently disenfranchised in Alabama, Florida, Iowa, Mississippi, New Mexico, Virginia, and Wyoming. Given that the current generation of children has a higher rate of contact with the criminal justice system, it is likely that as many as 30–40 percent of African American men will lose the right to vote for some or all of their adult lives. Thus, not only are criminal justice policies resulting in the disproportionate incarceration of African Americans; imprisonment itself reduces black political ability to influence these policies.

When the United States was founded, the franchise was restricted to a self-selected group of wealthy white men who excluded other groups such as women, blacks, felons, and the poor. After the Civil War and Reconstruction, restrictions were added, such as the poll tax and literacy requirements, specifically designed to disenfranchise blacks. Statutes were tailored to punish with disenfranchisement those offenses that blacks supposedly committed more frequently than whites.

Over time the poll tax, literacy requirements, and other restrictions have been erased—but not the exclusion of felons and ex-offenders. U.S. policies in regard to ex-offenders remain far out of line with international norms; no other democratic nation bars ex-offenders from voting for life or keeps such a significant proportion of its citizens from voting as a result of a felony conviction.

None of the preceding suggests, of course, that criminal behavior should be condoned or not have consequences. Indeed, removal of certain serious offenders from a community clearly has beneficial consequences for the community for the period of time that the offender is incarcerated. But any calculation of the impact of imprisonment that fails to take into account both the short-term and long-term consequences of massive incarceration is a deeply flawed analysis. Whether the objective is to produce community safety or a more inclusive society, the expansion of the prison system creates a more troubling set of consequences each day.

NOTES

1. Although prisons as institutions of punishment had not yet emerged in the new nation, jails for debtors and defendants awaiting trial had previously existed.
2. Negley K. Teeters and John D. Shearer, *The Prison at Philadelphia, Cherry Hill; The Separate System of Prison Discipline, 1829–1913* (New York: Columbia University Press, 1957), p. 84.
3. Nkechi Taifa, "Laying Down the Law, Race by Race," *Legal Times,* Oct. 10, 1994.
4. Michael Radelet and Margaret Vandiver, "Race and Capital Punishment: An Overview of the Issues," *Crime and Social Justice* 25, (1986), p. 98.
5. Clear, "Backfire," pp. 12–13.
6. Jamie Fellner and Marc Mauer, "Losing the Vote: The Impact of Felony Disenfranchisement Laws in the United States," The Sentencing Project and Human Rights Watch; October 1998.

A COMPUTER DIAGNOSIS OF PREJUDICE[1]

ERICA GOODE

Ask people if they have negative attitudes toward blacks, women or the elderly, and you are likely to hear a chorus of denials. But give those same individuals a simple test to tap unconscious beliefs, two psychologists say, and the results often tell a different story.

Prejudice can be so pervasive and so deeply rooted that many people are not consciously aware of their biases, say Dr. Anthony Greenwald of the University of Washington and Dr. Mahzarin Banaji of Yale University, developers of the Implicit Associations Test. The test, a series of word-pairing tasks, is intended to measure implicit or automatic associations to social groups. In one version, subjects are asked to pair random combinations of pleasant and unpleasant words—"peace" and "paradise" versus "hatred" and "violence"—with combinations of proper names common among white or black Americans—Brad and Peggy versus Jamal and Latisha. Other versions of the test address unconscious assumptions about women and older people. Still others focus on self-esteem and sex differences in preferences for math or art.

Drs. Greenwald and Banaji and their colleagues have given the test to hundreds of undergraduates, including more than 1,000 Yale freshmen this fall. Thousands of other people are taking the test on line, by visiting a web site (www.yale.edu/implicit) for the researchers. The site received 50,000 hits in its first week, the researchers said.

In studies using the race-based version of the test, 90 percent of white subjects took longer to pair pleasant words with black names and unpleasant words with white names than the other way around, a delay the psychologists interpret as an automatic or implicit preference for white names.

This discrepancy remained significant even when the researchers took into account the familiarity of the proper names, the order in which the words were presented, whether the pleasant words appeared on the right or left side, and other factors that might influence the results. Data from black subjects are still being collected, but Dr. Greenwald says many black people taking the test also show a preference for white names, though to a weaker degree.

SERVICE WITH A SNEER

HOWARD KOHN

U p top, front and center, is the familiar red script on a yellow background, and below is an "Open 24 Hours" sign. This is the Denny's
restaurant at the intersection of Highway 101 and Tully Road in San
Jose, Calif., where Robert Norton was assigned to work in 1990. It's the same
restaurant where, as Norton says, he watched with astonishment late one
night when young African-American customers stepped out of their cars into
the illuminated parking lot only to find themselves in a race to the front
doors. Denny's employees rushed to lock up, and the blacks were left to wonder at the boldfaced claim, "We're closed." Only after they had gone were the
doors reopened.

"I couldn't believe it," says Norton, who is white. "I said to the duty
manager: 'This is ludicrous. How can you be doing this?' But I was told this
was how the game was played."

Norton heard more detailed explanations during talks with his supervisors that occurred one on one at the Denny's on Tully Road or at regular district meetings for the eight restaurants in the area. According to Norton, he
was told that "A-A's"—in-house code for African-Americans—posed a problem because they could not be counted on to follow the protocols of restau-
rant-going: they offended other customers by being boisterous; they
alienated waitresses by leaving skin-flinty tips; they cost the company money
by skipping out on the bill.

"We were told we should take whatever measures we could to keep
A-A's to a minimum," Norton recalls. "You could seat white customers ahead
of A-A's. You could put A-A's in the rear and stall on serving them. You could
ask A-A's to pay before eating. Or, if you really wanted to get the job done,
you could lock them out." This practice was called "blackout," and the point
of it was to make African-Americans feel unwelcome. "You were to eliminate
them from your restaurant. No questions asked, just get it done."

The "blackout" practice in San Jose and dozens of other cities and towns
across the nation might never have come to light but for two special sets of
customers. In 1991, a group of 18 teen-agers, most of them members of the
N.A.A.C.P. Youth Council in San Jose, were told they would have to pay for
their food on ordering. While this is standard in fast-food restaurants like
McDonald's or Hardee's, where you pick up your order at a counter, it is not
at Denny's, which has table service.

The second incident, in 1993, involving six young black Secret Service officers, occurred at a Denny's in Annapolis, Md., and gave rise to Dan Rather's
one-sentence summation that these agents "put their lives on the line every
day, but they can't get served at Denny's."

In the past year and a half, following class-action lawsuits filed by the N.A.A.C.P. teen-agers and the Secret Service agents, thousands of complaints came in from around the country. Attorneys with the United States Justice Department concluded they were dealing with the largest case ever in the history of the public accommodations section of the 1964 Civil Rights Act.

While only the rare Denny's manager resorted to the extreme of locking out blacks, other variations of the "blackout" practice were commonplace: prepayments, minimum-purchase requirements, gratuities added to the bill, denials of free birthday meals previously advertised, interminable delays, back-room seating and service so disrespectful it would be hard to deny racist intent. Black customers were forced to pay in advance at as many as 150 to 200 Denny's in California, Illinois, Oregon, Oklahoma, Maryland, Ohio and Florida, according to plaintiffs' attorneys. The claimants included military officers, police officers, teachers, college administrators and government officials, as well as a teenager in a wheelchair.

That so many Denny's employees chose to treat customers in a fashion reminiscent of the Old South, a generation after the lunch-counter sit-ins, caught much of the country by surprise and raised a number of questions. For all the good intentions of civil rights laws, were America's black citizens still widely accorded second-class treatment? Or, as some of the evidence indicated, was there a deliberate corporate policy at work?

🌿 🌿 🌿

Jerome (Jerry) Richardson, 58, a physically imposing man with a big breakfast smile, is chairman and chief executive of Flagstar Companies, which owns the Denny's chain. In August, I accompanied Richardson as he toured several of his newly modernized restaurants around Houston. "Had you ever heard of the word 'blackout?' " Richardson asked a regional manager. "Before all the publicity, I mean, had you ever heard of 'blackouts' at Denny's?"

"No, never."

"I'll tell you, I've asked around, and I can't find anyone who'd ever heard of 'blackout' either," Richardson said. "Not before this all came out."

The regional manager reacted a little uneasily. "Well, I wouldn't swear we didn't have a few bad apples in the barrel. After all, we hire from the population. We get the bad with the good. But"—he gave Richardson a nod—"yeah, it makes you wonder if this wasn't blown way out of proportion."

From the beginning Richardson characterized the allegations against Denny's as isolated incidents. After reviewing the case of the N.A.A.C.P. teen-agers, he believed so strongly that "there was no intent to discriminate" that he spurned a chance to pay damages and perhaps cut short the escalation of complaints. Later, even as the evidence piled up nationwide, Richardson continued to take the position that very little wrong had actually been done. "If our African-American guests were mistreated, was it because of racism?" Richardson said to me. "I can't tell you. It's impossible to know what's in a person's heart."

Richardson decided not to contest the class-action litigation on the advice of Flagstar attorneys, who were not eager to face potential witnesses like the girl with paralyzed legs who tried to celebrate her prom night at a Denny's in Tampa and was kept waiting two hours without food. Flagstar eventually paid $54.4 million to settle the claims.

Richardson's own interest in getting to the bottom of things, he said, has now been superseded by a desire to "put this whole damn mess behind us." Because the case is settled, the official search for evidence has been cut off. Three company executives were interviewed under oath prior to the settlement, but their depositions remain confidential under court order.

To judge from the accounts of former and current employees and from court documents, however, there is little doubt that Denny's, a predominantly white organization, has had a longstanding problem with discrimination. It became a serious problem at least in part because of a cash-flow crisis that began in 1987, the year Richardson's company acquired Denny's.

Senior executives at headquarters reacted with a series of orders that were widely interpreted by employees to mean they had to improve profits or lose their jobs. The orders went from headquarters down a chain of command. Because about half of the 600 regional managers and higher executives were being laid off in a restructuring, the pressure to save money fell most heavily on about 140 district supervisors, who typically have charge of eight or nine locations in a metropolitan area, and on the individual restaurant managers. It appears that a number of those supervisors and managers then decided to scapegoat their African-American customers.

Today there is a reform era at Denny's. Employees must watch a 16-minute videotape about diversity, "What Color Am I?" Managers must attend sensitivity seminars that include a session on the business advantages of serving a multiracial clientele. Yet the real problem for so long at Denny's was the theory held by employees that black customers were bad for business. The fact is, the problem of discrimination at Denny's did not come out of the blue; it had existed for years.

🦅 🦅 🦅

Robert Norton was hired in 1988 by Denny's after 15 years with other discount-food chains and worked at several Denny's in the San Jose area until he was promoted in 1990 to manage the Tully Road restaurant. The routine in San Jose was for the district supervisors to meet two to four times a month with managers and assistant managers to discuss tasks like mixing pancake batter. At one of the meetings a supervisor declared what Norton took to be a state of emergency over corporate finances. "Headquarters was obsessed with saving money," says Norton. "It was either produce or we could kiss our jobs goodbye—that was the message."

Some Denny's managers in San Jose began to demand minimum purchases and to renege when customers asked for free birthday meals. The changes were applied primarily to black customers. At Denny's elsewhere in the country, other managers were adopting the same methods. It is plausible that certain changes were instituted locally without the knowledge of senior executives. On the other hand, prepayments and minimum-purchase requirements were known to Richardson, who had approved of them.

Of all the undesirable customers, the most undesirable were the walk-outs. In 1988, the installation of a computerized network gave Denny's exec-utives a new technological tool. As the computers came on line, executives could identify the restaurants where an above-average number of customers were eating without paying. Memos were sent to the district meetings. "Headquarters wanted us to crack down on walkouts," Norton says. "We had to find ways to get control of the situation." The solution for a number of managers was the "blackout."

"It didn't matter if a black kid walked in flashing money or not," Norton says. "He was presumed to be a walkout. The short of it was A-A's were not welcome. It was a business calculation. They were more trouble than they were worth. The company just didn't want to contend with walkouts. They trusted Caucasians, Hispanics and Asians, but they did not trust African-Americans."

Glenda Cappuccilli, a white assistant manager who had attended some San Jose meetings, confirmed Norton's basic account. "The first time I heard a man-ager make reference to 'blackout' I thought that there had been an electrical problem," Cappuccilli said in testimony submitted in the Denny's litigation. "As the meeting progressed, I began to understand that they were talking about reducing the black clientele." Cappuccilli's attempt to argue the point proved useless. "They just ignored me and went on with the meeting as usual." Norton also raised an objection to the policy, but it was "brushed under the carpet."

Although the district supervisors never clarified whether "blackouts" were authorized by someone higher up in the corporate structure, Norton assumed that. Certainly it seems to be more than coincidence that other supervisors in other districts used the same tactics. Tyrone Jackson, 39, a black man who was hired by Denny's to work in Los Angeles in 1987 and moved up to a manager's job in 1990, says his training included two instructions in regard to black cus-tomers: they were to pay in advance, and they were to be seated at whichever table was the farthest possible distance from the exits. Denise Perryman, a black former waitress in the college town of Champaign, Ill., said she had to operate under similar orders, and when she disobeyed in 1991, she was fired.

According to Richardson, the prepayment practice was supposed to be racially neutral. Nonetheless, as he acknowledges, it was put into effect on an "as needed" basis at "high risk" locations, which, for the most part, happened to be restaurants frequented by many young African-Americans.

🐾   🐾   🐾

It was shortly after midnight on Dec. 30, 1991, when 18 San Jose teen-agers ar-rived at a Denny's on Blossom Hill Road, hoping to wind down after taking part in a daylong forum sponsored by Tuskegee University. At first they did not know what to make of the manager's insistence on being paid in advance. "When we challenged this, the manager got hostile and threatened to call the police," says Rodney Braddock, then 18 and a Tuskegee freshman. Braddock is the kind of wisecracking kid who normally gets the rest of the crowd to lighten up. "But the way the manager was acting, I was starting to get mad."

Kristina Ridgeway, then 17 and a high-school senior, says, "The manager was adamant about having us pay first." While the group was arguing with the manager, Kristina recognized six white school-mates at a table. "I asked them, 'Did you have to pay before you got served,' and they said, 'No, of course not.' " Looking about, she noticed nine other teen-agers—whites and Latinos—and learned that they, too, had been able to order without prior restraints. By now Kristina and her friends understood that prepaying was designed for groups thought most likely to be walkouts, which only infuriated her further. "Here I was getting ready for college, planning to be an attorney, and Denny's saw me as a criminal who's going to eat and run."

In fact, many of the 18 are children of a white-collar, privileged world connected with San Jose's high-tech industries. Rodney's father, Reginald, 48, is a software engineer with 21 years at Lockheed; Kristina's father, William, 52, a marketing executive, has put in 27 years at I.B.M. Several of the 18 are also children of the civil rights movement. The elder Braddock was arrested in 1961, at age 16, for trying to buy a hamburger and french fries at the whites-only lunch counter in his native Ocala, Fla. Every summer from 1962 to 1967 he was a volunteer with voter registration drives in the South. In Alabama, he met his future wife, Vannette, whose two cousins were killed by a Ku Klux Klan bomb in a Birmingham church. The elder Ridgeway grew up in a rural area of Alabama where in the 1950's black sharecroppers were paid in currency minted by a white landowner.

William Ridgeway was awake, folding clothes, when Kristina came home, kicked off her shoes and began explaining what had happened at Denny's. "Put your shoes back on," he told her. "We're going to see about this." Tall like his daughter, he is a soft-spoken man with a silver-flecked goatee. At Denny's, he says, his questions were not treated seriously. "They asked me, did I want a free meal? I wanted answers, and they thought they could buy me for eggs and sausage!"

Reginald Braddock, a stocky man given to bursts of passion, was not told of the incident until a few days later. "My son chose not to bring it up, knowing it might touch a sore spot in our family. When I did hear about it, it really did hurt because it was the nightmare revisited. Here was the Old South, back in our face again."

An activist group of parents, many of whom already were friends, soon formed around the San Jose 18. They contacted attorneys and the news media.

A month after learning of the San Jose incident, Richardson formally did away with the prepayment practice as well as the minimum charges. In July 1992, nearly half a year later, however, Sylvia Skeeter, 35, a former Army captain training with Denny's in Orlando, Fla., was told by an instructor: "Please try to obtain money from young blacks as soon as they enter your store. This will discourage them from coming in, which is what you want. Most of them are going to be walkouts anyway." Skeeter, who is black, says: "I vividly recall the ease at which young blacks were equated with the criminal class. I was stunned into silence a minute, then I put up my hand and asked why does it have be just blacks, and the justification was, well, this applies to stores in predominantly black areas."

☙   ☙   ☙

On April 1, 1993, 21 members of the Secret Service stopped for breakfast at a Denny's near a U.S. 301 exit just outside Annapolis. Arriving about 7:30 A.M., the officers were working against a 9:30 deadline, by which time they had to set up portable metal detectors at the Naval Academy for a visit by President Clinton. Everything at the restaurant went according to routine, cups and glasses filled, plates of country breakfasts slapped down, except at the table occupied by Alfonso Dyson and five other black officers. At about 8:10, it was apparent that the waitress was bringing second helpings to the other tables while those at his table were still nursing coffee and juice. There could be no mistaking that the six officers were part of the Secret Service detail. Each agent was in full uniform—dark pants with wide gold stripes, white shirt with Presidential patch and gold badge, dark tie, pistols in flap holsters. "I had never before been to a restaurant where I became aware of being discriminated against," says Dyson.

The white, middle-aged waitress, he says, gave him only perfunctory replies to his three complaints about the poor service. With her back to the table, according to William Winans, a white officer, the waitress melodramatically rolled her eyes, then made a mocking comment. As of 8:20, Dyson's table still lacked the main course. A complaint to the manager elicited no satisfaction. The only explanation came from one of the cooks, who said steaming hot breakfasts for the six officers had been sitting for more than half an hour on a serving counter and had been pointedly ignored by the waitress.

The theory that prejudice was insinuated into the Denny's culture over a lengthy period is supported by Sandy Patterson, 55, a waitress in California for 15 years, beginning in 1974. She is white and was then married to a black man. All through her employment, she said in court papers, the hostility toward black people was such that she felt she couldn't have her husband pick her up at work or attend the company picnics. According to her, prepayments were required only for black customers "or other people of color" in the 1980's. She felt so intimidated she would not acknowledge her own mixed-race son when she served him and his friends. She was later reprimanded for not requiring prepayment from the group.

In Patterson's opinion, her supervisors were less concerned with crime than they were with keeping the restaurants as "white" as possible. To prevent black customers from lingering after their meals, she said, she was told to limit them to one complimentary refill of coffee, whereas white customers could have all the refills they wanted.

At a Denny's in downtown Portland, Ore., the issue seems not to have been security, nor concern over the decorum of customers. Kristen Siegrist, a white woman who sells perfume wholesale, inadvertently carried out a textbook test of the prepayment practice during two visits to the restaurant at the end of 1989. When in the company of her roommate, a black professional woman, Siegrist was required to prepay, she says, but then one night just before Christmas, acting spontaneously, she treated three unshaven, ill-dressed homeless men to meals at the same Denny's. She expected to be asked for money in advance, and was surprised to have food served without question. The only issue, it seems, was race: the homeless men were white.

🦅　🦅　🦅

A paradox of the Denny's case is that, while the company has become a symbol of race discrimination in the 1990's, the man in charge is seen in his own community as someone who has done pioneering work in race relations. Back in the 1960's Richardson's South Carolina Hardee's restaurants underwent a peaceful transition to integration. In July 1993 Richardson signed a "Fair Share" agreement with the national N.A.A.C.P., spanning a seven-year period at a cost to Flagstar of $1 billion. The agreement calls for Flagstar to add significant numbers of African-American managers, franchise owners and subcontractors, along with naming the first African-American to the board.

What has remained troubling, though, has been Richardson's inclination to avoid dealing with the central judgment of the case, namely that at the heart of the matter lies racism. In the official corporate rendering of the case, most of the complaints were written off as misunderstandings that are inevitable when a business has a million encounters a year with the public. While Denny's did fire the manager involved in the Secret Service incident, the stated reason was his "failure to report a complaint of alleged discrimination involving customer service." In the Denny's news release announcing resolution of the lawsuits, Richardson stated, "These settlements are not an admission that Denny's has had a policy or practice of discrimination against African-Americans." The terms of the settlements permit him to continue taking the same position.

When I inquired of Richardson why he does not simply make a clean breast of everything, his reply was legalistic. "My hands are tied. If I tell you our employees were guilty of civil rights violations, the employees will turn around and sue me." After hesitating, he added a few remarks. "Obviously there were situations where our customers did not get treated fairly, and it would be naïve of me to say nothing wrong happened. But the problems at Denny's came about because of the society we live in."

Only after I tried to get Richardson to be more forthcoming did he turn emotional. "I'll tell you the thing that bothered me the most, the thing that ate at me. All the stuff in the press about Denny's was so brutal on our employees, especially our African-American employees." His voice thickened. "We have thousands of good people working for us, black and white. They deserve the right to hold their heads high."

🦅　🦅　🦅

On Aug. 1, 1994, a federal judge in Baltimore issued a final approval of the $54.4 million settlement. The six Secret Service agents, seated in chairs reserved for plaintiffs, were told they will receive $35,000 apiece. The San Jose 18 are each to be paid $25,000, and other claimants are to divide the remainder.

A few days earlier several of the San Jose 18 and their parents had gathered to talk about their experience. Asked to define any lessons he learned, Reginald Braddock said: "I had gotten complacent in my life, and this woke me up. We didn't complete the job 30 years ago, and I realize now it's going to take more than my lifetime to complete it."

William Ridgeway interjected. "My daughter says my favorite expression is, 'Welcome to being black in America!' I don't know: Will there be a time when we can stop reliving the past and get on with the rest of our lives? I think back on the occasions I used to go to Denny's and sit there and justify the slow service as, well, the waitress is busy. Now, if I go into any restaurant, I have to wonder, am I being subjected to slow service because of what I look like? That's some of the baggage I carry. You try to shake it."

WHITE PRIVILEGE: UNPACKING THE INVISIBLE KNAPSACK

Peggy McIntosh

Through work to bring materials from Women's Studies into the rest of the curriculum, I have often noticed men's unwillingness to grant that they are over-privileged, even though they may grant that women are disadvantaged. They may say they will work to improve women's status, in the society, the university, or the curriculum, but they can't or won't support the idea of lessening men's. Denials which amount to taboos surround the subject of advantages which men gain from women's disadvantages. These denials protect male privilege from being fully acknowledged, lessened or ended.

Thinking through unacknowledged male privilege as a phenomenon, I realized that since hierarchies in our society are interlocking, there was most likely a phenomenon of white privilege which was similarly denied and protected. As a white person, I realized I had been taught about racism as something which puts others at a disadvantage, but had been taught not to see one of its corollary aspects, white privilege, which puts me at an advantage.

I think whites are carefully taught not to recognize white privilege, as males are taught not to recognize male privilege. So I have begun in an untutored way to ask what it is like to have white privilege. I have come to see white privilege as an invisible package of unearned assets which I can count on cashing in each day, but about which I was "meant" to remain oblivious. White privilege is like an invisible weightless knapsack of special provisions, maps, passports, codebooks, visas, clothes, tools and blank checks.

Describing white privilege makes one newly accountable. As we in Women's Studies work to reveal male privilege and ask men to give up some of their power, so one who writes about having white privilege must ask, "Having described it, what will I do to lessen or end it?"

After I realized the extent to which men work from a base of unacknowledged privilege, I understood that much of their oppressiveness was unconscious. Then I remembered the frequent charges from women of color that white women whom they encounter are oppressive. I began to understand why we are justly seen as oppressive, even when we don't see ourselves that way. I began to count the ways in which I enjoy unearned skin privilege and have been conditioned into oblivion about its existence.

My schooling gave me no training in seeing myself as an oppressor, as an unfairly advantaged person, or as a participant in a damaged culture. I was taught to see myself as an individual whose moral state depended on her individual moral will. My schooling followed the pattern my colleague Elizabeth Minnich has pointed out: whites are taught to think of their lives as morally neutral, normative, and average, and also ideal, so that when we work to benefit others, this is seen as work which will allow "them" to be more like "us."

I decided to try to work on myself at least by identifying some of the daily effects of white privilege in my life. I have chosen those conditions which I think in my case *attach somewhat more to skin-color privilege* than to class, religion, ethnic status, or geographical location, though of course all these other factors are intricately intertwined. As far as I can see, my African American co-workers, friends and acquaintances with whom I come into daily or frequent contact in this particular time, place, and line of work cannot count on most of these conditions.

1. I can if I wish arrange to be in the company of people of my race most of the time.
2. If I should need to move, I can be pretty sure of renting or purchasing housing in an area which I can afford and in which I would want to live.
3. I can be pretty sure that my neighbors in such a location will be neutral or pleasant to me.
4. I can go shopping alone most of the time, pretty well assured that I will not be followed or harassed.
5. I can turn on the television or open to the front page of the paper and see people of my race widely represented.
6. When I am told about our national heritage or about "civilization," I am shown that people of my color made it what it is.
7. I can be sure that my children will be given curricular materials that testify to the existence of their race.
8. If I want to, I can be pretty sure of finding a publisher for this piece on white privilege.
9. I can go into a supermarket and find the staple foods which fit with my cultural traditions, and into a hairdresser's shop and find someone who can cut my hair.
10. Whether I use checks, credit cards, or cash, I can count on my skin color not to work against the appearance of financial reliability.
11. I can arrange to protect my children most of the time from people who might not like them.
12. I can swear, or dress in second hand clothes, or not answer letters, without having people attribute these choices to the bad morals, the poverty, or the illiteracy of my race.
13. I can speak in public to a powerful male group without putting my race on trial.
14. I can do well in a challenging situation without being called a credit to my race.
15. I am never asked to speak for all the people of my racial group.
16. I can remain oblivious of the language and customs of persons of color who constitute the world's majority without feeling in my culture any penalty for such oblivion.
17. I can criticize our government and talk about how much I fear its policies and behavior without being seen as a cultural outsider.

18. I can be pretty sure that if I ask to talk to "the person in charge," I will be facing a person of my race.
19. If a traffic cop pulls me over or if the IRS audits my tax return, I can be sure I haven't been singled out because of my race.
20. I can easily buy posters, postcards, picture books, greeting cards, dolls, toys, and children's magazines featuring people of my race.
21. I can go home from most meetings of organizations I belong to feeling somewhat tied in, rather than isolated, out-of-place, outnumbered, unheard, held at a distance, or feared.
22. I can take a job with an affirmative action employer without having co-workers on the job suspect that I got it because of race.
23. I can choose public accommodation without fearing that people of my race cannot get in or will be mistreated in the places I have chosen.
24. I can be sure that if I need legal or medical help, my race will not work against me.
25. If my day, week, or year is going badly, I need not ask of each negative episode or situation whether it has racial overtones.
26. I can choose blemish cover or bandages in "flesh" color and have them more or less match my skin.

I repeatedly forgot each of the realizations on this list until I wrote it down. For me white privilege has turned out to be an elusive and fugitive subject. The pressure to avoid it is great, for in facing it I must give up the myth of meritocracy. If these things are true, this is not such a free country; one's life is not what one makes it; many doors open for certain people through no virtues of their own.

In unpacking this invisible knapsack of white privilege, I have listed conditions of daily experience which I once took for granted. Nor did I think of any of these perquisites as bad for the holder. I now think that we need a more finely differentiated taxonomy of privilege, for some of these varieties are only what one would want for everyone in a just society, and others give license to be ignorant, oblivious, arrogant and destructive.

I see a pattern running through the matrix of white privilege, a pattern of assumptions which were passed on to me as a white person. There was one main piece of cultural turf; it was my own turf, and I was among those who could control the turf. *My skin color was an asset for any move I was educated to want to make.* I could think of myself as belonging in major ways, and of making social systems work for me. I could freely disparage, fear, neglect, or be oblivious to anything outside of the dominant cultural forms. Being of the main culture, I could also criticize it fairly freely.

In proportion as my racial group was being made confident, comfortable, and oblivious, other groups were likely being made inconfident, uncomfortable, and alienated. Whiteness protected me from many kinds of hostility, distress, and violence, which I was being subtly trained to visit in turn upon people of color.

For this reason, the word "privilege" now seems to me misleading. We usually think of privilege as being a favored state, whether earned or conferred by birth or luck. Yet some of the conditions I have described here work to systematically overempower certain groups. Such privilege simply *confers dominance* because of one's race or sex.

I want, then, to distinguish between earned strength and unearned power conferred systemically. Power from unearned privilege can look like strength when it is in fact permission to escape or to dominate. But not all of the privileges on my list are inevitably damaging. Some, like the expectation that neighbors will be decent to you, or that your race will not count against you in court, should be the norm in a just society. Others, like the privilege to ignore less powerful people, distort the humanity of the holders as well as the ignored groups.

We might at least start by distinguishing between positive advantages which we can work to spread, and negative types of advantages which unless rejected will always reinforce our present hierarchies. For example, the feeling that one belongs within the human circle, as Native Americans say, should not be seen as privilege for a few. Ideally it is an *unearned entitlement*. At present, since only a few have it, it is an *unearned advantage* for them. This paper results from a process of coming to see that some of the power which I originally saw as attendant on being a human being in the U.S. consisted in *unearned advantage* and *conferred dominance*.

I have met very few men who are truly distressed about systemic, unearned male advantage and conferred dominance. And so one question for me and others like me is whether we will be like them, or whether we will get truly distressed, even outraged, about unearned race advantage and conferred dominance and if so, what we will do to lessen them. In any case, we need to do more work in identifying how they actually affect our daily lives. Many, perhaps most, of our white students in the U.S. think that racism doesn't affect them because they are not people of color; they do not see "whiteness" as a racial identity. In addition, since race and sex are not the only advantaging systems at work, we need similarly to examine the daily experience of having age advantage, or ethnic advantage, or physical ability, or advantage related to nationality, religion, or sexual orientation.

Difficulties and dangers surrounding the task of finding parallels are many. Since racism, sexism, and heterosexism are not the same, the advantaging associated with them should not be seen as the same. In addition, it is hard to disentangle aspects of unearned advantage which rest more on social class, economic class, race, religion, sex and ethnic identity than on other factors. Still, all of the oppressions are interlocking, as the Combahee River Collective Statement of 1977[1] continues to remind us eloquently.

One factor seems clear about all of the interlocking oppressions. They take both active forms which we can see and embedded forms which as a

---

[1] *Editor's note:* The Combahee River Collective Statement, drafted by a Boston-based group of Black feminists, describes the multiple dimensions of Black women's oppression.

member of the dominant group one is taught not to see. In my class and place, I did not see myself as a racist because I was taught to recognize racism only in individual acts of meanness by members of my group, never in invisible systems conferring unsought racial dominance on my group from birth.

Disapproving of the systems won't be enough to change them. I was taught to think that racism could end if white individuals changed their attitudes. But a "white" skin in the United States opens many doors for whites whether or not we approve of the way dominance has been conferred on us. Individual acts can palliate, but cannot end, these problems.

To redesign social systems we need first to acknowledge their colossal unseen dimensions. The silences and denials surrounding privilege are the key political tool here. They keep the thinking about equality or equity incomplete, protecting unearned advantage and conferred dominance by making these taboo subjects. Most talk by whites about equal opportunity seems to me now to be about equal opportunity to try to get into a position of dominance while denying that *systems* of dominance exist.

It seems to me that obliviousness about white advantage, like obliviousness about male advantage, is kept strongly enculturated in the United States so as to maintain the myth of meritocracy, the myth that democratic choice is equally available to all. Keeping most people unaware that freedom of confident action is there for just a small number of people props up those in power, and serves to keep power in the hands of the same groups that have most of it already.

Though systemic change takes many decades, there are pressing questions for me and I imagine for some others like me if we raise our daily consciousness on the perquisites of being light-skinned. What will we do with such knowledge? As we know from watching men, it is an open question whether we will choose to use unearned advantage to weaken hidden systems of advantage, and whether we will use any of our arbitrarily-awarded power to try to reconstruct power systems on a broader base.

Peggy McIntosh is Associate Director of the Wellesley College Center for Research on Women. This essay is excerpted from her working paper, "White Privilege and Male Privilege: A Personal Account of Coming to See Correspondences Through Work in Women's Studies," copyright © 1988 by Peggy McIntosh. Available for $8.00 from the SEED Project, Wellesley College Center for Research on Women, Wellesley MA 02481. The working paper contains a longer list of privileges. Permission to excerpt or reprint must be obtained from Peggy McIntosh.

What Did Your Grandfather Do?

I got into a long discussion with a white guy here at the Capitol . . . he was bellyaching about affirmative action, . . . saying, "You know, well I didn't have anything to do with what happened in the past, and I don't feel like I should suffer, and I should be penalized, and blah, blah, blah."

And I told him, "What did your grandfather do?"

"My grandfather was a mechanic. He worked a good union scale job back in the 1900s."

"Then, what did your dad do?"

"Well, my dad went to college, and got out of college, and he's an engineer now."

And I said, "Well, how do you know—we won't even go back four hundred years like we should, but let's just go back three generations—how do you know that because of Jim Crow and because of segregation and because of overt racial oppression, the mechanic that your grandfather was and the job he had wouldn't have been held by my grandfather, had he been allowed to? How do you know that my dad would not have been able to attend Georgia Tech and become an engineer, had he been allowed to and had his grandfather had a good union scale job and could afford to send him? How do you know?"

So, yes, white people today, even young white people today, are still benefiting from past segregation.

> —African-American legislative aide, quoted in Joe R. Feagin and Melvin P. Sikes, *Living with Racism: The Black Middle-Class Experience*, 1994

REFLECTIONS OF AFFIRMATIVE ACTION GOALS IN PSYCHOLOGY ADMISSIONS

JAMES AMIRKHAN, HECTOR BETANCOURT,
SANDRA GRAHAM, STEVEN REGESER LÓPEZ,
AND BERNARD WEINER

A moral and political tension exists in contemporary America between the ideal of meritocracy, wherein achievement is based on individual effort, and the reality of societal injustice, wherein groups of individuals have been denied an equal opportunity to pursue the meritocratic ideal. Because of this tension, few issues have generated as much controversy as affirmative action in higher education. Proponents view some form of preferential treatment based on gender and ethnicity as necessary at this time to ensure full participation of excluded groups. Opponents dismiss such policies as unfair to meritorious nontargeted groups and ultimately detrimental to the targeted beneficiaries themselves.

At issue are fundamental questions such as these: What kinds of affirmative action policies are truly effective in redressing past wrongs? Do the methods have unintended counterproductive outcomes? What kinds of burdens do the policies impose on other people, and are such policies fair?

Federal legislation has mandated that academic institutions adhere to some form of affirmative action in their student admission policies. Although most academics probably agree that steps should be taken to ensure that admissions procedures conform to established guidelines, they may be unaware of the assumptions that shape their adherence to these guidelines—assumptions as to the very goals of affirmative action. We argue that such goals, whether explicit or implicit, are not always completely compatible with one another, and that different goals may sometimes result in quite disparate admissions decisions.

For example, suppose that a psychology department at a large research university has committed itself to increasing its ethnic minority enrollment by 15% in the next academic year. A pool of eligible candidates is identified, and the process of selection begins. What criteria are most important? Should all nonwhite groups be equally represented? Should economic disadvantage be considered relevant? Should preference be afforded to applicants who express a desire to study minority issues over applicants with more traditional interests? One's answer to the first question, which focuses on ethnic differences, depends on whether one believes that some groups have stronger claims to preferential treatment than others. One's position on the second question, which calls attention to social status, is shaped by assumptions about the inclusiveness of affirmative action guidelines. And a response to the third question is partly determined by one's stance on the importance of a diversity of intellectual viewpoints. Because issues such as these capture much of the controversy surrounding affirmative action, the process as a whole stands to benefit from efforts to articulate what affirmative action policies are intended to accomplish.

In the following sections, we describe four prevalent goals of affirmative action, focusing on how each goal might lead to a differential weighting of various criteria for student admissions to graduate programs in psychology. Broadly conceived, these goals are defined as affirmative action to compensate for past injustices, correct present inequities, promote intellectual diversity, and enhance the presence of role models.

The Goals of Affirmative Action

Compensating for Past Injustice

One of the major goals of affirmative action is compensation for past injustice (e.g., Francis, 1993): Because ethnic minorities have been victimized by a history of discrimination, affirmative action procedures are necessary to balance the moral scales—that is, to position targeted individuals as much as possible in the situation they would have experienced had the injustice not occurred. In authorizing Executive Order 11246, which was the 1965 legislation that mandated affirmative action, President Johnson articulated a compelling case for the compensatory argument when he stated:

> You do not wipe away the scars of centuries by saying: Now you are free to go where you want, do as you desire, and choose the leaders you please. You do not take a man who has been hobbled by chains, liberate him, bring him to the starting line of a race, saying, "you are free to compete with all the others," and still justly believe that you have been completely fair. Thus it is not enough to open the gates of opportunity. (cited in Glasser, 1988, p. 348)

Affirmative action as compensation implies that individual victims of past discrimination can be identified and that consensus can be achieved regarding who should be compensated. Executive Order 11246 defined targeted minority groups as "Blacks, Spanish-surnamed Americans, American Indians, and Orientals." But if the defining feature of a compensatory argument is the cumulative effect of a history of victimization, then the case may be made that these four groups are not equally entitled to consideration under affirmative action guidelines. Without minimizing the plight of any of these groups, many readers might agree that the legacy of slavery endured by African Americans and the disenfranchisement suffered by Native Americans are unique and are not matched by the experiences of more recent and voluntary immigrant groups, such as Asians and most Latinos. Furthermore, although Asian Americans are a designated target group under Executive Order 11246, and the injustices toward Chinese immigrants in the 19th century and toward Japanese Americans during World War II are well known, many members of the academic community and lay public do not perceive Asians as a disadvantaged minority.

Even if consensus could be reached as to which minority groups have stronger cases for redress, affirmative action as compensation forces the issue of which individuals within a minority group are the rightful beneficiaries of preferential treatment. Is group membership alone sufficient? For example, should any qualified black applicant to graduate school be considered under affirmative action guidelines, or must a case be made that an individual applicant has been a victim of past discrimination? Although no serious scholar of affirmative action would claim that case summaries documenting individual histories of discrimination should become parts of admissions folders, it has been argued that socioeconomic status (SES) is at least a gross marker of individual victimization and should therefore become a relevant criterion for affirmative action, perhaps even superseding that of ethnicity (e.g., Simon, 1993). Affirmative action scholars sympathetic to this view, including some African American social scientists, have lamented that affirmative action programs have never been constructed to address the problems of the economically disadvantaged (e.g., Sowell, 1989; Wilson, 1987). Rather, such programs have favored minority group members who were from advantaged backgrounds and were in a position to compete for admission to college.

If these arguments have merit, and a generic category of "disadvantaged" should be used as a marker of past victimization, then a host of additional complexities arises in the application of affirmative action guidelines. Most obviously, a white applicant from an impoverished background might have a legitimate claim to preferential treatment over an affluent minority candidate. And how is one to evaluate minority subgroups, such as Latinos of South American descent, who have (relatively) little history of oppression in this country? It is common practice for Spanish-surname applicants to receive affirmative action consideration, as directed by Executive Order 11246, in the absence of information about their country of origin. A strict interpretation of affirmative action as compensation for past injustice might question the fairness of preferential treatment for members of minority groups that have not suffered economic disadvantage and have little or no history of injustice in this country.

Correcting Present Inequities

In contrast to the historical basis of affirmative action as compensation for past injustice, a second goal of affirmative action is grounded in the notion of correction and is more ahistorical in nature (see Francis, 1993). According to this argument, discriminatory practices have allowed some groups to receive a greater share of rewards than other groups, and this inequity must be corrected. Other than acknowledging that such inequality is attributable to characteristics such as race, the analysis does not rely on the historical bases of these inequalities.

How, then, does one determine the existence of present inequities without appealing to the historical argument? A straightforward argument, although not without controversy, is that of proportional representation (see Wolf-Devine, 1993). Ethnic minorities ought to be represented in the workforce and in academia to the same extent that they are represented in the general population. If they are not, there are inequities that need correction.

By all available indicators, ethnic minorities are markedly underrepresented in psychology. According to data recently reported in the *APA Monitor*, minorities constitute about 5% of all doctoral-level psychologists. Because the disparities between population statistics and representation in the discipline are so great, affirmative action goals based on correction are largely directed toward increasing opportunities for all ethnic minority groups, independent of particular group membership or characteristics of targeted individuals. In this sense, the goals of correction and compensation at times may seem incompatible, as when choices have to be made between two "equally qualified" members of different ethnic groups.

On the other hand, the distinction between compensation and correction may become blurred when SES is a relevant characteristic, inasmuch as economic disadvantage can also be linked to correcting present inequity. For example, consider the choice between a poor Asian American whose parents are Cambodian immigrants and an affluent first-generation Japanese American. In neither case is there a protracted history of victimization in this country. Yet affirmative action goals are likely to favor the disadvantaged Cambodian because present economic disparities no doubt will be salient. Thus, we cannot fully ascertain where compensation for past injustice leaves off and correction for present inequity begins.

Promoting Intellectual Diversity

The diversity argument is seemingly the one goal of affirmative action that is specific to academia. Education is an enterprise in which students learn by being exposed to different perspectives. Minority (and women) scholars have a special role in this endeavor because they are likely to be pursuing original work in areas not studied by mainstream scholars. Contributions in the areas of Afrocentricity and feminist theory are contemporary cases in point. Minorities in academia also have unique experiences with prejudice and discrimination that shape their thinking and research agendas in ways not possible for people not encountering these experiences directly.

As in the case of the two goals already discussed, some implicit assumptions guide admissions decisions when the affirmative action goal is intellectual diversity. Consider two equally qualified ethnic minority applicants to a doctoral program. Applicant A writes in her personal statement that she wants to study the role of ethnic identity in the formation of the self-concept, whereas Applicant B indicates an interest in structural theories of emotion. Applicant A links her interest to personal experiences with role conflict, whereas Applicant B refers exclusively to the need for theory-driven models of emotion with no suggestion of how these theories might have applicability to "socially relevant" issues. Which applicant should receive higher priority? If Applicant A is preferred over Applicant B, there is an implicit assumption that intellectual diversity is best fostered when minority scholars pursue race-relevant scholarship.

Of course, there is by no means universal agreement about this interpretation of diversity. For example, some ethnic scholars have argued that it is demeaning to expect members of minority groups to hold particular viewpoints or to think "differently" from whites, and that recruitment on either of these bases promotes intellectual conformity rather than diversity (e.g., Carter, 1991). Furthermore, there may be areas in psychology that are more amenable than others to intellectual diversity based on ethnic group membership. Surely an Afrocentric view is more important in the study of interpersonal relations than in the study of neuropsychology. In the latter case, intellectual diversity would appropriately be achieved by allowing for the representation of different viewpoints and methodologies using criteria that have nothing to do with ethnicity.

Enhancing the Presence of Role Models

A fourth goal of affirmative action is to increase the representation of minorities in academia so that successive cohorts of minority students can identify with minority scholars who are successful (Brooks, 1990). For all minority students, but particularly those on predominantly white campuses, it is essential to have the opportunity to observe faculty of color teaching classes, participating in hiring and student admissions decisions, sitting on committees, and otherwise visibly engaging in university business.

But even this seemingly noncontroversial goal might generate disagreement in admissions decisions depending on how one chooses to define the characteristics of a "good" role model. For example, does the Latino faculty member who came from an impoverished background and worked two jobs to put himself through college make a better role model than his Harvard-educated counterpart with professional parents who supported him throughout? Some of the same complex issues about individual suffering that surfaced in the discussion of affirmative action as compensation and correction are evident in the role model argument.

The role model goal might also be either compatible with or in conflict with the intellectual diversity goal. As indicated, a strict interpretation of the diversity argument suggests that candidates who study minority-relevant topics should receive preferential treatment over candidates who do not. However, in a strict interpretation of the role model argument, being a role model should not depend on one's research perspective. That is, for example, the black neuropsychologist and Latino biostatistician serve the same role model functions as do their counterparts studying topics more sensitive to race and ethnicity issues.

To summarize, four goals of affirmative action have been articulated as they relate to the graduate student admissions process. In some cases, the goals are compatible and overlapping, leading to general agreement about the criteria for student selection under affirmative action guidelines. In other instances, the goals may be contentious and divergent, resulting in potential lack of consensus about admissions policies.

REFERENCES

Brooks, R. (1990). *Rethinking the American race problem.* Berkeley: University of California Press.

Carter, S. (1991). *Reflections of an affirmative action baby.* New York: Basic Books.

Francis, L. (1993). In defense of affirmative action. In S. Cahn (Ed.), *Affirmative action and the university: A philosophical inquiry* (pp. 9–47). Philadelphia: Temple University Press.

Glasser, I. (1988). Affirmative action and the legacy of racial injustice. In P. Katz & D. Taylor (Eds.), *Eliminating racism* (pp. 341–357). New York: Plenum Press.

Simon, R. (1993). Affirmative action and the university: Faculty appointment and preferential treatment. In S. Cahn (Ed.), *Affirmative action and the university: A philosophical inquiry* (pp. 48–92). Philadelphia: Temple University Press.

Sowell, T. (1989). "Affirmative action": A world-wide disaster. *Commentary, 88,* 21–41.

Wilson, W. (1987). *The truly disadvantaged: The inner city, the underclass, and public policy.* Chicago: University of Chicago Press.

Wolf-Devine, C. (1993). Proportional representation of women and minorities. In S. Cahn (Ed.), *Affirmative action and the university: A philosophical inquiry* (pp. 223–232). Philadelphia: Temple University Press.

Two Supreme Court Views of Affirmative Action
Adarand Constructors v. Pena
June 12, 1995

Against Affirmative Action

I believe there is a "moral [and] constitutional equivalence" . . . between laws designed to subjugate a race and those that distribute benefits on the basis of race in order to foster some current notion of equality. . . . As far as the Constitution is concerned, it is irrelevant whether a government's racial classifications are drawn by those who wish to oppress a race or by those who have a sincere desire to help those thought to be disadvantaged. There can be no doubt that the paternalism that appears to lie at the heart of this program is at war with the principle of inherent equality that underlies and infuses our Constitution. . . . So-called "benign" discrimination teaches many that because of chronic and apparently immutable handicaps, minorities cannot compete with them without their patronizing indulgence. Inevitably, such programs engender attitudes of superiority or, alternatively, provoke resentment among those who believe that they have been wronged by the government's use of race. These programs stamp minorities with a badge of inferiority and may cause them to develop dependencies or to adopt an attitude that they are "entitled" to preferences.

> —Justice Clarence Thomas, Concurring with the Decision

In Favor of Affirmative Action

There is no moral or constitutional equivalence between a policy that is designed to perpetuate a caste system and one that seeks to eradicate racial subordination. Invidious discrimination is an engine of oppression, subjugating a disfavored group to enhance or maintain the power of the majority. Remedial race-based preferences reflect the opposite impulse: a desire to foster equality in society. No sensible conception of the Government's constitutional obligation to "govern impartially" . . . should ignore this distinction. . . . The consistency that the Court espouses would disregard the difference between a "No Trespassing" sign and a welcome mat. . . . It would equate a law that made black citizens ineligible for military service with a program aimed at recruiting black soldiers. An attempt by the majority to exclude members of a minority race from a regulated market is fundamentally different from a subsidy that enables a relatively small group of newcomers to enter that market.

> —Justice John Paul Stevens, Dissenting from the Decision

The Need for Compensatory Consideration

The nation must . . . incorporate in its planning some compensatory consideration for the handicaps [Negroes have] inherited from the past. . . . Whenever this issue of compensatory or preferential treatment for the Negro is raised, some of our friends recoil in horror. The Negro should be granted equality, they agree; but he should ask nothing more. On the surface, this appears reasonable, but it is not realistic. For it is obvious that if a man is entered at the starting line in a race three hundred years after another man, the first would have to perform some impossible feat in order to catch up with his fellow runner.

—Martin Luther King, Jr., *Why We Can't Wait*, 1964

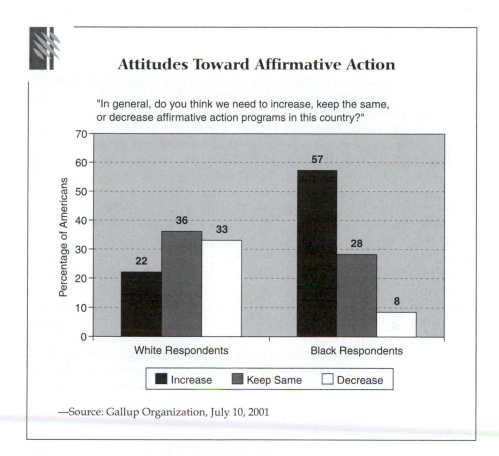

Attitudes Toward Affirmative Action

"In general, do you think we need to increase, keep the same, or decrease affirmative action programs in this country?"

—Source: Gallup Organization, July 10, 2001

TEN MYTHS ABOUT AFFIRMATIVE ACTION

SCOTT PLOUS

In recent years, affirmative action has been debated more intensely than at any other time in its 35-year history. Many supporters view affirmative action as a milestone, many opponents see it as a millstone, and many others regard it as both or neither—as a necessary, but imperfect, remedy for an intractable social disease. My own view is that the case against affirmative action is weak, resting, as it does so heavily, on myth and misunderstanding. Here are some of the most popular myths about affirmative action, along with a brief commentary on each one.

Myth 1: The only way to create a color-blind society is to adopt color-blind policies. Although this statement sounds intuitively plausible, the reality is that color-blind policies often put racial minorities at a disadvantage. For instance, all else being equal, color-blind seniority systems tend to protect White workers against job layoffs, because senior employees are usually White (Ezorsky, 1991). Likewise, color-blind college admissions favor White students because of their earlier educational advantages. Unless preexisting inequities are corrected or otherwise taken into account, color-blind policies do not correct racial injustice—they reinforce it.

Myth 2: Affirmative action has not succeeded in increasing female and minority representation. Several studies have documented important gains in racial and gender equality as a direct result of affirmative action (Bowen & Bok, 1998; Murrell & Jones, 1996). For example, according to a report from the U.S. Labor Department, affirmative action has helped 5 million minority members and 6 million White and minority women move up in the workforce ("Reverse Discrimination," 1995). Likewise, a study sponsored by the Office of Federal Contract Compliance Programs showed that between 1974 and 1980 federal contractors (who were required to adopt affirmative action goals) added Black and female officials and managers at twice the rate of noncontractors (Citizens' Commission, 1984). There have also been a number of well-publicized cases in which large companies (e.g., AT&T, IBM, Sears Roebuck) increased minority employment as a result of adopting affirmative action policies.

Myth 3: Affirmative action may have been necessary 30 years ago, but the playing field is fairly level today. Despite the progress that has been made, the playing field is far from level. Women continue to earn 76 cents for every male dollar (Bowler, 1999). Black people continue to have twice the unemployment rate of White people, twice the rate of infant mortality, and just over half the proportion of people who attend four years or more of college (see Figure 1). In fact, without affirmative action the percentage of Black students at many selective schools would drop to only 2% of the student body (Bowen & Bok, 1998). This would effectively choke off Black access to top universities and severely restrict progress toward racial equality.

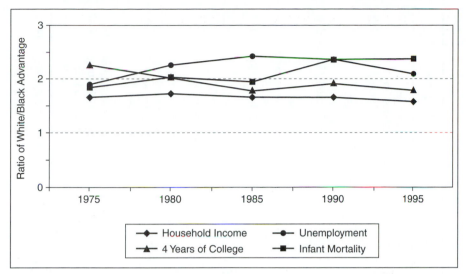

FIGURE 1   Common Standard of Living Indices
Despite Black gains in median family income and the number of students attending college during the past 25 years, the ratio of White-to-Black advantage has remained virtually unchanged with respect to several common standard-of-living indices (based on data from the U.S. Bureau of the Census, 1984, 1994, 2000).

Myth 4: The public doesn't support affirmative action anymore. Public opinion polls suggest that the majority of Americans support affirmative action, especially when the polls avoid an all-or-none choice between affirmative action as it currently exists and no affirmative action whatsoever (see Table 1). For example, a *Time*/CNN poll found that 80% of the public felt "affirmative action programs for minorities and women should be continued at some level" (Roper Center for Public Opinion, 1995a). What the public opposes are quotas, set-asides, and "reverse discrimination." For instance, when the same poll asked people whether they favored programs "requiring businesses to hire a specific number or quota of minorities and women," 63% opposed such a plan (Roper Center for Public Opinion, 1995b). As these results indicate, most members of the public oppose racial preferences that violate notions of procedural justice—they do *not* oppose affirmative action.

Myth 5: A large percentage of White workers will lose out if affirmative action is continued. Government statistics do not support this myth. According to the U.S. Commerce Department, there are 1.3 million unemployed Black civilians and 112 million employed White civilians (U.S. Bureau of the Census, 2000). Thus, even if every unemployed Black worker in the United States were to displace a White worker, only 1% of Whites would be affected. Furthermore, affirmative action pertains only to job-qualified applicants, so the actual percentage of affected Whites would be a fraction of 1%. The main sources of job loss among White workers have to do with factory relocations

TABLE 1 Survey Results Suggesting Majority Support for Affirmative Action

Item	Source[a]	Date	Sample size	Responses in %
Do you favor or oppose affirmative action programs for minorities and women for job hiring in the workplace?	Gallup[b]	8/01	1,523	Favor: 58 Oppose: 36 Don't know/Refused: 5
Do you favor or oppose affirmative action programs for minorities and women for admission to colleges and universities?	Gallup[c]	8/01	1,523	Favor: 56 Oppose: 39 Don't know/Refused: 6
In general, do you think we need to increase, keep the same, or decrease affirmative action programs in this country?	Gallup[d]	7/01	2,004	Increase: 27 Keep the same: 34 Decrease: 30 Don't know/Refused: 9
Do you generally favor or oppose affirmative action programs for women and minorities?	CNN/USA Today[e]	1/00	1,027	Favor: 58 Oppose: 33 Not sure: 9
What's the best thing to do with affirmative action programs giving preference to some minorities—leave the programs as they are, change the programs, or do away with the programs entirely?	CBS/New York Times[f]	12/97	1,258	Leave as are: 24 Keep but change: 43 Do away with: 25 Not sure: 8
What about affirmative action programs that set quotas ... Do you favor affirmative action programs with quotas, or do you favor affirmative action programs only without quotas, or do you oppose all affirmative action programs?	Associated Press[g]	7/95	1,006	Favor with quotas: 16 Favor without quotas: 47 Oppose all: 28 Don't know: 9

Source: [a]All polls are from the Roper Center for Public Opinion [RCPO]. [b]RCPO (2001a). [c]RCPO (2001b). [d]RCPO (2001c). [e]RCPO (2000). [f]RCPO (1997). [g]RCPO (1995c).

and labor contracting outside the United States, computerization and automation, and corporate downsizing (Ivins, 1995).

Myth 6: If Jewish people and Asian Americans can rapidly advance economically, African Americans should be able to do the same. This comparison ignores the unique history of discrimination against Black people in America. As historian Roger Wilkins has pointed out, Blacks have a 375-year history on this continent: 245 involving slavery, 100 involving legalized discrimination, and only 30 involving anything else (Wilkins, 1995). Jews and Asians, on the other hand, are populations that *immigrated* to North America and included doctors, lawyers, professors, and entrepreneurs among their ranks. Moreover, European Jews are able to function as part of the White majority. To expect Blacks to show the same upward mobility as Jews and Asians is to deny the historical and social reality that Black people face.

Myth 7: You can't cure discrimination with discrimination. The problem with this myth is that it uses the same word—*discrimination*—to describe two very different things. Job discrimination is grounded in prejudice and exclusion, whereas affirmative action is an effort to overcome prejudicial treatment through inclusion. The most effective way to cure society of exclusionary practices is to make special efforts at inclusion, which is exactly what affirmative action does. The logic of affirmative action is no different than the logic of treating a nutritional deficiency with vitamin supplements. For a healthy person, high doses of vitamin supplements may be unnecessary or even harmful, but for a person whose system is out of balance, supplements are an efficient way to restore the body's balance.

Myth 8: Affirmative action tends to undermine the self-esteem of women and racial minorities. Although affirmative action may have this effect in some cases (Heilman, Simon, & Repper, 1987; Steele, 1990), interview studies and public opinion surveys suggest that such reactions are rare (Taylor, 1994). For instance, a 1995 Gallup poll asked employed Blacks and employed White women whether they had ever felt others questioned their abilities because of affirmative action (Roper Center for Public Opinion, 1995d). Nearly 90% of respondents said no (which is understandable—after all, White men, who have traditionally benefited from preferential hiring, do not feel hampered by self-doubt or a loss in self-esteem). Indeed, in many cases affirmative action may actually *raise* the self-esteem of women and minorities by providing them with employment and opportunities for advancement. There is also evidence that affirmative action policies increase job satisfaction and organizational commitment among beneficiaries (Graves & Powell, 1994).

Myth 9: Affirmative action is nothing more than an attempt at social engineering by liberal Democrats. In truth, affirmative action programs have spanned nine different presidential administrations—six Republican and three Democratic. Although the originating document of affirmative action was President Lyndon Johnson's Executive Order 11246, the policy was significantly expanded in 1969 by President Richard Nixon and then Secretary of Labor George Schultz. President George Bush also enthusiastically signed the Civil Rights Act of 1991, which formally endorsed the principle of affirmative action. Thus, affirmative action has traditionally enjoyed the support of Republicans as well as Democrats.

Myth 10: Support for affirmative action means support for preferential selection procedures that favor unqualified candidates over qualified candidates. Actually, most supporters of affirmative action oppose this type of preferential selection. Preferential selection procedures can be ordered along the following continuum:

1. *Selection among equally qualified candidates.* The mildest form of affirmative action selection occurs when a female or minority candidate is chosen from a pool of equally qualified applicants (e.g., students with identical college entrance scores). Survey research suggests that three-quarters of the public does not see this type of affirmative action as discriminatory (Roper Center for Public Opinion, 1995e).

2. *Selection among comparable candidates.* A somewhat stronger form occurs when female or minority candidates are roughly comparable to other candidates (e.g., their college entrance scores are lower, but not by a significant amount). The logic here is similar to the logic of selecting among equally qualified candidates; all that is needed is an understanding that, for example, predictions based on an SAT score of 620 are virtually indistinguishable from predictions based on an SAT score of 630.

3. *Selection among unequal candidates.* A still stronger form of affirmative action occurs when qualified female or minority candidates are chosen over candidates whose records are better by a substantial amount.

4. *Selection among qualified and unqualified candidates.* The strongest form of preferential selection occurs when unqualified female or minority members are chosen over other candidates who are qualified. Although affirmative action is sometimes mistakenly equated with this form of preferential treatment, federal regulations explicitly prohibit affirmative action programs in which unqualified or unneeded employees are hired (Bureau of National Affairs, 1979).

Even though these selection procedures occasionally blend into one another (due in part to the difficulty of comparing incommensurable records), a few general observations can be made. First, of the four different procedures, the selection of women and minority members among equal or roughly comparable candidates has the greatest public support, adheres most closely to popular conceptions of fairness, and reduces the chances that affirmative action beneficiaries will be perceived as unqualified or undeserving (Kravitz & Platania, 1993; Nacoste, 1985; Turner & Pratkanis, 1994). Second, the selection of women and minority members among unequal candidates—used routinely in college admissions—has deeply divided the nation (with the strongest opposition coming from White males and conservative voters.) And finally, the selection of unqualified candidates is not permitted under federal affirmative action guidelines and should not be equated with legal forms of affirmative action. By distinguishing among these four different selection procedures, it becomes clear that opposition to stronger selection procedures need not imply opposition to milder ones.

Some writers have criticized affirmative action as a superficial solution that does not address deeper societal problems by redistributing wealth and developing true educational equality. Yet affirmative action was never proposed as a cure-all solution to inequality. Rather, it was intended only to redress discrimination in hiring and academic admissions. In assessing the value of affirmative action, the central question is merely this: In the absence of sweeping societal reforms—unlikely to take place any time soon—does affirmative action help counteract the continuing injustice caused by discrimination? The research record suggests, unequivocally, that it does.

REFERENCES

Bowen, W. G., & Bok, D. (1998). *The shape of the river: Long-term consequences of considering race in college and university admissions.* Princeton, NJ: Princeton University Press.

Bowler, M. (1999, December). Women's earnings: An overview. *Monthly Labor Review,* pp. 13–21.

Bureau of National Affairs. (1979). *Uniform guidelines on employee selection procedures.* Washington, DC: Author.

Citizens' Commission on Civil Rights. (1984, June). *Affirmative action to open the doors of job opportunity.* Washington, DC: Author.

Ezorsky, G. (1991). *Racism and justice: The case for affirmative action.* Ithaca, NY: Cornell University Press.

Graves, L. M., & Powell, G. N. (1994). Effects of sex-based preferential selection and discrimination on job attitudes. *Human Relations, 47,* 133–157.

Heilman, M. E., Simon, M. C., & Repper, D. P. (1987). Intentionally favored, unintentionally harmed? Impact of sex-based preferential selection on self-perceptions and self-evaluations. *Journal of Applied Psychology, 72,* 62–68.

Ivins, M. (1995, February 23). Affirmative action is more than black-and-white issue. *Philadelphia Daily News,* p. 28.

Kravitz, D. A., & Platania, J. (1993). Attitudes and beliefs about affirmative action: Effects of target and of respondent sex and ethnicity. *Journal of Personality and Social Psychology, 78,* 928–938.

Murell, A. J., & Jones, R. (1996). Assessing affirmative action: Past, present, and future. *Journal of Social Issues, 52,* 77–92.

Nacoste, R. W. (1985). Selection procedure and responses to affirmative action: The case of favorable treatment. *Law and Human Behavior, 9,* 225–242.

Newport, F., Ludwig, J., & Kearney, S. (2001, July 10). *Black-White relations in the United States.* Princeton, NJ: The Gallup Organization.

Reverse discrimination of whites is rare, labor study reports. (1995, March 31). *New York Times,* p. A23.

Roper Center for Public Opinion. (1995a). Question ID: USYANKP.95007, Q21 [Electronic database]. Available from Lexis-Nexis Academic Universe Web site, http://web.lexis-nexis.com/universe

Roper Center for Public Opinion. (1995b). Question ID: USYANKP.95007, Q18A [Electronic database]. Available from Lexis-Nexis Academic Universe Web site, http://web.lexis-nexis.com/universe

Roper Center for Public Opinion. (1995c). Question ID: USAP.927K, Q4 [Electronic database]. Available from Lexis-Nexis Academic Universe Web site, http://web.lexis-nexis.com/universe

Roper Center for Public Opinion. (1995d). Question ID: USGALLUP.950317, R31 [Electronic database]. Available from Lexis-Nexis Academic Universe Web site, http://web.lexis-nexis.com/universe

Roper Center for Public Opinion. (1995e). Question ID: USGALLUP.950317, R32 [Electronic database]. Available from Lexis-Nexis Academic Universe Web site, http://web.lexis-nexis.com/universe

Roper Center for Public Opinion. (1997). Question ID: USCBSNYT.121397, R47 [Electronic database]. Available from Lexis-Nexis Academic Universe Web site, http://web.lexis-nexis.com/universe

Roper Center for Public Opinion. (2000). Question ID: USGALLUP.00JA13, R16 [Electronic database]. Available from Lexis-Nexis Academic Universe Web site, http://web.lexis-nexis.com/universe

Roper Center for Public Opinion. (2001a). Question ID: USGALLUP.200127, Q35 [Electronic database]. Available from Lexis-Nexis Academic Universe Web site, http://web.lexis-nexis.com/universe

Roper Center for Public Opinion. (2001b). Question ID: USGALLUP.200127, Q34 [Electronic database]. Available from Lexis-Nexis Academic Universe Web site, http://web.lexis-nexis.com/universe

Roper Center for Public Opinion. (2001c). Question ID: USGALLUP.01RACE, R08 [Electronic database]. Available from Lexis-Nexis Academic Universe Web site, http://web.lexis-nexis.com/universe

Steele, S. (1990). *The content of our character: A new vision of race in America.* New York: St. Martin's Press.

Taylor. M. C. (1994). Impact of affirmative action on beneficiary groups: Evidence from the 1990 General Social Survey. *Basic and Applied Social Psychology, 15,* 143–178.

Turner, M. E., & Pratkanis, A. R. (1994). Affirmative action as help: A review of recipient reactions to preferential selection and affirmative action. *Basic and Applied Social Psychology, 15,* 43–69.

U.S. Bureau of the Census. (1984). *Statistical abstract of the United States: 1984* (104th ed.). Washington, DC: U.S. Government Printing Office.

U.S. Bureau of the Census. (1994). *Statistical abstract of the United States: 2000* (114th ed.). Washington, DC: U.S. Government Printing Office.

U.S. Bureau of the Census. (2000). *Statistical abstract of the United States: 2000* (120th ed.). Washington, DC: U.S. Government Printing Office.

Wilkins, R. (1995, May). Racism has its privileges: The case for affirmative action. *The Nation,* pp. 409–410, 412, 414–416.

V

Sexism

A woman, a spaniel, and a walnut tree,
The more you beat them the better they be.

—*The Annotated Mother Goose*, 1962

Although sexism is similar in many ways to racism, it is also different in important respects. For one thing, women constitute an integrated numeric majority rather than a segregated minority. For another, the perpetrators of sexism—unlike the perpetrators of racism—tend to be intimately involved with the targets of prejudice (e.g., as friends, family members, and romantic partners).

This section opens with an article on men listening to women, followed by a survey of history that includes statements from Plato and Aristotle, the Bible, the U.S. Supreme Court, Sigmund Freud, and others. These statements display both hostile and benevolent elements, reflecting what Peter Glick and Susan Fiske call "ambivalent sexism." There is also a list of dissonance-reducing statements on the topic of female suffrage, included for comparison with the earlier statements on slavery.

Next, articles on the Miss America Pageant, pornography, and slang show some of the ways that women have been physically scrutinized, objectified, and dehumanized. Finally, there are research reports on the effects of pornography and on the detection of sexism among women.

Take Special Notice

Throughout history, racial and gender stereotypes have converged to create a double burden for women of color. As you read the material in this section, consider how sexism and racism intersect and reinforce one another.

Questions Worth Pondering

- If you are male, did you hear any *clicks* when reading Sey Chassler's article "Listening"?
- How do the dissonance-reducing statements on female suffrage compare with the dissonance-reducing statements on slavery?
- Is the Miss America Pageant a form of pornography? Is there such a thing as nonviolent pornography, or is pornography inherently violent?
- Do media images influence whether you see someone as sexually attractive?
- How widespread is sexism among females? If there is undetected sexism among women, is there also undetected racism among people of color?

LISTENING

SEY CHASSLER

One morning, about 20 years ago, my wife and I were arguing about whether or not I ever listened to her. It was one of those arguments that grow into passion and pain and, often, for me at least, into a kind of hysteria. Suddenly, she threw something at me, and said: "From now on you do the shopping, plan the meals, take care of the house, everything. I'm through!"

I was standing in the kitchen looking at the shelves of food, at the oven, at the sink, at the refrigerator, at the cleaning utensils. At my wife.

My reaction was orgasmic. A volcanic gush of tears flooded my head and broke down over me. I shook and sobbed. I was terrified. No matter what, I knew I could not handle the burden. I could not do my job and be responsible for the entire household. How could I get through a day dealing with personnel, budgets, manuscripts, art departments, circulation statistics, phone calls, people, agents, management, writers, and *at the same time* plan dinner for tonight and tomorrow night and breakfast and a dinner party Thursday night and shopping for it all and making sure the house is in good shape and the laundry done and the children taken to the doctor, and the children taken care of? How could *any* one person do all that and stay sane? No one could do that properly. No one. Natalie simply watched me for a while. Finally she said: "Okay. Don't worry. I'll keep on doing it." She put on her coat and went to her office.

Despite her simple statement that she would go on doing it, I stood awhile telling myself that *no one* could do all of that. No one. There was a *click* in my head—and it dawned on me that *she* was doing it.

How invisible my wife's life was to me. How invisible to men women are.

Shortly afterward, not long after *The Feminine Mystique* was published, Betty Friedan and I were invited to speak to the nation's largest organization of home economists. As executive editor of *Redbook* magazine, I was asked to talk about the magazine's view of women. Betty was talking about the thesis of her book— that American women were trapped in their homebound positions and that women's magazines, among others, put out propaganda to keep them trapped.

I had read *The Feminine Mystique*, of course, and felt I was fully prepared to answer it and, thereby, to defend not only *Redbook* from Friedan's attack but to defend American women, as well.

In mid-speech I proclaimed that, despite what Friedan had written, women, in this day and in this country, were free to be whatever they wished to be, that they were not children to be told what they might and might not do, that they could work at whatever profession they chose or whatever job, that they were free to be wives if they wished, and truck drivers if they wished, and mothers if they wished or homemakers if they wished. The list was growing longer and the speech was getting more and more impassioned in its proclamation of freedoms. I paused and waited for the applause. I had, after all, just proclaimed freedom throughout the land! I looked out at the audience. The hall was silent.

My pause became a dark empty cavern, and I could feel myself groping for a way out, wondering what had gone awry. I felt naked, stripped bare before 800 women. I could not understand what I had said that was wrong. Looking for comfort, I thought of my wife, and—*click!* I suddenly realized that my wife was a woman who was free to choose a career and *had*—but who also had delayed that career until her children—*her* children!—were in school. She was not as free as I thought.

While my enthusiasm had diminished, I went on with my speech. But whatever it was that had clicked in my head first in the kitchen and then in Kansas City, stayed there. And for a long time afterward, there were things going on in my head that I couldn't quite get hold of.

I found myself listening for clicks in my head while thinking about, talking to, or dealing with women. And since I worked with more than 60 women every day and came home to my wife every night, I had a good deal of listening to do.

At home one night after dinner, I sat down to read the paper, as usual, while my wife went into the kitchen to do the dishes. I could see her in the kitchen. She looked happy, or at least not unhappy, there in the pretty kitchen she had designed—and she was probably appreciating the change of pace after a hard day as chief of service in a mental hospital dealing with a staff of three or four dozen employees and a hundred or more patients. I was feeling comfortably and happily married, when—*click!*—the view changed, and I saw a hardworking woman doing something she'd rather not be doing just now.

When my wife finished and sat down near me, I kissed her with a special tenderness, I thought. She didn't. As a matter of fact, she turned the other cheek. Something was going on in both our heads.

The next night *I* decided to do the dishes and she read the paper. At the sink, I began to think about male arrogance. Why did I have the choice of doing or not doing the dishes, while my wife did not? By the same token, why had she had to wait until our children were in school to exercise her "free" choice of working at her career? Our jobs were equally pressured and difficult (hers more harrowing than mine) and yet, if I chose to sit and read after dinner, I could. She could not, unless I decided she could by *offering* to do the dishes. My definition of freedom was based on a white male conception: the notion that because I am free, because I can make choices, anyone can make choices. I was defining "anyone" in my terms, in masculine terms. I am anyone, unqualified. She is anyone, gender female.

If you are one of those men who feel trapped by women, who think they are fine for sex but interfere with living, all of the above may not be very clear to you. Maybe the following will set some clicks off for you.

The other day I was reading *The Intimate Male,* by Linda Levine, ACSW, and Lonnie Barbach, Ph.D. It is one of those books in which men reveal all their sexual secrets, fantasies, and so on. It is supposed to help us understand each other, I guess. All I ever get out of such books is the discovery that other guys and I share the same fantasies. Well, in this one, I read about a guy who likes his wife to walk around the house without any underwear under her skirt. Innocent enough, you guess? But what he *really* likes is to "lay on the floor while my wife does the dishes, and look up her dress"!

I told this story to a couple of men I know, and they thought it beat all hell how he got his wife to walk around without her pants on. They loved it. Hey, what a crazy guy!

But wait. Let's try it from the wife's point of view: here is this nice woman who has spent her day working somewhere, either out on a job of some kind or taking care of this romantic fellow's house. She is about as beat as he is by the end of the day and maybe she'll be ready for sex later, but not right now. Right now her hands are full of dirty dishes and wet garbage, so what can she be thinking of? *He* doesn't have to do anything but work his eyeballs.

Everyone to her or his own kink, of course. But it isn't kink that is going on here. What is going on here is a neat exercise in power. The man on the floor is proving to his wife and to himself that he is the boss. He can take his pleasure while she works. Of course, she can tell him to knock it off and keep her pants on, but that is going to make him very unhappy. Unhappy enough maybe to go out for a few beers until she comes to her senses.

So the chances are she doesn't tell him to knock it off, because the implied threat of walking out for a while gains the husband the privilege of turning his wife into a dancing girl while she's doing the dishes. This is known as dominance—and you should have heard a click in your head.

My wife and I have been married 41 years. We think of ourselves as being happily married—and we are. But the dominance is there. If we make a plan together and she does most of the work on the plan, it is given to me for *approval.* If I do most of the work on the plan, I submit it to her for her *information.* If she agrees to the plan, she'll say "Good, should we do it?" If *I* agree to the plan, I'll say, "Good, let's go."

About eight years ago, my wife suggested that I must be hard of hearing because I never seemed to hear what she said, even though I answered all questions and conducted real conversations with her. She made me promise to see an ear doctor. I did. He found nothing wrong. When I told him that this whole idea was my wife's, he sent me home. "Most of my male patients," he said, "are here on the advice of their wives." I laughed. But . . . *click!*

We don't have to listen. As men we simply are in charge. It comes with the territory. Popeye sings "I am what I am." God said the same thing to Moses in the wilderness. Male images. They're built into us. Images of dominance.

What men see when they look out and about are creatures very like themselves—in charge of everything. What women see when they look out and about is that the creatures in charge of everything are *unlike* themselves.

If you are a man, think of a world, your world, in which for everything you own or do or think you are accountable to women. Women are presidents, bankers, governors, door holders, traffic cops, airline pilots, bosses, supervisors, landlords. Shakespeare. The whole structure is completely dominated by women. Your doctor, your lawyer, your priest, minister, rabbi are women. The figure on the cross is a woman. God is a woman. Every authoritative voice and every authoritative image is the image and voice of women: Buddha, Mohammed, Moses, Matthew, Luke, Paul, the guy who does the voice-over on the commercial and Ben Franklin—all are women. So are the Supreme Court, the head of the CIA, the mechanic who fixes your transmission, the editor of your daily newspaper. Think of yourself in such a world. Think of your father in it. Think of *him* as a woman. Think about it.

Don't just brush it off, for Mary's sake—think about it.

Some Ancient Views of Women

All those creatures generated as men who proved themselves cowardly and spent their lives in wrong-doing were transformed, at their second incarnation, into women.

    —Plato, *Timaeus*

We should look upon the female state as being as it were a deformity, though one which occurs in the ordinary course of nature.

    —Aristotle, *Generation of Animals*

Just as mankind is the most perfect of all animals, so within mankind the man is more perfect than the woman.

    —Galen, *On the Usefulness of the Parts of the Body*

A wife should have no feelings of her own, but share her husband's seriousness and sport, his anxiety and his laughter.

    —Plutarch, *Advice to the Bride and Groom*

Woman has been made for man.

    —Saint Augustine, *Confessions*

The male sex is more noble than the female.

    —St. Thomas Aquinas, *Summa Theologica*

More Recent Voices from History

The whole education of women ought to relate to men. To please men, to be useful to them, to make herself loved and honored by them, to raise them when young, to care for them when grown, to counsel them, to console them, to make their lives agreeable and sweet—these are the duties of women at all times, and they ought to be taught from childhood.

> —Jean-Jacques Rousseau, *Emile, or on Education,* 1762

A woman is embarrassed little that she does not possess certain high insights, that she is timid, and not fit for serious employments, and so forth; she is beautiful and captivates, and that is enough.

> —Immanuel Kant, *Observations on the Feeling of the Beautiful and Sublime,* 1763

A woman is but an animal; and an animal not of the highest order.

> —Edmund Burke, *Reflections on the Revolution in France,* 1790

Women . . . should not be regarded as the equals of men; they are, in fact, mere machines to make children.

> —Napoleon Bonaparte, in conversation, 1817

The wife is a piece of property, acquired by contract; she is part of your furniture, for possession is nine-tenths of the law; in fact, the woman is not, to speak correctly, anything but an adjunct to the man; therefore abridge, cut, file this article as you choose; she is in every sense yours. Take no notice at all of her murmurs, of her cries, of her sufferings; nature has ordained her for your use that she may bear everything—children, griefs, blows and pains from man.

> —Honoré de Balzac, *The Physiology of Marriage,* 1829

Women are defective in the powers of reasoning and deliberation. . . . [They] exist in the main solely for the propagation of the species, and are not destined for anything else.

> —Arthur Schopenhauer, *On Women,* 1851

Women want to serve, and therein lies their happiness.

> —Friedrich Nietzsche, Aphorism 432 of *Human, All Too Human,* 1878

Excerpts from the Bible

To the woman [God] said: "I will increase your labour and your groaning, and in labour you shall bear children. You shall be eager for your husband, and he shall be your master.

—*Genesis 3:16*

While every man has Christ for his Head, woman's head is man, as Christ's Head is God. . . . Man is the image of God, and the mirror of his glory, whereas woman reflects the glory of man. For man did not originally spring from woman, but woman was made out of man; and man was not created for woman's sake, but woman for the sake of man.

—*I Corinthians 11:3–4,7–9*

A woman must be a learner, listening quietly and with due submission. I do not permit a woman to be a teacher, nor must woman domineer over man; she should be quiet.

—*I Timothy 2:11–12*

Wives, be subject to your husbands as to the Lord; for the man is the head of the woman, just as Christ also is the head of the church. Christ is, indeed, the Saviour of the body; but just as the church is subject to Christ, so must women be to their husbands in everything.

—*Ephesians 5:22–24*

As in all congregations of God's people, women should not address the meeting. They have no license to speak, but should keep their place as the law directs. If there is something they want to know, they can ask their own husbands at home. It is a shocking thing that a woman should address the congregation.

—*I Corinthians 14:34–35*

Wives, be subject to your husbands; that is your Christian duty.

—*Colossians 3:18*

Other Religious Declarations

Islam

Men have authority over women because God has made the one superior to the other, and because they spend their wealth to maintain them. Good women are obedient.

> —*The Koran,* Chapter 4, Verse 34

Judaism

A person must recite three blessings every day: "Praised are you, O Lord, who has not made me a gentile," "Praised are you, O Lord, who did not make me a boor," and "Praised are you, O Lord, who did not make me a woman."

> —*The Talmud of Babylonia* (Menahot, 43B)

Buddhism

The female's defects—greed, hate, and delusion and other defilements—are greater than the male's.

> —*Sutra on Changing the Female Sex* (*Taishō,* Vol. 14, n. 564)

Hinduism

A girl, a young woman, or even an old woman should not do anything independently, even in (her own) house. In childhood a woman should be under her father's control, in youth under her husband's, and when her husband is dead, under her sons'. She should not have independence.

> —*The Laws of Manu* (Chapter 5, 147–148)

A Contemporary Statement

VI. The Church

. . . While both men and women are gifted for service in the church, the office of pastor is limited to men as qualified by Scripture. . . .

XVIII. The Family

. . . A husband is to love his wife as Christ loved the church. He has the God-given responsibility to provide for, to protect, and to lead his family. A wife is to submit herself graciously to the servant leadership of her husband even as the church willingly submits to the headship of Christ. She, being in the image of God as is her husband and thus equal to him, has the God-given responsibility to respect her husband and to serve as his helper in managing the household and nurturing the next generation. . . .

> —Excerpts from Articles VI and XVIII of Baptist Faith and Message. Copyright © 2000, Southern Baptist Convention. Used by permission.

Some Early Scientific Views on Women

The chief distinction in the intellectual powers of the two sexes is shewn by man's attaining to a higher eminence, in whatever he takes up, than can woman—whether requiring deep thought, reason, or imagination.

> —Charles Darwin, British naturalist, *The Descent of Man and Selection in Relation to Sex*, 1871

[There is] a somewhat earlier arrest of individual evolution in women than in men.

> —Herbert Spencer, British philosopher and sociologist, *Popular Science Monthly*, 1873

There are a large number of women whose brains are closer in size to those of gorillas than to the most developed male brains. . . . All psychologists who have studied the intelligence of women . . . recognize today that they represent the most inferior forms of human evolution.

> —Gustave Le Bon, French social psychologist, *Revue d'Anthropologie*, 1879

The masculine brain deals with new and complex matter . . . in a manner which the feminine method of direct intuition, admirably and rapidly as it performs within its limits, can vainly hope to cope with.

> —William James, third president of the American Psychological Association, *The Principles of Psychology*, 1890

Women are weaker in body and mind than men. . . . [Woman] in every fiber of her soul and body is a more generic creature than man.

> —G. Stanley Hall, first president of the American Psychological Association, *Adolescence: Its Psychology and Its Relations to Physiology, Anthropology, Sociology, Sex, Crime, Religion, and Education*, 1907

Direct thought is not at present an attribute of femininity. In this woman is now centuries, ages, even epochs behind man.

> —Thomas A. Edison, American inventor, *Good Housekeeping*, 1912

AN AMBIVALENT ALLIANCE: HOSTILE AND BENEVOLENT SEXISM AS COMPLEMENTARY JUSTIFICATIONS FOR GENDER INEQUALITY

PETER GLICK AND SUSAN T. FISKE

If woman had no existence save in the fiction written by men, one would imagine her a person . . . very various; heroic and mean; splendid and sordid; infinitely beautiful and hideous in the extreme.

—VIRGINIA WOOLF, *A Room of One's Own*

What Woolf saw as "astonishing extremes" in men's images of women date back to ancient texts. Pomeroy (1975), a social historian, suggested that classical representations of women fit into the polarized categories of goddesses, whores, wives, and slaves. Feminists who analyze contemporary society (e.g., Faludi, 1992) argue that similarly extreme characterizations of women are alive and well in popular culture, such as film depictions that divide women into faithful wives and murderous seductresses. Although what Tavris and Wade (1984) termed the *pedestal-gutter syndrome* (or the *Madonna-whore* dichotomy) has long been recognized by psychologists, historians, and feminists, most empirical researchers have identified sexism only with hostility toward women, ignoring the corresponding tendency to place (at least some) women on a pedestal.

This article reviews recent research on hostile and benevolent sexism. Hostile sexism is an adversarial view of gender relations in which women are perceived as seeking to control men, whether through sexuality or feminist ideology. Although *benevolent sexism* may sound oxymoronic, this term recognizes that some forms of sexism are, for the perpetrator, subjectively benevolent, characterizing women as pure creatures who ought to be protected, supported, and adored. This idealization of women simultaneously implies that they are weak and best suited for conventional gender roles; being put on a pedestal is confining, yet the man who places a woman there is likely to interpret this as cherishing, rather than restricting, her (and many women may agree).

In 19 nations, more than 15,000 participants have completed the Ambivalent Sexism Inventory (ASI; Glick & Fiske, 1996; Glick et al., 2000), a 22–item self-report measure of sexist attitudes with separate 11–item Hostile and Benevolent Sexism scales. Hostile and benevolent sexism are prevalent across cultures, and cross-cultural differences in ambivalent sexism are predictable and systematic, with both ideologies relating to national measures of gender inequality. What ASI research reveals about the nature of sexism challenges current definitions of prejudice as an unalloyed antipathy and draws attention to the manner in which subjectively benevolent, paternalistic prejudices may reinforce inequality between groups.

The Nature of Sexism

Allport (1954), in his foundational book *The Nature of Prejudice*, defined prejudice as "an antipathy based upon a faulty and inflexible generalization" (p. 9). Although some (e.g., Brown, 1995) have questioned the latter part of this definition, virtually all psychological theorists have likewise equated prejudice with antipathy. From antipathy, it is assumed, flow the discriminatory acts that disadvantage targets of prejudice. Simply put, men typically rule, dominating the highest status roles in government and business across the globe (United Nations Development Programme, 1998).

The standard model of prejudice would suggest, then, that attitudes toward women must be overwhelmingly hostile and contemptuous. Recent research, however, shows that overall attitudes toward women are quite favorable. Eagly and Mladinic (1993) found that both men and women have more favorable attitudes toward women than toward men, attributing an extremely positive set of traits to women. Known as the "women are wonderful" effect, this finding is extremely robust. The preference for women creates a conundrum for prejudice theorists: How can a group be almost universally disadvantaged yet loved?

Answers to this riddle come from several quarters. Eagly and Mladinic (1993) pointed out that the favorable, communal traits ascribed to women (e.g., nurturing, helpful, and warm) suit them for domestic roles, whereas men are presumed to possess traits associated with competence at high-status roles (e.g., independent, ambitious, and competitive). Furthermore, women's stereotypically communal attributes are also the traits that place a person in a subordinate, less powerful position (Ridgeway, 1992). Thus, the favorable traits attributed to women may reinforce women's lower status. Indeed, Jackman (1994), in her persuasive analysis of race, class, and gender relations, argued that subordination and affection, far from being mutually exclusive, often go hand-in-hand. Dominant groups prefer to act warmly toward subordinates, offering them patronizing affection as a reward for "knowing their place" rather than rebelling. Open antagonism is reserved for subordinates who fail to defer or who question existing social inequalities.

But can subjectively benevolent attitudes be a form of prejudice? By Allport's (1954) definition of prejudice as an antipathy, the answer is no. Yet, Allport immediately followed his definition by stating that "the net effect of prejudice . . . is to place the object of prejudice at some disadvantage" (p. 9). Allport's afterthought suggests that the crux of prejudice may not be antipathy but social inequality; if so, a patronizing but subjectively positive orientation toward women that reinforces gender inequality is a form of prejudice.

Why Benevolent Prejudices Matter

Benevolent sexism is a subtle form of prejudice, yet the ideology it represents may be far from trivial in promoting gender inequality. Both hostile and benevolent sexism are presumed to be "legitimizing ideologies," beliefs that help to justify and maintain inequality between groups (Sidanius, Pratto, & Bobo, 1994). Ideologies of benevolent paternalism allow members of dominant groups to characterize their privileges as well-deserved, even as a heavy responsibility that they must bear.

Equally important is the way in which benevolent paternalism may reduce women's resistance to patriarchy (cf. Jackman, 1994). Benevolent sexism is disarming. Not only is it subjectively favorable in its characterization of women, but it promises that men's power will be used to women's advantage, if only they can secure a high-status male protector. To the extent that women depend on men to be their protectors and providers, they are less likely to protest men's power or to seek their own independent status. For instance, Rudman and Heppen (2000) found that college women who implicitly associated male romantic partners with chivalrous images (e.g., Prince Charming) had less ambitious career goals, presumably because they were counting on a future husband for economic support. In a related study, Moya, Expósito, and Casado (1999) found, in a community sample of Spanish women, that those who did not have paid employment scored higher in benevolent sexism.

We believe that men who endorse both hostile and benevolent beliefs about women are likely to experience ambivalence toward individual women. Consider, for instance, the well-known pattern that occurs in domestic abuse with a husband reacting with violence when his authority is challenged but later expressing remorse and affection (the subsequent "honeymoon" period)—a pattern that suggests considerable sexist ambivalence. Furthermore, we strongly suspect that another form of ambivalence is likely when men who score high on both hostile and benevolent sexism find that an initial categorization of a woman does not hold. For example, a sexist man might initially place a woman in whom he is romantically interested on a pedestal but abruptly change his views when she rejects him, reclassifying her from "babe" to "bitch."

Women's Acceptance of Sexist Ideologies

A central part of our argument is that benevolent sexism is a particularly insidious form of prejudice for two reasons: (a) It does not seem like a prejudice to male perpetrators (because it is not experienced as an antipathy), and (b) women may find its sweet allure difficult to resist. Benevolent sexism, after all, has its rewards; chivalrous men are willing to sacrifice their own well-being to provide for and to protect women. In the 19 countries studied (Glick & Fiske, 1996; Glick et al., 2000), without exception, men's average hostile sexism scores are considerably higher than women's (see Figure 1). In contrast, in about half of the countries we have studied, women endorse benevolent sexism about as much as men do (see Figure 2). Most intriguing is the finding that in the 4 nations with the highest sexism scores (Cuba, Nigeria, South Africa, and Botswana), the gender gap in benevolent sexism was reversed, with women endorsing this form of sexism more strongly than men.

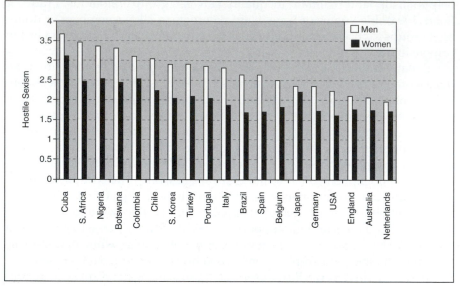

FIGURE 1   Hostile Sexism Across Countries

Note. From "Beyond Prejudice as Simple Antipathy: Hostile and Benevolent Sexism Across Cultures," by P. Glick et al., 2000, *Journal of Personality and Social Psychology, 79*, p. 770. Copyright 2000 by the American Psychological Association. Reprinted with permission.

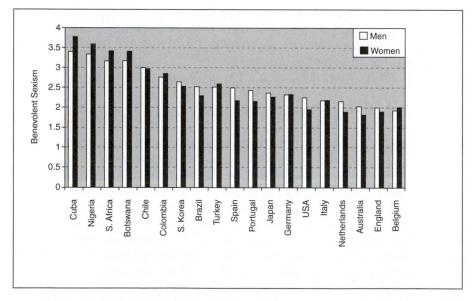

FIGURE 2   Benevolent Sexism Across Countries

Note. From "Beyond Prejudice as Simple Antipathy: Hostile and Benevolent Sexism Across Cultures," by P. Glick et al., 2000, *Journal of Personality and Social Psychology, 79*, p. 770. Copyright 2000 by the American Psychological Association. Reprinted with permission.

Virginia Woolf (1929/1981) argued that true gender equality will happen only when "womanhood has ceased to be a protected occupation" (p. 40). The irony is that women are forced to seek protection from members of the very group that threatens them, and the greater the threat, the stronger the incentive to accept benevolent sexism's protective ideology. This explains the tendency for women in the most sexist societies to endorse benevolent sexism more strongly than men. As sexist hostility declines, women may feel able to reject benevolent sexism without fear of a hostile backlash.

Implications for Theories of Prejudice: Paternalistic Versus Envious Prejudices

Although benevolent paternalism is most evident in sexist ideology, it is not unique to this form of prejudice. For example, some liberal Whites may have paternalistic attitudes toward African Americans, characterized by pity and an implicit belief that African Americans are incapable of helping themselves (Katz & Hass, 1988). Recent research that we have conducted with our colleagues suggests that paternalistic stereotypes are directed at a number of groups that are perceived to be low in status and capability but not threatening, such as people who are blind, people with handicaps, older individuals, and housewives (Fiske, 1998; Fiske, Glick, Cuddy, & Xu, 1999; Fiske, Xu, Cuddy, & Glick, 1999; Glick & Fiske, in press).

In contrast, the resentful tone evident in hostile sexism may be similar to prejudice directed toward socioeconomically successful minorities who are perceived as a competitive threat. Just as sexist men resent career women who succeed in traditionally male-dominated areas, minorities who are perceived to be successful (e.g., Jews or Asian Americans) may be envied and viewed as overly ambitious rivals. This can constitute another form of ambivalence—a grudging respect coupled with dislike and fear—that we have called "envious prejudice" (Glick & Fiske, in press).

Paternalistic and envious prejudices may be quite distinct in their causes and their consequences. The one-size-fits-all conception of prejudice, rooted in the idea that prejudice is pure hatred and contempt, has obscured these differences (Young-Breuhl, 1996). One commonality between envious and paternalistic stereotypes, however, is that seemingly favorable traits attributed to a group may only add fuel to the fire of prejudice. Paternalistic stereotypes assign the favorable traits of warmth to low-status groups, but this represents an amiable way of helping to ensure these groups' subordination. For example, the positive value placed on warm, communal traits also lends them a more prescriptive tone that sets up powerful norms for women's behavior. Likewise, even though envied groups (e.g., Jews or Asian Americans) may be attributed the normally positive traits of competence (e.g., ambitious or smart), these attributions often become part of the justification for discriminating against them; they are perceived to be too clever and manipulative.

Conclusion

Although sexist antipathy is the most obvious form of prejudice against women, our evidence suggests that sexist benevolence may also play a significant role in justifying gender inequality. Together, these ideologies represent a system of rewards and punishments that provide incentive for women to remain in conventional gender roles. More generally, we suggest parallels between the two forms of sexism and prejudice against other groups. Hostile sexism is similar to other forms of envious prejudice, directed at groups who are seen as threats to the in-group's status and power, whereas benevolent sexism corresponds to other paternalistic prejudices, directed at groups that are lower in status and viewed as cooperative or nonthreatening.

REFERENCES

Allport, G. W. (1954). *The nature of prejudice.* Reading, MA: Addison-Wesley.

Brown, R. (1995). *Prejudice: Its social psychology.* Oxford, England: Blackwell.

Eagly, A. H., & Mladinic, A. (1993). Are people prejudiced against women? Some answers from research on attitudes, gender stereotypes and judgments of competence. In W. Stroebe & M. Hewstone (Eds.), *European review of social psychology* (Vol. 5, pp. 1–35). New York: Wiley.

Faludi, S. (1992). *Backlash: The undeclared war against American women.* New York: Doubleday.

Fiske, S. T. (1998). Prejudice, stereotyping, and discrimination. In D. T. Gilbert, S. T. Fiske, & G. Lindzey (Eds.), *The handbook of social psychology* (4th ed., pp. 357–411). New York: McGraw-Hill.

Fiske, S. T., Glick, P., Cuddy, A. C., & Xu, J. (1999, July). *Ambivalent content of stereotypes, predicted by social structure: Status and competition predict competence and warmth.* Paper presented at the 22nd General Meeting of the European Association of Experimental Social Psychology, Oxford, England.

Fiske, S. T., Xu, J., Cuddy, A. C., & Glick, P. (1999). Respect versus liking: Status and interdependence underlie ambivalent stereotypes. *Journal of Social Issues, 55,* 473–489.

Glick, P., & Fiske, S. T. (1996). The Ambivalent Sexism Inventory: Differentiating hostile and benevolent sexism. *Journal of Personality and Social Psychology, 70,* 491–512.

Glick, P. & Fiske, S. T. (in press). Ambivalent stereotypes as legitimizing ideologies: Differentiating paternalistic and resentful prejudice. In J. T. Jost & B. Major (Eds.), *The psychology of legitimacy: Emerging perspectives on ideology, justice, and intergroup relations.* New York: Cambridge University Press.

Glick, P., Fiske, S. T., Mladinic, A., Saiz, J., Abrams, D., Masser, B., et al. (2000). Beyond prejudice as simple antipathy: Hostile and benevolent sexism across cultures. *Journal of Personality and Social Psychology, 79,* 763–775.

Jackman, M. R. (1994). *The velvet glove: Paternalism and conflict in gender, class, and race relations.* Berkeley: University of California Press.

Katz, I., & Hass, R. G. (1988). Racial ambivalence and value conflict: Correlational and priming studies of dual cognitive structures. *Journal of Personality and Social Psychology, 55,* 893–905.

Moya, M., Expósito, F., & Casado, P. (1999, July). *Women's reactions to hostile and benevolent sexist situations.* Paper presented at the 22nd General Meeting of the European Association of Experimental Social Psychology, Oxford, England.

Pomeroy, S. B. (1975). *Goddesses, whores, wives and slaves: Women in classical antiquity.* New York: Schocken.

Ridgeway, C. (1992). *Gender, interaction, and inequality.* New York: Springer-Verlag.

Rudman, L. A., & Heppen, J. (2000). *Some day my prince will come: Implicit romantic fantasies and women's avoidance of power.* Unpublished manuscript, Rutgers, The State University of New Jersey.

Sidanius, J., Pratto, F., & Bobo, L. (1994). Social dominance orientation and the political psychology of gender: A case of invariance? *Journal of Personality and Social Psychology, 67,* 998–1011.

Tavris, C., & Wade, C. (1984). *The longest war* (2nd ed.). San Diego, CA: Harcourt Brace Jovanovich.

United Nations Development Programme. (1998). *Human development report 1998.* New York: Oxford University Press.

Woolf, V. (1981). *A room of one's own.* New York: Harcourt Brace Jovanovich. (Original work published 1929)

Young-Breuhl, E. (1996). *The anatomy of prejudices.* Cambridge, MA: Harvard University Press.

Freud's Theory of Penis Envy

The psychical consequences of envy for the penis . . . are various and far-reaching. After a woman has become aware of the wound to her narcissism, she develops, like a scar, a sense of inferiority. When she has passed beyond her first attempt at explaining her lack of a penis as being a punishment personal to herself and has realized that that sexual character is a universal one, she begins to share the contempt felt by men for a sex which is the lesser in so important a respect. . . .

Character-traits which critics of every epoch have brought up against women—that they show less sense of justice than men, that they are less ready to submit to the great exigencies of life, that they are more often influenced in their judgments by feelings of affection or hostility—all these would be amply accounted for by the modification in the formation of their super-ego which we have inferred above. We must not allow ourselves to be deflected from such conclusions by the denials of the feminists, who are anxious to force us to regard the two sexes as completely equal in position and worth.

—Sigmund Freud, *Some Psychical Consequences of the Anatomical Distinction Between the Sexes*, 1925

A View from the U.S. Supreme Court

Civil law, as well as nature herself, has always recognized a wide difference in the respective spheres and destinies of man and woman. Man is, or should be, woman's protector and defender. The natural and proper timidity and delicacy which belongs to the female sex evidently unfits it for many of the occupations of civil life. . . . The paramount destiny and mission of woman are to fulfill the noble and benign offices of wife and mother. This is the law of the Creator.

—Justice Joseph P. Bradley, *Myra Bradwell v. State of Illinois,* 1873 (upholding an earlier decision by the Illinois Supreme Court to deny women licenses to practice law)

A Sampler of Dissonance–Reducing Statements
Opposition to Female Suffrage

The statements below were common justifications for denying women the vote. Note their resemblance to the rationales used to defend slavery (see Section III). All statements are taken from *The Works of Orestes A. Brownson* (1885).

Women Benefit from Subordination

"Women need a head, and the restraint of father, husband, or the priest of God."

Women Have It Good

"It would be hard to say how women could be more free than they are, or what rights the law can give them which they have not, or what legal disadvantage they labor under. . . . There is no country where women are so free, independent, and influential, as they are in the United States."

Women Do Not Suffer More Than Men

"Woman is not more a slave to man than man is to woman; and she tyrannizes over him even more than he does over her . . . . Men suffer as much from women as women do from men."

Suffrage Would Hurt Women

"Not only would the government or politics gain nothing by the so-called enfranchisement of women, but the women themselves would gain nothing, while they would unquestionably lose much. . . . They would lose most, if not all of the prerogatives hitherto claimed and enjoyed by them in society."

Religious Support for Inequality

"Revelation asserts, and universal experience proves that the man is the head of the woman, and that the woman is for the man, not the man for the woman."

Subordination Is Natural

"Woman was created to be a wife and a mother; that is her destiny. To that destiny all her instincts point, and for it nature has specially qualified her."

Subordination Is Necessary

"The political enfranchisement of women . . . would weaken and finally break up and destroy the Christian family . . . and the human race [would] be threatened with extinction."

Dissonance–Reducing Statements (continued)

Women Are Incompetent

"In the complicated questions of the state, where there is to be a conciliation of interests and even of duties . . . women fall far short of men, and really are incompetent."

Women Oppress Themselves

"The evils complained of are chiefly due to the women."

Women Prefer Not to Vote

"Women generally do not desire [enfranchisement]. Their present cares and burdens are as great as they can bear, and they feel that the proposed elevation would prove a degradation."

Male Self-Interest Protects Women

Man rarely, if ever, separates his private interest from that of woman—his mother, his sister, his wife, his daughter, or even his mistress. He always includes in his private interest that of some woman."

Men Are Caring

"Men [have a] chivalric respect for women [and] regard woman as placed in some sort under their protection."

Suffragists Are Fanatics

"Female suffrage and eligibility are desired by fanatics of every class, for women are by their very nature . . . far more susceptible of fanaticism than men."

Women's Rights Is Not the Issue

"The advocates of woman suffrage and eligibility are moved principally, whether men or women, by the desire to abolish Christian marriage and introduce in its place what is called FREE-LOVE. The whole movement, disguise it as we will, is a free-love movement."

Abuses Are Part of the System

"There is no doubt that women are exposed to many hardships and are compelled to bear many grievances, some through the fault of men, and some through their own fault; but they are beyond the reach of political power, administrative or legislative, to redress."

Equality Is Impossible

"You cannot make earth heaven, and there is no use in trying; and least of all can you do it by political means."

They Could Have Had a Girl

I think it was absolutely stupid...I've said several times, for the price they paid to rent the car, they could have had a girl.

—U.S. Admiral Richard C. Macke, explaining how three American service men accused of raping a 12-year-old Japanese girl in Okinawa could have avoided the incident by hiring a prostitute, *New York Times,* November 19, 1995

THE DEADLY SERIOUS GAME OF THE BEAUTY PAGEANT

Sandra McElwaine

Let's get it straight once and for all: The Miss America Pageant is not a beauty contest. Not at all. Despite the hype and hoopla, the nose jobs, breast implants, and fanny lifts, officials insist that Miss America is a Very Serious Person. They want you to forget the stereotype of a pageant that values pulchritude over personality, body more than brains, and instead see the annual Atlantic City ritual as a highly competitive scholarship program—a television extravaganza, certainly, but one in which the best and the brightest from fifty states match wit and talent as they vie for the coveted title.

The Miss America Pageant, of course, isn't the *Jeopardy* teen tournament, no matter what officials may say. In sum, it's a Cinderella story; broken down, it's equal parts sporting event, glamour contest, and fashion show, with a whisper of royalty, an air of purity, and an implication of forbidden sex. The spectacle, aimed at sixty million avid viewers, combines everything mainstream America loves and roots for, and it's as traditional as hot dogs and apple pie. It is also—as spokespeople never tire of telling us—the largest scholarship program for women in the country, offering $30,000 for tuition, plus $150,000 for a year of personal appearances.

According to Leonard Horn, pageant director, CEO, and chairman of the board, what counts is not that a woman be chaste but that she be "a thinking human being willing to put herself on the line for specific goals." The emphasis, he says, is on demonstrable talent, personality, and academic credentials.

Indeed, much of the competition is based on a highly personal interview that television audiences never get to see. Each woman, required by event guidelines to be between seventeen and twenty-six, is subjected to a grilling before a panel of preliminary judges. Contestants are questioned on the expected—career goals and philosophy of life—but are also asked to converse intelligently on such topics as national defense, the budget deficit, abortion, the impact of the Environmental Protection Agency.

By the time she takes the crown, Miss America will have been an old hand at the sport. Usually, she will have played at some point in the South, where pageantry is not just a sideline or a hobby but big business. For years, Dixie dominated the pageant scene. To a land where six-month-old babies battle for a title, hopeful young women flock in search of experts who hold the secrets of winning.

"There is no hidden formula," insists Randy Dimitt, who rose to fame in the pageant world in 1981, when, from his small shop in Russellville, Arkansas, he outfitted the victors of both the Miss America and the Miss USA pageants. "It's inside packaging along with outside packaging, and you better be good at both to win."

The word of his double win, coupled with contestants' growing reliance on professional "handlers," has turned Dimitt's specialty dress store, Randy's Another World, into a virtual pageant closet, a one-stop shop for thousands of contestants nationwide. At Randy's, entire contest wardrobes, and advice on how to choose them, are available under the same roof.

On the Miss America circuit alone, fifty thousand to sixty thousand young women start out on the local level each year, and they all need clothes. Many borrow or make their own, but those intent on winning a title must invest in an assortment of garments, the total cost of which may run into the stratosphere.

Dazzling a judge in the evening-gown event demands elaborate beading and perfect fit, both provided by Greenville, South Carolina, designer Stephen Yearick. Yearick caters to other glamorous women, including such luminaries as Dionne Warwick, Aretha Franklin, Joan Rivers, and Nancy Reagan. Priced from $2,500 to $10,000, Yearick's creations are sold at—where else?—Randy's Another World. "It's every girl's dream to own a Yearick," says Dimitt.

Yearick is quick to point out that although clothes don't make the winner, they do help a contestant "feel wonderful, like a million bucks onstage, to give her the *confidence* she needs to win."

A woman never needs that confidence more than when she's parading in front of a lineup of judges and sixty million television viewers in no more than stiletto heels and a bathing suit. Aficionados credit a solid-color Super Suit with the supernatural power of transforming wearers into winners. Made of cotton with three superstretch linings (hence its name), the suit, at a steep $150, is molded to the figure like a girdle, to prohibit all bouncing of breasts, stomach, and derriere.

It can, of course, be altered to meet individual needs. Dimitt creates the illusion of a longer leg by ensuring the suit has a V cut and ends one inch below the hip bone. Padding, made of foam rubber in varying thicknesses—thinner at the top of the bosom—emphasizes and enlarges the bust.

Of course, even after padding and shaping, much remains exposed. To perfect *those* parts, innumerable hopefuls trek to White Settlement, Texas, for the ministrations of the legendary bodybuilder Chuck Weisbeck, who holds the track record for coaching more pageant swimsuit winners than any other trainer in the country.

A consultation with Weisbeck costs just twenty-five dollars—one hundred less than he charges "civilians" for the same advice. "I really enjoy working with pageant girls," he explains. Many women fly in for only two and a half hours of orientation and instruction. Others spend a couple of days under Weisbeck's tutelage, and some return for a follow-up after a month. Those who live too far away phone in their questions. After a scan of figure flaws, which usually clump on thighs and buttocks, Weisbeck calculates a caloric maintenance diet, places each contender on a high-fiber, salt-, caffeine-, and fat-free regimen, and gives her an instruction packet explaining the details of an arduous aerobic weight-training program.

Although Weisbeck insists that "the best way to get it off is to do it naturally," more and more pageant contenders are opting for a quicker solution: the surgical knife. Contestants have had their ears pinned, their upper lips enlarged, buttocks tucked, cheeks and chins implanted, and eyes widened. One even had a rib removed to create a smaller waist. But most women who seek the services of James Billie, M.D., the head of the Cosmetic Surgery Center in Little Rock, Arkansas, want rhinoplasty—a nose job; it is by far his most requested operation. Liposuction, which has replaced the fanny tuck and leaves no unsightly scars, runs second, and breast implants of Meme (polyurethane-coated heat-vulcanized silicone gel) rank third.

Pageant women and their families, who now comprise up to 20 percent of his clientele, come because of Dr. Billie's reputation, but also because the price is right—$2,000 to $2,500 for any one of these operations, as compared to a national average of $4,000 to $6,000. Then, too, there is little chance of discovery in Little Rock. "We're really off the beaten track," notes Dr. Billie. "No one will run into any friends. It's like flying to Saudi Arabia or Japan."

The procedures are done on an outpatient basis, and patients are offered a selection of nearby hotels and motels that cost roughly $35 a night. One such inn offers a shuttle van that not only runs to and from the clinic but is available to pick up medications and such little luxuries as Kentucky Fried Chicken and pizza.

Does cosmetic surgery constitute cheating for a pageant aspirant? Dr. Billie says no: "It's easier to take an extremely talented girl and do a thirty-minute nasal operation than take a flawlessly beautiful girl and teach her to sing or play piano."

With the basic externals pulled, pushed, and sutured into place, contestants can turn their attention to saying and doing the right thing and learning to adapt to the complexities and rigors of pageant life. Needless to say, hired guns are on hand to help. June Graves, of Hurst, Texas, has been instructing competitors and serving as traveling companion to Miss America aspirants for more than twenty-five years. Her technique: three days—at $175 a day—of intensive training in poise, presentation, and etiquette. "Girls have to be sharp, able to think on their feet, walk into a room and feel comfortable talking with adults. Their personality has to come through," she says.

Critiquing begins the minute Graves picks up her charge at the airport and continues for the next seventy-two hours. Girls must master the challenging task of walking gracefully in a swimsuit and high heels.

In prepping them for the grueling interview, Graves insists that each girl read *Time,* the *Wall Street Journal,* and *People,* and watch the *Today* show and *Good Morning America* daily, to catch up on the news and form opinions. They even take brush-up pointers on table manners, proper grooming, and wardrobe selection.

Still, it's not over until it's over, and in the final, frenzied days and hours before the pageant proper, hair and makeup artists assume paramount importance. Jane White, makeup pro and official consultant to the Miss Arkansas pageant, expertly hides flaws, scars, tucks, and veins. A special beige-mint eye disguise, mortician's wax (to conceal large surgical wounds), and a corrective cosmetic called Dermablend are all stashed in her bag in Atlantic City as she zips from hotel to hotel.

Applying makeup for pageants is a unique challenge, says White; it must appear natural under the glaring stage lights, but differs from theatrical makeup in that it is applied solely for the judges sitting just *beyond* those foot-lights, not for the whole auditorium.

The face paint also tends to follow each year's fashion. Now, for instance, eyebrows are hot, false lashes are *not,* so White plucks the brows to conform to their natural shape and shows clients how to substitute rayon filaments be-tween coats of mascara to achieve a glamorous long-lashed look. She also teaches quick cosmetic changes to enhance different-colored outfits and is a wizard at the art of camouflage and makeup tricks. Basic tips: Preparation H to shrink eye bags; frozen tea bags to alleviate eye puffiness; a rolling pin to reduce saddlebags; Vaseline on the teeth for an easy smile; Clorox, lemon juice, and water, applied with a toothbrush, to lighten knees and elbows. White has been known to advise taking laxatives and diuretics the night be-fore a swimsuit contest, and suggests smearing the torso with Ben-Gay before wrapping it tightly in Saran Wrap to do away with any excess flab.

It's quite a lot of hullabaloo, and quite a wad of dough, to squander on one grand night, but as June Graves says, "What girls are doing is preparing for the rest of their lives. It's like getting ready for any job, and they'd better be on their toes. It's a tough, tough year, but if they make it, it's instant stardom."

Indeed, a win means a rise from obscurity that is as meteoric as it is re-warding, and luck and timing are as vital as any prepackaging that's taken place. Night after night during the preliminary judging, the Convention Hall crowd is packed with preening, ambitious, young girls. Many have been Miss Peachtree, Miss Magnolia Blossom, Junior Miss, Miss Teen. Each would like to land on the Atlantic City stage, to go for the big one: Miss America.

But with Miss America no longer on a pedestal—virginal, beautiful, and sexy—which way is she headed? Miss America, despite the sea change in em-phasis, will never be a woman who is *just* brainy and talented, and her pag-eant will never be a mere scholarship program or platform for ideas. Indeed, pageant director Leonard Horn has pushed to eliminate the swimsuit show-down—the very symbol of the pageant world's "cattle call" past—but other officials have loudly balked. Sniffed one executive director, "The general public does not want to see an ugly, fat lady singing opera."

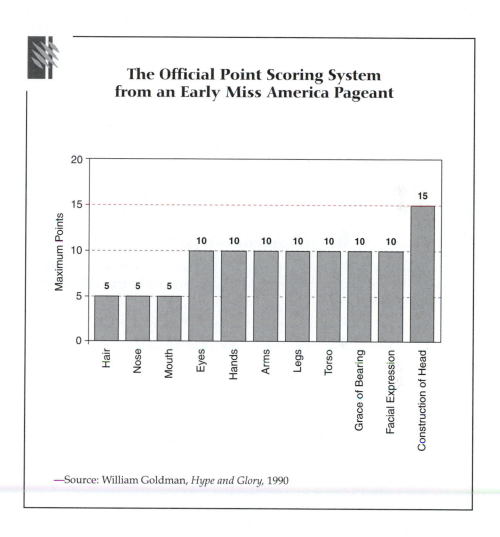

The Official Point Scoring System from an Early Miss America Pageant

—Source: William Goldman, *Hype and Glory,* 1990

Would You Encourage Her?

Percentage of Americans who say that if they had a daughter, they would "be proud and encourage her if she wanted to enter the Miss America pageant": 67%

Percentage of 18– to 29–year-olds who say they would: 82%

—*Source:* Gallup News Service, October 13, 2000

INFLUENCE OF POPULAR EROTICA AND JUDGMENTS OF STRANGERS AND MATES

DOUGLAS T. KENRICK, SARA E. GUTIERRES,
AND LAURIE L. GOLDBERG

What is the effect of exposure to soft-core erotica, like the nude centerfolds in *Playboy* and *Penthouse?* Exposure to magazines like *Playboy* may lead to a somewhat skewed perception of what an average person looks like naked. Such a skewed perception could lead to invidious comparisons between media beauties and "real world" lovers who are, on average, less attractive than models in *Playboy* or *Playgirl.*

There is indirect support for this line of reasoning. Kenrick and Gutierres (1980) found that exposure to attractive facial photographs lowered ratings of the attractiveness and dating desirability of an average looking female. Kenrick, Stringfield, Wagenhals, Dahl, and Ransdell (1980) suggested that such effects might be most important within the realm of erotica. Although standards of facial attractiveness might be raised by media beauties, those judgments should be brought "back to earth" just by looking at the less glamorous faces in the everyday world. Such reality testing is not available to the average looking college age male who has seen hundreds of beautiful nude women in *Playboy.* The women that he gets to see naked in "real life" are likely to be fewer and, like him, average looking. Thus, the media's skewed distribution would have more influence on his standards of beauty for naked bodies than for facial beauty.

In Experiment 1, male and female undergraduates judged an average looking nude female after exposure to nude female centerfolds.

Experiment 1

Method

Subjects One hundred seven males and 89 females participated to fulfill part of a course requirement at a large state university. Female experimenters ran subjects in same-sex groups of 2–8.

Procedure Subjects were told that they would participate in two separate experiments. The first experiment was, ostensibly, to address a controversy about whether particular works of art, photography, or cinema are artistically valuable or just offensive to "good taste." We explained that we were studying which characteristics separate "aesthetically pleasing from boring or unpleasant works" and that subjects would judge "materials which have aroused controversy with regard to their aesthetic significance." Since the materials might include nude photographs, subjects were told that they were free to withdraw by simply not joining the group in the experimental room (one female subject declined participation).

Stimulus Materials   Experimental subjects viewed 16 slides of highly attractive nude females from *Playboy* and *Penthouse* magazines. Two control conditions were run, in which subjects were shown either (a) 16 abstract art slides (e.g., Josef Albers' "Homage to the Square"), or (b) 16 photos of average-looking nude women, chosen from a men's magazine to which males supposedly submit photos of their wives or girlfriends (these had previously been judged as most nearly "average" by a group of five judges who rated 50 such photographs). Each slide was shown for 15 seconds and rated on 7-point scales tapping three dimensions: highly artistic/not at all artistic; unpleasant/pleasant; not at all socially valuable/socially valuable.

Rating of the Average Nude   After rating the 16 "aesthetic" slides, subjects were told they had completed the first experiment and were given a credit slip. They were told that they would now be participating in a second experiment that was not connected with the first one, but that was being conducted simultaneously because both required subjects who consented to view sensitive materials. A written description explained that we were examining an assumption of the encounter group movement:[1] that people can learn a great deal about another's personality by observing that person without clothing. Participants were told they would see a photograph of a person who took part in an encounter group workshop. Their task was to view the photo, and to try to accurately judge her personality (which had presumably been measured by "an extensive battery of psychological tests").

Subjects then viewed a slide of an average attractive nude woman (chosen in the same way as the average control photographs) for 60 seconds. They were then asked to rate her on a "Psychological Accuracy Inventory" that included 17 filler items and 3 items tapping her attractiveness. These were: (1) a bipolar scale anchored with "sexually unattractive/sexually attractive," and the questions (2) "How attractive is this person to males?," and (3) "How desirable would you imagine that males find this person as a date?" (anchored with "not at all/very much"). All were 9-point scales. The main dependent variable was a composite score including all three sexual attractiveness items.

Subjects next filled out a suspicion probe, and discussed any suspicions with the experimenters. Two subjects were dropped from the analysis. One was a female who suspected that there was a connection between looking at the first nudes and rating the target person. The other was a male subject in the art control condition whose friend had informed him that we were showing nudes in the other conditions. Subjects were fully debriefed regarding the true purpose of the study. Finally, they were asked to sign an agreement not to discuss the study.

───────────

[1]*Editor's note:* The encounter group movement was a humanistic psychology movement in which small groups of people "encountered" (interacted with) each other to learn about themselves through open communication and expression in a supportive social environment.

Results

Males found the centerfolds more pleasant than both controls, but did not differentiate between the two control conditions. Females found the centerfolds no more pleasant than controls, but did differentiate between art and average nudes, finding the latter less pleasant. As shown in Table 1, exposure to attractive centerfolds lowered judgments of the target's attractiveness compared to both the art and the average attractive controls. No effect of subject sex nor any interaction between type of prior stimuli and subject sex was found. A contrast pitting the centerfold condition against the two control conditions resulted in an $F(1, 191) = 9.49, p < .002$.

Discussion

In the first study, exposure to nudes from popular erotica produced a contrast effect on ratings of an average nude. That effect was similar for males and females. Given that subjects rated a stranger, these findings are most directly applicable to those crucial initial interactions, during which potential partners may lose interest in someone they judge to be unattractive (Walster, Aronson, Abrahams, & Rottmann, 1966).

Beyond first impressions, do these findings apply to judgments made within actual relationships? Attraction researchers have debated the extent to which processes found in laboratory encounters between strangers reflect on initial encounters as opposed to established relationships (e.g., Byrne, Ervin, & Lamberth, 1970; Levinger, 1972). The second study was designed to examine the effects of exposure to centerfold beauties on ratings of actual partners. It also differed from the first study in that females were exposed to attractive male centerfolds from *Playgirl* magazine.

TABLE 1   Cell Means: Experiment 1

Dependent Variables	Female Subjects			Male Subjects		
	Centerfolds	Average Nude	Art	Centerfolds	Average Nude	Art
Pleasantness of prior stimuli	3.2	2.4	3.8	4.9	3.6	3.8
Sexual attractiveness of target	11.6	13.7	12.9	9.6	14.1	11.8

Editor's note: Each number in this table represents an average rating for female or male subjects in the experimental (Centerfold) condition or the two control conditions (Average Nude or Art), with higher scores indicating greater pleasantness and attractiveness. The key finding is that a target person was rated as less attractive after subjects viewed centerfolds (average female rating = 11.6 and average male rating = 9.6) than after they viewed average nudes or art slides.

Experiment 2

Method

Subjects   Thirty males and 35 females enrolled at a large state university or a community college participated for partial fulfillment of course requirements. Subjects were run by female experimenters in same-sex groups of 2–8 persons.

Procedure   The experimental signup sheet stated that participants must either be married or involved in a similar live-in relationship with someone of the opposite sex. As in Experiment 1, a cover story indicated that we were studying standards of aesthetic and artistic judgment. The experimental males were first exposed to 16 female centerfold slides from *Playboy* and *Penthouse*. Experimental females were exposed to 16 male centerfold slides from *Playgirl*. Control subjects viewed the 16 abstract art slides.

Partner Ratings   After making the aesthetic judgments, subjects were told that there was some controversy about how relationships influenced responses to art. Subjects were told that some psychologists believe that being in a stable relationship enhances people's appreciation of art, others feel that the deep involvement interferes with aesthetic appreciation, and still others believe that it depends on the type of relationship. Subjects were then asked to rate their relationship on a questionnaire that included three filler items (rating the length of the relationship, partner's interest in art, and partner's conservatism). This questionnaire also included the three attractiveness items used in Study 1, which were aggregated to form one dependent variable. The other dependent variable was an aggregate of the 13 items from Rubin's (1970) Love Scale. All items were rated on 9-point scales.

After completing this questionnaire, subjects filled out a suspicion questionnaire (no subject indicated any awareness of the experimental ruse). Following this, subjects were fully debriefed regarding the purposes of the research and were asked to sign an agreement not to discuss the study.

Results

Subjects rated the nudes as more pleasant than the abstract art slides. As suggested by the means in Table 2, males' ratings of their mates' sexual attractiveness were significantly adversely affected by prior exposure to erotica, $F(1, 30) = 8.2$, $p < .001$. Females' ratings were not influenced by type of prior stimuli ($F < 1$). Love Scale items showed a marginally significant effect of type of stimuli. The tendency for subjects to indicate less love after exposure to centerfolds appears only for men's ratings, $F(1, 29) = 4.29$, $p < .05$. A comparable test for female subjects yielded an $F < 1$.

TABLE 2   Cell Means: Experiment 2

Dependent Variables	Female Subjects		Male Subjects	
	Centerfolds	*Art*	*Centerfolds*	*Art*
Pleasantness of prior stimuli	4.9	3.9	4.9	4.0
Sexual attractiveness of partner	22.2	22.5	22.1	26.2
Love for partner	82.3	85.0	87.2	98.8

Note. Higher scores indicate relatively more pleasantness, attractiveness, and love.

General Discussion

Experiment 1 found that exposure to attractive models from popular erotica decreased the rated attractiveness of a "normal" looking woman. Experiment 2 extended this finding to ratings of mates, but found the effect to hold only for males. Why the gender difference? One might speculate that females did not find the male centerfolds attractive or pleasant. However, pleasantness ratings suggest that females found the male centerfolds as pleasant as males found the female centerfolds. To further examine this possibility, we asked 28 female undergraduates from the same population to rate both the male and female centerfolds. They saw the male centerfolds as equal to female centerfolds in physical attractiveness and sexual attractiveness. Further, the females' ratings of the male centerfolds' attractiveness did not differ from 21 males' ratings of female centerfolds.

The gender difference found in Experiment 2 may fit with other findings on gender differences in mating behaviors (Hinde, 1984; Kenrick, 1987; Kenrick & Trost, 1987). That literature indicates that females are, on the average, likely to show a higher commitment to a monogamous relationship. Conversely, males are generally more inclined toward promiscuity. Finally, physical attractiveness appears to be a more central criterion for males' sexual responses than it is for females (Buss, 1985).

It would appear that it is the physical beauty of *Playboy* type stimuli, and not their erotic nature, that is responsible for the effects we obtained. Kenrick and Gutierres (1980) found similar attractiveness/contrast effects after subjects were exposed to media beauties that were fully dressed, whereas Dermer and Pyszcznski (1978) found that sexual arousal by itself enhanced males' ratings of their spouses. Also, female subjects showed the same contrast effects for ratings of a female stranger that males did, even though their affective reactions to those centerfolds were unpleasant. These findings make less of a case for avoiding sexually arousing materials than they do for avoiding the popular media in general.

REFERENCES

Buss, D. M. (1985). Sex differences in human mate selection: An evolutionary perspective. In C. Crawford et al. (Eds.), *Sociobiology and psychology: Issues, ideas, and findings.* Hillsdale, NJ: Erlbaum.

Byrne, D., Ervin, C. R., & Lamberth, J. (1970). Continuity between the experimental study of attraction and real-life computer dating. *Journal of Personality and Social Psychology, 16,* 157–165.

Dermer, M., & Pyszcznski, T. A. (1978). Effects of erotica upon men's loving and liking responses for women they love. *Journal of Personality and Social Psychology, 36,* 1302–1309.

Hinde, R. A. (1984). Why do the sexes behave differently in close relationships? *Journal of Social and Personal Relationships, 1,* 471–501.

Kenrick, D. T. (1987). Gender, genes, and the social environment: A biosocial interactionist perspective. In P. Shaver & C. Hendrick (Eds.), *Review of Personality & Social Psychology* (Vol. 7, pp. 14–43). Newbury Park, CA: Sage.

Kenrick, D. T., & Gutierres, S. E. (1980). Contrast effects and judgments of physical attractiveness: When beauty becomes a social problem. *Journal of Personality and Social Psychology, 38,* 131–140.

Kenrick, D. T., Stringfield, D. O., Wagenhals, W. L., Dahl, R. N., & Ransdell, H. J. (1980). Sex differences, androgyny, and approach responses to erotica: A new variation on the old volunteer problem. *Journal of Personality and Social Psychology 38,* 517–524.

Kenrick, D. T., & Trost, M. R. (1987). A biosocial model of heterosexual relationships. In K. Kelly (Ed.), *Males, females, and sexuality: Research and theory.* Albany, NY: SUNY Press.

Levinger, G. (1972). Little sand box and big quarry: Comment on Byrne's paradigmatic spade for research on interpersonal attraction. *Representative Research in Social Psychology, 3,* 3–19.

Rubin, Z. (1970). Measurement of romantic love. *Journal of Personality and Social Psychology, 16,* 265–273.

Walster, E., Aronson, V., Abrahams, D., & Rottman, L. (1966). Importance of physical attractiveness in dating behavior. *Journal of Personality and Social Psychology, 4,* 506–516.

MALE EPITHETS FOR ETHNIC WOMEN IN HISTORICAL AMERICAN SLANG

IRVING LEWIS ALLEN

In historical American English, over one thousand epithets or generic names have been coined and used for persons of about 50 different ethnic groups. All these words, which have accumulated since the Colonial period, may be found in the scholarly records of American slang and dialectal speech. Most of the terms are obsolete or obsolescent, though a few might be heard today. Also, most of the terms are generic of both men and women of an ethnic group; about one-fifth are gender specific, referring either to men or to women.

This study concerns the 96 terms that refer specifically to women of 20 different ethnic groups. Only a few of these words could be construed to be neutral to positive. The frequency distribution of the 96 terms by their targets indicates which particular ethnicities have been most variously, and probably most often, abused with such words. Table 1 lists all the terms as well as their etymologies when these are not self-evident. Some words, chiefly the older terms, are dated for their first appearance in American printed texts. Most of the undated words are probably of late nineteenth- and of twentieth-century origins.

Male Sex Roles, Anxiety, and Slang

Terms of abuse for ethnic women are chiefly a male vocabulary of slang. Historically, slang was generally a male vocabulary, and its social referents have tended to be stressful relations of all kinds (e.g., Flexner, 1975). Ethnic abuse is one of the most frequent social topics in American slang, growing out of ethnic conflict and reflecting the diversity of American society. Much ethnic conflict is the result of economic conflict, especially in male work roles and struggles over status hierarchies. In a similar way, the thousands of derogatory words for women, their bodies, and sexual acts of all kinds reflect the stresses and anxieties of traditional male sex roles. Each vocabulary is preeminently a political vocabulary that seeks to exert social control, maintain privilege, and wield power.

Ethnic slurs in general also parallel the abusive language that men have used against women. Ethnic epithets, as a vocabulary of psychological aggression, share with gender epithets clusters of phonetic elements, such as labial and velar occlusion, whose sound semantics perhaps universally or at least widely connote pejoration (cf. Wescott, 1971; Strainchamps, 1971; Miller & Swift, 1977, p. 109 et passim).

Terms for ethnic women, the intersection of the two vocabularies, spring from the dual anxieties—and subsequent aggressions—fostered by ethnic conflict, on the one hand, and traditional male sex roles with respect to women, on

TABLE 1   Terms in the Study

Ethnic Group	*Terms*
Appalachians	HILLNELLY (modeled on *hillbilly*).
Blacks	AUNT (early 1980s. Also auntie, -y. Used for older women); AUNT-JEMIMA (from a nineteenth-century minstrel song, later reinforced by the "Aunt Jemima" brand of pancake mix); BITCH (probably nineteenth century. Often *black-bitch*); BIT-OF-EBONY (nineteenth century); BLACK-CUNT; BLACK-DOLL; BLACK-MAMA; BROWN-SUGAR (also *sugar-brown*); CHARCOAL-BLOSSOM (also *charcoal-lily*); COAL; CHOCO-LATE-DROP (1912. Also *sweet-chocolate*). COVESS-DINGE (1850. From the feminine form of *cove,* an old slang term for a fellow, and *dinge,* a term for any black person); CULLUD-GAL (a dialectal, later burlesqued, rendering of *colored-girl*); DANGE-BROAD (from the old adjective *dange,* "sexy"); DARK-MEAT (also *piece-of-dark-meat, rare-piece-of-dark-meat; hot-piece-of-dark-meat*); DUSKY-DAME; FEMOKE (probably from *fem* or *femme,* a slang term for a woman, and *moke,* a term for any black person); GIN (originally a prostitute. Perhaps from *gin,* the liquor); HONEY; HOT-CHOCOLATE; INDIAN-PRINCESS; JIT (usually feminine. From *jitney,* a five-cent piece, hence anything of small value); LIZA (late nineteenth century. Also *lize*); LAUNDRY-QUEEN; MAMMY (late nineteenth century. Also *maumer.* Used for older women, especially nursemaids); MANDY (from the given name *Amanda*); MOCHA (usually feminine. Probably from *mocha,* the color and blend of coffee and chocolate); MONKEY-JANE (1920s); NEGRESS; NIGGERESS; NIGGER-GAL; POONTANG (1870s. From Louisiana French, *putain,* "whore"); RAVEN-BEAUTY (a pun); SAPPHIRE (from a supposedly common given name, popularized by a character in the "Amos and Andy" radio and television series); SCUTTLE-SAULT (*scuttle* alludes to coal-scuttle and *sault* is perhaps an old slang term for a woman, as an instance of sexual intercourse. Cf. *pale-sault,* a Black term for a White woman); SEAL (usually feminine); SHADY-LADY (a pun on *shade,* a term for any black person); SAUCER-LIP (also *ubangi*); WENCH (1765. Often *negro-* or *nigger-wench*). WOMAN-OF-COLOR (late eighteenth century. Also lady-of-color).
American Indians	SQUAW (from various Algonquian words for *woman.* Later used for any Native American woman).
Chinese	CHINA WOMAN (1872); CHING-DOLL; FORTUNE-COOKIE; SEGOONYA (origin is not known to me); SLOPIE-GAL (from *slope, slopie,* all from *slope-head,* a term for any Chinese).
Cornish	COUSIN-JENNY (counterpart of masculine *cousin-jack. Cousin-jack* is more often used for the Welsh in the United States).
English	JOAN-BULL (a modern variant of JOHN-BULL).
Eskimos	ESQUAW (perhaps from a variant of Algonquian, *squa,* "woman," hence *squaw,* or a blend of *Eskimo* and *squaw*); ESQUIMUFF (perhaps an alteration of *Eskimo* or Canadian French *Esquimau* or perhaps a blend of *Eskimo* and *muff,*

	which has been a slang term for a woman and for female genitalia, and is the name of a type of fur mitten); SQUAW.
Filipinos	PHILLIPEAN (or *philipeen*. Certainly influenced by sound and spelling of *Phillippine* and *Filipino*. But I conjecture, it is also for the unrelated *philopena, fillipeen, phillipina,* etc., which were all late nineteenth-century altered, Anglicized forms of German *Vielliebchen,* "darling, sweetheart." Possibly originated, in this application, in the Spanish-American War).
French	FROG-LEGS.
Germans	GRETCHEN; FRÄULEIN.
Irish	BRIDGET (Also diminutive *biddy*); GIRLEEN (diminutive of *girl*); PATESS (a feminine form of the generic nickname *pat,* from *Patrick*).
Japanese	CHERRY-BLOSSOM; SKIBBY (1910–1920. Perhaps originally a female prostitute, later applied to any Japanese. Probably from Japanese *sukebei,* "lewdness, lechery." It might have been heard as a salutation of prostitutes and the corruption was applied to them).
Jews	BAGEL-BABY; JEWESS; HEEBESS (a burlesque of *Hebrewess,* another epithet); JAP (acronym for Jewish American Princess); RACHEL; REBECCA; ZAFTIG (or *zoftig.* 1940. From nearly identical German and Yiddish adjectives, meaning "plump, well-rounded, buxom").
Koreans	MOOSE (originally a female prostitute, but later applied to any girl or woman. Probably from Japanese *musume,* "girl"); SLANT-EYE (usually feminine).
Mexicans	HOT-TAMALE (1929); MEXICAN-DISH (1930); SEXY-MEX.
Pacific Islanders	GEE-CHEE (often feminine. Perhaps from either Japanese *geisha,* a female entertainer, or *geechee,* a Bahamian Black person. It is also a generic term for a Eurasian woman); GOONEY-GAL (from *gooney,* a term of uncertain origin for any South Seas Islander, but possibly from the name of the Gooney bird); GRASS-SKIRT (a Hawaiian); HULA-LULA (a Hawaiian); MARY (Pidgin for "woman," originally any female household servant); PINEAPPLE; SQUACK (origin not known to me, but clearly a sound derogation).
Russians	STEPPE-SISTER (a pun on *step-sister* and the Russian *steppes*).
Southerners	REBEL (WWII army slang); SOUTHERN-BELLE (also *belle*).
Welsh	COUSIN-ANN (originally the wife of a Welsh miner working in the United States and the feminine counterpart of *cousin-Jack,* a Welshman).
Whites (used by blacks)	BALE-OF-STRAW (also *straw*); BLONDIE; GOLDEN-GIRL; GREY-BROAD; PALE-SAULT (cf. *scuttle-sault,* a White term for a Black woman); PINKIE, -Y; PINK-TOES; SILK-BROAD (silk is an allusion to finer, straight hair); CHARLENE (a term apparently chosen because it is cognate with *Charlie,* as in *mister-Charlie.* Probably 1960s); MISS-ANNE (1940s. Also *Miss-Annie.* Expressed a sentiment similar to *Charlene*); PEARLS (also *stars*); WHITE-MEAT.

the other. These terms derogate both ethnic and sex roles, each against the other, and they are revealing of the historical quality of these relations.

The Targets and Allusions of the Words

The 96 terms aimed at 20 different ethnic groups are chiefly interracial (73 of 96 terms), and most of the 73 interracial terms are directed at women of racial minorities (61 of 73). Forty terms refer to black women and 12 are black terms for white women. Twenty-one terms for women of other racial minorities refer to Native American, Asian, and Pacific groups. Most terms for Asian and Pacific groups originated in military slang during foreign wars.

Some of the terms are mild. About 10 names derive from stereotypical given names thought common in the group, such as *Liza* for Blacks, *Gretchen* for Germans, *Bridget* for the Irish, and *Rachel* for Jewish women. But many more terms allude to stereotypical physical traits of ethnic groups and deal in sexual insult.

Of the 73 interracial terms, 31 allude to physical differences, mostly of color, but also of hair texture and shape of eyes. Almost all the interracial terms using physical stereotypes (29 of 31) were used between Blacks and Whites. A word may sometimes have multiple allusions, combining perhaps a color reference and gender insult in the same term, such as the puns *raven-beauty*, *shady-lady*, and *white-meat*.

Todasco (1973) shows that the inventory of derogatory words for women trades heavily in animal metaphors and in the identity of female genitalia with women themselves. Words for ethnic women reflect the same themes. At least 20 of the 96 terms are highly derogatory allusions to women's bodies and to stereotypes of their sexuality. Most of the terms display the historical male inclination to depersonalize women as anonymous sex objects.

Some of the words combine bizarre allusions to sexuality and food, such as *brown-sugar*, *dark-meat* (and *white-meat*), *chocolate-drop*, *fortune-cookie*; *honey*, *hot-chocolate*, *frog-legs*, *hot-tamale*, *mexican-dish*, and perhaps *pineapple*. Flexner (1975, pp. xiii–xiv) notes the prominence of food references in American slang and, further, the "subconscious" relating of sex and food, as in *banana*, *cheesecake*, *cherry*, *jelly-roll*, *meal*, *cookie*, *peach*, *quail*, *tomato*. Speculations on the deep meaning of this association might be endless. Suffice to say that slang terms for ethnic women share this trait with American slang generally.

Another trait that terms for ethnic women share both with ethnic epithets and with terms of abuse for women is the use of animal metaphors. These metaphors also overlap with other allusions: *raven-beauty*, *seal*, *monkey-Jane*, *bitch*, *frog-legs*, *moose*, perhaps *gooney-gal*. Also another device connotes animalism. Pejoration is often done or increased with suffixes and modifiers. One morphemic element with an unfavorable connotation is the suffix -ess to make a name gratuitously feminine, such as *heebess*, *jewess*, *negress*, *niggeress*, and *patess*. This device, which is otherwise used to feminize words for roles that are normatively male, also suggests an animal metaphor, for the same suffix is used to feminize the names of feline species of animals, such as *lioness* and *tigress*.

Another order of words, in addition to those listed in Table 1, includes several that were used for racially mixed women, mostly women of Black-and-White parentage. One of the oldest terms is *métisse,* the feminine of Louisiana French *métis,* "mongrel, half-breed," which was a loanward in American English in the 1790s. *Mulatress,* in this feminine form, appeared at the beginning of the nineteenth century (from *mulatto,* ultimately from Portuguese and Spanish *mulato,* diminutive of *mulo,* "mule").

Conclusions

Epithets for ethnic women in historical American English are the intersection of the huge inventories of ethnic slurs, on the one hand, and abusive terms for women, on the other. All are chiefly male slang. When gender and ethnic insult combine, the words are disproportionately aimed at women of ethnic minorities, stereotype physical differences between groups, and make derogatory sexual allusions, often using food and animal metaphors.

REFERENCES

Flexner, S. B. Preface. In H. W. Wentworth & S. B. Flexner (Eds.), *Dictionary of American slang* (2nd suppl. ed.). New York: Crowell, 1975, Pp. vi-xv.

Miller, C., & Swift, K. *Words and women.* Garden City, N.Y.: Doubleday/Anchor, 1977.

Strainchamps, E. Our sexist language. In V. Gornick & B. K. Moran (Eds.), *Woman in sexist society.* New York: Basic Books, 1971, Pp. 240–250.

Todasco, R. (Ed.). *An intelligent woman's guide to dirty words. Volume one of the Feminist English Dictionary.* Chicago: Feminist English Dictionary, 1973.

Wescott, R. W. Labio-velarity and derogation in English: A study in phonosemic correlation. *American Speech,* 1971, *46,* 123–137.

Some Words Referring to Women and Prostitutes as Food

Apples	Breasts
Cake	Vagina
Cabbage	Vulva
Cauliflower	Vagina
Cheesecake	Sexually attractive young woman
Cherry	Attractive young woman; virgin; hymen
Cherries	Nipples
Cherry pie	Attractive young woman
Cookie	Vagina
Crumpet	Vagina; sexually available woman
Dish	Sexually attractive woman
Dumplings	Breasts
Honey pot	Vagina
Lemons	Breasts
Meat	Sexual intercourse; prostitute; vagina
Beefsteak	Prostitute
Beef buyer	Brothel customer
Fresh pink	New prostitute
Hot meat/beef	Fast or loose woman; prostitute; vagina
Meat house	Brothel
Meat market	Rendezvous of prostitutes; vagina; beauty contest
Meat merchant	Procuress
Meat salesman	Pimp
Meatball	Brothel customer
Pig meat	Prostitute
Melons	Large breasts
Muffins	Breasts
Mutton	Prostitute
Hot mutton	Sexually promiscuous woman; prostitute; vagina
Mutton-shunters	Police who keep street prostitutes moving along
Peaches	Breasts
Rib	Woman
Rib joint	Brothel
Spare rib	Woman; vagina
Strawberries	Nipples
Sweet potato pie	Vagina
Tart	Sexually promiscuous woman; prostitute
Tenderloin	Area with many brothels

—Sources: *Womanwords: A Dictionary of Words About Women,*1993; *Sexual Slang,* 1993; *The Lively Commerce: Prostitution in the United States,* 1971

I Was a Piece of Meat

I've done one picture, the cannibal picture, where I was a piece of meat being washed by two men. . . . I was just supposed to lay there and be unconscious, with them washing me as they're talking over the different parts of the body and what this meat is like and how it tastes.

　　—Pornography actress, quoted in *Porn: Myths for the Twentieth Century*, 1991

Some Words Referring to Women and Prostitutes as Animals

Beaver	Vagina
Bitch	Woman; prostitute; nasty person
Bunny	Sexy woman
Cathouse	Brothel
Cat	Prostitute
Chick	Young woman
Corral	Group of prostitutes working for the same pimp or madam
Cow	Ugly, old, or overweight woman
Dog	Ugly woman
Filly	Young woman
Fish	Vagina
To go fishing	Seek a prostitute; have sex
Fish market	Brothel
Fox	Sexually attractive woman
Foxy	Sexy
Fur	Female pubic hair
Hare	Prostitute
Heifer	An overweight woman
Hen	Woman
Moose	Prostitute; woman or girl
Nag	Prostitute; old woman
Oyster	Vagina
Pony girl	Call girl
Pussy	Vagina; sex
Selling pussy	Selling sex
Race track	Hotel area where prostitutes solicit customers
Ranch	Brothel
Chicken ranch	Brothel
Pigeon house	Brothel
Riding academy	Brothel
Shrew	A scolding, bad-tempered woman
Stable	Group of prostitutes working for the same pimp or madam
Stock	Young prostitutes
Fresh stock	Girls under the age of 15
Thoroughbred	Skilled prostitute
Vixen	Sexually aggressive woman
Wolves' den	Brothel
Zoo	Brothel

—Sources: *Womanwords,*1993; *Sexual Slang,* 1993; *Sex Roles,* 1984; *Love Locked Out,* 1963; *Bottom Feeders,* 1992; *New York Times,* May 11, 1994, and August 19, 2001; *The Lively Commerce,* 1971

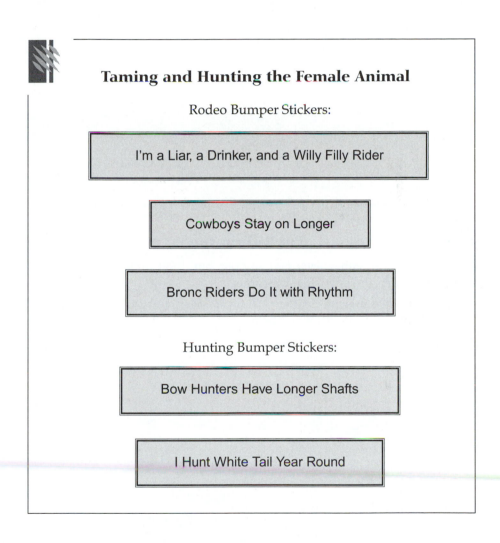

Taming and Hunting the Female Animal

Rodeo Bumper Stickers:

I'm a Liar, a Drinker, and a Willy Filly Rider

Cowboys Stay on Longer

Bronc Riders Do It with Rhythm

Hunting Bumper Stickers:

Bow Hunters Have Longer Shafts

I Hunt White Tail Year Round

I'm Riding You

I'm riding you with a slack rein, my pet, but don't forget that I'm riding with curb and spurs just the same.

—Rhett Butler to Scarlet O'Hara, in Margaret Mitchell's classic book *Gone with the Wind*, 1936

Stories of the Hunt

Man is the hunter; woman is his game;
The sleek and shining creatures of the chase,
We hunt them for the beauty of their skins;
They love us for it, and we ride them down.

> —Alfred Lord Tennyson, 1847, from his poem *The Princess*

I love to hunt. Prowling the streets looking for fair game—tasty meat. . . . I live for the hunt.

> —David Berkowitz, April 17, 1977, the "Son of Sam" serial killer who preyed on young women, initially using a hunting knife and later a gun

I am basically, as a male, a predator and all women look . . . like prey. I fantasize about the expression on a woman's face when I "capture" her and she realizes she cannot escape. It's like I won, I own her.

> —Rapist cited in *The Hite Report on Male Sexuality*, 1981

You know how you drag a deer by the horns or the neck, that's how I dragged her.

> —Stephen Francis Kuber, III, describing how he raped Kimberly Jaye Decker and slit her throat with a knife on July 30, 1990

Rape: Originally a Property Crime

Rape entered the law through the back door, as it were, as a property crime of man against man. Woman, of course, was viewed as the property. . . .

A female was allowed no independent status under Babylonian law. She was either a betrothed virgin, living in the house of her father, or else she was somebody's lawfully wedded wife and lived in the house of her husband. . . .

When Moses received his tablets from God on the top of Mount Sinai, "Thou shalt not rape" was conspicuously missing from the Ten Commandments, although Moses received a distinct commandment against adultery and another, for good measure, against the coveting of thy neighbor's wife, bracketed this second time around with thy neighbor's house, his field, his servant, ox and ass.

—Susan Brownmiller, *Against Our Will: Men, Women and Rape*, 1975

Every 13 Seconds

When women report being raped, physically assaulted, or stalked, nearly two thirds of the time the perpetrator is a current or former husband, partner, boyfriend, or date. In some hospitals, as many as one in three emergency room visits by women are the result of partner violence.

Averaging over time, an American woman is raped or physically assaulted by a partner or ex-partner once every 13 seconds. This means there is a high likelihood that in the time it took to read this page, a woman somewhere in the United States was just raped or assaulted by a current or former partner.

—Sources: *Full Report of the Prevalence, Incidence, and Consequences of Violence Against Women,* 2000; *Women at Risk,* 1996; *Behavioral Medicine,* 1997

DETECTING AND LABELING PREJUDICE: DO FEMALE PERPETRATORS GO UNDETECTED?

ROBERT S. BARON, MARY L. BURGESS,
AND CHUAN FENG KAO

Detecting prejudiced behavior is a neglected, but crucially important, research topic. Noticing and correctly categorizing prejudiced action is a key condition for changing such behavior. This is true regardless of whether the change is to occur through self-monitoring, social pressure, or legal procedures. Indeed, the failure to notice and/or rebut prejudiced behavior, when it occurs, often provides tacit support for prejudiced activity. Silence in such cases all too often implies agreement and complicity.

This article explores the possibility that prejudice is more likely to be detected when it is initiated by an expected than by an unexpected source. More specifically, this study examines the inferences individuals make when they observe gender bias against women committed either by a male or by a female. In this particular case, the prediction is that subjects will be less likely to categorize an action as an instance of sexism if it is initiated by a woman than by a man. This hypothesis can be derived from several theoretical perspectives.

If one assumes that males are stereotypically viewed as perpetrators of sexism while women are stereotypically viewed as victims, there is a good deal of evidence in the social cognition literature suggesting that this stereotype might have a self-fulfilling impact on perception of prejudice. Snyder (1981) reviewed a number of studies that suggest that an individual who adopts stereotyped beliefs about a target person will remember (e.g., Cohen, 1981) and interpret (e.g., Duncan, 1976) events about the target person in a way that will bolster and support the current stereotyped beliefs. For example, studies by Duncan (1976) and Sagar and Schofield (1980) indicate that the racial status of actors* affects the extent to which their action is viewed as hostile. These studies indicated that Black actors are generally rated as more aggressive than White actors given the same behavioral episode. Apparently, in these studies, racial stereotypes of Black actors lowered subjects' "threshold for labeling an act as violent" (Duncan, 1976, p. 596).

A related idea is that detection of prejudice might be influenced by subjects' expectations concerning in-group/out-group bias. Specifically, individuals may have strong expectations that members of a given gender category are unlikely to discriminate against other in-group members (at least on the basis of category membership). Any such expectations might also distort in-

---

*Editor's note: As used here, the term "actor" refers to a person who commits an act of behavior in a given setting; it does not refer to someone engaged in a theatrical performance.

terpretation and memory such that biased action from an unexpected source is unlikely to be labeled as discrimination.

In short, there are a number of conceptual reasons to predict that biased action from an unexpected source might be less likely to be labeled as such than similar behavior from an expected source. Although several of these explanations involve the assumption that base rate expectancies will bias judgment, the present study does not attempt to differentiate among such views by manipulating the presence or absence of such expectancies. Rather, it examines only the empirical validity of the key prediction—that is, that people are more likely to label acts discriminating against women as sexist if the acts corroborate their cultural expectations regarding the gender of the victim and perpetrator. This bias can have several important implications, not least of which is that witnesses, perpetrators, and even victims of sexist behavior may be less likely to recognize the prejudiced nature of such activity if it comes from an unexpected source.

An additional issue concerns the impact of subject gender. By using both male and female subjects, the authors were able to assess whether one gender is more likely than the other to interpret a given act as sexist. We expected that women would be more likely than men to readily recognize and label prejudiced behavior as sexist.

Method

Subjects

One hundred ninety-six students (105 females, 91 males) enrolled in an introductory psychology class at the University of Iowa volunteered to participate as one option for fulfilling a course requirement.

Procedure

The 196 subjects were told they were participating in a study involving how people react to differing communication styles. Two experimenters, one male and one female, administered the materials. Subjects were informed that they would read a series of different social encounters involving conversations between friends, acquaintances, and people at work and then rate the communication style of one of the individuals involved. Each subject received one of two forms of a booklet containing a series of 19 vignettes, 12 of which described a male or female perpetrator acting in a manner that could be interpreted as "sexist" toward a woman. The remaining 7 episodes described an interaction between two or more persons. These filler items did not involve biases toward either gender.

Stimulus Materials

As noted, 12 of the 19 vignettes described a perpetrator exhibiting sexist behavior toward a female. Of these critical vignettes, 6 described a female perpetrator and 6 described a male perpetrator. Though identical in content, vignette book-lets were presented in one of two forms to counterbalance the gender of the per-petrator for each of the 12 critical vignettes. For example, in Form 1, Vignette 1 described the actions of a male perpetrator, and in Form 2, the same actions were attributed to a female perpetrator.

The critical vignettes described actions commonly classified as demeaning to women. These items were developed on the basis of work with discussion groups and approximately 100 individual pilot subjects. In these vignettes, per-petrators react to and characterize women on the basis of stereotypes and tradi-tional sex roles. The vignettes described such things as women being expected to prepare food, a woman asked not to drive her own automobile in the snow, a woman being blamed for an unexpected pregnancy, women ignored as deci-sion makers, and a woman counseled to drop her premedical courses and trans-fer into nursing. An example of a sexist vignette follows, with the main actor's/actress's name in all capital letters (as in the actual booklets).

> *Sexist vignette:* Janice was 10 minutes early for her interview at Midwest-ern Unified Industries but was still second in line. She was applying for a position as yard jockey, one of the higher-paying hourly jobs. The yard jockey moved the large tractor trailer rigs in and out of loading bays as needed. The personnel officer, KEN (JILL) BANES, was 15 minutes late, and Janice had been waiting for close to an hour when she was finally called. After introductions, Ken (Jill) Banes examined Janice's résumé and said, "Why do you want this particular job, Janice?"
>
> Janice was amazed enough to be direct with her answer. "I'm sick of assembly line work. I really prefer to be outdoors. Second, jockeying rigs is challenging and I like that."
>
> Ken (Jill) Banes looked troubled. "I don't see here that you really have the relevant experience. This is a tough job. It takes a high level of skill and a good deal of strength."
>
> Janice wasn't worried. "I know I've never worked exactly moving rigs around a yard, but my first husband and I were codrivers for 6 years. We had our own rig. My dad was a trucker. I've been driving tractor trailers since I was seventeen, and I'm good. I can easily handle this job. No sweat."
>
> "I'm not so sure," answered Mr. (Ms.) Banes. "We have never had a woman in this position before."
>
> "Well, you probably never had a woman apply who had the qualifi-cations that I have."
>
> "That sounds fine, Janice, but it's my problem if I hire you and you aren't up to the position. This is a pressure job, a skill and strength job. I have a lot of people dying to try it because of the pay and the status. It's no skin off their noses if they try and then can't cut it, but it's the company's equip-ment that gets wrecked and the company's profits that are hurt if the yard jock can't come through and handle the pace. Also, it's my reputation that suffers if I make a bad choice. I'll be frank. Because of the pressure, I've al-ways viewed this as a man's job, and I still pretty much do. For right now,

I'm going to go on interviewing because I really doubt that you're going to be the best-qualified applicant that I can find. Lots of people can back up a semi, and I'm sure that you can, too. But not too many can handle the steady pressure involved in being a yard jockey for us. That's why the pay is so high. But don't worry. I'll definitely call you in for a road test if you prove to be my best applicant. Thanks for coming in."

Janice stood with a tired look on her face. "My pleasure. I just love job interviews," she said, and walked out.

The seven filler vignettes described interpersonal situations in which the main character did not act biased toward either gender. On the average, the fillers were the same length as the sexist vignettes. In the filler vignettes, all subjects read the same material and the gender of the main character was held constant. An example of a filler vignette is given below, with the main character's name capitalized.

> *Filler vignette:* JERRY and Ted are working together on an important project at work. Two days before the deadline, Ted fails to come to work and cannot be reached on the phone. At 4:30 he arrives at the office drunk and loud. He sees Jerry and says, "Here's old workaholic Jerry—Old Reliable—busting his hump as usual—how's it going, bean brain?" Jerry replies, "I don't appreciate that kind of talk, Ted. Can't you please hold it down? I have a lot of work to do." Ted says, "You're a jerk, you know that?" Jerry replies, "If you can't be polite, I'm just going to ignore you. Now please leave me alone."

Response Scale

After reading each vignette, subjects were asked, "In your opinion, what are the strongest qualities or traits exhibited by the actor/actress in this episode?" Subjects were asked to list at least two traits and to limit themselves to three traits. The actor/actress was always designated as the person whose name was spelled in all capital letters. This open-ended question was followed by three lines. A 7-point scale appeared under each of the three lines, allowing the subject to indicate the strength of each trait he or she identified (1 = *slightly displayed*, 7 = *extremely displayed*). This open-ended response format was used to minimize the strong experimental demand that would have resulted from employing a trait-rating index that included "How sexist" as a target trait. The seven filler items were used to further minimize such problems of demand.

Results

Interrater Reliability

The use of an open-ended response scale required that subject responses be coded in terms of whether they indicated sexist behavior on the part of the perpetrators. Two independent raters were instructed, "Based on your own personal experience, indicate those responses where you think the subject perceives the actor/actress as behaving in a sexist manner."[1] For the most part, those responses coded as sexist were obvious ones (e.g., *prejudiced, sexist, bigot, traditional*). Moreover, a reliability check on 30 randomly selected questionnaires indicated that coders generally agreed on what was considered sexist. Interrater agreement, correcting for chance agreement, was 86%.

Analyses

As noted, each booklet contained 7 filler and 12 critical vignettes. To assess the major hypothesis, an analysis procedure that held item content constant was employed. The 12 critical vignettes were divided into two groups: One block of 6 vignettes was composed of those items involving a male perpetrator, and the other block of 6 vignettes described all female perpetrators. Note, however, that the items in these "gender blocks" were not presented consecutively in the stimulus booklet. We analyzed the data in such a way that subjects who received Form 1 of the booklet had as their first gender block the 6 critical vignettes that involved a female perpetrator. The second block consisted of the 6 critical vignettes that involved a male perpetrator. Likewise, subjects receiving Form 2 of the booklet had their data analyzed in such a way that the first gender block contained the same content as the vignettes in Block 1 in Form 1, but the perpetrators were males. Organizing the results in this manner provided two replications of our basic design.

Frequency Data: Number of Vignettes Called "Sexist" A key dependent measure is the number of subjects who perceived sexist behavior in the critical vignettes. If a subject offered two sexist responses on a given vignette, they were counted as only one response, because the two responses characterized the same perpetrator. In short, the maximum score possible in each block was 6. Such a score would indicate that a subject's responses were coded as indicating awareness of gender bias on the part of the perpetrator in each of the six vignettes making up that gender block. The means are presented in Table 1. As expected, both male and female subjects were more likely to label a critical

TABLE 1   Mean Number of Sexist Vignettes Identified as Sexist as a Function of Subject Gender and Perpetrator Gender

	Replication 1 Perpetrator Gender		Replication 2 Perpetrator Gender	
	Male	*Female*	*Male*	*Female*
Male subjects	3.40 (42)	1.06 (49)	3.20 (49)	2.60 (42)
Female subjects	3.25 (52)	1.57 (53)	3.83 (53)	2.58 (52)
All subjects	3.32 (94)	1.32 (102)	3.53 (102)	2.59 (94)

Note: Means could range from 0 to 6. Numbers in parentheses indicate number of subjects per condition.
Editor's note: Replication 1 and Replication 2 refer to separate analyses of data collected with Form 1 and Form 2, which reversed the gender of perpetrators. In both replications, males were more likely than females to be viewed as sexist (averaging 3.32 versus 1.32 in Replication 1, and 3.53 versus 2.59 in Replication 2).

vignette as sexist if the perpetrator was male rather than female. Furthermore, there was no main effect for subject gender.

Intensity Data of "Sexist" Responses   The intensity scores were intended to reflect subjects' perceptions regarding the strength of sexist behavior. These scores were based on subjects' responses to a 7-point scale asking them to indicate how strongly a given trait was displayed. The intensity score reflected the subjects' response on this scale averaged over only those items on which they indicated the perpetrators' behavior was sexist.[2]

In this analysis, female subjects, compared with male subjects, gave more intense ratings to both male and female perpetrators when sexist behavior was detected. Furthermore, male perpetrators were seen as displaying more intense gender bias than female perpetrators. These results can be seen in Figure 1.

Intensity Ratings on Filler Items   To rule out the possibility that the higher intensity scores of women in rating sexist behavior merely reflected a tendency to give higher intensity scores in general, the intensity data for filler items were analyzed. Recall that the gender of the protagonist in the filler vignettes was held constant across forms. This analysis showed no significant effects for subject gender.

Discussion

The results clearly support the key predictions. The frequency data indicated that our subjects were more likely to label an action as sexist if the scenario corroborated cultural expectations regarding the gender of victims and perpetrators. Moreover, this effect was substantial. On the average, subjects were 8 times as

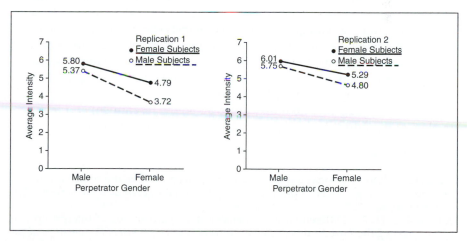

FIGURE 1
Average intensities of displayed sexist behavior (1=slightly displayed, 7=extremely displayed) seen in male and female perpetrators by male and female subjects.

likely to label an action as sexist when presented with a male perpetrator as when presented with a female one.[3] This effect was observed across both men and women. Consequently, these data do not appear to merely reflect some form of differential anti-male resentment on the part of our female subjects. The gender of the perpetrator also affected the intensity of the subjects' judgments. Both male and female subjects judged male perpetrators to display more extreme sexism than female perpetrators who were emitting the very same behavior.

The second prediction, that women would be more extreme in their ratings, was partially confirmed. Although men and women did not differ on the number of vignettes they identified as sexist, women did give higher intensity ratings to those sexist actions they did identify. In other words, women perceived the perpetrators of acts they categorized as sexist as displaying a greater degree of sexist behavior than men perceived. Moreover, this tendency of women to offer higher intensity ratings did not occur on filler items. These findings provide some evidence for the notion that women are more sensitive to potentially sexist material.

Note that we carefully camouflaged the purpose of the study in order to minimize experimental demand. If subjects had believed the study was one focusing on sexism, one could argue that the results were atypical or artifactual. For example, college students might have expressed atypically high awareness of and concern over gender prejudice if they had recognized the focus of the study. For this reason, we intentionally used a cover story, a set of instructions, and an open-ended response format that never mentioned sexism (or any other form of prejudice) as a likely or appropriate response. In addition, we included filler items having no obvious sexist content in order to further disguise the main focus of the research.

Aside from conceptual issues, the data have important pragmatic implications. Both men and women seem more likely to label a discriminating act against a woman as sexist when it is perpetrated by a male. This finding suggests that a good many prejudiced actions against women will go undetected and, therefore, will remain uncorrected if women themselves are the agents of bias. These data also raise the possibility that males, more than females, will be incorrectly perceived to have sexist intent in an ambiguous setting where nonsexist motives might be operative. Men, far more than women, need to exercise care in what they say and do if they are to avoid the resentment and interpersonal friction produced when gender bias is assumed or suspected.

REFERENCES

Cohen, C. E. (1981). Person categories and social perception: Testing some boundaries of the processing effects of prior knowledge. *Journal of Personality and Social Psychology, 40,* 441–452.

Duncan, B. L. (1976). Differential social perception and attribution of Intergroup violence: Testing the lower limits of stereotyping of blacks. *Journal of Personality and Social Psychology, 34,* 590–598.

Sagar, H. A., & Schofield, J. W. (1980). Racial and behavioral cues in black and white children's perceptions of ambiguously aggressive acts. *Journal of Personality and Social Psychology, 39,* 590–598.

Snyder, M. (1981). On the self-perpetuating nature of social stereotypes. In D. L. Hamilton (Ed.), *Cognitive processes in stereotyping and intergroup behavior* (pp. 183–212). Hillsdale, NJ: Lawrence Erlbaum.

NOTES

1. Note that whether or not these subjects' one-word responses implied that the subject perceived the perpetrator to be sexist could be inferred only if one considered the content of each vignette. For example, the response "prejudiced" would not imply "sexist" if it were used to characterize a Republican perpetrator who vilified a Democrat. But when a perpetrator vilified a female job applicant because of her gender, describing that perpetrator as "prejudiced," "biased," or "narrow-minded" strongly implies awareness of gender prejudice. Because vignette context was important in determining the meaning of subjects' responses, raters read each vignette before coding these responses. However, coders were kept blind to the gender of the subject and the perpetrator. This was accomplished by covering the vignette text in each subject's questionnaire booklet with a piece of paper and having the coder read the content from a master copy. As a result, there is no way in which coder expectations could have affected the treatment differences presented in the text.

2. The intensity ratings presented in the text average the strength of sexist responses only over those items where a sexist response was coded. One can also average these scores over all six sexist vignettes presented in each replication by entering zeros as the strength scores for those vignettes where no sexist response was coded. This form of analysis yields the same pattern of significant differences reported in the text.

3. This number was derived by computing ratios comparing the number of subjects offering a sexist interpretation to a given vignette when the perpetrator was male versus female. These ratios were then averaged across the 12 vignettes.

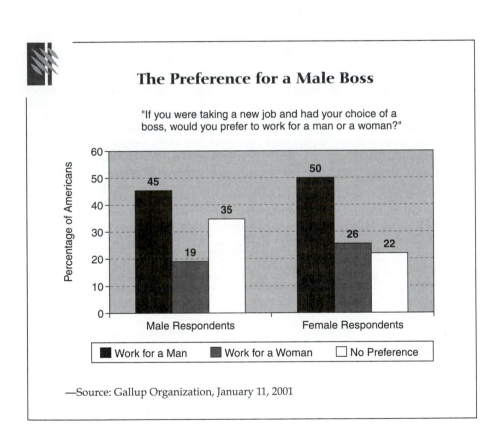

The Preference for a Male Boss

"If you were taking a new job and had your choice of a boss, would you prefer to work for a man or a woman?"

—Source: Gallup Organization, January 11, 2001

On the Feminist Movement

In the last 25 years, we've convinced ourselves and a majority of the country that women can do what men can do. Now we have to convince the majority of the country—and ourselves—that men can do what women can do. If we don't, the double burden of working inside and outside the home—always a reality for poor women, and now one for middle-class women, too—will continue to be the problem most shared by American women nationwide. Let's face it: until men are fully equal inside the home, women will never really be equal outside it.

For the last 25 years, we've fought for equal pay, pensions, and benefits—to equalize the amount of money we earn—all of which must continue. For the next 25 years, however, we need to add a focus on how we spend. Are we spending more on our outsides (clothing and appearance) than our insides (health and learning)? Are we tithing to patriarchal religions but not to feminist groups? Supporting women-owned businesses? In other words, are we using our dollars as consciously as we would our votes?

—Adapted from Gloria Steinem, *Ms.*, September/October, 1997

VI

Anti–Semitism

 One of the least helpful ways of understanding the Holocaust is to regard the destruction process as the work of a small group of irresponsible criminals who were atypical of normal statesmen and who somehow gained control of the German people, forcing them by terror and the deliberate stimulation of religious and ethnic hatred to pursue a barbaric and retrograde policy that was thoroughly at odds with the great traditions of Western civilization. On the contrary, we are more likely to understand the Holocaust *if we regard it as the expression of some of the most profound tendencies of Western civilization in the twentieth century.*

—Richard L. Rubenstein, *The Cunning of History: Mass Death and the American Future,* 1975

VI

SECTION OVERVIEW

Although Adolf Hitler was the central figure of the Holocaust, his campaign against the Jews would not have been possible without the active participation of thousands of people and the passive indifference of millions more. This section examines anti-Semitism with special attention to America's role in the Holocaust.

The Holocaust was centuries in the making, and as the material in this section shows, Germany used language and imagery to dehumanize Jews in much the same way that White Southerners used it to dehumanize Black slaves. For example, Jews were often described as animals, and in some cases, Jewish prisoners were requisitioned as "war supplies" for medical experiments. In fact, Hitler explicitly cited America's racial practices as precedents for Nazi policies toward the Jews, and he was emboldened by the anti-Semitism he saw in America, Europe, and elsewhere. Postwar investigations also found that several countries knew of Hitler's plans early on and were silent or even benefited financially from the plundering of Jewish property.

Since the days of World War II, American anti-Semitism has greatly diminished. As the last reading in this section shows, however, more than a thousand anti-Semitic incidents still occur each year in the United States.

Take Special Notice

This section includes a comparison of 1940s German public opinion toward Jews with White American public opinion toward Blacks. Such cross-cultural comparisons can be instructive as long as their limitations are kept in mind (for example, German citizens at that time may not have felt as free as Americans to express their views).

Questions Worth Pondering

- If you had been a fly on the wall of Nazi Germany, what would you have seen?
- How did the daily routine of German citizens in the early 1940s compare with the daily routine of most Americans today?
- Is a high degree of prejudice among citizens necessary for a Holocaust to occur?
- Why isn't the relationship between Hitler and Henry Ford common knowledge?
- How does America's response to the Holocaust compare with its response to the Rwandan genocide 50 years later?

The Holocaust: Centuries in the Making

Thirteenth Century

The "Jew hat," shaped like a cone or a funnel, and the yellow Jewish badge, shaped like a ring or a wheel, were officially mandated in Germany during the 13th century. . . .

There were exact specifications for the yellow badge: it had to be two fingers' breadths wide and four fingers' breadths long, and it had to be worn on the outer garment.

The purpose of these identifying marks was to set the Jews apart from the non-Jews. All male Jews twelve years of age and older were obliged to wear them.

—Gertrude Hirschler, *Ashkenaz: The German Jewish Heritage,* 1988

Twentieth Century

At the height of fighting in Poland, in September 1939, local German military and civilian authorities [ordered Jews] to wear a yellow badge on the left side of their breast, bearing the inscription *Jude*. . . . As of December 1, 1939, all "Jews and Jewesses" over the age of twelve living in [occupied Poland had] to wear, on the right sleeve of their jacket or dress and on their overcoat, a white band at least 4 inches (10 cm) in width, with a blue Star of David inscribed on it.

—*Encyclopedia of the Holocaust,* 1990 (entry for "Badge, Jewish")

Five Centuries Before Hitler

We decree and order that from now on, and for all time, Christians shall not eat or drink with Jews, nor admit them to feasts, nor cohabit with them, nor bathe with them. Christians shall not allow Jews to hold civil honors over Christians, or to exercise public offices in the state.

—Pope Eugenius IV, 1442

Four Centuries Before Hitler

Be on your guard against the Jews, knowing that wherever they have their synagogues, nothing is found but a den of devils in which sheer self-glory, conceit, lies, blasphemy, and defaming of God and men are practiced most maliciously. . . .

I shall give you my sincere advice: First, to set fire to their synagogues or schools and to bury and cover with dirt whatever will not burn. . . . Second, I advise that their houses also be razed and destroyed. . . . Third, I advise that all their prayer books and Talmudic writings, in which such idolatry, lies, cursing, and blasphemy are taught, be taken from them. Fourth, I advise that their rabbis be forbidden to teach henceforth on pain of loss of life and limb. . . . Fifth, I advise that safe-conduct on the highways be abolished completely for the Jews. . . . Sixth, I advise that usury be prohibited to them, and that all cash and treasure of silver and gold be taken from them. . . .

If we wish to wash our hands of the Jews' blasphemy and not share in their guilt, we have to part company with them. They must be driven from our country.

> —Martin Luther, German founder of Lutheran Christianity (the largest Protestant denomination in the world), *On the Jews and Their Lies,* 1543

Three Centuries Before Hitler

Jews who are to be found in this our kingdom will be required, on pain of death and the confiscation of all their property, to depart and to withdraw from the same, at once and within the time and term of a month.

—Parliament of Paris, 1615

Two Centuries Before Hitler

Our loyal subjects can expect nothing but evil from the haters of our Savior Christ. We therefore order the deportation abroad of all Jews, male and female, together with their property. In the future only those Jews shall be permitted to enter the country who will consent to embrace the Greek Orthodox faith.

> —Empress Elizabeth Petrovna of Russia, *The Ukase on Zhids,* December 2, 1742 [*Note:* A *Ukase* is a proclamation or imperial order; *Zhid* is a derogatory term for "Jew."]

A Century Before Hitler

What is the secular cult of the Jew? Haggling. What is his secular god? Money. Money is the jealous god of Israel before whom no other god may stand.

> —Karl Marx, German political philosopher, in his essay "On the Jewish Question," 1844

Decades Before Hitler

Owing to their obstinacy and their failure to believe, [Jews] have become *dogs*. . . . We have today in Rome unfortunately too many of these dogs, and we hear them barking in all the streets, and going around molesting people everywhere.

> —Pope Pius IX, speaking to a Catholic women's group, 1871
> [*Note:* On September 3, 2000, Pope John Paul II beatified Pope Pius IX, placing him one step from sainthood.]

Greetings to Hitler from the New Pope

To the Illustrious Herr Adolf Hitler, Führer and Chancellor of the German Reich! Here at the beginning of Our Pontificate We wish to assure you that We remain devoted to the spiritual welfare of the German people entrusted to your leadership. . . . During the many years we spent in Germany, We did all in Our power to establish harmonious relations between Church and State. Now that the responsibilities of Our pastoral function have increased Our opportunities, how much more ardently do We pray to reach that goal. May the prosperity of the German people and their progress in every domain come, with God's help, to fruition!

—From a letter drafted by Pope Pius XII to Adolf Hitler shortly after the Pope was elected, March, 1939

THE DESTRUCTION
OF THE EUROPEAN JEWS:
DEHUMANIZATION AND CONCEALMENT

RAUL HILBERG

Since Auschwitz was a receiving station, always on call, it was necessary to have a dependable gas supply.* The enterprises that furnished it specialized in large-scale fumigations of buildings, barracks, and ships; disinfected clothes in specially constructed gas chambers; and deloused human beings, protected by gas masks.[1] In short, this industry used very powerful gases to exterminate rodents and insects in enclosed spaces. That it should have become involved in an operation to kill off Jews by the hundreds of thousands is no mere accident. In German propaganda, Jews had frequently been portrayed as insects.

A number of Nazis, including the chief of the German SS and Police Himmler, the Generalgouverneur of Poland Hans Frank, and Justice Minister Thierack, inclined to the view that Jews were a lower species of life, a kind of vermin, which upon contact infected the German people with deadly diseases. Himmler once cautioned his SS generals not to tolerate the stealing of property that had belonged to dead Jews. "Just because we exterminated a bacterium," he said, "we do not want, in the end, to be infected by that bacterium and die of it."[2] Frank frequently referred to the Jews as "lice." When the Jews in his Polish domain were killed, he announced that now a sick Europe would become healthy again.[3]

The commanders of the mobile killing units attempted to cope systematically with the psychological effects of the killing operations. Even while they directed the shooting, they began to repress as well as to justify their activities. The repressive mechanism is quite noticeable in the choice of language for reports of individual killing actions. The reporters tried to avoid the use of direct expressions such as "to kill" or "murder." Instead, the commanders employed terms that tended either to justify the killings or to obscure them altogether. The following is a representative list:

liquidiert: liquidated
erledigt: finished (off)
Aktionen: actions
Sonderaktionen: special actions
sonderbehandelt: specially treated
Säuberung: cleansing

Editor's note: Auschwitz, located in Oswiecim, Poland, was the largest Nazi concentration camp. It included more than 40 subcamps, including Birkenau, where gas chambers were used to kill untold numbers of people.

Ausschaltung: elimination
Aussiedlung: resettlement
Vollzugstätigkeit: execution activity
Exekutivmassnahme: executive measure
entsprechend behandelt: treated appropriately
der Sondermassnahme zugeführt: conveyed to special measure
Lösung der Judenfrage: solution of the Jewish question
judenfrei gemacht: (area) made free of Jews

The most important and possibly the most misleading term used for the killing centers collectively was the "East." This phrase was employed again and again during the deportations. When reference to an individual death camp was necessary, the term used was *Arbeitslager* (labor camp) or *Konzentrationslager* (concentration camp). Birkenau, the Auschwitz killing site, was called *Kriegsgefangenenlager* (PW camp) in accordance with its originally intended purpose.[4]

The gas chamber and crematorium units in Auschwitz were known as *Spezialeinrichtungen* (special installations), *Badeanstalten* (bath houses), and *Leichenkeller* (corpse cellars).[5] The diesel engine operated in Belzec was located in a shack called the "Hackenholt Foundation." The primary term for the killing operation itself was the same that had been employed for killings in Russia—*Sonderbehandlung* (special treatment).

🍂　🍂　🍂

Among the closest participants, it was considered bad form to talk about the killings. This is what Himmler had to say on the subject in his speech of October 4, 1943:

> I want to mention here very candidly a particularly difficult chapter. Among us it should be mentioned once, quite openly, but in public we will never talk about it. . . . It was with us, thank God, an inborn gift of tactfulness, that we have never conversed about this matter, never spoken about it. Every one of us was horrified, and yet every one of us knew that we would do it again if it were ordered and if it were necessary. I am referring to the evacuation of the Jews, to the extermination of the Jewish people.[6]

This then was the reason why that particular "page of glory" was never to be written. There are some things that can be done only so long as they are not discussed.

We know, of course, that among those who were not quite so close to the killing operations the sensations of the destructive process were irresistible. The rumor network was spread all over Axis Europe. One Foreign Office official stationed in Rome mentions that he discussed details of the killings with at least thirty of his colleagues.[7] But the urge to talk was not so deep in men who were heavily involved in the destructive process. Höss, the Auschwitz commander, says that he never spoke about his job even to his wife. She found out about what he was doing because of an inadvertent remark by a family friend, Gauleiter Bracht.[8] The Treblinka guard Hirtreiter never spoke of his task at all.[9]

The final stage in the process of repression was to omit mention of "killings" or "killing installations" even in the secret correspondence in which such operations had to be reported. The reader of these reports is immediately struck by their camouflaged vocabulary: *Endlosüng der Judenfrage* ("final solution of the Jewish question"), *Lösungsmöglichkeiten* ("solution possibilities"), *Sonderbehandlung* or *SB* ("special treatment"), *Evakuierung* ("evacuation"), *Aussiedlung* (same), *Umsiedlung* (same), *Spezialeinrichtungen* ("special installations"), *durchgeschleusst* ("dragged through"), and many others.

NOTES

1. Lectures by Dr. Gerhard Peters and Heinrich Sossenheimer (gas experts), February 27, 1942, NI-9098.
2. Speech by Himmler, October 4, 1943, PS-1919 [*Editor's note:* PS-1919 refers to a Nuremberg document. For the meaning of citation abbreviations, see Appendix C ("Notation on Sources") of Raul Hilberg, *The Destruction of the European Jews* (New York, 1985).]
3. Generalgouvernement Health Conference, July 9, 1943, Frank Diary, PS-2233. Remarks by Frank recorded verbatim.
4. Jan Sehn, "Concentration and Extermination Camp at Oswięcim," Central Commission for Investigation of German Crimes in Poland, *German Crimes in Poland* (Warsaw, 1946–1947), vol. 1, p. 32.
5. Sehn, "Oswięcim," *German Crimes in Poland,* vol. 1, p. 32.
6. Himmler speech, October 4, 1943, PS-1919.
7. Affidavit by Ulrich Dörtenbach, May 13, 1947, NG-1535.
8. Testimony by Höss, *Trial of the Major War Criminals,* XI, 396–411.
9. "Ein Wachmann von Treblinka," *Frankfurter Zeitung,* November 11, 1950, p. 3.

Die Spinne

Manch Opfer blieb im Netze hangen / Von Schmeicheltönen eingefangen
Zerreißt das Netz der Heuchelei / Ihr macht die deutsche Jugend frei

In Nazi Germany, Jews were often portrayed as spiders, lice, and other types of vermin that might bite, trap, or infect the German population. The example above comes from *Der Stürmer,* one of the most popular German newspapers of the 1930s [Source: Die Spinne ("The Spider"). (1934). *Der Stürmer,* No. 26, p. 1.]

In this *Der Stürmer* illustration, Jews are depicted as bloodthirsty vampires. This caricature builds upon centuries-old "blood libel" myths charging that Jews use the blood of sacrificial Christians and Muslims when baking bread or preparing holiday pastries [Source: Der Vampire ("The Vampire"). (1934). *Der Stürmer*, No. 31, p. 1.]

Nazi propaganda frequently compared Jews with apes and monkeys, implying that Jews were unevolved and animal-like [Source: Die Weltpest ("The Plague"). (1932, March). *Der Stürmer*, No. 10, p. 1.]

Supply Orders for Nazi Experiments

- "In contemplation of experiments with a new soporific drug, we would appreciate your procuring for us a number of women."

- "We received your answer but consider the price of 200 marks a woman excessive. We propose to pay not more than 170 marks a head. If agreeable, we will take possession of the women. We need approximately 150."

- "We acknowledge your accord. Prepare for us 150 women in the best possible health conditions, and as soon as you advise us you are ready, we will take charge of them."

- "Received the order of 150 women. Despite their emaciated condition, they were found satisfactory. We shall keep you posted on developments concerning this experiment."

- "The tests were made. All subjects died. We shall contact you shortly on the subject of a new load."

  —From business correspondence found at the Auschwitz concentration camp, *Time,* November 24, 1947

None of Our Business

As to obstacles placed in the way of Jewish athletes or any others in trying to reach Olympic ability, I would have no more business discussing that in Germany than if the Germans attempted to discuss the Negro situation in the American South or the treatment of the Japanese in California.

> —Brigadier General Charles Sherrill, American representative on the International Olympic Committee, defending America's participation in the 1936 Berlin games, *New York Times,* October 22, 1935

Racial Politics in America

We must preserve our Aryan nationality in the state, and admit to its membership only such non-Aryan race-elements as shall have become Aryanized in spirit and in genius by contact with it.

>—From an article on the "ideal American commonwealth," *Political Science Quarterly*, 1895

America, which leads all other countries in the strong counter-movement, has least of all had reason for the protest. The American people were the first to draw practical political consequences from the differentiation of races. Through its immigration law America has inhibited the unwelcome influx of such races as it has been unable to tolerate within its midst. Nor is America ready now to open its doors to Jews "fleeing from Germany."

>—Adolf Hitler, responding to American protests against anti-Semitic German policies, *New York Times*, April 7, 1933

As for the racial problem and America, we merely wish to state that the United States possesses rigorous immigration laws while Germany has had absolutely none thus far. We further point to American relations with Negroes—social and political. And finally, certain American universities have long since excluded Jews.

>—*Völkische Beobacher*, Hitler's house organ, responding to American criticism of German policies toward Jews, *New York Times*, July 15, 1933

The question of Jewish persecution in Europe is being given top news priority by the English and the Americans. . . . At bottom, however, I believe both the English and the Americans are happy that we are exterminating the Jewish riff-raff.

>—Diary Entry of Dr. Joseph Goebbels, German Minister for Public Enlightenment and Propaganda, December 13, 1942

Jewish Expulsion Orders
During the U.S. Civil War

I. The Jews, as a class, violating every regulation of trade established by the Treasury Department, and also Department orders, are hereby expelled from the Department [the "Department of the Tennessee," a Union Army administrative district of occupation that included Tennessee, Kentucky, and Mississippi].

II. Within twenty-four hours from the receipt of this order by Post Commanders, they will see that all of this class of people are furnished with passes and required to leave, and any one returning after such notification, will be arrested and held in confinement until an opportunity occurs of sending them out as prisoners . . .

—General Orders No. 11, issued by General Ulysses S. Grant, December 17, 1862. In an attempt to curb the Southern cotton trade, Grant directed that "Jews should receive special attention" in baggage searches, and on November 10, 1862, he ordered that "no Jews are to be permitted to travel on the Rail Road southward from any point." After a national uproar ensued over General Orders No. 11, President Abraham Lincoln had the order revoked.

A Madison Square Garden Rally

The years from 1938 through 1945 saw antisemitism in America reach a peak. Groups such as Father Charles E. Coughlin's Social Justice movement and the German-American Bund contributed to this atmosphere.

The German-American Bund, composed mainly of lower-middle-class German-born residents of the United States, in effect formed the American Nazi movement. Uniforms, swastika armbands, Nazi flags, Storm Troop units, the Nazi salute, goose-step marching, a score of camps for drill and for youth indoctrination served notice of the plans that these Hitlerites had for America.

At a 1939 Americanism rally in honor of George Washington's birthday, 20,000 Nazi sympathizers met in New York's Madison Square Garden to heil Hitler, boo President Roosevelt, and thunder applause at the mention of Father Coughlin.

—Adapted from David S. Wyman, *Paper Walls*, 1968

ANTISEMITISM IN AMERICA

LEONARD DINNERSTEIN

The aftermath of the First World War left Americans frightened that foreigners would corrupt the nation's values and traditions. A majority seemed tired of almost two decades of domestic reform and longed for what the 1920 Republican presidential nominee, Warren G. Harding, termed "normalcy." And to most people "normalcy" meant remaking the United States into what it symbolized in the minds of old stock Americans. The Secretary of the Chamber of Commerce of one community in Florida captured an extreme expression of this feeling in 1924 when he advocated expelling all Jews and foreigners from St. Petersburg to make the community "a 100% American Gentile City."[1] More specifically, "Gentile" meant "Protestant." In rural and urban areas alike Catholics and Jews were regarded as outcasts intent on undermining American values rather than as groups longing to accept them.[2]

In the 1920s Jews, more than the offspring of any of the other southern and eastern European minorities who entered America between the 1880s and the First World War, seemed prepared to enter the elite Protestant world in terms of schooling, employment, housing, and recreation. Efforts to acculturate, however, were met with strong resistance from members of the middle and upper classes who had little inclination to associate with Jews.

Such disinclinations were not new. Antisemitic traditions had existed in this country for centuries. Nevertheless, the antagonism toward Jews increased alarmingly during the postwar decade. Articles published in the popular periodical, *Literary Digest,* reinforced the views that the terms "Jews" and "Bolsheviks" were synonymous. Poles in Chicago also equated Bolshevism and Judaism, denounced President Woodrow Wilson as a dupe, and labeled the Treaty of Versailles a product of "Jewish internationalists."[3] By 1924 Chicago's *Polonia,* written in Polish, observed:

> Practically the whole world knows that the Jews direct socialism, Jews who through socialism are striving to stir up in various countries ferment and social unrest which always results in harm to Christian society and in profit and gain for the Jews.[4]

Another scurrilous association of Jews, radicalism, and subversion that emerged from the war came packaged in the form of a book: The *Protocols of the Elders of Zion.* Concocted by members of the Russian secret police at the turn of the century, this spurious work, based on European Christian mythology, purported to show that Jews, agents of the devil, were secretly plotting a world revolution to undermine Christian civilization. The document received little attention until after the Bolshevik Revolution when it soon made its way into western Europe and then into the United States. For those needing an explanation for the Russian upheaval the book provided a great deal of information, albeit preposterous. Published in London early in 1920, it took only a few weeks before *The Protocols* appeared in Boston. An American publisher then put out an edition entitled, *The Cause of World Unrest.*[5]

On May 22, 1920, an article entitled "The International Jew: The World's Problem" reproduced the essence of *The Protocols* and dominated page one of Henry Ford's newspaper, *The Dearborn Independent.* This piece inaugurated a series of attacks upon Jews that the newspaper ran for 91 consecutive weeks, and then intermittently until 1927. When the essays began, *The Dearborn Independent* had a circulation of about 72,000 copies a week. By 1922 that figure had increased to 300,000. It peaked in 1924 at 700,000, only 50,000 fewer than that of the largest daily paper in the United States at that time, *New York City's Daily News.*[6] The outlandish tales of alleged Jewish vices were read by millions of Americans, mostly in rural areas, who knew little or nothing about Jews except what they had already absorbed from religious teachings, gossip, and *The Dearborn Independent.*

Exactly what motivated Henry Ford to launch an attack upon Jews is unclear. He had grown up on a farm in rural Michigan during the Populist era when there was a general wariness of Jews, especially about their alleged greed and control of wealth. But not until 1915 did Ford publicly express antisemitic thoughts. He took a group of people to Europe on a "Peace Ship" that year with the hope of influencing the European powers to end the war. The mission failed and Ford attributed this to Rosika Schwimmer, a Jewish woman of Hungarian birth who had encouraged him to proceed, and to Jews in general. In his later virulent antisemitic campaigns, Ford would repeatedly return to the ill-fated Peace Ship incident and Rosika Schwimmer's influence on him at that time. As Ford recalled it later, that event introduced him to the connection between radicalism and Jews. By 1918, when he ran as the Democratic nominee for U.S. Senator from Michigan and lost, Ford was attributing almost everything that went wrong with his political fortunes to Jews and Jewish capitalism.[7]

In 1919 Ford purchased *The Dearborn Independent.* "Let's have some sensationalism," in the form of a strong and forceful series on a major topic, suggested a consultant brought in to help improve sales. Given Ford's increasing hostility toward Jews, the publication of *The Protocols* in the United States in 1920 provided him with a vehicle that brought national attention to his fledgling weekly. In 1921 when asked for his rationale for the series on "The International Jew" Ford responded that he was

> only trying to awake the Gentile world to an understanding of what is going on. The Jew is a mere huckster, a trader who doesn't want to produce, but to make something out of what somebody else produces.[8]

The first of the essays on "The International Jew" in *The Dearborn Independent* described the Jew as the world's enigma. Poor in his masses, he yet controls the world's finances. Scattered abroad without country or government, he yet presents a unit of race continuity no other people has achieved. Living under legal disabilities in almost every land, he has become the power behind many a throne. There are ancient prophecies to the effect that the Jew will return to his own land and from that center rule the world, though not until he has undergone an assault by the united nations of mankind.

> The single description which will include a larger percentage of Jews than members of any other race is this: He is in business. It may be only gathering rags and selling them, but he is in business. From the sale of old clothes to the control of international trade and finance, the Jew is supremely gifted for business.

"In America alone," *The Dearborn Independent* went on,

> most of big business, the trusts and the banks, the natural resources and the chief agricultural products, especially tobacco, cotton and sugar, are in the control of Jewish financiers or their agents. Jewish journalists are a large and powerful group here. "Large numbers of department stores are held by Jewish firms," says the Jewish Encyclopedia, and many if not most of them are run under Gentile names. Jews are the largest and most numerous landlords of residence property in the country. They are supreme in the theatrical world. They absolutely control the circulations of publications throughout the country. . . . Werner Sombart, in his "Jew and Modern Capitalism," says: "If the conditions of America continue to develop along the same lines as in the last generation, if the immigration statistics and the proportion of births among all nationalities remain the same, our imagination may picture the United States of fifty or a hundred years hence as a land inhabited only by Slavs, Negroes and Jews."[9]

These ideas were old but *The Protocols of the Elders of Zion* added an international twist to the myths already perpetuated. What Henry Ford and *The Dearborn Independent* did was to merge these accusations against Jews into one series on "The International Jew" and run the articles for almost two years. Had the topic not won reader approval, it would certainly have been abandoned.

Articles on Jews in *The Dearborn Independent* evoked widespread and enthusiastic comment in the years 1920 to 1924. The series also won plaudits overseas. Copies of "The International Jew" were translated into several languages and circulated in Europe and Latin America throughout the 1920s and 1930s. The work is widely credited with influencing the writing of Adolf Hitler's *Mein Kampf*.[10] Hitler kept a picture of Ford on the wall of his office in Munich, praised the automobile magnate in *Mein Kampf,* and later told a *Detroit News* reporter, "I regard Henry Ford as my inspiration."[11] On Ford's 75th birthday, in 1938, Hitler sent personal greetings and bestowed on him the highest honor the German government could grant a foreigner: the Grand Cross of the German Eagle.[12]

Despite widespread acceptance of Ford's writings about the Jews it would be a mistake to conclude that his antisemitism or the repetitious attacks in *The Dearborn Independent* won universal approval. Articles in *The Century, Current Opinion, The Independent, The Outlook,* and *Harper's Weekly* strongly denounced the *Protocols*, Ford, and the series on "The International Jew."[13] Samuel Walker McCall, Governor of Massachusetts from 1916 to 1919, wrote:

> The so-called "Protocols of the Elders of Zion" have recently been brought forward among us as a basis for anti-Jewish agitation. And this has been done after they have been fully discredited in Europe, where scholars of independence and character had no difficulty in penetrating into their fraudulent character.[14]

The Nation also noted that same wave of antisemitism sweeping the world in 1920 and agreed that "the chief responsibility for the survival of this hoary shame among us in America attaches to Henry Ford."[15] A few weeks later 119 prominent Americans, including Woodrow Wilson and William Howard Taft, signed a statement denouncing what they described as "an organized campaign of anti-Semitism, conducted in close conformity to and co-operation with similar campaigns in Europe."[16]

Despite the disclaimer, many genteel Americans questioned the wisdom of allowing Jews too many opportunities in the United States. President A. Lawrence Lowell, for example, thought that Harvard University had a "Jewish problem" because the percentage of Jewish undergraduates had tripled from 6 percent in 1908 to 22 percent in 1922. He suggested that a limit be placed on the number of them who would later be admitted to the university. Lowell feared that too many Jews at Harvard would result in the institution's losing "its character as a democratic, national university, drawing from all classes of the community and promoting a sympathetic understanding among them."[17]

Not only the Harvard President, but members of the Board of Governors, alumni, students, faculty, and other administrators shared this concern. The subject of what to do with an increasing number of Jewish students had been previously discussed at Harvard as well as at other schools, and it affected significant areas of university life outside the classroom as well. In 1920, for example, a year after Judge Julian Mack became the first Jew to win election to Harvard's Board of Overseers, a colleague on the Board, Jack Morgan, of the J. P. Morgan investment bank, communicated his concerns to President Lowell about another vacancy on that body:

> I think I ought to say that I believe there is a strong feeling among the Overseers that the nominee should by no means be a Jew or a Roman Catholic, although, naturally, the feeling in regard to the latter is less than in regard to the former.[18]

Morgan's views represented those of a broad spectrum of individuals. Few, if any, of those associated with the university wanted, as historian Frederick Jackson Turner wrote, a "New Jerusalem" at Harvard.[19]

The Harvard president knew the sentiments of various members of the university community before he made his announcement, and he was not expressing a view that came uneasily to him.[20] Lowell had been an officer of the Boston-based Immigration Restriction League and shared other members' values about the superiority of the Anglo-Saxon culture and their anxieties about it being undermined in the United States by hordes of foreigners with "inferior" backgrounds. Of all of those so-called lesser groups, none seemed more threatening to the reigning elite in America than the immigrant Jews. "The Jews," as Lewis Gannett noted in *The Nation* in 1923, were "the most eager to get the benefit of all that the Anglo-Saxon has to offer him. No other group flocks to our colleges with the same pathetic thirst for learning."[21]

Never before had any secular American university openly acknowledged that it wished to limit the number of its Jewish students. Lowell's announcement, however, publicly signaled that the increase in Jewish undergraduates alarmed him, as well as the faculty, students, and alumni of the university. The action taken at Harvard inspired other institutions. The Association of New England Deans, meeting in Princeton in May 1918, had already discussed the "problem" of having too many Jewish students[22] but reached no conclusion about how to deal with that dilemma. Once Harvard took the lead, however, many of the nation's most prestigious private colleges and universities, along with less distinguished academies throughout the country, established their own allotments. These schools included Columbia, Princeton, Yale, Duke, Rutgers, Barnard, Adelphi, Cornell, Johns Hopkins, Northwestern, Penn State, Ohio State, Washington and Lee, and the Universities of Cincinnati, Illinois, Kansas, Minnesota, Texas, Virginia, and Washington. As the 1920s admissions moved from selective to restrictive fewer places became available for Jews.[23]

Many universities found unique ways of handling what they perceived of as "the Jewish problem." The Dean at Colgate wanted only six Jews in the university so that if charges of antisemitism were raised the six could be trotted out to disprove the assertion. At Syracuse University, where a Ku Klux Klan chapter existed, Jews were also excluded from most social organizations and, from 1927 to 1931, were housed separately from Christians. Ohio State segregated Jews in some female dormitories while Gentile students at the Universities of Michigan and Nebraska were advised against associating with Jewish males. Columbia College's application wanted to know the student's "religious affiliation," whether he or his parents had ever been known by another name, parents' place of birth, mother's full maiden name, and father's occupation. Harvard came up with the idea of geographical diversity, assuming that outside of the major cities in the East and Midwest one would find few Jews.[24] The President of Dartmouth, Ernest Hopkins, summed up the general reasons for these questions and policies when he said: "Any college which is going to base its admissions wholly on scholastic standing will find itself with an infinitesimal proportion of anything else than Jews eventually."[25]

An antisemitic atmosphere also existed at the U.S. Naval Academy in Annapolis where Jews were harassed, excluded, and psychologically ostracized. In the class of 1922 the editors of the school yearbook humiliated the Jewish cadet who ranked second academically by printing his picture on a perforated page so that it could be removed without defacing the rest of the volume.[26] When asked about his college experiences a half century later, Democratic party chairman and later U.S. Ambassador to the Soviet Union Robert Strauss recalled, "Not many things happened to me at the University of Texas. I discovered I was Jewish, which meant that you were ostracized from certain things."[27]

Universities had even less desire for Jewish faculty than for Jewish students. In 1927 the faculties of Yale, Princeton, Johns Hopkins, and the Universities of Chicago, Georgia, and Texas each included one Jew. There were two each at Berkeley and Columbia, three at Harvard, and four at the City College of New York. Tales of the rare Jews who succeeded are usually accompanied by the caveat that they were specifically chosen because of their unusual qualities rather than as a sign that barriers were being dropped. Letters of recommendation for historians Oscar Handlin, Bert Lowenberg, and Daniel Boorstin, for example, bore phrases like "has none of the offensive traits which people associate with his race," "by temperament and spirit . . . measure up to the whitest Gentile I know," and "is a Jew, though not the kind to which one takes exception."[28] A professor of mathematics at the University of Chicago, commenting about a mathematical astronomer, noted, "He is one of the few men of Jewish descent who does not get on your nerves and really behaves like a gentile to a satisfactory degree." Many academics, however, believed that people of the "Jewish race" should be totally barred from the academic world.[29]

NOTES

1. Quoted in Carey McWilliams, *A Mask for Privilege: Anti-Semitism in America* (New York: Little, Brown and Company, 1948), p. 38; see also Leo P. Ribuffo, *The Old Christian Right* (Philadelphia: Temple University Press, 1983), p. 12.

2. David O. Levine, *The American College and the Culture of Aspiration, 1915–1940* (Ithaca: Cornell University Press, 1985), pp. 147–148.

3. Edward R. Kantowicz, *Polish-American Politics in Chicago, 1880–1940* (Chicago: University of Chicago Press, 1975), p. 124.

4. Quoted in ibid., p. 124.

5. Rosemary Radford Ruether, "Anti-Semitism and Christian Theology," in Eva Fleischner, ed., *Auschwitz: Beginning of a New Era? Reflections on the Holocaust* (New York: KTAV Publishing House, Inc., 1977), p. 90; Morton Rosenstock, *Louis Marshall, Defender of Jewish Rights* (Detroit: Wayne State University Press, 1965), p. 119ff.; Baron S. A. Korff, "The Great Jewish Conspiracy," *The Outlook,* 127 (February 2, 1921), 181; Burton J. Hendrick, "The Jews in America;" *World's Work,* 45 (1922–23), 266; David Brian Davis, *The Fear of Conspiracy* (Ithaca: Cornell University Press, 1971), p. 26; Leo P. Ribuffo, "Henry Ford and *The International Jew,*" *American Jewish History,* 69 (June, 1980), p. 441.

6. "Mr. Ford Retracts," *Review of Reviews,* 76 (August, 1927), 197; Rosenstock, Louis Marshall, p. 145.

7. David Levering Lewis, "Henry Ford's Anti-Semitism and Its Repercussions," *Michigan Jewish History,* 24 (1984), 3; Leonard Dinnerstein, "When Henry Ford Apologized to the Jews," *Moment,* 15 (February, 1990), 24; Henry Feingold, *A Time for Searching: Entering the Mainstream, 1920–1945* (Baltimore: The Johns Hopkins Press, 1992), pp. 8–9.

8. Ibid., pp. 26–27; quote on page 27.

9. "The International Jew", a reprint of the series appearing in *The Dearborn Independent* from May 22 to October 2, 1920 (no city: n. p., n. d.), pp. 10–11; "Mr. Ford Retracts," *Review of Reviews,* 76 (August, 1927), p. 197.

10. Dinnerstein, "When Henry Ford," pp. 27, 54; Robert Lacey, *Ford: The Men and the Machine* (Boston: Little, Brown, 1986), p. 218; Samuel Walker McCall, *The Patriotism of the American Jew* (New York: Plymouth Press, Inc., 1924), p. 36; Rosenstock, *Louis Marshall*, p. 197.

11. Quote in Albert Lee, *Henry Ford and the Jews* (New York: Stein and Day, 1980), p. 47; see also Robert Lacey, *Ford: The Men and the Machine* (Boston: Little, Brown, 1986), p. 218.

12. *New York Times*, July 31, 1938, p. 31, December 1, 1938, p. 12; Lacey, *Ford*, p. 386; Lee, *Henry Ford*, p. 113.

13. Rosenstock, *Louis Marshall*, p. 125; Bernard G. Richards Oral History Memoir, Columbia University Oral History Collection, p. 183; "Anti-Jewish Propaganda," *The Outlook*, 127 (January 26, 1921), 125; Herbert Adams Gibbon, "The Jewish Problem," The Century, 102 (September, 1921), 786–787.

14. McCall, *The Patriotism of the American Jew*, p. 28.

15. "Reaction and the Jew," *The Nation*, 111 (November 3, 1920), 493.

16. "Anti-Jewish Propaganda," p. 125; Rosenstock, *Louis Marshall*, p. 154ff.; "Wilson and Harding Defend Jews," *The Independent*, 105 (January 29, 1921), 118.

17. Henry Aaron Yeomans, *Abbot Lawrence Lowell* (Cambridge: Harvard University Press, 1948), p. 209; Feingold, *A Time for Searching*, p. 17; Oliver B. Pollak, "Anti-semitism, the Harvard Plan, and the Roots of Reverse Discrimination, " Jewish Social Studies, 45 (Spring, 1983), 114.

18. Yeomans, *Abbot Laurence Lowell*, p. 209; William T. Ham, "Harvard Student Opinion on the Jewish Question," *The Nation*, 115 (September, 6, 1922), 225; Marcia Graham Synnott, *The Half-Opened Door: Discrimination and Admissions at Harvard, Yale, and Princeton, 1900–1970* (Westport, Conn.: Greenwood Press, 1979), p. 15ff.; Morgan's letter quoted in Ron Chernow, *The House of Morgan: An American Banking Dynasty and the Rise of Modern Finance* (New York: Atlantic Monthly Press, 1990), pp. 214–215.

19. Ray Allen Billington, *Frederick Jackson Turner* (New York: Oxford University Press, 1973), p. 437; Levine, *The American College*, p. 150.

20. Dan A. Oren, *Joining the Club: A History of Jews and Yale* (New Haven: Yale University Press, 1985), p. 47.

21. Lewis S. Gannett, "Is America Anti-Semitic?" *The Nation*, 116 (March 21, 1923), 331.

22. Synnott, *Half-Opened Door*, p. 15ff.

23. Jerold Auerbach, "From Rags to Robes: The Legal Profession, Social Mobility and the American Jewish Experience," *American Jewish History Quarterly*, 66 (October, 1976), 252; Harold S. Wechsler, *The Qualified Student* (New York: John Wiley and Sons, 1977), p. 163; "May Jews Go to College?" *The Nation*, 114 (June 14, 1922), 708; Heywood Broun and George Britt, *Christians Only* (New York: The Vanguard Press, 1931), pp. 89–90, 118–119; Ruth Marcus Platt, *The Jewish Experience at Rutgers* (East Brunswick, N.J.: Jews Historical Society of Central Jersey, 1987), p. 21; Oren, *Joining the Club*, pp. 51, 54–55; Garry T. Greenebaum, "The Jewish Experience in the American College and University" (unpublished Ph.D., 1978, Small Collections, American Jewish Archives), p. 110; *The Nation and the Atheneum*, 32 (January 27,1923), 635; Minutes, V (1932), pp. 1608–1609; McWilliams, *Mask for Privilege*, p. 135; John Higham, *Strangers in the Land* (New Brunswick: Rutgers University Press, 1955; this edition: New York: Atheneum, 1974), p. 278; Levine, *The American College*, pp. 146, 154ff; Michael Greenberg and Seymour Zenchelsky, "Private Bias and Public Responsibility: Anti-Semitism at Rutgers in the 1920s and 1930s," *History of Education Quarterly*, 33 (Fall, 1993), 311.

24. Broun and Britt, *Christians Only*, pp. 74, 88, 92; Harvey Strum, "Louis Marshall and Anti-Semitism at Syracuse University," *American Jewish Archives* 35 (April, 1983), 8,

10; Paula S. Fass, *The Damned and the Beautiful: American Youth in the 1920's* (New York: Oxford University Press, 1977), p. 152; L. B. Rose, "Secret Life of Sarah Lawrence," *Commentary*, 75 (May, 1983), 54; Pollak "Antisemitism," p. 1129.

25. Quoted in Levine, *The American College*, p. 156.

26. Norman Polmar and Thomas B. Allen, *Rickover* (New York: Simon & Schuster, 1982), pp. 51, 52–53; Robert Wallace, "A Deluge of Honors for an Exasperating Admiral," *Life*, 45 (September 8, 1958), 109.

27. Quoted in Elizabeth Drew, "Profile of Robert Strauss," *The New Yorker*, May 17, 1979, p. 117.

28. Quoted in Peter Novick, *That Noble Dream* (Cambridge: Cambridge University Press, 1988), pp. 172–173.

29. Quoted in Nathan Reingold, "Refugee Mathematicians in the United States of America, 1933–1941: Reception and Reaction," in *Annals of Science*, 38 (May, 1981), 320, 321.

Signs at Employee Parking Gates
of the Ford Motor Company
(Dearborn, Michigan, 1939)

> Jews are traitors to America and should not be trusted—buy Gentile.

> - Jews Teach Communism
> - Jews Teach Atheism
> - Jews Destroy Christianity
> - Jews Control the Press
> - Jews Produce Filthy Movies
> - Jews Control Money

—Source: Lee, A. (1980). *Henry Ford and the Jews.* New York: Stein & Day.

***New York Times* Headlines**
50 Years After World War II:
Stories of Complicity and Silence

11/19/96: *Files Suggest British Knew Early of Nazi Atrocities Against Jews*

12/14/96: *Swiss Acknowledge Profiting from Nazi Gold*

12/19/96: *Red Cross Admits Knowing of the Holocaust During the War*

2/3/97: *Canada Called Haven for Nazi Criminals*

5/29/97: *New Records Show the Swiss Sold Arms Worth Millions to Nazis*

7/16/97: *Allies Linked to Swapping of Nazi Gold*

8/23/97: *Croatia Apologizes to Jews for Nazi-Era Crimes*

10/8/97: *Red Cross Admits Failing to Condemn Holocaust*

10/12/97: *Nazi-Era Apology by French Doctors*

12/1/97: *U.S. Melted Down Gold Items from Nazis*

5/23/98: *Switzerland Said to Have Backed Nazi Trade in Looted Gold*

5/26/98: *Report Says Swiss Knew Some Nazi Gold Was Stolen*

6/21/98: *U.S. Details 6 Neutral Countries' Role in Aiding Nazis*

12/1/98: *U.S. Shifts from Nazi Gold to Art, Land and Insurance*

3/17/99: *French Detail Vichy Looting of Jews' Assets*

7/29/99: *U.S. Knew Early of Nazi Killings in Asylums, Official Documents Show*

10/15/99: *G.I.'s Are Called Looters of Jewish Riches*

12/3/99: *Swiss Holocaust Accounts Reportedly Have $250 Million*

12/7/99: *54,000 Swiss Accounts Tied to the Nazis' War Victims*

12/11/99: *Historians' Report Blames Swiss for Barring Jews During War*

12/14/99: *G.M. Opel Unit Says It's Likely to Pay Nazi-Era Slaves*

4/29/00: *A Fund Is Planned by U.S. Companies for Nazis' Victims*

1/17/01: *Report on Holocaust Assets Tells of Items Found in U.S.*

12/2/01: *Swiss Were Part of Nazi Economic Lifeline, Historians Find*

3/7/02: *Vienna Skewered as a Nazi-Era Pillager of Its Jews*

[*Note:* Full citations are given in Source Notes.]

WHILE SIX MILLION DIED:
A CHRONICLE OF AMERICAN APATHY

ARTHUR D. MORSE

Introduction

The Nazi destruction of six million Jews, as chronicled to date, is essentially a history of the killers and the killed. It is as if there were no other world, as if two circling antagonists, one armed, the other unarmed, inhabited an otherwise vacant planet.

Many books have examined the administrative techniques and physical acts by which the Nazis accomplished the slaughter of the innocent. This volume concentrates on the bystanders rather than the killers or the killed. It attempts to answer two fundamental questions:

1. What did the rest of the world and, in particular, the United States and Great Britain, know about Nazi plans for the annihilation of the Jews?
2. What was their reaction to this knowledge?

To answer these questions, two types of information have been examined—materials published openly from 1933 to 1945 and, most important, government documents which were denied to the public. These official records are quoted extensively; many have never been published before.

Some may wonder why this volume focuses on the plight of the Jews. After all, the total number of civilian victims of the Nazis was several times the estimated six million Jewish deaths. The Czechs of Lidice, the Yugoslav school children of Kragujevac, the Russians of countless villages, the Catholic priests imprisoned in Dachau, all these were equally precious and the loss of their lives is as significant an indictment of Germany as the death of the Jews.

But Jewish destruction was to be total. Hitler's indiscriminate attack began the moment he assumed power in 1933. The subsequent social and economic debasement of the Jews was unique and therefore the world's response was unique. In contrast to the selective murder of members of other ethnic, religious and racial groups, the Nazis' blatant announcement that they intended to destroy every Jew in Europe presented the United States and its allies with a clear-cut challenge. How this challenge was met is the subject of this report.

If genocide is to be prevented in the future, we must understand how it happened in the past—not only in terms of the killers and the killed but of the bystanders.

1938: Evian

"We really didn't know what the Nazis were doing at the time" is a familiar refrain in contemporary American discussions of the murder of six million Jews and of the specific events which preceded their final journey to the gas chambers.

Memory is clouded by time. The events of 1938, which foreshadowed mass murder, were widely publicized. They made headlines day after day in the United States and Great Britain, were described on the radio and filled the pages of the mass magazines.

The German annexation of Austria in March 1938 triggered the most savage anti-Semitism since the rise of Hitler. Following the fall of the Schuschnigg government, the 200,000 Jews of Austria were subjected to torments which made the persecution in Germany seem moderate. The following are brief excerpts from the *New York Times* during the first days after the German takeover:

March 16

"Adolf Hitler has left behind him in Austria an anti-Semitism that is blossoming far more rapidly than ever it did in Germany. This afternoon the Jewish quarter of Leopoldstadt was invaded by triumphant crowds that called families from their houses and forced them to kneel and try to scrub from the pavements slogans such as 'Hail Schuschnigg' which were part of the former Chancellor's plebiscite campaign. This humiliation was carried out under the supervision of Storm Troopers wearing swastika armlets. The crowds were . . . shouting, 'Perish Jewry!' 'Out with the Jews!' "

March 18

"There have been many cases of men in Storm Troop and Elite Guard uniforms entering Jewish-owned shops and carrying off whatever goods they fancied as well as money, and going into private houses and demanding large sums of money, or in default of personal jewelry, other valuables. In other cases not only are automobiles removed but their owners are also asked to hand over money for gasoline."

March 23

"Whereas in Germany the first Nazi victims were the Left political parties—Socialists and Communists—in Vienna it is the Jews who are to bear the brunt of the Nazis' revolutionary fire . . . . That is why the daily list of suicides is so great, for the Jews are exposed to arrest, plunder, deprivation of their opportunity for a livelihood, and mob fury."

🙰   🙰   🙰

The world's press reported that suicides among Jews in Vienna had risen to two hundred daily and that Austria had closed the frontiers to her Jewish citizens. Italy, Switzerland and Czechoslovakia sealed their own borders and thus double-locked the gates of their neighbor.

On March 22, ten days after the first German troops had marched into Austria, the United States launched what appeared to be a bold plan of action. The President invited thirty-three governments to join in a cooperative effort to aid the emigration of political refugees from Germany and Austria. They included twenty Latin American republics, plus Great Britain, France, Italy, Belgium,

Switzerland, Sweden, Norway, The Netherlands, Denmark, Canada, Australia, New Zealand and South Africa. The invitation specified that no country "would be expected or asked to receive a greater number of emigrants than is permitted by its existing legislation," but it emphasized that the freedom-loving nations must work together to solve the tragic problem.

The day the conference was announced, the President held an informal press conference at Warm Springs, Georgia. He reaffirmed the traditional role of the United States as a haven for the politically oppressed of all nations, but assured his listeners that the new proposal would not result in an increase or revision of U.S. immigration quotas. He added that it would be up to private groups rather than governments to finance any movement of refugees.

There was an instantaneous, massive reaction from church, civic and women's groups, with generous offers of funds, assistance and encouragement. The Federal Council of Churches of Christ in America "hailed with appreciation" the U.S. proposal; the Hebrew Sheltering and Immigrant Aid Society called it "one of the great humanitarian acts of the twentieth century." Even the American Federation of Labor responded warmly, and its president, William Green, went so far as to say that "refugees have proved themselves through the years to be our finest citizens. It would be cruel, illogical and entirely out of keeping with our American principles if we were to close our doors to them now." Green had only one small reservation. The United States should admit no more than the number of immigrants provided by law, because of the competition for jobs.

The reaction to Roosevelt's proposal might have been less exuberant had the public known the motives behind it. An internal State Department memorandum prepared later in 1938 by an official of the Division of European Affairs described the origins of the Evian Conference with cold detachment.[1]

The Nazi absorption of Austria had brought about increased public demand for State Department action in behalf of refugees. "Dorothy Thompson and certain Congressmen with metropolitan constituencies were the principal sources of this pressure," said the memorandum.

To counteract this outcry, Secretary Hull, Undersecretary Welles and two lesser colleagues had decided that it was preferable for the department to "get out in front and attempt to guide the pressure, primarily with a view toward forestalling attempts to have the immigration laws liberalized."

It was Summer Welles who had come up with the idea of an international conference, and the President had approved. On this noble note the Evian Conference was born. It would be months in planning, would silence the critics of apathy, and if all worked well, would divert refugees from the United States to the other cooperating nations.

The Germans responded to the U.S. refugee plan with contempt. Chancellor Hitler, never losing an opportunity to deflate democratic pretense, said in a speech at Königsberg, "I can only hope and expect that the other world, which has such deep sympathy for these criminals, will at least be generous enough to convert this sympathy into practical aid. We, on our part, are ready to put all these criminals at the disposal of these countries, for all I care, even on luxury ships."[2]

On April 26, Vienna's *Völkischer Beobachter* commented on President Roosevelt's impending refugee conference: "We cannot take seriously President Roosevelt's appeal to the nations of the world as long as the United States maintains racial quotas for immigrants."

The Nazis demonstrated malevolent efficiency in utilizing these immigration restrictions to rob the Jews materially and torture them emotionally. In Vienna they first imprisoned their victims. After a number of weeks of brutality and starvation they offered to release them. In return the Jews were required to pledge that they would relinquish their property and leave the country within four to six weeks.

Three thousand Jews a day waited in vain for visas at the American consulate in Vienna, while ten thousand applications lay unanswered at the Australian consulate. The Nazis now enjoyed what for them was the best of all possible worlds—they were able to acquire valuable property while retaining the impoverished former owners as hostages.

At the same time that Americans were reading about the assault on the Jews in Austria, Berlin newspaper correspondents quoted from a new German textbook, Julius Streicher's *First Reader.*[3] In the opening chapter a mother tells her son what Jews are like:

"Just as one poisonous mushroom can kill a whole family," she explains, "so can one Jew ruin a whole city—even a whole nation" (see Figure 1).

In a section on religion, the Streicher textbook exhorts its young readers: "Remember that the Jews are children of the devil and murderers of mankind. . . . Whoever is a murderer deserves to be killed himself."

❦ ❦ ❦

On May 12 France approved of Evian-les-Bains as the site of the refugee conference. The luxurious resort on the French shore of Lake Geneva would provide excellent accommodations for representatives of the thirty-two nations which would attend. Only Italy and South Africa had declined, and the latter was sending an observer. The conference would not begin until July, so there was plenty of time for preparation.

The United States announced that Myron C. Taylor, former chairman of the U.S. Steel Corporation, would be its principal representative at the conference. With thirty-two nations compiling material for the conference, the precarious situation of the Jews was held in abeyance between May and July. Nothing was done to ease the rigidity of the immigration procedures, which proved particularly tragic for a thirty-six-year-old German Jewish woman named Luise Wolf.

Luise Wolf had arrived in New York on a six-week visitor's permit. During her stay she hoped to obtain an affidavit attesting to her means of support so she could assure the United States of America that she would not become one of its public charges. Then she would become a bonafide immigrant.

In Munich she had worked as a saleswoman to support her sick mother and herself, but was discharged as a non-Aryan. At the Clara de Hirsch Home for Working Girls, where she lived in New York, she was regarded as a well-educated, quiet person, but somehow she had not been able to obtain her affidavit. She was scheduled to return to Germany on May 27. On May 25 Luise

„Die Judennase ist an ihrer Spitze gebogen. Sie sieht aus wie ein Sechser..."

FIGURE 1
This figure shows a page from the 1938 book Der Giftpilz ("The Poisonous Mushroom"), published by Julius Streicher. The caption reads: "The Jewish nose is bent at its tip. It looks like the numeral six . . ." Inset: Detail from the book's cover.

Wolf leaped to her death from a fifth-floor window of the Home. A return ticket to Germany and $15 were found in her purse.[4]

Such tragedies seemed needless to many Americans, especially since U.S. immigration quotas were unfilled. On June 7, 1938, a delegation of the Jewish People's Committee for United Action Against Fascism and Anti-Semitism visited the White House and presented 120,000 signatures on petitions proposing that the unused quotas from any country be made available for the admission of refugees from other countries. Presidential secretary Marvin McIntyre met the group, accepted the petitions and then sent a note to Sumner Welles:

"Personally I do not see much necessity for any reply except that a more or less courteous but stereotyped answer signed by me may head off insistence in the future for a specific reply. What do you think."[5]

Welles thought so too.

On June 19, two weeks before Evian, the London *Times*'s Vienna correspondent wrote: "Men and women, young and old, are taken each day and each night from their houses or in the streets and carried off, the more fortunate to Austrian prisons, and the rest to Dachau and other concentration camps in Germany. . . . The Jews would welcome evacuation, but for most it is impossible. . . . Thousands stand outside the consulates of America, England and other countries, waiting through the night for admission so that they may register their names."

Perhaps no one described the challenge of Evian more eloquently than Anne O'Hare McCormick, columnist of the *New York Times*. Two days before the conference opened, she wrote: "It is heartbreaking to think of the queues of desperate human beings around our consulates in Vienna and other cities. . . . Can America live with itself if it lets Germany get away with this policy of extermination, allows the fanaticism of one man to triumph over reason, refuses to take up this gage of battle against barbarism?"

❧   ❧   ❧

On July 6, 1938, the highly publicized Evian Conference was called to order. When the delegates finally turned to substantive issues it became clear that it would take more than the dedication of a Myron Taylor to rescue the conference: one after another the nations made clear their unwillingness to accept refugees.[6] Since the business meetings were closed to the press, they did not risk public exposure.

Australia, with vast, unpopulated areas, announced: "As we have no real racial problem, we are not desirous of importing one." New Zealand was unwilling to lift its restrictions. The British colonial empire, reported Sir John Shuckburgh, contained no territory suitable to the large-scale settlement of Jewish refugees. Canada wanted agricultural migrants and none others. The same was true of Colombia, Uruguay and Venezuela.

Peru was particularly opposed to the immigration of doctors and lawyers. The Peruvian delegate pointedly remarked that the United States had given his country an example of "caution and wisdom" by its own immigration restrictions.

France, whose population already included two hundred thousand refugees and three million aliens, stressed that it had reached its saturation point.

Nicaragua, Honduras, Costa Rica and Panama issued a joint statement saying that they could accept no "traders or intellectuals." Argentina, with a population one-tenth that of the United States, reported that it had welcomed almost as many refugees as the United States and hence could not be counted on for large-scale immigration.

The Netherlands and Denmark reflected their traditional humanitarianism. Though Holland had already accepted twenty-five thousand Jewish refugees, it offered itself as a country of temporary sojourn. Denmark, so densely populated that its own citizens were forced to emigrate, had already taken in a disproportionately large number of German exiles. Within its narrow limits, it would continue to do so.

And the United States, the nation at whose initiative the conference had convened, what would it offer? The answer was soon in coming. The United States, with its tradition of asylum, its vast land mass and its unlimited resources, agreed, for the first time, to accept its full, legal quota of 27,370 immigrants annually from Germany and Austria. That was the major American concession made at Evian.

Although Myron Taylor lacked the power to vitalize American immigration policy, participants in the Evian Conference established the Intergovernmental Committee on Refugees, with permanent headquarters in London. Unfortunately, its leadership would consist of the same personalities who had dominated the Evian meeting. They would accomplish just as little.

🌿 🌿 🌿

The Evian Conference adjourned on July 15 and it was announced that the new Intergovernmental Committee would meet in London in August. Its first task was to commence negotiations with Germany for an orderly solution of the refugee problem. Judging by the reactions of that nation's newspapers to the Evian discussions, the task would not be easy.

The *Danziger Vorposten,* aware that no new gates had been opened to the Jews, commented: "We see that one likes to pity the Jews as long as one can use this pity for a wicked agitation against Germany, but that no state is prepared to fight the cultural disgrace of central Europe by accepting a few thousand Jews. Thus the conference serves to justify Germany's policy against Jewry." The *Nationalsozialistische Parteikorrespondenz* stated that Evian had revealed "the danger which world Jewry constitutes."

American and British press reactions were almost as bitter, though for different reason. Several publications pointed out that "Evian" spelled backwards is "naïve," and *Time* magazine observed wryly, "Evian is the home of a famous spring of still and unexciting table water. After a week of many warm words of idealism and few practical suggestions, the Intergovernmental Committee on Political Refugees took on some of the same characteristics."

Although some of the British press felt that Evian had been useful in establishing machinery which might ultimately help the refugees, the *Daily Herald* disagreed, "If this is coming to the help of the refugees, then what would the nations do if they meant to desert them?"

NOTES

1. Division of European Affairs undated memo on refugee problems, attached to Division of the American Republics memo of November 15, 1938 (National Archives of the United States, Calamities—Relief—Europe—Refugees, 840.48/900 ½).
2. Quoted in *N.Y. Times,* March 27, 1938.
3. Quoted in *N.Y. Times,* April 7, 1938.
4. *N.Y. Times,* May 26, 1938.
5. Franklin D. Roosevelt Library, Hyde Park, New York (Official File 3186).
6. *Wiener Library Bulletin* (London), No. 3, 1961; also, memo from Sumner Welles to President Roosevelt, November 28, 1938; Franklin D. Roosevelt Library, Hyde Park, New York (President's Personal File); and Norman Bentwich, "The Evian Conference and After," *The Fortnightly,* September 1938.

We Can Delay

Response to the Holocaust, 1940

We can delay and effectively stop for a temporary period of indefinite length the number of immigrants into the United States. We could do this by simply advising our consuls to put every obstacle in the way and to require additional evidence and to resort to various administrative devices which would postpone and postpone and postpone the granting of the visas.

> —Memo from U.S. Assistant Secretary of State Breckinridge Long, June 26, 1940, outlining ways to restrict the granting of U.S. visas to Jewish refugees and others. According to Long's diary, he discussed his thoughts on immigration with President Roosevelt on October 3, 1940, and the President was "100% in accord with my ideas."

Response to the Rwandan Genocide, 1994

Be careful. Legal at State was worried about this yesterday—Genocide finding could commit [the U.S. government] to actually "do something."

> —Discussion paper on Rwanda, U.S. Office of the Secretary of Defense, May 1, 1994, warning that a finding of "genocide" could, according to State Department lawyers, commit the U.S. government to act

American Public Opinion on Admitting Refugees

Asked in 1938: *Should we allow a larger number of Jewish exiles from Germany to come to the United States to live?*

Yes:	17%
No:	75%
Don't know:	8%

Asked in 1939: *If you were a member of Congress, would you vote yes or no on a bill to open the doors of the U.S. to a larger number of European refugees than now admitted under our immigration quotas?*

Yes:	9%
No:	83%
Don't know:	8%

Asked in 1939: *It has been proposed that the government permit 10,000 refugee children from Germany to be brought into this country and taken care of in American homes. Do you favor this plan?*

Yes:	26%
No:	66%
No opinion:	8%

Asked in 1943: *Do you think it would be a good idea or a bad idea to let more immigrants come into this country after the war?*

Good idea:	13%
Bad idea:	78%
Don't know:	9%

—Source: Charles Stember, *Jews in the Mind of America*, 1966

U.S. Immigration During the Holocaust

In 1943 immigration to the United States totaled 23,725, the lowest figure in 110 years except for 1933. In 1943 alone, 130,000 legal entry certificates went unused. While thousands of Jews were gassed daily in
Europe, only 4,705 Jews entered the United States that year.

—Saul S. Friedman, *No Haven for the Oppressed: United States Policy Toward Jewish Refugees, 1938–1945, 1973*

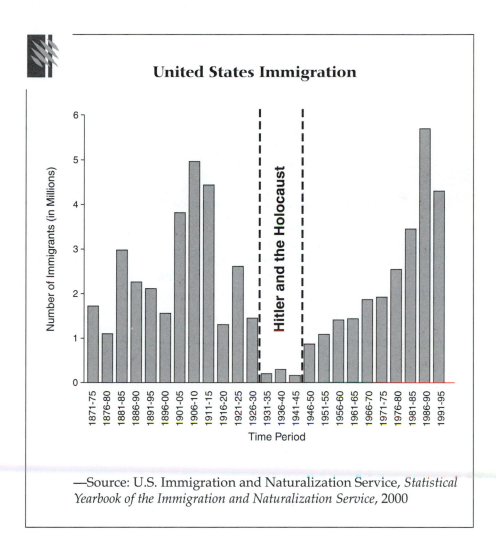

United States Immigration

Number of Immigrants (in Millions)

Hitler and the Holocaust

Time Period

—Source: U.S. Immigration and Naturalization Service, *Statistical Yearbook of the Immigration and Naturalization Service*, 2000

Inscription on the Statue of Liberty

Give me your tired, your poor,
Your huddled masses yearning to breathe free,
The wretched refuse of your teeming shore.
Send these, the homeless, the tempest-tossed to me,
I lift my lamp beside the golden door!

—Emma Lazarus, *The New Colossus*, 1883

Apathy^I = Insanity^M

Apathy at the individual level translates into insanity at the mass level.

—Douglas R. Hofstadter, *Metamagical Themas: Questing for the Essence of Mind and Pattern*, 1985

Postwar German Attitudes About Jews and White American Attitudes About Blacks

German Surveys		American Surveys	
1946: "Jews should have the same legal rights as members of the Aryan race."	Yes: 85% No: 10% Other: 5%	1945: "Do you favor or oppose a law in this state which would require an employer to hire a person if he is qualified for the job, regardless of his race or color?"	Favor: 43% Oppose: 44% Other: 13%
1946: Would you work with a Jew?"	Yes: 73% No: 11% Other: 16%	*1958: "Would you be willing to work next to members of the other race?"	White <u>Southerners</u> Yes: 48% No: 46% Other: 6% White <u>Northerners</u> Yes: 79% No: 17% Other: 4%
1946: "Should Jews be allowed to go to the same restaurants as non-Jews?"	Yes: 64% No: 12% Other: 24%	1942: "Do you think there should be separate restaurants for Negroes and white people?"	Yes: 69% No: 27% Other: 4%
1946: Do you agree with the following statement? "If a pure German marries a non-Aryan wife, he should be looked down on and criticized."	Yes: 10% No: 85% Other 5%	†1958: "Do you approve or disapprove of marriages between white and colored people?"	Approve: 4% Disapprove: 94% Other: 2%
1946: "Would you have anything against Jews living on the same street with you?"	Yes: 5% No: 73% Other: 22%	1942: "If a Negro with just as much income and education as you have, moved into your block, would it make any difference to you?"	Yes: 62% No: 35% Other: 3%

*From Erskine, 1968.
†From Gallup, 1972. All other questions are from Cantril, 1951.

A Jewish Perspective on Anti–Semitism

If the world were reduced to 1,000 people, with the same population proportions that currently exist, there would be 331 Christians, and only 3 Jews. Whereas Christians are approximately 33% of the world's population, Jews are approximately one third of 1%.

The sense of being a minority, combined with a knowledge of the history of Jewish persecution, makes it difficult for Jews to take their safety for granted. Outwardly it may look as if Jews are perfectly at home in America, but this is misleading. As Paul Stallsworth wrote in *The Story of an Encounter:*

> There is one thing that every Jew knows: Jewish history has been a succession of rises and falls. So you wait for the other shoe to drop. We are now on an upswing, but all of Jewish history guarantees that there will be a downswing.

To non-Jews this may seem paranoid. To Jews, however, who are more familiar with the history of anti-Semitism, this "paranoia" has, all too often, been justified.

—Adapted from Peter F. Langman, *Journal of Multicultural Counseling and Development,* 1995

ADL 2000 AUDIT OF ANTI–SEMITIC INCIDENTS

ANTI–DEFAMATION LEAGUE

The Anti-Defamation League was founded in 1913 "to stop the defamation of the Jewish people and to secure justice and fair treatment to all citizens alike." The *ADL Audit of Anti-Semitic Incidents*, published annually since 1979, is an account of overt acts and expressions of anti-Jewish bigotry or hostility. It reflects the number of incidents reported to ADL, and to law enforcement agencies when such figures are made available. It is not, and does not claim to be, a scientific measure of anti-Semitism in all of its forms.

Many incidents reported in the *Audit* are not crimes. For example, distributing neo-Nazi pamphlets and making slurs against Jewish individuals are both protected free speech. Therefore, there will most likely be discrepancies between the total numbers of anti-Semitic incidents reported in the *Audit* and in official law enforcement bias-crime statistics.

The *Audit* is not only a catalog of anti-Jewish acts that take place in a given year. It seeks also to uncover trends in anti-Semitic activity, especially trends in the types of activity reported, such as changes in the proportion of attacks against Jewish institutions. Toward the end of 2000, turmoil in the Middle East appeared to have been connected to a spate of anti-Semitic violence in the United States. At least 34 politically related incidents were reported in New York State alone. In one of the incidents, a rabbi and his wife were attacked and beaten by a group of men in Brooklyn, NY, including one who reportedly yelled, "This is for the Palestinians." That incident was followed by another beating in Brooklyn, where two assailants yelled anti-Semitic and pro-Palestinian slogans while hitting and slashing an Orthodox Jew with a sharp object. Other incidents of assault or harassment have been reported in Chicago, Nashville, San Francisco, Cleveland and Berkeley, including threatening phone calls to Jewish organizations from people claiming to be representatives of Palestinian and Islamic groups.

One of the most high profile acts of vandalism was the attempted firebombing of a synagogue in Riverdale, NY, which led to four arrests, including two Arab-Americans, both adults; a 17–year-old from Jordan and an unidentified 15-year-old. Two of the suspects became the first to be charged under New York State's new hate crimes statute. Meanwhile, police are investigating an explosion and fire that gutted a synagogue in Syracuse, NY. Other incidents involving vandalism or property damage possibly related to recent events in the Mideast have been reported in Philadelphia, Charlotte, Oakland, and elsewhere.

Main Findings

- In 2000, 44 states and the District of Columbia reported 1,606 anti-Semitic incidents to the Anti-Defamation League. This marks approximately a 4 percent increase in anti-Jewish incidents over 1999. Anti-Semitic activity reported in 2000 comprises 877 acts of harassment (intimidation, threats and assaults) and 729 of vandalism (property damage as well as arson and cemetery desecration).

- The small increase in anti-Semitic incidents is partly attributable to acts apparently related to the turmoil in the Middle East, which began at the end of September. While there is usually an increase in anti-Semitic incidents during the Jewish High Holy Days, when Jews are more visible, in 2000 there were at least 42 incidents that were linked by their perpetrators to the unrest in the Middle East.

- The five states reporting the most anti-Semitic incidents in 2000 are New York (481), California (257), New Jersey (213), Massachusetts (128), and Florida (81). Together, these states (with the largest Jewish populations and thus the most targets of opportunity) account for 1,160 of the 1,606 incidents reported (72 percent).

- Sixty-nine incidents of anti-Semitism occurred on college campuses, a 15 percent increase over 1999, when there were 60. This increase halts a five-year general trend of decline during which such incidents dropped by 50 percent. More than a third of these incidents involved the publication of Holocaust-denial materials in campus newspapers, a growing problem.

- In addition to their mass mailings of anti-Semitic propaganda and printings of anti-Jewish and racist publications, extremist groups continue to find in the Internet a growing vehicle for their hate. As a medium that is inexpensive and almost impossible to regulate, the Internet has become an increasingly active component of the anti-Semitic propaganda machine.

Anti–Semitism on the Internet

While some bigots mail anti-Semitic letters to or shout hateful slurs at their victims, others transmit their hate electronically. Anti-Semitic propaganda or threats directed to a specific person and received by e-mail, in a chat room, or sent via an instant-messaging program are considered anti-Semitic harassment by the *Audit*. These messages are deliberately directed to a particular person in an effort to intimidate.

E-mail messages are essentially electronic letters. Nearly anyone with access to the Internet can send and receive e-mail messages anonymously and free of charge. A mailing list can easily be compiled from public sources such as online e-mail address directories.

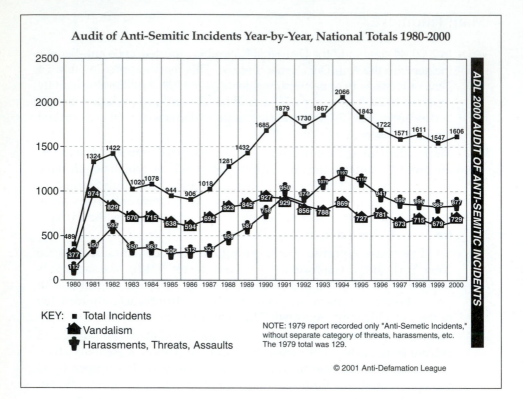

Audit of Anti-Semitic Incidents Year-by-Year, National Totals 1980-2000

KEY: ■ Total Incidents
      🏠 Vandalism
      👤 Harassments, Threats, Assaults

NOTE: 1979 report recorded only "Anti-Semetic Incidents," without separate category of threats, harassments, etc. The 1979 total was 129.

© 2001 Anti-Defamation League

ADL 2000 AUDIT OF ANTI-SEMITIC INCIDENTS

In a chat room, an Internet user can communicate in real time with one or many other users. The text that the user types almost immediately appears on the screens of the other users in the room. Haters enter chat rooms, sometimes those specifically devoted to Jewish interests, and aim anti-Semitic comments at other users. Their victims resemble friends conversing on a street corner who are hassled by bigots shouting hateful comments.

Instant-messaging software enables Internet users to create a private chat room with another individual. Functionally, an instant-messaging session is similar to a telephone call. Haters can use directories of instant-messaging users to find targets for their attacks, just as they might find Jews to target with harassing telephone calls by looking in the telephone book. An unsuspecting victim might receive a disturbing instant message just as he or she might pick up the telephone and hear a hateful voice on the other end of the line.

Measuring Internet Incidents

From year to year, ADL strives to maintain a consistent policy of evaluating anti-Semitic incidents in an effort to make accurate and reliable comparisons. There are times, however, when a significant shift in the types of anti-Semitism reported emerges, which requires a rethinking of *Audit* procedure. In response to the explosion of Internet use in the past few years, ADL has instituted the following policy on evaluating Internet-related incidents.

Anti-Semitic hate messages, threats or harassment received by electronic mail are treated as if they were sent by traditional mail and are therefore considered anti-Semitic harassment. These messages are sent deliberately from one person to another in an effort to intimidate. As with mass mailings or local distribution of hate literature, an anti-Semitic e-mail sent to a large number of recipients is classified as one incident.

Hate-oriented sites on the World Wide Web are not included as anti-Semitic incidents in the *Audit*. The presence of such a web site is comparable to the publication of a KKK or neo-Nazi newspaper, the mere existence of which, while of ongoing concern, would not be considered an anti-Semitic incident for purposes of the *Audit*.

Examples of Internet Threats and Harassment Incidents

The following is a representative sampling of anti-Semitic incidents of harassment on the Internet (some wording has been edited).

- Florida—6/12/00: A woman received an instant message stating, "f—king jew ill kill your mother f—king ass you dum f—king jew."
- Maryland—7/2/00: A Jewish woman received an instant message that read, "r u really the chepest kike in the world?"
- Florida—7/7/00: After a man requested payment for the item he had auctioned online, the winning bidder sent him an e-mail that read, "Your probably Jewish, yep gotta be. Ya Hebrew bastard! Ya sheeny dirty hebe jew!"
- Illinois—8/18/00: A Jewish teenager was targeted by anti-Semitic instant messages including "you grandparents can fit in my ash tray," "you killed Christ on your own time . . . you little kyke," and "i CAN'T WAIT TO SEE YOU BURN IN HELL . . . FOR KILLING OUR SAVIOR."
- New Jersey—8/28/00: A 14-year-old Jewish girl received an instant message stating, "u oven burining jew lemme throw u n the oven u stupid jew."

Conclusion

The 2000 figure of 1,606 represents a small increase in anti-Semitic incidents over those reported to ADL in 1999, when there were 1,547 incidents. At the same time, the 2000 figure is lower than the average of the previous five years (1,658), and lower still than the average of the previous 10 years (1,752). To be sure, any increase is troubling—but the 2000 totals are within the approximate range of 1,550–1,600 incidents reflected in the *Audits* of the last several years.

Yet, while the five- and ten-year trends inspire cautious optimism, they should not invite complacency. Anti-Semitism in the U.S. cannot be viewed as merely the sum total of incidents reported to ADL. These incidents are part of a larger picture, which must be placed in a broader context. According to the FBI's most recent annual reports on hate crimes, over 75 percent of all such acts per-petrated on the basis of religion were directed against Jewish individuals and institutions. Further, as always, anti-Semitic and racist organizations such as The World Church of the Creator, The National Alliance, and the Ku Klux Klan continue to recruit members and advertise their hatred to as many eyes and ears as possible.

Extremism and the hostilities it generates persist in America. Dozens of organizations and movements on the extreme fringes of American society have gained access to much wider audiences by building web sites that pro-mote their propaganda. Numbering in the hundreds and growing, these sites are relatively easy and inexpensive to build and maintain, and because the Internet is virtually impossible to regulate, they can influence Web surfers, es-pecially young people.

A realistic perspective on anti-Semitism in America further recognizes that the *Audit* does not tell the full story reflected by each individual incident: behind each statistic lies a real person or community in pain. The lasting ef-fect of anti-Semitism and racism on individuals and communities is impossi-ble to quantify, but should not be overlooked.

Community leaders have a significant role to play in relieving the effects of anti-Jewish incidents, and in helping prevent similar acts in the future. In their distinct spheres of influence, educators, clergy, law enforcement per-sonnel and parents have the opportunity to act and speak out against hateful speech and behavior, while promoting education that encourages tolerance and respect for differences. Over time, preventive measures such as educa-tion, anti-bias and diversity training and hate crimes legislation can reduce hate activity.

State Hate Crimes Statutory Provisions

Provision	AL	AK	AZ	AR	CA	CO	CT	DC	DE	FL	GA	HI	ID	IL	IN	IA	KS	KY	LA	ME	MD	MA	MI	MN	MS	MO	MT	NE	NV	NH	NJ	NM	NY	NC	ND	OH	OK	OR	PA	RI	SC	SD	TN	TX	UT	VT	VA	WA	WV	WI	WY
Bias-Motivated Violence and Intimidation	✓	✓	✓		✓	✓	✓	✓	✓	✓	✓		✓	✓		✓		✓	✓	✓	✓	✓	✓	✓	✓	✓	✓	✓	✓	✓	✓		✓	✓	✓	✓	✓	✓	✓	✓		✓	✓	✓[1]	✓[2]	✓	✓	✓	✓	✓	
Civil Action		✓	✓	✓	✓	✓	✓	✓	✓	✓	✓		✓	✓		✓			✓			✓	✓	✓	✓	✓		✓			✓						✓	✓	✓	✓		✓	✓			✓	✓	✓		✓	
Criminal Penalty	✓	✓	✓		✓	✓	✓	✓	✓	✓			✓	✓		✓		✓	✓	✓	✓	✓	✓	✓	✓	✓		✓	✓	✓	✓		✓	✓	✓	✓	✓	✓	✓	✓		✓	✓	✓	✓	✓	✓	✓	✓	✓	
Race, Religion[3], Ethnicity	✓	✓	✓		✓	✓	✓	✓	✓	✓	✓		✓	✓		✓		✓	✓	✓	✓	✓	✓	✓	✓	✓	✓	✓	✓	✓	✓		✓	✓	✓	✓	✓	✓	✓	✓		✓	✓			✓	✓	✓	✓	✓	
Sexual Orientation			✓		✓		✓	✓	✓	✓				✓		✓			✓	✓		✓		✓		✓		✓		✓	✓		✓					✓								✓		✓		✓	
Gender		✓			✓			✓						✓		✓			✓	✓	✓				✓			✓		✓	✓		✓													✓		✓	✓		
Other[4]		✓			✓			✓	✓	✓	✓	✓		✓	✓		✓					✓	✓	✓						✓	✓		✓	✓	✓		✓									✓					
Institutional Vandalism	✓		✓		✓	✓	✓	✓	✓					✓		✓	✓	✓	✓	✓	✓	✓	✓	✓	✓	✓	✓		✓		✓	✓	✓	✓	✓	✓	✓	✓	✓	✓	✓		✓	✓			✓	✓	✓	✓	
Data Collection[5]			✓		✓	✓	✓	✓		✓			✓	✓		✓		✓	✓	✓	✓	✓	✓	✓				✓			✓		✓				✓		✓	✓				✓			✓	✓		✓	
Training for Law Enforcement Personnel[6]			✓		✓									✓								✓		✓														✓										✓			

1 The Texas Statute refers to victims selected "because of the defendant's bias or prejudice against a person or group."

2 The Utah Statute ties penalties for hate crimes to violations of the victim's constitutional or civil rights.

3 The following states also have statutes criminalizing interference with religious worship: CA, DC, FL, ID, MD, MA, MI, MN, MS, MO, NV, NM, NY, NC, OK, RI, SC, SD, TN, VA, WV.

4 "Other" includes mental and physical disability or handicap (AL, AK, AZ, CA, DC, DE, IL, IA, LA, ME, MA, MN, MO, NE, NV, NH, NJ, NY, OK, RI, VT, WA, WI), political affiliation (DC, IA, LA, WV) and age (DC, IA, LA, VT).

5 States with data collection statutes which include sexual orientation are AZ, CA, CT, DC, FL, IL, IA, MD, MI, MN, NV, OR, and WA; those which include gender are AZ, DC, IL, IA, MI, MN, WA.

6 Some other states have regulations mandating such training.

Anti–Semitism in the Middle East

On the Holocaust

[Jews] are the plague of the generation and the bacterium of all time. Their history always was and always will be stained with treachery, falseness, and lying. . . . [The Holocaust] is no more than a fabrication, a lie, and a fraud.

> —Fatma Abdallah Mahmoud, writing in the Egyptian government daily *Al-Akhbar,* April 29, 2002

The success of the Jews has not been a mere coincidence. It resulted from long and arduous years of planning, which preceded their cunning control of the world's media. . . . They concocted horrible stories of gas chambers which Hitler, they claimed, used to burn them alive. . . . The truth is that such persecution was a malicious fabrication by the Jews. It is a myth which they named "The Holocaust" in order to rouse empathy.

> —Seif 'Ali Al-Jarwan, writing in *Al-Hayat Al-Jadida* (the largest daily in the Palestinian Authority), July 2, 1998

On Jews Consuming Blood

The Jews spilling human blood to prepare pastry for their holidays is a well-established fact. . . . the victim must be a mature adolescent who is, of course, a non-Jew—that is, a Christian or a Muslim.

> —Dr. Umayma Ahmad Al-Jalahma of King Faysal University, writing in the Saudi government daily *Al-Riyadh,* March 10, 2002

On Getting Rid of Jews

[Jews] must be butchered and killed, as Allah the Almighty said: "Fight them: Allah will torture them at your hands, and will humiliate them and will help you to overcome them". . . . Have no mercy on the Jews, no matter where they are, in any country. Fight them, wherever you are. Wherever you meet them, kill them. Wherever you are, kill those Jews and those Americans who are like them.

> —Dr. Ahmad Abu Halabiya, member of the Palestinian Authority appointed "Fatwa Council" and former acting Rector of the Islamic University in Gaza, in a sermon broadcast live on the official Palestinian Authority television, October 13, 2000

Bin Laden defended the oppressed. We warn the U.S. and advise her to get rid of the Jews.

> —Abdallah Bin Matruk Al-Haddal of the Saudi Arabia Ministry of Islamic Affairs, on *Al-Jazeera TV,* January 22, 2002

> —Source: Middle East Media Research Institute (www.MEMRI.org)

VII

Genocide in America

> We can send from here, in the name of the Holy Trinity, all the slaves and brazil-wood which could be sold. If the information I have is correct, we can sell 4,000 slaves, who will be worth, at least, 20 millions, and 4,000 hundred-weight of brazil-wood, which will be worth just as much. . . . one Indian is worth three Negroes. . . . So that, from these two commodities it seems we can get at least forty millions.
>
> —Christopher Columbus to Ferdinand and Isabella, King and Queen of Spain, 1496

VII
SECTION OVERVIEW

In the centuries following Christopher Columbus's arrival in the "New World," the number of Native Americans killed (both in absolute numbers and percentage of the population) exceeded the number of Jews killed in the Holocaust. Nonetheless, scores of American cities, buildings, highways, and monuments are named in honor of Christopher Columbus, and Columbus Day continues to be celebrated as a U.S. national holiday.

As the readings in this section show, prejudice against American Indians has been held at the highest levels of government, and the extermination of Indians was for many years an explicit national policy. Moreover, the appropriation of Native American culture and property is not merely historical—it continues to this day, often unnoticed by non-Indians. As you read this section, consider how Native American language, ideas, foods, art, and customs are woven into everyday life in the United States.

Take Special Notice

Much of the historical material in this section is absent from American history textbooks, even though textbooks often cover American slavery and the Holocaust in some detail. What accounts for the difference? Are the reasons psychological?

Questions Worth Pondering

- Would you agree with Ward Churchill that genocide was committed against Native Americans?
- Is genocide *currently* being committed against Native Americans?
- How is the destruction of American Indian nations similar to what took place during the Holocaust of World War II? How is it different?
- Why is it acceptable to name and market products such as Red Man chewing tobacco, Big Chief writing tablets, Land O'Lakes butter, Jeep Cherokees, Cadillacs, and Pontiacs when other minority group names and logos would be considered racist?
- Is the use of American Indian mascots in sports a form of legalized discrimination against a minority group?
- Is the appropriation of Native American culture a modern form of colonialism? If so, have you been an accomplice? A passive bystander? A resistance fighter?

A Christopher Columbus Day Parable

Suppose some hungry, homeless people suddenly appear in your neighborhood, and you decide to take them into your home and care for them. You give them rooms of their own and treat them as members of your family. After they regain their strength, you show them how to be self-reliant.

But then, rather than moving out on their own, the homeless people decide they want to stay in your home. They take over your den, your kitchen, and your living room. Soon you are forced to live in the garage. Then they discover that your garage contains a car, which they decide they need, and you are banished to live in the backyard.

Your friends and neighbors come to your defense, asking the homeless people to return your property. The homeless people respond by killing them and taking their property, too.

You appeal to the courts for justice, but because the homeless people possess your property, the judge rules that it is theirs by law. You are forced to beg in the streets, and you watch, helplessly, as your children die of disease and malnutrition.

Now imagine one final nightmare. Imagine that you are asked to celebrate this event. If you understand how impossible such a celebration would be, you understand how Native Americans feel about celebrating the 500th anniversary of Christopher Columbus' arrival in North America. Asking Native Americans to celebrate this anniversary is like asking the Jews to celebrate the Holocaust.

—Adapted from Tom Trimmer, *Fourteen Hundred and Ninety-Two: Owosh-Keday-So-Quay's Story*, 1991

American Indian Stereotypes and Realities

Stereotype	Reality
Native Americans were uncivilized and unsophisticated before Europeans arrived.	Native Americans had already cultivated corn, beans, potatoes, tomatoes, cacao (chocolate), peppers, and many other foods. They had also developed cures for amoebic dysentery, scurvy, intestinal worms, and other maladies.
Native Americans were "wild Indians" who had no form of government until Europeans arrived.	The American Constitution was predated and in part based on the Iroquois Confederacy's "Great Law of Peace," which included ideas such as equal representation, checks and balances, impeachment, democracy, and freedom.
As suggested by the children's game "Cowboys and Indians," cowboys were the main enemy of Native Americans.	The main enemy of Native Americans was the U.S. army, not cowboys. In fact, some of the first cowboys were Mexican Indians.
Native Americans invented the practice of scalping their enemies.	Scalping dates back to ancient Greece and was introduced in America by the Dutch. The Massachusetts and Pennsylvania colonies offered bounties for Indian scalps.
Native Americans lived in tipis before Europeans arrived.	Although Plains Indians often lived in tipis, most North American Indians never saw a tipi, let alone lived in one.
Native Americans died mainly because their bows and arrows were no match for the guns used by the U.S. army.	Native Americans died mainly from the introduction of European diseases. In some cases, the diseases were spread deliberately. For example, in 1763 Lord Jeffrey Amherst (namesake of Amherst, Massachusetts) sent blankets infected with smallpox to the Ottawa people.
Pocahontas was an Indian princess.	There is no such thing as an American Indian princess; the lexicon of royalty was imposed by Europeans. Pocahontas was the daughter of Wahunsonacock, chief of the Powhattan confederacy.
Today, most Native Americans in the United States live on reservations.	Most Native Americans live outside U.S. reservations. During much of the 1800s Native Americans were forced to live on reservations, but this restriction was eliminated long ago.
Native Americans are not U.S. citizens.	In 1924, the Indian Citizenship Act declared all Native Americans U.S. citizens. Native Americans 18 or older are eligible to vote in all U.S. elections.

Source: Adapted from Mihesuah, American Indians: Stereotypes and Reality, 1996; U.S. Department of Health and Human Services, Mental health: Culture, Race, and Ethnicity—A Supplement to Mental Health: A Report of the Surgeon General, 2001

How Native Americans Were Described

"... the merciless Indian savages, whose known rule of warfare is an undistinguished destruction of all ages, sexes, and conditions ..."

—U.S. Declaration of Independence, July 4, 1776

A Half–Filled Outline of Humanity

[Indians] are extreamly apt to get drunk, and, when so, are very quarrelsome and disorderly. . . . if it be the design of Providence to extirpate these savages in order to make room for cultivators of the earth, it seems not improbable that rum may be the appointed means.

　　—Benjamin Franklin, 1771

Look at the aboriginal inhabitants of the land we occupy. It pleased the Creator to call into existence this half-filled outline of humanity; this sketch in red crayons of a rudimental manhood; to keep the continent from being a blank until the true lord of creation should come to claim it. Civilization and Christianity have tried to humanize him. . . . But instinct has its way sooner or later; the partridge makes but a troublesome chicken, and the Indian but a sorry Master of Arts. . . . Then the white man hates him, and hunts him down like the wild beasts of the forest, and so the red-crayon sketch is rubbed out, and the canvas is ready for a picture of manhood a little more like God's own image.

　　—Oliver Wendell Holmes, 1855

The people of the pueblos [are] Indians in race, customs, and domestic government. Always living in separate and isolated communities, adhering to primitive modes of life, largely influenced by superstition and fetichism, and chiefly governed according to the crude customs inherited from their ancestors, they are essentially a simple, uninformed, and inferior people.

　　—U.S. Supreme Court, in *United States v. Felipe Sandoval*, 1913

U.S. Presidents Speak

Attempting to drive [Indians] by force of arms out of their Country . . . is like driving the wild Beasts of ye forest . . . the gradual extension of our settlements will as certainly cause the savage, as the wolf, to retire; both being beasts of prey, tho' they differ in shape.

—George Washington, 1783

[Indians] have neither the intelligence, the industry, the moral habits, nor the desire of improvement which are essential to any favorable change in their condition. Established in the midst of another and a superior race, and without appreciating the causes of their inferiority or seeking to control them, they must necessarily yield to the force of circumstances and ere long disappear.

—Andrew Jackson, 1833

[The American government's] dealings with the Indian tribes have been just and friendly throughout; its efforts for their civilization constant, and directed by the best feelings of humanity.

—Martin Van Buren, 1838

It is our glory that whilst other nations have extended their dominions by the sword we have never acquired any territory except by fair purchase or, as in the case of Texas, by the voluntary determination of a brave, kindred, and independent people to blend their destinies with our own.

—James Buchanan, 1857

I don't go so far as to think that the only good Indians are the dead Indians, but I believe nine out of every ten are, and I shouldn't like to inquire too closely into the case of the tenth.

It is nonsense to talk about our having driven most of these Indians out of their lands. They did not own the land at all, in the white sense; they merely occupied it.

—Theodore Roosevelt, 1886 and 1893

U.S. Army Generals Speak

I want no peace till the Indians suffer more.

> —Samuel R. Curtis, 1864

[Do] not receive overtures of peace or submission . . . attack and kill every male Indian over twelve years of age.

> —Patrick E. Connor, giving orders to a field officer, 1865

We must act with vindictive earnestness against the Sioux, even to their extermination, men, women and children.

> —William Tecumseh Sherman, 1866

The whites are a numerous people, and they are spreading out. They require room, and cannot help it.

> —Winfield Scott Hancock, 1867

The only good Indians I ever saw were dead.

> —Philip Sheridan, 1869

It is useless to suppose that thousands of wild savages thoroughly armed and mounted can be controlled by moral [per]suasion.

> —Nelson A. Miles, 1879

I wanted no other occupation in life than to ward off the savage and kill off his food until there should no longer be an Indian frontier in our beautiful country.

> —John McAllister Schofield, 1897

Definition of Genocide

Genocide means any of the following acts committed with intent to destroy, in whole or in part, a national, ethnical, racial or religious group, as such:

(a) Killing members of the group;
(b) Causing serious bodily or mental harm to members of the group;
(c) Deliberately inflicting on the group conditions of life calculated to bring about its physical destruction in whole or in part;
(d) Imposing measures intended to prevent births within the group;
(e) Forcibly transferring children of the group to another group.

—Convention on the Prevention and Punishment of the Crime of Genocide, Article II, *United Nations Treaty Series*, 1951

How Does Genocide Happen?

With prolonged exposure to violence and killing, human beings have the capacity to regard such acts as nothing extraordinary. Some perpetrators may feel sick and disgusted when killing large numbers of people, as they might feel in slaughtering animals, but often even they will proceed to kill for a "good" reason, for a "higher" cause. How do they come to this? In essence, difficult life conditions, real or perceived conflicts of interest, and certain cultural characteristics—such as aggressiveness, ethnocentrism, and obedience to authority—generate psychological processes and motives that lead one group to turn against another group. The perpetrators change, individually and collectively, as they progress along a continuum of destruction that ends in genocide.

—Adapted from Ervin Staub, *The Roots of Evil: The Origins of Genocide and Other Group Violence,* 1989

They Have Not the Same Sensibilities

They have not the same acute and tender sensibilities with the other races of men. . . . Their impassible fortitude and endurance of suffering, which have been so much vaunted, are after all, in my mind, the result of a greater degree of physical insensibility. It has been told me, with how much truth I know not, but I believe it, that in amputation, and other surgical operations, their nerves do not shrink, do not show the same tendency to spasm, with those of the whites. . . . This increasing insensibility, transmitted from generation to generation, finally becomes inwrought with the whole web of animal nature, and the body of the savage seems to have little more sensibility than the hoof of horses.

—Clergyman Timothy Flint, describing Native Americans in *Recollections of the Last Ten Years*, 1826

What Was Promised

The utmost good faith shall always be observed towards the Indians; their lands and property shall never be taken from them without their consent; and, in their property, rights, and liberty, they shall never be invaded or disturbed, unless in just and lawful wars authorized by Congress; but laws founded in justice and humanity, shall from time to time be made for preventing wrongs being done to them, and for preserving peace and friendship with them.

> —*The Northwest Ordinance*, Article III, adopted by the Congress of the Confederacy on July 13, 1787

The general government will never consent to your being defrauded. But it will protect you in all your just rights. . . . If any man brings you evil reports of the intentions of the United States, mark that man as your enemy, for he will mean to deceive you and lead you into trouble. The United States will be true and faithful to their engagements.

> —George Washington, addressing chiefs of the Seneca Nation, December 29, 1790

Your lands are your own; your right to them shall never be violated by us; they are yours to keep or to sell as you please. . . . When a want of land in a particular place induces us to ask you to sell, still you are always free to say "No."

> —Thomas Jefferson, addressing the Ottawas, Senecas, and other American Indian nations, April 22, 1808

What Took Place

The indigenous peoples of the United States once possessed exclusive tenure to all the lands. Today they are left with only 2.3% of the land which was once their exclusive possession.

—Klaus Frantz, *Indian Reservations in the United States: Territory, Sovereignty, and Socioeconomic Change,* 1999

Within no more than a handful of generations following their first encounters with Europeans, the vast majority of the Western Hemisphere's native peoples were exterminated (an overall decline of 95 percent has become a working rule of thumb). The destruction of the Indians of the Americas was, far and away, the most massive act of genocide in the history of the world, with numbers that eventually totaled close to 100,000,000.

—Adapted from David E. Stannard, *American Holocaust: Columbus and the Conquest of the New World,* 1992

The Current State of Affairs

Indians are about twice as likely as non-Indians to be murdered. Their death rate from alcoholism is four times the national average, and the rate of fetal alcohol syndrome among their children is thirty-three times higher than for whites. Indian babies are three times as likely as white babies to die of sudden infant death syndrome (SIDS). Indians smoke more than non-Indians, and smoking is their leading cause of cancer death. They commit suicide at rates that in certain circumstances approach the epidemic. The American Medical Association says that one in five Indian girls and one in eight boys attempts suicide by the end of high school.

—Ian Frazier, *On the Rez,* 2000

A Good Break

I don't feel we did wrong in taking this great country away from [the American Indians]. . . . Our so-called stealing of this country from them was just a matter of survival. There were great numbers of people who needed new land, and the Indians were selfishly trying to keep it for themselves. . . . you can't whine and bellyache 'cause somebody else got a good break and you didn't, like these Indians are.

    —John Wayne, in a *Playboy* interview (May, 1971)

I Don't Know What Their Complaint Might Be

Let me tell you just a little something about the American Indian in our land. We have provided millions of acres of land for what are called preservations—or reservations, I should say. . . . And [the Indians are] free also to leave the reservations and be American citizens among the rest of us, and many do. Some still prefer, however, that way—that early way of life. And we've done everything we can to meet their demands as to how they want to live. Maybe we made a mistake. Maybe we should not have humored them in that wanting to stay in that kind of primitive lifestyle. Maybe we should have said, no, come join us; be citizens along with the rest of us. As I say, many have; many have been very successful. . . .

And you'd be surprised: Some of them became very wealthy because some of those reservations were overlaying great pools of oil, and you can get very rich pumping oil. And so, I don't know what their complaint might be.

> —Ronald Reagan, speaking to students and faculty at Moscow State University (apparently unaware that the Citizenship Act of 1924 had already granted citizenship to American Indians), May 31, 1988

Court Ruling: "Irresponsibility in Its Purest Form"

It would be difficult to find a more historically mismanaged federal program than the Individual Indian Money (IIM) trust. . . . The court knows of no other program in American government in which federal officials are allowed to write checks—some of which are known to be written in erroneous amounts—from unreconciled accounts—some of which are known to have incorrect balances. Such behavior certainly would not be tolerated from private sector trustees. It is fiscal and governmental irresponsibility in its purest form.

The United States' mismanagement of the IIM trust is far more inexcusable than garden-variety trust mismanagement. . . . As the government concedes, the purpose of the IIM trust was to deprive plaintiffs' ancestors of their native lands. . . . [Yet now the government] cannot provide an accounting of plaintiffs' money, which the United States has forced into the IIM trust. This problem . . . imposes far more than pecuniary costs, although those are clear and cannot be overstated. Plaintiffs' class includes some of the poorest people in this nation.

> —Judge Royce Lamberth, February 22, 1999, holding the U.S. Secretary of the Interior in contempt for "flagrant disregard" of court orders and "lack of candor in concealing their wrongdoing" [*Note:* The funds involve $500 million in annual payments owed to nearly 40,000 Indians for business leases and other uses of their land. Among other things, the government allegedly used Indian funds to help bail out New York City during its 1975 fiscal crisis, save the Chrysler Corporation from going under, and reduce the national debt.]

NAMING OUR DESTINY: TOWARD A LANGUAGE OF AMERICAN INDIAN LIBERATION

WARD CHURCHILL

"What's your tribe?" This familiar query, typically coming after introductory greetings between American Indians, or extended by non-Indians when introduced to Indians, is hardly as innocuous as it may seem. Nor is the usual reply, offered reflexively and consisting of only a few words: "I'm a member of the Kiowa Tribe," or "the Mohawk Tribe," or any of several hundred comparable designations popularly, anthropologically, and often legally recognized as describing the status of the many distinct peoples indigenous to North America. Although the question and its response may appear harmless enough, they are actually charged with political content, all of it implicitly negative in terms of native rights and dignity. Indeed, the vernacular of "tribalism" goes a long way toward foreclosing on the potential for positive changes in the socioeconomic and political situation of American Indians in the future.

The principles at issue are both fundamental and straightforward. How one is perceived by others does much to determine the nature of the respect—or lack of it—they are likely to accord you. By the same measure, how one sees oneself is a crucial element by which one ultimately defines the type and extent of respect (and attendant rights) one asserts as one's due. Only when one's self-concept is at odds with the views of others does the foundation exist for one to challenge and resist the treatment which results from it.

Such matters are, of course, as relevant to the dynamics of interactive group processes as they are to the realm of interpersonal relations: how a group is seen by others, and how it sees itself, are factors that in many ways define the conditions under which the group will live, and the options it will be able to exercise in affecting these conditions. It is, for example, one thing to see oneself as being part of a social or political movement, quite another to be lumped in as a member of a "gang." Hence, it seems self-evident that how individuals and groups are labeled or named—and, perhaps more importantly, how they name themselves—is vital to the circumstances of their existence. In naming ourselves, both individually and collectively, we in effect name not only our reality, but our destiny.

Words such as "nation" and "tribe" are *not* interchangeable in either political or legal contexts. To the contrary, phrases such as "tribal sovereignty" add up to near-perfect politico-judicial oxymorons, logical impossibilities designed to distort and confuse rather than to inform or clarify discussion of indigenous rights. Referring to someone, or to oneself, as a "member of an Indian tribe" is not, and has never been, a friendly or value-neutral act. This essay will endeavor to explain why.

"Tribes" Versus "Peoples"

The ongoing significance of Europeans' bestowal of the term "tribes" upon the native peoples they encountered during the period of their expansion across the globe may be apprehended in a meaning of the word which was being developed concurrently. According to the definitive *Oxford English Dictionary* (OED), a tribe is a "group in the classification of plants, animals, etc., used as superior and sometimes inferior to a family; also, loosely, any group or series of animals."[1] There is thus little disparity between categorizing indigenous peoples as tribes, and classifying them as being aggregated into herds, packs, gaggles, coveys, flocks, or any other mode of "lower" animal organization. When applied to human groups, the term takes as its primary focus the lineage of the people included within its rubric, in much the same manner that cattle breeders concern themselves with the pedigree of their livestock. In fact, *Webster's New Collegiate Dictionary* continues to associate the term with *"Stock Breeding"* (emphasis in the original), as in "a group of animals descended from some particular female progenitor, through the female line."[2] It is in this light that the balance of the OED's current definition of "tribe" should be considered:

> A group of persons forming a community and claiming common ancestry. . . . A particular race of recognized ancestry: a family. . . . A race of people; now esp. to a primary aggregate of people in a primitive or barbarous condition, under a headman or chief.

Or, examine the pertinent language in *Webster's*: "[A]ny aggregation of people, esp. in a primitive or nomadic state, believed to be of a common stock." No matter which way one twists it, to be addressed as "tribal" by English-speaking people—and by speakers of all other major European languages as well—is to be demeaned. Not only is one's society definitionally restricted from having achieved any level of cultural attainment beyond that of "primitivism" or "barbarism"—both pejoratives in the Western lexicon—but one is reduced to being construed as no more than the product of one's gene pool. Suffice it to say that a more racist construction would be difficult to conceive.[3]

No native language in North America contains a word which translates accurately as "tribe." The literal translation of most American Indian people's names for themselves was, traditionally, exactly that: "people." The consistency with which what is at best a mistranslation has been substituted for more accurate terminology cannot be dismissed as something either benign or inadvertent. Consider the relevant portion of *Webster's* definition of most native groups' own self-descriptor:

> **Peo'ple...1.** A body of persons united by a common character, culture, or sentiment: the individuals collectively of any characteristic group, conceived apart from the unity of the group as subject to common government (that is, as a *state*) or as issued from a common stock (that is, as a *race* or *tribe*). **2.** A race, tribe, or nation; as, the *peoples* of Europe [emphases in the original].

There is nothing positive which can be said to be intrinsic to the meaning of "tribe" and not encompassed within the term "people." The significance of the Euroamerican's continuing insistence upon referring to native societies as tribes rather than as peoples can thus be located primarily—though not necessarily exclusively, as will be explained below—in the animalistic emphasis embodied in the former, a matter readily contrasted to the fact that the latter relates, as the OED puts it, specifically and *"emphatically* [to] Human beings" (emphasis in the original). It follows that, when indigenous peoples are passed off as tribes, and conditioned to view themselves this way, they are effectively cast as being subhuman. From the imposition of such linguistic subordination, it is but the easiest of steps, both psychologically and physically, to the wholesale expropriation of American Indian assets.[4]

The Meaning of "Nation"

Nor has "people" been the only terminological alternative to "tribe." The word "nation," for example, is defined by *Webster's* as being applicable to a "people connected by supposed ties of blood generally manifested by a community of language, religion, customs, etc. . . . Any aggregation of people having institutions and customs and a sense of social homogeneity and mutual interest. . . . The body of inhabitants of a country united under a single independent government." Or, to take the meaning formulated by the OED, a nation is:

> An extensive aggregate of persons, so closely associated with one another by common descent, language, or history, as to form a distinct race or people, usually organized as a separate political state and occupying a definite territory. In early examples the racial idea is usually stronger than the political; in recent use the notion of political unity and independence is more prominent . . . a country. . . . The whole people of a country, freq. in contrast to some smaller or narrower body within it [such as a community, clan, family or "tribe"].

This would, in a number of important ways, seem to be the most accurate English-language depiction of American Indian societies. Indeed, almost as an afterthought, *Webster's* acknowledges that nation is a term which might be correctly applied to any "one of a group of Indian tribes; as, the *Six Nations*" (the reference being to the Haudenosaunee, or Iroquois Six Nations Confederacy, as it is called in English; emphasis in the original). The OED goes a bit further, observing that the word "nation" might best serve to supplant certain archaic or inappropriate terminology, like "Irish Clans" or "tribes of North American Indians," with a more satisfactory and fitting explanation of the social contexts involved.

In the real world, however, suggestions that Indians should be referred to as composing nations rather than tribes are often met with flippant dismissal as being "rhetorical," "polemical" or, to borrow a catch phrase presently in vogue among reactionaries, "politically correct."[5] It is frequently asserted that attempting to apply contemporary concepts of nationhood to historical indigenous societies is an exercise in revisionism, a *post hoc* effort to inject a form and dignity into native settings in which it was never really present.[6]

The idea that the concept of national identity is somehow too modern to be applicable to indigenous societies is itself a revision of historical fact. Even the most cursory reading of the literature of the European colonial period in North America reveals that the colonists and their respective governments understood very well that when dealing with indigenous peoples, they were dealing with other nations. The Spanish record is marked by the Dominican priest Bartolomé de Las Casas's early sixteenth century declaration that "no one may deny that these people are fully capable of governing themselves, and of living like men of good intelligence, and that they are more than others well ordered, sensible, prudent, and rational."[7] The French are known to have entered into a whole series of formal alliances with a large number of Algonkian-speaking peoples—the Montagnais, Micmacs, Etchemins, Hurons, Abenakis, and Algonquins among them—of the sort explicitly reserved for the realm of international affairs.[8] Regarding the brief extension of Dutch colonialism onto the continent, it has been observed that:

> [Colonists and Indians] treated each other as separate powers, equal in theory and practice. The Dutch came to America for trade and empire: in seeking these they dealt with the Indians as . . . political and military powers to be negotiated with, fought as enemies, or courted as allies.[9]

The English Crown in particular, despite an abundant usage of terms such as "tribes" and "savages" (or "salvages," as it was most often spelled in those days) to describe Indians in popular literature, consistently referred to native peoples as constituting nations in their own right.[10] This was intended, not metaphorically, but in a precise and legalistic sense. Examples are legion, but citation of only a few should serve to illustrate the point. In 1624, for instance, Plymouth colonist William Wood remarked that, among the native societies he encountered in Massachusetts, there were both laws and a relative absence of criminal conduct: "[A]s their evill courses come short of many other Nations, so they have not so many Lawes, though they are not without some."[11] Somewhat later, an anonymous chronicler of Indian/white relations in Maryland recorded native "ambassadors" seeking to school their English counterparts in "ye law of Nations."[12] "No people in the world," wrote English Superintendent for Southern Indian Affairs Edmund Atkin in 1754, "understand and pursue their true National Interest, better than the Indians."[13]

England officially and repeatedly affirmed the genuinely national character of most of eastern North America's indigenous societies, forging a complex set of diplomatic relations with them which included numerous trade agreements and military alliances. Career diplomats were committed by the Crown to such purposes—Atkin in the south, for example, and Sir William Johnson in the north—their efforts consummating in a lengthy series of treaties between England and an array of American Indian peoples. What is important to note in this connection is that the prevailing international custom and convention to which

England was then bound held that treaties were instruments of understanding and agreement which could exist *only* between fully sovereign nations.[14] In other words, each treaty legally signified England's formal and unequivocal recognition that its native counterparts embodied the same attributes of nationality evidenced by England itself. As Atkin put it at the time, "[I]n their publick Treaties no People on earth are more open, explicit, and Direct [than Indian nations]. Nor are they excelled by any in the observance of them."[15]

After 1776, the newly-emergent United States followed the English example, conducting its relations with Indians on an explicitly nation-to-nation basis involving formal treaties and other accoutrements of international diplomacy.[16] Between 1778 and 1868, the federal government entered into more than 370 ratified treaties (and several hundred more which were never ratified), each of them conveying direct legal recognition by the United States that one or more indigenous peoples constituted nations in exactly "the same sense as any other."[17] Given that many of these international instruments entailed land cessions by the native peoples involved, and thus constitute the basic title to most of what the U.S. now claims as its own territory, the majority of the treaties remain in force at the present time despite the government's official suspension of treaty-making with Indians in 1871.[18]

Although it has become fashionable in some circles to insist U.S./Indian treaties never "really" implied any genuine acknowledgement of the national status of the latter peoples, the statements of the federal government's most preeminent legal authorities at the time point to the exact opposite. As Chief Justice of the Supreme Court John Marshall observed in 1831 with regard to the Cherokees: "The numerous treaties made with them by the United States recognize them as a people capable of maintaining the relations of peace and war, of being responsible for their political character for any violation of their engagements, or for any aggression committed on the citizens of the United States, by any individual of their community. . . . [Hence, the] acts of our government plainly recognize the Cherokee nation as a state, and the courts are bound by those acts."[19] More broadly, Attorney General William Wirt framed the matter in the following way in an opinion written in 1828:

> The point . . . once conceded, that the Indians are independent to the purpose of treating, their independence is, to that purpose, as absolute as that of any other nation. Nor can it be conceded that their independence as a nation is a limited independence. Like all other independent nations, they are governed solely by their own laws. Like all other independent nations, they have the absolute power of war and peace. Like all other independent nations, their territory is inviolable by any other sovereignty. . . . They treat, or refuse to treat, at their pleasure; and there is no human power that can rightfully control them in the exercise of their discretion in this respect. In their treaties, in all their contracts with regard to their property, they are as free, sovereign, and independent as any other nation.[20]

This was by no means a transient or atypical viewpoint. A generation later, there was still no disagreement among U.S. policymakers as to whether treaty-making with Indian peoples entailed recognition of them as nations. As Indian Commissioner Ely S. Parker stated in 1869, "A treaty involves the idea of a compact between two or more sovereign powers,"[21] a matter which led Commissioner Edward P. Smith to conclude in 1873 that, "we have in theory over sixty-five independent nations within our borders, with whom we have entered into treaty relations as being sovereign peoples."[22]

"Nits Make Lice"

That the popular European/Euroamerican discourse on American Indians— most of it government-sanctioned—continued to rely upon the vernacular of tribalism even while the governments themselves were evolving policies in which Indians were recognized as nations may seem contradictory on its face. This apparent paradox can, however, be reconciled by the simple suggestion that the governments involved never intended to honor the commitments they were making to indigenous nations. It was mainly tactical, to gain certain advantages over them.[23] In effect, native nations could be acknowledged as such because their national rights would, in the future, be extinguished via their physical liquidation (at least as early as 1830, federal statutes are known to contain clauses stipulating Indian lands would "revert" to the U.S. "if the Indians become extinct").[24] Once this end result had been attained by extralegal means, the means could be legitimated through denials that those liquidated had ever possessed bona fide national rights in the first place (the dead, after all, are in no position to debate the point). Small wonder that Adolf Hitler would later expressly base his own notions of diplomacy and foreign policy on the example offered by "the Nordics of North America."[25]

As a rule, it was the population-at-large—average colonists, "pioneers," and "settlers," not the formal apparatus of European states—which was expected to carry out the actual expropriation of native property and corresponding eradication of indigenous populations.[26] In order for this to work, it was imperative that the citizenry of Europe be inculcated with a view of those to be exterminated as something less than themselves, or, preferably, less than human.[27] To this purpose, the nomenclature of tribalism, with its emphasis on the animalism of those thus classified, was ideally suited.

Thus, during the sixteenth century, the Spanish could lead the way, customarily referring to Indians as "beasts" and treating them as such.[28] In the Caribbean, this led to the unremitting horrors documented by Las Casas and the reduction of the regional indigenous population from as many as 14 million to extinction in barely a generation.[29] On the mainland, the story was much the same; in central Mexico, for example, "the population fell by almost 95 percent within seventy-five years following the Europeans' first arrival—from more than 25,000,000 in 1519 to barely 1,300,000 in 1595."[30] In Peru, the drop was from as many as 14 million to about one-half million between 1520 and 1620.[31] And so it went, throughout "Latin" America.

The means and attitudes by which this was accomplished are instructive: "To many of the conquerors, the Indian was merely another savage animal, and [so] dogs were trained to pursue and rip apart their human quarry with the same zest as they felt when hunting wild beasts."[32] In one instance, involving men under command of the celebrated "Discoverer of the Pacific," Vasco Núñez de Balboa:

> The Spaniards cut off the arm of one, the leg or hip of another, and from some their heads at one stroke, like butchers cutting up beef or mutton for market. Six hundred, including the cacique, were thus slain like brute beasts. . . . Vasco ordered forty of them to be torn to pieces by dogs.[33]

Such scenes were the norm rather than the exception in Spanish practice, as historian David E. Stannard recounts:

> Just as the Spanish soldiers seem to have particularly enjoyed testing the sharpness of their yardlong rapiers on the bodies of Indian children, so their dogs seemed to find the soft bodies of infants especially tasty, and the accounts of the invading conquistadors and the padres who traveled with them are filled with detailed descriptions of young Indian children routinely taken from their parents and fed to the hungry animals.[34]

Meanwhile, the English—who had already acquired considerable recent experience in dealing with "Tribes of Wild Irish," whom they correspondingly described as "unreasonable beasts"—began their invasion of North America.[35] Soon, colonial militias were "running amok," to quote one New Englander who was there, "killing . . . wounded men, women, and children indiscriminately, firing their camps, burning the Indians alive or dead in their huts [which were elsewhere likened to "kennels"]."[36] Puritan leader Cotton Mather directly linked the latter activity to the cooking of meat, jubilantly referring to the burning of Indians as "a barbeque."[37] Just as in New Spain, "Hunting redskins became . . . a popular sport in New England."[38] It could be profitable, too, as a bounty was paid by local governments for Indian scalps until there were simply no Indians left to kill.[39] Like their Spanish counterparts, although perhaps to a lesser extent, the English also exhibited a penchant for feeding their "game" to dogs. Massachusetts colonist John Easton, for example, records how the capture of "a very decrepit and harmless [old] Indian" by Puritans precipitated a debate among them: "[S]ome would have had him devoured by dogs," wrote Easton, "but the tenderness of some of them prevailed to cut off his head."[40] In Virginia and Maryland, another writer described how, as a rule, "blood-Hounds were used to draw after" Indian quarry, and "Mastives to seaze them."[41]

By 1763, when Lord Jeffrey Amherst issued his infamous written order to "extirpate this execrable race" through bacteriological means—thereby proving beyond all reasonable doubt that the devastation of native societies by disease was never so unintended by European colonists as their apologists like to pretend[42]—the indigenous peoples of North America's Atlantic Seaboard, once numbering as many as 2.2 million, had been reduced by approximately 99 percent.[43]

After it successfully broke away from England, the new U.S. not only perpetuated, but expanded and accelerated the process. Referring to Indians as "wolves"—"both being beasts of prey, tho' different in shape"—George Washington ordered in 1783 that those remaining within the areas of the initial thirteen states be "hunted like beasts," and that a "war of extermination" be waged against those barring U.S. access to certain desired areas, notably the Ohio River Valley.[44] Or, as Thomas Jefferson put it in 1812, Euroamericans should drive every Indian in its path "with the beasts of the forests into the stony mountains"; alternatively, as he'd already stated in 1807, the U.S. should "pursue [the Indians] into extermination, or drive them to new seats beyond our reach"; national policy should be to wage war against each native people it encountered "until that tribe is exterminated, or driven beyond the Mississippi."[45]

Over the next forty years, even as the federal government was acknowledging by treaty hundreds of times that the peoples at issue were in fact nations of human beings, the "private" sentiments of Washington and Jefferson concerning the implications of their "tribal" nature were being worked out at a more popular level. Andrew Jackson, to take one notorious example, rode into the White House in 1828 on the breadth of public approval attending his characterization of Indians as "wild dogs" and his frequent boasts that, in the manner of a trophy hunter, he had "on all occasions preserved the scalps" of the many native people he'd personally murdered.[46] Jackson was, of course, far more than an individual butcher; he was a grassroots Euroamerican leader:

> [He was the] same Andrew Jackson who had supervised the mutilation of 800 or so Creek Indian corpses—the bodies of men, women, and children that he and his men had massacred [at a place called Horseshoe Bend, in Alabama]—cutting off their noses to count and preserve a record of the dead, slicing long strips of flesh from their bodies to tan and turn into bridle reins. The same Andrew Jackson who—after his Presidency was over—still was recommending that American troops specifically seek out and systematically kill Indian women and children who were hiding: to do otherwise, he wrote, was equivalent to pursuing "a wolf in the hamocks without knowing first where her den and whelps are."[47]

By the 1850s, such phenomena had been consolidated into what analyst David Svaldi has termed an outright "rhetoric of extermination," a discourse in which Indians were not simply dehumanized as "beasts," "dogs," and "wolves" in the popular consciousness, but as "vermin."[48] Although such sensibilities were to be, and had been, concretized through an unrelenting series of massacres like that at Horseshoe Bend, nowhere was it better epitomized than in Colorado Territory. There, in 1863, a local newspaper, the *Rocky Mountain News,* launched an all-out campaign to create a climate in which the citizenry would "exterminate . . . the red devils," in this case Cheyennes and Arapahoes, whom editors of the *News* described as being "a dissolute, vagabondish, brutal, and ungrateful race" which should be "wiped from the face of the earth."[49] The paper threw its enthusiastic support behind Colonel John Milton Chivington, a former Methodist minister who served as commander of the territory's volunteer militia.

Several months earlier Chivington, who [by 1864] was also a candidate for Congress, had announced in a speech that his policy was to "kill and scalp all, little and big." "Nits make lice," he was fond of saying—indeed, the phrase became a rallying cry for his troops; since Indians were lice, their children were nits—and the only way to get rid of lice was to kill the nits as well. Clearly, Colonel Chivington was a man ahead of his time. It would take more than half a century, after all, before Heinrich Himmler would think to describe the extermination of another people as "the same thing as delousing."[50]

Chivington was, however, hardly alone. After he and some 750 of his men staged a surprise attack on a peaceful Cheyenne encampment on November 29, 1864—killing somewhere between 150 and 300 women and children who were there under ostensible government protection, and who had displayed a white flag of surrender when the militia approached—they mutilated the bodies, returned to Denver, and then conducted a triumphal march through the center of the city, proudly displaying "trophies" which included not only scalps, but whole heads and genitalia.[51] The citizens of Denver went wild with applause, while the *News* proclaimed the whole affair to have been "a brilliant feat of arms" and chuckled that "Cheyenne scalps are getting thick as toads in Egypt. . . . Everybody has got one and is anxious to get another to send east."[52] Three separate congressional and military investigating committees, convened to affect the proper official posture of concern about the "excess" which had occurred in Colorado, condemned what had happened but failed to recommend a single prosecution. President Theodore Roosevelt later went out of his way to rehabilitate Chivington's "honor"—the colonel himself having gone on to become a favorite on the after-dinner lecture circuit—by proclaiming the massacre to have been "as righteous and beneficial a deed as ever took place on the frontier."[53]

It is in this context that a tidbit of Americana, General Phil Sheridan's 1869 observation that the "only good Indians I ever saw were dead," must be understood.[54] The reality bound up in the general's phrasing was a near-insatiable bloodlust in which another army officer, Alfred Sully, ordered the skulls of Teton Lakotas mounted as decorations on his headquarters wall;[55] where scalp bounties paid better than buffalo hides for "enterprising citizens" in Texas and the Dakotas until the 1880s;[56] where the entire Navajo Nation was interned in a concentration camp at the Bosque Redondo in New Mexico in 1864, until, after four years and the death of half their number by starvation and disease, they were finally released;[57] where, for "sport," the settlers and miners in California drove the state's Indian population (which had once been over a million) downward from 100,000 in 1849 to a nadir of barely 15,000 in the 1890s.[58]

Even after the last great massacre—the Seventh Cavalry's slaughter of about 300 unarmed Minneconjou Lakotas at Wounded Knee in 1890—the popular sentiments demanding total extermination persisted.[59] The *Aberdeen Saturday Pioneer* in South Dakota, to take but one example, recommended in the aftermath of Wounded Knee that "we had better, in order to protect our civilization, follow it up . . . and wipe these untamed and untamable creatures from the face of the earth."[60] The editor, L. Frank Baum, later to win acclaim as the "kind and decent soul" who authored the *Wizard of Oz*, went on to explain that:

> [Indians are merely] a pack of whining curs who lick the hand that smites them. The Whites, by law of conquest, by justice of civilization, are masters of the American continent, and the best safety of the frontier settlements will be secured by the total annihilation of the few remaining Indians. Why not annihilation? . . . [B]etter they should die than live as the miserable wretches that they are.[61]

In sum, there can be no question but that the mantle of tribalism has contributed greatly to the ill-treatment, often quite literally genocidal, we have suffered since our fifteenth-century "discovery" by Europeans. While it is true that the most overt pattern of behavior by which this was expressed is primarily historical, at least in North America,[62] there is no shortage of indication that certain effects continue to linger: witness the sign on the door of a bar in Scenic, South Dakota—removed only during the late 1980s—which read "No Dogs or Indians Allowed." More importantly, the evidence is overwhelming that much of what was worst in the historical interactions between Europeans/Euroamericans and Indians is being continued in more covert fashion, as a matter of official policy, and under the time-tested rubric of indigenous tribalism.

NOTES

1. *The Compact Edition of the Oxford English Dictionary* (London/New York: Oxford University Press, 1985). Although the initial meaning of "tribe" pertained to the original three groups of Romans, and later to the Hebrew clans of ancient Israel, by the time it began to be applied to indigenous peoples outside the flow of European history it was beginning to be applied to the "animal kingdom" as well. The relationship between these last two applications in the European mind is thus quite clear.

2. I've used the dictionaries immediately before me on my desk for purposes of this essay. This includes my trusty Webster's dictionary, given to me by my grandfather while I was in high school: *Webster's New Collegiate Dictionary* (Springfield, MA: G.&C. Merriam Co., Publisher, 1949). It was suggested that I cross-reference the "old" definitions obtained therein with those in newer iterations of the same dictionary, to see whether there have been changes. There have, insofar as the language has been rendered in a more "technical" (sterile) manner.

3. In essence, what is at issue is a direct continuation of the sort of nineteenth century American "scientific" racism exemplified in Samuel George Morton's *Crania Americana; or, A Comparative View of the Skulls of Various Aboriginal Nations of North and South America*, to which is *Prefixed an Essay on The Varieties of the Human Species* (Philadelphia: John Pennington Publisher, 1839); for an excellent overview, see William Stanton, *The Leopard's Spots: Scientific Attitudes toward Race in America, 1815–59* (Chicago: University of Chicago Press, 1960). This body of work had a significant influence upon the formation of the subsequent racial perspectives of nazism; see Robert Cecil, *The Myth of the Master Race: Alfred Rosenberg and Nazi Ideology* (New York: Dodd, Mead & Co., 1972).

4. Arguably, this is a crucial dimension of all colonial contexts. A particularly lucid psychological explanation is offered in Albert Memmi, *The Colonizer and the Colonized* (Boston: Beacon Press, 1965). Also see Frantz Fanon, *The Wretched of the Earth* (New York: Grove Press, 1965).

5. See, for example, Donald A. Grinde's analysis in his newly revised and expanded edition of *The Iroquois and the Founding of the American Nation* (Niwot: University Press of Colorado, forthcoming) of the controversy attending his contention, corroborated by John Adams and other "Founding Fathers" in their own handwriting, that the form of governance exhibited by the Iroquois Six Nations Confederacy influenced the drafting of the U.S. Constitution and consequent establishment of the American republic.

6. A prime example of each category will be found in James A. Clifton, ed., *The Invented Indian: Cultural Fictions and Government Policies* (New Brunswick, NJ: Transaction Books, 1990); see especially, Allan van Gestel, "When Fictions Take Hostages," pp. 291–312.

7. Quoted in Lewis Hanke, "The Dawn of Conscience in America: Spanish Experiments and Experiences with Indians in the New World," *American Philosophical Society Proceedings*, No. 107, 1963, p. 90. For elaboration of the legal implications of Las Casas's position, see James Brown Scott, *The Spanish Origins of International Law* (Oxford: Clarendon Press, 1934).

8. Mason Wade, "The French and the Indians," in Howard Peckham and Charles Gibson, eds., *Attitudes of the Colonial Powers toward the American Indian* (Salt Lake City: University of Utah Press, 1969, pp. 61–80). Wade observes on page 71 that, by 1622, "an ever increasing amount" of the time of Samuel de Champlain, Governor of Nouvelle France (as the French New World colony was called), was consumed by "Indian diplomacy," and that in that year he negotiated on behalf of his Crown a formal treaty—an incontrovertibly international instrument—with what he termed "ambassadors" of the Iroquois Confederacy.

9. Allen W. Trelease, "Dutch Treatment of the Indian, with Particular Reference to New Netherland," in Peckham and Gibson, *op. cit.*, p. 51.

10. K. Knorr, *British Colonial Theories, 1570–1850* (Cambridge, MA: Cambridge University Press, 1944).

11. William Wood, *New England's Prospect* (London, 1624, p. 80).

12. Anonymous, *A Relation to Maryland* (London, 1635, p. 43).

13. Quoted in Wilbur R. Jacobs, *The Appalachian Indian Frontier: The Edmund Atkin Report and the Plan of 1755* (Lincoln: University of Nebraska Press, 1967, p. 38).

14. Alden T. Vaughn, *Early American Indian Documents: Treaties and Laws, 1607–1789* (Washington, D.C.: University Publications of America, 1979).

15. Quoted in Jacobs, *op. cit.*, p. 38.

16. The United States became the first country to commit to black letter law the relevant international customs pertaining to the making of treaties. Article I, Section 10 of the U.S. Constitution follows Article IX of the Articles of Confederation in reserving treaty-making prerogatives to the federal government exclusively, and then only with other fully sovereign national entities. The Articles of Confederation make specific reference to American Indian relations in this regard.

17. The phrasing comes from Attorney General William Wirt, Opinion of the Attorney General 110 (1828). Texts of 371 of the ratified treaties appear verbatim in Charles J. Kappler, *Indian Treaties, 1778–1883* (New York: Interland Publishers, 1973). Lakota scholar Vine Deloria, Jr., in conducting an as yet unfinished treaty study of his own, has uncovered the texts of a further eight ratified treaties which are not included in Kappler, and has compiled the texts of approximately 400 unratified treaties upon which the United States predicates portions of presumed land title.

18. To abrogate the treaties out-of-hand would have served—and would still serve—to void most U.S. land title in North America. The Act of March 3, 1871 (16 Stat. L. 566), by which U.S. treaty-making with Indians was ended, was therefore very carefully worded: "*Provided,* That hereafter no Indian nation or tribe within the territory of the United States shall be recognized as an independent nation, tribe, or power with whom the United States may contract by treaty; *Provided further,* That nothing herein contained shall be construed to invalidate or impair the obligation of any treaty heretofore lawfully made and ratified with any Indian nation or tribe." The best intentions of its framers to play both ends against the middle notwithstanding, the statute obviously adds up to a juridical contradiction of the first order: one of the primary obligations lawfully incurred by—indeed, constitutionally required of—the government in ratifying its many treaties with Indians was/is to recognize them as *precisely* the sort of independent entities with which it could continue to treat. There is simply no legal basis for one nation, having recognized the sovereignty of another, to arbitrarily and unilaterally "unrecognize" it, even if it no longer wishes to enter into new treaties with it.

19. *Cherokee Nation v. Georgia*, 30 U.S. (5 Pet.) 1, 16 (1831). See Chapter 14, sec. 3.

20. Opinion of the Attorney General 110 (Washington, D.C.: U.S. Department of Justice, 1828).

21. *Report of the Commissioner of Indian Affairs* (Washington, D.C.: U.S. Department of Interior, 1869, p. 6).

22. *Report of the Commissioner of Indian Affairs* (Washington, D.C.: U.S. Department of Interior, 1873, p. 3).

23. We have this in so many words. During the early 1600s, the Council of Virginia advised its diplomats to enter into treaty relations with Indians so that, when the natives grew "secure upon the treatie, we shall have the better Advantage both to surprise them, & cutt down their Corne"; quoted in George Percy, "A Trewe Relacyon of the Procedeings and Occurrentes of Momente which have hapned in Virginia," *Tyler's Quarterly Historical and Genealogical Magazine.* No. 3, 1922, pp. 272–3. Overall, see Dorothy V. Jones, *License for Empire: Colonialism by Treaty in Early America* (Chicago: University of Chicago Press, 1982).

24. Act of May 28, 1830 ("Indian Removal Act"), 4 Stat. 411, Sec. 3.

25. "Neither Spain nor Britain should be models of German expansion, but the Nordics of North America, who had ruthlessly pushed aside an inferior race to win for themselves soil and territory for the future"; Norman Rich, *Hitler's War Aims: Ideology, the Nazi State, and the Course of Expansion* (New York: W.W. Norton Publisher, 1973, p. 8). For Hitler's own statements in this regard, see his *Mein Kampf* (Boston: Houghton Mifflin Publishers, 1971, pp. 403, 591); and *Hitler's Secret Book* (New York: Grove Press, 1961, pp. 44–8). Also see the memorandum prepared by Hitler's adjutant, Colonel Friedrich Hossbach, summarizing the contents of a so-called Fuhrer Conference conducted on November 5, 1937; International Military Tribunal, *Trial of the Major War Criminals before the International Military Tribunal: Proceedings and Documents,* Vol. 25, 386–PS (Nuremberg: Office of the International Military Tribunal, 1947–1949, pp. 402–13).

26. A classic example of this sort of duplicity occurred in 1875 when President Ulysses S. Grant secretly instructed his military commanders not to meet the army's legal obligation, incurred under the 1868 Fort Laramie Treaty, to prevent U.S. citizens from trespassing in the territory of the Lakota Nation (the trespassing itself having been fostered by false but widely publicized reports, written under pseudonyms by George Armstrong Custer and other officers, that an illegal army expedition into the Lakota homeland in 1874 had turned up evidence of major gold deposits therein). The resulting presence of large numbers of U.S. citizens in Lakota country by 1876, and an alleged "need to protect their safety,"

was then used as a pretext by which the Grant administration could claim to be "compelled" to wage a war of conquest against the Indians. On Grant's order and related maneuvering, see the report by E.T. Watkins listed as Executive Document 184 (Washington, D.C.: 44th Cong., 1st Sess., 1876, pp. 8–9). Overall, see John E. Gray, *The Centennial Campaign: The Sioux Wars of 1876* (Norman: University of Oklahoma Press, 1988).

27. A good case can be made that such sentiments, at least insofar as they were cast along racial lines, were a new thing, coming into being only at the point—*circa* 1450–1500—that Europe was consolidating its notion of itself as a distinct cultural/geographic entity, and discovering that it possessed the capacity, potentially at least, of expanding outward at the expense of other peoples. An interesting examination of this thesis may be found in Ronald Sanders, *Lost Tribes and Promised Lands: The Origins of American Racism* (New York: Harper Perennial Publishers, 1992). A somewhat obtuse, but nonetheless useful analysis of the same ideas is offered by Steven Greenblatt in his *Marvelous Possessions: The Wonder of the New World* (Chicago: University of Chicago Press, 1991).

28. In "Indians and Spaniards," Hanke recounts how in 1935, "on my way home from archival work, I visited the ancient silver mining center of Potosi and there observed a Bolivian army officer viciously kicking Indian recruits. . . . This officer also called the Indians 'dogs' and other unpleasant names. Later, when philosophically-minded historians eager to split hairs denied that any Spaniard had ever called Indians 'beasts' in the full scientific and philosophical sense of the word, I found it difficult to follow their subtle reasoning."

29. Bartolomé de Las Casas, *The Devastation of the Indies: A Brief Account* (Baltimore: Johns Hopkins University Press, 1992). For population estimates, see Sherburn F. Cook and Woodrow Borah, *Essays in Population History, Vol. I: Mexico and the Caribbean* (Berkeley: University of California Press, 1971); esp. "The Aboriginal Population of Hispaniola," pp. 376–410.

30. David E. Stannard, *American Holocaust: Columbus and the Conquest of the New World* (London/New York: Oxford University Press, 1992, p. 85).

31. Nobel David Cook, *Demographic Collapse: Peru, 1520–1620* (Cambridge, MA: Cambridge University Press, 1981, p. 114).

32. John Grier Varner and Jeanette Johnson Varner, *Dogs of Conquest* (Norman: University of Oklahoma Press, 1983, pp. 192–3).

33. This is from a contemporaneous account by Peter Martyr, quoted in Tzvetan Todorov, *The Conquest of America: The Conquest of the Other* (New York: Harper and Row Publishers, 1984, p. 141).

34. Stannard, *op. cit.*, pp. 83–4.

35. See, for example, the descriptions of the supposedly "bestial" nature of the "tribal" Irish offered by William Thomas during the 1550s; quoted in Howard Mumford Jones, *O Strange New World: American Culture—The Formative Years* (London: Chatto and Windus Publishers, 1964, p. 169). It is worth noting that, to the extent the more educated English viewed the Irish as being human at all, they emphatically denied that such "wild men" might be considered "White." Hence, until the late nineteenth century, the Irish were officially categorized as being "Black" by their colonizers.

36. Quoted in Richard Slotkin and James K. Folsom, eds., *So Dreadful a Judgement: Puritan Responses to King Philip's War, 1676–1677* (Middletown, CT: Wesleyan University Press, 1978, p. 381). The description of Indian homes as being "nothing more than kennels" comes from Sarah Kembel Knight, *The Journal of Madam Knight* (Boston: David R. Godine Publisher, 1972, p. 22).

37. Quoted in Slotkin and Folsom, *op. cit.*

38. Douglas Edward Leach, *Flintlock and Tomahawk: New England in King Philip's War* (New York: W.W. Norton Publisher, 1958, p. 237).

39. Contrary to myth, scalping was not an Indian practice, but rather something imported by the English. Its origin may be found in Ireland, where the taking of heads was used as a means of identifying slain resistance leaders. The heads were then used to terrorize the population; they were, according to Gilbert Humphrey, who thought up the idea, "laide on the ground by eche side of the waie ledynge to [English encampments] so that none could come . . . for any cause but commonly he muste passe through a lane of heddes which [were] used *ad terrorem*" (quoted in Nicholas P. Canny, "The Ideology of English Colonization: From Ireland to America," *William and Mary Quarterly*, 3rd Ser., No. 30, 1973, p. 582). In the comparatively vast and forested reaches of the New World, the taking of whole heads often proved too cumbersome, and so scalping was evolved as proof the "beasts" had been killed.

40. See "John Easton's Relacion," in Charles H. Lincoln, ed., *Narratives of the Indian Wars, 1675–1699* (New York: Charles Scribner's Sons, Publishers, 1913, pp. 14, 16).

41. Quoted in James Axtell, "The Rise and Fall of the Powhatan Empire," in James Axtell, ed., *After Columbus: Essays in the Ethnohistory of Colonial North America* (London/New York: Oxford University Press, 1988, pp. 218–9).

42. For the purpose indicated, Amherst (in whose honored memory a town and university campus in Massachusetts are presently named) ordered a subordinate, Bouquet, to distribute items taken from a smallpox infirmary as "gifts" during a peace parley with Pontiac's Confederacy. The following day, Bouquet reported, also in writing, that this had been done and that he hoped the measure would "obtain the desired result." Upwards of 100,000 Indians died of smallpox in the ensuing epidemic. Although this is history's first documentable instance of biological warfare, the familiarity with requisite techniques displayed by Amherst and his men strongly suggest that the British had engaged in similar methods before; E. Wagner Stearn and Allen E. Stearn, *The Effects of Smallpox on the Destiny of the Amerindian* (Boston: Bruce Humphries, Publisher, 1945, pp. 44–5). Chemical means—poisons—were also regularly employed by English colonists for purposes of mass extermination, from at least as early as 1623; see, for example, "Bennetes Welcome," *William and Mary Quarterly*, 2nd Ser., No. 13, 1933, p. 122.

43. The pre-invasion population estimate comes from Henry F. Dobyns, *Their Numbers Become Thinned: Native American Population Dynamics in Eastern North America* (Knoxville: University of Tennessee Press, 1983, p. 41); attrition is estimated by Stannard, *op. cit.*, pp. 120–1.

44. Quoted in Richard Drinnon, *Facing West: The Metaphysics of Indian Hating and Empire Building* (New York: Schocken Books, 1990, pp. 65, 331–2).

45. Quoted in Ronald T. Takaki, *Iron Cages: Race and Culture in 19th-Century America* (New York: Alfred A. Knopf, 1979, pp. 61–5). Also see Drinnon, *op. cit.*, pp. 96, 98, 116. As Stannard aptly remarks (at p. 120), "Had these same words been enunciated by a German leader in 1939, and directed at European Jews, they would be engraved in modern memory. Since they were uttered by one of America's founding fathers, however, the most widely admired of the South's slaveholding philosophers of freedom, they conveniently have become lost to historians in their insistent celebration of Jefferson's wisdom and dignity."

46. Quoted in Takaki, *op. cit.*, p. 96. As President, Jackson remained true to his (and Jefferson's) views, overseeing the removal of virtually all Indians east of the Mississippi to points west. This was accomplished by forced march at bayonet-point—called the "Trail of Tears" by its victims—often in the dead of winter, and without adequate food, shelter, or medical care. The toll on native lives

was predictably horrendous, with up to 55 percent of all Cherokees perishing as a result, about half of all Creeks and Seminoles, etc. See Russell Thornton, "Cherokee Population Losses on the Trail of Tears: A New Perspective and a New Estimate." *Ethnohistory,* No. 31, 1984, pp. 289–300.

47. Stannard, *op. cit.,* p. 123. The massacre at Tohopeka (Horseshoe Bend) occurred on March 27, 1814. The slaughter—in which 557 Creek men and 250–300 women and children died by official count—was immortalized as a "great battle" by the Walt Disney Studios in its 1950s movie series about Davy Crockett, one of the volunteers serving under Jackson, who was cast in the film as a "genuine American hero." In reality, Crockett was a sadist who could write glowingly in his diary about "stewing the grease out of" a 12–year-old Creek boy whose arm and leg had already been shattered by musket balls; see Jimmie Durham, "Cowboys and . . . Notes on Art, Literature, and American Indians in the Modern American Mind," in *The State of Native America, op. cit.,* p. 423.

48. David Svaldi, *Sand Creek and the Rhetoric of Extermination: A Case Study in Indian-White Relations* (Washington, D.C.: University Press of America, 1989).

49. Quoted in *ibid.,* pp. 149–50, 172.

50. Stannard, *op. cit.,* p. 131. The quote from Himmler appears in Robert Jay Lifton, *The Nazi Doctors: Medical Killing and the Psychology of Genocide* (New York: Basic Books, 1986, p. 477).

51. For details on all this, see Stan Hoig, *The Sand Creek Massacre* (Norman: University of Oklahoma Press, 1961).

52. Quoted in Svaldi, *op. cit.,* pp. 298–9. It should be noted that, as late as 1991, members of the American Indian Movement in Colorado discovered that two Cheyenne scalps taken at Sand Creek were still being displayed as a "tourist attraction" in a resort near Denver.

53. Quoted in Thomas G. Dyer, *Theodore Roosevelt and the Idea of Race* (Baton Rouge: Louisiana State University Press, 1980, p. 79).

54. Quoted in Edward S. Ellis, *The History of Our Country: From the Discovery of America to the Present Time, Vol. 6* (Cincinnati: Bartlett Publishing, 1900, p. 1483).

55. Edward Lazarus, *Black Hills, White Justice: The Sioux Nation versus the United States, 1775 to the Present* (New York: Harper-Collins Publishers, 1991, p. 29). Despite its inclusion of this sort of useful information, the book is a work of anti-Indian revisionism.

56. On Texas, see Stiffarm and Lane, *op. cit.,* p. 35. On the Dakotas, see Lazarus, *op. cit.,* p. 28.

57. Lawrence Kelly, *Navajo Roundup* (Boulder, CO: Pruett Publishing Co., 1970).

58. Sherburn F. Cook, *The Conflict Between the California Indian and White Civilization* (Berkeley: University of California Press, 1976, pp. 284). Also see Robert F. Heizer, ed., *Destruction of the California Indians* (Salt Lake City/Santa Barbara: Peregrine Smith, Inc., 1974).

59. For details on the massacre, see Dee Brown, *Bury My Heart at Wounded Knee: An Indian History of the American West* (New York: Henry Holt & Co., 1970, pp. 415–45). A number of Congressional Medals of Honor for "bravery" and "gallantry" were awarded to the troops who gunned down defenseless women and children.

60. Quoted in Elliot J. Gorn, Randy Roberts, and Terry D. Bilhartz, *Constructing the American Past: A Source Book of a People's History* (New York: Harper-Collins Publishers, 1991, p. 99).

61. *Ibid.*

62. The contemporary situation in Central and South America continues to display the same sorts of direct physical genocide of native peoples which marks the historical reality of North America. In Guatemala, for example, it is estimated that perhaps 60,000 Mayan Indians have been killed, and another 100,000 turned into refugees, since 1970; Amnesty International, *Guatemala: The Human Rights Record* (London: Amnesty International Publications, 1987); Jean-Marie Simon, *Guatemala: Eternal Spring, Eternal Tyranny* (New York: W.W. Norton, 1987). In Paraguay, during the 1960s and early 70s, the bulk of the Aché people were exterminated through the time-honored expedient of hunting them down with dogs, dispatching them with machetes, and selling the survivors into slavery; Richard Arens, ed., *Genocide in Paraguay* (Philadelphia: Temple University Press, 1976). In Brazil, some 150 distinct peoples are presently confronted with the prospect of genocide because of "development" of the homelands in the Amazon Basin; *The Indian People in Brazil, Vols. 1–18* (Sao Paulo: Center for Documentation and Information, 1978–1981).

LET'S SPREAD THE "FUN" AROUND: THE ISSUE OF SPORTS TEAM NAMES AND MASCOTS

WARD CHURCHILL

People should remember that an honor isn't born when it parts the honorer's lips, it is born when it is accepted in the honoree's ear.
—GLENN T. MORRIS
COLORADO AIM

During the past few seasons, there has been an increasing wave of controversy regarding the names of professional sports teams like the Atlanta Braves, Cleveland Indians, Washington Redskins, and Kansas City Chiefs. The issue extends to the names of college teams like Florida State University Seminoles, University of Illinois Fighting Illini, and so on, right on down to high school outfits like the Lamar (Colorado) Savages. Also involved has been the adoption of team mascots, replete with feathers, buckskins, beads, spears, "warpaint," and pep gestures like the "Tomahawk Chop."

American Indians have protested that the use of native names, images, and symbols as sports team mascots is, by definition, a virulently racist practice. Given the historical relationship between Indians and non-Indians during what has been called the "Conquest of America," American Indian Movement leader Russell Means has compared the practice to contemporary Germans naming their soccer teams the "Jews," "Hebrews," and "Yids," while adorning their uniforms with grotesque caricatures of Jewish faces taken from the nazis' antisemitic propaganda of the 1930s.[1]

In response to these objections, a number of players—especially African-Americans and other minority athletes—have been trotted out by professional team owners like Ted Turner, as well as university and public school officials, to announce that they mean not to insult, but instead to "honor," native people. They have been joined by the television networks and most major newspapers, many of which have editorialized that Indian discomfort with the situation is "no big deal," insisting that the whole thing is just "good, clean fun." The country needs more such fun, they've argued, and "a few disgruntled Native Americans" have no right to undermine the nation's enjoyment of its leisure time by complaining. This is especially the case, some have contended, "in hard times like these." It has even been contended that Indian outrage at being degraded—

---

[1] My use of lower case letters for the term "nazi" is not accidental. In my view, the word does not deserve the dignity of capitalization.

rather than the degradation itself—creates "a serious barrier to the sort of inter-group communication so necessary in a multicultural society such as ours."

Okay, let's communicate. Just for the sake of argument, let's accept the premise that they are sincere. If what they are saying is true, then isn't it time we spread such "good cheer" around among *all* groups? Simple consistency demands that anyone who thinks the Tomahawk Chop is a swell pastime must be just as hearty in their endorsement of the following ideas.

First, as a counterpart to the Redskins, we need an NFL team called "Niggers" to "honor" Afroamerica. Halftime festivities for fans might include a simulated stewing of the opposing coach in a large pot while players and cheerleaders dance around it, garbed in leopard skins and wearing fake bones in their noses. This concept goes along with the actions of the Kansas City Chiefs, whose team members lately appeared on a poster looking "fierce" and "savage" by way of wearing Indian regalia.

So that the newly-formed "Niggers" sports club won't end up too out of sync while honoring Afroamericans, a baseball franchise—let's call this one the "Sambos"—should be formed. How about a basketball team called the "Spearchuckers"? A hockey team called the "Jungle Bunnies"? Maybe the essence of these teams could be depicted by images of tiny black faces adorned with huge pairs of lips. The players could appear on TV gnawing on chicken legs and spitting watermelon seeds at one another. Catchy, eh? Well, there's "nothing to be upset about," according to those who love wearing "war bonnets" to the Super Bowl or having "Chief Illiniwik" dance around the sports arenas of Urbana, Illinois.

And why stop there? There are plenty of other groups to include. Hispanics could be represented by the Galveston "Greasers" and San Diego "Spics," at least until the Wisconsin "Wetbacks" and Baltimore "Beaners" get off the ground. Asian Americans? How about the "Slopes," "Dinks," "Gooks," and "Zipperheads"? Owners of the latter teams might get their logo ideas from editorial page cartoons printed in the nation's newspapers during World War II: slant-eyes, buck teeth, big glasses, but nothing racially insulting or derogatory, according to the editors and artists involved at the time.

Let's see. Who's been left out? Teams like the Kansas City "Kikes," Hanover "Honkies," San Leandro "Shylocks," Daytona "Dagos," and Pittsburgh "Polacks" will fill a certain social void among white folk. Issues of gender and sexual preference can be addressed through creation of teams like the Boston "Bimbos," Detroit "Dykes," and the Fresno "Faggots." How about the Gainesville "Gimps" and Richmond "Retards," so the physically and mentally impaired won't be excluded from our fun and games?

None of this is demeaning or insulting, at least when it's being done to Indians. Just ask the folks who are doing it. They'll tell you that there's been no harm done, regardless of what their victims think, feel, or say. Those with precisely the same mentality used to insist that Step'n'Fetchit was okay, or Charlie Chan, the Frito Bandito, or other symbols making up the lexicon of American racism.

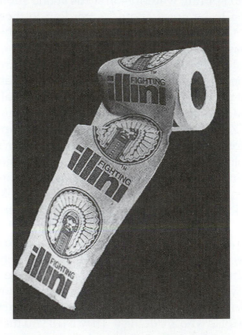

The notion of "fun" embodied in rituals like the Tomahawk Chop must be understood for what it is. There's not a single non-Indian example mentioned above which can be considered socially acceptable in even the most marginal sense. The reasons are obvious enough. So why is it different where American Indians are concerned?

Fortunately, a few teams and their fans have gotten the message and have responded appropriately. One illustration is Stanford University, which opted to drop the name "Indians" with regard to its sports teams (and Stanford has experienced no resulting drop-off in attendance at its games). Meanwhile, the local newspaper in Portland, Oregon, recently decided its long-standing editorial policy prohibiting use of racial epithets should include derogatory sports team names. The Redskins, for instance, are now simply referred to as being "the Washington team," and will continue to be described in this way until the franchise adopts an inoffensive moniker (newspaper sales in Portland have suffered no decline as a result). Such examples are to be applauded and encouraged. They stand as figurative beacons in the night, proving beyond all doubt that it is quite possible to indulge in the pleasure of athletics without accepting racism into the bargain.

—Reprinted with permission from the National Conference for Community and Justice, Washington, D.C.

Making Room for Education

The U.S. Commission on Civil Rights calls for an end to the use of Native American images and team names by non-Native schools. . . . Since the civil rights movement of the 1960s many overtly derogatory symbols and images offensive to African Americans have been eliminated. However, many secondary schools, postsecondary institutions, and a number of professional sports teams continue to use Native American nicknames and imagery. . . .

It is particularly disturbing that Native American references are still to be found in educational institutions. . . . The stereotyping of any racial, ethnic, religious or other groups when promoted by our public educational institutions, teach all students that stereotyping of minority groups is acceptable, a dangerous lesson in a diverse society. . . .

The elimination of Native American nicknames and images as sports mascots will benefit not only Native Americans, but all Americans. The elimination of stereotypes will make room for education about real Indian people, current Native American issues, and the rich variety of American Indian cultures in our country.

—Statement of the U.S. Commission on Civil Rights on the Use of Native American Images and Nicknames as Sports Symbols, April 16, 2001

BATTLE RAGES OVER A 5–LETTER FOUR–LETTER WORD[1]

ERIC SCHMITT

TWO HARBORS, Minn.—Minnesota's enactment of a law last year ordering counties to rename any natural geographic place identified by the word "squaw" was a victory for the state's 55,000 American Indians, many of whom had campaigned for the change.

A number of such places in Minnesota, like others similarly named across the United States, got their designations in the 19th century, at a time when whites commonly used "squaw" to describe an American Indian woman. But the word has now long been considered offensive, and, Indian linguists say, for good reason: originally a French corruption of Algonquin words for "woman," it soon became, they say, an obscenity describing female genitals.

Now, as a result of the new state law, Squaw Pond in Cass County is officially Scout Camp Pond. Squaw Lake in Itasca County is now Natures Lake. And Squaw Creek in Carlton County will soon become Fond du Lac Creek. Indeed, virtually all 11 Minnesota counties that were home to places called "squaw"—a total of 19 of them—met the state deadline to rename their offending lakes, streams, points and ponds.

But not Lake County, a thinly populated swath of forest, lakes and streams in northern Minnesota that stretches from the pebbly shores of Lake Superior to a watery border with Canada. Many of the county's 10,000 residents say the state's effort to do away with names more than a century old is a weak-kneed bow to a small but vocal minority who are upset over a word that should not be considered offensive at all.

"The term 'squaw' is in common use throughout North America, far beyond its Algonquin origin," Sharon K. Hahn, head of the Lake County Board of Commissioners, said in a letter to the state. "We find nothing derogatory in continued use of this term."

County officials, who say the changes would cost tens of thousands of dollars for new maps, offered in protest to rename Squaw Creek and Squaw Bay, in northern Lake County, Politically Correct Creek and Politically Correct Bay.

Minnesota officials were not amused. They rejected the proposal, and now a showdown of sorts is shaping up as the state and the county plot their next moves.

"Our residents are saying it's about time we have a county board standing up to the state," said Miss Hahn, who is running for re-election this fall along with one of the five other commissioners.

Indians say the commissioners are being arrogant and disrespectful.

"It's equivalent to having the New York Mets called the New York Jews," said Larry Aitken, tribal historian for the Chippewa nation's Leech Lake band, one of 11 Chippewa and Sioux tribes in Minnesota.

The state is mulling court action against officials of the recalcitrant county.

"They're trying to bill this as political correctness, but it's a matter of civility," said Glen Yakel, geographic namekeeper of the Minnesota Department of Natural Resources. "Political correctness changes. Words that are offensive do not."

If Mr. Yakel is right, then the United States has a lot of places known by an offensive word. There are 1,050 natural or man-made locales around the country whose names include "squaw," according to the United States Geological Survey's Board on Geographic Names.

But the new Minnesota statute may have set off a cultural consciousness-raising. Arizona is now debating whether to strike the word from its "squaw" places, and California is preparing to change the name of Squaw Gulch in Siskiyou County to Taritsi Gulch (although no one has yet tinkered with the name of Squaw Valley, the ski resort). Not since 1967, when the Board on Geographic Names directed that 143 places named Nigger be changed to Negro, and 26 places named Jap be switched to Japanese, has one term drawn such wide opprobrium.

The Minnesota statute was overwhelmingly approved by the State Legislature and signed by Gov. Arne Carlson after two Chippewa high school girls took an American Indian culture class, traced the word's origins and lobbied lawmakers across the state.

"It's too offensive to even write or say out loud," said Muriel Litzau, the mother of one of the girls, adding that she had grown up ashamed of "the S word."

For now the law applies only to natural places, partly at the request of Indian leaders in the small village of Squaw Lake in north-central Minnesota, who did not want the issue to divide their residents, some of whom are Indians, others whites.

Lake County, which has Indian reservations on its borders but none within its jurisdiction, responded to the enactment by deciding that the naming of Squaw Creek and Squaw Bay, two tiny places on the edge of the Boundary Waters Canoe Area that are accessible only by boat, should be left to Fall Lake Township, the nearest populated community.

"Locally it wasn't considered offensive," said Lee Hotaling, chairman of the Fall Lake Town Board. "It was just accepted. It's been around for years, and years and years."

Bob Cary, editor of *The Ely Echo*, a weekly newspaper that covers Lake County issues, said, "I don't think anyone here gives a hoot one way or another."

As far as the Lake County commissioners were concerned, the people had spoken: "squaw" was staying put.

"Until our people agree to change the names, we won't be doing it," Miss Hahn said. "We're elected by the people to represent the people, not the state bureaucracy."[2]

―――――――

[2]*Editor's note:* Sharon Hahn was subsequently reelected to the Lake County Board of Commissioners. In 1999, against her vote, Squaw Creek and Squaw Bay were renamed Fall Creek and Mist Bay. As of April, 2002, the U.S. Geological Survey listed more than 900 place names that use the word "squaw," including Squaw Bosom (Maine), Squaw Nipple (Montana), Squaws Tit (Montana), Squaw Tits (Arizona), Squat Tit Canyon (New Mexico), Squawtit (Idaho), Squaw Humper Dam (South Dakota), Squaw Teats (Wyoming), and Squawteat Peak (Texas).

NEW PROSPERITY BRINGS NEW CONFLICT TO INDIAN COUNTRY[1]

TIMOTHY EGAN

SKULL VALLEY, Utah—Not long after the Goshute Indians stopped resisting the Mormons who had poured into the sun-cracked bowl of the Great Basin, the tribe seemed to disappear, gone like most natives into sepia tones of the past, their poses ever frozen—noble, doomed, vanquished.

But then, nearly a century and a half after the first state lines were stamped on an area once known as the Great American Desert, the Goshutes reappeared. Suddenly, last year, the most powerful politicians in the West became deeply concerned about the actions of a tiny tribe that had been left in the alkaline dust of central Utah.

With barely 100 members, the Skull Valley Band of Goshutes declared what few people outside the reservation had taken seriously: that they were a sovereign nation. As such, the Goshutes—looking for a multimillion-dollar infusion—have offered to lease part of their reservation as the temporary storage ground for high-level civilian nuclear waste. Utah's Governor and Congressional representatives are outraged, vowing to block the border of Indian country to any shipments.

The Goshute proposal is a very un-Indian-like thing to do, critics say; native people are supposed to be keepers of the earth, not protectors of its poisons.

But in fact, the Goshutes say that what they are doing is the most characteristic action a tribe can take in the modern era—asserting itself to be a nation within a nation, free to make its own decisions.

The clash in a forgotten valley of the unwatered West is but one awakening of sovereignty by hundreds of American Indian tribes. From the smallest bands in the desert to groups that govern from glass towers in the East, native tribes are actively shoring up the bonds of nationhood.

What is happening in Indian country, an archipelago of 554 nations within the boundaries of the United States, goes far beyond the popular image of modern tribes.

Between two extremes of Indian life—the poverty of the Pine Ridge Reservation in South Dakota, which includes the poorest county in America, and the gambling gusher at the Foxwoods Casino in Connecticut, where Mashantucket Pequots are running the biggest casino in the country—is a forceful drive for independence from the states.

"Some people think we're living in teepees out here," said Leon Bear, the Goshute tribal chairman. "They come up to my house and see a satellite dish

---

[1]From "New Prosperity Brings New Conflict to Indian Country" by Timothy Egan, *The New York Times*, March 8, 1998. Copyright© 1998 The New York Times Co. Reprinted by permission.

and a big color TV, it surprises them. We are alive and well and a sovereign nation. And we're using that sovereignty to attract the only business you can get to come here."

A new generation of Indian leaders, schooled in the nascent sovereignty movement of the 1970's, has come to power at the same time that many tribes are getting their first taste of prosperity, through tribal casinos. Now, there is a convergence of economic strength, legal muscle and political will.

The number of Indian lawyers has increased more than ten-fold to about 1,000 in the last 20 years, and there has been a four-fold increase to just over 300 in the number of tribal courts.

"What we've seen is simply the civil rights movement for Native Americans," said John Echohawk, executive director of the Native American Rights Fund, a nonprofit legal defense group based in Boulder, Colo. "Tribal rights are finally being enforced because more and more tribes have the resources to have their own lawyers."

"What most people don't understand is that we are governments first, and racial entities second," said Anthony Pico, chairman of the Viejas Band of Kumeyaay Indians in Southern California.

People who have rarely given a second thought to the natives in their midst suddenly find there really are four major levels of government in America: Federal, state, local and tribal. Until recently, one of them was nearly always invisible.

A Power Restored: Decreeing Nations Within Nations

Congress ratified 371 treaties with native people, the first in 1778 with the Delaware, the last in 1871 with the Nez Perce. In most cases, Indians were forced to give up land in return for self-governing rights and a tribal homeland. But those rights were often ignored, and the homelands, or reservations, were sliced up or overrun.

When Georgia declared Indian laws on designated Indian land within the state to be null and void, the Cherokees sued—and won. Writing in 1830, Chief Justice John Marshall held that the Cherokees were "a distinct political society, separated from others, capable of managing its own affairs and governing itself."

It was one of three Supreme Court decisions in the 1830's that established the right of American Indian tribes to be free from state control, while they remained subordinate to the will of Congress. A century and a half later, this remains the governing framework.

Indian nations were not judged to be stand-alone countries. Instead, the Supreme Court defined them as "domestic, dependent nations"—a unique status that is still subject to much contention. Indian country is an evolving political experiment, trying to live the oxymoron of being nations that are still subject to a greater political power.

For more than a hundred years after the last treaty, virtually every census found Indian lands to be islands of squalor and poverty, with chronic unemployment and rates of disease and early death unmatched in the country.

Then came the "new buffalo"—gambling operations on Indian land, approved by Congress in 1988. A third of all tribes now operate some form of gambling enterprise, and though the windfall is unevenly spread, it generates more than $6 billion a year.

"The Indians in California have been poverty stricken for 150 years," Mr. Pico said of the Viejas band. "We've never been to a point where we could exercise our rights. Now we have an economic base, and suddenly we're on people's radar screens."

Indian country came alive, in ways both unintended and planned, with gambling. Suddenly, little patches of long-forgotten ground blossomed into cash centers in neon, which gave rise to cultural programs, language revival, scholarships, better schools.

The venture into gambling also changed the average American's view of Indians, prompting talk of "rich Indians," even though an overwhelming majority of the tribes have seen no windfall from gambling.

The tribes with money started to buy into the political process, giving more than $2 million in campaign contributions, mostly to Democrats, in the 1996 election.

But even the tribes without money have seen their sons and daughters—educated at law schools from Stanford to Dartmouth—return to the reservations. They are well-versed in court rulings, treaties and laws passed in the 1970's and 1980's that gave the tribes more independence.

More than ever, the tribes are acting like states and counties, levying their own taxes, enforcing their own land use regulations, building codes and criminal statutes. Some tribes are thinking of issuing their own driver's licenses.

"I remember my dad used to take me out in a pickup truck, and he'd say, 'This is our land, only the people around us have changed,'" said Roy Bernal, chairman of the All-Indian Pueblo Council, which represents tribes in New Mexico. "Over the years, we have had sovereign recognition from Spain, from Mexico and the United States."

But just as the full consequence of the nation-within-a-nation architecture designed by the Supreme Court is being realized, the sovereignty movement is bumping into a wall of opposition.

Members of Congress from California, Utah, Washington and Montana, alarmed by the latest assertions of Indian nationhood within their states, ask: What right does a small minority have to ignore their neighbors' concerns?

"I don't think this is what the Founding Fathers had in mind," said Representative Merrill Cook, Republican of Utah, referring to new tribal ventures like casinos and nuclear storage proposals. "It's just not right, this use of sovereignty. The implications are frightening for us as a nation."

Nearly half the American states have no Indian tribes or reservations within their borders. But elsewhere, tribal land is etched in shades all over the national map, most of it in the West.

Indian country today is 56 million acres, 314 reservations and about 1.4 million people living on or near tribal land—less than 1 percent of the overall population of the United States spread over a bit more than 2 percent of the land. An additional 500,000 or so people who listed themselves as Indian in the last census live mostly in urban areas.

The Government was supposed to hold tribal lands in trust, acting as guardian to the nations it had warred against. But instead Congress opened up tribal lands to sale, trying to make commercial landowners out of individual Indians. From the 1880's to the 1930's, the reservations lost more than 90 million acres—nearly two-thirds of the land base—as big pieces of Indian country were sold to non-Indians.

The low point, for many tribes, was in the 1950's, when more than 100 Indian governments were dismantled under an Eisenhower Administration policy known as termination. Erased from official recognition in exchange for cash, many tribes simply ceased to exist.

Flash Points: When Tribal Law and Others Collide

But in the last quarter century, there has been a strong rebound, as Indians have defiantly rejected assimilation. There are now 554 tribes, each recognized by the Federal Government as a sovereign entity with varying degrees of power.

"Sovereignty sounds like something from the King of England, but all it really boils down to is the right to make your own laws and be ruled by them," said Kevin Gover, a Pawnee who is the new Assistant Secretary of the Interior for Indian Affairs.

By any measure, Indian country is deep in social problems. Unemployment is more than 30 percent. Among people who have jobs, nearly a third earned less than $10,000 a year in 1995—the last full year surveyed.

Indians have the highest rates of alcoholism, suicide and child abuse in the country, though some progress is being made.

More than 250 languages are spoken in Indian country. There are courts and statutes that are grounded more in tribal and family customs than English common law, but basic American Constitutional rights supersede. In 1924, Congress declared that all Indians were American citizens, though many reject the label.

"I don't belong to two nations," Mr. Bear said, strolling on Goshute land in central Utah. "I belong to one—the Skull Valley Goshute Nation."

Today, governments collide with greater frequency, particularly where Indian country rubs up against major urban areas. And tribes are doing what any corporation or government with something to protect has done: they have hired top-tier lobbyists, publicists and legal talent to make their case.

"They want us to be traditional," Leon Bear said. "Sure, we'd like to be traditional. But you can't eat wild rice anymore because those lands are polluted. And you can't hunt around here—they've poisoned the watering holes up in those mountains." He motioned toward a range with two commercial toxic waste dumps.

In Salt Lake City, Mr. Cook, the Congressman whose district borders Skull Valley, sees a collision ahead. Nobody wants the nuclear waste site but a handful of Indians trying to get rich, he says. Plus, parts of Utah may be Indian country, but it is also earthquake country—a potential safety problem, he says.

"Something is dead wrong when a small group of people can ignore the will of 90 percent of our state," Mr. Cook said.

It is possible, Mr. Cook said, that parallel nations may never work, a feeling shared by some experts. The sovereignty movement "is creating a hodgepodge of economically and perhaps politically unviable states whose role in the United States is glaringly undefined in the United States constitution," Fergus M. Bordewich wrote in a recent book, *Killing the White Man's Indian* (Anchor, 1997; Doubleday, 1996).

Mr. Bordewich took a journalistic tour of Indian country and came away greatly worried. He imagines a future where nearly every major city has a tribal casino, and passports are needed to travel from one area to the next.

The Indians scoff at such suggestions. For more than two centuries, the tribes have been in retreat. They once had a peak population of perhaps as high as 10 million people living 500 years ago in what is now the United States, according to the estimates of some historians. The population fell to barely 300,000 by the 1920's.

"I believe we will be here as long as the United States will exist," Mr. Gover said. "By sheer tenacity, we have held on." The grip of life, he said, is the very sovereignty movement that scares non-Indians.

But what about casinos? What do these have to do with being an Indian, with living the old way? Leon Bear and other Indians have a ready reply.

"We have our traditional values," he said. "Sovereignty—that's what we've held onto."

Never Sell Your Parents' Bones

Always remember that your father never sold his country. You must stop your ears whenever you are asked to sign a treaty selling your home. A few years more, and white men will be all around you. They have their eyes on this land. My son, never forget my dying words. This country holds your father's body. Never sell the bones of your father and your mother.

—Final words of Chief Joseph of the Nez Percé Nation, spoken to his son Joseph, 1871

VIII

Heterosexism

 I put prostitutes and gays at about the same level. . . . I'd be hard put to give somebody life for killing a prostitute.

—A State District Judge in Texas, explaining why he gave a lighter sentence to a murderer whose victims were gay, December, 1988

In the United States, it is illegal to discriminate on the basis of race, color, religion, sex, or national origin. In most states, however, the law permits discrimination based on a person's sexual orientation. Thus, heterosexism differs from racism, sexism, and anti-Semitism in that it is often legally permissible.

This section's readings begin by reviewing the history of heterosexism, including the role of religion, medicine, and government. Until 1973 the American Psychiatric Association grouped homosexuality with sexual deviations such as pedophilia and exhibitionism (still done in the *International Classification of Diseases*), and in 1986 the U.S. Supreme Court referred to homosexuality as a "crime against nature."

The section also includes a laboratory investigation linking male homophobia with homosexual arousal—a result interpreted by the authors as evidence that homophobic men may have hidden homosexual impulses. Finally, the readings move beyond the traditional gender categories of female and male to consider transgender issues. For example, recent laws against same-sex marriage raise unique legal questions about "heterosexual" marriages involving intersexuals (people whose sex is neither female nor male). On a more general note, the section concludes by describing several ways that heterosexism and rigid gender roles harm heterosexuals.

Take Special Notice

As a graph in this section shows, the American public has become nearly unanimous in favoring equal rights in the workplace for homosexuals, even though it remains divided on whether homosexual relations should be legal. What accounts for this change in public opinion?

Questions Worth Pondering

- Are equal rights possible when homosexuality is illegal?
- What is the difference between heterosexism and homophobia?
- How is homophobia similar to antifat prejudice?
- Why does the American Psychological Association recommend using the term "sexual orientation" rather than "sexual preference"?
- In light of the fact that millions of people are born intersexual, is it prejudiced to behave as though "female" and "male" are the only two sex categories?

Biblical Statements on Homosexuality

If a man has intercourse with a man as with a woman, they both commit an abomination. They shall be put to death.

—Leviticus 20:13

No fornicator or idolater, none who are guilty either of adultery or of homosexual perversion, no thieves or grabbers or drunkards or slanderers or swindlers, will possess the kingdom of God.

—I Corinthians 6:9–10

A Biblical Statement on Cross-Dressing

No woman shall wear an article of man's clothing, nor shall a man put on a woman's dress; for those who do these things are abominable to the Lord your God.

—Deuteronomy 22:5

Do You Believe It?

Sure, I believe it. I believe everything the Bible says.

> —Reverend Eugene Lumpkin of the San Francisco Human Rights Commission, when asked on TV whether he believed that homosexuals should be stoned to death, *New York Times,* August 20, 1993

Homosexual conduct is, and has been, considered abhorrent, immoral, detestable, a crime against nature, and a violation of the laws of nature and of nature's God. . . . Homosexual behavior is . . . an inherent evil, and an act so heinous that it defies one's ability to describe it. . . . Any person who engages in such conduct is presumptively unfit to have custody of minor children under the established laws of this State.

> —Roy Moore, Chief Justice of the Alabama Supreme Court, in a 9–0 ruling that awarded custody of three children to their heterosexual father rather than to their lesbian mother, February 15, 2002

Moral Trespassing

With grief we must tell you that as long as you are living as a homosexual, you, of course, would not be welcome on the campus and would be arrested for trespassing if you did visit.

> —Excerpt from a letter to a gay alumnus from the Dean of Students at Bob Jones University, a Christian evangelical school in South Carolina, *New York Times*, October 25, 1998

Scripture and our confessions teach that God's intention for all people is to live either in fidelity within the covenant of marriage between a man and a woman or in chastity in singleness.

> —Amendment approved by the Presbyterian Church's General Assembly on June 30, 2000, forbidding ministers from performing same-sex unions

Ceremonies that celebrate homosexual unions shall not be conducted by our ministers and shall not be conducted in our churches.

> —Rule adopted in 1996 and affirmed in 1998 by the United Methodist Church (the second largest Protestant denomination in the United States)

We don't allow pedophiles, transvestites or cross-dressers, either.

> —Robert Black, Texas Republican Party Spokesperson, explaining the party's decision to ban the Log Cabin Republicans (a gay organization) from its state convention, *New York Times*, June 30, 1998

BIBLICAL VERSE: IS IT A REASON
OR AN EXCUSE?

DEB PRICE

An engineering professor is treating her husband, a loan officer, to dinner for finally giving in to her pleas to shave off the scraggly beard he grew on vacation.

His favorite restaurant is a casual place where they both feel comfortable in slacks and cotton-polyester blend golf shirts. But, as always, she wears the gold and pearl pendant he gave her the day her divorce to her first husband was final.

They're laughing over their menus because they know he always ends up diving into a giant plate of ribs, but she won't be talked into anything more fattening than shrimp.

Quiz: How many biblical prohibitions are they violating? Well, wives must be "submissive" to their husbands (I Peter 3:1). And all women are forbidden to teach men (I Timothy 2:12), wear gold or pearls (I Timothy 2:9) or dress in clothing that "pertains to a man" (Deuteronomy 22:5).

Shellfish and pork are definitely out (Leviticus 11:7, 10), as are usury (Deuteronomy 23:19), shaving (Leviticus 19:27) and clothes of more than one fabric (Leviticus 19:19). And since the Bible rarely recognizes divorce, they're committing adultery, which carries the rather harsh penalty of death by stoning (Deuteronomy 22:22).

So why are they having such a good time? Probably because they wouldn't think of worrying about rules that seem absurd, anachronistic or—at best—unrealistic.

Yet this same modern-day couple easily could be among the millions of people who never hesitate to lean on the Bible to justify their own anti-gay attitudes.

Bible verses have long been used selectively to support many kinds of discrimination. Somewhere along the way, Jesus' second-greatest commandment gets lost: "You shall love your neighbor as yourself."

Once a given form of prejudice falls out of favor with society, so do the verses that had seemed to condone it. It's unimaginable today, for example, that anyone would use the Bible to justify slavery.

Yet when the abolitionist movement began to gain momentum in the early 19th century, many Southern ministers defended the owning of human beings as a divinely approved system: "Slaves, obey in everything those who are your earthly masters" (Colossians 3:22).

In an influential anti-abolitionist essay, South Carolina Baptist leader Richard Furman declared in 1822 that "the right of holding slaves is clearly established in the Holy Scriptures."

Nearly 100 years after the Emancipation Proclamation, a Virginia court defended racial segregation by saying, "The Almighty God created the races white, black, yellow, Malay and red, and He placed them on separate continents. . . . He did not intend for the races to mix." The U.S. Supreme Court rejected that reasoning in 1967 when it struck down laws in 16 states forbidding interracial marriage.

Like advocates of racial equality, suffragists found the literal reading of the Bible was their biggest stumbling block. Many ministers even condemned using anesthesia during labor because pain in childbirth was punishment for Eve's bite of forbidden fruit (Genesis 3:16).

Susan B. Anthony eventually declared in frustration: "I distrust those people who know so well what God wants them to do, because I notice it always coincides with their own desires."

Studying the Bible is often akin to looking at Rorschach ink blots, says biblical scholar Joe Barnhart.

"What we get out of it is sometimes what we put into it," he explains.

The punishment the Bible metes out to all men for Adam's downfall is toiling "in the sweat of your face" (Genesis 3:19).

Yet, Barnhart notes with a laugh, there's one bit of progress never denounced by preachers hot under the clerical collar: air conditioning.

A Monster in Human Shape

American homosexuals have been legally condemned to death by choking, burning, and drowning; they have been executed, jailed, pilloried, fined, court-martialed, fired, disinherited, declared insane; and they have been castrated, lobotomized, and treated with electroshock therapy. Here are some events from early American history:

- In 1646, John Winthrop, the first governor of the Massachusetts Bay Colony, referred to a gay man as a "monster in human shape" and had him executed.

- In the New Netherland Colony (Manhattan Island), the following entry appears for June 25, 1646: "Court proceedings. Fiscal [public prosecutor] vs. Jan Creoli, a negro, sodomy; second offense; this crime being condemned of God (Gen., c. 19; Levit., c. 18: 22, 29) as an abomination, the prisoner is sentenced to be conveyed to the place of public execution, and there choked to death, and then burnt to ashes."

- In 1655, the New Haven Colony published a sodomy statute that included lesbianism, male homosexuality, heterosexual anal intercourse, and masturbation as crimes punishable by death.

- In Bill #64, submitted on June 18, 1779, Thomas Jefferson proposed revising Virginia law so that instead of calling for death, the penal code for homosexuality would, more leniently, read as follows: "Whosoever shall be guilty of Rape, Polygamy, or Sodomy with man or woman shall be punished, if a man, by castration, if a woman, by cutting thro' the cartilage of her nose a hole of one half inch diameter at the least." The proposal was never enacted.

— Source: Jonathan Katz, *Gay American History: Lesbians and Gay Men in the U.S.A.,* 1976

VIOLENCE TOWARD HOMOSEXUALS

KAREN FRANKLIN AND GREGORY M. HEREK

Anthropologists and historians have located examples from many time periods and geographic settings of individuals being punished for violating the gender and sexual norms of their particular culture. Widespread institutionalized violence against homosexuals appears to be a relatively recent historical phenomenon, however, emerging in Europe in the 13th and 14th centuries during the rise of the modern nation-state. The Christian Crusades and the Holy Inquisition of this period saw unprecedented vilification and persecution of homosexuals and other previously tolerated social groups, including Jews, Muslims, religious dissidents, witches, lepers, moneylenders, and the poor.

Public antagonism during this period was exacerbated by homosexuality's linkage with Islamic cultures and religious heretics. Trials of heretics frequently mentioned their alleged practice of sodomy, and Muslims were accused during the Crusades of sodomy, effeminacy, transvestitism, and the sexual corruption of Christian youth. Indeed, the earliest legislation against homosexual behavior, proscribing death by burning for sodomites, was enacted by Europeans attempting to wrest Jerusalem from the Muslims.

During the latter half of the 13th century, the pendulum regarding homosexuality swung from complete legality to punishment by death in most of Europe. In Spain, a new law proscribed castration followed by death by hanging from the legs. In France, male sodomites were punishable by castration for the first offense, dismemberment for the second, and burning for the third, whereas women were punishable by dismemberment for the first and second offenses and burning for the third.

The extent to which these laws were actually enforced is difficult to determine. Contemporaneous records suggest that accusations of homosexuality were widely used during religious and political crusades. The Church accused wealthy noblemen of homosexuality in order to seize their lands. Pagans who practiced ritualized homosexuality and cross-dressing were executed at so-called "witch" trials; these antiwitch campaigns continued until the end of the 18th century, with estimates of the number of people killed ranging from several hundred thousand to several million.

The legal persecution of homosexuals continued for several centuries in Europe and North America. Records from 17th and 18th century England, France, and the Netherlands reveal that gatherings of homosexual men in parks and taverns were met with arrests, torture, and executions. In colonial New England, executions for sodomy occurred as early as 1646. A statute passed in 1655 by the New Haven colony mandated the death penalty for lesbianism as well as male homosexuality. Anti-homosexual epithets such as faggot, fairy, punk, and bugger date back to this era, which set the stage for contemporary violence toward homosexuals.

Although laws in Europe and the United States proscribing the death penalty for homosexuality were largely abolished by the end of the 19th century, hostility toward homosexuality reached a tragic climax in Nazi Germany. An estimated 50,000 to 63,000 suspected male homosexuals were convicted of homosexuality under the infamous Paragraph 175[1] between 1933 and 1944. Between 5,000 and 15,000 are thought to have died in concentration camps. Gay men were forced to wear a pink triangle or letter "A" (for *Arschficker*) as a badge of identity, and were singled out for violence including beating, rape, castration, and medical experimentation. (Although a small number of lesbians were ensnared in the Nazi juggernaut, lesbianism was not illegal under Paragraph 175.) At the war's end, other surviving prisoners were liberated but the homosexuals were not; Germany's anti-homosexual law remained in effect until 1969.

In the United States, the end of World War II signaled the emergence of the homosexual subculture as a definable, self-conscious social minority in the United States. The birth of modern gay culture coincided with the anti-communist hysteria of the McCarthy era, which ushered in a resurgence of anti-homosexual discrimination through legal codes, military regulations, mass firings, and arrests. As early as 1950, the Republican National Chairman announced that "the sexual perverts who have infiltrated our government" were "perhaps as dangerous as the actual communists." By April of that year, 91 alleged homosexuals had been fired from the State Department alone. The branding of homosexuals as traitors and security risks led to an upsurge of antigay violence as police across the United States routinely engaged in bar raids, blackmail, entrapment, and other abuses.

Contemporary Overview

Globally, state-sanctioned violence by law enforcement authorities appears to be the most prevalent form of violence experienced by homosexuals. In many countries, the police routinely raid gay and lesbian meeting places. Suspected homosexuals are rounded up and detained, frequently without formal charges. These detentions are often marked by beatings, torture, attempted blackmail, and other forms of abuse. Examples include a June, 1996, discotheque raid in Halle, Germany, in which patrons were beaten with batons and bar stools by 160 masked police, and mass roundups around Bulgaria in July, 1996, at gay beaches, magazine offices, and bars. Routine police beatings and torture of arrested homosexuals have been reported in numerous other countries. Countries garnering extensive international attention due to such incidents in the 1990s included Albania, Greece, and Romania.

Violence against lesbians is less well documented than that against gay men, due in part to the social invisibility of lesbians within both the dominant

---

[1] *Editor's note:* Paragraph 175 was an anti-sodomy law adopted by Germany in 1871.

culture and homosexual subcultures. Lesbians most typically are victimized when their behaviors interfere with male privileges or property rights. For example, women who will not marry, who request divorces, or who refuse to terminate same-sex love affairs face punishment by male suitors, husbands, or family members. Frequent forms of punishment are rape and beating. For example, a Zimbabwean woman reported that when her parents learned of her lesbianism, they locked her in a room with an older man who raped her daily, in order that she become pregnant and be forced to marry.[2] Similarly, an Iranian woman who refused to curtail her lesbian relationship was severely beaten by her father and brothers and then repeatedly raped by the man whom they forced her to marry. In addition to physical abuse, one of the most severe punishments faced by lesbians is state-sanctioned theft of their children based on judicial decisions that their sexuality makes them unfit parents.

Cultural Context

Because heterosexism has been promulgated by major societal institutions such as the courts, medicine, religion, and the mass media, it is ubiquitous in most parts of the world. This cultural climate of denigration allows widespread violence against homosexuals to go largely unpunished, clearly conveying the message that gay people do not deserve full legal protection and justice.

The legal tradition of heterosexism was cogently expressed in *Bowers v. Hardwick,* the 1986 U.S. Supreme Court decision permitting states to outlaw homosexual behavior, which held that condemnation of homosexuality "is firmly rooted in Judeo-Christian moral and ethical standards." In 1997, approximately 84 countries and nearly half of the U.S. states had laws on the books prohibiting sex between two men and, in many cases, two women. By defining homosexuals as criminals and deviants, these laws provided moral justification for violence against gay men and lesbians.

Judicial disdain for homosexual victims also encourages perpetrators to believe they will face no significant consequences if caught. The so-called "homosexual panic defense," in which assailants claim they acted in self-defense against homosexual overtures, has resulted in lenient sentences and even acquittals in U.S. courts. By shifting responsibility from the perpetrator to the victim, this defense appeals strongly to the cultural stereotype of gay people as sexually predatory. Judges have often perpetuated this victim-blaming. In a Florida murder trial, for example, the judge joked, "That's a crime now, to beat up a homosexual?"

In the field of medicine, homosexuals have been victimized since the 19th century by attempted "cures" such as castration, hysterectomy, lobotomy, drug therapies, and shock treatment. Although homosexuality was

---

[2]*Editor's note:* The President of Zimbabwe later urged citizens to arrest homosexuals, declaring that homosexuality "is sub-animal behaviour and we will never allow it here."

removed from the Diagnostic and Statistical Manual of the American Psychiatric Association in 1973, the International Classification of Diseases has continued to label homosexuality as a mental illness, and many medical practitioners outside the United States continue to regard homosexual behavior as pathological. Homosexuals—especially adolescents—are still disproportionately hospitalized in mental institutions, where they are often physically and emotionally abused due to their sexuality.

In religion, luminaries in both Christian and Jewish faiths have vociferously condemned homosexuality for centuries. Although some denominations began to express more tolerance during the 1980s and 1990s, others maintained a strong antigay stance. In 1986, for example, a Roman Catholic proclamation opposing civil rights protections for homosexuals was widely interpreted as condoning antigay violence.

Most virulent among modern religious institutions are the fundamentalist movements of the late 20th century. Both Christian and Islamic fundamentalist leaders have publicly advocated execution of homosexuals.[3] Christian fundamentalists in particular have used homosexuality as a primary organizing issue. Casting civil rights for homosexuals as "special rights" for perverts and child molesters, they have warned that homosexual proselytizers are "on the advance" against heterosexuals. The Internet provides a far-reaching forum for dissemination of inflammatory propaganda through World Wide Web sites with titles such as "Homosexuals: A Clear and Present Danger to Our Children," "AIDS and God's Wrath," and "The True Objective of 'Gay Rights': Total Domination!"

Prevention Strategies

The 1980s and 1990s saw a dramatic upswing in organizing efforts by lesbians and gay men against violence. These efforts took a number of forms, including legislative drives, educational outreach, community mobilizations, and increased data collection and research efforts.

International Campaigns

Internationally, efforts to reduce violence and public hostility toward homosexuals have focused on legislative drives for anti-discrimination laws, repeal of sodomy statutes, and efforts to publicize and put an end to basic human rights violations. Considerable progress has been made in all three

---

[3]*Editor's note:* Homosexual behavior is punishable by death in several Islamic nations, including Iran, Afghanistan, and Saudi Arabia. In Iran, this penalty has been meted out to approximately 4,000 people since 1979; in Afghanistan, at least six men were reportedly crushed to death publicly after being convicted of sodomy in 1998 and 1999; and on January 1, 2002, three men in Saudi Arabia were publicly beheaded for committing homosexual acts.

areas. In 1996, for example, South Africa took the historic step of becoming the first country in the world to ban all forms of discrimination against homosexuals. An international campaign for the repeal of sodomy laws—which have set a social tone of tolerance for both legal and extralegal violence against homosexuals—met with significant success during the 1990s. And increasing scrutiny by international human rights agencies helped curtail some of the more extreme cases of mass arrests, torture, and police abuse of suspected homosexuals. In the wake of this heightened international focus, several countries—including Australia, Canada, and the United States—began granting refugee status to homosexuals attempting to escape violence and other types of persecution in their home countries.

United States Efforts

In the United States, a combination of local and national efforts led to dramatic legislative and public policy changes, combined with significant changes in public opinion, during the 1990s. Intensive lobbying by antiviolence activists, civil rights organizations, and concerned professionals led to the inclusion of homosexuals in the 1990 Hate Crimes Statistics Act, a modest law that encouraged local law enforcement agencies to voluntarily report hate crimes to the Federal Bureau of Investigation. Subsequent federal and state laws mandated enhanced sentencing for a variety of hate crimes, including those based on sexual orientation. By 1997, 16 U.S. states required stiffer penalties for crimes committed on the basis of sexual orientation.

Many lesbian and gay activists believe that the most effective long-term method of reducing violence is to change the cultural stereotypes that make homosexuals a permissible target, especially for adolescents and young adults. With this in mind, they have launched public opinion campaigns in the schools and the mass media. Efforts to teach school children about homosexuality have been introduced into larger antibias curricula in several school districts around the United States. Teachers lead discussions aimed at correcting inaccurate beliefs, and gay and lesbian speakers are brought into classrooms to answer questions and counteract negative stereotypes. "Gay/Straight Student Alliances" and support groups for gay and lesbian youth also have been established in dozens of schools across the country. Research indicating that antigay assailants are more influenced by peers' opinions than parents' opinions about homosexuality suggests that such school-based interventions have utility.

One effect of school-based interventions is that they frequently encourage gay and lesbian teachers in those schools to be more open about their identities. Research indicating that personal contact with gay men and lesbians is correlated with more tolerant attitudes toward homosexuality suggests that the increasing public visibility of gay and lesbian teachers—and indeed homosexuals more generally—may ultimately contribute to a decrease in antigay violence.

BIBLIOGRAPHY

Boswell, J. (1980). *Christianity, social tolerance, and homosexuality.* Chicago: University of Chicago Press.

Cohen, H. S. (Producer), & Chasnoff, D. (Producer/Director). (1996). *It's Elementary: Talking about gay issues in school.* [Film]. (Available from Women's Educational Media, 2180 Bryant Street, Suite 203, San Francisco, CA 94110)

Comstock, G. D. (1991). *Violence against lesbians and gay men.* New York: Columbia University Press.

Dong, A. (Producer/Director). (1997). *Licensed to Kill.* [Film]. (Available from DeepFocus Productions, c/o Film Arts Foundation, 346 Ninth Street, San Francisco, CA 94103)

Franklin, K. (1996). Hate crime or rite of passage? Assailant motivations in antigay violence. Unpublished doctoral dissertation, California School of Professional Psychology.

Franklin, K. (1998). Unassuming motivations: Contextualizing the narratives of antigay assailants. In G. M. Herek (Ed.), *Stigma and sexual orientation: Understanding prejudice against lesbians, gay men, and bisexuals* (pp. 1–23). Thousand Oaks, CA: Sage.

Herek, G. M., & Berrill, K. T. (1992). *Hate crimes: Confronting violence against lesbians and gay men.* Newbury Park, CA: Sage.

Herek, G. M., Gillis, J. R., Cogan, J. C., & Glunt, E. K. (1997). Hate crime victimization among lesbian, gay, and bisexual adults: Prevalence, psychological correlates, and methodological issues. *Journal of Interpersonal Violence, 12,* 195–215.

Pharr, S. (1988). *Homophobia: A weapon of sexism.* Inverness, CA: Chardon Press.

Plant, R. (1986). *The pink triangle: The Nazi war against homosexuals.* New York: Henry Holt.

Rosenbloom, R. (1995). *Unspoken rules: Sexual orientation and women's human rights.* San Francisco, CA: International Gay and Lesbian Human Rights Commission.

Arrested Development

Homosexuality is ... produced by a certain arrest of sexual development....

[You ask] if I can abolish homosexuality and make normal hetero-sexuality take its place. The answer is, in a general way we cannot promise to achieve it. In a certain number of cases we succeed in developing the blighted germs of heterosexual tendencies, which are present in every homosexual; in the majority of cases it is no more possible. It is a question of the quality and the age of the individual. The result of treatment cannot be predicted.

—Sigmund Freud, in a letter to a woman whose son was homo-sexual, April 9, 1935

Diagnostic Category 302.0: Homosexuality

302   Sexual deviations

This category is for individuals whose sexual interests are directed primarily toward objects other than people of the opposite sex, toward sexual acts not usually associated with coitus, or toward coitus performed under bizarre circumstances as in necrophilia, pedophilia, sexual sadism, and fetishism. Even though many find their practices distasteful, they remain unable to substitute normal sexual behavior for them. This diagnosis is not appropriate for individuals who perform deviant sexual acts because normal sexual objects are not available to them.

302.0 Homosexuality

302.1 Fetishism

302.2 Pedophilia

302.3 Transvestitism

302.4 Exhibitionism

—Reprinted with permission from the *Diagnostic and Statistical Manual of Mental Disorders, Second Edition.* Copyright © 1968 American Psychiatric Association.

302   SEXUAL DEVIATIONS AND DISORDERS—

Abnormal sexual inclinations or behavior which are part of a referral problem. The limits and features of normal sexual behavior have not been stated absolutely in different societies and cultures, but are broadly such as serve approved social and biological purposes. The sexual activity of affected persons is directed primarily either towards people not of the opposite sex, or towards sexual acts not associated with coitus normally, or towards coitus performed under abnormal circumstances. . . . *See also* Exhibitionism, Fetishism, Homosexuality, Nymphomania, Pedophilia, Satyriasis, Sexual masochism, Sexual sadism, Transvestism, Voyeurism, and Zoophilia.

—Reprinted with permission from the *Diagnostic and Statistical Manual of Mental Disorders, Second Edition.* Copyright © 1968 American Psychiatric Association.

The AIDS Epidemic: Don't Ask, Don't Tell

1981

335 cases have been diagnosed in the United States; 158 people have died.

- The U.S. Centers for Disease Control publishes the first account of a cluster of peculiar deaths from a syndrome that would later be named AIDS.

- The phenomenon is initially called "gay cancer," and then "gay-related immune deficiency," or GRID.

1982

1,580 cases have been diagnosed in the United States; 603 people have died.

- *The Wall Street Journal* reports that GRID is now appearing in women and male heterosexual drug users. It becomes apparent that the disease is caused by an infectious agent linked to blood, and it is given a new name—Acquired Immune Deficiency Syndrome, or AIDS.

- President Ronald Reagan has not yet mentioned the word "AIDS" in public.

1983

4,788 cases have been diagnosed in the United States; 2,137 people have died.

- Dr. Luc Montagnier and his colleagues in France isolate what would later become known as the human immunodeficiency virus, or HIV.

- Outbreaks begin to appear in Britain, France, Australia and Africa; altogether, 33 countries have reported cases of the disease.

- President Reagan has still not explicitly acknowledged AIDS in public.

1984

11,148 cases have been diagnosed in the United States; 5,655 people have died.

- Among the platform planks adopted at the Democratic Convention is a call to increase funding and attention "to learn the cause and cure for AIDS, and to provide treatment for people with AIDS."

- The Republican Party platform is silent on HIV/AIDS. President Reagan has yet to say the word "AIDS" in public.

The AIDS Epidemic (continued)

1985

23,174 cases have been diagnosed in the United States; 12,652 people have died.

- A *Los Angeles Times* poll finds that 51 percent of those surveyed support a quarantine of AIDS patients, 48 percent approve of identity cards for people who test positive for HIV, and 15 percent support tattooing people with AIDS.

- The first International Conference on AIDS is held in Atlanta. Sponsored by the World Health Organization, it attracts 2,000 attendees from 26 countries.

- Film star Rock Hudson dies of AIDS.

- Cases of AIDS have been reported in 51 countries.

- Still no public acknowledgement of the epidemic from President Reagan.

1986

42,546 cases have been diagnosed in the United States; 24,806 people have died.

- The World Health Organization launches a global AIDS strategy that includes needle exchange programs to reduce the spread of the virus among drug users.

- HIV-positive children are barred from schools.

- U.S. Surgeon General C. Everett Koop releases a report on AIDS calling for comprehensive sex education.

1987

71,616 cases have been diagnosed in the United States; 41,262 people have died.

- The World Health Organization estimates that up to 150,000 cases exist worldwide.

- The U.S. Immigration and Naturalization Service refuses entry to HIV-positive immigrants and visitors.

- For the first time—six years and 40,000 deaths in the United States after the first signs of an epidemic—President Reagan publicly uses the word "AIDS."

—Source: Human Rights Campaign, *HIV/AIDS & HRC: Two Decades of Fighting for Life*, 2001

U.S. Supreme Court Decisions

The issue posed in this case is the extent to which a self-governing democracy, having made [sodomy] criminal, may prevent or discourage individuals from engaging in speech or conduct which encourages others to violate those laws. . . . [The question is] akin to whether those suffering from measles have a constitutional right, in violation of quarantine regulations, to associate together and with others who do not presently have measles, in order to urge repeal of a state law providing that measles sufferers be quarantined.

> —Justice William Rehnquist, 1978, likening homosexuality to a contagious disease. In the case, a gay-rights student group was trying to overturn a Missouri law that mandated a prison sentence for anyone convicted of "the detestable and abominable crime against nature, committed with mankind or beast, with the sexual organs or with the mouth."

Decisions of individuals relating to homosexual conduct have been subject to state intervention throughout the history of Western civilization. Condemnation of those practices is firmly rooted in Judeao-Christian moral and ethical standards. . . . Blackstone described "the infamous crime against nature" as an offense of "deeper malignity" than rape, a heinous act "the very mention of which is a disgrace to human nature." . . . To hold that the act of homosexual sodomy is somehow protected as a fundamental right would be to cast aside millennia of moral teaching.

> —Chief Justice Warren Burger, 1986, upholding the constitutionality of a Georgia state law that punished consensual sodomy with up to 20 years' imprisonment

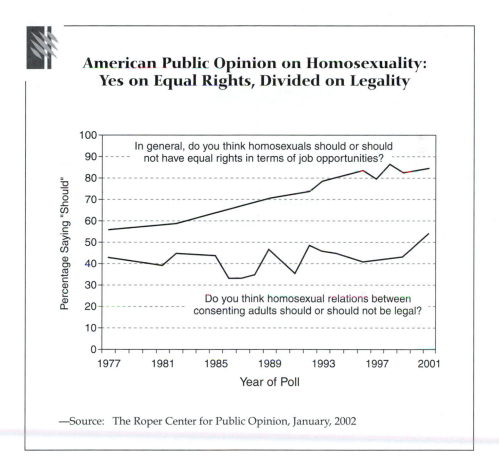

American Public Opinion on Homosexuality: Yes on Equal Rights, Divided on Legality

—Source: The Roper Center for Public Opinion, January, 2002

Is Homosexuality a Sin?

Yeah, it is. . . . You should still love that person. You should not try to mistreat them or treat them as outcasts. You should try to show them a way to deal with that problem, just like alcohol . . . or sex addiction . . . or kleptomaniacs.

—Trent Lott, former U.S. Senate Majority Leader, June 15, 1998

Is Homosexuality a Disease?

It is a pathology. It is a sickness, and it needs to be treated. It doesn't need to be taught in the classroom as a preferred way of life.

Acceptance of homosexuality is the last step in the decline of Gentile civilization.

—Pat Robertson, Founder of the Christian Broadcasting Network
First quote source: *700 Club,* March 7, 1990
Second quote source: *Time,* October 26, 1998

Is Homosexuality Unnatural?

We've got to have some common sense about a disease transmitted by people engaging in unnatural acts.

—Senator Jesse Helms, discussing AIDS in an interview with the *New York Times*, July 5, 1995

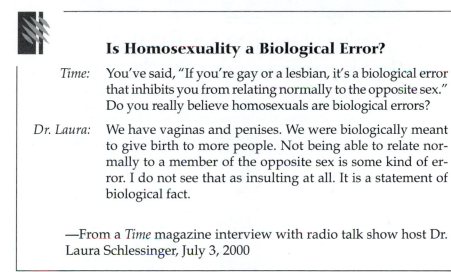

Is Homosexuality a Biological Error?

Time: You've said, "If you're gay or a lesbian, it's a biological error that inhibits you from relating normally to the opposite sex." Do you really believe homosexuals are biological errors?

Dr. Laura: We have vaginas and penises. We were biologically meant to give birth to more people. Not being able to relate normally to a member of the opposite sex is some kind of error. I do not see that as insulting at all. It is a statement of biological fact.

—From a *Time* magazine interview with radio talk show host Dr. Laura Schlessinger, July 3, 2000

—Full-page advertisement appearing in the *Washington Post* and other newspapers, July 14, 1998. Reprinted with permission of the Center for Reclaiming America.

Sexual Orientation vs. Sexual Preference

The term *sexual orientation* is preferred to *sexual preference* for psychological writing and refers to sexual and affectional relationships of lesbian, gay, bisexual, and heterosexual people. The word *preference* suggests a degree of voluntary choice that is not necessarily reported by lesbians and gay men and that has not been demonstrated in psychological research.

—Committee on Lesbian and Gay Concerns, American Psychological Association, *American Psychologist,* 1991

IS HOMOPHOBIA ASSOCIATED WITH HOMOSEXUAL AROUSAL?

HENRY E. ADAMS, LESTER W. WRIGHT, JR.,
AND BETHANY A. LOHR

Hostility and discrimination against homosexual individuals are well-established facts (Berrill, 1990). On occasion, these negative attitudes lead to hostile verbal and physical acts against gay individuals with little apparent motivation except a strong dislike (Herek, 1989). In fact, more than 90% of gay men and lesbians report being targets of verbal abuse or threats, and more than one-third report being survivors of violence related to their homosexuality (Fassinger, 1991). Although negative attitudes and behaviors toward gay individuals have been assumed to be associated with rigid moralistic beliefs, sexual ignorance, and fear of homosexuality, the etiology of these attitudes and behaviors remains a puzzle (Marmor, 1980). Weinberg (1972) labeled these attitudes and behaviors *homophobia,* which he defined as the dread of being in close quarters with homosexual men and women as well as irrational fear, hatred, and intolerance by heterosexual individuals of homosexual men and women.

It has been argued that the term *homophobic* may not be appropriate because there is no evidence that homophobic individuals exhibit avoidance of homosexual persons (Bernstein, 1994; Rowan, 1994). Nevertheless, the only necessary requirement for the label of phobia is that phobic stimuli produce anxiety. Whether the individual exhibits avoidance or endures the anxiety often depends on the nature of the stimuli and the environmental circumstances. MacDonald's (1976) suggestions are consistent with this analysis because he defined *homophobia* as anxiety or anticipatory anxiety elicited by homosexual individuals. O'Donahue and Caselles (1993) noted that McDonald's definition parallels the diagnostic criteria of the *Diagnostic and Statistical Manual of Mental Disorders (DSM-IV;* American Psychiatric Association, 1994) for simple phobia and captures the negative emotional reactions toward homosexuality that seem to have motivated use of the term.

Although the causes of homophobia are unclear, several psychoanalytic explanations have emerged from the idea of homophobia as an anxiety-based phenomenon. Psychoanalytic theories usually postulate that homophobia is a result of repressed homosexual urges or a form of latent homosexuality. *Latent homosexuality* can be defined as homosexual arousal which the individual is either unaware of or denies (West, 1977). Psychoanalysts use the concept of repressed or latent homosexuality to explain the emotional malaise and irrational attitudes displayed by some individuals who feel guilty about their erotic interests and struggle to deny and repress homosexual impulses. The relationship between homophobia and latent homosexuality has not been empirically investigated and is one of the purposes of the present study.

Specifically, the present study was designed to investigate whether homophobic men show more sexual arousal to homosexual cues than nonhomophobic men. As O'Donahue and Caselles (1993, p. 193) have noted, an investigation of whether those who "aggress against homosexuals become sexually aroused to homosexual stimuli (as certain psychoanalytic theories might predict)" would contribute to our understanding of homophobia. A secondary goal was to evaluate whether homophobic individuals are persons who are more generally hostile or aggressive than nonhomophobic men. The present investigation was designed to evaluate these two hypotheses.

Method

Participants

Caucasian heterosexual male volunteers ($n = 64$) recruited from the Psychology Department Research Subject Pool at the University of Georgia participated in the study. They were screened during large group testing during which time they completed the modified version of the Kinsey Heterosexual-Homosexual Rating Scale (Kinsey, Pomeroy, & Martin, 1948), the Index of Homophobia (IHP; Hudson & Ricketts, 1980), and the Aggression Questionnaire (Buss & Perry, 1992). They were contacted by telephone at a later date to schedule the laboratory portion of the study. All participants received partial course credit. The mean age of the men was 20.3 years (range = 18 to 31 years).

Screening Measures

Kinsey Heterosexual-Homosexual Rating Scale   A modified version of the Kinsey Heterosexual-Homosexual Rating Scale was used to assess sexual arousal and prior sexual experiences. This version of the Kinsey is a 7-point scale on which individuals separately rated their sexual arousal and experiences from *exclusively homosexual* to *exclusively heterosexual*. Only participants who reported exclusively heterosexual arousal and experiences (i.e., 1s on both sections) were selected for participation.

IHP   The IHP is the most widely used measure of homophobia (O'Donahue & Caselles, 1993). The items of the IHP assess affective components of homophobia. The scale contains 25 items, and scores range from 0 to 100: 0–25, high-grade nonhomophobic; 26–50, low-grade nonhomophobic; 51–75, low-grade homophobic; and 76–100, high-grade homophobic. The score obtained is a measure of "dread" when placed in close quarters with a homosexual; a low score equals low dread, and a high score equals high dread. Because most of the items contain the terms *comfortable* or *uncomfortable*, dread can be assumed to mean anticipatory anxiety about interacting with a homosexual person. For example, one item states "I would feel nervous being in a group of homosexuals."

The men were divided into two groups on the basis of their scores on the IHP: 0–50 = nonhomophobic men, $n = 29$, $M = 30.48$; 51–100 = homophobic men, $n = 35$, $M = 80.40$. This split was necessary because of an inability to find an adequate number of exclusively heterosexual men who scored in the high-grade nonhomophobic range (0–25).

Response Measures

Penile plethysmography[1]   A mercury-in-rubber (MIR) circumferential strain gauge (Bancroft, Jones, & Pullan, 1966) was used to measure erectile responses to the sexual stimuli. When attached, changes in the circumference of the penis caused changes in the electrical resistance of the mercury column, which were detected by a Parks Model 270 Plethysmograph. The pre-amplifier output was channeled into a Grass polygraph. Tumescence responses were recorded on the polygraph and were channeled to an IBM computer. Penile plethysmographic responses to sexually explicit stimuli have been shown to discriminate between homosexual and heterosexual men (Tollison, Adams, & Tollison, 1979). Zuckerman (1971) described penile plethysmography as the most specific measure of sexual arousal because significant changes occur only during sexual stimulation and sleep.

Aggression Questionnaire   Buss and Perry's (1992) 29-item scale was used to assess an overall trait of aggression. The men rated each item on a scale of 1 (*extremely uncharacteristic of me*) to 5 (*extremely characteristic of me*). Items targeted four aspects of aggression: physical aggression, verbal aggression, anger, and hostility. This overall score of aggression was used as the dependent variable.

Stimulus Materials

The stimuli were 4-minute segments of explicit erotic videotapes depicting consensual adult heterosexual activity, consensual male homosexual activity, and consensual female homosexual activity. The sexual activity in the videos included sexual foreplay (e.g., kissing and undressing), oral-genital contact (e.g., fellatio or cunnilingus), and intercourse (i.e., vaginal penetration, anal penetration, or tribadism in the lesbian film). The lesbian videotape was included because it has been shown to be highly sexually arousing to heterosexual men and is a better discriminator between heterosexual and homosexual men than other stimuli (Mavissikalian, Blanchard, Abel, & Barlow, 1975).

———————————————
[1] *Editor's note:* A plethysmograph is an instrument that measures variations in the size of an organ or other body part based on how much blood is present or passing through it. In the present study, a plethysmograph measured the degree of tumescence, or penile erection, that participants had while being shown experimental stimuli. Greater tumescence scores indicated a higher degree of engorgement (erection).

Procedure

The procedure was explained to the participant on arrival at the laboratory. He was informed that he could terminate participation at any time, and he signed informed consent. The participant was accompanied to a soundproof chamber, where he was seated in a comfortable reclining chair and was given instructions on the proper placement of the MIR strain gauge. After the experimenter's departure from the experimental chamber into the adjoining equipment room, the participant attached the penile strain gauge. The adjoining equipment room housed the polygraph, the videotape player, an IBM-compatible computer, and the two-way intercom. Once the participant indicated that the apparatus was in place by way of the intercom, a 4-minute baseline was recorded in the absence of any stimuli. Next, the three sexually explicit videos were presented to the participant. Following each videotaped presentation, he rated his level of subjective sexual arousal (i.e., how "turned on" he was) and the degree of penile erection (i.e., from no change to 100% erection) on a scale of 0 to 10. The participant's penile circumference was allowed to return to baseline levels before the next stimulus was presented. The sequence of presentation was counterbalanced across participants to avoid order effects.

Data Reduction

A change score was used to analyze the penile plethysmographic data where the mean penile circumference (in millimeters) in the first second of time was subtracted from subsequent seconds for each video presentation. These scores were divided into six 40-second time blocks. The average change score in penile circumference for each time block was then analyzed.

Results

Penile Plethysmography

The data were analyzed using analysis of variance (ANOVA). Data for each time block for the two groups are presented separately for each stimulus type in Figure 1. For the heterosexual and lesbian videos, both groups showed significant engorgement. For the male homosexual video, results indicate that the homophobic men showed a significant increase in penile circumference to the male homosexual video but that the control men did not.

Another way of evaluating these data is to calculate the percentage of men who demonstrated no significant tumescence (i.e., 0-6 mm), modest tumescence (i.e., > 6-12 mm), and definite tumescence (i.e., > 12 mm) based on their mean tumescence score to the homosexual video. In the homophobic group, 20% showed no significant tumescence, 26% showed moderate tumescence, and 54% showed definite tumescence to the homosexual video; the corresponding percentages in the nonhomophobic group were 66%, 10%, and 24%, respectively.

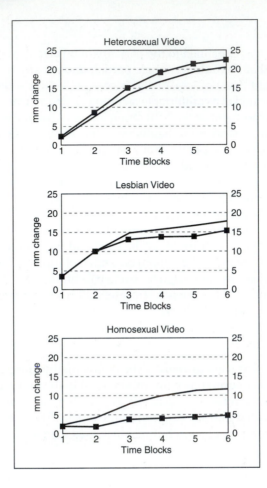

FIGURE 1
Stimulus presentations by groups across time blocks. The only significant difference between groups is with the homosexual video. The blocked line represents the nonhomophobic group; the solid line represents the homophobic group.

Subjective Ratings

Subjective estimates of sexual arousal and penile erection were analyzed with a mixed model ANOVA. The main effect of stimulus type was significant, $F(2, 124) = 90.93$, $p < .001$, indicating significantly greater arousal and erection ratings to the heterosexual and lesbian videos than to the male homosexual video. These means are shown in Table 1.

Correlation coefficients were computed between the penile response measures and subjective ratings of arousal and erection, as shown in Table 1. These correlations ranged from .53 to .66 and indicate that participants' ratings were generally in agreement with their penile responses. Correlations coefficients were also computed with subjective ratings of arousal and erection ratings for

TABLE 1   Means and Correlations of Subjective Ratings with Penile Response

	Arousal		Erection	
Video	*M*	r^a	*M*	*r*
Heterosexual	7.14	.57*	7.10	.64*
Lesbian	6.28	.63*	6.31	.66*
Male homosexual	2.03	.53*	2.79	.64

[a]Subjective ratings were correlated with mean penile response across time blocks.
* $p < .01$.

TABLE 2   Correlations Between Subjective Arousal and Subjective Erection Ratings

		Video		
Group	*N*	*Heterosexual*	*Lesbian*	*Male homosexual*
Homophobic	35	.91	.95	.90
Nonhomophobic	29	.93	.94	.78

each group, as shown in Table 2. These correlations are quite high and are all significant at the $p < .01$ level of confidence, indicating that these two ratings are essentially measuring the same event. The correlation of erection and arousal to the homosexual video in the nonhomophobic group was significantly smaller when compared to other correlations. The decreased consistency between erection and arousal may have been due to the smaller changes in penile responses in this group, making subjective estimates more difficult.

Aggression Questionnaire

A *t*-test between groups was conducted on the Aggression Questionnaire. The difference between the scores for the homophobic ($M = 58.37$) and the nonhomophobic men ($M = 55.96$) was not statistically significant. This result indicates that these groups did not differ in aggression as measured by this questionnaire.

Discussion

The results of this study indicate that individuals who score in the homophobic range and admit negative affect toward homosexuality demonstrate significant sexual arousal to male homosexual erotic stimuli. These individuals were selected on the basis of their report of having only heterosexual arousal and experiences. Furthermore, their ratings of erection and arousal to homosexual stimuli were low and not significantly different from nonhomophobic men who demonstrated no significant increase in penile response to homosexual stimuli. These data are consistent with various psychoanalytic theories, which have generally explained homophobia as a threat to an individual's own homosexual impulses causing repression, denial, or reaction formation (or all three; West, 1977). Generally, these explanations conceive of homophobia as one type of latent homosexuality where persons either are unaware of or deny their homosexual urges.

The hypothesis that homophobic men are merely aggressive individuals is not supported by the present data. There were no differences in aggression scores between groups as measured by the Aggression Questionnaire. However, this questionnaire is a general measure of aggression and does not address the possibility of situational aggression or hostility where the situation involves homosexuality or interacting with a homosexual person. It is possible that aggressiveness in homophobic individuals is specific to homosexual cues.

These data also indicate that subjective estimates of arousal and erection are largely consistent with physiological indices of penile erections, with correlation coefficients ranging from .53 to .66. Because the relationships between subjective measures of erection and arousal were quite high, ranging from .78 to .95, it is likely that these two estimates are measures of similar or identical events. Most of these latter correlations were in the .90 range with the exception of nonhomophobic individuals' ratings of arousal and erection to homosexual stimuli, which was .78. As noted before, these results were probably due to the small penile responses to this stimulus, making subjective estimates more difficult and less consistent.

A major difficulty in this area of research is in defining and measuring homophobia. For example, with the scale used in the present study, we found it difficult to find heterosexual men who scored in the high-grade nonhomophobic range (0–25). The issue of whether homophobia is specific to men or may also occur in women has not been addressed systematically, nor is it clear whether homophobic women may show sexual arousal to erotic lesbian stimuli. With answers to these and similar issues, a clearer understanding of the nature of homophobia will be possible.

REFERENCES

American Psychiatric Association. (1994). *Diagnostic and statistical manual of mental disorders* (4th ed.). Washington, DC: Author.

Bancroft, J. H., Jones, H. G. & Pullan, B. R. (1966). A simple transducer for measuring penile erection with comments on its use in the treatment of sexual disorders. *Behaviour Research and Therapy, 4,* 230–241.

Bernstein, G. S. (1994). A reply to Rowan. *Behavior Therapist, 17,* 185–186.

Berrill, K. T. (1990). Anti-gay violence and victimization in the United States: An overview. *Journal of Interpersonal Violence, 5,* 274–294.

Buss, A. H. & Perry, M. (1992). The aggression questionnaire. *Journal of Personality and Social Psychology, 63,* 452–459.

Fassinger, R. (1991). The hidden minority: Issues and challenges in working with lesbian women and gay men. *Counseling Psychologist, 19,* 157–176.

Herek, G. M. (1989). Hate crimes against lesbians and gay men: Correlates and gender differences. *American Psychologist, 44,* 948–955.

Hudson, W. W. & Ricketts, W. A. (1980). A strategy for the measurement of homophobia. *Journal of Homosexuality, 5,* 356–371.

Kinsey, A. C., Pomeroy, W. B. & Martin, C. E. (1948). *Sexual behavior in the human male.* Philadelphia: W. B. Saunders.

MacDonald, A. P. Jr. (1976). Homophobia: Its roots and meanings. *Homosexual Counseling Journal, 3,* 23–33.

Marmor, J. (1980). Overview: The multiple roots of homosexual behavior. In J. Marmor (Ed.), *Homosexual behavior–A modern reappraisal* (pp. 3–22). New York: Basic Books.

Mavissikalian, N., Blanchard, E. D., Abel, G. G. & Barlow, D. H. (1975). Responses to complex erotic stimuli in homosexual and heterosexual males. *British Journal of Psychiatry, 126,* 252–257.

O'Donahue, W. & Caselles, C. E. (1993). Homophobia: Conceptual, definitional, and value issues. *Journal of Psychopathology and Behavioral Assessment, 15,* 177–195.

Rowan, A. (1994). Homophobia: A new diagnosis for DSM-V? *Behavior Therapist, 17,* 183–184.

Tollison, C. D., Adams, H. E., & Tollison, J. W. (1979). Cognitive and physiological indices of sexual arousal in homosexual, bisexual, and heterosexual males. *Journal of Behavioral Assessment, 1,* 305–314.

Weinberg, G. (1972). *Society and the healthy homosexual.* New York: St. Martin's Press.

West, D. J. (1977). *Homosexuality re-examined.* Minneapolis: University of Minnesota Press.

Zuckerman, M. (1971). Physiological measures of sexual arousal in the human. *Psychological Bulletin, 75,* 297–329.

Club Faggots Not Seals!

—From a T-shirt distributed by a fraternity at Syracuse University. On the side of the shirt with this statement, a cartoon depicted a person who had been clubbed unconsciousness and a nearby seal hoisting a mug of beer. The opposite side of the shirt said "Homophobic and Proud of It!" (*New York Times,* June 26, 1991)

Some Gender Differences In . . .

Same-Sex Behavior

- Percentage of pre-adolescent American girls who report sex play with other girls, according to Alfred Kinsey's classic study: 33%
- Percentage of pre-adolescent American boys who report sex play with other boys: 60%
- Percentage of American females who report having had at least 1 homosexual experience that resulted in an orgasm, according to Kinsey's research: 13%
- Equivalent percentage for American males: 37%

Attitudes

- Percentage of American women who favor extending civil rights protection to homosexuals, according to a Gallup poll: 56%
- Equivalent percentage for American men: 35%

Antigay Violence

- Percentage of antigay hate crime perpetrators who are female, according to a study by the National Coalition of Anti-Violence Programs: 15%
- Percentage who are male: 85%

—Sources: *Sexual Behavior in the Human Female*, 1953; *Sexual Behavior in the Human Male*, 1948; *Gallup Poll Monthly*, 1993; *Anti-Lesbian, Gay, Transgender and Bisexual Violence in 2000: A Report of the National Coalition of Anti-Violence Programs*, 2001

The Inescapable Conclusion

As far back as 1948, sex researcher Alfred Kinsey showed that sexual orientation should be viewed in terms of a continuum rather than as a rigid choice between heterosexuality and homosexuality. His studies found that "37 percent of the total male population has at least some overt homosexual experience to the point of orgasm between adolescence and old age," and that between 8 percent and 20 percent of females (depending on marital status and education) has experienced homosexual contact or responses.

The inescapable—but often escaped—conclusion from Kinsey's research is that a mix of homosexual and heterosexual behavior in a person's erotic biography is a common occurrence; it is entirely possible to engage in anywhere from a little to a great deal of homosexual behavior without categorizing oneself as homosexual. Even the label "bisexual" is somewhat misleading, suggesting, as it does, a person in the middle, equidistant from heterosexuality and from homosexuality, equally attracted to one gender or the other. Data on human sexuality show that few people come so neatly packaged.

—Adapted from Philip W. Blumstein and Pepper Schwartz, *Bisexuality: Some Social Psychological Issues*, 1993

A One–Drop Rule for Sexual Orientation?

It is a characteristic of the human mind that it tries to dichotomize in its classification of phenomenon. Things either are so, or they are not so. Sexual behavior is either normal or abnormal, socially acceptable or unacceptable, heterosexual or homosexual; and many persons do not want to believe that there are gradations in these matters from one to the other extreme.

In regard to sexual behavior it has been possible to maintain this dichotomy only by placing all persons who are exclusively heterosexual in a heterosexual category, and all persons who have any amount of experience with their own sex [in another category]. It would be as reasonable to rate all individuals heterosexual if they have any heterosexual experience, and irrespective of the amount of homosexual experience which they may be having. The attempt to maintain a simple dichotomy on these matters exposes the traditional biases which are likely to enter whenever the heterosexual or homosexual classification of an individual is involved.

—Alfred C. Kinsey, Wardell B. Pomeroy, Clyde E. Martin, and Paul H. Gebhard, *Sexual Behavior in the Human Female,* 1953

As Unique as Fingerprints

The latest research shows that people's erotic and affectional "personalities" are as varied and unique as a fingerprint or someone's voice. Studies show a wide variety of overlapping possibilities—the woman who identifies herself as a bisexual but never develops a strong attraction to a man, for instance, or the heterosexual man who uses homoerotic fantasies when having sex with his female partner—that point to more complex realities. As one bisexual woman put it, "My sexual orientation is toward creative people of color who can cook."

—Tori DeAngelis, from a research summary published in the American Psychological Association magazine *Monitor on Psychology,* April, 2001

TRANSGENDER IDENTITIES:
LIKE STARS IN THE SKY[1]

VANESSA BAIRD

"Is it a boy or a girl?" tends to be the first question asked when a baby is born. And a cursory look at the genitals usually provides the answer.

Most of us are heavily conditioned to categorize sex and gender in this binary, dimorphic way. But actually life and nature are a lot more complex than that.

Until recently most public knowledge of transgender issues came from shock-horror style newspaper articles. They might be revelations of women who had "passed" most of their lives as men and vice-versa. Or, in less sensational mode, they might be autobiographical accounts by people who had had "sex change" operations, as gender reassignment was commonly called. Usually those who told their stories were male-to-female transsexuals who spoke of having felt, since an early age, that they were "trapped in the wrong body."

Today more and more transgendered (or trans) people are coming out. In so doing they have revealed the extent to which the human rights of transgendered individuals have been—and continue to be—violated.

The variety of people coming out includes female-to-male (FTMs) and male-to-female (MTFs) transsexuals, transvestites or cross-dressers, intersexuals or hermaphrodites (born with ambiguous genitalia), eunuchs (in India, *hijras*). It includes people who are transgendered in the sense that they live their lives as a gender different from their biological sex but have done nothing to alter their biology; people who have had partial or total gender reassignment through surgery and hormone therapy; others who have elected for hormone therapy alone. It includes people of various sexual orientations— gay, straight, bisexual.

Anthropological studies reveal transgender expressing itself in ways that are culturally quite distinct, with frames of reference that are not always translatable. Transgender in Peru is not the same as in Indonesia; being trans in North America may bear little resemblance to the experience in Namibia. What is certain, however, is that transgender is widespread and in its emergence from the closet is challenging fixed ideas about gender more than ever before.

The Law and the Knife

An accepting approach to gender ambiguity has not been the pattern in most of the Western world. Far from it: binary is the rule. We are, in the words of trans activist Leslie Feinberg, faced with "two narrow doorways—female and male." But some people just don't fit those doorways. When faced with official forms to fill in they cannot tick either the "M" box or the "F" one. They do not officially exist, unless they fit the binary model—or are made to fit it.

Since the routine practice of correcting the ambiguous genitalia of inter-sexed children began in the U.S. and Europe in the late 1950s, debates have raged about whether gender identity and roles are biologically determined or culturally determined.

Intersexuals, popularly referred to as "hermaphrodites," are usually born with genitals somewhere between male and female. The number of such births is more common than most people realize, with the highest estimates in the U.S. at four per cent of births. That's some ten million children, annually."[2]

The standards which mark maleness allow penises as short as one inch; and for femaleness, clitorises only as large as about a quarter of an inch. In-fants with appendages between ¼–1 inch are, according to psychologist Suzanne Kessler, considered unacceptable and require surgical intervention. In some cases where parents haven't even noticed a problem, doctors still in-sist on surgery. Baby girls as young as six weeks may be operated upon to deepen their vaginas, even though the surgery is not always successful and has to be repeated at various stages as they grow up.[3] Suzanne Kessler notes that genital ambiguity is "'corrected' because it threatens not the infant's life but the culture the infant is born into."

Complex Genders

Identifying a person's gender is far more complex than most people imagine. There are no absolutes in nature, only statistical probabilities. We all begin life with a common anatomy which then differentiates if there is a Y chromosome present. This activates the production of testosterone, appropriate receptors in the brain and the formation of testes.

Several factors can be taken into account in determining a person's bio-logical sex. They include chromosomal sex (X and Y, for example); hormonal sex (estrogen and testosterone); gonadal sex (ovaries and testes); genital sex (vagina and penis, for example); reproductive sex (sperm-carrying and in-seminating; gestating and lactating); and other associated internal organs (such as the uterus or the prostate).

These factors are not always consistent with each other. In fact everyone falls somewhere along a continuum. But few people would know if they were 100 percent male or 100 percent female, chromosomally or hormonally, as there are not many cases in everyday practice in which this would be tested. Other indicators of sex are subject to similar variations. Even the capacity to reproduce is not a clear indicator: some intersexuals have had children. The so-called biological line between male and female is fuzzy.

Sex is not gender. Sex is biological. Gender is social, cultural, psycholog-ical and historical. It is used to describe people and their roles in society, the jobs they do and the way they dress, how they are meant to behave.

A person's gender is usually assigned at birth. The "boy" or "girl" which is documented on the birth certificate affects almost everything else that happens to that child socially for the rest of his or her life.

The Third Gender

Responses to ambiguous genitals vary from culture to culture. The two-sex/two-gender model is by no means universal. One of the most humane and enlightened approaches was observed in the 1930s among the Native American Navajo people. The Navajo recognized three physical categories: male, female and hermaphrodite or *nadle*. *Nadles* had a special status, specific tasks and clothing styles, and were often consulted for their wisdom and skills. Also known as *berdache*, these existed in other Native American groups. *Berdache* would move into the third gender for spiritual and personal reasons. They did not change their bodies. They changed gender without changing sex—a change that was culturally acceptable, without concern for biology. No stigma was attached to them or their partners.

In India the *hijras* have a 2,500–year-old history. Known as a "third gender" caste, *hijra* translates as hermaphrodite or eunuch or "sacred erotic female-man." Some are born intersexual, others are castrated.

Elsewhere, among the Samba people in the Eastern highlands of Papua New Guinea, third-sex people are known as *kwolu-aatmwol* or "female thing transforming into male thing." Medically they are like the *guevedoche* in the Dominican Republic—they have rare form of hermaphroditism. While doing fieldwork among the Samba people in the 1970s anthropologist Gilbert Herdt found that, although in some instances they may be killed at birth, most *kwolu-aatmwol* are accepted as such and their unique identity does not prevent them from becoming respected shamans or war leaders. There are other examples of "thirdness"—of the *bayot* or *lakin-on* people in Cebuen society in the Philippines, the Indonesian "third-sex" role of *waria,* or the *mahu* of Tahiti.[4]

Violence and Vulnerability

Transgender people are vulnerable in a number of ways. They are discriminated against in employment—most countries do not protect the rights of trans people. A comparatively high number of male-to-female transsexuals go into prostitution—partly because of the difficulty in getting other employment, partly to raise cash for operations. This makes trans people more vulnerable to HIV infection and violence.

The violence to which trans people are subjected is extreme, especially in some Latin American countries. Sexual and physical abuse are common; those arrested may be stripped, beaten and forced to perform sexual acts. According to Amnesty International, transgender people are often attacked in ways that strike at key manifestations of their identity. For example, in numerous cases male-to-female trans people have been beaten on their cheekbones or breasts to burst their implants, sometimes causing the release of toxic substances with severe health consequences.[5]

Using health services can be an ordeal—reports of humiliation and worse are common. As a result many avoid seeking medical help when sick. And in many countries trans people cannot get important documents altered to reflect their gender following reassignment—denying the possibility of marriage and causing humiliation, aggravation and arrest on suspicion of using false documents.

The Challenge

Challenging the two-gender model and the human-rights abuses that arise from it is the Transgender Movement, a broad alliance of people who cross the gender line.

Zachary Nataf explains: "As a transgendered man (female-to-male transsexual) I do not 'pass' as simply male but am 'out' in order to campaign for non-discrimination and Transgender Pride. I did not choose to be transsexual, nor did I change gender roles in protest against society's oppressive gender system. I did it to achieve an authenticity and outward expression of a deeply abiding sense of myself as a gendered being. During transition I became more fully and truly myself, suspending the symbolic hold society's rules had over my body in order to achieve it. The rigidity of the rules is what is not natural." In Britain, for example, post-operative transsexuals are legally padlocked to the gender written on their birth certificates, even though this contravenes the European Charter on Human Rights.

The two-sex system is not inevitable. Activist Michael Hernandez says: "I am more than male and more than female. I am neither man nor woman, but the circle encompassing both . . . Gender and behavior are as variable as the stars in the sky."[6]

The struggle has the potential to liberate all of us, whatever our gender or sex, from rigid, stereotypical ways of being masculine and feminine.

NOTES

1. This chapter draws extensively from Zachary I. Nataf's article "Whatever I feel," *New Internationalist*, April 1998.
2. Quelle Difference? Biology Dooms the Defense of Marriage Act, David Berreby, High Concept (web site: http://www.pfc.org.uk/news/1996/biodoma.htm).
3. *Hermaphrodites with Attitude Quarterly*, Bo Laurent, Fall/Winter, 1995–96.
4. *Third Sex, Third Gender*, Gilbert Herdt ed., Zone Books, NY, 1994.
5. *Crimes of Hate, Conspiracy of Silence*, Amnesty International, 2001.
6. *Trans Liberation*, Leslie Feinberg, Beacon Press, 1998.

Females Who Test "Male"

Both the scientific and social interpretations of gender are complicated and controversial. The International Olympic Committee has found itself at the center of the uncertainty. The first shock came when Hermann Ratjen, who ran as Dora Ratjen for Germany in the 1930s, confessed in 1957 that he had disguised himself at the request of the Nazi Youth Movement. So in 1966, as the opportunities for women to compete expanded rapidly, a panel of judges began checking female athletes for vaginal openings, oversized clitorises, a penis, or testicles. By 1968, chromosome testing replaced these "nude parades," and in 1992, a more sophisticated instrument to hunt for the sex-determining SRY gene was adopted.

But as the technology advanced, so did the confusion. Five women out of 2,406 tested "male" in the 1992 Barcelona Olympics. Eight women in the 1996 Atlanta games didn't pass as females. And in February of 1999, the Athletes' Commission of the International Olympics Committee urged its parent organization to do away with sex analysis entirely and rely instead on observed urination during drug testing to pinpoint any likely imposters.

—Adapted from Sally Lehrman, salon.com, April 5, 1999

The Problem with Categories

Legislators throughout the nation, trying to prevent recognition of "gay marriage," have introduced legislation that would grant official recognition only to marriages between "a man and a woman." Legislation embodying this language has already been passed or proposed in 30 states and may become law in more.

Perhaps lawmakers who are pushing these bills don't realize it, but such legislation would unwittingly nullify or prevent millions of supposedly heterosexual marriages. Why? Because the marriage partners are intersexuals who will not meet the medical definition of being "a man and a woman."

Between 3 million and 10 million Americans are neither male nor female at birth. Additionally, as adults they may differ genetically from the sex that they and their parents believe them to be. Consequently, many of these couples will not even know that they are illegally married.

Our social, religious, and legal institutions typically categorize people as either male and female, but in reality there is no foolproof, unambiguous definition for these categories. At the very least a person's sex depends upon anatomy, genes, hormones, and behavior, any of which may lean toward male, female, or somewhere in between. Sex, like race and sexual orientation, is socially constructed.

—Adapted from William O. Beeman, *Transgender Tapestry,* Fall 1999

SUIT OVER ESTATE CLAIMS
A WIDOW IS NOT A WOMAN[1]

JODI WILGOREN

LEAVENWORTH, Kansas—J'Noel Gardiner is hardly the first widow to be accused of marrying a man twice her age for money instead of love, with a stepson she first met at her husband's funeral trying to block her inheritance.

But Mrs. Gardiner has much more at stake than a share in a $2.5 million estate. Her stepson, Joe Gardiner, hopes to nullify the 11–month marriage, claiming his father's widow is not actually a woman.

"There's not a widow alive who wouldn't fight to defend her marriage," said Mrs. Gardiner, 44, who was born male but has had a series of surgeries to make her body conform to the female identity she says she has always felt. "I am anatomically, biologically, socially and, most important, spiritually, female."

At its core, the unusual case revolves around the question of what makes a man a man and a woman a woman. It could have profound implications on the debate over same-sex marriage and on the emerging issue of transsexuals' rights.

Since marriage is seen as a fundamental right, several legal experts said that if transsexuals like Mrs. Gardiner were barred from marrying men, they would probably be allowed to marry women. Indeed, after a Texas court invalidated a similar marriage in 1999, at least two male-to-female transsexuals have married women in that state.

"We're talking 'Brave New World' here," said Edward White of the Thomas More Center for Law and Justice, a public interest law firm that focuses on traditional values and is one of several national groups that have filed briefs on behalf of either side in the case. "If a determination is made that a transsexual can marry, the next step would be homosexual marriage and lesbian marriage."

But Jennifer Middleton of the Lambda Legal Defense and Education Fund, a gay rights group, says courts and legislatures lag behind science and society. "How much of what we think of as appropriate for a woman or a man is biologically determined versus socially constructed?" she said. "It's very difficult when the law tries to draw clear-cut lines saying that it's O.K. for a woman to do something but not a man, or vice versa."

Mrs. Gardiner was born Jay Noel Ball with what she calls a birth defect—a penis and testicles. As Jay Ball, she was married to a woman for five years, but at age 34 embarked on a transformation that included hormone therapy, a vocal-cord shave and cheek implants. After operations to create a vagina, Mr. Ball in 1994 changed his Wisconsin birth certificate to reflect a new name, J'Noel Ball, and sex, female.

In 1997, Ms. Ball, who has a Ph.D. in business from the University of Georgia, took a job at a college outside Kansas City, Mo., now called Park University. The following May, she met Marshall G. Gardiner, a former state legislator and chairman of the Kansas Democratic Party. They married four months later.

"We were soul mates," Mrs. Gardiner said of her 86–year-old husband, who died of heart failure aboard an airplane in August 1999.

Joe Gardiner, Mr. Gardiner's only child, learned of the marriage after the fact in a phone conversation. Nobody mentioned medical history.

After the funeral, Joe Gardiner discovered an incomplete prenuptial agreement and a one-sentence document signed by J'Noel Ball before the wedding that appeared to waive her rights to his father's estate. He hired a private detective, and hundreds of pages of medical records on the sex change were added to the court file.

Because Marshall Gardiner had no will, Kansas law dictates that his estate be split between wife and son. Joe Gardiner's half is not in dispute.

In legal documents, Mr. Gardiner says in a footnote he is using the feminine pronoun only as a courtesy, and argues that the widow suffers from a mental disorder.

"It's an illusion, it's an image she's trying to project, but it doesn't change the laws of God," he said at the home where he and his father grew up.

Mrs. Gardiner refused to discuss transsexuality.

"If Marshall were still alive, I wouldn't have to be explaining that I'm a woman," she said. "He would be standing here saying, 'How dare you ask my wife these questions?' "

Heterosexism Doesn't Just Hurt Sexual Minorities—It Also Hurts Heterosexuals by . . .

- *Locking them into rigid gender roles.* Males must be careful not to act too feminine, and females must be careful not to act too masculine.
- *Inhibiting intimacy and affection among members of the same sex.* For example, many heterosexual males cannot put an arm around each other or tell each other they look good without having their sexuality questioned.
- *Limiting school-based sex education to heterosexuality,* thereby omitting vital information that could help prevent the transmission of AIDS.
- *Encouraging premature or superficial sexual involvement* in order to prove one's heterosexuality. Early sexual activity increases the chances of teen pregnancy and the spread of sexually transmitted diseases.
- *Delaying and reducing the government's response to AIDS.* Because AIDS was originally thought to be a strictly "gay" disease, the government was slow to respond and the disease quickly spread to many heterosexuals.
- *Restricting family communication.* Children, fearing negative parental reactions, frequently withhold information about themselves. Parents, not wanting to learn about their child's sexual or gender identity, may never get to know their children.
- *Stigmatizing the friends and family members of a lesbian, gay, or bisexual person.* In some cases, this leads friends and family members to enter a closet of their own, hiding the truth from others.
- *Preventing heterosexuals from accepting the contributions of sexual minorities* in areas such as art, religion, military service, and family life.
- *Encouraging heterosexuals to put aside their integrity and treat other people badly.* When this happens, all of humanity loses.

—Adapted from Warren J. Blumenfeld, *Homophobia: How We All Pay the Price,* 1992

IX

Making Connections

From an interview with the Dalai Lama:

Q: I understand that you were very angry during the 1990 gulf war, as angry as you've ever been.

A: Angry? No. But one thing, when people started blaming Saddam Hussein, then my heart went out to him.

Q: To Saddam Hussein?

A: Yes. Because this blaming everything on him—it's unfair. He may be a bad man, but without his army, he cannot act as aggressively as he does. And his army, without weapons, cannot do anything. And these weapons were not produced in Iraq itself. Who supplied them? Western nations! So one day something happened and they blamed everything on him—without acknowledging their own contributions. That's wrong."

—*New York Times Magazine*, November 28, 1993

IX

SECTION OVERVIEW

"**W**e cannot just be," wrote Thich Nhat Hanh in *Peace Is Every Step*. "We can only inter-be. We are responsible for everything around us."

If Thich Nhat Hanh is correct, what does the notion of "interbeing" imply about the nature of prejudice? And equally important, what does it imply about ways to *reduce* prejudice?

Many of the world's most respected advocates of peace and social justice have embraced a worldview similar to Nhat Hanh's philosophy of interbeing, including Mohatma Gandhi, Nelson Mandela, and Martin Luther King, Jr. This section of the anthology focuses on that worldview by making connections among people, prejudices, and social justice movements.

In addition to an excerpt from *Peace Is Every Step*, the readings include a passage from Gordon Allport's classic book *The Nature of Prejudice,* in which Allport notes that people who harbor prejudices against one group are likely to harbor them against others. The section also has a reading on environmental justice—a social movement that links racism, classism, and environmental degradation.

Take Special Notice

A few of the readings focus on general principles rather than on prejudice specifically. In these cases, you will need to apply the principles to prejudice.

Questions Worth Pondering

- Does social justice require the existence of prejudice and discrimination?
- Nhat Hanh discusses the way that garbage and flowers "inter-are." If prejudice and discrimination are garbage, what are the flowers?
- If Nhat Hanh's philosophy of interbeing is correct, what are the implications for prejudice reduction?
- As a quote in this section shows, Nazi leader Heinrich Himmler was homophobic as well as anti-Semitic. Why does having one type of prejudice increase the chances of having others?
- Does the presence of environmental racism in the energy and petrochemical industries mean that wasting electrical energy and consuming unnecessary plastic products are acts of racial discrimination?

A Single Garment of Destiny

All life is interrelated. We are all caught in an inescapable network of mutuality, tied into a single garment of destiny. Whatever affects one directly, affects all indirectly. . . . Did you ever stop to think that you can't leave for your job in the morning without being dependent on most of the world? You get up in the morning and go to the bathroom and reach over for the sponge, and that's handed to you by a Pacific islander. You reach for a bar of soap, and that's given to you at the hands of a Frenchman. And then you go into the kitchen to drink your coffee for the morning, and that's poured into your cup by a South American. And maybe you want tea: that's poured into your cup by a Chinese. Or maybe you're desirous of having cocoa for breakfast, and that's poured into your cup by a West African. And then you reach over for your toast, and that's given to you at the hands of an English-speaking farmer, not to mention the baker. And before you finish eating breakfast in the morning, you've depended on more than half of the world. This is the way our universe is structured, this is its interrelated quality. We aren't going to have peace on earth until we recognize this basic fact of the interrelated structure of all reality.

—Martin Luther King, Jr., *The Trumpet of Conscience*, 1967

Putting Oneself in Chains

No man can put a chain about the ankle of his fellow man, without at last finding the other end of it fastened about his own neck.

—Frederick Douglass, October 22, 1883

No Hierarchy of Oppression

There can be no hierarchies of oppression. I have learned that sexism (a belief in the inherent superiority of one sex over all others and thereby its right to dominance) and heterosexism (a belief in the inherent superiority of one pattern of loving over all others and thereby its right to dominance) both arise from the same source as racism—a belief in the inherent superiority of one race over all others and thereby its right to dominance. . . .

Any attack against Black people is a lesbian and gay issue, because I and thousands of other Black women are part of the lesbian community. Any attack against lesbians and gays is a Black issue, because thousands of lesbians and gay men are Black. There is no hierarchy of oppression.

—Audre Lorde, *Interracial Books for Children Bulletin*, 1983

Beyond Equality: A Latina Perspective

Liberation has similar meanings for all people of color engaged in struggle. It means an end to oppression, the birth of collective self-respect and genuine hope of the social justice that we sometimes call equality. The tendency to frame U.S. racial issues in strictly Black-white terms makes little sense when the U.S. Census projects that 33% of our population will be Asian/Pacific Island-American, Latino, Native American/Indigenous (which includes Hawaiian) and Arab-American by the year 2050—in other words, neither white nor Black.

With greater solidarity, justice for people of color could be won. And an even bigger prize would be possible: a U.S. society that advances beyond "equality," beyond granting people of color a respect equal to that given to white Americans. Too often "equality" leaves whites still at the center, still embodying the Americanness by which others are judged.

We also need to look at the often stunning commonalities of racist experience. When some 120,000 Japanese—most of them U.S. citizens—were packed off to "internment" camps during World War II, this should have rung an old, familiar bell. We have lived with the internment camp under so many other names: reservation, plantation, migrant labor camp. We must recognize our interdependence, and the need to build on it, as a fundamental, live-saving strategy.

—Adapted from Elizabeth Martínez, *De Colores Means All of Us: Latina Views for a Multi-Colored Century*, 1998

PEACE IS EVERY STEP: THE PATH OF MINDFULNESS IN EVERYDAY LIFE

THICH NHAT HANH

Editor's Introduction[1]

As I walked slowly through a green oak forest this morning, a brilliant red-orange sun rose on the horizon. It immediately evoked for me images of India, where a group of us joined Thich Nhat Hanh the year before last to visit the sites where the Buddha taught. On one walk we stopped in a field surrounded by rice paddies and recited this poem:

> Peace is every step.
> The shining red sun is my heart.
> Each flower smiles with me.
> How green, how fresh all that grows.
> How cool the wind blows.
> Peace is every step.
> It turns the endless path to joy.

These lines summarize the essence of Thich Nhat Hanh's message—that peace is not external. Living mindfully, slowing down and enjoying each step and each breath, is enough. Peace is already present in each step, and if we walk in this way, a flower will bloom under our feet with every step. In fact the flowers will smile at us and wish us well on our way.

I met Thich Nhat Hanh in 1982. I was one of the first American Buddhists he had met, and it fascinated him that I looked, dressed, and, to some extent, acted like the novices he had trained in Vietnam for two decades. When my teacher, Richard Baker-roshi, invited him to visit our meditation center in San Francisco the following year, he happily accepted, and this began a new phase in the extraordinary life of this gentle monk, whom Baker-roshi characterized as "a cross between a cloud, a snail, and a piece of heavy machinery—a true religious presence."

Thich Nhat Hanh was born in central Vietnam in 1926 and was ordained a Buddhist monk in 1942, at the age of sixteen. Just eight years later, he co-founded what was to become the foremost center of Buddhist studies in South Vietnam, the An Quang Buddhist Institute.

In 1961, Nhat Hanh came to the United States to study and teach comparative religion at Columbia and Princeton Universities. But in 1963, his monk-colleagues in Vietnam telegrammed him to come home to join them in their work to stop the war. He immediately returned and helped lead one of the great nonviolent resistance movements of the century, based entirely on Gandhian principles.

---

[1]This introduction is an abridged version of Arnold Kotler's original introduction in *Peace Is Every Step.*

In 1966, at the urging of his fellow monks, he accepted an invitation from the Fellowship of Reconciliation and Cornell University to come to the U.S. He had a densely packed schedule of speaking engagements and private meetings, and spoke convincingly in favor of a ceasefire and a negotiated settlement. Martin Luther King, Jr. was so moved by Nhat Hanh and his proposals for peace that he nominated him for the 1967 Nobel Peace Prize, saying, "I know of no one more worthy of the Nobel Peace Prize than this gentle monk from Vietnam." Largely due to Thich Nhat Hanh's influence, King came out publicly against the war at a press conference, with Nhat Hanh, in Chicago.

When Thomas Merton, the well-known Catholic monk and mystic, met Thich Nhat Hanh at his monastery, Gethsemani, near Louisville, Kentucky, he told his students, "Just the way he opens the door and enters a room demonstrates his understanding. He is a true monk." Merton went on to write an essay, "Nhat Hanh Is My Brother," an impassioned plea to listen to Nhat Hanh's proposals for peace and lend full support for Nhat Hanh's advocacy of peace. After meetings with Senators Fullbright and Kennedy, Secretary of Defense McNamara, and others in Washington, Thich Nhat Hanh went to Europe, where he met with a number of heads of state and officials of the Catholic church, including two audiences with Pope Paul VI, urging cooperation between Catholics and Buddhists to help bring peace to Vietnam.

In 1969, Thich Nhat Hanh set up the Buddhist Peace Delegation to the Paris Peace Talks. After the Peace Accords were signed in 1973, he was refused permission to return to Vietnam, and he established a small community a hundred miles southwest of Paris, called "Sweet Potato." In 1976–77, Nhat Hanh conducted an operation to rescue boat people in the Gulf of Siam, but hostility from the governments of Thailand and Singapore made it impossible to continue. So for the following five years, he stayed at Sweet Potato in retreat—meditating, reading, writing, binding books, gardening, and occasionally receiving visitors.

In June 1982, Thich Nhat Hanh visited New York, and later that year established Plum Village, a retreat center near Bordeaux, surrounded by vineyards and fields of wheat, corn, and sunflowers. Since 1983 he has travelled to North America every other year to lead retreats and give lectures on mindful living and social responsibility, "making peace right in the moment we are alive."

Peace Is Every Step was assembled from Thich Nhat Hanh's lectures, published and unpublished writings, and informal conversations. This book is the clearest and most complete message yet of a great bodhisattva, who has dedicated his life to the enlightenment of others. Thich Nhat Hanh's teaching is simultaneously inspirational and very practical. I hope the reader enjoys this book as much as we have enjoyed making it available.

Arnold Kotler
Thenac, France
July 1990

Interbeing

If you are a poet, you will see clearly that there is a cloud floating in this sheet of paper. Without a cloud, there will be no rain; without rain, the trees cannot grow; and without trees, we cannot make paper. The cloud is essential for the paper to exist. If the cloud is not here, the sheet of paper cannot be here either.

So we can say that the cloud and the paper *inter-are.* "Interbeing" is a word that is not in the dictionary yet, but if we combine the prefix "inter-" with the verb "to be," we have a new verb, inter-be.

If we look into this sheet of paper even more deeply, we can see the sunshine in it. Without sunshine, the forest cannot grow. In fact, nothing can grow without sunshine. And so, we know that the sunshine is also in this sheet of paper. The paper and the sunshine inter-are. And if we continue to look, we can see the logger who cut the tree and brought it to the mill to be transformed into paper. And we see wheat. We know that the logger cannot exist without his daily bread, and therefore the wheat that became his bread is also in this sheet of paper. The logger's father and mother are in it too. When we look in this way, we see that without all of these things, this sheet of paper cannot exist.

Looking even more deeply, we can see ourselves in this sheet of paper too. This is not difficult to see, because when we look at a sheet of paper, it is part of our perception. Your mind is in here and mine is also. So we can say that everything is in here with this sheet of paper. We cannot point out one thing that is not here—time, space, the earth, the rain, the minerals in the soil, the sunshine, the cloud, the river, the heat. Everything co-exists with this sheet of paper. That is why I think the word inter-be should be in the dictionary. "To be" is to inter-be. We cannot just *be* by ourselves alone. We have to inter-be with every other thing. This sheet of paper is, because everything else is.

Suppose we try to return one of the elements to its source. Suppose we return the sunshine to the sun. Do you think that this sheet of paper will be possible? No, without sunshine nothing can be. And if we return the logger to his mother, then we have no sheet of paper either. The fact is that this sheet of paper is made up only of "non-paper" elements. And if we return these non-paper elements to their sources, then there can be no paper at all. Without non-paper elements, like mind, logger, sunshine and so on, there will be no paper. As thin as this sheet of paper is, it contains everything in the universe in it.

Flowers and Garbage

Defiled or immaculate. Dirty or pure. These are concepts we form in our mind. A beautiful rose we have just cut and placed in our vase is pure. It smells so good, so fresh. A garbage can is the opposite. It smells horrible, and it is filled with rotten things.

But that is only when we look on the surface. If we look more deeply we will see that in just five or six days, the rose will become part of the garbage. We do not need to wait five days to see it. If we just look at the rose, and we look deeply, we can see it now. And if we look into the garbage can, we see that in a few months its contents can be transformed into lovely vegetables, and even a rose. If you are a good organic gardener, looking at a rose you can see the garbage, and looking at the garbage you can see a rose. Roses and garbage inter-are. Without a rose, we cannot have garbage; and without garbage, we cannot have a rose. They need each other very much. The rose and the garbage are equal. The garbage is just as precious as the rose. If we look deeply at the concepts of defilement and immaculateness, we return to the notion of interbeing.

In the city of Manila there are many young prostitutes; some are only fourteen or fifteen years old. They are very unhappy. They did not want to be prostitutes, but their families are poor and these young girls went to the city to look for some kind of job, like street vendor, to make money to send back to their families. Of course this is true not only in Manila, but in Ho Chi Minh City in Vietnam, in New York City, and in Paris also. After only a few weeks in the city, a vulnerable girl can be persuaded by a clever person to work for him and earn perhaps one hundred times more money than she could as a street vendor. Because she is so young and does not know much about life, she accepts and becomes a prostitute. Since that time, she has carried the feeling of being impure, defiled, and this causes her great suffering. When she looks at other young girls, dressed beautifully, belonging to good families, a wretched feeling wells up in her, a feeling of defilement that becomes her hell.

But if she could look deeply at herself and at the whole situation, she would see that she is the way she is because other people are the way they are. How can a "good girl," belonging to a good family, be proud? Because the "good family's" way of life is the way it is, the prostitute has to live as a prostitute. No one among us has clean hands. No one of us can claim that it is not our responsibility. The girl in Manila is that way because of the way we are. Looking into the life of that young prostitute, we see the lives of all the "non-prostitutes." And looking at the non-prostitutes and the way we live our lives, we see the prostitute. Each thing helps to create the other.

Let us look at wealth and poverty. The affluent society and the deprived society inter-are. The wealth of one society is made of the poverty of the other. "This is like this, because that is like that." Wealth is made of non-wealth elements, and poverty is made by non-poverty elements. It is exactly the same as with the sheet of paper. So we must be careful not to imprison ourselves in concepts. The truth is that everything contains everything else. We cannot just be, we can only inter-be. We are responsible for everything that happens around us.

Only by seeing with the eyes of interbeing can that young girl be freed from her suffering. Only then will she understand that she is bearing the burden of the whole world. What else can we offer her? Looking deeply into ourselves, we see her, and we will share her pain and the pain of the whole world. Then we can begin to be of real help.

Waging Peace

Many people are aware of the world's suffering; their hearts are filled with compassion. They know what needs to be done, and they engage in political, social, and environmental work to try to change things. But after a period of intense involvement, they may become discouraged if they lack the strength needed to sustain a life of action. Real strength is not in power, money, or weapons, but in deep, inner peace.

Practicing mindfulness in each moment of our daily lives, we can cultivate our own peace. I have seen this peace in people of various religious and cultural backgrounds who spend their time and energy protecting the weak, struggling for social justice, lessening the disparity between rich and poor, fighting against discrimination, and watering the trees of love and understanding throughout the world.

There is no phenomenon in the universe that does not intimately concern us, from a pebble resting at the bottom of the ocean, to the movement of a galaxy millions of light-years away. Walt Whitman said, "I believe a leaf of grass is no less than the journey-work of the stars. . . ." These words are not philosophy. They come from the depths of his soul. He said, "I am large, I contain multitudes."

A Love Letter to Your Congressman

In the peace movement there is a lot of anger, frustration, and misunderstanding. People in the peace movement can write very good protest letters, but they are not so skilled at writing love letters. We need to learn to write letters to the Congress and the President that they will want to read, and not just throw away. The way we speak, the kind of understanding, the kind of language we use should not turn people off. The President is a person like any of us.

Can the peace movement talk in loving speech, showing the way for peace? I think that will depend on whether the people in the peace movement can "be peace." Because without being peace, we cannot do anything for peace. If we cannot smile, we cannot help other people smile. If we are not peaceful, then we cannot contribute to the peace movement.

I hope we can offer a new dimension to the peace movement. The peace movement often is filled with anger and hatred and does not fulfill the role we expect of it. A fresh way of being peace, of making peace is needed. That is why it is so important for us to practice mindfulness, to acquire the capacity to look, to see, and to understand.

Citizenship

As citizens, we have a large responsibility. Our daily lives, the way we drink, what we eat, have to do with the world's political situation. Every day we do things, we are things, that have to do with peace. If we are aware of our lifestyle, our way of consuming, of looking at things, we will know how to make peace right in the moment we are alive. We think that our government is free to make any policy it wishes, but that freedom depends on our daily life. If we make it possible for them to change policies, they will do it.

You may think that if you were to enter government and obtain power, you would be able to do anything you wanted, but that is not true. If you became President, you would be confronted by this hard fact—you would probably do almost exactly the same thing as our current President, perhaps a little better, perhaps a little worse.

As we ourselves begin to live more responsibly, we must ask our political leaders to move in the same direction. We have to encourage them to stop polluting our environment and our consciousness. We should help them appoint advisors who share our way of thinking about peace, so that they can turn to these people for advice and support. It will require some degree of enlightenment on our part to support our political leaders, especially when they are campaigning for office. We have the opportunity to tell them about many important things, instead of choosing leaders by how handsome they look on television and then feeling discouraged later by their lack of mindfulness.

Ecology of Mind

Peace is based on respect for life, the spirit of reverence for life. Not only do we have to respect the lives of human beings, but we have to respect the lives of animals, vegetables, and minerals. The destruction of our health by pollution of the air and water is linked to the destruction of the minerals. The way we farm, the way we deal with our garbage, all these things are related to each other.

Ecology should be a deep ecology. Not only deep but universal, because there is pollution in our consciousness. Television, for instance, is a form of pollution for us and for our children. Television sows seeds of violence and anxiety in our children, and pollutes their consciousness, just as we destroy our environment by chemicals, tree-cutting, and polluting the water. We need to protect the ecology of the mind, or this kind of violence and recklessness will continue to spill over into many other areas of life.

Like a Leaf, We Have Many Stems

One autumn day, I was in a park, absorbed in the contemplation of a very small, beautiful leaf, shaped like a heart. Its color was almost red, and it was barely hanging on the branch, nearly ready to fall down. I spent a long time with it, and I asked the leaf a number of questions. I found out the leaf had been a mother to the tree. Usually we think that the tree is the mother and the leaves are children, but as I looked at the leaf I saw that the leaf is also a mother to the tree. The sap that the roots take up is only water and minerals, not sufficient to nourish the tree. So the tree distributes that sap to the leaves, and the leaves transform the rough sap into elaborated sap and, with the help of the sun and gas, send it back to the tree for nourishment. Therefore, the leaves are also the mother to the tree. Since the leaf is linked to the tree by a stem, the communication between them is easy to see.

We do not have a stem linking us to our mother anymore, but when we were in her womb, we had a very long stem, an umbilical cord. The oxygen and the nourishment we needed came to us through that stem. But on the day we were born, it was cut off, and we received the illusion that we became in-dependent. That is not true. We continue to rely on our mother for a very long time, and we have many other mothers as well. The Earth is our mother. We have a great many stems linking us to our Mother Earth. There are stems link-ing us with the clouds. If there are no clouds, there will be no water for us to drink. We are made of at least seventy percent water, and the stem between the cloud and us is really there. This is also the case with the river, the forest, the logger, and the farmer. There are hundreds of thousands of stems linking us to everything in the cosmos, supporting us and making it possible for us to be. Do you see the link between you and me? If you are not there, I am not here. This is certain. If you do not see it yet, please look more deeply and I am sure you will.

I asked the leaf whether it was frightened because it was autumn and the other leaves were falling. The leaf told me, "No. During the whole spring and summer I was completely alive. I worked hard to help nourish the tree, and now much of me is in the tree. I am not limited by this form. I am also the whole tree, and when I go back to the soil, I will continue to nourish the tree."

That day there was a wind blowing and, after a while, I saw the leaf leave the branch and float down to the soil, dancing joyfully, because as it floated it saw itself already there in the tree. It was so happy. I bowed my head, knowing that I have a lot to learn from that leaf.

Call Me by My True Names

In Plum Village, where I live in France, we receive many letters from the refugee camps in Singapore, Malaysia, Indonesia, Thailand, and the Philip-pines, hundreds each week. It is very painful to read them, but we have to do it, we have to be in contact. We try our best to help, but the suffering is enor-mous, and sometimes we are discouraged. It is said that half the boat people die in the ocean. Only half arrive at the shores in Southeast Asia, and even then they may not be safe.

There are many young girls, boat people, who are raped by sea pirates. Even though the United Nations and many countries try to help the govern-ment of Thailand prevent that kind of piracy, sea pirates continue to inflict much suffering on the refugees. One day we received a letter telling us about a young girl on a small boat who was raped by a Thai pirate. She was only twelve, and she jumped into the ocean and drowned herself.

When you first learn of something like that, you get angry at the pirate. You naturally take the side of the girl. As you look more deeply you will see it differently. If you take the side of the little girl, then it is easy. You only have to take a gun and shoot the pirate. But we cannot do that. In my meditation I saw that if I had been born in the village of the pirate and raised in the same conditions as he was, there is a great likelihood that I would become a pirate. I saw that many babies are born along the Gulf of Siam, hundreds every day, and if we educators, social workers, politicians, and others do not do something about the situation, in twenty-five years a number of them will become sea pirates. That is certain. If you or I were born today in those fishing villages, we may become sea pirates in twenty-five years. If you take a gun and shoot the pirate, you shoot all of us, because all of us are to some extent responsible for this state of affairs.

After a long meditation, I wrote this poem. In it, there are three people: the twelve-year-old girl, the pirate, and me. Can we look at each other and recognize ourselves in each other? The title of the poem is "Please Call Me by My True Names," because I have so many names. When I hear one of these names, I have to say, "Yes."

Do not say that I'll depart tomorrow
because even today I still arrive.

Look deeply: I arrive in every second
to be a bud on a spring branch,
to be a tiny bird, with wings still fragile,
learning to sing in my new nest,
to be a caterpillar in the heart of a flower,
to be a jewel hiding itself in a stone.

I still arrive, in order to laugh and to cry,
in order to fear and to hope.
The rhythm of my heart is the birth and
death of all that are alive.

I am the mayfly metamorphosing on the surface of the river,
and I am the bird which, when spring comes, arrives in time
*   to eat the mayfly.*

I am the frog swimming happily in the clear pond,
and I am also the grass-snake who, approaching in silence,
*   feeds itself on the frog.*

I am the child in Uganda, all skin and bones,
my legs as thin as bamboo sticks,
and I am the arms merchant, selling deadly weapons to
*   Uganda.*

I am the twelve-year-old girl, refugee on a small boat,
who throws herself into the ocean after being raped by a sea
*   pirate,*
and I am the pirate, my heart not yet capable of seeing and
*   loving.*

I am a member of the politburo, with plenty of power in my
*   hands,*
and I am the man who has to pay his "debt of blood" to my
*   people,*
dying slowly in a forced labor camp.

My joy is like spring, so warm it makes flowers bloom in all
*   walks of life.*
My pain is like a river of tears, so full it fills the four oceans.

Please call me by my true names,
so I can hear all my cries and laughs at once,
so I can see that my joy and pain are one.

Please call me by my true names, so I can wake up,
and so the door of my heart can be left open,
the door of compassion.

Love in Action

During our journey together, I have presented a number of practices to help us maintain mindfulness of what is going on inside us and immediately around us. Now, as we make our way through the wider world, some additional guidelines can help us and protect us. Several members of our community have been practicing the following principles, and I think you may also find them useful in making choices as to how to live in our contemporary world. We call them the fourteen precepts of the Order of Interbeing.

1. Do not be idolatrous about or bound to any doctrine, theory, or ideology. All systems of thought are guiding means; they are not absolute truth.
2. Do not think that the knowledge you possess is changeless, absolute truth. Avoid being narrow-minded and bound to present views. Learn and practice non-attachment from views in order to be open to receive others' viewpoints. Truth is found in life and not merely in conceptual knowledge. Be ready to learn throughout your entire life and to observe reality in yourself and in the world at all times.
3. Do not force others, including children, by any means whatsoever, to adopt your views, whether by authority, threat, money, propaganda, or even education. However, through compassionate dialogue, help others renounce fanaticism and narrowness.

4. Do not avoid contact with suffering or close your eyes before suffering. Do not lose awareness of the existence of suffering in the life of the world. Find ways to be with those who are suffering, by all means, including personal contact and visits, images, and sound. By such means, awaken yourself and others to the reality of suffering in the world.

5. Do not accumulate wealth while millions are hungry. Do not take as the aim of your life fame, profit, wealth, or sensual pleasure. Live simply and share time, energy, and material resources with those who are in need.

6. Do not maintain anger or hatred. Learn to penetrate and transform them while they are still seeds in your consciousness. As soon as anger or hatred arises, turn your attention to your breathing in order to see and understand the nature of your anger or hatred and the nature of the persons who have caused your anger or hatred.

7. Be in touch with what is wondrous, refreshing, and healing, both inside and around yourself. Plant the seeds of joy, peace, and understanding in yourself in order to facilitate the work of transformation in the depths of your consciousness.

8. Do not utter words that can create discord and cause the community to break. Make every effort to reconcile and resolve all conflicts, however small.

9. Do not say untruthful things for the sake of personal interest or to impress people. Do not spread news that you do not know to be certain. Do not criticize or condemn things that you are not sure of. Always speak truthfully and constructively. Have the courage to speak out about situations of injustice, even when doing so may threaten your own safety.

10. Do not use the religious community for personal gain or profit, or transform your community into a political party. A religious community should, however, take a clear stand against oppression and injustice, and should strive to change the situation without engaging in partisan conflicts.

11. Do not live with a vocation that is harmful to humans and nature. Do not invest in companies that deprive others of their chance to live. Select a vocation that helps realize your ideal of compassion.

12. Do not kill. Do not let others kill. Find whatever means possible to protect life and prevent war.

13. Possess nothing that should belong to others. Respect the property of others but prevent others from enriching themselves from human suffering or the suffering of other beings.

14. Do not mistreat your body. Learn to handle it with respect. Sexual expression should not happen without love and commitment. In sexual relationships, be aware of future suffering that may be caused. To preserve the happiness of others, respect the rights and commitments of others. Be fully aware of the responsibility of bringing new lives into the world.

The Twenty–First Century

The word "policy" is very much in use these days. There seems to be a policy for just about everything. I have heard that the so-called developed nations are contemplating a garbage policy to send their trash on huge barges to the Third World.

I think that we need a "policy" for dealing with our suffering. We do not want to condone it, but we need to find a way to make use of our suffering, for our good and for the good of others. There has been so much suffering in the twentieth century: two world wars, concentration camps in Europe, the killing fields of Cambodia, refugees from Vietnam, Central America, and elsewhere fleeing their countries with no place to land. We need to articulate a policy for these kinds of garbage also. We need to use the suffering of the twentieth century as compost, so that together we can create flowers for the twenty-first century.

When we see photographs and programs about the atrocities of the Nazis, the gas chambers and the camps, we feel afraid. We may say, "I didn't do it; they did it." But if we had been there, we may have done the same thing, or we may have been too cowardly to stop it, as was the case for so many. We have to put all these things into our compost pile to fertilize the ground.

The flower of tolerance to see and appreciate cultural diversity is one flower we can cultivate for the children of the twenty-first century. Another flower is the truth of suffering—there has been so much unnecessary suffering in our century. If we are willing to work together and learn together, we can all benefit from the mistakes of our time, and, seeing with the eyes of compassion and understanding, we can offer a beautiful garden and a clear path.

Take the hand of your child and invite her to go out and sit with you on the grass. The two of you may want to contemplate the green grass, the little flowers that grow among the grasses, and the sky. Breathing and smiling together—that is peace education. If we know how to appreciate these beautiful things, we will not have to search for anything else. Peace is available in every moment, in every breath, in every step.

I have enjoyed our journey together. I hope you have enjoyed it too. We shall see each other again.

Quiet Rhythms

Last month
A pregnant thunder cloud
Broke water
High above Brazil,
Pouring sheets of wet glass
Over desiccated orange trees.

At breakfast this morning
You drank the juice of those trees,
And rivulets of Brazilian rainwater
Began flowing
Through your veins.

Who says
The environment
Is faceless?

Listen closely
To the quiet rhythms
Of your heart;
Each beat contains the echo
Of a distant thunder clap.

      —Anonymous

Your 50th Cousin

No human being (of any race) can be less closely related to any other human than approximately fiftieth cousin, and most of us (no matter what color our neighbors) are a lot closer. . . .

It is virtually certain therefore that you are a direct descendant of Muhammad and every fertile predecessor of his, including Krishna, Confucius, Abraham, Buddha, Caeser, Ishmael, and Judas Iscariot. . . .

There is no end to interrelations anywhere. . . . Even this book, written by an American, is made of paper invented by Chinese and printed with ink evolved out of India and from type developed largely by Germans using Roman symbols modified from Greeks who got their letter concepts from Phoenicians who had adapted them partly from Egyptian hieroglyphs.

—Guy Murchie, *The Seven Mysteries of Life,* 1978

PREJUDICE AS A GENERALIZED ATTITUDE

GORDON W. ALLPORT

One of the facts of which we are most certain is that people who reject one out-group will tend to reject other out-groups. If a person is anti-Jewish, he is likely to be anti-Catholic, anti-Negro, anti any out-group.

An ingenious demonstration of this point was made by E. L. Hartley in an investigation of college students.[1] He ascertained their attitudes toward 32 nations and races, asking them to judge each in respect to the items on the Borgardus Social Distance Scale. In addition to the 32 familiar nations and races he included three fictitious ethnic groups—the "Daniereans," "Pireneans," and the "Wallonians." The students were fooled, and thought these "nonesuch" groups were real. It turned out that students prejudiced against familiar ethnic groups were also prejudiced against the nonesuch peoples. The correlation between their social distance scores for the 32 real groups and these three nonesuch groups was around +.80, a high correlation indeed.[2]

One student, intolerant of many real groups, wrote on his paper regarding nonesuch peoples, "I don't know anything about them; therefore I would exclude them from my country." At the same time, another student, generally unprejudiced, wrote, "I don't know anything about them; therefore I have no prejudices against them."

The comments of these two students are revealing. To the first any strange group represented a vague menace, and he therefore rejected it in advance of experience or evidence. The second, lacking apprehensiveness in his nature, would suspend judgment until the facts are known. He would give "Daniereans," for example, the benefit of a doubt and regard them innocent (and welcome) until they are proved guilty. Obviously there is a pervasive quality of mind in a student that disposes him to be prejudiced in general, or tolerant in general.

Looking at some additional results from Hartley's study, we find correlations between various specific negative attitudes as follows:

Negro—Jew	.68
Negro—Catholic	.53
Catholic—Jew	.52
Nonesuch—Jew	.63
Nonesuch—Communist	.68
Nonesuch—labor union member	.58

Why a person who is distrustful of labor unions should also distrust, say, "Pireneans" is a psychological puzzle indeed.

The same tendency is seen in the tirades of agitators. One delivered himself of the following composite blast. "When will the plain, ordinary, sincere, sheeplike people of America awaken to the fact that their common affairs are being arranged and run for them by aliens, communists, crackpots, refugees, renegades, socialists, termites, and traitors?"[3]

People who dislike both Negroes and the federal administration sometimes condense their hostilities into the phrase "nigger-loving bureaucrats." The familiar expression, "Jewish international banker" reflects two fused negative attitudes—in defiance of the simple truth that few Jews are international bankers and few such bankers are Jews. In Latin America, where Catholicism is the dominant religion, one hears of a "Jewish-Protestant alliance" that threatens the world. But in lands where both anti-Catholicism and anti-Semitism are common, the result is condemnation in a single breath for the "Vatican and the Jews." The fact that scapegoats of different breeds are so often harnessed together shows that it is the *totality* of prejudice that is important rather than specific accusations against single groups.

NOTES

1. E. L. Hartley, *Problems in Prejudice,* New York: Kings Crown Press, 1946.
2. Occasionally in this volume we shall express a degree of relationship with the aid of coefficients of correlation. For those who are not familiar with this simple statistical device, it is necessary only to know that the coefficients range between +1.00 and –1.00. The first figure represents a perfect positive relationship; the latter a perfect negative relationship. The closer the decimal figure comes to either extreme the more significant is the relationship indicated. Zero (or coefficients in that neighborhood) tell us that no significant relationship obtains.
3. This agitator is quoted by Leo Lowenthal and Norman Guterman in *Prophets of Deceit,* New York: Harper, 1949, 1.

Antigay Prejudice in Nazi Germany

We mean to get rid of homosexuals root and branch. They're a danger to the national health. Just think how many children will never be born because of this, and how a people can be broken in nerve and spirit when such a plague gets hold of it. If a man has an affair with his pretty secretary, at most she will exert some influence over him, but she won't affect his ability to work. In certain circumstances there will be a child. But when a man in the Security Service, in the SS or in the Government has homosexual tendencies, then he abandons the normal order of things for the perverted world of the homosexuals. Such a man always drags ten others after him, otherwise he can't survive. We can't permit such a danger to the country; the homosexuals must be entirely eliminated.

Our forefathers knew what they were doing when they had their own homosexuals drowned in a bog, but let those belonging to conquered peoples, the Romans for instance, go unpunished and even encouraged them. Politically speaking, these were wise measures which we should do well to copy. The homosexual is a traitor to his own people and must be rooted out.

—Heinrich Himmler, Reich Leader of the SS, head of the Gestapo, and the most powerful Nazi leader after Hitler, November 10, 1940

The Bars of Prejudice

It was during those long and lonely years [in prison] that my hunger for the freedom of my own people became a hunger for the freedom of all people, white and black. I knew as well as I knew anything that the oppressor must be liberated just as surely as the oppressed. A man who takes away another man's freedom is a prisoner of hatred, he is locked behind the bars of prejudice and narrow-mindedness. I am not truly free if I am taking away someone else's freedom, just as surely as I am not free when my freedom is taken from me. The oppressed and the oppressor alike are robbed of their humanity.

—Nelson Mandela, *Long Walk to Freedom: The Autobiography of Nelson Mandela,* 1994 [*Note:* After spending decades imprisoned under apartheid, Mandela went on to become president of South Africa from 1994 to 1999.]

ENVIRONMENTAL JUSTICE FOR ALL

ROBERT D. BULLARD AND BEVERLY H. WRIGHT

In 1967, students at predominantly African American Texas Southern University in Houston were involved in a campus riot triggered by the death of an eight-year-old African American girl who had drowned at a garbage dump. Student protesters questioned why a garbage dump was located in the middle of the mostly African American Sunnyside neighborhood.[1] The protests got out of hand. Police were met with rocks and bottles. Gunshots were fired. A police officer, struck by a ricocheting bullet, was killed. Nearly 500 male students were cleared from the dormitories, and many of the leaders were arrested.

In 1968, Reverend Martin Luther King, Jr., went to Memphis on an environmental justice mission—better working conditions and pay for striking African American garbage workers. King was killed in Memphis before he could complete this mission. Nevertheless, garbage and landfills did not disappear as an environmental justice issue.

In 1979, residents of Houston's Northwood Manor subdivision (a suburban neighborhood of African American home owners) filed the first lawsuit charging environmental discrimination. Residents charged Browning-Ferris Industries with locating a municipal solid waste landfill in their community. An early attempt to place a similar facility in the same area in 1970—when the area was mostly white—had been defeated by the Harris County Board of Supervisors.

Houston has a long history of locating its solid waste facilities in communities of color, especially in African American neighborhoods. From the early 1920s through the late 1970s, all five of the city-owned sanitary landfills and six of its eight municipal solid waste incinerators were located in mostly African American neighborhoods. Similarly, three of the four privately owned solid waste landfills were located in mostly African American communities during this period. African Americans, however, made up only 28 percent of the city's population. Despite the overwhelming statistical evidence, the plaintiffs lost their lawsuit, and the Whispering Pines landfill was built in Northwood Manor.[2]

Some proponents of the Whispering Pines landfill suggested that the African American neighborhood would benefit from the waste facility by way of the jobs and taxes it would provide. However, Charles Streadit, president of Houston's Northeast Community Action Group, addressed the benefits and liabilities associated with the landfill in his neighborhood:

> Sure, Browning-Ferris Industries [owner of the Whispering Pines landfill] pays taxes, but so do we. We need all the money we can get to upgrade our school system. But we shouldn't have to be poisoned to get improvements for our children. When my property values go down, that

means less for the schools and my children's education. . . . It's hard enough for blacks to scrape and save enough money to buy a home, then you see your dream shattered by a garbage dump. That's a dirty trick. No amount of money can buy self-respect.[3]

The aforementioned examples show a clear link between civil rights and environmental justice. However, it was not until the early 1980s that a national movement for environmental justice took root in several mainstream civil rights organizations. The environmental justice movement took shape out of protests in Warren County, North Carolina. This mostly African American and rural county had been selected as the burial site for 30,000 cubic yards of soil contaminated with highly toxic PCBs (polychlorinated biphenyls). Oil laced with PCBs had been illegally dumped along roadways in fourteen North Carolina counties in 1978; the roadways were cleaned up in 1982.[4]

More than 500 protesters were jailed over the siting of the Warren County PCB landfill. Demonstrations were led by a number of national civil rights advocacy groups, including the United Church of Christ Commission for Racial Justice, the Southern Christian Leadership Conference, and the Congressional Black Caucus. Although the demonstrations were unsuccessful in halting construction of the landfill, the protests marked the first time African Americans had mobilized a national, broad-based group to oppose what they defined as environmental racism. The demonstrations also prompted District of Columbia delegate Walter Fauntroy, who was chairman of the Congressional Black Caucus, to initiate the 1983 U.S. General Accounting Office (GAO) study of hazardous waste landfill siting in the Environmental Protection Agency's Region IV.[5] Fauntroy had been active in the protests and was one of many who went to jail over the landfill.

The GAO study found a strong relationship between the location of off-site hazardous waste landfills and the race and socioeconomic status of the surrounding communities. The study identified four off-site hazardous waste landfills in the eight states that constitute the EPA's Region IV (Alabama, Florida, Georgia, Kentucky, Mississippi, North Carolina, South Carolina, and Tennessee). In 1983, African Americans were clearly overrepresented in communities with waste sites, since they made up only about one-fifth of the region's population, yet African American communities contained three-fourths of the off-site landfills.

In October 1991, the First National People of Color Environmental Leadership Summit was held in Washington, DC. The Summit demonstrated that it is possible to build a multi-issue, multiracial environmental movement around *justice*. The four-day Summit was attended by more than 650 grass-roots and national leaders representing more than 300 environmental groups of color. Delegates came from all fifty states, including Alaska and Hawaii, as well as from Puerto Rico, Chile, Mexico, and the Marshall Islands. Grass-roots groups organized themselves around a number of environmental issues, ranging from the siting of landfills and incinerators to lead pollution.

The Environmental Justice Framework

There is general agreement that the nation's environmental problems need immediate attention. The head of the U.S. Environmental Protection Agency, writing in the agency's *EPA Journal,* stressed that "environmental protection should be applied fairly."[6] However, the nation's environmental laws, regulations, and policies are not applied uniformly, resulting in some individuals, neighborhoods, and communities being exposed to elevated health risks.

Environmental decision making operates at the juncture of science, technology, economics, politics, and ethics. A 1992 study by staff writers from the *National Law Journal* uncovered glaring inequities in the way the federal EPA enforces its laws. The authors wrote:

> There is a racial divide in the way the U.S. government cleans up toxic waste sites and punishes polluters. White communities see faster action, better results and stiffer penalties than communities where blacks, Hispanics and other minorities live. This unequal protection often occurs whether the community is wealthy or poor.[7]

After examining census data, civil court dockets, and the EPA's own record of performance at 1,177 Superfund toxic waste sites, the *National Law Journal* report revealed the following:

1. Penalties under hazardous waste laws at sites having the greatest white population were 500 percent higher than penalties with the greatest minority population, averaging $335,566 for white areas, compared to $55,318 for minority areas.
2. The disparity occurs by race alone, not income.
3. For federal environmental laws aimed at protecting citizens from air, water, and waste pollution, penalties in white communities were 46 percent higher than in minority communities.
4. Under the giant Superfund cleanup program, abandoned hazardous waste sites in minority areas take 20 percent longer to be placed on the national priority list than those in white areas.[8]

These findings suggest that unequal environmental protection places communities of color at special risk. The environmental justice framework attempts to uncover underlying assumptions that may influence environmental decision making. It also rests on an analysis of strategies to eliminate unfair, unjust, and inequitable conditions and decisions. The basic elements of the framework consist of five characteristics:

1. Incorporates the principle of the right of all individuals to be protected from environmental degradation,
2. Adopts a public health model of prevention (elimination of the threat before harm occurs) as the preferred strategy,
3. Shifts the burden of proof to polluters and dischargers who do harm or discriminate or who do not give equal protection to racial and ethnic minorities and other "protected" classes,

4. Allows disparate impact and statistical weight, as opposed to "intent," to infer discrimination,
5. Redresses disproportionate risk burdens through targeted action and resources.

The goal of an environmental justice framework is to make environmental protection more democratic. Environmental and health laws have not provided equal protection for all Americans. Numerous studies, dating back to the 1970s, reveal that communities of color have borne greater health and environmental risk burdens than has society at large.[9]

Nationally based conservation and environmental groups have played an instrumental role in shaping this nation's environmental laws and regulations. It was not until recently, however, that these nongovernmental organizations paid attention to environmental and health threats to poor, working-class persons and to communities of color. The environmental justice movement defines environment in very broad terms, as the places where people live, work, and play. The question of environmental justice is not anchored in a scientific debate but rests on an ethical analysis of environmental decision making.

Endangered Communities

Millions of Americans live in housing and physical environments that are over-burdened with environmental problems including older housing with lead-based paint, congested freeways that criss-cross their neighborhoods, industries that emit dangerous pollutants into the area, and abandoned toxic waste sites.

Virtually all of the studies of exposure to outdoor air pollution have found significant differences by income and race.[10] African Americans and Latino Americans are more likely than whites to live in areas with reduced air quality. For example, National Argonne Laboratory researchers D. R. Wernette and L. A. Nieves found the following:

> 57 percent of whites, 65 percent of African Americans, and 80 percent of Hispanics live in 437 counties with substandard air quality. Out of the whole population, a total of 33 percent of whites, 50 percent of African Americans, and 60 percent of Hispanics live in the 136 counties in which two or more air pollutants exceed standards.[11]

The public health community has very little information to explain the magnitude of some of the health problems related to air pollution. However, we do know that persons suffering from asthma are particularly sensitive to the effects of carbon monoxide, sulfur dioxides, particulate matter, ozone, and nitrogen oxides.[12] African Americans, for example, have a significantly higher prevalence of asthma than does the general population.[13]

In the heavily populated Los Angeles basin, more than 71 percent of African Americans and 50 percent of Latino Americans live in areas with the most polluted air, while only 34 percent of whites live in highly polluted areas.[14] A "green" initiative will need to incorporate strategies employing residents in cleanup efforts that adopt environmentally sound technologies.

Industrial encroachment into Chicago's South Side neighborhoods is another example of endangered communities. Chicago is one of the most racially segregated cities in the country; more than 92 percent of the city's 1.1 million African American residents live in racially segregated areas. The Altgeld Gardens housing project, located on the city's Southeast Side, is one of these segregated enclaves.

Altgeld Gardens is encircled by municipal and hazardous waste landfills, toxic waste incinerators, grain elevators, sewer treatment facilities, smelters, steel mills, and a host of other polluting industries. Because of the physical location, Hazel Johnson, a community organizer in the neighborhood, has dubbed the area a "toxic doughnut." The Southeast Side neighborhood is home to 150,000 residents, of whom 70 percent are African American and 11 percent are Latino American. It also has 50 active or closed commercial hazardous waste landfills, 100 factories (including seven chemical plants and five steel mills), and 103 abandoned toxic waste dumps.[15]

Environmental justice advocates have sought to persuade the government to adopt a framework that addresses distributive impacts, enforcement, and compliance concerns. They have taken their fight to city halls, state capitals, and the U.S. Congress. In 1990, New York City adopted a "fair share" legislative model designed to ensure that every borough and every community within each borough bear its fair share of noxious facilities. Proceedings from a hearing on environmental disparities in the Bronx point to concerns raised by African Americans and Puerto Ricans who see their neighborhoods threatened by garbage transfer stations, salvage yards, and recycling centers:

> A policy whereby low-income and minority communities have become the "dumping grounds" for unwanted land uses works to create an environment of disincentives to community-based development initiatives. It also undermines existing businesses.[16]

In 1992, Chicago congresswoman Cardiss Collins offered an amendment to the bill reauthorizing the Resource Conservation and Recovery Act (RCRA), requiring "community information statements" that assess the demographic makeup of proposed waste site areas and the cumulative impact a new facility would have on the existing environmental burden. In a similar vein, in 1992 Georgia congressman John Lewis, a longtime civil rights activist, and former senator Al Gore introduced their version of an Environmental Justice Act. The act was designed to "establish a program to ensure nondiscriminatory compliance with environmental, health, and safety laws and to ensure equal protection of the public health."

Some communities form a special case for environmental justice and risk reduction. Because of more stringent state and federal environmental regulations, Native American reservations, from New York to California, have become prime targets. Few reservations have infrastructures to handle the risky technologies that are being proposed for their communities, and more than 100 waste disposal facilities have been proposed for Native American lands.[17]

Coping with Poisons in Cancer Alley

The South has always been an important battleground for African Americans' struggle for social justice. Southerners, both African American and white, have less education, lower incomes, higher infant mortality, and shorter life expectancy than Americans elsewhere. It should be no surprise that the environmental quality Southerners enjoy is markedly different from that in other regions of the country. Lax enforcement of environmental regulations has left the region's air, water, and land the most industry-befouled in the United States.

African Americans have always constituted a sizable share of the population in southern states where the plantation economy was dominant—as in Louisiana. Louisiana has tagged itself a "sportsman's paradise." However, in the early 1900s the state's economy slowly began to change from an agricultural and fishing economy, based on its cypress swamps, waterways, and fertile soil, as oil exploration led to the construction of a refinery in Baton Rouge. By the 1970s, Louisiana's industrial corridor, an 85-mile stretch along the Mississippi River from Baton Rouge to New Orleans, was producing 60 percent of the nation's vinyl chloride and nitrogen fertilizer and 26 percent of the nation's chlorine.

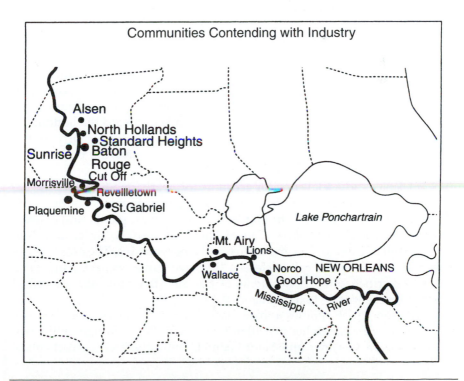

In 2001, African Americans made up nearly a third of Louisiana's population. How have African Americans fared under this new system, in which the petrochemical industry is king? Many of these industries are located next to African American communities that were settled by former slaves—areas that were unincorporated and where the land was cheap. Local residents had few political rights (most African Americans were denied the right to vote or to hold public office). While the promise of jobs was the selling point for industries coming to towns along the Mississippi River, only a few jobs were actually offered to African American residents—and these were usually the dirtiest jobs, at the lowest wages.

The petrochemical industry has played an important role in the state's economy, especially in southern Louisiana. This single industry accounts for one out of three tax dollars collected by the state.[18] Even though Louisiana is a poor state, many of the giant corporations get special tax breaks. For example, thirty large corporations, many of which are major polluters, received $2.5 billion in Louisiana property tax exemptions in the 1980s.

Louisiana is not a large state; it ranks thirty-first in land area for all of the states. Yet despite its compact size, Louisiana has become a hazardous waste "importer" state. It disposed of 819 million pounds of hazardous waste shipped from other states in the latest year for which Louisiana Department of Environmental Quality figures are available.[19] On the other hand, Louisiana sent 307 million pounds of hazardous waste to other states for disposal, giving the state a net import of 512 million pounds of hazardous waste.

In 1992, the Institute for Southern Studies' "Green Index" ranked Louisiana forty-ninth of fifty states in overall environmental quality. The Green Index is based on seventy-seven federal and state policy indicators.[20] Louisiana ranked fiftieth in toxic release to surface water, high-risk cancer facilities, per capita toxic underground injection, and oil spills in state waters. On community and work force health, it also ranked toward the bottom: infant mortality, forty-ninth; households with only septic tanks, forty-fourth; households without plumbing, forty-third; doctors delivering patient care, forty-first; and workers in high-risk jobs, fortieth.[21]

Louisiana's industrial corridor accounts for nearly one-fourth of the nation's petrochemical production. Some 125 companies in this corridor manufacture a range of products including fertilizers, gasoline, paints, and plastics. This corridor has been dubbed "Cancer Alley" because the air, ground, and water are full of carcinogens, mutagens, and embryotoxins. The area was described in a *Washington Post* article as a "massive human experiment" and a "national sacrifice zone."[22] Residents of Cancer Alley have also described their environment as a "toxic gumbo."

Ascension Parish typifies a toxic "sacrifice zone." The rural and mostly African American parish lies just 10 miles south of Baton Rouge. In the two parish towns of Geismer and Saint Gabriel, some eighteen petrochemical plants are crammed into a 9.5-square-mile area. Companies such as BASF, Vulcan, Triad, CF Industries, Liquid Airbonic, Bordon Chemical, Shell, Uniroyal, Rubicon, Ciba-Geigy, and others discharge 196 million pounds of pollutants annually into the water and air.[23]

It takes Amos Favorite to describe the hellish nightmare in his hometown of Geismer, a small, mostly African American river town: "You ought to see this place at night. . . . When these companies burn off their waste the air lights up like a battlefield. I'm telling you it's scary. Nighttime around here is like an evil dream."[24]

Buyouts, Push–Outs, and Sellouts

Many of these threatened communities were there long before the petro-chemical industry came to the region. Reveilletown, a community founded by former slaves after the Civil War, is located across the Mississippi River from Baton Rouge. The entire community was poisoned by vinyl chloride emissions released from Georgia Gulf's manufacture of plastics.

After traces of vinyl chloride were found in the blood of local children in 1987, thirteen Reveilletown property owners filed a lawsuit against Georgia Gulf. The case was later settled out of court. Twenty other families subsequently agreed to sell to Georgia Gulf for a reported $1.2 million, and the company completed a program in 1990 to move a total of fifty families away from its vinyl chloride plant.[25]

Morrisonville, founded in the 1870s by former slaves, is another community that was bought out. The town's founder, Robert Morrison, was a minister who struggled to create this community around the church he led, the Nazarene Baptist Church. The community survived flooding from the Mississippi and it survived Jim Crow, but it could not survive Dow Chemical.

Some Morrisonville residents can still recall when the land that Dow stands on was part of a huge sugarcane empire owned by the Mayflower and Union Plantation. The plantation house is still standing and can be seen inside the fence owned by Dow. In 1959, the community sold some land to Dow. Many of the residents now see this transaction as the mistake that marked the beginning of their demise as a community. The land sold to Dow created a greenbelt, but Dow expanded and built on the land—up to the property lines of some Morrisonville residents.[26]

The Morrisonville chemical plant is Dow's largest facility in Louisiana. "Dow built right out to the fence until they were on top of us," says Jack Martin, a longtime Morrisonville resident. The buyout has brought sadness to the community. Doretha Thompson sums up the demise of her community: "It's like a big death taking place. . . . I always thought I'd spend the rest of my life in Morrisonville with my relatives. But it seems like what Dow wants, Dow gets."[27]

The chemical conglomerate spent more than $10 million in a voluntary buyout of the town's 250 home owners—the first of its kind in the absence of a lawsuit. Dow compensated people for the cost of their homes, but the "community" is lost forever. Presently, the town's residents have moved upriver, downriver, and to Baton Rouge. Many of them return every Sunday to worship in the Nazarene Baptist Church, the only surviving symbol of the community.

The community of Sunrise was purchased in 1874 from a white land-owner by Alexander Banes, a former slave. In the 1930s, Sunrise was inhab-ited by mostly white residents, but by 1970, the community was 83 percent African American. Sunrise is the home of Placid Refining Company, an inde-pendent oil-refining and oil-marketing company. In 1979, Placid initiated a program to purchase the property of employees of the refining company who lived in Sunrise. The program resulted in Placid's acquiring more than 100 parcels of land—about one-third of the lots in Sunrise. However, African American Sunrise residents were not offered the same opportunities to be bought out as their white counterparts. White residents who lived closest to the plant at the time of the buyout and other white residents were bought out first. In 1985, some African American property owners in Sunrise were told that the company would get back to them. This, however, did not occur.

The remaining residents of Sunrise who lived in the shadow of Placid filed a lawsuit against the company in 1990. In response, Placid initiated its "Sunrise program," which offered to buy the homes of any nonplaintiff own-ers in Sunrise. An offer was made to property owners to purchase homes at prices that would allow owners to buy or build new homes that were similar in size and materials to the ones they owned in Sunrise. In addition to the purchase price, owners were provided $5,000 per household. This program resulted in Placid's acquiring more than 90 percent of the homes of the non-plaintiff owners. Placid and the plaintiffs finally reached an out-of-court set-tlement under which Placid would purchase all property of the plaintiffs.

Toxic Waste Time Bombs

The roughly 2 billion pounds of poisons put into the air, land, and water in Cancer Alley find their way sooner or later into the homes of all Americans. In about three days, ethylene and thousands of other lethal gases make their way from Cancer Alley refineries to the Great Lakes and the Northeast. A few more days, and those same gases, although somewhat diluted, poison the air of Europe, Asia, Africa, and the other continents. Many of the pesticides and fertilizers produced here poison us first and farm workers second, then fi-nally wind up on America's and the world's dinner tables.

Likewise, fish and seafood from Louisiana's waters find their way to most dinner tables. Louisiana is the second largest seafood-exporting state in the United States. Fish in Louisiana's largest river system, the Calcasieu Es-tuary, have been studied and found to be poisoned with cancer-causing chemicals. The state and federal governments have said and done very little to protect the public except to post advisories warning people against fishing and consuming fish caught in this estuary.

The hazardous waste problem continues to be one of the most "serious problems facing the industrial world."[28] Toxic time bombs are not randomly scattered across the urban landscape. In New Jersey (a state with one of the highest concentrations of uncontrolled toxic waste dumps), hazardous waste sites are often located in communities that have high percentages of poor, elderly, young, and minority residents.[29]

The United Church of Christ Commission for Racial Justice, a church-based civil rights organization, conducted the first national study on this topic.[30] The Commission for Racial Justice's landmark study, *Toxic Wastes and Race in the United States,* found race to be the single most important factor (i.e., more important than income, home ownership rate, and property values) in the location of abandoned toxic waste sites.[31] The study also found that (1) three out of five African Americans live in communities with abandoned toxic waste sites; (2) 60 percent (15 million) African Americans live in communities with one or more abandoned toxic waste sites; (3) three of the five largest commercial hazardous waste landfills are located in predominantly African American or Latino American communities and account for 40 percent of the nation's total estimated landfill capacity; and (4) African Americans are heavily overrepresented in the populations of cities with the largest number of abandoned toxic waste sites.[32]

In metropolitan Chicago, for example, more than 81.3 percent of Latino Americans and 76 percent of African Americans live in communities with abandoned toxic waste sites, compared with 59 percent of whites. Similarly, 81.3 percent of Latino Americans and 69.8 percent of African Americans in the Houston metropolitan area live in communities with abandoned toxic waste sites, compared with 57.1 percent of whites. Latino Americans in the Los Angeles metropolitan area are nearly twice as likely as their Anglo counterparts to live in a community with an abandoned toxic waste site.[33]

The mounting waste problem is adding to the potential health threat to environmental high-impact areas. Incineration has become the leading technology for disposal of this waste. This technology is also becoming a major source of dioxin, as well as lead, mercury, and other heavy metals released into the environment. For example, millions of pounds of lead per year will be emitted from the nation's municipal solid waste incinerators in the next few years. All of this lead is being released despite what we know about its hazards to human health.

Hazardous waste incinerators are not randomly scattered across the landscape. A 1990 Greenpeace report, *Playing with Fire,* found that (1) the minority portion of the population in communities with existing incinerators is 89 percent higher than the national average; (2) communities where incinerators are proposed have minority populations 60 percent higher than the national average; (3) average income in communities with existing incinerators is 15 percent less than the national average; (4) property values in communities that are hosts to incinerators are 38 percent lower than the national average; and (5) average property values are 35 percent lower in communities where incinerators are proposed.[34]

The Politics of Lead Poisoning

Why has so little been done to prevent lead poisoning in the United States? Overwhelming scientific evidence exists on the ill effects of lead on the human body. However, very little has been done to rid the nation of lead poisoning—a preventable disease tagged the "number one environmental health threat to children" by the federal Agency for Toxic Substances and Disease Registry.[35]

Lead began to be phased out of gasoline in the 1970s. In 1971, a child was not considered at risk for lead poisoning unless he or she had 400 micrograms of lead per liter of blood (or 40 micrograms per deciliter [$\mu g/dl$]). Since that time, the amount of lead that is considered safe has continually dropped. In 1991, the U.S. Public Health Service changed the official definition of an unsafe level to 10 $\mu g/dl$. Even at that level, a child's IQ can be slightly diminished and physical growth stunted. Lead poisoning is correlated with both income and race (see Table 1)[36]

Conclusion

If the United States is to achieve environmental justice, the environment in urban ghettos, barrios, reservations, and rural poverty pockets must be given the same protection as that provided to the suburbs. All communities—African American or white, rich or poor—deserve to be protected from the ravages of pollution.

The current emphasis on waste management and pollution control regulations encourages dependence on disposal technologies, which are them-

TABLE 1 **Estimated Percentages of Children (Living in Cities with Population over 1 Million) 0.5–5 Years Old with Lead Blood Levels Greater than 15 $\mu g/dl$, by Race and Income**

Race	Income		
	<$6,000	*$6,000–$15,000*	*>$15,000*
African American	68%	54%	38%
White	36%	22%	12%

Source: Agency for Toxic Substances and Disease Registry, *The Nature and Extent of Lead Poisoning in Children in the United States: A Report to Congress* (Atlanta: U.S. Department of Health and Human Services, 1988).

selves sources of toxic pollution. Pushing incinerators and risk technologies off on people under the guise of economic development is not a solution to this nation's waste problem.

An environmental justice framework needs to be incorporated into a national policy on facility siting. In addition to the standard technical requirements, environmental justice proposals will need to require implementation of some type of "fair share" plan that takes into account sociodemographic, economic, and cultural factors of affected communities. It is clear that current environmental regulations and "protectionist" devices (zoning, deed restrictions, and other land use controls) have not had the same impact on all segments of society.

No segment of society should be allowed to become a dumping ground because of economic vulnerability or racial discrimination. We need a holistic methodology in documenting, remediating, and preventing environmental health problems. Prevention is the key. Environmental justice demands that lead poisoning—the number one environmental health problem affecting children—be given the attention and priority it deserves. The poorest among the nation's inhabitants are being poisoned at an alarming rate. Many of these individuals and families have little or no access to regular health care.

The solution lies in leveling the playing field and protecting all Americans. Environmental decision makers have failed to address "justice" questions of who gets help and who does not, why some communities get cleaned up at a faster rate than others, and why industry poisons some communities and not others. Federal, state, and local legislation is needed to target resources for those areas where societal risk burdens are the greatest. It is time for environmental justice to become a national priority.

NOTES

1. Robert D. Bullard, *Invisible Houston: The Black Experience in Boom and Bust* (College Station: Texas A & M University Press, 1987), pp. 110–111.
2. See Robert D. Bullard, *Dumping in Dixie: Race, Class, and Environmental Quality* (Boulder, CO: Westview Press, 1990), chap. 3.
3. Interview with Charles Streadit, president of the Houston Northeast Community Action Group, May 30, 1988.
4. Ken Geiser and Gerry Waneck, "PCBs and Warren County," *Science for the People* 15 (July–August 1983): 13–17.
5. General Accounting Office, *Siting of Hazardous Waste Landfills and Their Correlation with Racial and Economic Status of Surrounding Communities* (Washington, DC: General Accounting Office, 1983), p. 1.
6. William K. Reilly, "Environmental Equity: EPA's Position," *EPA Journal* 18 (March–April 1992): 18.
7. Marianne Lavelle and Marcia Coyle, "Unequal Protection," *National Law Journal*, September 21, 1992, pp. S1–S2.
8. Ibid., p. S2.
9. See W. J. Kruvant, "People, Energy, and Pollution," pp. 125–167 in *The American Energy Consumer*, ed. D. K. Newman and Dawn Day (Cambridge, MA: Ballinger, 1975); Robert D. Bullard, "Solid Waste Sites and the Black Houston Community,"

Sociological Inquiry 53 (Spring 1983): 273–288; United Church of Christ Commission for Racial Justice, *Toxic Wastes and Race in the United States: A National Study of the Racial and Socioeconomic Characteristics of Communities with Hazardous Waste Sites* (New York: United Church of Christ Commission for Racial Justice, 1987); Michel Gelobter, "The Distribution of Air Pollution by Income and Race" (paper presented at the Second Symposium on Social Science in Resource Management, Urbana, Illinois, June 1988); Dick Russell, "Environmental Racism," *Amicus Journal* 11 (Spring 1989): 22–32; Bullard, *Dumping in Dixie*; Paul Ong and Evelyn Blumenberg, "Race and Environmentalism" (Los Angeles: University of California, Los Angeles, Graduate School of Architecture and Urban Planning, March 1990); Eric Mann, *L.A.'s Lethal Air: New Strategies for Policy, Organizing, and Action* (Los Angeles: Labor/Community Strategy Center, 1991); Leslie A. Nieves, "Not in Whose Backyard? Minority Population Concentrations and Noxious Facility Sites" (paper presented at the annual meeting of the American Association for the Advancement of Science, Chicago, February 1991); D. R. Wernette and L. A. Nieves, "Breathing Polluted Air: Minorities Are Disproportionately Exposed," *EPA Journal* 18 (March–April 1992): 16–17; Robert D. Bullard, "In Our Backyards: Minority Communities Get Most of Dumps," *EPA Journal* 18 (March–April 1992): 11–12; Bunyan Bryant and Paul Mohai, eds., *Race and the Incidence of Environmental Hazards* (Boulder, CO: Westview Press, 1992).

10. See Gelobter, "The Distribution of Air Pollution."

11. Wernette and Nieves, "Breathing Polluted Air," pp. 16–17.

12. See Mann, *L.A.'s Lethal Air*.

13. See H. P. Mak, H. Abbey, and R. C. Talamo, "Prevalence of Asthma and Health Service Utilization of Asthmatic Children in an Inner City," *Journal of Allergy and Clinical Immunology* 70 (1982): 367–372; I. F. Goldstein and A. L. Weinstein, "Air Pollution and Asthma: Effects of Exposure to Short-Term Sulfur Dioxide Peaks," *Environmental Research* 40 (1986): 332–345; J. Schwartz, D. Gold, D. W. Dockey, S. T. Weiss, and F. E. Speizer, "Predictors of Asthma and Persistent Wheeze in a National Sample of Children in the United States," *American Review of Respiratory Disease* 142 (1990): 555–562.

14. Ong and Blumenberg, "Race and Environmentalism"; Mann, *L.A.'s Lethal Air*.

15. Greenpeace, "Home Street, USA," *Greenpeace* (October–November 1991): 8–13.

16. Fernando Ferrer, "Testimony by the Office of Bronx Borough President," *Proceedings of the Public Hearing on Minorities and the Environment: An Exploration into the Effects of Environmental Policies, Practices, and Conditions on Minority and Low-Income Communities* (Bronx, NY: Bronx Planning Office, September 20, 1991), p. 27.

17. Bradley Angel, *The Toxic Threat to Indian Lands: A Greenpeace Report* (San Francisco: Greenpeace, 1992).

18. Bob Anderson, Mike Dunn, and Sonny Alabarado, "Prosperity in Paradise: Lousiana's Chemical Legacy," *Morning Advocate,* April 25, 1985.

19. James O'Byrne and Mark Schleifstein, "Dumping Ground: State a Final Stop for Nation's Toxic Waste," *Times Picayune,* March 26, 1991.

20. See Institute for Southern Studies, *1991–1992 Green Index: A State-by-State Guide to the Nation's Environmental Health* (Durham, NC: Institute for Southern Studies, 1992).

21. For a discussion of Lousiana's environmental and economic problems, see Paul H. Templet and Stephen Farber, "The Complementarity between Environmental and Economic Risk: An Empirical Analysis" (Baton Rouge: Louisiana State University, Institute for Environmental Studies, 1992).

22. Quoted in David Maraniss and Michael Weisskopf, "Jobs and Illness in Petrochemical Corridor," *Washington Post,* December 22, 1989.

23. Conger Beasley, "Of Pollution and Poverty: Keeping Watch in 'Cancer Alley,'" *Buzzworm* 2 (July–August 1990): 39–45 (see p. 41).

24. Ibid., p. 39.

25. See Beverly H. Wright and Florence Robinson, "Voluntary Buy-Outs as an Alternative Damage Claims Arrangement: A Comparative Analysis of Three Impacted Communities" (Baton Rouge: Southern University, Institute for Environmental Issues and Policy Assessment, December 15, 1992), pp. 10–11.

26. Ibid., pp. 8–10.

27. Quoted in James O'Byrne, "The Death of a Town: A Chemical Plant Closes In," *Times Picayune,* February 20, 1991, p. A12.

28. Samuel S. Epstein, Lester O. Brown, and Carl Pope, *Hazardous Waste in America* (San Francisco: Sierra Club Books, 1983), pp. 33–39.

29. Michael R. Greenberg and Richard F. Anderson, *Hazardous Waste Sites: The Credibility Gap* (New Brunswick, NJ: Rutgers University, Center for Urban Policy Research, 1984), pp. 158–159; Bullard, *Dumping in Dixie,* pp. 4–5.

30. United Church of Christ Commission for Racial Justice, *Toxic Wastes and Race.*

31. Ibid., pp. xiii–xiv.

32. Ibid., pp. 18–19.

33. United Church of Christ Commission for Racial Justice, *Toxic Wastes and Race.*

34. Pat Costner and Joe Thornton, *Playing with Fire* (Washington, DC: Greenpeace, 1990).

35. Agency for Toxic Substances and Disease Registry, *The Nature and Extent of Lead Poisoning in Children in the United States: A Report to Congress* (Atlanta: U.S. Department of Health and Human Services, 1988).

36. Agency for Toxic Substances and Disease Registry, *Nature and Extent of Lead Poisoning.*

The Web of Life

You must teach your children that the ground beneath their feet is the ashes of our grandfathers. So that they will respect the land, tell your children that the earth is rich with the lives of our kin. Teach your children what we have taught our children, that the earth is our mother. Whatever befalls the earth befalls the sons of the earth. If men spit upon the ground, they spit upon themselves.

This we know. The earth does not belong to man; man belongs to the earth. This we know. All things are connected like the blood which unites one family. All things are connected.

Whatever befalls the earth befalls the sons of the earth. Man does not weave the web of life, he is merely a strand in it. Whatever he does to the web, he does to himself.

—Chief Seattle, 1854

X

Reducing Prejudice

 A young man was picking up objects off the beach and tossing them out into the sea. A second man approached him, and saw that the objects were starfish.

"Why in the world are you throwing starfish into the water?"

"If the starfish are still on the beach when the tide goes out, they will die," replied the young man.

"That's ridiculous. There are thousands of miles of beach and millions of starfish. You can't really believe that what you're doing could possibly make a difference!"

The young man picked up another starfish, paused thoughtfully, and remarked as he tossed it out into the waves, "It makes a difference to this one."

—Based on Loren Eiseley's story *The Star Thrower,* 1978

Wistful do the trick? Will empathy? What about direct confrontation? This section examines individual and group strategies aimed at prejudice reduction.

The first article, by Fletcher Blanchard, Teri Lilly, and Leigh Vaughn, demonstrates that even one public condemnation of prejudice—made by one college student—is enough to move other people in that direction. And the next article, by Milton Rokeach, shows that enduring changes can result when people are simply made aware of inconsistencies in their values and attitudes. Taken together, these studies suggest that small actions taken by individuals may be surprisingly effective agents of change.

Walter Stephan and Krystina Finlay then discuss the importance of empathy, and Sam Gaertner and his colleagues observe that prejudice is sometimes driven more by ingroup favoritism than outgroup rejection. Accordingly, Gaertner et al. recommend "recategorizing" outgroup members so they are in the ingroup. Finally, a brief article by Martin Luther King, Jr., explains the power of nonviolent resistance.

Take Special Notice

The articles by Martin Luther King, Jr., and Milton Rokeach are "modern classics" that first appeared in the 1960s and 1970s. As you read these articles, see if you can apply the material to contemporary events.

Questions Worth Pondering

- If you could snap your fingers and eliminate all prejudice, would you do it?
- What is the most effective way to respond when you hear someone make a prejudiced comment?
- Walter Stephan and Krystina Finlay propose that prejudice can be reduced by increasing cognitive empathy, parallel empathy, and reactive empathy. When is one type of empathy more important than another?
- In the "Racism Then" section of this book, Anne Moody compared students in the 1960s to interns who would become "the best doctors in the world for social problems." Are students in the twenty-first century also interns? Why or why not?

What Individuals Can Do for Social Justice

What can any individual do? Of that, every individual can judge. There is one thing that every individual can do,—they can see to it that *they feel right*. An atmosphere of sympathetic influence encircles every human being; and the man or woman who *feels* strongly, healthily, and justly on the great interests of humanity, is a constant benefactor to the human race. See, then, to your sympathies in this matter!

—Harriet Beecher Stowe, *Uncle Tom's Cabin*, 1852

Going North

The problem is whether we are determined to go in the direction of compassion or not. If we are, then can we reduce the suffering to a minimum? If I lose my direction, I have to look for the North Star, and I go to the north. That does not mean I expect to arrive at the North Star. I just want to go in that direction.

—Thich Nhat Hanh, *Being Peace*, 1987

REDUCING THE EXPRESSION OF RACIAL PREJUDICE

FLETCHER A. BLANCHARD, TERI LILLY,
AND LEIGH ANN VAUGHN

M uch of the intergroup relations research over the last 35 years has been organized around the goal of reducing the individual prejudice levels of whites. An alternative approach might focus instead upon the goal of creating social settings that minimize the public expression of discriminatory or otherwise interracially insensitive behavior (Blanchard, 1989). A focus upon the immediate social context would emphasize the elimination of *behavior* that has the effect of discriminating or offending regardless of the intentions or associated prejudices of the actor. Such an approach is analogous to antismoking norms and regulations that have largely achieved the elimination of smoke from public places, while ignoring the personal feelings, attitudes, and out-of-context behavior of the smokers. In a manner parallel to the way in which antismoking norms have freed nonsmokers from noxious smoke, blacks might escape the averseness of discriminatory and insensitive behavior if strong social pressure and negative sanctions against such behavior were introduced and proved similarly effective (Pettigrew, 1985).

Normative influence[1] offers considerable promise for guiding the interracial behavior of whites. Theorists and researchers suggest that effective normative influence sometimes emanates from persons in authority (Pettigrew, 1961; Weigel & Howes, 1985) and sometimes from peers (Cook, 1978; Stephan & Stephan, 1984). For the most part, however, experimental evidence of the effects of norms that prescribe harmonious interracial interaction or condemn racism remains incomplete. Those few investigations that evaluate the consequences of norms favoring egalitarian intergroup behavior (e.g., Cohen, 1982; Cook, 1978, 1984; Sherif & Sherif, 1953; Yarrow et al., 1958) have treated norms as one part of gross manipulations intended to produce favorable interracial outcomes.

The current and widespread problem of racism on college campuses (Farrell & Jones, 1988) provides the context for the present studies. One form of attack against black students, faculty, and administrators observed on many American campuses has consisted of threats and racial epithets delivered in anonymous letters and notes. The anonymous character of these attacks exaggerates the negative effects on the recipients by calling into question previously trusted white friends and acquaintances, any one of whom might have been the author of such a letter. We believed that opinions about anonymous racist notes constituted a personally relevant domain for the white participants in this study because recent incidents of this type had occurred on their campus and at nearby colleges and universities.

---

[1]*Editor's note:* Normative influence occurs when people are influenced by expectations or rules (norms) for acceptable behavior.

Experiment 1

Method

Subjects   Research participants were 72 white, undergraduate women who were interviewed as they walked between classes. The experimental team approached every white student walking alone as she passed a designated reference point. No one declined to participate over three days of interviewing. Subjects were debriefed immediately after their participation.

Design and Procedure   We manipulated four independent variables in the context of what appeared to be an opinion poll about the problem of racism on college campuses. Experimental confederates assisted with the manipulation of the first two variables, direction of normative influence (favorable to egalitarian behavior, neutral, negative) and number of influencing agents (one or two). Either one or two white female confederates, posing as students walking to class, approached the white interviewer so that they arrived at the same time as a naive participant. The interviewer gained agreement to participate anonymously in "an opinion poll conducted for a psychology class," read a brief introduction, and then administered to the subject and confederate(s) five questions about how their college should respond to anonymous racist notes. Subjects and confederate(s) responded orally after each item. The experimenter instructed the confederate(s) to answer each question before the subject in the favorable and unfavorable normative influence conditions. In the neutral condition, the experimenter designated the subject as the first to respond. Confederates answered each opinion item consistently with either the most antiracist end of the response continuum (favorable normative influence), the midpoint of the five-point response continuum (neutral normative influence), or the least antiracist end of the response continuum (unfavorable normative influence).

We manipulated the other two independent variables by altering the introductory remarks that preceded administration of the opinion items. Individuating information (present or absent) described a target of anonymous racist notes as a black student at the same college as the respondents, cited her major, year in school, and mentioned her participation in extracurricular activities. The self-interest invocation (present or absent) described the possibility that press coverage of racism might negatively affect the public image of the college. The order of experimental conditions was randomized.

The five opinion items were: (1) "The person who is writing these notes should be expelled"; (2) "[the institution] . . . is making too big an issue of this incident, thereby causing divisiveness on campus" (reversed); (3) "We need to have more affirmative action policies instituted at . . . [the institution]"; (4) "The person who is receiving these notes must have done something to make the author mad" (reversed); and (5) "The investigators should be allowed to take handwriting samples from everyone who lives in the house where the incident occurred." The experimenter displayed a card containing the response continuum that ranged from "strongly agree" to "strongly disagree." Subjects responded orally by providing the letter corresponding to one of the five points on the continuum. Because they were highly correlated, responses to the five items were summed to form a composite reaction to racism index.

Results

The normative influence manipulation very strongly affected reactions to racism. Participants expressed significantly more strongly antiracist sentiment when normative influence was favorable ($M = 23.54$) than when it was either neutral ($M = 18.83$), Bonferroni[2] $t(48) = 5.78$, $p < .001$, or unfavorable ($M = 18.38$), $t(48) = 6.34$, $p < .001$. The neutral and unfavorable normative influence conditions did not differ significantly. No other reliable effects were observed.

Discussion

Hearing at least one other person express strongly antiracist opinions produced dramatically more antiracist public reactions to racism than hearing others express equivocal opinions or opinions more accepting of racism. Consistent with the suggestions of others (Dovidio & Gaertner, 1983; Gaertner & Dovidio, 1986; Weigel & Howes, 1985), it appears that favorable normative influence can contribute to the establishment of a social climate that condemns racism. Hearing one or two persons express opinions more accepting of racism failed to produce significantly less-condemning responses to racism than did the neutral normative influence condition. It is possible, however, that the neutral condition may have artificially suppressed scores on the reactions to racism index by inducing responses toward the midpoint of the scale. The mean score in the neutral influence condition may simply reflect an artifact of the experimental procedures.

Experiment 2

We conducted the second experiment to clarify two issues regarding the effects of normative influence. First, Experiment 2 introduced a manipulation that allows us to discern whether conformity like that observed in Experiment 1 constitutes mere compliance (a laudable goal in and of itself) or something closer to private acceptance. Half the subjects in Experiment 2 responded to the opinion items publicly as they had in Experiment 1; the other half responded privately.

Second, in Experiment 1 the procedures for the neutral-influence condition may have inadvertently exerted some normative pressure toward the midpoint of the response continuum. Recall that we required confederates to respond to each item with the scale midpoint after the naive subject had

---

[2] *Editor's note:* A Bonferroni *t*-test adjusts statistically for the increased chances of finding a significant result when multiple *t*-tests are conducted, and is therefore a more conservative test than an unadjusted *t*-test.

provided her opinion on that item. Thus, instead of creating a neutral, no-influence condition as intended, the procedures may have produced normative pressure toward the middle of the response scale. We altered Experiment 2 so that no confederates were present in the neutral, no-influence condition. Subjects' responses to the opinion items in the revised no-influence condition should more closely parallel their personal opinions regarding antiracism policies, especially in the private-response condition.

Method

Subjects   Research participants were 72 white, undergraduate women who were interviewed in the same way as in Experiment 1. Fifteen people declined to participate over six days of interviewing, in all cases before they discovered the survey topic. We debriefed each subject immediately.

Design and Procedure   We manipulated two independent variables. One white female confederate helped orchestrate the direction of normative influence conditions (favorable, no influence, unfavorable). The interviewer read the same five opinion items used in Experiment 1 to the subject alone, in the no-influence condition, or to a subject and confederate, in the favorable and unfavorable normative-influence conditions. In the favorable and unfavorable conditions, the experimenter told the confederate to respond orally to each question before the subject. The confederate always provided the most antiracist response in the favorable normative-influence condition and the least antiracist response in the unfavorable normative-influence condition.

We manipulated the second independent variable, response format (public or private), by requiring the subject either to answer the questions orally or to write the answers on a form. The public-response condition was identical with the procedure used in Experiment 1. In the private-response condition, the experimenter handed the subject a clipboard containing the response form and an envelope. The experimenter instructed subjects to place the completed form in the envelope and seal it before returning it to her. In conditions where a confederate was present, as she handed the clipboard to the subject, the experimenter said, "I only have one clipboard. Here, you take this [to the subject] and write your answers on the form. You [to the confederate] can just tell me your answers and I'll write them down for you." The public and private conditions were identical in every other way.

Results

Changing the neutral-influence condition to a no-influence condition altered the pattern of differences among the three levels of normative influence. In contrast to Experiment 1, participants expressed significantly less antiracist sentiment when normative influence was unfavorable ($M = 17.58$) than when either there was no normative influence ($M = 20.38$), Bonferroni $t(66) = 2.61$, $p < .05$, or favorable normative influence ($M = 22.08$), $t(66) = 4.21$, $p < .001$ (see Table 1). The difference between the favorable and neutral conditions observed

TABLE 1   Mean Reactions to Racism Scores as a Function of Direction of Normative Influence and Public vs. Private Response Format

Response Format	Direction of Normative Influence		
	Favorable	*None*	*Unfavorable*
Public	23.17	20.08	16.58
Private	21.00	20.67	18.58

Note. High scores indicate more strongly antiracist sentiments on a scale that ranges from 5 to 25. There are 12 subjects per cell.

in Experiment 1 was no longer significant. Response format exerted no significant effects on reactions to racism.

Discussion

Hearing only one other person express strongly antiracist opinions produced much more strongly antiracist reactions than hearing someone express opinions more accepting of racism. The large effect of normative influence encompassed both the public-response condition, wherein especially powerful normative influence might be expected, and the private-response condition, wherein normative influence is typically more difficult to observe (Moscovici, 1985).

We were especially interested in whether the procedural alteration introduced in Experiment 2 would change the pattern of differences between the no-influence condition, on the one hand, and the favorable and unfavorable direction of normative-influence conditions, on the other. In contrast to Experiment 1, wherein the mean for the neutral condition fell much closer to the mean of the unfavorable than the favorable condition, in Experiment 2, the mean was closer to the middle of the interval.

The results of Experiment 2 clearly indicate that unfavorable normative pressure does affect the expression of antiracist sentiments. Subjects who observed another person voice opinions more accepting of racism expressed significantly less antiracist opinions than those who observed no one else offer opinions. This effect of overheard opinions parallels other research findings in the area of intergroup relations showing that overhearing another member of the ingroup apply a derogatory ethnic label to a member of the outgroup results in less-favorable evaluations of the target of the label and of any ingroup persons associated with the target (Greenberg & Pyszczynski, 1985; Kirkland, Greenberg, & Pyszczynski, 1987).

Conclusions

Antiracist sentiment is malleable. The goal of creating social settings that maximize the public expression of strong, antiracist opinions and minimize the expression of discriminatory and insensitive behavior might be advanced by the efforts of a few outspoken persons who vigorously advocate antiracist positions and by the presence of norms consistent with those views. It is just as clear, however, that the presence of voices antagonistic to the goals of eliminating racism produces the opposite effect. Our findings suggest that attention to the normative features of the social settings where blacks and whites interact is warranted.

REFERENCES

Blanchard, F. A. (1989). Effective affirmative action programs. In F. A. Blanchard & F. J. Crosby (Eds.), *Affirmative action in perspective* (pp. 193–208). New York: Springer-Verlag.

Cohen, E. G. (1982). Expectation states and interracial interaction in school settings. In R. H. Turner & J. F. Short (Eds.), *Annual Review of Sociology* (Vol. 8, pp. 209–235). Palo Alto, CA: Annual Reviews, Inc.

Cook, S. W. (1978). Interpersonal and attitudinal outcomes in cooperating interracial groups. *Journal of Research and Development in Education, 12*, 97–113.

Cook, S. W. (1984). Cooperative interaction in multiethnic contexts. In N. Miller & M. B. Brewer (Eds.), *Groups in contact: The psychology of desegregation* (pp. 155–185). Orlando, FL: Academic Press.

Dovidio, J. F., & Gaertner, S. L. (1983). Race, normative structure, and help seeking. In B. M. DePaulo, A. Nadler, & J. P. Fisher (Eds.), *New directions in helping* (Vol. 2, pp. 285–303). New York: Academic Press.

Farrell, W. C., & Jones, C. K. (1988). Recent racial incidents in higher education: A preliminary perspective. *The Urban Review, 20*, 211–226.

Gaertner, S. L., & Dovidio, J. F. (1986). The aversive form of racism. In J. F. Dovidio & S. L. Gaertner (Eds.), *Prejudice, discrimination, and racism* (pp. 61–89). Orlando, FL: Academic Press.

Greenberg, J., & Pyszczynski, T. (1985). The effects of an overheard ethnic slur on evaluations of the target: How to spread a social disease. *Journal of Experimental Social Psychology, 21*, 61–72.

Kirkland, S. L., Greenberg, J., & Pyszczynski, T. (1987). Further evidence of the deleterious effects of overheard derogatory ethnic labels: Derogation beyond the target. *Personality and Social Psychology Bulletin, 13*, 216–227.

Moscovici, S. (1985). Social influence and conformity. In G. Lindzey & E. Aronson (Eds.), *Handbook of Social Psychology* (3rd ed., Vol. 2, pp. 347–412). New York: Random House.

Pettigrew, T. F. (1985). New Black-White patterns: How best to conceptualize them? In R. H. Turner & J. F. Short (Eds.), *Annual Review of Sociology* (Vol. 11, pp. 329–346). Palo Alto, CA: Annual Reviews, Inc.

Pettigrew, T. F. (1961). Social psychology and desegregation research. *American Psychologist, 16*, 105–112.

Sherif, M., & Sherif, C. W. (1953). *Groups in harmony and tension*. New York: Harper.

Stephan, W. G., & Stephan, C. W. (1984). The role of ignorance in intergroup relations. In N. Miller & M. B. Brewer (Eds.), *Groups in contact: The psychology of desegregation* (pp. 229–255). Orlando, FL: Academic Press.

Weigel, R. H., & Howes, P. W. (1985). Conceptions of racial prejudice: Symbolic racism reconsidered. *Journal of Social Issues, 41(3)*, 117–138.

Yarrow, M. R., Campbell, J. D., & Yarrow, L. J. (1958). Acquisition of new norms: A study of racial desegregation. *Journal of Social Issues, 14(1)*, 8–28.

The Part of You That Chooses

Every time you make a choice you are turning the central part of you, the part of you that chooses, into something a little different from what it was before.

—C. S. Lewis, 1943

LONG–RANGE EXPERIMENTAL MODIFICATION OF VALUES, ATTITUDES, AND BEHAVIOR

MILTON ROKEACH

Since the summer of 1966, a major portion of the research effort at Michigan State University has been devoted to a systematic investigation of the effects of experimentally induced feelings of self-dissatisfaction on long-range changes in values, attitudes, and behavior. To date, a number of experiments have been carried out in which states of self-dissatisfaction have been induced concerning one's values, attitudes, and behavior, and in which the long-range effects of such induced states have been objectively ascertained. The general procedure employed in all these experiments is basically the same, as follows:

The experimental subjects (college students at Michigan State University, 97% of whom are white[1]) are first asked to rank 18 values (see Table 1) in order of importance, and also to state their position in writing toward civil rights demonstrations. They are then shown Table 1 and Table 2 which are reproduced here. Table 1, the subjects are informed, shows the average rankings that had been previously obtained from Michigan State University students. The experimenter draws specific attention to two target values—equality and freedom. More precisely, their attention is drawn to the finding that previously tested college students had ranked freedom first and equality eleventh on the average. To arouse feelings of self-dissatisfaction, the experimenter then interprets these findings to mean that "Michigan State University students, in general, are much more interested in their own freedom than they are in the freedom for other people." The experimental subjects are then invited to compare their own rankings of the same 18 values with the results shown in Table 1.

Then, to increase the level of self-dissatisfaction to an even greater degree, subjects are asked to state the extent of their sympathy with the aims of civil rights demonstrators as follows: (a) "Yes, and I have personally participated in a civil rights demonstration"; (b) "Yes, but I have not participated in a civil rights demonstration"; (c) "No." Immediately afterward, they are shown Table 2 which displays a highly significant positive relationship between attitude toward civil rights demonstrations and value for equality.

The experimenter then interprets the results shown in Table 2 as follows:

This raises the question as to whether those who are *against* civil rights are really saying that they care a great deal about *their own* freedom but are

---

[1]*Editor's note:* A figure of 97% was not unusual for American universities in 1971, when this article was first published. The current percentage of White students at Michigan State University is approximately 80%.

TABLE 1   Rank Order of Importance to 298 Michigan State University Students

Rank	Value
13	A comfortable life
12	An exciting life
6	A sense of accomplishment
10	A world at peace
17	A world of beauty
11	Equality
9	Family security
1	Freedom
2	Happiness
8	Inner harmony
5	Mature love
16	National security
18	Pleasure
14	Salvation
15	Social recognition
4	Self-respect
7	True friendship
3	Wisdom

TABLE 2   Average Rankings of Freedom and Equality by Michigan State University Students for and Against Civil Rights

Value	Yes, and have participated	Yes, but have not participated	No, not sympathetic to civil rights
Freedom	6	1	2
Equality	5	11	17
Difference	+1	−10	−15

indifferent to other people's freedom. Those who are *for* civil rights are perhaps really saying they not only want freedom for themselves, but for other people too.

Once again the subjects are invited to compare their own rankings of equality and freedom and their own position on the civil rights issue with the results shown in Table 2.

By this self-confrontation procedure, many of the experimental subjects become aware for perhaps the first time in their lives of certain inconsistencies existing within their own value-attitude systems. For example, some subjects discover to their dismay that they had placed a high value on freedom but a low value on equality; others discover that they had expressed a pro-civil-rights attitude, yet had ranked equality relatively low in their value hierarchy, etc.

At the end of the experimental treatment, measurements of self-dissatisfaction are obtained by having the subjects rate, on an 11–point scale, how satisfied or dissatisfied they are in general with what they had found out about their values and attitudes. They also indicate whether they are satisfied or dissatisfied with their ranking of each of the 18 values considered separately.

The control group merely fill out the value and attitude scales and are then dismissed. They are not shown Tables 1 and 2 and thus have no opportunity to think about or to discover that they might hold incompatible values, or an attitude that is incompatible with one or more of their values, or that they had engaged in behavior that is incompatible with their values or attitudes.

Experimental and control subjects are typically tested in groups of 20–25 at a time. The experimental session lasts for about 30–40 minutes and the control session for about 20 minutes.

Experiment 1

A preliminary report of Experiment 1 has already been published (Rokeach, 1968a, 1968b). The major findings were (a) that induced states of self-dissatisfaction concerning one's values and attitudes led to highly significant changes in values and attitudes that were evident 3–5 months after the experimental treatment. Moreover, (b) measures of self-satisfaction-dissatisfaction, obtained at the end of the experimental session, predicted the value changes that were observed 3 weeks and 3–5 months afterward.

We were extremely reluctant, however, to accept these experimental findings as evidence of real, genuine long-range changes in values and attitudes because it seems unlikely that any single and brief experimental session could have resulted in such long-range changes. More convincing evidence that such changes are indeed real would require additional data concerning behavioral effects as well as effects on values and attitudes (measured by paper-and-pencil tests), following the experimental treatment. Experiments 2 and 3 were therefore carried out in order to determine the long-range effects of procedures designed to induce feelings of self-dissatisfaction on real-life behavior as well as on values and attitudes.

Experiments 2 and 3

These two experiments are basically identical to Experiment 1 except that unobtrusive measures of behavioral effects were obtained as well as measures of value and attitude change. Moreover, posttest measures were extended to include a much longer time interval following the experimental treatment. Dependent measures (values, attitudes, and behavior) were obtained 3 weeks, 3–5 months, 15–17 months, and 21 months after the experimental treatment.

The subjects of Experiments 2 and 3 were entering freshmen of two newly founded small residential colleges at Michigan State University: James Madison College, for students interested in the social sciences (Experiment 2); Lyman Briggs College, for students interested in the natural sciences (Experiment 3). Experiments 2 and 3 were identical in all respects except that they were carried out with these two different types of college freshmen. As already described, the experimental treatment was designed to induce feelings of self-dissatisfaction by making the subjects consciously aware that they held certain incompatible values or that they held an attitude that is incompatible with certain of their values. And, as already stated, the only difference in the treatment of the experimental and control subjects was that the experimental subjects were exposed to Tables 1 and 2, and to brief interpretations of these tables, while control subjects were not.

Pretest measures of values and attitudes showed no significant differences between experimental and control groups. More specifically, experimental and control subjects were not significantly different from one another in their pretest rankings of equality or freedom or position on civil rights. Posttest measures were obtained not only for values and attitudes, but also for various kinds of behavior. The best unobtrusive measure, obtained 3–5 months after and also 15–17 months after the experimental treatment, involved a direct solicitation by first-class letter from the National Association for the Advancement of Colored People (on NAACP letterhead) addressed to each subject individually. The letter invited the subject to join the NAACP. To join, the subject had to (a) fill out an application blank, (b) enclose $1, and (c) drop the prestamped return envelope into a United States mailbox.

The results pertaining to value and attitude change for the three posttest periods are shown in Table 3.

Table 3 shows that significant increases in value for equality and freedom were found for the experimental subjects on all three posttests. Fifteen to 17 months after the experimental session, for example, the experimental group had increased its ranking of equality an average of 2.68 units (on an 18–point ranking scale), while the control group had increased its ranking of equality only .32 units. Similarly, 15–17 months after the experimental session, the experimental group had increased its ranking of freedom an average of 1.59 units, while the control group had increased its ranking of freedom only .22 units. These findings, therefore, suggest long-range value change as a result of the experimental treatment.

TABLE 3 **Mean Increases in Value for Equality and Freedom and in Pro-Civil-Rights Attitude for Experimental and Control Groups**

	Posttest 1 (3 weeks later)		Posttest 2 (3–5 months later)		Posttest 3 (15–17 months later)	
Value	Experimental	Control	Experimental	Control	Experimental	Control
Equality	1.91**	.68	2.80**	.71	2.68**	.32
Freedom	1.48**	.20	1.16*	.21	1.59**	.22
Equal rights for Negroes	−.46	−.69	2.09*	.20	2.79**	.86

Note.—Madison and Briggs data combined.
*$p < .01$.
**$p < .001$.

Consider next the findings concerning attitude change (equal rights for Negroes). The findings at Posttest 1—three weeks after the experimental session—showed a "sleeper" effect: no change in the experimental group at Posttest 1, and in fact, a slight "backlash effect." But significant increases in pro-civil-rights attitude were found for the experimental group at Posttests 2 and 3, suggesting long-range attitude change as well as value change. In contrast, no significant value or attitude changes were observed in control subjects for any of the three posttest measures. After 15–17 months in college, the subjects in the control groups had essentially the same values for equality and freedom and the same attitude toward civil rights they had started with.

Consider next the results shown in Table 4 that pertain to the first NAACP solicitation initiated 3–5 months after the experimental treatment. Forty subjects responded to this solicitation by joining the NAACP, and an additional 13 subjects responded by writing a sympathetic, pro-civil-rights letter asking for more literature or information about the NAACP as a civil rights organization. Thus, a total of 53 persons out of 366 responded to the NAACP solicitation. Of these 53, 39 were experimental subjects, and only 14 were control subjects. This difference between experimental and control groups is statistically significant at the .002 level of confidence.

Table 5 shows the results of an identical NAACP solicitation initiated a full year after the first solicitation—15–17 months after the experimental treatment. All experimental and control subjects still in school were once again invited to join the NAACP or, if they had previously joined, to renew their membership by paying their $1 annual dues. This second solicitation resulted in 6 new NAACP members—5 experimental and 1 control. It moreover yielded 11 additional letters, all favorable in tone, requesting more information about the NAACP, 7 coming from experimental subjects and 4 from control subjects. Six subjects renewed their membership, 3 renewals coming from experimental subjects and 3 from control subjects. Finally, 2 subjects who had joined the previous year wrote indignant letters complaining that they had not heard from the NAACP all year. Both of these letters came from experimental subjects. All told, a total of 17 experimental subjects responded to this second NAACP solicitation as against 8 control subjects. While these findings fall somewhat short of statistical significance, they are highly consistent with those obtained from the first solicitation (Table 4).

TABLE 4   Number of Persons Responding to First NAACP Solicitation: 3–5 Months After Experimental Treatment

Group	Joined NAACP	Wrote positive letter asking for more information about NAACP	No response	Total
Experimental	29	10	158	197
Control	11	3	155	169
Total	40	13	213	366

TABLE 5   Number of Persons Responding to Second NAACP Solicitation: 15–17 Months After Experimental Treatment

Group	Joined NAACP	Wrote positive letter asking for more information about NAACP	Renewed membership	NAACP member wrote letter complaining he had not heard from NAACP all year	No response	Total
Experimental	5	7	3	2	159	176
Control	1	4	3	0	139	147
Total	6	11	6	2	298	323

TABLE 6   Number of Persons Responding to First and Second NAACP Solicitations

Group	Responded to NAACP appeal	No response	Total
Experimental	51	146	197
Control	18	151	169
Total	69	297	366

When the results of the NAACP solicitations from both years are combined, the findings shown in Table 6 are obtained. A total of 69 persons out of 366—about 20%—had responded to the NAACP solicitations. Fifty-one of these were experimental subjects, and only 18 were control subjects.[2] This represents a response rate of about 1 out of 10 for the control subjects compared with 1 out of 4 for the experimental subjects. These findings are significant beyond the .001 level. When considered along with the findings previously presented, they suggest long-range behavioral effects as well as long-range value and attitude changes as a result of the experimental treatment.

Conclusions

Obviously, the finding that relatively enduring changes in values, attitudes, and behavior can be brought about as a result of a rather brief experimental treatment has important implications for the fields of political science and propaganda, as well as for the fields of education and therapy. If we have indeed learned how to bring about changes in values, attitudes, and behavior, as I think the experiments described here suggest, we must make certain that this kind of knowledge will be put to use for the benefit

---

[2]One subject wrote letters requesting more information in response to both NAACP solicitations.

rather than the detriment of mankind. At the same time, it is also necessary to ensure that scientific research will continue to be encouraged on what is perhaps the most distinctively human of all human problems, namely, the nature of human value systems and how they affect social attitudes and social behavior.

REFERENCES

Rokeach, M. (1968). *Beliefs, attitudes, and values.* San Francisco: Jossey-Bass. (a)
Rokeach, M. (1968). A theory of organization and change within value-attitude systems. *Journal of Social Issues, 24,* 13–33. (b)

THE ROLE OF EMPATHY IN IMPROVING INTERGROUP RELATIONS

WALTER G. STEPHAN AND KRYSTINA FINLAY

Granma said you couldn't love something you didn't understand

—CARTER, 1976, p. 38

The study of empathy has a long and rich history in the social sciences (Cooley, 1902; Coutu, 1951; Mead, 1934; Piaget, 1932; Turner, 1956). In general, researchers and theorists agree there are two basic types of empathy: cognitive empathy and emotional empathy (Davis, 1994; Duan & Hill, 1996). Although many terms are used to label these two types of empathy, the first clearly refers primarily to taking the perspective of another person, whereas the second refers primarily to emotional responses to another person that either are similar to those the other person is experiencing (parallel empathy) or are a reaction to the emotional experiences of the other person (reactive empathy).

To illustrate the distinction between reactive and parallel empathy, imagine that you are observing a member of an ethnic outgroup as an ethnic ugly slur is uttered. If you sympathize with this person's pain and discomfort, you are experiencing reactive empathy (your emotional reaction to the other's situation), whereas if you respond with feelings of indignation and resentment toward the person who uttered the slur, you are more likely experiencing parallel empathy (feeling emotions similar to those of the outgroup member). What we will refer to as cognitive empathy has often been labeled perspective taking and role taking, and what we are referring to as emotional empathy has often been labeled as sympathy, affective empathy, or emotional responsiveness.

Research indicates that empathy has a host of beneficial effects on attitudes and behavior, whereas a lack of empathy has a host of negative effects on attitudes and behavior. A well-established finding is that empathic concern causes helping (Batson, 1991; Davis, 1994; Oswald, 1996). The standard paradigm involves having people read about the plight of another person under varying types of instructions. People are then given an opportunity to assist the person in need. When people read about the plight of others under instructions to engage in emotional empathy, they subsequently offer more help than those who read about the plight of others under instructions that blunt empathic responding.

Although studies done in this tradition have not generally explored attitudes toward the people who are suffering, several recent studies have done so. In one set of studies, Batson and his colleagues asked students to read scenarios involving individuals who were suffering and then measured attitudes toward the groups of which these individuals were members (Batson, Polycarpou et al., 1997). They found that reading these scenarios under emotional empathy instructions led to more favorable attitudes than did reading the same materials under instructions designed to minimize empathy. Using this procedure, they found changes in attitudes toward people suffering from HIV/AIDS or homelessness, as well as for prisoners on death row. In one of these studies the attitude changes were present 2 weeks after the students read the scenarios, suggesting that the attitude changes may be lasting.

We have conducted research in a related vein, using a racial group as the target group (Finlay & Stephan, 2000). The White students in this study read a series of vignettes depicting everyday acts of discrimination directed toward African Americans. The vignettes were presented to students as a set of short essays written in the first person by African American freshmen attending college. The vignettes included instances of African Americans being falsely accused of wrongdoing, being denied check-writing privileges, overhearing racially slanderous remarks, and being perceived as a threat simply because of their race. In the empathy condition the students were asked to "imagine how each writer feels . . . [and] identify with their feelings and responses to the situation." As part of a separate study, the students were then asked to evaluate both African Americans and Whites. The central finding was that reading vignettes about African Americans who had suffered from discrimination, under instructions to empathize with the victims, eliminated the differences between evaluations of African Americans and Whites that were found in the control condition. Students in this condition also reported experiencing more of the parallel empathic emotions (anger, annoyance, hostility, discomfort, and disgust) than students in the control condition.

Nonexperimental studies have shown that a lack of empathy is associated with sexual aggression among men (Lisak & Ivan, 1995), child abuse (Letourneau, 1981), antisocial behaviors (Eysenck, 1981), and negative attitudes toward homosexuals (Johnson, Brems, & Alford-Keating, 1997). At the opposite end of the spectrum, studies of empathic concern have found that it is related to prosocial behavior. For instance, one study found that for children both empathic concern and perspective taking were related to teacher ratings of the students' helpfulness (Litvack-Miller, McDougall, & Romney, 1997). In another study it was found that perspective taking skills were associated with the inhibition of aggression (Richardson, Hammock, & Smith, 1994). Thus, both situational and dispositional empathy are related to prosocial attitudes and behaviors, whereas a lack of empathy is linked to antisocial behaviors.

A number of studies have shown that it is possible to increase levels of empathy through training programs (Crabb, Morocco, & Bender, 1983; Goldstein & Michaels, 1985). For instance, one program found that training social work students by having them imagine the emotional responses of their clients increased levels of empathy (Erera, 1997). In another study it was found that an empathy-oriented rape awareness training program that included discussions of case histories increased empathy for victims of rape (Pinzone-Glover, Gidycz, & Jacobs, 1998). A third study found that training medical students in empathy for the elderly led to increases in empathy and more favorable attitudes toward the elderly (Pacala, Boult, Bland, & O'Brien, 1995).

Feshbach (1989) developed a program in which children aged 7–11 were provided with 30 hours of training in cognitive and emotional empathy. This training led to reductions in aggression and increases in prosocial behavior and self-esteem. A developmental study by Doyle and Aboud (1995) measured children's role-taking abilities and their attitudes toward racial outgroups in kindergarten and again in the third grade. The children who improved the most in role-taking abilities displayed the greatest reductions in prejudice. In this study naturally occurring changes in cognitive empathy abilities were associated with reduced prejudice in children, which suggests that increasing empathy may improve intergroup relations.

Intergroup Relations Programs That Incorporate Empathy

Despite the widespread use of empathy in intergroup relations programs, few programs actually measure empathy as either a mediating or outcome variable. One exception consists of studies of the "jigsaw classroom." The jigsaw classroom and other cooperative learning techniques involve bringing children of different racial and ethnic groups together to work cooperatively on academic materials. Bridgeman (1981) believes that when children work interdependently with children from other groups, they learn to take the role of the other students and learn to view the world from their perspectives. In her study, the empathy scores of children in cooperative jigsaw groups increased over the course of the study (8 weeks), whereas the empathy scores of children in control classes did not. Aronson and Bridgeman (1979) argue that the improvements in intergroup relations that occur in jigsaw classrooms (Aronson, Blaney, Stephan, Sikes, & Snapp, 1978; Aronson & Patnoe, 1997) are due in part to empathy.

Other intergroup relations programs explicitly use empathy-oriented techniques. For instance, empathy is an explicit component of the conflict resolution workshops that have been used to foster mutual understanding between members of opposing groups (Burton, 1986, 1987; Doob, 1974; Kelman, 1990; Kelman & Cohen, 1986; Rouhana & Kelman, 1994). In these workshops, conflict is presented as a problem to be solved, not a contest to be won. The participants are urged to engage in role taking so they can learn to view the conflict from the perspective of people on the other side. The goal of these workshops is to improve relations between the opposing parties by generating changed perceptions and new ideas for resolving the conflict.

Most multicultural education programs involve empathy. Students typically read material about different groups, watch movies and videos, and engage in exercises designed to give them insight into the values, norms, and behaviors of other groups. Only a limited number of studies of the effects of multicultural education exist. For instance, Litcher and Johnson (1969) examined the use of a multiethnic reader by White second-grade students. This program led to more favorable attitudes toward African Americans. Colca and her colleagues (Colca, Lowen, Colca, & Lord, 1982) examined the effects of a semester-long program for fourth and fifth graders that included small group discussions, films, role playing, games, and experiential exercises. The program led to improved racial attitudes and decreased social distance among both African American and White students.

Theoretical Accounts of Empathy as a Mediator of Attitudes and Behavior

Researchers have proposed several explanations to account for the mediational role of empathy in improving intergroup relations. The effects of cognitive empathy on prejudice may be mediated by reductions in perceptions of dissimilarity and feelings of threat. Prejudice toward outgroups is often associated with exaggerated perceptions of intergroup differences and high levels of fear and threat (Rokeach & Mezei, 1966; Stephan & Stephan, 2000; Triandis & Davis, 1965). Cognitive empathy may reduce prejudice because it leads people to see that they are less different from members of the other group than they thought they were. In laboratory studies, creating a sense of a common identity has been found to reduce prejudice and discrimination (Gaertner, Mann, Dovidio, Murrell, & Pomare, 1990). Understanding the ways that others view the world has the potential to make them seem less alien and frightening and thus to break down the perceived barriers between the ingroup and the outgroup.

Parallel empathy leads to attitude change by arousing feelings of injustice (Finlay & Stephan, 2000). Feelings of injustice can counteract prejudice, particularly if the prejudice is based on beliefs in a just world (Lerner, 1980). People who believe the world is just and that others receive what they deserve tend to blame the suffering of outgroup members on negative traits they possess. However, empathizing with victims may lead people to reappraise their assumptions concerning blame, and they may come to believe that the victims do not deserve the mistreatment to which they are being subjected.

There may also be an element of cognitive dissonance involved in the changes in attitude brought about by empathy. Empathizing with a member of an outgroup toward which one has previously held negative attitudes may create dissonance due to the discrepancy between the individual's current empathic concern and his or her prior negative attitudes. As a means of reducing this dissonance, the person may change his or her attitudes toward the previously disliked outgroup. A similar process has been suggested for people who engage in exercises that involve actively playing the role of outgroup members (McGregor, 1993). Role playing seems to require both cognitive and emotional empathy.

Each of these explanations suggests reasons why it is difficult to hate the people with whom you empathize. In the following section we consider the ways in which empathy can be incorporated into intergroup relations programs, and we employ these mediational explanations to help us understand the role empathy can play.

The Role of Empathy in Improving Intergroup Relations

In intergroup relations programs it is often assumed that reading information about the experiences of another group or listening to the members of an outgroup describe their experiences creates empathy for that group. This may well be the case for people who have high levels of empathy, but even for these people and certainly for others, empathic responses could probably be strengthened by explicitly encouraging participants to empathize with the members of the other group (e.g., Batson, Polycarpou et al., 1997; Finlay & Stephan, 2000). Suggestions to empathize could be offered by group facilitators and could stress emotional empathy, cognitive empathy, or both.

As the research on empathy training programs indicates, empathy can also be explicitly taught (Barak, 1990; Erera, 1997; Pinzone-Glover et al., 1998). For example, in a simulation game designed to create empathy, third-grade students were divided into two groups and asked to wear either orange or green armbands. The orange-banded children then experienced a day in which they were negatively stereotyped, discriminated against, and not praised by the teacher. The roles were reversed on a second day. The students exposed to this experience were less prejudiced than a comparison group, and the changes in attitude persisted for at least 2 weeks (Weiner & Wright, 1973).

When people do empathize with outgroups, their empathic reactions can take three forms: cognitive empathy, reactive empathy, and parallel empathy. Cognitive empathy is likely to be useful in acquiring knowledge about the outgroup, including coming to understand the worldview of members of the other group and learning about their cultural practices, norms, values, beliefs, and rules, as well as learning about the way the outgroup views the ingroup. Cognitive empathy may be more effective in changing stereotypes than either type of emotional empathy.

Reactive empathy can lead to two different types of emotional responses (Davis, 1994). One consists of compassion-related emotions that arise from a feeling of concern for the suffering of the other, usually labeled empathic concern. These emotions tend to be predominantly positive and are likely to lead to favorable changes in attitudes toward the outgroup. The other type of reactive empathy consists primarily of negative emotions evoked by the suffering of the other. These emotions can include feelings of anxiety, threat, and revulsion and are unlikely to lead to improvements in intergroup relations. Therefore, reactive empathy can lead to either positive or negative emotional reactions.

The emotional responses elicited by parallel empathy may also be positive or negative. For instance, outgroup members are likely to respond to an ethnic slur with negative emotions, but they are likely to respond to favorable outcomes (e.g., winning a competitive game) with positive emotions. Thus, reactive and parallel emotions may share the same valence (e.g., both positive), or they may differ in valence (one type being positive and the other negative). Learning about the suffering caused by discrimination may lead to the reactive emotional responses of compassion and concern along with the parallel emotional reactions of dread, confusion, and perhaps anger toward one's own ingroup.

When empathy creates dissonance, people are caught in an uncomfortable dilemma. Rokeach (1971) demonstrated that when White students were confronted with the discrepancy between their attitudes and behavior toward minorities and their beliefs in freedom, they responded by changing both their attitudes and their behaviors toward minority group members. Similarly, when reactive empathy creates dissonance, participants may change their attitudes to be consistent with the feelings of compassion they are experiencing toward the outgroup.

Recommendations for the Use of Empathy in Intergroup Relations Programs

Although a great many intergroup relations programs have employed procedures designed to create empathy, most have done so without a careful consideration of the subtleties of the process or an explicit understanding of what they are trying to accomplish. Thus, our first recommendation is that intergroup relations trainers, facilitators, and educators devote some careful attention to deciding what their goals are and how to achieve them. Then they can match their procedures to their goals. If the goal is greater understanding, cognitive empathy may be called for, but if it is social action, parallel empathy is more likely to prove successful.

Our second recommendation is to beware of the pitfalls of empathy. The literature is replete with studies of unsuccessful intergroup relations programs (see Bigler, 1999). Also, empathy can be introduced in ways that blunt its impact. In discussing this issue, Boler (1997) suggests that techniques designed to activate empathy run the risk of creating compassion without simultaneously leading participants to recognize that they themselves are implicated in the social forces responsible for the suffering with which they are empathizing. Another risk of activating empathy is that the greater the identification with the victim, the greater the possibility that the participants will fear that similar suffering could befall them, which may lead to defensive avoidance. If people feel threatened, this may distance them from the victims of discrimination and could actually lead to more negative attitudes.

Our third recommendation is that trainers implement empathy in ways that are most likely to maximize its impact. We urge trainers not to leave the induction of empathy up to chance. Invite participants to identify with members of the other group as they read about them or listen to them. Pose questions to the participants that they can ask themselves while reading or listening, such as, "What emotions are the members of the other group feeling, what are they thinking, how are they viewing the world, and how do you feel about their responses to the situation?" One way to achieve a more active stance toward empathy consists of role-playing exercises or paraphrasing exercises in which people actively take the role of the other and write about or speak from the perspective of the other.

The fourth recommendation is that intergroup relations trainers who are contemplating the use of empathy interventions attend to a host of issues that may influence its effectiveness. What is the age of the participants (for a developmental analysis of the relationship of prejudice to role-taking skills, see Doyle & Aboud, 1995)? How similar are members of the two groups in terms of social class and other status variables that might be relevant in the context? What are the attitudes of the participants toward the other group and the intervention itself (for a discussion of these and other issues related to implementation, see Bargal, 1992)?

A Caveat . . .

Most of this discussion has assumed that the participants are members of the majority group and the groups to be empathized with are minority groups. We emphasized this pairing because in hierarchical social systems it is typically the prejudices, stereotypes, and discriminatory behavior of majority group members that is the greatest problem. However, many intergroup relations programs also include members of minority groups, and it is reasonable to ask if empathy is also useful in helping them to understand and interact with members of the majority group. We believe the answer to this question is a definite "yes," but we would qualify it by saying that perhaps it is more important to emphasize cognitive empathy with minority participants than it is to emphasize reactive and parallel empathy. Generally speaking, members of the majority group do not suffer from discrimination at the hands of minority group members, but they may well be the targets of stereotypes and prejudice, and their worldview, values, beliefs, norms, and practices often do differ from those of the minority group.

. . . and a Conclusion

We have argued that empathy takes three forms, cognitive, reactive, and parallel. Empathy can be induced through simple instructions, and training can be used to increase it. Its presence is associated with prosocial behavior and its absence with antisocial behavior. Empathy is widely used as a technique to improve intergroup relations, but usually without clear goals or an understanding of how it operates. It can be created through a variety of means, its effects are mediated by several different processes, and it can have a positive effect on both attitudes and behaviors. Empathy can also have negative consequences, so attention must be given to maximizing its beneficial effects. This involves being consciously aware of the goals one is attempting to achieve, carefully selecting means that will accomplish these goals, and explicitly assessing this process so that it can be improved in the future. We believe that used effectively, empathy shows great promise of increasing the beneficial effects of intergroup relations programs.

REFERENCES

Aronson, E., Blaney, N., Stephan, C., Sikes, J., & Snapp, M. (1978). *The jigsaw classroom.* Beverly Hills, CA: Sage.

Aronson, E., & Bridgeman, D. (1979). Jigsaw groups and the desegregated classroom: In pursuit of common goals. *Personality and Social Psychology Bulletin, 5,* 438–446.

Aronson, E., & Patnoe, S. (1997). *The jigsaw classroom.* New York: Longman.

Barak, A. (1990). Counselor training in empathy by a game procedure. *Counselor Education and Supervision, 29,* 170–186.

Bargal, D. (1992). Conflict management workshops for Arab and Palestinian youth—A framework for planning, intervention, and evaluation. *Social Work With Groups, 15,* 51–68.

Batson, C. D. (1991). *The altruism question: Toward a social psychological answer.* Hillsdale, NJ: Erlbaum.

Batson, C. D., Polycarpou, M. P., Harmon-Jones, E., Imhoff, H. J., Mitchener, E. C., Bednar, L. L., Klein, T. R., & Highberger, L. (1997). Empathy and attitudes: Can feeling for a member of a stigmatized group improve feelings toward the group? *Journal of Personality and Social Psychology, 72,* 105–118.

Bigler, R. S. (1999). The use of multicultural curricula and materials to counter racism in children. *Journal of Social Issues, 55,* 687–705.

Boler, M. (1997). The risks of empathy: Interrogating multiculturalism's gaze. *Cultural Studies, 11,* 253–273.

Bridgeman, D. (1981). Enhanced role taking through cooperative interdependence: A field study. *Child Development, 52,* 1231–1238.

Burton, J. W. (1986). The procedures of conflict resolution. In E. E. Azar and R. W. Burton (Eds.), *International conflict resolution: Theory and practice* (pp. 92–116). Boulder, CO: Lynne Reiner.

Burton, J. W. (1987). *Resolving deep-rooted conflict.* Lanham, MD: University Press of America.

Carter, F. (1976). *The education of Little Tree.* Albuquerque, NM: University of New Mexico Press.

Colca, C., Lowen, D., Colca, L. A., & Lord, S. A. (1982). Combating racism in the schools: A group work pilot project. *Social Work in Education, 5,* 5–18.

Cooley, G. H. (1902). *Human nature and social order.* New York: Scribner's.

Coutu, W. (1951). Role playing versus role taking: A request for clarification. *American Sociological Review, 16,* 180–187.

Crabb, W. T., Moracco, J. C., & Bender, R. C. (1983). A comparative study of empathy training with programmed instruction for lay helpers. *Journal of Counseling Psychology, 30,* 221–226.

Davis, M. H. (1994). *Empathy: A social psychological approach.* Madison, WI: Brown and Benchmark.

Doob, L. W. (1974). A Cyprus workshop: An exercise in intervention methodology. *Journal of Social Psychology, 84,* 161–178.

Doyle, A. B., & Aboud, F. E. (1995). A longitudinal study of White children's racial prejudice as a social-cognitive development. *Merrill-Palmer Quarterly, 41,* 209–228.

Duan, C., & Hill, C. E. (1996). The current state of empathy research. *Journal of Counseling Psychology, 43,* 261–274.

Erera, P. I. (1997). Empathy training for helping professionals: Model and evaluation. *Journal of Social Work Education, 33,* 245–260.

Eysenck, S. B. G. (1981). Impulsive and antisocial behavior in children. *Current Psychological Research, 1,* 31–37.

Feshbach, N. D. (1989). Empathy training and prosocial behavior. In J. Groebel and R. A. Hinde (Ed.), *Aggression and war: Their biological and social bases* (pp. 101–111). Cambridge, England: Cambridge University Press.

Finlay, K. A., & Stephan, W. G. (2000). Improving intergroup relations: The effects of empathy on racial attitudes. *Journal of Applied Social Psychology, 30,* 1720–1737.

Gaertner, S. L., Mann, J., Dovidio, J. F., Murrell, A., & Pomare, M. (1990). How does cooperation reduce intergroup bias? *Journal of Personality and Social Psychology, 59,* 692–704.

Goldstein, A. P., & Michaels, G. Y. (1985). *Empathy: Development, training, and consequences.* Hilldsale, NJ: Erlbaum.

Johnson, M. E., Brems, C., & Afford-Keating, P. (1997). Personality correlates of homophobia. *Journal of Homosexuality, 34,* 57–69.

Kelman, H. C. (1990). Interactive problem-solving: A social psychological approach to conflict resolution. In J. Burton and F. Dukes (Eds.), *Conflict: Readings in management and resolution* (pp. 199–215). New York: St. Martin's Press.

Kelman, H. C., & Cohen, S. P. (1986). Resolution of international conflict: An international approach. In S. Worchel and W. G. Austin (Eds.), *Psychology of intergroup relations* (pp. 323–432). Chicago: Nelson Hall.

Lerner, M. J. (1980). *Beliefs in a just world: A fundamental illusion.* New York: Plenum.

Letourneau, C. (1981). Empathy and stress: How they affect parental aggression. *Journal of Social Work, 26,* 383–389.

Lisak, D., & Ivan, C. (1995). Deficits in intimacy and empathy in sexually aggressive men. *Journal of Interpersonal Violence, 10,* 296–308.

Litcher, J. H., & Johnson, D. W. (1969). Changes in attitudes toward Negroes of White elementary school students after use of multiethnic readers. *Journal of Educational Psychology, 60,* 148–152.

Litvack-Miller, W., McDougall, D., & Romney, D. M. (1997). The structure of empathy during middle childhood and its relationship to prosocial behavior. *Genetic, Social, and General Psychology Monographs, 123,* 303–324.

McGregor, J. (1993). Effectiveness of role playing and antiracist teaching in reducing student prejudice. *Journal of Educational Research, 86,* 215–226.

Mead, G. H. (1934). *Mind, self, and society from the standpoint of a social behaviorist.* Chicago: University of Chicago Press.

Oswald, P. A. (1996). The effects of cognitive and affective perspective taking on empathic concern and altruistic helping. *Journal of Social Psychology, 136,* 613–623.

Pacala, J. T., Boult, C., Bland, C., & O'Brien, J. (1995). Aging game improves medical students caring for elders. *Gerontology and Geriatrics Education, 15,* 45–57.

Piaget, J. (1932). *The moral judgment of the child.* London: Kegan Paul, Trench, Trubner.

Pinzone-Glover, H. A., Gidycz, C. A., & Jacobs, C. D. (1998). An acquaintance rape prevention program. *Psychology of Women Quarterly, 22,* 605–621.

Richardson, D. R., Hammock, G. S., & Smith, S. M. (1994). Empathy as a cognitive inhibitor of interpersonal aggression. *Aggressive Behavior, 20,* 275–289.

Rokeach, M. (1971). Long-range experimental modification of values, attitudes and behavior. *American Psychologist, 26,* 453–459.

Rokeach, M., & Mezei, L. (1966). Race and shared belief as factors in social choice. *Science, 151,* 167–172.

Rouhana, N. N., & Kelman, H. C. (1994). Promoting joint thinking in international conflicts: An Israeli-Palestinian continuing workshop. *Journal of Social Issues, 50,* 157–178.

Stephan, W. G., & Stephan, C. W. (2000). An integrated threat theory of prejudice. In S. Oskamp (Ed.), *Reducing prejudice and discrimination* (pp. 23–45). Mahwah, NJ: Erlbaum.

Triandis, H. C., & Davis, E. (1965). Race and beliefs as determinants of behavioral intentions. *Journal of Personality and Social Psychology, 2,* 715–725.

Turner, R. (1956). Role taking, role standpoint and reference group behavior. *American Journal of Sociology, 61,* 316–328.

Weiner, M. J., & Wright, F. E. (1973). Effects of undergoing arbitrary discrimination upon subsequent attitudes toward a minority group. *Journal of Applied Social Psychology, 3,* 94–102.

A Home Inventory

Our homes are less separable from the greater community than they have ever been. They are connected to the outside world through television and cable channels, the Internet, toys, music, books, magazines, the daily newspaper, and direct market catalogs. Each of these provide vehicles for prejudice to enter your home and opportunities to respond to it.

Do the calendars, pictures, and posters on your walls reflect the diverse society we live in? Are there books by women and men, lesbian, straight, and gay people from many different cultures? Are there magazines from communities of color? Paying attention to our environment broadens our perspective and counters the stream of negative stereotypes that otherwise enter our home through the media.

—Adapted from Paul Kivel, *Uprooting Racism,* 2002

THE CHALLENGE OF AVERSIVE RACISM: COMBATING PRO–WHITE BIAS

SAMUEL L. GAERTNER, JOHN F. DOVIDIO, BRENDA S. BANKER, MARY C. RUST, JASON A. NIER, GARY R. MOTTOLA, AND CHRISTINE M. WARD

How do we explain the persistence of discrimination among "liberal" whites who claim no prejudice against blacks? If, indeed, these whites are not prejudiced against blacks, is it possible that they discriminate due to *pro-white* attitudes? And, what difference does it make why whites discriminate?

Prejudice has traditionally been considered to be an unfavorable attitude toward another group, involving both negative feelings and beliefs. For example, Allport (1954) defined prejudice as "an antipathy based on faulty and inflexible generalization." Ashmore (1970, p. 253) described it as "a negative attitude toward a socially defined group and any person perceived to be a member of that group." Perhaps as a consequence of this perspective, the prejudice of whites toward blacks has typically been measured using attitude scales reflecting whites' degree of endorsement of statements about negative attributes of blacks, negative feelings toward the group, and support for policies that restrict opportunities for blacks (Brigham, 1993; McConahay, 1986; Sears, 1988).

In our earlier work on "aversive" racism, however, we challenged the assumption that whites who appear non-prejudiced on these questionnaires, and who may truly believe that they possess egalitarian principles, are nonracist. Specifically, our research on aversive racism revealed that many of these presumably non-prejudiced whites have not entirely escaped cultural and cognitive forces that promote racial bias (see Dovidio, Mann, & Gaertner, 1989; Gaertner & Dovidio, 1986; Kovel, 1970). Rather, individuals who appear nonracist on these measures do discriminate in subtle, rationalizable ways that insulate them from awareness of their own prejudice (see Crosby, Bromley, & Saxe, 1980; Devine, 1989). Ironically, these people believe that if everybody's racial attitudes were like theirs, racism would not be a problem.

In this article, we review our work on aversive racism and explore the flip side of the conventional assumption that the racial bias of whites primarily reflects anti-black (or anti-outgroup) attitudes. We consider the possibility that modern forms of bias—such as aversive racism—involve a significant component of pro-white (i.e., pro-ingroup) attitudes which do not seem racist to the individual himself or herself.

Aversive Racism

Whereas traditional forms of prejudice are direct and overt, contemporary forms are often indirect and subtle. Aversive racism occurs when a white

person's egalitarian value system is brought into conflict with unacknowledged negative racial beliefs and feelings from (1) historical and contemporary culturally racist contexts, and (2) biases that result when people are
categorized into ingroups and outgroups (see Hamilton & Troiler, 1986).
Relative to symbolic (see Sears, 1988) or modern racism (see McConahay,
1986), aversive racists are more liberal and egalitarian. Aversive racists are
motivated by the desire to not see themselves as harboring negative feelings about blacks. To the contrary, awareness of such beliefs and feelings
would seriously threaten their non-prejudiced, non-discriminatory self-
images. When the context is normatively impoverished, however, with the
distinction between appropriate and inappropriate behavior more ambiguous, or when the context permits unfavorable behavior to be attributed to non-race related factors, aversive racists reveal their intergroup
biases.

Anti–Black vs. Pro–White Attitudes

In many circumstances, behavior that favors members of one's own group or
family is regarded as appropriate and does not necessarily denote negative
feelings toward others. Inviting only members of one's immediate family to
a holiday dinner, for example, would not be interpreted as expressing ill will
toward people outside of family. Given the normative appropriateness of
inviting only family to such an event, the failure to invite others may only inform us, at best, about attitudes toward family. If invitations were issued to
some non-family members, or if invitations were withheld from some family
members, the implications would be clear. These events would inform us
about the positive feelings toward invited non-family members and the likely
negative feelings toward uninvited family members.

As we review our earlier experiments, we use an attributional framework that considers whether the racial discrimination that we observed
among our white subjects most likely resulted from either anti-black or
pro-white feelings. We argue that when the social pressure to help is weak
(e.g., the fire department has already arrived), a bystander's *not helping*
would not be particularly revealing of his or her feelings toward the victim
(see also Campbell, 1963). However, taking action by *helping* the victim under these circumstances may inform us about the bystander's positive attitude toward the victim. Only when social forces strongly promote
intervention would *not helping* reveal the bystanders' possibly negative
feelings toward the victim.

In general, the pattern we observed in our research is that whites treated
blacks and whites differently only when helping, but not the failure to help,
could inform us about the bystander's attitude toward the victim. In the next
section, we describe some of our earlier studies in view of their potential to
reflect pro-white sentiments among people with liberal, egalitarian values—
but who do discriminate on the basis of race.

The Wrong-Number Study

The first study, which initiated our interest in aversive racism, was a field experiment that examined the likelihood of black and white persons obtaining non-emergency assistance from white Liberal Party and Conservative Party members residing in Brooklyn, New York (Gaertner, 1973). Members of these political parties received apparent wrong-number telephone calls from black and white members of the research staff whose race was clearly identifiable from their dialects. Each caller explained that his or her car was disabled and that he or she was trying to reach a service station from a parkway telephone. Nearly all subjects explained that our caller had reached the wrong number. Then our "motorist" explained that he or she did not have more coins to make another call and asked if the subject would telephone the garage to report the problem.

Conservative Party members who learned of the motorist's entire dilemma telephoned the garage significantly less often for black than for white motorists (65 percent vs. 92 percent). Liberal Party members, in contrast, helped black and white motorists equivalently (75 percent vs. 85 percent). Not every subject, though, stayed on the line long enough to learn of the full dilemma; indeed, many subjects hung up "prematurely" immediately after the opening greeting, "Hello, Ralph's Garage? This is George Williams. I'm stuck out here on the highway. . . ." Hanging up prematurely was particularly characteristic of Liberal Party members—and we soon discovered that they did not ignore the "motorist's" race in this regard. Rather, Liberal Party members hung up prematurely much more frequently on blacks (19 percent of the time) than on whites (3 percent of the time), while the premature hang-up rate for Conservative Party members was very low (about 5 percent).

Initially, we assumed that both Liberal and Conservative Party members discriminated against blacks, but in different ways. We believed that learning of the motorist's full dilemma would arouse a sense of social responsibility—a norm suggesting that a person usually should help others in need of assistance. In the presence of this norm, Conservatives, but not Liberals, were more likely to refuse help to blacks than whites.

But why did Liberals discriminate by hanging up prematurely more frequently on blacks than on whites? Initially, we believed that Liberals unwittingly expressed anti-black feelings in this way. At the stage of the encounter when premature hang-ups occurred there was no clear norm for appropriate behavior. Thus, Liberals could hang up prematurely on blacks because it would be difficult to self-attribute this decision to negative racial attitudes. We believed that hanging up prematurely permitted Liberals to express anti-black feelings and also protected their non-prejudiced self-images.

The attributional reanalysis of this behavior that we are proposing in this article, however, suggests that because norms to stay on the phone were so weak, hanging up would not necessarily be informative about a person's attitude toward the caller. Instead, staying in the interaction can be regarded as behavior beyond the call of duty. From this perspective, white Liberals remaining in the encounter more frequently with other whites than with blacks could be reflective of their positive attitudes toward whites rather than reflective of anti-black attitudes. Just as the failure to invite non-family members to holiday dinner does not inform us of the host's attitude toward them, Liberals hanging up prematurely more frequently on blacks than on whites may not indicate their attitudes toward blacks. Liberals just did not treat blacks as *positively* as they treated family.

If the responses of aversive racists reflect primarily ingroup favoritism, these actions should be most apparent when they have the opportunity to benefit the person even when there is ample reason not to help. The premature hang-ups in the telephone study suggested that in the absence of clear norms for helping, Liberals were more responsive to whites than blacks. In effect, however, blacks end up not being helped by white Liberals at anywhere near the rate they could have been.

Diffusion of Responsibility

Gaertner and Dovidio (1977) engaged white students in a laboratory experiment in which a simulated emergency involving a black or a white student was overheard. A stack of heavy chairs ostensibly fell on another participant, who was located in a different room than the subject. This experiment systematically varied the victim's race (using picture ID cards) and also the presence or absence of two other white bystanders, each located in separate rooms. In their classic study, Darley and Latané (1968) discovered that when a person is alone at the time of an emergency all of the responsibility for helping is focused on this one bystander, but as the number of additional bystanders is increased the responsibility for helping becomes diffused. In the multiple bystander condition, the forces propelling any one bystander to intervene become weaker.

Gaertner and Dovidio introduced the presence of other bystanders in their study to provide subjects with a non-race-related justification that would allow them to rationalize their failure to intervene. The presence of other bystanders, not bigoted intent, could be used by subjects to explain their failure to help. Thus, there should be hardly any awareness that the victim's race influenced the subjects' behavior. When subjects were the only bystander, however, the situation was quite different. In view of the clarity of the emergency, failure of the single bystander to help a black victim could very easily be self-attributed to bigoted intent. Therefore, the forces propelling action were expected to be especially strong and effective on behalf of black victims when the bystander was alone.

The results supported these predictions. White subjects believing themselves to be the only bystander helped black victims somewhat more than white victims (94 percent vs. 81 percent). White bystanders who believed that two other bystanders could also intervene, however, helped white victims more frequently than they helped black victims (75 percent vs. 38 percent). But, again we ask, does this difference reflect subjects' anti-black sentiment as we initially believed? Alternatively, as we are proposing in this article, the tendency to diffuse responsibility more readily for black victims than for white victims may likely inform us about subjects' positive attitudes toward fellow whites and does not necessarily suggest that subjects were anti-black.

In summary, evidence originally interpreted as indicating subtle anti-black prejudice may instead represent pro-white bias. This attributional analysis may similarly account for the results of other studies, examined in the next section, that have revealed asymmetries in the associations of positive and negative characteristics to blacks and whites.

Positive and Negative Associations

The assumption that the expression of aversive racism may be more subtle than traditional forms led us to explore alternative ways to assess prejudice. Evidence has demonstrated that aversive racists do not express their bias openly on self-report scales in which the assessment of negative racial attitudes is obvious. For example, when we asked college students to evaluate black and white people on bipolar scales (e.g., good _ _ _ _ _ _ bad), we found no differences in the evaluative ratings of blacks and whites (Dovidio & Gaertner, 1991).

To assess ingroup favoritism and outgroup favoritism independently, we modified the rating-scale instrument by creating separate scales for positive characteristics (e.g., good) and negative characteristics (e.g., bad). No racial bias appeared on the negative scales. However, on the positive scales, whites were evaluated more favorably than blacks. This pattern is consistent with the thesis that contemporary bias may primarily reflect pro-white attitudes.

Because self-reports are susceptible to impression management, we followed up these studies with a series of response latency experiments (see Dovidio & Gaertner, 1993). For example, in one study participants were asked to decide whether two strings of letters presented simultaneously were both words (Gaertner & McLaughlin, 1983). Faster response times reflected greater association between the words. The results were consistent with the self-report study. Participants did not respond differently to negative words paired with the racial categories "blacks" and "whites," but they did respond faster to positive words appearing with "whites" than with "blacks."

This distinction may have relevance for theories that propose how interracial biases can be reduced. If mere social categorization results largely in pro-ingroup biases and if aversive racism reflects primarily pro-white rather than anti-black orientations, then the process of social categorization may play a central role in contemporary forms of racism and perhaps should be the process that is targeted for change. Factors that induce an ingroup social identity that is inclusive of both blacks and whites should prime more positive feelings, beliefs, and behaviors toward people who would otherwise be regarded as outgroup members.

Reducing Subtle Bias: The Common Ingroup Identity Model

Although there has been some agreement about the utility of undoing the rigidity of social categories to reduce intergroup bias, different strategies have been developed to accomplish this goal. The decategorization strategy attempts to erase members' perceptions of the intergroup boundary by inducing members to conceive of one another as individuals, in more personalized terms, rather than as group members (see Wilder, 1986). Alternatively, the Common Ingroup Identity Model proposes a strategy of re-categorization to reduce intergroup bias by restructuring a definition of who is in the ingroup (Gaertner, Dovidio, Anastasio, Bachman, & Rust, 1993; Anastasio, Bachman, Gaertner, & Dovidio, 1996). Specifically, the Common Ingroup Identity Model proposes that if members of different groups come to see themselves as a single group rather than as separate ones, attitudes toward former outgroup members will become more positive through processes involving pro-ingroup bias (see Social Identity Theory, Tajfel & Turner, 1979; and Self-Categorization Theory, Turner et al., 1987).

A Game They Came to Watch

The major proposition of the Common Ingroup Identity Model is that outgroup members will be treated more favorably in the context of a common ingroup identity than they would be if they were regarded only as outgroup members. To test this idea experimentally in a natural context, our research team was composed of eight students (black and white, male and female) who visited the University of Delaware football stadium shortly before a game between the University of Delaware (UD) and West Chester State University (WSU). Claiming to be surveyors of fans' food preferences, our student researchers systematically varied their apparent university affiliation by wearing either a UD or WSU hat. Only white fans whose clothing revealed a UD or WSU affiliation were approached by our students (of the same sex as the fan) with a request to complete a survey.

When the surveyors and fans did not share the same university identity, black and white surveyors, contrary to our prediction, received equivalent levels of compliance (38 percent vs. 40 percent). Nevertheless, the findings pertaining to the effect of a common university ingroup identity received some support. Although the presence or absence of a common university identity did not affect compliance with a white surveyor (43 percent vs. 40 percent), fans who shared a common university identity with black surveyors complied more frequently (60 percent) than when they had a different university identity with the black surveyor (38 percent). Thus, consistent with the major proposition of the Common Ingroup Identity Model, white fans treated blacks more favorably when they shared a common ingroup identity with these surveyors than when they did not.

It is difficult to know with certainty why the black surveyors who shared a common university identity with the fans elicited somewhat more compliance than comparable white surveyors. We suspect, however, that although many of these fans regarded themselves as unprejudiced, they rarely felt a sense of connection or common identity with blacks and thus, they felt especially positive when they had the opportunity to share an important ingroup identity with them. In any event, this study offers further support for the idea that outgroup members will be treated more favorably in the context of a common ingroup identity. Apparently, ingroup forces that usually foster intergroup discrimination can be used to increase positive behaviors toward outgroup members.

Conclusion

This article has examined the possibility that racial bias, particularly in its contemporary manifestations, may reflect a pro-white, not simply anti-black, sentiment. This does not mean, however, that anti-black intentions do not drive interracial behavior among many whites. Not all racists are aversive types.

Considering pro-whiteness as an important element in intergroup relations has both theoretical and applied value for understanding, assessing, and addressing issues of racism in our society. Our analysis suggests that traditional prejudice scales that measure primarily anti-black attitudes, either directly or indirectly, are limited in the extent to which they can capture whites' racial attitudes. They may provide relatively accurate assessments of the intergroup attitudes of traditional racists, whose attitudes are composed mainly of anti-black sentiments, but they offer relatively poor estimates of the attitudes of aversive racists, whose interracial attitudes have a significant pro-white emphasis.

Appreciating the impact of pro-white attitudes in contemporary racism also offers insight into legal, social, and personal actions that can eliminate racial bias. Current anti-discrimination laws are based largely on the premise that racial discrimination by whites is primarily the result of anti-black attitudes and actions. For example, the second author of this article served as an expert witness for the plaintiff in an employment discrimination case. The plaintiff, a black man, was placed on probationary status by his employer because of some deficiencies in his performance. After a review of his performance during the probationary period, the employer terminated his appointment with the company. The plaintiff's claim was not that his treatment violated the company's procedure but that another person—a white man—who was also on probation and whose performance during this time was comparable to that of the plaintiff's was retained and reassigned within the company. The argument was that this represents different and unfair treatment for equivalent performance. The defense countered that although the plaintiff was indeed treated differently for equivalent performance, he was not treated unfairly. Special treatment toward the white (ingroup) worker, the defense claimed, does not demonstrate unfair and discriminatory treatment toward the black (outgroup) employee. The plaintiff's case was dismissed. Thus, laws designed to protect disadvantaged individuals and groups from discrimination based on anti-outgroup actions may be ineffective for addressing biased treatment based on ingroup favoritism. Awareness of the changing nature of contemporary racism may require a reconceptualization of policies and laws to address the consequences of persistent, if changing, racism.

REFERENCES

Allport, G. W. (1954). *The nature of prejudice.* Cambridge, MA: Addison-Wesley.

Ashmore, R. D. (1970). Prejudice: Causes and cures. In B. E. Collins (Ed.), *Social psychology: Social influence, attitude change, group processes and prejudice* (pp. 245–339). Reading, MA: Addison-Wesley.

Anastasio, P. A., Bachman, B. A., Gaertner, S. L., & Dovidio, J. F. (1996). Categorization, recategorization and common ingroup identity. In R. Spears, P. J. Oakes, N. Ellemers, and S. A. Haslam (Eds.), *The social psychology of stereotyping and group life.* Oxford: Blackwell.

Brigham, J. C. (1993). College students' racial attitudes. *Journal of Applied Social Psychology, 23,* 1933–1967.

Campbell, D. T. (1963). Social attitudes and other acquired behavioral dispositions. In S. Koch (Ed.), *Psychology: A study of science* (vol. 6). New York: McGraw-Hill.

Crosby, F., Bromley, S., & Saxe, L. (1980). Recent unobtrusive studies of black and white discrimination and prejudice: A literature review. *Psychological Bulletin, 87,* 546–563.

Darley, J. M., & Latané, B. (1968). Bystander intervention in emergencies: Diffusion of responsibility. *Journal of Personality and Social Psychology, 8,* 377–383.

Devine, P. (1989). Stereotypes and prejudice: Their automatic and controlled components. *Journal of Personality and Social Psychology, 56,* 5–18.

Dovidio, J. F., & Gaertner, S. L. (1991). Changes in the expression and assessment of racial prejudice. In H. J. Knopke, R. J. Norrell, and R. W. Rogers (Eds.), *Opening Doors: Perspectives of Race Relations in Contemporary America.* Tuscaloosa, AL: University of Alabama Press.

Dovidio, J. F., & Gaertner, S. L. (1993). Stereotypes and evaluative intergroup bias. In D. M. Mackie and D. L. Hamilton (Eds.), *Affect, cognition and stereotyping.* Orlando, FL: Academic Press.

Dovidio, J. F., Mann, J., & Gaertner, S. L. (1989). Resistance to affirmative action: The implications of aversive racism. In F. A. Blanchard and F. J. Crosby (Eds.), *Affirmative action in perspective* (pp. 83–102). New York: Springer-Verlag.

Gaertner, S. L. (1973). Helping behavior and racial discrimination among liberals and conservatives. *Journal of Personality and Social Psychology, 25,* 335–341.

Gaertner, S. L., & Dovidio, John F. (1977). The subtlety of white racism, arousal and helping behavior. *Journal of Personality and Social Psychology, 35*(10), 691–707.

Gaertner, S. L., & Dovidio, J. F. (1986). The aversive form of racism. In J. F. Dovidio and S. L. Gaertner (Eds.), *Prejudice, discrimination, and racism* (pp. 61–89). Orlando, FL: Academic Press.

Gaertner, S. L., Dovidio, J. F., Anastasio, P. A., Bachman, B. A., & Rust, M. C. (1993). The common ingroup identity model: Recategorization and the reduction of intergroup bias. In W. Stroebe and M. Hewstone (Eds.), *The European Review of Social Psychology* (Vol. 4, pp. 1–25). London: Wiley.

Gaertner, S. L., & McLaughlin, J. (1983). Racial stereotypes: Associations and ascriptions of positive and negative characteristics. *Social Psychology Quarterly, 46,* 23–30.

Hamilton, D. L., & Trolier T. K. (1986). Stereotypes and stereotyping: An overview of the cognitive approach. In J. F. Dovidio and S. L. Gaertner (Eds.), *Prejudice, discrimination, and racism* (pp. 127–163). Orlando, FL: Academic Press.

Kovel, J. (1970). *White racism: A psychohistory.* New York: Pantheon.

McConahay, J. B. (1986). Modern racism, ambivalence, and the Modern Racism Scale. In J. F. Dovidio and S. L. Gaertner (Eds.), *Prejudice, discrimination, and racism* (pp. 91–125). Orlando, FL: Academic Press.

Sears, D. O. (1988). Symbolic racism. In P. Katz and D. Taylor (Eds.), *Towards the elimination of racism: Profiles in controversy* (pp. 53–84). New York: Plenum.

Tajfel, H., & Turner, J. C. (1979). An integrative theory of intergroup conflict. In W. G. Austin and S. Worchel (Eds.), *The social psychology of intergroup relations* (pp. 33–47). Monterey, CA: Brooks/Cole.

Turner, J. C., Hogg, M. A., Oakes, P. J., Reicher, S. D., & Wetherell, M. S. (1987). *Rediscovering the social group: A self-categorization theory.* Oxford: Blackwell.

Wilder, D. A. (1986). Social categorization: Implications for creation and reduction of intergroup bias. In L. Berkowitz (Ed.), *Advances in Experimental Social Psychology* (vol. 19, pp. 291–355). Orlando, FL: Academic Press.

MARTIN LUTHER KING EXPLAINS
NONVIOLENT RESISTANCE

MARTIN LUTHER KING, JR.

During my freshman days in 1944 at Atlanta's Morehouse College I read Henry David Thoreau's essay *On Civil Disobedience* for the first time. Here, in this courageous New Englander's refusal to pay his taxes and his choice of jail rather than support a war that would spread slavery's territory into Mexico, I made my first contact with the theory of nonviolent resistance. Fascinated by Thoreau's idea of refusing to cooperate with an evil system, I was so deeply moved that I reread the work several times.

A few years later I heard a lecture by Dr. Mordecai Johnson, President of Howard University. Dr. Johnson had just returned from a trip to India and he spoke of the life and teachings of Mahatma Gandhi. His message was so profound and electrifying that I left the meeting and bought a half-dozen books on Gandhi's life and works.

Before reading Gandhi, I had believed that Jesus' "turn the other cheek" philosophy and the "love your enemies" philosophy could only be useful when individuals were in conflict with other individuals—when racial groups and nations were in conflict, a more realistic approach seemed necessary. But after reading Gandhi, I saw how utterly mistaken I was.

During the days of the Montgomery bus boycott, I came to see the power of nonviolence more and more. As I lived through the actual experience of this protest, nonviolence became more than a useful method; it became a way of life.

Nonresistance attacks the forces of evil rather than the persons who happen to be doing the evil. As I said to the people of Montgomery: "The tension in this city is not between white people and Negro people. The tension is at bottom, between justice and injustice, between the forces of light and the forces of darkness. And if there is a victory, it will be a victory not merely for fifty thousand Negroes but a victory for justice and the forces of light. We are out to defeat injustice and not white persons who may be unjust."

It must be emphasized that nonviolent resistance is not for cowards. *Nonviolent resistance does resist.* If one uses this method because he is afraid or merely because he lacks the weapons of violence, he is not truly nonviolent. That is why Gandhi often said that if cowardice is the only alternative to violence, it is better to fight. He made this statement knowing that there is always another choice we can make: There is the way of nonviolent resistance. No individual or group need submit to any wrong, nor need they use violence to right a wrong. This is ultimately the way of the strong man.

The nonviolent resistance of the early Christians shook the Roman Empire. The nonviolence of Mahatma Gandhi and his followers had muzzled the guns of the British Empire in India and freed more than three hundred and fifty million people from colonialism. It brought victory in the Montgomery bus boycott.

The phrase "passive resistance" often gives the false impression that this is a sort of "do-nothing method" in which the resister quietly and passively accepts evil. But nothing is further from the truth. For while the nonviolent resister is not physically aggressive toward his opponent, his mind and emotions are always active, constantly seeking to persuade his opponent that he is wrong—constantly seeking to open the eyes of blind prejudice. This is not passive nonresistance to evil, it is active nonviolent resistance to evil.

Nonviolence does not seek to defeat or humiliate the opponent, but to win his friendship and understanding. The nonviolent resister not only refuses to shoot his opponent but he also refuses to hate him. To strike back in the same way as his opponent would do nothing but increase the existence of hate in the universe. Along the way of life, someone must have sense enough and morality enough to cut off the chain of hate.

Together Action

If you practice with others, your good and bad actions already help other people. We call this together action. Together action is like washing potatoes. When people wash potatoes in Korea, instead of washing them one at a time, they put them all in a tub full of water. Then someone puts a stick in the tub and pushes it up and down, up and down. This makes the potatoes rub against each other; as they bump into each other the hard crusty dirt falls off. If you wash potatoes one at a time, it takes a long time to clean each one, and only one potato gets clean at a time. If they are all together, the potatoes clean each other.

—Korean Zen Master Seung Sahn, *Only Don't Know*, 1982

Like a Blowtorch on Steel

[Effective activism is] like applying a blowtorch to a piece of steel. If you try to cover the whole piece, everything gets lukewarm. But if you target the heat in one spot, you can cut it in half.

—Activist Henry Spira, *Effective Strategies of Social Protest*, 1979

$1 for Every Minute of Hate

Most gay men and lesbians greet the news that anti-gay demonstrator Fred Phelps is coming to their town with chagrin or a protest or both. But when Keith Orr, co-owner of the Aut Bar in Ann Arbor, Michigan, discovered his establishment was about to be the target of a Phelps demonstration, he found an ingenious way to fight back. Orr sent out 270 e-mails to friends and acquaintances, announcing that he intended to pledge $1 for every minute Phelps protested in front of the bar. He encouraged others to make some kind of pledge too. Any money collected would go to a local gay and lesbian community group. By the time Phelps and his group packed up, Orr had collected $7,500 for the town's gay and lesbian community center.

Thanks to the power of the Internet, word of Orr's clever plan spread quickly, and now lesbian and gay organizations across the country are cashing in on Phelps sightings. Orr, who has taken on the unofficial role of adviser to the growing number of pledge drives, says he receives e-mails daily asking for advice on how to pull off a fundraiser. But the momentum behind the idea, Orr says, is only marginally about raising money. "It gives people a constructive way to combat a destructive person," he says. It may also give Phelps a reason to think twice before he stages too many more hate vigils.

—Adapted from *The Advocate*, August 14, 2001 [*Note:* In 1998, Fred Phelps received national media attention for displaying picket signs such as "God hates fags" at the funeral of hate-crime victim Matthew Shepard.]

No Such Thing as Means and Ends

There is no such thing as means and ends. Everything that we do is an end, in itself, that we can never erase. That is why we must make all our actions the kind we would like to be judged on. . . . That is why we will not let ourselves be provoked by our adversaries into behaving hatefully.

—César Chávez, cofounder of the United Farm Workers, speaking at a union meeting, 1969

In Closing . . .

I would like to tell you in closing the story of an old man. This old man was very wise, and he could answer questions that [were] almost impossible for people to answer. So some people went to him one day, two young people, and said, "We're going to trick this guy today. We're going to catch a bird, and we're going to carry it to this old man. And we're going to ask him, 'This that we hold in our hands today, is it alive or is it dead?' If he says 'Dead,' we're going to turn it loose and let it fly. But if he says, 'Alive,' we're going to crush it."

So they walked up to this old man, and they said, "This that we hold in our hands today, is it alive or is it dead?"

He looked at the young people and he smiled. And he said, "It's in your hands."

—Fannie Lou Hamer, in a speech before the NAACP Legal Defense Fund Institute, May 7, 1971

Appendix
Animals as an Outgroup

I shoot and she drops her head. As she kicks her final shudders I go to her, sitting with my hip against her spine, my hand on her flank, feeling her warmth, her pulse, her life, changing states. She is enormous, and beautiful, and my throat constricts. Her right cheek lies on the snow; her nose is moist; her eye stares into the heaven, now blue with the morning. . . . Taking out my knife, I slit the hide on her belly. . . . After I pull out her stomach and intestines, I open her pelvic girdle with the saw, being careful not to rupture her bladder or rectum. As I start skinning her I discover a piece of meat on my finger. I put it in my mouth, chew it, and swallow it. She tastes like warm, raw elk. . . . Kneeling by her hooves and head, I stroke her long brown hair.

—Hunting account from Ted Kerasote, *Bloodties: Nature, Culture, and the Hunt*, 1993

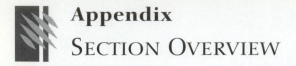

Appendix

SECTION OVERVIEW

At first it may seem strange to include animals as an outgroup when considering prejudice and discrimination. Prejudice is normally thought of in strictly human terms, and the idea of being "prejudiced" against animals appears out of place. Yet animals have suffered in many ways from human prejudice. For example, animals have been treated as though they do not feel pain. They have been treated as though they do not have thoughts, feelings, or family bonds. They have been commodified, advertised, and sold without regard to their individual identity or welfare. And in many cases, these prejudices have been psychologically maintained in much the same way as are prejudices against human outgroups.

The first reading of this section describes several psychological mechanisms involved in the human use of animals. This article is followed by a list of dissonance-reducing statements in support of harming animals (compare these statements with earlier ones on slavery and female suffrage).

Next, the section contains some intriguing speculations by Richard Dawkins on the conceptual origins of animal prejudice—sometimes referred to as "speciesism." Finally, the section concludes with Gail Eisnitz's disturbing exposé on the treatment of animals in the U.S. meat industry. In this report, Eisnitz explores not only the physical effects on animals but the psychological and health effects on workers and their families.

Take Special Notice

All of us use animal products to some extent, so if this section's readings lead you to feel cognitive dissonance, pay special attention to how you reduce that dissonance. If you find yourself wanting to discount or avoid the readings, ask yourself why.

Questions Worth Pondering

- Are there areas of your life in which you display prejudice toward animals?
- If you eat meat, do you think of it coming from a some*thing* or some*one?*
- If you eat dairy products, do you associate them with a lactating animal?
- Is speciesism more defensible than racism and sexism? Why or why not?
- Is it possible to eliminate prejudice against humans (e.g., racism, sexism) without eliminating prejudice against animals?

IS THERE SUCH A THING AS PREJUDICE TOWARD ANIMALS?

SCOTT PLOUS

Prejudice toward animals? The very notion seems odd. Prejudice is a term usually reserved for human relations, and it feels wrong on at least three counts to speak of prejudice against nonhuman animals (commonly referred to as "speciesism"). First, speciesism appears to fly in the face of the love many people have for animals.[1] Second, speciesism runs the risk of trivializing scourges such as racism and sexism. And third, speciesism suggests a demeaning equivalence between human targets of prejudice (e.g., people of color) and animals. Let us consider each point in turn.

On the first point, it is unquestionably true that many people love animals. In the United States alone, people live with half a billion companion animals, and when asked, roughly 90% report regarding their animals as family members (Gallup, 1997; Siegel, 1993). According to Jasper and Nelkin (1992), 10–15 million Americans belong to an animal welfare group, and one in five claims to have contributed money to an animal protection organization. One study even found that among families with companion animals, 38% of respondents indicated feeling closer to their dog than to any other family member (Barker & Barker, 1988).

As George Orwell put it in *Animal Farm,* however, some animals are "more equal" than others. Of the 10 billion or so farm animals raised annually in the United States, many are consigned to live the full measure of their lives in intensive confinement systems (Robbins, 2001). For example, at least 90% of pigs and egg-laying chickens in the United States live in small indoor cages or stalls (Mason & Singer, 1990; Fox, 1997). Likewise, millions of animals on "fur farms" are reared in cages and ultimately electrocuted or gassed (Scientific Committee, 2001; McKenna, 1998). In many cases, fur-bearing animals and farm animals are made to suffer or die for reasons no more important than trimming a coat with fur or topping a pizza with pepperoni.

If the core of prejudice and discrimination amounts to prejudging and treating others poorly based on their group membership, there is no question that certain types of animals qualify as targets of discrimination. Throughout history, millions of animals have been treated as though they experience little or no pain, as though they do not feel emotions, as though they have no family bonds, and as though they have no vested interest in living. To take but a few examples, animals have been injured and killed in bullfights, fox hunts, rodeos, and cockfights, all staged for human entertainment. If these practices do not fall within the ken of prejudice and discrimination, their exclusion is merely semantic.

---

[1] As used in this article, the term "animals" refers to nonhuman animals.

At the same time, speciesism is clearly not equivalent to racism and sexism. There are important differences between the subjugation of people and the subjugation of animals, and people are capable of suffering in many ways that animals are not. But why should this difference be seen as trivializing racism or sexism? We do not rank-order prejudices aimed at humans and say that the existence of one form of prejudice trivializes the others or demeans its victims.

With respect to speciesism, this reaction is an understandable result of historic attempts to portray human targets of prejudice as animal-like. African Americans have been depicted as apes, Jews as vermin, women as prey, homosexuals as beasts, fat people as cows and pigs. Yet the very act of "treating people like animals" would lose its meaning if animals were treated well. Just as racism, sexism, and other prejudices share a similar mindset, many of the psychological factors that underlie speciesism serve to reinforce and promote prejudice against humans. These factors include power, privilege, dominance, control, entitlement, and the need to reduce cognitive dissonance when committing harmful acts.

For example, dissonance-reducing statements now made about animal use are strikingly similar to the dissonance-reducing statements once made about human slavery. Animals are often described as benefiting from being used, as being content with their lot, as being insensitive to pain, unintelligent, unaware, or wanting to be used. Animal use is frequently described as natural, economically necessary, or inevitable. Religious scriptures are invoked to support various practices. And people whose livelihood depends on the use of animals often stress that they love animals, that their own economic interests prevent widespread cruelty, and that abolitionism amounts to fanaticism.

Indeed, the parallels between slavery and animal use extend well beyond dissonance reduction. For instance, American slaves were often auctioned, branded, had their ears cropped, and were bred "like other live stock" (Weld, 1839/1968, p. 183). Slaves were explicitly referred to as "stock" or "cattle," childbearing female slaves were called "breeders," children were referred to as the "increase," and slave overseers were called "drivers." Field hands were frequently forced into labor with whips, collars, yokes, fetters, and chains, and they were often fed a corn meal diet (food thought sufficient for animals of burden). House servants, in some ways the counterpart of modern-day companion animals, were fed corn meal along with assorted table scraps such as unwanted bones and fat.

Afro-American parents had as little control over the disposition of their children "as have domestic animals over the disposal of their young," and slaves were used as test subjects for all manner of surgical techniques and experimental treatments (Weld, 1839/1968, pp. 45, 56). In fact, the prospectus of one Southern medical college even boasted that: "Some advantages of a peculiar character are connected with this Institution, which it may be proper to point out. No place in the United States offers as great opportunities for the acquisition of anatomical knowledge, subjects being obtained from among the colored population in sufficient number for every purpose, and proper dissections carried on without offending any individuals in the community" (Weld, 1839/1968, p. 169). Until 1821, the laws governing slaves and animals bore much in common; killing another person's slave and killing another person's draft animal were both considered misdemeanors.

In 1906, the line between outgroup biases toward humans and outgroup biases toward animals was blurred in a particularly dramatic way. That year, the New York Zoological Park (now the Bronx Zoo) set up a monkey exhibit that included a 23-year-old African Pigmy named Ota Benga. A sign on the cage read, "The African Pigmy, 'Ota Benga.' Age, 23 years. Height, 4 feet 11 inches. Weight, 103 pounds. Brought from the Kasai River, Congo Free State, South Central Africa, by Dr. Samuel P. Verner. Exhibited each afternoon during September" ("Man and monkey show," 1906). One of the most telling aspects of this episode is that the zoo director, William T. Hornaday, used many of the same dissonance-reduction strategies that are found in connection with the use of animals. According to Hornaday, Ota Benga "begged to accompany Mr. Verner to America, and even threatened to drown himself otherwise" (Hornaday, 1906, p. 302). Hornaday also told the *New York Times* that: "The little black man is really very comfortable . . . [and] seems happy" ("Man and monkey show," 1906, p. 2). The truth of these statements was subsequently belied when Ota Benga committed suicide (Bridges, 1974).

Several years later, the Ringling Brothers Circus created a similar display called "The Monkey Man." In this instance, a male African American was caged with a female chimpanzee who had been taught to wash clothes and hang them on a line (Bradna & Spence, 1952). And in 1980, the racism-speciesism line was blurred when two White hunters fatally shot a deaf Black man who was walking along some railroad tracks in California (Turner, 1980). According to the story, both hunters stated that they had "decided to shoot a black person" because they had "failed to bag a deer after a day-long hunting trip." In the words of these hunters, they were hunting "dark meat" and bagging "critters" (Ellena, 1980). After killing the deaf man, the hunters drove to a nearby town and shot at four other Black people.

The question these episodes raise is whether parallels between speciesism and other forms of prejudice are psychologically meaningful, or whether their resemblance is largely superficial. Is it significant that the word *mulatto*—often used in the Old South as a synonym for "half-breed"—shares its etymology with *mule*? Or that *race* emerged from terms for animal breeding? Does it mean anything that the word *husband* shares a common origin with animal *husbandry,* or that rape was originally classified as a property crime? Why is homosexuality grouped with zoophilia (beastiality) in the *International Classification of Diseases?* And even if prejudices "animalize" human outgroups, does that imply the existence of prejudice toward animals themselves?

The thesis of this article is that these parallels are far from coincidental. On the contrary, they tell us something fundamental about how prejudice operates and how people balance their desire to be fair with their desire to maintain an inequitable status quo (regardless of whether the outgroup is human or another species). In the following sections, I turn to a discussion of several psychological factors that allow people to use animals without feeling that their actions are unfair or prejudiced.

Dissociation

A number of psychological factors serve to dissociate, or distance, consumptive practices from the infliction of pain or suffering. In his classic article "The Case for Certain Cruelties," Gwynn (1924, p. 913) argued that "it is healthy to keep our imaginations so disciplined that we can eat roast chicken without thinking of the fowl's death struggles." Although a dissociation between the use of animals and the infliction of pain may at times be intentional, it is more often the result of structural variables such as the language surrounding animal use, the physical appearance of animal products, the remoteness of animal industries, and the way people are socialized to think about animals (Serpell, 1986; Wood, 1971).

Language

Consider the following excerpt from a market report:

> Harvest levels this past season were off markedly. This is partly a result of last summer's drought, but mostly a function of market price. While some areas reported near normal harvests, my colleagues estimate that many areas harvested only 10–25 percent of the harvest of last season. (Shroeder, 1989, p. 54)

Nothing in this passage indicates that the crop being harvested is, in fact, a crop of live animals—that the commodity is raw fur. Yet animals are commonly referred to as crops by hunters, trappers, and the fur industry (Baker, 1985; Swan, 1995, p. 75). In the words of one hunter, "Deer have to be harvested. . . . It's not a whole lot different than going into the field and harvesting apples every year. You cultivate animals for what their purpose is, the same as cultivating a crop" (quoted in Mitchell, 1979, pp. 25–26). Or, in the words of a former Canadian minister of mines and energy: "I see little difference between someone in Florida harvesting oranges and someone in northeast Newfoundland engaging in the seal hunt" (Johnston, 1979). One trapper writing on behalf of the National Trappers Association even argued that "There are more fur animals now than when I started. I have simply taken a yearly harvest leaving plenty of seed for the next year" (Hoyt, 1979, p. 3). In hunting and trapping, consumptive practices are dissociated from the infliction of pain by using euphemisms for killing such as "harvesting," "bagging," "thinning," "managing," and "controlling." Similarly, animals are described impersonally as "crops," "seed," "game," "trophies," "surpluses," and "renewable resources."

The American legal system is particularly explicit in describing animals as inanimate objects. Whereas children and mentally disabled adults have "guardians" and are technically considered "wards," animals have "owners" and are legally considered "chattel" or "personal property" (McCarthy, 1982).[2] This difference is not attributable to legal necessity, for there are instances in which nonhuman entities have been granted legal standing. According to former U. S. Supreme Court Justice William O. Douglas, "A ship has a legal personality, a fiction found useful for maritime purposes [and] the ordinary corporation is a 'person' for purposes of the adjudicatory processes" (*Sierra Club versus Morton,* 1974, p. 1370). Animals are also treated as inanimate within the Dewey Decimal library classification system; books on naming animals do not fall under section 929.4 ("Personal Names"), but rather, under section 929.97 ("Forms of Insignia and Identification"), along with books on naming houses and books on naming ships (Comaromi, 1989).

Finally, dissociation is apparent in language relating to food consumption (Adams, 1990; Sahlins, 1976). In many cases, the use of animals is divorced from the infliction of pain by using different names for the consumed animal and the live animal. Cows are "beef," calves are "veal," pigs are "pork," and so on. Even when the same word is used to indicate the consumed animal and live animal—as in chicken, turkey, shrimp, or lobster—the consumed animal is usually indicated by a singular noun without an article, whereas the live animal is represented by a plural noun or a singular noun with an article. People do not eat chickens; they eat *chicken.* The fact that plants are not generally given dual names suggests that such distinctions are more than useful conventions.

Although the dual naming of consumed and live animals did not originate specifically in order to foster dissociation (the etymology is more complicated than that), this duality serves to distance animal products from live animals. Moreover, in some cases language *is* deliberately manipulated in order to depersonalize animals. For example, the "4-H Plan for Prevention" distributed by the 4-H Club warns animal fair participants to "be aware of the terminology you use; don't humanize the animals:

chicks, calves, lambs . . . . not babies

farrow, hatch, foal, bear . . . . . not giving birth

process . . . . not kill or slaughter

health products . . . . not drugs

family farm . . . . not factory farm

beak trimming . . . . not debeaking."

Lederer (1992) has documented similar word substitutions in the biomedical literature dating as far back as the early 1900s, when the Council on the Defense of Medical Research asked medical journal editors to eliminate

---

[2] It is worth noting in this regard that the word *cattle* shares the same etymological root as *chattel,* and that the Latin word for money, *pecunia,* comes from *pecus,* which means cattle (Rifkin, 1992).

"expressions which are likely to be misunderstood." The *Journal of Experimental Medicine* (*JEM*), for example, maintained in-house publication guidelines that suggested substituting *intoxicant* for *poison, fasting* for *starving,* and *hemorrhaging* for *bleeding. JEM* also explicitly counseled authors not to refer to animals by name or initials, and when large numbers of animals were involved, the journal often renumbered subjects to give the appearance that fewer animals were used (e.g., rabbit 10-2 instead of rabbit 102).

Appearance

Many Americans find it difficult to eat animal products if the consumed animal closely resembles the live animal. As a consequence, body parts that are associated with life or personality—such as the eyes, face, or brain—are rarely eaten, and most animals are marketed without their heads or feet. This need for dissociation was summarized quite well by novelist John Updike, who once remarked in an interview, "I'm somewhat shy about the brutal facts of being a carnivore. . . . I don't like meat to look like animals. I prefer it in the form of sausages, hamburgers and meatloaf, far removed from the living thing" (Sheraton, 1982, p. C8).

The importance of this form of dissociation is widely recognized within the animal industries. For example, *Meat Trades Journal* ("Meat," 1977, May 5, p. 12) warned that "to acquaint a customer with the knowledge that the lamb chops she has just purchased were part of the anatomy of one of those pretty little creatures we see gamboling in the fields at springtime is probably the surest way of turning her into a vegetarian." Even more directly, the popular paperback *Raising a Calf for Beef* cautioned readers that:

> There may be a moment of trauma the day the calf is sent away, but the packages of processed beef that are brought home are not easily associated with the animal. Many families buy another small calf just before the older calf is sent to the butcher. And many people refuse to give a name to any animal they intend later to butcher on the theory that the name gives it a personality. But if members of the family—especially children—still object to the idea of butchering an animal, it may be a good idea to explain that livestock which are raised for food are the same as vegetables in the garden. (Hobson, 1983, p. 63)

The importance of dissociation is equally evident in the clothing industry. For example, in an article entitled "How to Talk About Fur Farming," a prominent trade publication for the fur industry advised:

> When you are holding a mink for photographs or for TV, do not allow zoom-in-pictures or shots made very close to the head of our animals. This type of picture shows our animals to be cute, lovable, cuddly, and adorable to the uninitiated urban viewer. . . . [The] reason you can give to avoid the situation described above could be, that you are afraid that strangers and unusual commotion will disturb and upset your animals. (Althouse, 1985, p. 88)

Remoteness

The dissociation between using animals and inflicting pain or suffering is additionally reinforced by the physical remoteness of animal industries. Intensive farming operations, livestock auctions, slaughterhouses, animal laboratories, and fur farms are typically remote or inaccessible (Fox, 1997; Wood, 1971). Farm animals also receive far less media attention than do other types of animals, and virtually all of the popular magazines and educational television shows about animals focus on wildlife rather than farm animals or intensive farming (Singer, 2002; Steinhart, 1988).

Partly as a result of this remoteness, public awareness concerning animal products is often minimal. For example, when 143 college students were tested with the true-false items in Table 1, the most common score was 0 items correct out of 8, and less than one fourth of respondents answered more than 1 item correctly (Plous, 1993). Similarly, a national survey found that only 54% of respondents could answer correctly whether "veal comes from lamb" (Kellert & Berry, 1980). Many people are unsure whether foods such as veal come predominantly from male animals or female animals, and a large percentage of well-educated adults do not associate cow's milk with the animal's pregnancy (Schleifer, 1985).

Indeed, a survey in the 1990s found that one in three adults did not know that butter, cheese, and ice cream come from cows (Plous, 1993). In this survey,

TABLE 1   Survey on Knowledge About the Use of Animals for Food and Clothing

	% saying "True"	% saying "False"	% saying "Don't know"
Leather from alligators and snakes is usually made by skinning the animals alive.	2	18	80
The unwanted chicks of laying hens are often ground alive to make pet food.	6	7	87
Most goose down comes from geese that have been plucked alive.	15	6	79
To make "kid" gloves, young goats are sometimes boiled alive.	0	12	88
To harvest silk, live silkworms are typically boiled in their cocoons.	20	6	75
In the United States, pigs and cows usually die from having their throats slit with a knife.	49	8	43
It is common practice in the United States to castrate pigs, sheep, and cattle without anesthesia.	34	1	65
Animals used for food are not protected by the United States Animal Welfare Act.	20	8	73

Note: Figures indicate the percentage of respondents giving each answer (the percentages are rounded off and do not always add up to 100). The correct answer to all items is "True."

117 respondents were asked whether any of the following 13 items were commonly made with animal products: butter, margarine, crayons, phonograph records, photographic film, ice cream, shaving cream, chewing gum, cheese, wallpaper adhesive, cellophane, linoleum, and marshmallows. Respondents were also asked to identify the animal of origin for any items they thought contained animal products.

The correct answer is that all 13 items are commonly made with products that come from cows[3] (and some items, such as cheese, are made from other animals as well). The highest score anyone achieved, however, was six correct items, and the mean number of correct answers was 2.8. Twenty-two percent of the respondents did not know where butter comes from, 22% did not know where cheese comes from, and 24% did not know where ice cream comes from (all told, 34% of the respondents failed to identify at least one dairy product). None of the respondents answered correctly when asked about photographic film, shaving cream, chewing gum, cellophane, and linoleum, and many expressed surprise that such a wide variety of household items are made with animal products.

Although the remoteness of animal industries is often a result of practical constraints rather than a deliberate strategy aimed at maintaining dissociation, there are some cases in which temporal and spatial distancing is intentionally used to insulate the public. For instance, in a policy statement issued by the Acting Director of the Bureau of Sport Fisheries and Wildlife (now the U.S. Fish and Wildlife Service), regional directors were instructed that:

> Scheduling and zoning should be judiciously employed in hunting programs to buffer the non-hunting public from the sights and sounds of the hunt. The roar of shotguns with geese falling out of the sky may be offensive—and confusing—to persons who visit refuges while hunts are in progress. Likewise, large numbers of deer carcasses hanging at a check-station may create an unpleasant atmosphere if viewed by visitors not kindly disposed to hunting. . . . Aggressive competent public relations initiatives must be an integral part of a hunting program. . . . If hunting is to survive on national wildlife refuges we must take whatever steps as are necessary to place our hunting programs in a firm, defensible posture. (Schmidt, 1973, pp. 4–6, 13)

Socialization

From childhood, Americans are taught both to love and to consume animals. Conflict between these practices is avoided in part by deemphasizing consumed animals as objects of affection (Singer, 2002). Conflict is also minimized by socializing children to believe that meat comes from happy farm animals who live in idyllic settings (see Figure 1). As a result of such messages, children

---

[3] This information comes from an informational brochure entitled "When Is a Cow More Than a Cow?" published by the American National CattleWomen, and can also be found in Rifkin (1992).

FIGURE 1

This figure compares farm animals as they are depicted in children's books with farm animals as they actually live in intensive confinement. (Henhouse illustration reprinted with permission of Scholastic Press from *Old MacDonald,* copyright © 1999 by Amy Schwartz. Pig illustration reprinted with permission of McIntosh and Otis, Inc., from *The Pig Who Saw Everything,* published by Seabury Press, © 1978 by Dick Gackenbach. Photographs reprinted with permission of Jim Mason.)

are often left with the impression that farm animals lead untroubled lives. For example, one study found that elementary school children rated farm animals as less likely than other types of animals to experience unhappiness (Plous, 1993). In this study, only 26% of students said that farm animals sometimes feel unhappy, compared with 46% who thought companion animals at times feel unhappiness and 53% who thought wild animals feel unhappiness.

In addition, many students were unaware of the uses to which farm animals are put. In the second half of the study, children were shown pictures of nine common animal products (along with four decoy items not made from animals) and were asked to identify the animal of origin, if any. The animal products, along with the overall percentage of students who correctly identified them, were as follows: bacon (88%), hotdog (77%), cheese (74%), butter (72%), wool blanket (67%), ice cream (49%), hamburger (46%), leather jacket

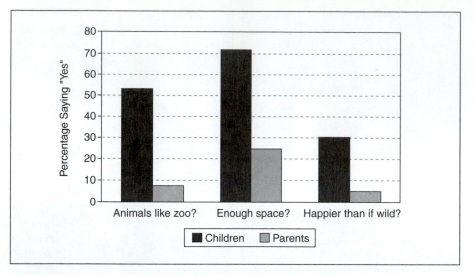

FIGURE 2
In a study conducted at the National Zoo, children were significantly more likely than their parents to believe that animals enjoy being in the zoo, that the animals have enough space, and that zoo animals are happier than their wild counterparts.

(21%), and silk tie (5%). First graders averaged 4.1 items correct, third graders averaged 4.4 correct, and fifth graders averaged 6.0 correct. Thus, first and third graders missed roughly half the items, and fifth graders missed an average of one in three. These findings suggest that even through age 10 or 11, children frequently fail to link common animal products with live animals.

Many young children are also taught that zoo animals lead happy lives, despite the fact that parents often believe the opposite. In an onsite study of zoo visitors, for example, children were significantly more likely than their parents to see the animals as content (Plous, 1993). This study was conducted at the National Zoo in Washington, DC, and included interviews with 50 children (21 girls and 29 boys, with a mean age of 7.9 years) and surveys of adults who were accompanying the children. The children and their parents/guardians answered three key questions, among others: (1) Do you think most zoo animals like being in the zoo? (2) Do you feel that most of the animals here have enough space to be happy? and (3) Are zoo animals happier than animals like them living in the wild? In answer to all three questions, children were far likelier than adults to view the animals as happy.[4] For example, the majority of children thought that zoo animals liked being in the zoo, whereas only 1 adult in 14 felt this way (see Figure 2).

---

[4] Because all three questions were worded so that a positive response indicated greater zoo animal welfare, an alternative explanation for these findings is that children simply answered "yes" more often than did adults. Survey data from negatively worded questions rendered this explanation unlikely, however.

Conflict Reduction

Because consumptive practices are ordinarily dissociated from the infliction of pain, people rarely experience emotional conflict over their use of animals. In some instances, however, the infliction of harm is unusually salient. In such cases, people employ a number of mechanisms to reduce the dissonance between perceptions of themselves as compassionate and the realization that they are hurting animals. Probably the most common of these mechanisms is simply to avoid the topic when it comes up. Other ways of reducing conflict include asserting that the use of animals is necessary for survival,[5] downplaying one's own use of animals, belittling the issue through the use of humor, and claiming that the use of animals causes no more suffering than its alternatives.

One of the most common means of dissonance reduction is to deny that animals feel pain in the same way that humans do. The historical roots of this position go back to the French philosopher René Descartes, who likened animals to machines (Regan & Singer, 1989). In contemporary society, this view is particularly ironic given the prominent role of animal experimentation in pain research (Perl & Kruger, 1996). The way most nonhuman mammals react to pain is remarkably similar in physiology, behavior, and evolutionary purpose to the way that humans react to pain. For example, nonhuman mammals commonly respond with increases in pulse rate, changes in blood pressure, perspiration, pupil dilation, and releases of endogenous opiates that can be blocked by naloxone (Rollin, 1986). Animals and humans also display many of the same behaviors in response to pain, such as writhing, grimacing, crying out, cringing before being struck, and attempting to avoid the source of pain. In fact, many nonhuman mammals may feel even *more* pain than humans; their senses are often more acute than human senses, and their modern-day survival depends more heavily upon sensory information (Serjeant, 1969). Nonetheless, animals are frequently treated as though they do not feel pain. For instance, in the United States cattle are usually branded, dehorned, and castrated without anesthesia (Fox, 1980; Rifkin, 1992).

---

[5] In contrast to the thesis that meat is necessary for human survival, the anthropological and historical record suggests that the earliest hominids were not prodigious hunters, but rather were limited to opportunistic scavenging of carcass remnants abandoned by carnivores (Speth, 1989). According to the American Dietetic Association, "Most of mankind for much of human history has subsisted on near-vegetarian diets. The vast majority of the population of the world today continues to eat vegetarian or semi-vegetarian diets for economic, ecologic, philosophical, religious, cultural, or other reasons" (1980, p. 62). Moreover, human physiology departs significantly from the physiology of most mammalian carnivores (Cox, 1980). Humans have long bowels well suited for fermentative bacteria, rather than short bowels adapted for rapid expulsion of putrefactive bacteria. Humans have short teeth and no claws, rather than long teeth and retractable claws. Humans jaws move laterally rather than strictly up and down, and unlike carnivores, humans secrete relatively little hydrochloric acid to dissolve bones. Human saliva also differs from the saliva of most carnivores in containing ptyallin for predigestion of starches.

An extreme variant of the Cartesian position is that animals are not only immune to suffering, but that they actually *prefer* to be used—that they freely present themselves to be used, and that people do them a favor by using them (see Figure 3). For example, for many years a famous series of advertisements featured a tuna named Charlie who was disappointed at not being eaten. Another well-known advertising campaign implied that being made into a wiener was something to be wished for. Smiling and laughing cows are often used to promote dairy products, and a rooster was used to promote the largest retail restaurant chain specializing in fried chicken. A leading producer of chickens even advertised that its animals lived in "chicken heaven" (Feder, 1989). These advertisements claimed that the

FIGURE 3
This figure shows an example of how laboratory animals have been portrayed as wanting to be used (from *Laboratory Animal Science*, 1980, December, p. 1049).

chickens "lead such a soft life they can't help but turn out tender. They live in $60,000 houses, get eight hours sleep and eat princely meals that include cookies for dessert."

Hunting and trapping are two other animal uses that have been portrayed as a favor to animals. As John Mitchell (1979, p. 20) reported in his study of hunters: "I have talked with hunters from every region of the nation and sooner or later there is one in every crowd who attempts to convince me that hunting is a public service to wild animals." In his book *In Defense of Hunting,* for example, James Swan (1995) argued that hunters were "heroes" who spared animals from the ravages of starvation and disease. According to Swan (p. 160), "If all hunting in America were to stop tomorrow, the consequences for many species would be devastating."

In much the same way, trappers routinely portray their activities as a kindness to animals. For instance, a leading trapper periodical published an article from "the red fox" that said:

> When you see a fox hunter or trapper, which is a predator to us, think about what he stands for. He takes the sick, the weak and the excess to keep us from getting overpopulated so we don't starve. . . . So maybe the next time you see such a guy, you could thank him for what he is doing for us. (Eldridge, 1991, p. 9)

There are several reasons to believe that hunting and trapping are not performed as a service to animals. First, if overpopulation were the reason for these activities, wildlife authorities would work to lower the birth rate of the animals in question. Instead, wildlife managers often strive to *increase* the population of many hunted and trapped species (Dommer, 1989; U.S. Department of the Interior, 1993, 1996). Second, if it were in the collective interest of animals to have their numbers reduced, sharpshooters could be hired to humanely kill diseased members of the population. Currently, millions of animals are wounded each year by unskilled shooters, thousands die painful deaths during special seasons for bow and arrow or by being caught in leghold traps, and the majority of hunters work against natural selection by killing the largest and healthiest members of the population (Motavalli, 1995; Regenstein, 1975).

Another common way people reduce conflict over their use of animals is to acknowledge that animals feel pain but to deny that animals are intelligent or self-aware. One of the earliest proponents of this position was Saint Augustine, who wrote 16 centuries ago: "We can perceive by their cries that animals die in pain, although we make little of this since the beast, lacking a rational soul, is not related to us by a common nature" (Augustine, 390/1966, p. 105).

Yet ever since Kohler (1925) documented the extraordinary problem-solving abilities of chimpanzees in *The Mentality of Apes,* research has steadily revealed greater animal intelligence and awareness than previously assumed (for overviews, see Hauser, 2000; Page, 1999). For example, Koko—a gorilla who was taught American Sign Language and had a working vocabulary of

375 signs by age seven—consistently scored between 85 and 95 on the Stanford-Binet Intelligence Scale (Patterson, 1978). Several studies on self-awareness have documented that chimpanzees, orangutans, and pigeons are capable of using mirrors to locate body markings that cannot be seen directly (Epstein, Lanza, & Skinner, 1981; Gallup, 1977). Chimpanzees in the wild, when ill, have been observed to seek out bitter-tasting medicinal plants and medicate themselves in appropriate dosages (Huffman & Seifu, 1989), and there is now compelling evidence of culturally learned behaviors among chimpanzee groups (Whiten et al., 2001).

Research on nonprimates has yielded equally surprising results. For instance, Pepperberg (1990) taught an African gray parrot to verbally identify the name, shape, and color of objects chosen from a set of 100 possible combinations. Research has also shown that rats are able to discriminate among their own behaviors and press levers corresponding to whether they are face-washing, walking, rearing, or immobile (Beninger, Kendall, & Vanderwolf, 1974). Pigeons are able to exchange information on their level of arousal by pecking keys that correspond to different drug-induced mood states (Lubinski & Thompson, 1987), and have been trained to discriminate among human facial expressions of happiness, anger, surprise, and disgust (Browne, 1989).

Research aside, though, the use of animals depends not so much on issues of intellect or self-awareness as on species membership itself. Society does not consume mentally impaired people, nor does it assume that because such people lack speech and reason, they also lack the ability to feel pain—quite the contrary, it typically extends extra protection to individuals who are unable to speak for themselves (e.g., infants, toddlers, people with mental disabilities). The next section explores whether research findings on human intergroup biases can be fruitfully applied to human-animal relations.

The Similarity Principle

Parallels between prejudice against human outgroups and prejudice against animals have long been recognized by such prominent thinkers as Jeremy Bentham, Charles Darwin, John Stuart Mill, Harriet Beecher Stowe, Frederick Douglass, Albert Schweitzer, and Ashley Montagu. Erik Erikson (1985) even went so far as to describe human outgroup biases as "pseudospeciation." As Spiegel (1988) pointed out, American slaves were sometimes hunted just as animals are hunted today, and not long ago, African Americans served as laboratory animals in medical experiments. For example, in the Tuskegee syphilis study—begun in 1932 and funded by the U.S. Public Health Service—Black men were not told that they had syphilis and were left untreated for up to forty years (Jones, 1981).

Early in American history, it was also assumed by many White people that other races had higher pain thresholds than Whites (Pernick, 1985). For instance, one 18th-century author declared, "What would be the cause of unsupportable pain to a white man, a Negro would almost disregard" (cited in Winchell, 1880, p. 178). Likewise, another prominent writer claimed, "Among your red Indian and other uncivilized tribes, the parturient female does not suffer the same amount of pain during labour, as the female of the white race" (Simpson, 1849, p. 246). Members of racial minorities have often been described explicitly as animals (e.g., "Judge says," 1991; Plous & Williams, 1995; Reinhold, 1991), and for a time, some authors even attempted to prove scientifically that Black people are apes (e.g., Carroll, 1900/1969).

If animals are viewed as an outgroup in the same sense that members of another race, religion, or nationality are regarded as an outgroup, then psychological research on intergroup relations may be relevant to how people perceive animals. Such research has shown that ingroup members tend to see outgroup members as inferior (Brewer, 1979) and more homogeneous than ingroup members (Park & Rothbart, 1982). Research has also shown that the very act of categorization itself leads to an overestimation of between-group differences and an underestimation of within-group differences (Tajfel & Wilkes, 1963; Wilder, 1986), which suggests that perceived differences between humans and animals (e.g., in the capacity to feel pain) may be exaggerated. Although there are obviously profound differences between humans and other species, outgroup biases against animals may foster the impression that individual animals are not unique and irreplaceable in the same way people are (see, for example, Adler, 1985).

A common denominator between outgroup biases based on species membership and outgroup biases based on racial or ethnic membership can be summarized in the following rule, which might be called the "Similarity Principle": *In general, people give more consideration to others who are perceived as similar to themselves than to those who are perceived as dissimilar.*[6] For example, people are more physiologically aroused when watching a person with similar traits suffer than when watching a dissimilar person suffer (Krebs, 1975), and there is some evidence that people empathize more readily with others of the same sex (e.g., Feshbach & Roe, 1968). Studies also suggest that identical twins grieve at the loss of a co-twin more intensely than do fraternal twins (Segal, 1990), and that parents grieve more intensely for children who resemble their side of the family (Littlefield & Rushton, 1986).

Returning to human-animal relations, research indicates that perceived similarity may affect physiological reactions to animal abuse (Plous, 1993). In this study, the skin conductance[7] of 89 college students was monitored as they watched a videotape of apparent animal abuse (the videotape was actually

---

[6] In a very different context, Sherman, Chassin, Presson, and Agostinelli (1984) discussed a "similarity principle," but the principle they proposed was the following: "People who are generally good and toward whom I am oriented positively are similar to me. People who are generally bad are dissimilar to me" (p. 1246). This principle is conversely related to the Similarity Principle advanced here.

[7] Skin conductance tends to increase with sweating and is therefore a popular measure of physiological arousal.

staged without harming an animal). Prior to the videotape, students were instructed as follows:

> The purpose of today's experiment is to get your reactions to an emotional scene. In particular, you'll be watching a 6–7 minute videotape that was filmed at a nearby animal rehabilitation center known as CARE—the Center for Animal Rehabilitation and Education. CARE helps to heal or find homes for all sorts of animals—from farm animals to wildlife to exotic species such as chimpanzees and baboons. As part of their educational program for young children, they also maintain a petting zoo and a collection of snakes, frogs, and so on.
>
> The scene you are about to see involves animal abuse. A female worker at CARE heard some firecrackers go off near the edge of the property, went to see what was happening, and saw a group of people (mostly men) who had broken in and were injuring one of the animals. . . . She wanted to intervene, but because she was the only worker on duty and felt afraid of the men, she ran to get a video camera which CARE uses in its education program. She then returned and secretly videotaped the people as they injured the animal. CARE would like to use footage from this tape in an anti-cruelty campaign, but because the footage is so graphic, they have blocked out the animal with a black box (like you see in interviews when a person's identity is protected, only much larger).

Participants were told that the experimenters wanted to see whether the videotape would be more effective when supplemented with a color slide of the animal before it was injured (all participants were told that they had been assigned to the "slide condition"). Then the laboratory lights were dimmed, and a slide of one of four animals was projected onto a screen: a vervet monkey, a raccoon, a pheasant, or a bullfrog. These animals were selected for several reasons: (1) pilot tests indicated that they differed reliably in perceived similarity to humans, (2) they represented a wide range of animals (i.e., a primate, nonprimate mammal, bird, and amphibian), (3) they were all medium-sized animals that could plausibly appear obscured by the black box, and (4) none had a privileged status (e.g., chimpanzees, dogs) or were routinely harmed by humans (e.g., chickens, pigs).

Using this procedure, the same videotape was shown in all four experimental conditions; the only element that varied was the animal *thought* to be the victim of abuse. The main results of the study, as shown in Figure 4, were consistent with the Similarity Principle. Perceived similarity was directly related to average skin conductance scores, maximum skin conductance scores, and self-reports of how difficult it was to watch the videotape (with students in the monkey condition reporting the most difficulty watching the tape). Thus, people found it most upsetting to witness the abuse of others who were similar to them, even when the others were not human.

Of course, it is worth noting that the Similarity Principle does not mean that perceived similarity *always* makes a difference or that outgroup biases are based on dissimilarity *alone*, for there is abundant evidence that the

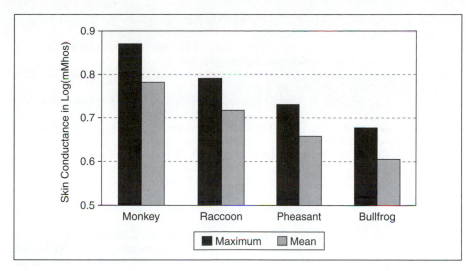

FIGURE 4
When participants in a laboratory study watched scenes of what appeared to be animal abuse, their skin conductance (a measure of physical arousal) decreased with the animal's perceived similarity to humans.

perception and treatment of outgroups also depends on factors such as beauty, familiarity, economic value, status, and potential harmfulness (e.g., Burghardt & Herzog, 1980; Kellert, 1979, 1980).[8] Rather, the Similarity Principle merely suggests that speciesism shares certain psychological features with other forms of prejudice. Because of this correspondence—and because animals are important in their own right—speciesism deserves greater attention than it has heretofore received.

REFERENCES

Adams, C. (1990). *The sexual politics of meat: A feminist-vegetarian critical theory.* New York: Continuum.

Adler, M. J. (1985). *Ten philosophical mistakes.* New York: Macmillan.

Althouse, D. (1985, September). How to talk about fur farming. *The Trapper,* p. 88.

American Dietetic Association. (1980). Position paper on the vegetarian approach to eating. *Journal of the American Dietetic Association, 77,* 61–69.

Augustine, S. (390/1966). *The Catholic and Manichaean ways of life.* Washington, DC: Catholic University of America Press.

Baker, R. (1985). *The American hunting myth.* New York: Vantage Press.

Barker, S. B., & Barker, R. T. (1988). The human-canine bond: Closer than family ties? *Journal of Mental Health Counseling, 10,* 46–56.

Beninger, R. J., Kendall, S. B., & Vanderwolf, C. H. (1974). The ability of rats to discriminate their own behaviours. *Canadian Journal of Psychology, 28,* 79–91.

---

[8] For example, many people would undoubtedly give greater consideration to an endangered species of butterfly than an endangered species of rat, even if they perceived the rat as more similar to humans.

Bradna, F., & Spence, H. (1952). *The big top: My forty years with the Greatest Show on Earth.* New York: Simon & Schuster.

Brewer, M. B. (1979). In-group bias in the minimal intergroup situation: A cognitive-motivational analysis. *Psychological Bulletin, 86,* 307–324.

Bridges, W. (1974). *Gathering of animals: An unconventional history of the New York Zoological Society.* New York: Harper & Row.

Browne, M. W. (1989, May 2). A smile or a grimace? Ask a pigeon's opinion. *New York Times,* p. 22.

Burghardt, G. M., & Herzog, H. A., Jr. (1980). Beyond conspecifics: Is Brer Rabbit our brother? *Bioscience, 30,* 763–768.

Carroll, C. (1900/1969). *The negro a beast.* Miami, FL: Mnemosyne Publishing Co.

Comaromi, J. P. (Ed.). (1989). *Dewey decimal classification and relative index: Devised by Melvil Dewey* (Ed. 20, Vol. 3). Albany, NY: Forest Press.

Cox, M. (1980). *The subversive vegetarian.* Santa Barbara, CA: Woodbridge Press.

Dommer, L. A. (1989, April). A hunter's delusions: Saving the deer from starvation. *Animal's Voice,* pp. 82–84.

Eldridge, F. (1991, January). The red fox. *Trapper and Predator Caller,* pp. 8–9.

Ellena, N. (1980, February 28). Youths sent to prison. *Chico Enterprise-Record,* pp. 1A, 4A.

Epstein, R., Lanza, R. P., & Skinner, B. F. (1981). "Self-awareness" in the pigeon. *Science, 212,* 695–696.

Erikson, E. H. (1985). Pseudospeciation in the nuclear age. *Political Psychology, 6,* 213–215.

Feder, B. J. (1989, November 26). Pressuring Perdue. *New York Times Magazine,* pp. 32–33, 60, 72.

Feshbach, N. D., & Roe, K. (1968). Empathy in six- and seven-year-olds. *Child Development, 39,* 133–145.

Fox, M. W. (1980). *Factory farming.* Washington, DC: Humane Society of the United States.

Fox, M. W. (1997). *Eating with conscience: The bioethics of food.* Troutdale, OR: NewSage Press.

Gallup, G., Jr. (1997). *The Gallup poll: Public opinion 1996.* Wilmington, DE: Scholarly Resources Inc.

Gallup, G. G., Jr. (1977). Self-recognition in primates: A comparative approach to the bidirectional properties of consciousness. *American Psychologist, 32,* 329–338.

Gwynn, S. (1924). The case for certain cruelties. *The Spectator, 132,* 912–913.

Hauser, M. D. (2000). *Wild minds: What animals really think.* New York: Henry Holt and Company.

Hobson, P. (1983). *Raising a calf for beef.* Pownal, VT: Garden Way Publishing.

Hornaday, W. T. (1906). An African pigmy. *Zoological Society Bulletin, 23,* 301–302.

Hoyt, D. (1979). *Fact or fallacy? A trapper tells the truth.* Marshall, MI: National Trappers Association.

Huffman, M. A., & Seifu, M. (1989). Observations on the illness and consumption of a possibly medicinal plant *Vernonia amygdalina* (DEL.), by a wild chimpanzee in the Mahale Mountains National Park, Tanzania. *Primates, 30,* 51–63.

Jasper, J. M., & Nelkin, D. (1992). *The animal rights crusade: The growth of a moral protest.* New York: The Free Press.

Johnston, L. (1979, January 10). Newfoundland seal harvest in March stirs early storm. *New York Times,* p. B6.

Jones, J. H. (1981). *Bad blood: The Tuskegee syphilis experiment.* New York: The Free Press.

Judge says remarks on 'Gorillas' may be cited in trial on beating. (1991, June 12). *New York Times,* p. A24.

Kellert, S. R. (1979). *Public attitudes toward critical wildlife and natural habitat issues* (U.S. Fish and Wildlife Report No. PB-80-138332). Washington, DC: U.S. Government Printing Office.

Kellert, S. R. (1980). American attitudes toward and knowledge of animals: An update. *International Journal for the Study of Animal Problems, 1,* 87–119.

Kellert, S. R., & Berry, J. K. (1980). *Knowledge, affection and basic attitudes toward animals in American society* (U.S. Fish and Wildlife Service Report No. PB-81-173106). Washington, DC: U.S. Government Printing Office.

Kohler, W. (1925). *The mentality of apes.* New York: Harcourt, Brace & Company.

Krebs, D. (1975). Empathy and altruism. *Journal of Personality and Social Psychology, 32,* 1134–1146.

Lederer, S. E. (1992). Political animals: The shaping of biomedical research literature in twentieth-century America. *Isis, 83,* 61–79.

Littlefield, C. H., & Rushton, J. P. (1986). When a child dies: The sociobiology of bereavement. *Journal of Personality and Social Psychology, 51,* 797–802.

Lubinski, D., & Thompson, T. (1987). An animal model of the interpersonal communication of interoceptive (private) states. *Journal of the Experimental Analysis of Behavior, 48,* 1–15.

Man and monkey show disapproved by clergy. (1906, September 10). *New York Times,* pp. 1–2.

Mason, J. & Singer, P. (1990). *Animal factories* (revised and updated). New York: Harmony Books.

McCarthy, V. P. (1982). The changing concept of animals as property. *International Journal for the Study of Animal Problems, 3,* 295–300.

McKenna, C. (1998). *Fashion victims: An inquiry into the welfare of animals on fur farms.* London: World Society for the Protection of Animals.

Meat has many mysteries. (1977, May 5). *Meat Trades Journal,* p. 12.

Mitchell, J. G. (1979). *The hunt.* New York: Penguin Books.

Motavalli, J. (1995, September–October). The killing game: A slow fade. *E: The Environmental Magazine,* p. 36.

Page, G. (1999). *Inside the animal mind.* New York: Doubleday.

Park, B., & Rothbart, M. (1982). Perception of out-group homogeneity and levels of social categorization: Memory for the subordinate attributes of in-group and out-group members. *Journal of Personality and Social Psychology, 42,* 1051–1068.

Patterson, F. (1978). Conversations with a gorilla. *National Geographic, 154,* 438–465.

Pepperberg, I. M. (1990). Cognition in an African gray parrot (*Psittacus erithacus*): Further evidence for comprehension of categories and labels. *Journal of Comparative Psychology, 104,* 41–52.

Perl, E. R., & Kruger, L. (1996). Nociception and pain: Evolution of concepts and observations. In L. Kruger (Ed.), *Pain and touch* (pp. 179–211). San Diego, CA: Academic Press.

Pernick, M. S. (1985). *A calculus of suffering: Pain, professionalism, and anesthesia in nineteenth-century America.* New York: Columbia University Press.

Plous, S. (1993). Psychological mechanisms in the human use of animals. *Journal of Social Issues, 49,* 11–52.

Plous, S., & Williams, T. (1995). Racial stereotypes from the days of American slavery: A continuing legacy. *Journal of Applied Social Psychology, 25,* 795–817.

Regan, T., & Singer, P. (Eds.). (1989). *Animal rights and human obligations* (2nd ed.). Englewood Cliffs, NJ: Prentice Hall.

Regenstein, L. (1975). *The politics of extinction.* New York: Macmillan.

Reinhold, R. (1991, July 10). Study of Los Angeles police finds violence and racism are routine. *New York Times,* pp. A1, A14.

Rifkin, J. (1992). *Beyond beef: The rise and fall of the cattle culture.* New York: Dutton.

Robbins, J. (2001). *The food revolution: How your diet can help save your life and the world.* Berkeley, CA: Conari Press.

Rollin, B. E. (1986). Animal pain. In M. W. Fox & L. D. Mickley (Eds.), *Advances in animal welfare science 1985* (pp. 91–106). Boston: Martinus Nijhoff Publishers.

Sahlins, M. (1976). *Culture and practical reason.* Chicago: University of Chicago Press.

Scientific Committee on Animal Health and Animal Welfare, European Commission Health and Consumer Protection Directorate-General. (2001, December 12–13). *The welfare of animals kept for fur production: Report of the Scientific Committee on Animal Health and Animal Welfare*. Retrieved February 8, 2002, from the European Commission Web site at http://europa.eu.int/comm/food/fs/sc/scah/out67_en.pdf

Schleifer, H. (1985). Images of death and life: Food animal production and the vegetarian option. In P. Singer (Ed.), *In defense of animals* (pp. 63–73). New York: Harper & Row.

Schmidt, V. (1973). *Policy on public hunting on lands and waters within the national wildlife refuge system* (Policy Update No. 4). Washington, DC: Bureau of Sport Fisheries and Wildlife.

Segal, N. L. (1990, June). *Grief associated with twin loss exceeds grief associated with other relatives*. Paper presented at the meeting of the American Psychological Society, Dallas, TX.

Serjeant, R. (1969). *The spectrum of pain*. London: Rupert Hart-Davis.

Serpell, J. (1986). *In the company of animals: A study of human-animal relationships*. New York: Basil Blackwell.

Sheraton, M. (1982, December 15). John Updike ruminates on matters gustatory. *New York Times*, pp. C1, C8.

Sherman, S. J., Chassin, L., Presson, C. C., & Agostinelli, G. (1984). The role of the evaluation and similarity principles in the false consensus effect. *Journal of Personality and Social Psychology, 47,* 1244–1262.

Shroeder, G. (1989, March). Raw fur markets. *Fur-Fish-Game*, p. 54.

Siegel, J. (1993). Companion animals: In sickness and in health. *Journal of Social Issues, 49,* 157–167.

Sierra Club v. Rogers C. B. Morton. (1974). *Supreme Court Reporter, 405–408,* 1361–1378.

Simpson, J. Y. (1849). *Anaesthesia, or the employment of chloroform and ether in surgery, midwifery, etc.* Philadelphia, PA: Lindsay & Blakiston.

Singer, P. (2002). *Animal liberation: A new ethics for our treatment of animals*. New York: Ecco, HarperCollins.

Speth, J. D. (1989). Human evolution: New questions. *Science, 243,* 241–242.

Spiegel, M. (1988). *The dreaded comparison: Race and animal slavery*. Philadelphia, PA: New Society Publishers.

Steinhart, P. (1988, November). Electronic intimacies. *Audubon*, pp. 10, 12–13.

Swan, J. A. (1995). *In defense of hunting*. San Francisco, CA: HarperSanFrancisco.

Tajfel, H., & Wilkes, A. L. (1963). Classification and quantitative judgement. *British Journal of Psychology, 54,* 101–114.

Turner, W. (1980, February 28). Two white men get 25 years in random murder of a black. *New York Times*, p. A16.

U.S. Department of the Interior. (1993, September). *Big game habitat management*. Washington, DC: Bureau of Land Management.

U.S. Department of the Interior. (1996). *Adaptive harvest management: Considerations for the 1996 duck hunting season*. Laurel, MD: U.S. Fish and Wildlife Service.

Weld, T. D. (1839/1968). *American slavery as it is: Testimony of a thousand witnesses*. New York: Arno Press.

Whiten, A., Goodall, J., McGrew, W. C., Nishida, T., Reynolds, V., Sugiyama, Y., et al. (2001). Cultures in chimpanzees. *Nature, 399,* 682–685.

Wilder, D. A. (1986). Social categorization: Implications for creation and reduction of intergroup bias. In L. Berkowitz (Ed.), *Advances in Experimental Social Psychology* (Vol. 19, pp. 291–355). New York: Academic Press.

Winchell, A. (1880). *Preadamites*. Chicago: S. C. Griggs and Company.

Wood, D. (1971). Strategies. In S. Godlovitch, R. Godlovitch, & J. Harris (Eds.), *Animals, men and morals: An enquiry into the maltreatment of non-humans* (pp. 193–212). New York: Taplinger Publishing Company.

A Sampler of Dissonance–Reducing Statements in Support of Harming Animals

The statements below are common justifications for using or harming animals. Note their resemblance to the rationales used to defend slavery (see Section III) and to deny women voting rights (see Section V).

Animals Benefit from Being Used

Hunting

"We [of the Fish and Wildlife Service] allow hunting where it benefits the species" (Satchell, 1987, p. 26).

"Wildlife cannot be stockpiled. . . . Predation is needed to cull and crop wildlife populations to keep them healthy. This is done by managed sport hunting" (*Archery World*, 1989, p. 159).

Trapping

"Starvation is an every-day fact in too many parts of the world. . . . Wild animals can no longer be ignored. Some must be protected to preserve them from becoming extinct and to allow their numbers to increase. Others must be trapped for their sakes and the sakes of humans who need food and the land to grow it" (Fur Information and Fashion Council, undated pamphlet, p. 19).

Cockfighting

"As a chicken he is brought up with the tenderest care and attention; as a young cock he is kept in luxury and freedom, monarch of all he surveys; after two years he is given the joy of battle, and if he dies, what more could a brave heart ask?" (Fitz-Barnard, 1921, p. 12).

Farming

"In some cases, animals are restrained to avoid injuring themselves, other animals or the farmer. All forms of restraint are designed for the welfare of the animal as well as efficiency of production" (Animal Industry Foundation, 1989, p. 109).

"Today's chicken has a diet far superior to any human diet today. . . . All of us older people should envy the chicken" (Babcock, 1987, p. 27).

Dissonance–Reducing Statements (continued)

Animals Are Happy and Do Not Suffer

"Cage chickens are happy chickens. When you go in a cage house, the singing is almost deafening to a human" (Babcock, 1987, p. 27).

"Cage layers [chickens] are immeasurably better off than millions of humans dwelling in the underprivileged sections of the world and certainly better than some American citizens" (Muller, 1981, p. 22A).

"Most animals in biomedical research do not suffer" (Dodds, 1983, p. 67).

"The clamping effect of a properly matched trap does no damage. . . . The trap and drag merely restrict the animal's movements. A properly constructed drowning set dispatches the animal very quickly. Dry land sets that use the leghold trap do not cause great suffering either" (Geary, 1989, p. 176).

"[High-step] pads don't hurt the horses, and eliminating them is like asking women to stop wearing high heels. . . . As for the action devices, those chains are no more weight or annoyance to the horse than your wristwatch is to you" (Smothers, 1990, p. A8).

Economics Prevent Cruelty

"A farmer would compromise his or her own welfare if animals were mistreated. . . . It is in the farmer's own best interest to see the animals in his charge treated humanely, guaranteeing him a healthy, high quality animal, a greater return on his investment, and a wholesome food product" (Animal Industry Foundation, 1989, p. 108).

"For business reasons as well as humane ones, abuse and neglect occur infrequently in animal operations" (Curtis, 1987a, p. 372).

"The producer who keeps his cattle in an improper manner will suffer a loss in production. For that reason alone, most livestock producers will treat their animals as well as possible" (Miller, 1983, p. 98).

"Basically they're treated well. . . . It's in the farmers' interest to take good care of the mink" (Hochswender, 1989, p. 1).

"You won't get a quality pelt without good care of the animal" (Johnson, 1990, p. A14).

"All good researchers insist that animals be treated humanely—not only out of compassion but also because valid work depends on clean, healthy research subjects that are not victims of physical or emotional stress" (White, 1988, p. 130).

Dissonance–Reducing Statements (continued)

Animals Are Machines/Property

"The modern layer [chicken] is, after all, only a very efficient converting machine, changing the raw materials—feedingstuffs—into the finished product—the egg—less, of course, maintenance requirements" (Kennedy, 1962, p. 39).

"The breeding sow should be thought of, and treated as, a valuable piece of machinery whose function is to pump out baby pigs like a sausage machine" (British observer praises U.S. boars, 1978, p. 27).

"Pigs should make admirable production factories for proteins such as hemoglobin" (Moffat, 1991, p. 34).

"Forget the pig is an animal. Treat him just like a machine in a factory. Schedule treatments like you would lubrication. Breeding season like the first step in an assembly line. And marketing like the delivery of finished goods. In other words approach building a pig just like building an automobile or anything else. Except instead of shiny new cars or a new fangled widget your product is feeder pigs" (Byrnes, 1976, p. 30).

"There is nothing immoral or improper about creating cows which produce unnatural and prodigious quantities of milk and treating them as a 'milk factory' because that is what we intended them to be. We breed them artificially, we feed them artificially, and we milk them artificially" (Miller, 1983, p. 98).

Animals Don't Suffer As People Do

"Pain is associated with 'higher' faculties. . . . There are good reasons for questioning the traditional view that animals feel pain. . . . Animals' reactions to painful stimuli should not be viewed as expressions of pain, but rather as examples of adaptive behaviours to dangerous stimuli" (Harrison, 1989, pp. 86–87, 91).

"Pain exists only in a conscious ego. [It] is almost literally the price man pays for the possession of a conscious ego. . . . The higher up in the evolutionary scale the organism is, the more likely that organism is to possess anything that can be identified as pain" (Bakan, 1968, pp. 70–71).

"I have the impression, based on field observations, that many shot animals do not especially show feeling or pain, and may be protected from anguish by going into physiological shock" (Van Gelder, 1972, p. 59).

"Horses suffer very little pain from broken bones" (Paget, 1960, p. 6).

Dissonance–Reducing Statements (continued)

"Domesticated animals have been bred by man to be adaptable to confinement and suffer only minimal stress in their lives from not being able to participate in social and other instinctual behavior that no longer has survival value when animals are reared under confinement" (Jacobs, 1984, pp. 1344–1345).

Animals Lack Intelligence

"I cannot share the opinion of [people] who attribute understanding or thought to animals. . . . The reason animals do not speak as we do is not that they lack the organs but that they have no thoughts" (Descartes, 1646–1649/1989, pp. 16–17, 1989).

"I do not think animals can have desires. My reasons for thinking this turn largely upon my doubt that animals can have beliefs, and my doubts in this regard turn partially though in large part, upon the view that having beliefs is not compatible with the absence of language and linguistic ability" (Frey, 1979, p. 235).

Religious Support for Animal Use

"It is indifferent how [man] behaves towards animals, since God has given him dominion over all, as it is written, Thou has subjected all things under his feet. It is in this sense that St. Paul says that God has no care for oxen, since he does not judge a man on how he has acted with regard to oxen or other animals" (Saint Thomas Aquinas, 1273/1969, p. 225).

"There are levels of creation with man at the top. There should be no question of man's right to life above the animal world because he bears the Creator's image and has a spiritual nature" (Smick, 1973, pp. 22–23).

"Cruelty is an offence against that holy Law which our Maker has written on our hearts, and is displeasing to Him. But they [animals] can claim nothing at our hands; into our hands they are absolutely delivered. We may use them, we may destroy them at our pleasure, not our wanton pleasure, but still for our own ends, for our own benefit or satisfaction" (Cardinal John Henry Newman, 1900, p. 80).

Animal Use Is Necessary

"If we stopped eating animals and using them in research the human race would be decimated" (Levin, 1977, p. 12).

"Our relationship with animals as food-providers is a very old and natural thing. . . . That relationship has, I feel, imprinted on us a basic need to rely on animals to give us the food values we need to live at top form" (Rodale, 1980, p. 21).

Dissonance–Reducing Statements (continued)

"We are right to keep [farm animals], both because we are basically omnivorous animals, and to insure a well-fed nation without providing meat would be pretty difficult" (Tudge, 1973, p. 181).

"Hunting [is] a necessary farming service" (James & Stephens, 1960, p. ix).

Animal Consumption Is Natural

"Herbivorous animals eat the plants and carnivorous animals eat the plant-eaters. Nature imposes no limitations on how one species may exploit another for survival, and I submit that humans have a natural 'right' to exploit other species for our survival and benefit" (Simmonds, 1986, March, p. 36).

"A propensity to hunt is part of our humanity or 'humaneness'. . . . Hunting, I claim, is part of our human inheritance. . . . Our natural diet includes meat" (Robinson, 1987, p. 275).

"Man evolved as a meat-eater" (Ardrey, 1976, p. 12).

"Humans instinctively love meat" (Eaton, 1987, p. 44).

Animals Want to Be Used

"A cock had rather fight than to eat. Cocks love to fight, and they don't care about death. It would be cruel to keep them from fighting" (Pridgen, 1938, pp. 146–147).

"[With certain Pit Bulls] it is cruel to prevent them from fighting, in the way it is cruel to put birds in cages, or at least in cages that are too small for them" (Hearne, 2000, p. 220).

"Most horses enjoy racing enormously" (Francis, 1960, p. 123).

"Far from an example of man's domination, our relationship with [domesticated] animals is a product of nature—initiated by the animals themselves as a strategy for survival" (Budiansky, 1989, p. 76).

Reducing Animal Use Would Hurt the Animals

"If you were to abolish hunting, farmers would fire on the deer—usually with inadequate weapons—and the countryside would be strewn with wounded deer dying painfully and miserably" (Paget, 1960, p. 5).

"More vegetarians would mean more demand for prairie potholes to be converted to grainfields, and, consequently, less wild ducks. Thus, indirectly, vegetarians become more efficient killers of waterfowl than duck hunters, because the former attack the resource base while the hunters harvest the surplus" (Reiger, 1977, p. 20).

Dissonance–Reducing Statements (continued)

"Would the fox be worse off if he were not hunted? In practice he would cease to exist. The fox is preserved because he is an object of sport. [Fox-hunting] does not, in fact, increase the total of animal suffering" (Paget, 1960, p. 4).

Animal Users Are Caring

"Animal producers are at least as humane as members of society in general. Any representation to the contrary comprises a calumny. . . . If animal producers have adopted inhumane production technologies, it has been because they and those who advise them have been ignorant" (Curtis, 1987b, pp. 253–254).

"Nobody cares as much as the farmer. The animal is his livelihood" (Hendrickson, 1989, p. 15).

"The unorganized fraternity of cock fighters contains more brotherly love than any other society anywhere, be it political, religious or secret order" (Pridgen, 1938, p. 153).

"The hunter loves the animal he kills. . . . Hunters are first and foremost ecologists" (Eaton, 1987, pp. 147–148).

"Most of those involved in [wound ballistic] experimentation and instruction are 'fond of dogs' if not actual 'dog lovers' " (Swan & Swan, 1984, p. 349).

Animal-Lovers Hate Animals

"An excessive and unnatural display of love actually represents an underlying animosity. . . . Rather than the sympathetic and compassionate animal-lover, we may perhaps frequently expect to find an individual with underlying tendencies for cruelty and sadism" (Barahal, 1946, p. 8).

Animal Rights Is Fanaticism and Is Only the First Step

"If we do this [give up fur coats], then we have to stop eating meat, no leather shoes, nothing. Then you're back to nature completely" (Designer Karl Lagerfeld, cited in Kasindorf, 1990, p. 32).

"Vegetarianism [is] an eccentric fad which, although not definitely in the domain of the abnormal, attracts to its colors a great many cranks, fanatics, and others who may be considered to be on the fringe of mental imbalance. . . . In short, the average vegetarian is definitely not 'a lunatic,' but he certainly fringes on it" (Barahal, 1946, p. 5).

"This preoccupation with the alleged pain and suffering of the animals used in medical research may well represent, at the very least, social prejudice against medicine or, more seriously, true psychiatric aberrations" (White, 1971, p. 504).

Dissonance–Reducing Statements (continued)

Animal Use Is Not the Issue

"Can all this skirmishing actually be about meat? Probably not. Whatever the merits of the vegetarian-carnivore dispute, the parent-child version looks suspiciously like a reprise of old food battles in the home. 'Kids have always used food as a focus for rebellion,' says Anthropologist Lionel Tiger. 'The vegetarian conflict is only the latest form of the rebellion' " (Leo, 1979, p. 112).

Abuses Are Part of the System

"There is no doubt that the actual treatment of animals used for food is immoral, that animals are made to suffer needlessly. The question that must be raised, however, is how the conclusion not to eat meat follows from this" (Martin, 1976, p. 27).

Animal Consumption Is Inevitable

"There has to be a realistic balance between what we can postulate as an intellectual existence and what that same human mind will believe as it is housed in the body of a predatory animal—and in his profound essence man will forever be partly a predator" (Anthony, 1957, p. 40).

[*Note:* Full citations are given in Source Notes.]

Our Moral Schizophrenia About Animals

Suppose "Simon the Sadist" proposes to torture a dog by burning the dog with a blowtorch. Simon's only reason for torturing the dog is that he derives pleasure from this activity. Most of us, I think, would say that blowtorching the dog is morally wrong.

Our objection may stem partly from the negative effect Simon's behavior has on people who see it or on Simon himself, but that is not our primary reason for objecting. After all, we would condemn the act even if Simon tortured the animal in private, or if the act had no discernible effect on Simon.

The main reason we find Simon's action morally wrong is its direct effect on the dog. Like us, the dog feels pain and therefore has an interest in not being burned. No other characteristic—such as rationality, self-consciousness, or language ability—is necessary. Simply because the dog can experience pain and suffering, we require a justification for any infliction of harm. We may disagree about whether a particular justification suffices, but we agree that some justification is needed beyond Simon's pleasure.

When it comes to how we treat animals in daily life, however, our behavior reveals a deep moral schizophrenia. Contrary to our beliefs about what is moral, we often harm animals with no justification beyond human pleasure. A key question posed by the animal rights movement is this: if it is morally wrong to hurt or kill a dog strictly for human gratification, why is it acceptable to hurt or kill a pig for pizza toppings?

—Adapted from Gary L. Francione, *Introduction to Animal Rights: Your Child or the Dog?*, 2000

GAPS IN THE MIND

RICHARD DAWKINS

Sir,

You appeal for money to save the gorillas. Very laudable, no doubt. But it doesn't seem to have occurred to you that there are thousands of *human* children suffering on the very same continent of Africa. There'll be time enough to worry about gorillas when we've taken care of every last one of the kiddies. Let's get our priorities right, *please*!

This hypothetical letter could have been written by almost any well-meaning person today. In lampooning it, I don't mean to imply that a good case could not be made for giving human children priority. I expect it could, and also that a good case could be made the other way. I'm only trying to point the finger at the *automatic,* unthinking nature of the speciesist double standard. To many people it is simply self-evident, *without any discussion,* that humans are entitled to special treatment. To see this, consider the following variant on the same letter:

Sir,

You appeal for money to save the gorillas. Very laudable, no doubt. But it doesn't seem to have occurred to you that there are thousands of *aardvarks* suffering on the very same continent of Africa. There'll be time enough to worry about gorillas when we've saved every last one of the aardvarks. Let's get our priorities right, *please*!

This second letter could not fail to provoke the question: What's so special about aardvarks? A good question, and one to which we should require a satisfactory answer before we took the letter seriously. Yet the first letter, I suggest, would not for most people provoke the equivalent question: What's so special about humans? As I said, I don't deny that this question, unlike the aardvark question, very probably has a powerful answer. All that I am criticising is an unthinking failure to realise in the case of humans that the question even arises.

The speciesist assumption that lurks here is very simple. Humans are humans and gorillas are animals. There is an unquestioned yawning gulf between them such that the life of a single human child is worth more than the lives of all the gorillas in the world. The "worth" of an animal's life is just its replacement cost to its owner—or, in the case of a rare species, to humanity. But tie the label *Homo sapiens* even to a tiny piece of insensible, embryonic tissue, and its life suddenly leaps to infinite, uncomputable value.

This way of thinking characterises what I want to call the discontinuous mind. We would all agree that a six-foot woman is tall, and a five-foot woman is not. Words like "tall" and "short" tempt us to force the world into qualitative classes, but this doesn't mean that the world really is discontinuously distributed. Were you to tell me that a woman is five feet nine inches tall, and ask me to decide whether she should therefore be called tall or not, I'd shrug and say "She's five foot nine, doesn't that tell you what you need to know?" But the discontinuous mind, to caricature it a little, would go to court (probably at great expense) to decide whether the woman was tall or short. Indeed, I hardly need to say caricature. For years, South African courts have done a brisk trade adjudicating whether particular individuals of mixed parentage count as white, black or coloured.

The discontinuous mind is ubiquitous. Recently, after giving a public lecture, I was cross-examined by a lawyer in the audience. He brought the full weight of his legal acumen to bear on a nice point of evolution. If species A evolves into a later species B, he reasoned, there must come a point when a mother belongs to the old species A and her child belongs to the new species B. Members of different species cannot interbreed with one another. I put it to you, he went on, that a child could hardly be so different from its parents that it could not interbreed with their kind. So, he wound up triumphantly, isn't this a fatal flaw in the theory of evolution?

But it is we that choose to divide animals up into discontinuous species. On the evolutionary view of life there must have been intermediates, even though, conveniently for our naming rituals, they are usually extinct: usually, but not always. The lawyer would be surprised and, I hope, intrigued by so-called "ring species." The best-known case is herring gull versus lesser black-backed gull. In Britain these are clearly distinct species, quite different in colour. Anybody can tell them apart. But if you follow the population of herring gulls westward round the North Pole to North America, then via Alaska across Siberia and back to Europe again, you will notice a curious fact. The "herring gulls" gradually become less and less like herring gulls and more and more like lesser black-backed gulls until it turns out that our European lesser black-backed gulls actually are the other end of a ring that started out as herring gulls. At every stage around the ring, the birds are sufficiently similar to their neighbours to interbreed with them. Until, that is, the ends of the continuum are reached, in Europe. At this point the herring gull and the lesser black-backed gull never interbreed, although they are linked by a continuous series of interbreeding colleagues all the way round the world. The only thing that is special about ring species like these gulls is that the intermediates are still alive. *All* pairs of related species are potentially ring species. The intermediates must have lived once. It is just that in most cases they are now dead.

The lawyer, with his trained discontinuous mind, insists on placing individuals firmly in this species or that. He does not allow for the possibility that an individual might lie half-way between two species, or a tenth of the way from species A to species B. Self-styled "pro-lifers," and others that indulge in debates about exactly when in its development a foetus "becomes human," exhibit the same discontinuous mentality. It is no use telling these people that, depending upon the human characteristics that interest you, a foetus can be "half human" or "a hundredth human." "Human," to the discontinuous mind, is an absolute concept. There can be no half measures. And from this flows much evil.

The word "apes" usually means chimpanzees, gorillas, orang-utans, gibbons and siamangs. We admit that we are like apes, but we seldom realise that we *are* apes. Our common ancestor with the chimpanzees and gorillas is much more recent than their common ancestor with the Asian apes—the gibbons and orang-utans. There is no natural category that includes chimpanzees, gorillas and orang-utans but excludes humans. The artificiality of the category "apes," as conventionally taken to exclude humans, is demonstrated by Figure 1. This family tree shows humans to be in the thick of the ape cluster; the artificiality of the conventional category "ape" is shown by the stippling.

In truth, not only are we apes, we are African apes. The category "African apes," if you don't arbitrarily exclude humans, is a natural one. The stippled area in Figure 2 doesn't have any artificial "bites" taken out of it.

"Great apes," too, is a natural category only so long as it includes humans. We are great apes. All the great apes that have ever lived, including ourselves, are linked to one another by an unbroken chain of parent-child bonds. The same is true of all animals and plants that have ever lived, but there the distances involved are much greater. Molecular evidence suggests that our common ancestor with chimpanzees lived, in Africa, between five and seven million years ago, say half a million generations ago. This is not long by evolutionary standards.

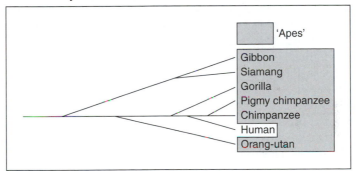

FIGURE 1
Artificiality of the conventional category "Ape".

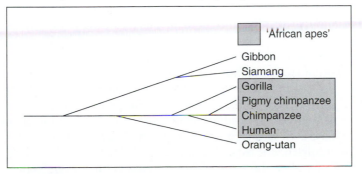

FIGURE 2
The category "African apes" without artificial bites.

Happenings are sometimes organised at which thousands of people hold hands and form a human chain, say from coast to coast of the United States, in aid of some cause or charity. Let us imagine setting one up along the equator, across the width of our home continent of Africa. It is a special kind of chain, involving parents and children, and we will have to play tricks with time in order to imagine it. You stand on the shore of the Indian Ocean in southern Somalia, facing north, and in your left hand you hold the right hand of your mother. In turn she holds the hand of her mother, your grandmother. Your grandmother holds her mother's hand, and so on. The chain wends its way up the beach, into the arid scrubland and westwards on towards the Kenya border.

How far do we have to go until we reach our common ancestor with the chimpanzees? It is a surprisingly short way. Allowing one yard per person, we arrive at the ancestor we share with chimpanzees in under 300 miles. We have hardly started to cross the continent; we are still not half way to the Great Rift Valley. The ancestor is standing well to the east of Mount Kenya, and holding in her hand an entire chain of her lineal descendants, culminating in you standing on the Somali beach.

The daughter that she is holding in her right hand is the one from whom we are descended. Now the arch-ancestress turns eastward to face the coast, and with her left hand grasps her other daughter, the one from whom the chimpanzees are descended (or son, of course, but let's stick to females for convenience). The two sisters are facing one another, and each holding their mother by the hand. Now the second daughter, the chimpanzee ancestress, holds her daughter's hand, and a new chain is formed, proceeding back towards the coast. First cousin faces first cousin, second cousin faces second cousin, and so on. By the time the folded-back chain has reached the coast again, it consists of modern chimpanzees. You are face to face with your chimpanzee cousin, and you are joined to her by an unbroken chain of mothers holding hands with daughters. If you walked up the line like an inspecting general—past *Homo erectus, Homo habilis,* perhaps *Australopithecus afarensis*—and down again the other side (the intermediates on the chimpanzee side are unnamed because, as it happens, no fossils have been found), you would nowhere find any sharp discontinuity. Daughters would resemble mothers just as much (or as little) as they always do. Mothers would love daughters, and feel affinity with them, just as they always do. And this hand-in-hand continuum, joining us seamlessly to chimpanzees, is so short that it barely makes it past the hinterland of Africa.

Our chain of African apes, doubling back on itself, is in miniature like the ring of gulls round the pole, except that the intermediates happen to be dead. The point I want to make is that, as far as morality is concerned, it should be incidental that the intermediates are dead. What if they were not? What if a clutch of intermediate types had survived, enough to link us to modern chimpanzees by a chain, not just of hand-holders, but of interbreeders? Remember the song, "I've danced with a man, who's danced with a girl, who's danced with the Prince of Wales"? We can't (quite) interbreed with modern chimpanzees, but we'd need only a handful of intermediate types to be able to sing: "I've bred with a man, who's bred with a girl, who's bred with a chimpanzee."

It is sheer luck that this handful of intermediates no longer exists. But for this chance, our laws and our morals would be very different. We need only discover a single survivor, say a relict *Australopithecus* in the Budongo Forest, and our precious system of norms and ethics would come crashing about our ears. The boundaries with which we segregate our world would be all shot to pieces. Racism would blur with speciesism in obdurate and vicious confusion. Apartheid, for those that believe in it, would assume a new and perhaps a more urgent import.

But why, a moral philosopher might ask, should this matter to us? Isn't it only the discontinuous mind that wants to erect barriers anyway? So what if, in the continuum of all apes that have lived in Africa, the survivors happen to leave a convenient gap between *Homo* and *Pan?* Surely we should, in any case, not base our treatment of animals on whether or not we can interbreed with them. If we want to justify double standards—if society agrees that people should be treated better than, say, cows (cows may be cooked and eaten, people may not)—there must be better reasons than cousinship.

The discontinuous gap between humans and "apes" that we erect in our minds is arbitrary, the result of evolutionary accident. If the contingencies of survival and extinction had been different, the gap would be in a different place. Ethical principles that are based upon accidental caprice should not be respected as if cast in stone.

Moral Progress

The greatness of a nation and its moral progress can be judged by the way its animals are treated.

—Mohandas Gandhi, *The Moral Basis of Vegetarianism*, 1931

UNHEARD VOICES: INSTITUTIONALIZED PREJUDICE TOWARD ANIMALS IN THE U.S. MEAT INDUSTRY

GAIL A. EISNITZ

Prologue

The men Carol Taylor dates all seem to have at least one tattoo and hair that's either razor short or very long. She hangs out with crooks and brawlers in bars and roadhouses, and has been chased at 120 mph in the middle of the night by thugs trying to kill her.

Right now Carol Taylor is sitting with a man she met an hour ago, the cop who caught serial killer Ted Bundy. They are in the Florida mobile home of Gibb and Jean Gibson,* the four of them drinking Scotch and telling jokes.

The Gibsons train greyhounds to race. They've welcomed her into their circle and think of her as a dear friend. Carol Taylor, for her part, thinks of the Gibsons as the people she's about to have arrested.

🌿   🌿   🌿

I, Gail Eisnitz, prefer to spend my evenings at home with my cat, a cup of tea, and a good book. "Carol Taylor" is my undercover identity and persona. I have been working on and off for months to have Gibb Gibson arrested for the torture and death of thousands of rabbits used as live bait in his dog-training business.

At five-thirty the next morning Jeannie Gibson is cooking us breakfast inside the trailer. Outside, my "boyfriend" Capt. David Lee and I watch Gibb tie a live rabbit to the track's mechanical arm. Some of the country's leading greyhound owners are standing at the edge of the track to see how this round of training goes.

The arm takes off around the track and the dogs leap after it, biting at the helpless rabbit dangling from it upside down. I'm shooting photos as fast as I can—supposedly of the dogs, for portraits, but actually of the people.

Captain Lee ducks his head to speak into his shirt collar.

"Takedown. Takedown."

Seven police cars come tearing down the road, and ten officers move out from behind trees around the track. I slip away, ostensibly to point the police in the direction of the evidence, but mainly because I don't want to face the Gibsons.

After the court releases Gibson and the others on their own recognizance, pending trial, the Gibsons spot me dumpster-diving for more evidence close to their dog track. They pull over, shaking their fists and screaming obscenities. We're all by ourselves on this lonely stretch of road, just me and my former friends. Then Captain Lee pulls up.

---

*Some names of individuals have been changed to protect their privacy.

The Gibsons drive off, yelling at me as if they would beat me to a pulp first chance they get.

🐾   🐾   🐾

The Gibsons aren't the only reason I'm in Florida. As Gail Eisnitz, I've also come to interview a man named Timothy Walker who has written me a letter claiming firsthand knowledge of atrocities so horrific that I would have dismissed them as ravings if it weren't for his sane and sober tone.

His letter will start me on an investigation that will nearly kill me, an investigation into cruelty so deep and broad, to humans and animals, that it touches every person in this country.

One Man's Cry for Help

Timothy Walker is a troublemaker.

In the 1980s, when employed as a Kansas City weights and measures inspector, he found that for the previous thirty years gas stations had been shortchanging their customers. Instead of keeping his mouth shut like everyone else, he blew the whistle. The case made headlines all over Missouri.

Later, as an energy auditor for the city, he tried to get officials to do something about the poverty he saw in the course of duty. The city, claiming budget constraints, refused to act. Walker ended up buying storm windows for low-income families out of his own pocket, paying one elderly woman's real-estate taxes, and bringing Thanksgiving dinner to another.

I first heard of Timothy Walker back in 1989 when, as a field investigator with a Washington, D.C.-based animal protection organization, I received a letter from him. He wrote that he had firsthand knowledge that Kaplan Industries, a slaughterhouse in Bartow, Florida, was skinning cattle while they were still alive.

Skinning live cattle? As a cruelty investigator, I would sometimes receive crank letters about cows butchered by aliens, or messages channeled from manatees, or telepathic chickens. But something about this letter seemed genuine.

"This is not only extremely cruel," he wrote, "but also very dangerous for the plant personnel who have to skin these kicking animals." Plant management knew about the problem, he said, but didn't want to correct it because that would mean slowing down the production line. "I have contacted a number of federal agencies but have been told there is nothing they can do. They also told me that the problems I described exist all over the country, that they are just a little worse at Kaplan's."

🐾   🐾   🐾

In my line of work, I've seen just about every imaginable kind of cruelty to animals, from the mundane to the exotic: dogs trained to rip each other apart for the amusement of people; ritual sacrifice of chickens, goats, sheep, and cattle; cockfighting, where birds wearing razor-sharp spurs fight to a slow, bloody death; puppy mills where inbred, genetically deformed puppies suffer from overcrowding, malnutrition, exposure to the elements.

But who in their right mind would attempt to skin conscious cows, particularly right under the noses of United States Department of Agriculture (USDA) meat inspectors? Sometimes involuntary reflexes in stunned or dead animals can look like conscious kicking. And there was always the possibility that Walker might not be telling the truth. Perhaps he was just a disgruntled employee. I needed to dig deeper.

🦅 🦅 🦅

I learned that Kaplan was slaughtering about six hundred head of cattle a day. Not as many as some of the nation's newer high-speed mega-operations, but still high enough to make it the largest beef slaughterhouse in Florida. Next I called the USDA and requested an immediate investigation. Four days later a USDA official called me back with her findings. She said that no cattle were being skinned alive at Kaplan.

"Though I wouldn't have been surprised if they were, at *that* plant," she added.

"How come?" I asked.

"Oh, they have a reputation around here."

"Reputation for what?" I asked.

She wouldn't elaborate.

🦅 🦅 🦅

I decided it was time to contact Walker by phone. He was soft-spoken and articulate. When I asked for the source of his inside information, he admitted it was himself. He was, as it turned out, a USDA employee.

Unlike USDA meat inspectors who examined carcasses and body parts elsewhere in the plant, Walker worked in what's known as the "blood pit." Part of Walker's job was to take blood samples from cows to test for bovine brucellosis, a highly contagious disease which causes abortions in cattle and has a major financial impact on the beef industry. He was stationed on a catwalk between two head-skinners and a man who used a pneumatic dehorner and huge cleaver to cut off the animals' horns and front legs.

In theory, cattle in a slaughterhouse are either prodded along a chute into a "knocking box" or up to a conveyor/restrainer, which then carries them up to the "stun operator." The stun operator, or "knocker," shoots each animal in the forehead with a compressed-air gun that drives a steel bolt into the cow's skull and then retracts it. If the knocking gun is properly used by the operator, it knocks the cow unconscious or kills the animal on the spot.

The next man on the line, the "shackler," wraps a chain around one of the stunned cow's hind legs. Once shackled, the animal is automatically lifted onto a moving overhead rail. The cow, now hanging upside down by a leg, is sent to the "sticker," the worker who cuts the carotid arteries and a jugular vein in the neck.

Next the cow travels along the "bleed rail" and is given several minutes to bleed out. The carcass then proceeds to the head-skinners, the leggers, and on down the line where it is skinned, eviscerated, and split in half.

That's the way it's supposed to be done, according to federal law. But according to Walker, that's not at all what was happening at Kaplan Industries.

🦅 🦅 🦅

In 1906 Upton Sinclair published *The Jungle,* an account of an immigrant family's struggle to survive amidst the appalling conditions of Chicago's stockyards and slaughterhouses. *The Jungle* revealed slaughterhouse conditions so shocking and meat so filthy that meat sales plummeted more than fifty percent and President Theodore Roosevelt personally crusaded for enactment of the Federal Meat Inspection Act of 1906. That law and subsequent legislation established standards for plant sanitation and required federal inspection of all meat shipped interstate or out of the country.

Today, USDA employees inspect meat in much the same way as they did back in 1906. According to federal law, all animals in slaughterhouses must be examined before and after they are killed. These inspections are conducted by government veterinarians or trained inspectors. Veterinarians, knowledgeable in animal physiology and health, have general oversight in slaughterhouses. Inspectors, who receive classroom and on-the-job training, learn how to detect lesions, signs of illness, and contamination in animals. When an abnormal carcass or organ is detected, it is tagged and retained for examination by the USDA veterinarian.

Congress passed the Humane Slaughter Act (HSA) in 1958 and broadened it in 1978. Among the HSA's most important provisions is the requirement that all animals be rendered unconscious with just *one* application of an effective stunning device by a trained person *before* being shackled and hoisted up on the line.

🦅 🦅 🦅

For months before contacting me, Walker had pleaded with his USDA supervisors to correct the problems at the plant. "I can safely say someone is going to be killed if conditions at Kaplan's are not changed," Walker had written in a letter to a supervisor. To another he wrote, "You cannot begin to know what the conditions are at this plant unless you have worked on the kill floor and seen them for yourself. I have almost had my clock stopped [been killed] a number of times by live cows kicking wildly as they were skinned while still conscious." To a third supervisor he wrote, "The situation calls for immediate action."

Will We Get Out of Here Alive?

Timothy Walker lived in Naples, Florida, a sunny town sandwiched between the Gulf of Mexico and Big Cypress Swamp. I met him in a small seafood restaurant. He looked to be in his late forties, of average height and build, with a pleasant, self-effacing air. To get acquainted, we swapped a little personal information before I turned on the tape recorder.

Having dreamed of living in Florida, Walker had left his job as an energy auditor a year earlier and moved south. He thought he'd lined up a job with the USDA's animal welfare division, the unit that inspects conditions in research labs, commercial dog-breeding establishments, and zoos. He never expected to find himself inside a beef slaughterhouse collecting blood samples.

"Last Saturday," he said, "the line was smoking. There were more live cows coming through than I've ever seen before. The skinners were cussing. We were cussing. The whole line was going crazy. Just about every cow that come down the line—at least a hundred of them—was alive that afternoon."

Often, he said, improperly stunned cattle regained consciousness after they'd been shackled and hoisted onto the overhead rail. In addition to kicking and thrashing as they hung upside down, he told me, "they'd be blinking and stretching their necks from side to side, looking around, really frantic."

Regardless, the cattle moved down the line to the sticker.

"A lot of times the sticker just can't do his job right," Walker said. "He doesn't get a good bleed." Still, within seconds of being stuck, the cows arrived at the two head-skinners, who stripped all the hide from the animals' heads.

"A lot of times the skinner finds out an animal is still conscious when he slices the side of its head and it starts kicking wildly. If that happens, or if a cow is already kicking when it arrives at their station, the skinners shove a knife into the back of its head to cut the spinal cord."

This practice paralyzes the cow from the neck down but doesn't deaden the pain of head skinning or render the animal unconscious; it simply allows workers to skin or dismember the animal without getting kicked.

"I asked my boss if I had the authority to stop the line. He said it was Dr. Tecsan's problem [the USDA veterinarian at Kaplan]. 'She's in charge.' In order to tell Tecsan I'd have to leave my station, and if I do that, I'm not taking blood samples. So I'd tell her after I got off the line that they were skinning live cows. Sometimes she'd say something, sometimes she was too busy."

Walker named about twenty different people he'd contacted at the USDA, the VA, and the U.S. Congress. By the time we finished talking that evening, we had tallied up fourteen different federal humane and safety regulations that were routinely violated at Kaplan.

☙ ☙ ☙

The next morning I drove north to Frostproof to speak with Kenneth Sandborne, one of Walker's co-workers. Sandborne, like Walker a USDA brucellosis tester, told me that all the problems on Walker's list had been around long before he'd come to work at the plant. When I pressed him for details and for observations of his own, he told me a story.

Before Walker had even hired on with the USDA, Sandborne and another brucellosis tester had stopped the slaughter operation at Kaplan when conscious cattle were being skinned alive. The plant vice president rushed out to the floor.

"He chewed us out," Sandborne said. "Said we weren't there to stop the line, and if we didn't like what was going on we'd be asked to leave. I don't know how he could threaten us with our jobs when we didn't even work for the plant. We worked for the USDA—the government." Nevertheless, Sandborne had backed down.

Still afraid that he might lose his job, he didn't allow me to tape the interview, wouldn't commit to signing an affidavit, but did say enough to corroborate Walker's statements.

🍃   🍃   🍃

Over the next few days, I spoke with two more brucellosis testers who'd been temporarily stationed at the plant. The first, Ronnie Watson, lived with his wife and children on a pretty farm in the Florida countryside. With the family horse looking on and a kitten rubbing up against my feet, I asked him about Walker's statements.

"Don't get me wrong. Tim's good people, but he's out of his element," Watson spoke slowly with a Southern twang. "Nobody likes to see animals hung up alive, but Tim's too sensitive to the animals' suffering. Me, I was scared. I got whacked a few times."

I asked if he was sure the cows were really still alive.

"Kicking can be muscle reaction," he said. "If they're bellowing or making noise they're alive. When the eyes are blinking and you've got eye movement, they're alive."

"Did you complain about the live ones?" I asked.

"I complained to Dr. Tecsan two or three times. I'd say, 'Dr. Tecsan, the cattle are coming in alive. They're dangerous!' She'd go and chew out the knocker, but that wouldn't solve the problem. I wrote a letter—a lot of us wrote letters."

🍃   🍃   🍃

There was enough corroborative evidence now to make me believe Walker's claims. But all of the people I'd questioned were USDA employees.

I went back to Kaplan Industries in Florida.

There were about 260 employees at Kaplan. The majority of them were of Mexican descent. I knew that there were a few Spanish-speaking communities about twenty-five miles south of Kaplan. I got in my car and headed south.

Perhaps it was luck or just good old-fashioned detective work that led me to a low-income housing project in Bowling Green. I hung around until dusk, when I saw a couple climbing out of a car with two small children and their arms full of grocery bags. I followed them into their apartment while introducing myself.

Albert Cabrera, a tall, slim man of about twenty with dark curly hair and huge brown eyes, invited me to sit down. A small electric fan nudged the hot, humid air around the room. I turned on my tape recorder.

"In the morning the big holdup was the calves," he said. "To get done with them faster, we'd put eight or nine of them in the knocking box at a time. As soon as they start going in, you start shooting, the calves are jumping, they're all piling up on top of each other. You don't know which ones got shot and which ones didn't get shot at all, and you forget to do the bottom ones. They're hung anyway, and down the line they go, wriggling and yelling. The baby ones—two, three weeks old—I felt bad killing them so I just let them walk past.

"But it wasn't just the calves that went through conscious. It was a serious problem with the cows, and the bulls have even harder skulls. A lot I had to hit three or five times, ten times before they'd go down. There were plenty of times you'd have to make a big hole in their head, and still they'd be alive.

"I remember one bull with really long horns. I knocked it twice," he said. "That bull must have felt the shackle going on its leg, it got up like nothing ever happened to it, it didn't even wobble, and took off out the back door, started running down Route 17 and just wouldn't stop. They went out and shot it with a rifle, dragged it back with the tractor.

"See, they got a little poster that shows you a little X on its head," Cabrera explained. "And that's where you're supposed to hit them—right there on the center of the X."

"And that's what you tried to do?" I asked.

"That's what I *did* do. But they were always complaining I wasn't doing my job."

"What about the USDA people?" I asked.

"They used to watch the animals stand up after I knocked them. They'd complain but they never did anything about it," he said. "They don't slow that line down for nothing or nobody."

🦃 🦃 🦃

I headed back to Washington. A few days later, Timothy Walker called me with some bad news: The USDA had fired him for speaking to me.

The Man with the Scar

As for me, I was working like mad transcribing the interviews I'd taped and turning them into affidavits. This was all very powerful, but I was concerned that the meat industry might try to explain Kaplan away as a backwater anachronism. I suspected, however, that Kaplan was representative of slaughterhouses across the country. So I decided to broaden my investigation's scope and started researching the entire U.S. meat industry.

I obtained statistics from various government sources. The slaughter figures were staggering. Ninety-three million pigs are slaughtered each year in the United States. Thirty-seven million cattle. Two million calves. Six million horses, goats, and sheep. And eight *billion* chickens and turkeys. In all, annually in the United States farmers produce 43 billion pounds of pork and beef, 43 billion pounds of poultry, and 76 billion eggs.

Lax enforcement of antitrust laws during the Reagan and Bush administrations, I learned, had allowed a consolidation of meatpacking power to levels higher than at any time in history, and a corresponding deregulation of slaughterhouse procedures. According to the USDA, between 1984 and 1994, a few large, high-speed slaughter operations had driven roughly 2,000 small to mid-sized packers out of business—one-third of all packers in the United States. They also reduced the workforce while cranking up the killing speeds. Fewer employees were slaughtering more animals, and, according to the United Food and Commercial Workers International Union, which represents thousands of slaughterhouse employees, the worker turnover rate in high-speed plants approached 100 percent per year.*

---

*According to the USDA, in 1980, it took the country's 50 largest beef packing companies and 103 individual plants to slaughter two-thirds of the nation's cattle. By 1992, *three* firms were already slaughtering that percentage of animals in 29 plants. In 1996 more than 40 percent of the nation's cattle were killed in a mere 11 plants that slaughter more than one million animals each year. Similarly, more than 40 percent of the nation's hogs were killed in 10 plants.

I glanced through the pile of complaints on my desk that had gathered as I worked on my slaughterhouse case. A guy in North Carolina strangled a hundred puppies for fun; a New Yorker collected two hundred homeless pets and then starved them to death. Just when I thought I'd seen it all, some new way to torture animals would land in my in-box.

I thumbed through *Animal's Voice*, an animal protection magazine I found buried among the complaints and tossed it aside. Then something I'd flipped past registered and I opened it up again. It was an article about one of the huge, high-speed meat packers I'd just been researching. The main difference between the abuses described there and those at Kaplan was that the animals depicted were not cattle, but hogs—and they were reportedly being immersed in the plant's scalding tank and boiled alive.

According to the story, a union official at the John Morrell & Company slaughterhouse in Sioux City, Iowa, claimed that hogs at that plant were not being properly stunned and were still fully conscious as they were submerged in the plant's scalding tank. "What the public sees is fancy labels," said the official who'd had twenty-four years' experience in the packing industry. "But those of us inside the walls can tell the truth about what the vast majority have never seen—living hell in John Morrell's slaughterhouse."

I contacted the magazine for more information, threw some clothes into a suitcase, and headed for the airport.

Mike Huntsinger, the union official quoted in the magazine, was a burly man with a direct manner. He told me that while John Morrell & Company had the capacity to slaughter seventy-five thousand hogs a week at the breakneck speed of one hog every four seconds, line speed was only part of the problem.

Hogs were stunned electrically rather than mechanically; electrodes held to the hog's head and back sent a three-second jolt of current through its body, knocking the animal out. But if the animal was excessively prodded on its way to the stunner, or if the stun operator improperly applied the electrodes, the jolt would burst capillaries in the hog's back. The result—"bloodsplash" or "blown loins"—made the meat look bruised and bloody, thus lowering its value.

Plant managers preferred to lower the current to the stunning equipment. The weaker jolt prevented bloodsplash but often stunned the hogs only momentarily, if at all.

I wanted to talk to the sticker, the man on the scene whose photo had appeared in the magazine. He'd been hurt on the job, Huntsinger told me, and no longer worked at Morrell. Huntsinger gave me his new address and I headed out. A ten-hour drive would bring me to a quiet mobile home community in southwestern Kansas.

Tommy Vladak, a sandy-haired man in his mid-twenties, reminded me of Hollywood's Brad Pitt—except for the puckered scar that ran from his forehead, across his eye and nose, and over his lips to his jaw.

Because he worked the evening shift at his new job, my first interview with Vladak didn't start until almost midnight. Despite the hour, he seemed wired when he walked into my motel room. He sat down, declined my offer of a soda, and said he was ready to talk. I turned on my tape recorder. Vladak seemed proud of his nine years' experience in the packing industry. Originally from Texas, Vladak and his wife and kids had moved to Sioux City to be closer to his in-laws.

"What was it like, being a sticker at Morrell?" I asked.

"Dangerous," Vladak said. "I was kicked, bitten, stabbed in the forearm, had a tooth knocked out, an eardrum punctured, and finally got my face slashed. And that was *after* I'd complained about live hogs to almost every level of management, and had shut the chain off a bunch of times trying to deal with the problem.

"I was a good sticker. I could do the job at any chain speed. At Morrell's I was sticking about nine hundred hogs an hour, which wouldn't be that hard if they were stunned right. But when most of them are fully conscious, kicking and biting at you, it's like . . ."

"Tell me about the kill line," I said.

"I've seen hogs stunned up to twelve times. Like, a big boar would come through, they'd hit him with the stunner, he'd look up at them, go RRRAAA! Hit him again, the son of a bitch wouldn't go, wouldn't go. It's amazing the willpower these animals have.

"One night I asked somebody on the kill floor how many loins we'd blown out that night. Two or three. How come they lowered the stunner voltage for just two or three out of thousands? Two or three's still too many, they said."

"What happens after you stick them?" I asked.

"After they left me, the hogs would go up a hundred-foot ramp to a tank where they're dunked in 140° water [a standard procedure in pork processing]. That's to scald their hair off," he explained. "Water any hotter than that would take the meat right off the bones. You stick a live hog, it tightens up the muscles around that slit and holds the blood in. There's no way these animals can bleed out in the few minutes it takes to get up the ramp. By the time they hit the scalding tank, they're still fully conscious and squealing. Happens all the time. . . .

"There was one night I'll never forget as long as I live," he continued. "A little female hog was coming through the chutes. She got away and the supervisor said, 'Stick that bitch!' I grabbed her and flipped her over. She looked up at me. It was like she was saying, 'Yeah, I know it's your job, do it.' That was the first time I ever looked into a live hog's eyes. And I stuck her."

The phone rang, jerking me back to the drab room. Vladak's wife was calling, probably wondering just what kind of an interview was going on in a motel room at two o'clock in the morning. Tommy and I arranged to meet at his place later in the day, and he left.

The Vladaks' mobile home was clean and tidy, with children's drawings taped to the walls here and there. Vladak was alone when I arrived. We sat down at the kitchen table next to the one big window. Country music played on the radio.

Last night I'd pretty much gotten all the factual information I'd wanted from him, but I wondered what kind of a person would take on a job like his, and what effect it had had on him.

"You get just as sadistic as the company itself. When I was sticking down there, I was a sadistic person. By the end of the night everybody would be yelling at everybody else. The stunner would be yelling at the hog drivers to stop prodding the hogs so much. The shackler would be yelling at the stunner to quit sending him live hogs. I'd be yelling at all three of them. Then at the end of the shift we'd hit the local bar and talk about it."

A car pulled up outside. I could see a woman and a child inside.

"The worst part," he continued, "was what happened to my family life. I'd come home, my wife would ask me how my night went, and instead of being happy to see her I'd say, 'What the hell do you care?' We'd get into arguments about stupid things. Or else I'd come in so drunk I'd wonder how in the hell I made it home."

We watched a blonde woman climb out of the car. The child, a little girl, ran from the car out of sight around the trailer.

"My wife and I finally separated in early July," Vladak said, "about two weeks before I cut my face. She couldn't take the bitching any more. I'd blow up at the drop of a hat, come home every night and find something to complain about, take my frustrations from work out on my family."

Vladak's wife, Lisa, came in and gave me a warm welcome.

"I was just telling Gail about my attitude when I worked at Morrell's," Vladak said. "What I was like to live with, and that you finally left me."

"Did you tell her *why* I left you?"

He nodded and looked away. "Somewhat. My attitude."

"No," Lisa said.

"Oh." He was looking at his hands on the table now. "Me slapping her around."

"You were hitting her?" I said.

"Yup."

Vladak glanced out the window at his daughter, now playing on a swing. He let out a loud sigh.

Pangs of Conscience

I decided to cross-check Vladak's story by questioning his replacement at Morrell. Steve Jansson was a polite young man with no ax to grind.

"You're talking to someone who loves this job," said Jansson when we first spoke.

Soon I was hearing about the same conscious hogs, worker injuries, and blind-eyed management—recounted this time as the natural perils of a life of adventure.

It turned out that the same stun operator who'd sent Vladak to the hospital was now stunning for Jansson.

"This stunner," Jansson said, "he already got one guy stabbed in the face. Everybody knows he stinks at his job. But when that hog comes at me alive,

I don't care where I hit him—whether I hit him high or I hit him low. I just poke a hole in him and get out as fast as I can. That's all that's required of me. I don't care if he bleeds good or not."

🍃   🍃   🍃

Ed Van Winkle's name kept popping up in conversations around Morrell's, usually in a tone that let you know you were hearing about a living legend. Since the 1960s, he'd worked just about every kill-floor job at ten different plants.

We met at the Holiday Inn coffee shop in Sioux City. A husky man in his early forties with bushy, brown hair and a beard, he was polite but distant at first. As soon as I asked about working in the blood pit he brought up the same thing—conscious, struggling hogs.

"Do you think the problem is a function of the stun operators?" I asked him. "Or the equipment?"

"I think the whole problem is the attitude," he replied. "Management doesn't care whether the hog is stunned or conscious, or whether the sticker is injured in the process. All Morrell cares about is getting those hogs killed.

"When I first started driving hogs for Morrell back in 1985, we used leather slappers to prod them. But whipping the hogs hard with these slappers left marks on the animals and damaged the meat, so management started issuing hotshots. One touch of that electric prod gets an animal to move, but at Morrell's they were vicious with them."

The coffee shop smelled of bacon and sausage.

Van Winkle was quiet for a few moments. "This is kind of hard to talk about," he said softly. "You're under all this stress, all this pressure. And it really sounds mean but," he was speaking almost in a whisper, "I've taken prods and stuck them in their eyes. And held them there."

"What else do the drivers do?" I asked.

"The preferred method of handling a cripple at Morrell's is to beat him to death with a lead pipe before he gets into the chute. It's called 'piping.' All the drivers use pipes to kill hogs that can't go through the chutes. Or if you get a hog that refuses to go in the chutes and is stopping production, you beat him to death. Then push him off to the side and hang him up later."*

"How often does that happen?" I asked.

"I've beaten eleven to death in one day."

"You'd think management would want a good stun," I said.

"I went to the foremen about it," he replied. "We kept telling them we were slaughtering conscious hogs. We asked them to set the stunner voltage high enough to knock the hogs out. We said we could try this, try that. The main foreman would agree to take care of the problem then just walk away. Five minutes later, when we knew he was in another area, we'd run upstairs to the control room and turn up the voltage. What does management do? Puts a lock on the control-room door."

🍃   🍃   🍃

---

*Humane slaughter regulations prohibit the use of pipes, sharp objects, and other dangerous devices to prod animals.

Ed Van Winkle no longer worked at Morrell, and Vladak and Jansson could only speak for the night shift. I wanted to find someone who could document conditions on the day shift.

On a bitterly cold night, eleven degrees with a blustery north wind, I drove the hilly streets of Sioux City, Iowa, looking for the address of Donny Tice, the day-shift sticker Tommy Vladak had told me about. When I knocked at his apartment, a tall, thin man in his mid-thirties with a receding hairline opened the door. He smiled and let me into his homey, nicely furnished living room, put on some soft music, and offered me a beer. I said no thanks and unpacked my tape recorder.

I noticed a purplish bruise among the tattoos on his arm.

"How'd you get that?"

"A hog I was sticking kicked me."

"Don't they get stunned before they come to you?"

"Some are completely missed by the stunners," he said. "Sometimes they get doubled up in the restrainer and the stunner misses the bottom hog. Sometimes the stun operator dozes off—I've actually seen him fall asleep on the job. . . .

"Sometimes the stunner likes to play games with the shackler. He purposely doesn't stun hogs right so they'll be hard to shackle. He'll give the shackler a hog that's just a little testy so when he tries to hang it it'll kick and fall down into the pit."

"Isn't that dangerous for you?" I asked. "What do you do?"

"Sometimes I grab it by the ear and stick it right through the eye. I'm not just taking its eye out, I'll go all the way to the hilt, right up through the brain, and wiggle the knife. Instant rag doll."

Tice was on autopilot now.

"Another thing that happens is that you don't care about people's pain anymore. I used to be very sensitive about people's problems—willing to listen. After a while, you become desensitized. And as far as animals go, they're a lower life-form. They're maybe one step above a maggot.

"Like, one day the live hogs were driving me nuts and the kill-floor superintendent was playing his power games, yelling at me about something. I threw my knife on the floor, I'm screaming at him, 'Come on, you little pimple. You want a piece of me? Come on! Right now!' If he'd come down there I would've slit his throat. Could've taken a human life and not given it one thought or had one regret for it."

Tice had his beer bottle clasped in both hands in his lap and was staring straight ahead. A smooth, perfectly vertical column of smoke rose like incense from the cigarette in the ashtray.

"It's the same thing with an animal who pisses you off, except it *is* in the stick pit, you *are* going to kill it. Only you don't just kill it, you go in hard, push hard, blow the windpipe, make it drown in its own blood."

Tice looked at me again, and seemed to snap out of his confessional trance.

"But I wasn't the only guy doing this kind of stuff," he said. "One guy I work with actually chases hogs into the scalding tank. And everybody—hog drivers, shacklers, utility men—uses lead pipes on hogs. Everybody knows it, all of it."

"Including management?" I asked.

"Right. They make sure everything's by the book when anybody official visits. Whenever OSHA comes to check on things, the stick pit runs like a jewel. As soon they're gone it's back to business as usual.

"How come you're willing to tell me these things'?" I asked.

"Like they say," Tice replied, "if you're not part of the solution, you're part of the problem."

I turned off the tape recorder and got ready to leave. I didn't hate Donny Tice. But I hated what he was doing. I probably should have been afraid to be alone with him. For his part he seemed relieved to have gotten his sins off his chest.

I said good night and left.

Other Nations

We need another and a wiser and perhaps a more mystical concept of animals. Remote from universal nature, and living by complicated artifice, man in civilization surveys the creature through the glass of his knowledge and sees thereby a feather magnified and the whole image in distortion. We patronize them for their incompleteness, for their tragic fate of having taken form so far below ourselves. And therein we err, and greatly err. For the animal shall not be measured by man. In a world older and more complete than ours they move finished and complete, gifted with extensions of the senses we have lost or never attained, living by voices we shall never hear. They are not brethren, they are not underlings; they are other nations, caught with ourselves in the net of life and time, fellow prisoners of the splendour and travail of the earth.

—Henry Beston, *The Outermost House: A Year of Life on the Great Beach of Cape Cod*, 1956

Glossaries

The following three glossaries should help decode some of the technical language that appears in this book. The first glossary contains terms from psychology, sociology, research methodology, and other social sciences. The second glossary contains terms related specifically to prejudice. And the third glossary contains statistical terms commonly found in research reports.

The best way to use these glossaries is to look through the first two before starting to read the book, and then consult all three on an as-needed basis while reading the rest of the book.

I. Social Science and Research Terms

affective   Affective is synonymous with "emotional." Psychologists sometimes describe a person's mood and emotional expressiveness as the person's *affect* (e.g., "His affect was flat").

attribution   An attribution, in the language of social psychology, is a causal explanation for behavior. A dispositional attribution is an explanation based on personal characteristics (e.g., "She scored well because she's smart"), and a situational attribution is an explanation based on environmental factors (e.g., "She scored well because the teacher gave her extra help").

attribution theory   Attribution theory is a social-psychological theory about how people explain the causes of their behavior and the behavior of others.

attributional ambiguity   Attributional ambiguity occurs when the causes of behavior are unclear. Under conditions of attributional ambiguity, people are prone to misattribute the causes of behavior.

cognitive   Cognitive factors, variables, or activities are those related to beliefs and thoughts ("cognition").

cognitive dissonance   Cognitive dissonance is a feeling of tension that arises from simultaneously holding psychologically incompatible thoughts (e.g., "I'm an honest person, yet I just told a lie"). According to the theory of cognitive dissonance, people are motivated to reduce feelings of dissonance whenever possible.

confederate   A confederate is a research assistant who plays a specific role in a study (most often, appearing to be an experimental participant).

conformity   Conformity is the adoption of attitudes or behaviors in order to fit in with others.

control group   A control group is an "untreated" group that serves as a baseline, or comparison, with groups that are exposed to some kind of experimental treatment. For example, in a study on the effectiveness of a vaccination, the control group would consist of unvaccinated participants.

correspondent inference theory   Correspondent inference theory is a theory about how people infer the causes of behavior. The term is somewhat rare now; most social psychologists use "attribution theory" when discussing the way people explain behavior. See *attribution theory.*

debriefing   A debriefing is an explanation given to research participants after a study is over, disclosing details about the research objectives and the techniques used.

dependent variable   A dependent variable is a variable that a researcher measures to see whether it is affected by (depends on) another variable. For instance, in a study on the effectiveness of an AIDS vaccine, a dependent variable might be the likelihood of contracting AIDS.

dissonance   See *cognitive dissonance.*

filler items   Filler items are questions or problems (e.g., on a questionnaire) that a researcher asks but does not intend to analyze. Filler items are often used to disguise the focus of a study. For example, a questionnaire on drug usage might include filler items on diet, exercise, and smoking so that respondents are unaware that the study is specifically concerned with drugs.

fundamental attribution error   The fundamental attribution error is the tendency for people to attribute someone's behavior to dispositional causes (e.g., laziness) when the behavior was actually caused by situational factors.

hypothesis   A hypothesis is a researcher's prediction of a study's results. Typically, researchers form one or more hypotheses based on past results or theories. They then collect data to test whether their hypotheses are supported.

independent variable   An independent variable is a variable that a researcher manipulates to see whether it has an effect on another variable. For instance, in a study on the effectiveness of an AIDS vaccine, an independent variable might be the amount of vaccine a person receives.

informed consent   Informed consent refers to a research participant's willingness to take part in a study after being made aware of its requirements and any serious risks involved.

negative affect   Negative affect refers to negative mood or emotion (e.g., "The subject reacted with negative affect when asked to remember a sad event").

norms   Norms are expectations or rules for acceptable behavior in a given situation. For example, in the United States it is now normative (normal) to disapprove of prejudice.

null hypothesis   A null hypothesis is a hypothesis that two or more groups (e.g., an experimental group and a control group) do not differ with respect to a dependent variable.

positive affect   Positive affect refers to positive mood or emotion (e.g., "The subject reacted with positive affect when asked to remember a happy event").

primary literature   Primary literature refers to books or articles written by researchers reporting the results of their investigations. In contrast, secondary sources (e.g., textbooks, magazine articles) describe or interpret primary research reports.

priming   Priming takes place when an idea, image, or association is activated or made salient. For example, stereotypes can be primed by mentioning social categories such as race and gender.

research participant   A research participant, or subject, is a person who takes part in a study.

respondent   A respondent is a research participant who answers a survey.

salience   The salience of a person or stimulus refers to how prominent, noticeable, or attention-getting it is.

schema   A schema is a belief, expectation, or organizing framework that guides how people perceive, think about, and remember information.

secondary literature   See *primary literature.*

self-esteem   Self-esteem refers to a person's feeling of self-worth.

social cognition   Social cognition refers to the thoughts, beliefs, perceptions, and memories that people have about others. Social cognition also refers to an area of research that combines social and cognitive psychology.

stimulus materials   Stimulus materials (sometimes referred to as experimental materials, study materials, or stimuli) are materials that a researcher uses in the course of a study. For instance, a researcher may use music in a study of sound perception, photographs in a study of social perception, problems in a study of decision making, and so on.

subject   See *research participant.*

II. Prejudice–Related Terms

affirmative action   Affirmative action is a set of policies designed to level the playing field in higher education and the workplace. Affirmative action beneficiaries include women, people with disabilities, and designated racial and ethnic minorities.

ambivalent sexism   Ambivalent sexism refers to a combination of "hostile sexism" (antipathy toward women) and "benevolent sexism" (a chivalrous ideology that offers protection and affection to women).

aversive racism   Aversive racism is a subtle form of contemporary racism in which people believe in egalitarian principles but harbor an aversion toward racial outgroups.

concentration camp   A concentration camp is a facility where political prisoners, minority members, religious groups, or other targeted subpopulations are held, or concentrated, against their will.

contact hypothesis   The contact hypothesis, as formulated by Gordon Allport in his 1954 classic book *The Nature of Prejudice,* predicts that prejudice will diminish as groups have equal-status contact with each other in pursuit of common goals.

desegregation   Desegregation is the reduction of segregation. For example, school desegregation refers to the creation of racially integrated classrooms.

discrimination   Discrimination occurs when members of a group are disadvantaged or treated unfairly as a result of their group membership.

egalitarian   Egalitarian values, behaviors, and norms are those that favor equality, especially with respect to social, political, and economic rights and opportunities.

genocide   Genocide refers to a program of action intended to destroy an ethnic or racial group.

ingroup   An ingroup is the group that one is a member of (the opposite of an *outgroup*). [*Note:* One person's ingroup may be another person's outgroup, and vice versa.]

integration   Integration takes place when ethnic, racial, or otherwise distinct groups live, work, study, or spend time together. The opposite of *segregation.*

intersexual   An intersexual is someone whose genitalia, genes, and other sex-related biological characteristics are not clearly female or male (a person who is "between the sexes").

jigsaw classroom   The jigsaw classroom is a cooperative learning technique designed to reduce prejudice by dividing students into racially integrated groups and making each student indispensable to the group.

minimal group procedure   The minimal group procedure is an experimental technique in which participants are randomly divided into groups that appear to have little or no actual differences. Research suggests that even when people are divided into "minimal groups," they often favor members of their own group.

modern racism   Modern racism is a subtle form of contemporary racism in which people see racial prejudice as wrong but view racial minorities as making unfair demands or receiving too many resources.

NAACP   The National Association for the Advancement of Colored People (NAACP) is a U.S. civil rights organization founded by a multiracial group of activists in 1909.

outgroup   An outgroup is a group that one is not a member of (the opposite of an *ingroup*). Outgroup members are often the recipients, or "targets," of prejudice.

outgroup homogeneity effect   The outgroup homogeneity effect is a tendency to see outgroup members as more alike than ingroup members.

prejudice   Prejudice is a prejudgment, usually negative, about a group or its members.

realistic group conflict theory   Realistic group conflict theory, sometimes called "realistic conflict theory," is the theory that group conflict and prejudice result from competition over limited resources.

segregation   Segregation takes place when ethnic, racial, or otherwise distinct groups are physically or geographically separated from each other. The opposite of *integration.*

self-enhancement bias   A self-enhancement bias occurs when people view themselves as better than they are or than others judge them to be.

social identity theory   Social identity theory is a theory that people derive self-esteem in part from their group memberships, and as a result, tend to favor ingroups over outgroups.

stereotype   A stereotype is a generalization (or, often, an overgeneralization) about the members of a group.

stereotype threat   Stereotype threat occurs when members of a group fear that their behavior might confirm a negative stereotype about them.

stigma   A stigma is a mark of inferiority or shame. Stigmatized groups are usually looked down upon or avoided.

subtle racism   Subtle racism is a type of prejudice in which people hold racist views but avoid obvious displays of bias (and may not even realize they harbor prejudice).

ultimate attribution error   The ultimate attribution error is a tendency to attribute outgroup members' negative behaviors to their disposition, and to attribute their positive behaviors to situational factors or other uncharitable causes.

III. Statistical Terms

analysis of variance   Analysis of variance is a statistical technique that psychologists use to assess the independent and interactive effects of multiple variables.

ANOVA   ANOVA is an acronym for "analysis of variance."

bonferroni correction   A Bonferroni correction adjusts statistically for the increased chances of finding a significant result when multiple tests (e.g., *t*-tests) are conducted.

chi-square   Chi-square is a statistic used with frequency data. For example, a chi-square statistic might show whether the frequency of car accidents is significantly higher when drivers use cell phones than when they do not.

correlation coefficient   A correlation coefficient is a statistic that describes how strongly two variables are related. The Pearson correlation coefficient, *r,* is the most commonly used correlation coefficient. A Pearson correlation runs from -1.00 (a perfect negative correlation, in which one variable increases as the other decreases) to 0 (no relationship between two variables) to $+1.00$ (a perfect positive correlation, in which one variable increases as the other increases). To take an example, if a study were to find a $+.20$ correlation between happiness and income, this would mean that the two variables are positively related, though not very strongly.

data   Data are observations or measurements that a researcher uses to make inferences. Most often, researchers collect data from a sample in order to make inferences about a population. [*Note: Data* is a plural word; the singular term is *datum.*]

F   *F* is an abbreviation for *F*-ratio, the main statistic involved in analysis of variance. See *analysis of variance.*

M   *M* is an abbreviation for "mean" average. See *mean.*

mean   The mean, or arithmetic average, of a set of scores is calculated by adding up all the scores and dividing the number of scores. For example, the mean of 5, 7, and 18 is 10, because $5 + 7 + 18 = 30$, and 30 divided by 3 equals 10.

median   The median of a set of scores is the number above which half the scores lie and below which the remaining scores lie. The median bisects a distribution of scores just as the median of a highway bisects traffic lanes.

meta-analysis   Meta-analysis is a statistical technique that analyzes the combined results from multiple independent studies.

N   *N* refers to the size of an entire population (e.g., the total number of homeless people in New York City). Sometimes survey researchers will also use *N* to refer to the number of respondents in their sample.

n   *n* refers to the size of a sample, subsample, or subgroup (e.g., the number of homeless people participating in a study).

nonsignificance   See *ns* and *statistical significance.*

ns   *ns* is an abbreviation for "not significant." Sometimes a statistical significance level above .05 is simply described as *ns* rather than giving the specific *p* value. See *p.*

p   *p* refers to the probability that a research result occurred by chance alone. See *statistical significance.*

Pearson correlation coefficient   See *correlation coefficient.*

r   *r* is an abbreviation for the Pearson correlation coefficient. See *correlation coefficient.*

regression   Regression is a statistical technique that can be used for a wide variety of purposes, such as examining the relationship among variables or predicting the score of one variable based on scores from other variables (e.g., predicting college grade point averages based on SAT scores and high school grade point averages).

sd   *sd* is an abbreviation for standard deviation. See *standard deviation.*

significance   See *statistical significance.*

standard deviation   The standard deviation is a measure of how much a set of numbers varies (how spread out they are). A small standard deviation indicates that there is relatively little variability, and a large standard deviation indicates that there is a high degree of variability. The lowest standard deviation possible is zero, which indicates no variability at all (e.g., everyone scoring the same).

statistical significance   Statistical significance refers to the probability that a research result occurred by chance alone. In psychology, results are usually considered significant when their chance probability is less than 5% (represented as $p < .05$). [*Note:* The significance of a finding is *not* the same thing as the importance of a finding. In the context of statistics, significance refers only to the probability of obtaining a result— not to the result's importance.]

t-**test**   The *t*-test, or *t* statistic, is used to see whether two groups differ significantly. For example, a *t*-test might show whether women and men differ in income when hired for the same job. The higher *t* is, the more likely it is that the two groups differ significantly.

χ^2 χ^2 is an abbreviation for the chi-square statistic. See *chi-square.*

Source Notes

I. *Homo Stereotypus:* **Wired for Trouble**
Page 20 of Allport, G. W. (1954). *The nature of prejudice*. Reading, MA: Addison-Wesley.

The Psychology of Prejudice, Stereotyping, and Discrimination: An Overview
This article was written specifically for the current anthology and has not been published previously. Thanks go to Chun Luo for suggesting the square-diamond illustration that appears under "Categorical Thinking." Copyright © 2003, S. Plous.

Who Is Black? One Nation's Definition
Davis, F. J. (1991). *Who is black? One nation's definition* (pp. 1–23). University Park, PA: Pennsylvania State University Press.

Why Oppression Is Hard to See
Pages 4–5 of Frye, M. (1983). *The politics of reality: Essays in feminist theory*. Freedom, CA: The Crossing Press.

II. **Stigmatization**
An act in amendment to the various acts relative to immigration and the importation of aliens under contract or agreement to perform labor, 26 Stat 1084 (1891).

The Stigma of Physical Disabilities
From Biblical Times: Pages 159–160 of *The New English Bible: The Old Testament*. (1970). Oxford, England: Oxford University Press.

Centuries Later: Pages 863–864 of Burgdorf, M. P., & Burgdorf, R., Jr. (1975). A history of unequal treatment: The qualifications of handicapped persons as a "suspect class" under the equal protection clause. *Santa Clara Lawyer, 15*, 855–910.

Disabled Children in Ancient Greece
Page 192 of Everson, S. (Ed.). (1996). *Aristotle: The politics and the constitution of Athens*. New York: Cambridge University Press.

A Defective Race of Human Beings
Pages 41 and 45 of Bell, A. G. (1884). *Memoir upon the formation of a deaf variety of the human race*. Washington, DC: National Academy of Sciences.

Eliminating the Unfit
Pages 359 and 377 of Cattell, J. M. (1902). A statistical study of eminent men. *Popular Science Monthly, 62*, 359–377.

Page 1002 of Carrie Buck v. J. H. Bell. (1928). *Cases argued and decided in the Supreme Court of the United States: October Term, 1926* (Lawyer's ed., Book 71, pp. 1000–1002). Rochester, NY: Lawyers Co-operative Publishing Co.

No Pity: People With Disabilities Forging a New Civil Rights Movement
Pages 3–8, 30–34, 271–274, 280, 281, and 333–350 of Shapiro, J. P. (1993). *No pity: People with disabilities forging a new civil rights movement*. New York: Times Books.

Exhibiting the Insane
Pages 63–65 of Deutsch, A. (1949). *The mentally ill in America: A history of their care and treatment from colonial times* (2nd ed.). New York: Columbia University Press.

Dwarfs as Pets and Presents
Pages 187–188 of Thompson, C. J. S. (1968). *The mystery and lore of monsters: With accounts of some giants, dwarfs and prodigies.* New Hyde Park, NY: University Books.

In Europe, Outcry Is Loud Over a Sport Called Dwarf-Tossing
Hemp, P. (1985, November 4). In Europe, outcry is loud over a sport called dwarf-tossing. *Wall Street Journal,* pp. 1, 21.

As Much Fun as Playing Grumpy or Sleepy
Royko, M. (1985, March 5). A little bar fun: The dwarf toss. *Chicago Tribune,* p. 3.

An Offshoot: Dwarf Bowling
Cuomo signs bill to ban dwarf tossing. (1990, July 25). *Los Angeles Times,* p. A12.

Avoidance of the Handicapped: An Attributional Ambiguity Analysis
Snyder, M. L., Kleck, R. E., Strenta, A., & Mentzer, S. J. (1979). Avoidance of the handicapped: An attributional ambiguity analysis. *Journal of Personality and Social Psychology, 12,* 2297–2306.

The Management of Stigma
Page xiii of Gallagher, H. G. (1985). *FDR's splendid deception.* New York: Dodd, Mead & Company.

Citing Intolerance, Obese People Take Steps to Press Cause
Goldberg, C. (2000, November 5). Citing intolerance, obese people take steps to press cause. *New York Times,* pp. 1, 36.

Race and the Schooling of Black Americans
Steele, C. M. (1992, April). Race and the schooling of black Americans. *Atlantic Monthly,* pp. 68–78.

The Stereotype Trap
Begley, S. (2000, November 6). The stereotype trap. *Newsweek,* pp. 66–68.

III. Racism Then

Page 234 of Labaree, L. W., & Bell, W. J., Jr. (Ed.). (1961). *The papers of Benjamin Franklin* (vol. 4: July 1, 1750, through June 30, 1753). New Haven, CT: Yale University Press.

The Hottentot Venus
Gould, S. J. (1985). The Hottentot Venus. In *The flamingo's smile: Reflections in natural history* (pp. 291–305). New York: W. W. Norton & Company.

Molasses and Rum
For example, Thomas Jefferson: Page 154 of Boyd, J. P. (Ed.). (1961). *The papers of Thomas Jefferson* (vol. 16, 30 November 1789 to 4 July 1790). Princeton, NJ: Princeton University Press.

Likewise, Andrew Jackson: Pages 87, 148, and 244 of Bassett, J. S. (Ed.). (1933). *Correspondence of Andrew Jackson* (vol. VI, 1839–1845). Washington, DC: Carnegie Institution of Washington.

And in 1766, George Washington wrote: Pages 211–212 of Ford, W. C. (Ed.). (1889). *The writings of George Washington* (vol. 2, 1758–1775). New York: G. P. Putnam's Sons.

In the last year of his life: Pages 130–131 and 138 of Dalzell, R. F., Jr., & Dalzell, L. B. (1998). *George Washington's Mount Vernon: At home in revolutionary America.* New York: Oxford University Press.

Peak Slave Holdings of U.S. Presidents
Note: Every effort has been made to construct this graph with the most definitive estimates available, but the historical record of presidential slave holdings is in some cases fragmentary and open to differing interpretations. In such cases the graph shows the most

conservative (lowest) credible estimate on record. If you believe a number in the graph is in error, feel free to send the editor, Scott Plous, a reference citation for what you believe to be the correct number.

George Washington: Pages 130–131 of Dalzell, R. F., Jr., & Dalzell, L. B. (1998). *George Washington's Mount Vernon: At home in revolutionary America.* New York: Oxford University Press. [Washington's 317 slaves, enumerated in a 1799 inventory entitled "NEGROES Belonging to George Washington in his own right and by Marriage," included "dower" slaves from his wife's family and 40 slaves attached to a lifetime rental property. See pages 18–19 of Hirschfeld, F. (1997). *George Washington and Slavery: A documentary portrayal.* Columbia, MO: University of Missouri Press.]

John Adams: Page 134 of McCullough, D. (2001). *John Adams.* New York: Simon & Schuster. [See also page 380 of Adams, C. F. (Ed.). (1856). *The works of John Adams, second president of the United States* (vol. 10). Boston: Little, Brown and Company.]

Thomas Jefferson: Slave Demographic Database, Monticello Research Department, as compiled by Monticello Senior Research Historian Lucia C. Stanton, March 28, 2002 [*Note:* According to historian Paul Finkelman, Jefferson owned roughly 200 slaves at the time of his death and at least 330 over his lifetime. See page 218, note 108 of Finkelman, P. (1993). Jefferson and slavery. In P. S. Onuf (Ed.), *Jeffersonian legacies* (pp. 181–221). Charlottesville, VA: University of Virginia Press.]

James Madison: Page 12 of Ketcham, R. (1971). *James Madison: A biography.* New York: Macmillan.

James Monroe: 1830 Federal Census of Virginia, Loudoun County, Cameron, family of James Monroe family (unpaginated), retrieved February 1, 2002, from http://www.ancestry.com

John Quincy Adams: Page 430 of Nevins, A. (Ed.). (1960). *The diary of John Quincy Adams, 1794–1845: American diplomacy, and political, social, and intellectual life, from Washington to Polk.* New York: Frederick Ungar Publishing Co. [See also page 33 of Booker, C. B. (2000). *African-Americans and the presidency: A history of broken promises.* New York: Franklin Watts.]

Andrew Jackson: Page 30 of Walker, A. (1943). Andrew Jackson: Planter. *East Tennessee Historical Society's Publications, 15,* 19–34.

Martin Van Buren: Page 385 of Niven, J. (1983). *Martin Van Buren: The romantic age of American politics.* New York: Oxford University Press.

William Henry Harrison: Page 434 of Green, J. A. (1941). *William Henry Harrison: His life and times.* Richmond, VA: Garrett and Massie.

John Tyler: Page 300 of Seager, R., Jr. (1963). *And Tyler too: A biography of John & Julia Gardiner Tyler.* New York: McGraw-Hill.

James Knox Polk: Personal communication from Wayne Cutler, Professor of History and Editor of the Polk Project, University of Tennessee—Knoxville, January 25, 2002 [*Note:* Professor Cutler's estimate is based on an 1843 tax record (the last available before Polk died in 1849). A somewhat higher estimate is contained in Bassett, J. S. (1925/1968). *The Southern plantation overseer as revealed in his letters.* Westport: Negro Universities Press.]

Zachary Taylor: Page 27 of Smith, E. B. (1900). *The presidencies of Zachary Taylor & Millard Fillmore.* Lawrence, KS: University Press of Kansas. [*Note:* Taylor is quoted as claiming to own 300 slaves on page 208 of McKinley, S. B., & Bent, S. (1946). *Old rough and ready: The life and times of Zachary Taylor.* New York: Vanguard Press. This claim is contradicted, however, by several other credible sources, including: Page 320 of Bauer, K. J. (1985). *Zachary Taylor: Soldier, planter, statesman of the old southwest.* Baton Rouge, LA: Louisiana State University Press. Page 145 of Currie, S. (Ed.). (1984). Zachary Taylor, plantation owner. *Civil War History, 30,* 144–156. Pages 18, 31, 33, and 180 of Holman, H. (1951). *Zachary Taylor: Soldier in the White House.* Indianapolis, IN: Bobbs-Merrill Company.]

Millard Fillmore: Page 431 of Severance, F. H. (Ed.). (1907). *Millard Fillmore papers* (vol. 1). Buffalo, NY: Buffalo Historical Society.

Franklin Pierce: Page 24 of Bell, C. I. (1980). *They knew Franklin Pierce (and others thought they did).* Springfield, VT: April Hill Publishers.

James Buchanan: Page 100 of Klein, P. S. (1962). *President James Buchanan: A biography.* University Park, PA: Pennsylvania State University Press. [*Note:* Buchanan bought two slaves from his brother-in-law in order to free them. The terms stipulated that one of the slaves would be free after a 7–year period of service to Buchanan, and the other would be free after a 23–year period of service.]

Abraham Lincoln: Page 24 of Donald, H. D. (1995). *Lincoln.* New York: Simon & Schuster.

Andrew Johnson: Page 45 of Trefousse, H. L. (1989). *Andrew Johnson: A biography.* New York: W.W. Norton.

Ulysses Simpson Grant: Page 62 of McFeely, W. S. (1981). *Grant: A biography.* New York: Norton.

Some Presidential Statements on Race

Thomas Jefferson: Pages 140 and 143 of Jefferson, T. (1787/1972). *Notes on the state of Virginia.* New York: W. W. Norton.

James Buchanan: Pages 40–41 of Moore, J. B. (Ed.). (1909). *The works of James Buchanan* (vol. 6). Philadelphia, PA: J. B. Lippincott Company.

Abraham Lincoln: Page 235 of Angle, P. M. (Ed.). (1958). *Created equal? The complete Lincoln-Douglas debates of 1858.* Chicago: University of Chicago Press.

Andrew Johnson: Page 368 of Moore, F. (Ed.). (1865). *Speeches of Andrew Johnson, President of the United States.* Boston, MA: Little, Brown, and Company.

James A. Garfield: Page 185 of Fredrickson, G. M. (1971). *The black image in the white mind: The debate on Afro-American character and destiny, 1817–1914.* New York: Harper & Row.

Rutherford Hayes : Page 522 of Williams, C. R. (Ed.). (1924). *Diary and letters of Rutherford Birchard Hayes: Nineteenth president of the United States* (vol. 3). Columbus, OH: Ohio State Archeological and Historical Society.

Woodrow Wilson: Page 51 of Link, A. S. (Ed.). (1967). *The papers of Woodrow Wilson* (vol. 2). Princeton, NJ: Princeton University Press. Wilson also made the following statement as a presidential candidate in 1912: "I stand for the national policy of exclusion. We cannot make a homogeneous population out of a people who do not blend with the Caucasian race . . . . Oriental coolieism will give us another race problem to solve and surely we have had our lesson." [Page 55 of Daniels, R. (1966). *The politics of prejudice: The anti-Japanese movement in California and the struggle for Japanese exclusion.* Gloucester, MA: Peter Smith.]

Herbert C. Hoover: Page 150 of Hoover, H. (1902, August 2). The Kaiping coal mines and coal-field, Chihle Province, North China. *Engineerng and Mining Journal,* pp. 149–150.

Theodore Roosevelt: Page 226 of Morison, E. E. (Ed.). (1952). *The letters of Theodore Roosevelt* (vol. 5). Cambridge, MA: Harvard University Press.

Harry S. Truman: Pages 56–57 of Leuchtenburg, W. E. (1991). The conversion of Harry Truman. *American Heritage,* 55–58, 60, 62, 64, 66, 68. [*Note:* In the original, William Leuchentburg added "[sic]" after the misspelled word "negros."]

Calvin Coolidge: Page 14 of Coolidge, C. (1921, February). Whose country is this? *Good Housekeeping,* pp. 13–14, 106, 109.

Warren G. Harding: Pages 421–422 of Podell, J., & Anzovin, S. (Eds.). (1988). *Speeches of the American presidents.* New York: H. W. Wilson Company.

Dwight D. Eisenhower: Page 127 of Larson, A. (1968). *Eisenhower: The president nobody knew.* New York: Charles Scriber's Sons.

Punishment for Stealing and Destroying Property

Page 355 of McCord, D. J. (1840). *The statutes at large of South Carolina.* Columbia, SC: A. S. Johnston.

Insurance for Slave Owners

Savitt, T. L. (1977). Slave life insurance in Virginia and North Carolina. *Journal of Southern History, 43,* 583–600.

Staples, B. (2000, July 24). How slavery fueled business in the North. *New York Times,* p. A18.

See also: O'Donnell, T. (1935, June). A bona-fide replica of a slave policy. *American Conservationist,* pp. 13–17.

A Sampler of Dissonance-Reducing Statements in Support of Slavery

Calhoun, J. C. (1853). *The works of John C. Calhoun* (vol. II). New York: D. Appleton and Company.

Carroll, C. (1900). *The negro a beast.* Miami: Mnemosyne Publishing Co.

Cartwright, S. A. (1851). Report on the diseases and physical peculiarities of the negro race. *New Orleans Medical and Surgical Journal, 7,* 691–715.

Christy, D. (1860). Cotton is king: Or, slavery in the light of political economy. In E. N. Elliott (Ed.), *Cotton is king, and pro-slavery arguments.* Augusta, GA: Pritchard, Abbott, & Loomis.

Cobb, T. R. R. (1858). *An inquiry into the law of negro slavery in the United States of America* (vol. I). Philadelphia: T. & J. W. Johnson & Co.

Collins, Dr. (1811/1971). *Practical rules for the management and medical treatment of negro slaves, in the sugar colonies.* Freeport, NY: Books for Libraries Press.

Dew, T. R. (1832/1970). *Review of the debate in the Virginia legislature of 1831 and 1832.* Westport, CT: Negro Universities Press.

Fitzhugh, G. (1854). *Sociology for the South, or the failure of free society.* Richmond, VA: A. Morris.

Fitzhugh, G. (1857/1960). *Cannibals all! Or slaves without masters.* Cambridge, MA: Belknap Press.

Hammond, J. H. (1866/1978). *Selections from the letters and speeches of the Hon. James H. Hammond, of South Carolina.* Spartanburg, SC: The Reprint Company.

Hecht, M. B. (1972). *John Quincy Adams: A personal history of an independent man.* New York: Macmillan.

Holmes, G. F. (1852). Uncle Tom's Cabin. *Southern Literary Messenger, 18,* 721–731.

Hughes, H. (1854). *Treatise on sociology, theoretical and practical.* Philadelphia, PA: Lippincott, Grambo & Co.

Jefferson, T. (1794/1955). *Notes on the state of Virginia.* Chapel Hill, NC: University of North Carolina Press.

Nolan, A. T. (1991). *Lee considered: General Robert E. Lee and Civil War history.* Chapel Hill, NC: University of North Carolina Press.

Ruffin, E. (1853). *The political economy of slavery; Or, the institution considered in regard to its influence on public wealth and the general welfare.* Washington, DC: Lemuel Towers.

White, C. (1799). *An account of the regular gradation in man, and in different animals and vegetables.* London: C. Dilly.

The Use of Blacks for Medical Experimentation and Demonstration in the Old South

Savitt, T. L. (1982). The use of Blacks for medical experimentation and demonstration in the Old South. *Journal of Southern History, 48,* 331–348.

An Early Entry for "Negro" from The Encyclopædia Britannica

Pages 316–318 of *The Encyclopædia Britannica.* (1884). (9th ed., vol. 17). New York: Charles Scribner's Sons. [*Note:* All footnotes have been eliminated from the original text.]

Spoken on the Floor of the U.S. Congress

John C. Calhoun: Page 98 of U.S. Congress. (1848). *The congressional globe: New series: Containing sketches of the debates and proceedings of the first session of the thirtieth Congress.* Washington, DC: Blair & Rives.

John Franklin Miller: Page 1487 of U.S. Congress. (1882). *Congressional record: Containing the proceedings and debates of the forty-seventh Congress, first session* (vol. XXXIII, part II). Washington, DC: Government Printing Office.

David A. De Armond: Page 362 of U.S. Congress. (1898). *Congressional record: Containing the proceedings and debates of the fifty-fifth Congress, second session* (vol. XXXI, part VIII). Washington, DC: Government Printing Office.

John Sharp Williams: Page 342 of U.S. Congress. (1899). *Congressional record: Containing the proceedings and debates of the fifty-fifth Congress, third session* (vol. XXXII, part I). Washington, DC: Government Printing Office.

Ben Tillman: Pages 2244–2245 of U.S. Congress. (1900). *Congressional record: Containing the proceedings and debates of the fifty-sixth Congress, first session* (vol. XXXIII, part III). Washington, DC: Government Printing Office.

An Early Aunt Jemima Advertisement

Page 71 of Kern-Foxworth, M. (1994). *Aunt Jemima, Uncle Ben, and Rastus: Blacks in advertising, yesterday, today, and tomorrow.* Westport, CT: Greenwood Press.

Some Examples of Jim Crow

South Carolina: Page 39 of Carnes, J. (1995). *Us and them: A history of intolerance in America.* Montgomery, AL: Southern Poverty Law Center.

Montgomery, Alabama: Page 341 of Katz, W. L. (1967). *Eyewitness: The negro in American history.* New York: Pitman Publishing.

Coming of Age in Mississippi

Moody, A. (1968). *Coming of age in Mississippi* (pp. 263–267). New York: Dell Publishing Co.

"Operation Wetback"

Page 11 of United States Commission on Civil Rights. (1980). *The tarnished golden door: Civil rights issues in immigration.* Washington, DC: U.S. Government Printing Office.

The American Concentration Camps: A Cover-Up Through Euphemistic Terminology

Okamura, R. Y. (1982). The American concentration camps: A cover-up through euphemistic terminology. *Journal of Ethnic Studies, 10,* 95–109.

Instructions to All Persons of Japanese Ancestry

United States Government poster reprinted courtesy of the California State Library, California History Section.

How to Tell Japanese from Chinese People

How to tell your friends from the Japs. (1941, December 22). *Time,* p. 33.

Not Normal Human Beings

Buna vital to foe, declares Blamey. (1943, January 9). *New York Times,* p. 4.

Signs of the Times

Page 131 of McWilliams, C. (1971). *Prejudice: Japanese-Americans: Symbol of racial intolerance.* Hamden, CT: Archon Books.

Scalping in World War II

Adapted with permission from pages 64–65 and 82 of Dower, J. (1986). *War without mercy: Race and power in the Pacific War.* New York: Pantheon.

The Japanese Internment: An Epilogue

President Harry Truman: Page 421 of Miller, M. (1974). *Plain speaking: An oral biography of Harry S. Truman.* New York: Berkeley Publishing Group.

Supreme Court Justice Tom Clark: Page C-5 of An interview with Supreme Court Justice Tom Clark: 'That's why we have courtrooms: To debate the issues, the cases.' (1966, July 10). *San Diego Union,* pp. C4–C5.

Civil Liberties Act of 1988: Civil Liberties Act of 1988, Public Law No. 100–383, § 2, 102 Stat. 903 (1988).

IV. Racism Now

Page 154 of Sniderman, P. M., & Piazza, T. (1993). *The scar of race.* Cambridge, MA: Harvard University Press.

Five Myths About Immigration: The New Know-Nothingism

Cole, D. (1994, October 17). Five myths about immigration. *The Nation, 410, 412.*

Typical Neighborhood Diversity for Each Group: U.S. Metropolitan Averages

Page 3 of Logan, J. (2001, December 18). *Ethnic diversity grows, neighborhood integration lags behind* (report by the Lewis Mumford Center). Albany, NY: University at Albany.

Mixing That Which God Separated

In 1998 South Carolina repealed: O'Driscoll, P. (1998, November 5). Voters had their say in 44 states. *USA Today,* p. 8A.

Yet in that same year: Date, S. V. (2000, February 3). Bush opponents describe campaign stop at college as 'racist.' Cox News Service. Retrieved January 18, 2002, from Lexis-Nexis Academic Universe [http://web.lexis-nexis.com/universe/].

More than 100 years earlier: Page 110 of Young, B. (1865). *Journal of Discourses* (reported by G. D. Watt and J. V. Long, vol. 10). Liverpool, England: Daniel H. Wells.

Three days later: Parents' note needed for interracial dates. (2000, March 8). *New York Times,* p. A20.

Another Ban Repealed

Adapted with permission from Prejudice takes a hit. (2000, November 11). *Times-Picayune* (New Orleans), p. B-6.

An Inside Look at Multiracial Identities within a Mexican-American Family

Adapted with permission from pages 159–160 and 172 of Johnson, K. R. (1999). *How did you get to be Mexican? A White/Brown man's search for identity.* Philadelphia, PA: Temple University Press.

Once Appalled by Race Profiling, Many Find Themselves Doing It

Verhovek, S. H. (2001, September 23). Once appalled by race profiling, many find themselves doing it. *New York Times,* pp. A1, B13.

American Opinion in the Month After the Terrorist Attacks of September 11, 2001

Poll data from the Roper Center for Public Opinion. Retrieved January 1, 2002, from Lexis-Nexis Academic Universe [http://web.lexis-nexis.com/universe/].

Race to Incarcerate

Adapted with permission from pages 1–4, 14, 124–126, and 181–188 of Mauer, M. (1999). *Race to incarcerate.* New York: New Press.

A Computer Diagnosis of Prejudice

Goode, E. (1998, October 13). A computer diagnosis of prejudice. *New York Times,* p. F7.

Service With a Sneer

Kohn, H. (1994, November 6). Service with a sneer. *New York Times Magazine,* pp. 42–47, 58, 78, 81.

White Privilege: Unpacking the Invisible Knapsack

Adapted with permission from McIntosh, P. (1989, July/August). White privilege: Unpacking the invisible knapsack. *Peace and Freedom,* pp. 10–12.

What Did Your Grandfather Do?

Adapted with permission from pages 340–341 of Feagin, J. R., & Sikes, M. P. (1994). *Living with racism: The Black middle-class experience.* Boston: Beacon Press.

Reflections on Affirmative Action Goals in Psychology Admissions

Amirkhan, J., Betancourt, H., Graham, S., López, S. R., & Weiner, B. (1995). Reflections on affirmative action goals in psychology admissions. *Psychological Science, 6,* 140–148.

Two Supreme Court Views of Affirmative Action

Against Affirmative Action: Pages 190–191 of 132 L Ed 2d.

In Favor of Affirmative Action: Pages 192–193 of 132 L Ed 2d.

The Need for Compensatory Consideration

Pages 146–147 of King, M. L., Jr. (1964). *Why we can't wait.* New York: Harper & Row.

Attitudes Toward Affirmative Action

Gallup Organization. (2001, July 10). *The Gallup Poll Social Audit on Black/White relations in the United States: 2001 update.* Princeton, NJ: Author.

Ten Myths About Affirmative Action

Updated version of Plous, S. (1996). Ten myths about affirmative action. *Journal of Social Issues, 52,* 25–31.

V. Sexism

Page 289 of Baring-Gould, W. S., & Baring-Gould, C. (1962). *The annotated Mother Goose.* New York: Clarkson N. Potter, Inc.

Listening

Chassler, S. (1984, August). Listening. *Ms.,* pp. 51–53, 98–99.

Some Ancient Views of Women

Plato: Page 249 of Plato. (1929). *Timaeus* (91A). London: William Heinemann Ltd.

Aristotle: Page 461 of Peck, A. L. (1943). *Aristotle: Generation of animals.* Cambridge, MA: Harvard University Press.

Galen: Page 630 of May, M. T. (Trans.). (1968). *On the usefulness of the parts of the body* (vol. II). Ithaca, NY: Cornell University Press.

Plutarch: Page 7 of Pomeroy, S. (Ed.). (1999). *Plutarch's advice to the bride and groom* and *a consolation to his wife.* New York: Oxford University Press.

Saint Augustine: Page 344 of Pine-Coffin, R. S. (Trans.). (1961). *Saint Augustine: Confessions.* New York: Penguin Books.

St. Thomas Aquinas: Page 2182 of St. Thomas Aquinas. (1981). *Summa Theologica: Complete English edition in five volumes* (vol. 4; Third Part, Question 31, Article 4). (Trans. by Fathers of the English Dominican Province). Westminster, MD: Christian Classics.

More Recent Voices from History

Jean-Jacques Rousseau: Page 365 of Rousseau, J.-J. (1762/1979). *Emile, or on education* (A. Bloom, Trans.). New York: Basic Books.

Immanuel Kant: Page 93 of Kant, I. (1763/1965). *Observations on the feeling of the beautiful and sublime* (J. T. Goldthwait, Trans.). Berkeley: University of California Press.

Edmund Burke: Page 77 of Burke, E. (1790/1993). *Reflections on the revolution in France* (L. G. Mitchell, Ed.). Oxford: Oxford University Press.

Napoleon Bonaparte: Page 14 of Herold, J. C. (1955). *The mind of Napoleon: A selection from his written and spoken words.* New York: Columbia University Press.

Honoré de Balzac: Page 140 of McSpadden, J. W. (Ed.). (1901). The physiology of marriage (vol. 33 of *The works of Honoré de Balzac).* Philadelphia: Avil Publishing Co.

Arthur Schopenhauer: Pages 449–450 of Durant, W. (Ed.). (1928). *The works of Schopenhauer, abridged.* New York: Simon & Schuster.

Friedrich Nietzsche: Page 207 of Nietzsche, F. (1909). *Human, all too human: A book for free spirits* (M. Faber, with S. Lehmann, Trans.). Lincoln, NE: University of Nebraska Press.

Excerpts from the Bible

The New English Bible. (1970). Cambridge: Cambridge University Press.

Other Religious Declarations

Islam: Page 64 of Dawood, N. J. (Trans.). (1995). *The Koran: Translated with notes.* London: Penguin Books.

Judaism: Page 29 of Neusner, J. (Trans.). (1991). *The Talmud of Babylonia: An American translation* (vol. 29B: Tractate Menahot, Chapters 4–7). Atlanta, GA: Scholars Press.

Buddhism: Page 308 of Paul, D. Y. (1979). *Women in Buddhism: Images of the feminine in Mahāyāna tradition.* Berkeley, CA: Asian Humanities Press.

Hinduism: Page 115 of Doniger, W., & Smith, B. K. (1991). *The laws of Manu.* London: Penguin Books.

A Contemporary Statement

Rogers, A. (2000, June 14). *Report of the Baptist Faith and Message Study Committee to the Southern Baptist Convention.* Nashville, TN: Southern Baptist Convention. Copyright © 2000 Southern Baptist Convention. Used by permission. [See also: Page A24 of Niebuhr, G. (1998, June 10). Southern Baptists declare wife should "submit" to her husband. *New York Times,* pp. A1, A24. Southern Baptist Convention passes resolution opposing women as pastors. (2000, June 15). *New York Times,* p. A22.]

Some Early Scientific Views on Women

Charles Darwin: Page 858 of Darwin, C. (1906). *The descent of man and selection in relation to sex* (2nd ed.). London: John Murray.

Herbert Spencer: Page 32 of Spencer, H. (1873). Psychology of the sexes. *Popular Science Monthly, 4,* 30–38.

Gustave Le Bon: Pages 104–105 of Gould, S. J. (1981). *The mismeasure of man.* New York: W.W. Norton.

William James: Page 991 of James, W. (1890/1981). *The principles of psychology* (vol. 2). Cambridge, MA: Harvard University Press.

G. Stanley Hall: Pages 579 and 616 of Hall, G. S. (1907). *Adolescence: Its psychology and its relations to physiology, anthropology, sociology, sex, crime, religion, and education* (vol. 2). New York: D. Appleton and Co.

Thomas A. Edison: Page 440 of Edison, T. A. (1912, October). The woman of the future. *Good Housekeeping,* pp. 436–444.

An Ambivalent Alliance: Hostile and Benevolent Sexism

Glick, P. & Fiske, S. T. (2001). An ambivalent alliance: Hostile and benevolent sexism as complementary justifications for gender inequality. *American Psychologist, 56,* 109–118.

Freud's Theory of Penis Envy

Pages 253 and 258 of Strachey, J. (Ed. and Trans.). (1966). *The standard edition of the complete psychological works of Sigmund Freud* (vol. 19). London: Hogarth Press.

A View from the U.S. Supreme Court

Page 446 of Myra Bradwell v. State of Illinois (1883). *Cases argued and decided in the Supreme Court of the United States* (Lawyer's ed., Book 21, pp. 442–446). Rochester, NY: Lawyers Co-operative Publishing Co.

A Sampler of Dissonance-Reducing Statements in Opposition to Female Suffrage

All statements taken from Brownson, H. F. (Ed.). (1885). *The works of Orestes A. Brownson* (vol. 18). Detroit, MI: Thorndike Nourse, Publisher.

Women benefit from subordination: Page 403.

Women have it good: Pages 405, 412.

Women do not suffer more than men: Page 404.

Suffrage would hurt women: Pages 404, 412.

Religious support for inequality: Page 403.

Subordination is natural: Page 389.

Subordination is necessary: Pages 388–389.

Women are incompetent: Page 412.

Women oppress themselves: Page 392.

Women prefer not to vote: Page 404.

Male self-interest protects women: Pages 385, 403.

Men are caring: Page 390.

Suffragists are fanatics: Page 412.

Women's rights is not the issue: Page 407.

Abuses are part of the system: Page 409.

Equality is impossible: Page 386.

They Could Have Had a Girl

Schmitt, E. (1995, November 19). Admiral's gaffe pushes Navy to new scrutiny of attitudes. *New York Times,* p. 14.

The Deadly Serious Game of the Beauty Pageant

McElwaine, S. (1989, September). The deadly serious game of the beauty pageant. *Cosmopolitan,* pp. 218–221.

The Official Point System from an Early Miss America Pageant

Page 32 of Goldman, W. (1990). *Hype and glory*. New York: Villard Books.

Would You Encourage Her?

Carlson, D. K. (2000, October 13). Most Americans would be proud to have daughter in Miss America Pageant. [http://www.gallup.com/poll/releases/pr001013b.asp]

Influence of Popular Erotica on Judgments of Strangers and Mates

Kenrick, D. T., Gutierres, S. E., & Goldberg, L. L. (1989). Influence of popular erotica on judgments of strangers and mates. *Journal of Experimental Social Psychology, 25,* 159–167.

Male Epithets for Ethnic Women in Historical American Slang

Allen, I. L. (1984). Male sex roles and epithets for ethnic women in American slang. *Sex Roles, 11,* 43–50. [*Note:* For a more extensive treatment of this topic, see Allen, I. L. (1990). *Unkind words. Ethnic labeling from Redskin to Wasp.* New York: Bergin and Garvey.]

Some Words Referring to Women and Prostitutes as Food

Mills, J. (1993). *Womanwords: A dictionary of words about women.* New York: Henry Holt.

Richter, A. (1993). *Sexual slang.* New York: HarperPerennial.

Winick, C., & Kinsie, P. M. (1971). *The lively commerce: Prostitution in the United States.* Chicago, IL: Quadrangle Books.

I Was a Piece of Meat

Page 100 of Stoller, R. J. (1991). *Porn: Myths for the twentieth century.* New Haven, CT: Yale University Press.

Some Words Referring to Women and Prostitutes as Animals

Allen, I. L. (1984). Male sex roles and epithets for ethnic women in American slang. *Sex Roles, 11,* 43–50.

Cleugh, J. (1963). *Love locked out: An examination of the irrepressible sexuality of the Middle Ages.* New York: Crown Publishers.

Hubner, J. (1992). *Bottom feeders: From free love to hard core.* New York: Doubleday.

Mills, J. (1993). *Womanwords: A dictionary of words about women.* New York: Henry Holt.

Nieves, E. (2001, August 19). Anxious days in bordello country. *New York Times*, p. 18.

Richards, D. (1994, May 11). Musical visit to Southwestern bordello. *New York Times*, pp. C13–C14.

Richter, A. (1993). *Sexual slang.* New York: HarperPerennial.

Winick, C., & Kinsie, P. M. (1971). *The lively commerce: Prostitution in the United States.* Chicago, IL: Quadrangle Books.

Taming and Hunting the Female Animal

Rodeo Bumper Stickers: Page 96 of Lawrence, E. A. (1985). *Hoofbeats and society: Studies of human-horse interactions.* Bloomington: Indiana University Press.

Hunting Bumper Stickers: Page 233 of Cartmill, M. (1993). *A view to a death in the morning: Hunting and nature through history.* Cambridge: Harvard University Press.

I'm Riding You

Page 850 of Mitchell, M. (1936/1973). *Gone with the wind.* New York: Avon Books.

Stories of the Hunt

Alfred Lord Tennyson: Page 95 of Tennyson, A. L. (1896). *The princess: A medley.* New York: American Book Co.

David Berkowitz: Pages 141–142 of Klausner, L. D. (1981). *Son of Sam.* New York: McGraw-Hill.

Stephen Francis Kuber, III: Page B1 of DeMare, C. (1991, May 9). Killer gets 23 years to life, arsonist 62$^{1}/_{2}$–125. *Times Union* (Albany, NY), pp. B1, B8.

Rapist cited in *The Hite Report:* Page 781 of Hite, S. (1981). *The Hite report on male sexuality.* New York: Alfred Knopf.

Rape: Originally a Property Crime

Pages 8–10 of Brownmiller, S. (1975). *Against our will: Men, women and rape.* New York: Bantam Books.

Every 13 Seconds

When women report: Page 46 of Tjaden, P., & Thoennes, N. (2000, November). *Full report of the prevalence, incidence, and consequences of violence against women: Findings from the National Violence Against Women Survey* (National Institute of Justice Research Report No. NCJ-183781). Washington, DC: U.S. Department of Justice.

In some hospitals: Page 10 of Stark, E., & Flitcraft, A. (1996). *Women at risk: Domestic violence and women's health.* Thousand Oaks, CA: Sage Publications. Page 55 of Acierno, R., Resnick, H. S., & Kilpatrick, D. G. (1997). Health impact of interpersonal violence 1: Prevalence rates, case identification, and risk factors for sexual assault, physical assault, and domestic violence in men and women. *Behavioral Medicine, 23,* 53–64.

Averaging over time: Pages 15 and 46 of Tjaden, P., & Thoennes, N. (2000, November). *Full report of the prevalence, incidence, and consequences of violence against women: Findings from the National Violence Against Women Survey* (National Institute of Justice Research Report No. NCJ-183781). Washington, DC: U.S. Department of Justice. [*Note:* The figure of 13 seconds was calculated by dividing 54,864,000 (60 seconds × 60 minutes × 24 hours × 365 days) by 64.0% of 6,807,117, which is the percentage of rapes and physical assaults of women per year committed by intimate partners, based on Exhibits 5 and 26 of the report.]

Detecting and Labeling Prejudice: Do Female Perpetrators Go Undetected?

Adapted with permission from Baron, R. S., Burgess, M. L., & Kao, C. F. (1991). Detecting and labeling prejudice: Do female perpetrators go undetected? *Personality and Social Psychology Bulletin, 17,* 115–123.

The Preference for a Male Boss

Simmons, W. W. (2001, January 11). *When it comes to choosing a boss, Americans still prefer men: Even women prefer a male boss by two-to-one margin* (Poll Analyses). Retrieved January 1, 2002, from http://www.gallup.com/poll/releases/pr010111.asp [*Note:* Figure excludes approximately 2% of respondents who had no opinion].

On the Feminist Movement

Adapted with permission from pages 83–84 of Steinem, G. (1997, September/October). Revving up for the next 25 years. *Ms.*, pp. 82–84.

VI. Anti-Semitism

Page 21 of Rubenstein, R. L. (1975). *The cunning of history: Mass death and the American future.* New York: Harper & Row. [Emphasis in original]

The Holocaust: Centuries in the Making

13th Century: Page 305 of Hirschler, G. (Ed.). (1988). *Ashkenaz: The German Jewish Heritage.* New York: Yeshiva University Museum.

20th Century: Page 139 of Gutman, I. (1990). *Encyclopedia of the Holocaust* (vol. 1). New York: Macmillan.

Five Centuries Before Hitler

Page 11 of Langer, H. (1997). *The history of the Holocaust: A chronology of quotations.* Northvale, NJ: Jason Aronson, Inc.

Four Centuries Before Hitler

Pages 172, 268–270, and 288 of Sherman, F. (Ed.). (1971). *Luther's works* (vol. 47, The Christian in Society: IV, "On the Jews and Their Lies"). Philadelphia, PA: Fortress Press.

Three Centuries Before Hitler

Page 176 of Poliakov, L. (1965). *The History of Anti-Semitism* (vol. 1). New York: Vanguard Press.

Two Centuries Before Hitler

Page 122 of Vishniak, M. (1946). Antisemitism in Tsarist Russia. In K. S. Pinson (Ed.), *Essays on antisemitism* (vol 2, pp. 121–144). New York: Conference on Jewish Relations.

A Century Before Hitler

Pages 110 and 112 of McLellan, D. (Trans. and Ed.). (1971). *Karl Marx: Early texts.* New York: Barnes & Noble.

Decades Before the Hitler

Owing to their obstinacy: Page 130 of Kertzer, D. I. (2001). *The popes against the Jews: The Vatican's role in the rise of modern anti-Semitism.* New York: Alfred A. Knopf.

On September 3: Page 166 of Kertzer, D. I. (2001). *The popes against the Jews: The Vatican's role in the rise of modern anti-Semitism.* New York: Alfred A. Knopf.

Greetings to Hitler from the New Pope

Page 208 of Cornwall, J. (1999). *Hitler's Pope: The secret history of Pius XII.* New York: Viking.

The Destruction of the European Jews: Dehumanization and Concealment

Pages 20, 328–329, 886, 962–963, and 1015–1016 of Hilberg, R. (1985). *The destruction of the European Jews* (revised and definitive edition). New York: Holmes & Meier.

Die Spinne

Die spinne. (1934). *Der Stürmer*, No. 26, p. 1.

Der Vampire

Der vampire. (1934). *Der Stürmer*, No. 31, p. 1.

Die Weltpest
Die weltpest. (1932, March). *Der Stürmer,* No. 10, p. 1.

Supply Orders for Nazi Experiments
War crimes. (1947, November 24). *Time,* p. 33.

None of Our Business
Page 1 of Sherrill rebuffs Olympic ban plea; scores agitation. (1935, October 22). *New York Times,* pp. 1, 10.

Racial Politics in America
We must preserve our Aryan nationality: Page 407 of Burgess, J. W. (1895). The ideal of the American commonwealth. *Political Science Quarterly, 10,* 404–425.

America, which leads all other countries: Hitler challenges American protests. (1933, April 7). *New York Times,* p. 10.

As for the racial problem: Dodd denies orders to help Reich Jews. (1933, July 15). *New York Times,* p. 4.

The question of Jewish persecution: Page 241 of Lochner, L. P. (Ed. and Trans.). (1948). *The Goebbels diaries 1942–1943.* Garden City, NY: Doubleday & Co.

Jewish Expulsion Orders During the U.S. Civil War
General Orders No. 11: Page 50 of Simon, J. Y. (Ed.). (1979). *The papers of Ulysses S. Grant* (vol. 7: December 9, 1862–March 31, 1863). Carbondale, IL: Southern Illinois University Press. [For an overview of General Orders No. 11 and its aftermath, see Chapter 6 of Korn, B. W. (2001). *American Jewry and the Civil War.* Philadelphia, PA: Jewish Publication Society.]

In an attempt: Page 238 of Simon, J. Y. (Ed.). (1973). *The papers of Ulysses S. Grant* (vol. 5: April 1–August 31, 1862). Carbondale, IL: Southern Illinois University Press.

On November 10, 1862: Page 283 of Simon, J. Y. (Ed.). (1977). *The papers of Ulysses S. Grant* (vol. 6: September 1–December 8, 1862). Carbondale, IL: Southern Illinois University Press.

A Madison Square Garden Rally
Adapted with permission from pages 14–15 of Wyman, D. S. (1968). *Paper walls: America and the refugee crisis 1938–1941.* Amherst, MA: University of Massachusetts Press.

Antisemitism in America
Pages 78–89 of Dinnerstein, L. (1994). *Antisemitism in America.* New York: Oxford University Press.

Signs at Employee Parking Gates of the Ford Motor Company
Pages 100–101 of Lee, A. (1980). *Henry Ford and the Jews.* New York: Stein & Day.

New York Times Headlines 50 Years After the War: Stories of Complicity and Silence
Cowell, A. (1996, November 19). Files suggest British knew early of Nazi atrocities against Jews. *New York Times,* pp. A1, A6.

Cowell, A. (1996, December 14). Swiss acknowledge profiting from Nazi gold. *New York Times,* p. 3.

Molotsky, I. (1996, December 19). Red Cross admits knowing of the Holocaust during the war. *New York Times,* p. B17.

DePalma, A. (1997, February 3). Canada called haven for Nazi criminals. *New York Times,* p. A6.

Cowell, A. (1997, May 29). New records show the Swiss sold arms worth millions to Nazis. *New York Times,* p. A8.

DePalma, A. (1997, July 16). Allies linked to swapping of Nazi gold. *New York Times,* p. A9.

Croatia apologizes to Jews for Nazi-era crimes. (1997, August 23). *New York Times,* p. 4.

Red Cross admits failing to condemn Holocaust. (1997, October 8). *New York Times,* p. A10.

Nazi-Era apology by French doctors. (1997, October 12). *New York Times,* p. 4.

Sanger, D. E. (1997, December 1). U.S. melted down gold items from Nazis. *New York Times,* p. A8.

Cowell, A. (1998, May 23). Switzerland said to have backed Nazi trade in looted gold. *New York Times,* p. A4.

Olson, E. (1998, May 26). Report says Swiss knew some Nazi gold was stolen. *New York Times,* p. A6.

Risen, J. (1998, June 21). U.S. details 6 neutral countries' role in aiding Nazis. *New York Times,* p. 11.

Sanger, D.E. (1998, December 1). U.S. shifts from Nazi gold to art, land and insurance. *New York Times,* p. A6.

French detail Vichy looting of Jews' assets. (1999, March 17). *New York Times,* p. A8.

Stout, D. (1999, July 29). U.S. knew early of Nazi killings in asylums, official documents show. *New York Times,* p. A14.

Golden, T. (1999, October 15). G.I.'s are called looters of Jewish riches. *New York Times,* pp. A1, A22.

Olson, E. (1999, December 3). Swiss Holocaust accounts reportedly have $250 million. *New York Times,* p. A5.

Sanger, D. E. (1999, December 7). 54,000 Swiss accounts tied to the Nazis' war victims. *New York Times,* p. A15.

Olson, E. (1999, December 11). Historians' report blames Swiss for barring Jews during war. *New York Times,* p. A10.

Andrews, E. L. (1999, December 14). G.M. Opel unit says it's likely to pay Nazi-era slaves. *New York Times,* p. A3.

Kahn, J. (2000, April 29). A fund is planned by U.S. companies for Nazis' victims. *New York Times,* pp. A1, A5.

Sanger, D. E. (2001, January 17). Report on Holocaust assets tells of items found in U.S. *New York Times,* p. A12.

Olson, E. (2001, December 2). Swiss were part of Nazi economic lifeline, historians find. *New York Times,* p. 24.

Erlanger, S. (2002, March 7). Vienna skewered as a Nazi-era pillager of its Jews. *New York Times,* p. A3.

While Six Million Died: A Chronicle of American Apathy

Pages ix–x, 199–215, and 397 of Morse, A. D. (1968). *While six million died: A chronicle of American apathy* (Introduction and Chapter 11). New York: Random House.

We Can Delay

Memo from Assistant Secretary of State Breckinridge Long: Page 173 of Wyman, D. S. (1968). *Paper walls: America and the refugee crisis 1938–1941.* Amherst, MA: University of Massachusetts Press.

According to Long's diary: Page 134 of Israel, F. L. (Ed.). (1966). *The war diary of Breckinridge Long.* Lincoln, NE: University of Nebraska Press.

Discussion paper on Rwanda: Page 96 of Power, S. (2001, September). Bystanders to genocide: Why the United States let the Rwandan tragedy happen. *Atlantic Monthly,* pp. 84–108.

American Public Opinion on Admitting Refugees

Pages 145–149 of Stember, C. (1966). *Jews in the mind of America.* New York: Basic Books.

U.S. Immigration During the Holocaust

Page 172 of Friedman, S. S. (1973). *No haven for the oppressed: United States policy toward Jewish refugees, 1938–1945.* Detroit, MI: Wayne State University Press.

United States Immigration

U.S. Immigration and Naturalization Service. (2000). *Statistical Yearbook of the Immigration and Naturalization Service, 1998* (Table 1). Washington, DC: Government Printing Office.

Inscription on the Statue of Liberty

Page 1028 of Foner, E., & Garraty, J. A. (Eds.). (1991). *The reader's companion to American history.* Boston: Houghton Mifflin Company.

Apathy[I] = Insanity[M]

Page 757 of Hofstadter, D. R. (1985). *Metamagical themas: Questing for the essence of mind and pattern.* New York: Basic Books.

Postwar German Attitudes About Jews and White American Attitudes About Blacks

Page 137 of Erskine, H. (1968). The polls: Negro employment. *Public Opinion Quarterly, 32,* 132–153.

Page 1572 of Gallup, G. H. (1972). *The Gallup poll: Public opinion 1935–1971* (vol. 2). New York: Random House. [*Note:* Figures are approximate.]

Pages 384–385, 477, 703, and 988–989 of Cantril, H. (1951). *Public opinion: 1935–1946.* Princeton: Princeton University Press.

A Jewish Perspective on Anti-Semitism

Adapted with permission from pages 223–224 of Langman, P. F. (1995). Including Jews in multiculturalism. *Journal of Multicultural Counseling and Development, 23,* 222–236.

ADL 2000 Audit of Anti-Semitic Incidents

Adapted with permission from pages pp. 1–6, 8–9, 17–18, and 30–31 of Anti-Defamation League. (2001). *ADL 2000 audit of anti-Semitic incidents.* New York: Author.

Anti-Semitism in the Middle East

All quotes retrieved May 19, 2002, from the Middle East Media Research Institute web site, http://www.memri.org and reprinted with permission [See also: Sachs, S. (2002, April 27). Anti-Semitism is deepening among Muslims. *New York Times,* pp. B9, B11. Kertzer, D. I. (2002, May 9). The modern use of ancient lies. *New York Times,* p. A39.]

VII. Genocide in America

Page 57 of Williams, E. (1963). *Documents of West Indian history* (vol. 1, 1492–1655). Port-of-Spain, Trinidad: PNM Publishing Co.

A Christopher Columbus Day Parable

Trimmer, T. (1991). Fourteen hundred and ninety-two: Owosh-Keday-So-Quay's story. *Episcopal Peace Fellowship Newsletter.*

American Indian Stereotypes and Reality

Mihesuah, D. A. (1996). *American Indians: Stereotypes and reality.* Atlanta, GA: Clarity Press.

U.S. Department of Health and Human Services. (2001). *Mental health: Culture, race, and ethnicity—A supplement to mental health: A report of the Surgeon General.* Rockville, MD: U.S. Department of Health and Human Services. [*Note:* The statistic that 1 in 5 Native Americans live on U.S. reservations was taken from page 81 of this report.]

How Native Americans Were Described

Page 1190 of Foner, E., & Garraty, J. A. (Eds.). (1991). *The reader's companion to American history.* Boston: Houghton Mifflin Company. [*Note:* Other reference volumes transcribe this passage with slightly different capitalization and punctuation, such as: "the merciless Indian Savages, whose known rule of warfare, is an undistinguished destruction of all ages, sexes and conditions."]

A Half-Filled Outline of Humanity

Benjamin Franklin: Pages 375–376 of Symth, A. H. (1907). *The writings of Benjamin Franklin* (vol. 1). New York: Macmillan.

Oliver Wendell Holmes: Page 298 of Holmes, O. W. (1901). Oration, 1855. In C. Brainerd & E. W. Brainerd (Eds.), *The New England Society Orations* (vol. 2) (pp. 271–302). New York: The Century Company.

U.S. Supreme Court: Page 111 of United States v. Sandoval. (1914). *Cases argued and decided in the Supreme Court of the United States: October Term, 1913* (Book 58, Lawyer's ed., pp. 107–115). Rochester, NY: Lawyers Co-operative Publishing Co.

U.S. Presidents Speak

George Washington: Page 65 of Drinnon, R. (1980). *Facing West: The metaphysics of Indian-hating and empire-building.* New York: New American Library.

Andrew Jackson: Page 33 of Jackson, A. (1900). Fifth annual message (1833, December 3). In J. D. Richardson (Ed.), *A compilation of the messages and papers of the presidents, 1789–1897* (vol. 3, pp. 19–35). New York: Bureau of National Literature and Art.

Martin Van Buren: Page 499 of Van Buren, M. (1900). Second annual message (1838, December 3). In J. D. Richardson (Ed.), *A compilation of the messages and papers of the presidents, 1789–1897* (vol.3, pp. 483–505). New York: Bureau of National Literature and Art.

James Buchanan: Page 116 of Buchanan, J. (1961). Inaugural Address: March 4, 1857. In *Inaugural address of the presidents of the United States* (pp. 111–117). Washington, DC: United States Government Printing Office.

Theodore Roosevelt, "I don't go so far as": Page 355 of Hagedorn, H. (1921). *Roosevelt in the Bad Lands.* Boston, MA: Houghton Mifflin.

Theodore Roosevelt, "It is nonsense to talk": Page 18 of Roosevelt, T. (1893, February 25). *Report of Honorable Theodore Roosevelt made to the United States Civil Service Commission.* Philadelphia, PA: Indian Rights Association.

U.S. Army Generals Speak

Samuel R. Curtis: Page 462 of United States War Department. (1893). *The war of the rebellion: A compilation of the official records of the union and confederate armies* (series 1, vol. 41, part 3). Washington, DC: U.S. Government Printing Office. [correspondence with Colonel J. M. Chivington on September 28, 1864]

Patrick E. Connor: Page 1049 of United States War Department. (1896). *The war of the rebellion: A compilation of the official records of the union and confederate armies* (series 1, vol. 48, part 2). Washington, DC: U.S. Government Printing Office. [correspondence with Colonel N. Cole on July 4, 1865]

William Tecumseh Sherman: Page 99 of Athearn, R. G. (1995). *William T. Sherman and the settlement of the West.* Norman, OK: University of Oklahoma Press.

Winfield Scott Hancock: Page 77 of Hancock, W. S. (1867). *Reports of Major General W. S. Hancock upon Indian affairs, with accompanying exhibits.* Washington, DC: McGill & Witherow.

Philip Sheridan: Page 1483 of Ellis, E. S. (1900). *History of our country: From the landing of the Norsemen to the present time.* New York: Francis R. Niglutsch.

Nelson A. Miles: Pages 309–310 of Miles, N. A. (1879, March). The Indian problem. *North American Review, 128,* 304–314.

John McAllister Schofield: Page 428 of Schofield, J. M. (1897). *Forty-six years in the army.* New York: The Century Co.

Definition of Genocide

Page 280 of United Nations. (1951). Convention on the prevention and punishment of the crime of genocide. *Treaty Series, 78,* 277–287.

How Does Genocide Happen?

Adapted with permission from page 13 of Staub, E. (1989). *The roots of evil: The origins of genocide and other group violence.* Cambridge: Cambridge University Press.

They Have Not the Same Sensibilities
Pages 133–135 of Flint, T. (1826/1932). *Recollections of the last ten years.* New York: Alfred A. Knopf.

What Was Promised
The Northwest Ordinance: Page 131 of Commager, H. S. (Ed.). (1968). *Documents of American history.* New York: Appleton-Century-Crofts.

George Washington: Pages 773 and 776 of Washington, G. (1997). *Writings.* New York: Library of America.

Thomas Jefferson: Page 429 of Bergh, A. E. (Ed.). (1907). *The writings of Thomas Jefferson* (definitive edition, vol. 16). Washington, DC: Thomas Jefferson Memorial Association.

What Took Place
Klaus Frantz: Page 39 of Frantz, K.(1999). *Indian reservations in the United States: Territory, sovereignty, and socioeconomic change.* Chicago, IL: University of Chicago Press.

David E. Stannard: Adapted with permission from pages x and 151 of Stannard, D. E. (1992). *American Holocaust: Columbus and the conquest of the New World.* New York: Oxford University Press.

The Current State of Affairs
Page 73 of Frazier, I. (2000). *On the Rez.* New York: Farrar, Straus and Giroux.

A Good Break
Page 82 of Playboy interview: John Wayne. (1971, May). *Playboy,* pp. 75–76, 78, 80, 82, 84, 86, 88, 90, 92.

I Don't Know What Their Complaint Might Be
Pages 690–691 of Reagan, R. (1990). Remarks and a question-and-answer session with the students and faculty at Moscow State University, May 31, 1988. In *Public papers of the presidents of the United States: Ronald Reagan, 1988* (Book 1, pp. 683–692). Washington, DC: United States Government Printing Office.

Court Ruling: "Irresponsibility in Its Purest Form"
"It would be difficult to find": Pages 4–6 of Memorandum opinion: Findings of fact and conclusions of law. *Cobell v. Babbitt,* Civil No. 96-1285, February 22, 1999.

"Flagrant disregard" and "lack of candor": Page 3 of Memorandum opinion. *Cobell v. Babbitt,* Civil No. 96-1285, February 22, 1999.

"The funds involve": Egan, T. (2002, February 14). A computer shutdown plays havoc at Interior. *New York Times,* p. A20.

"Among other things": Maas, P. (2001, September 9). The broken promise. *Parade Magazine,* pp. 4–6.

Naming Our Destiny: Toward a Language of American Indian Liberation
Churchill, W. (1994). *Indians are us? Culture and genocide in Native North America* ("Naming our destiny: Toward a language of American Indian liberation," pp. 291–357). Monroe, ME: Common Courage Press.

Let's Spread the "Fun" Around: The Issue of Sports Team Names and Mascots
Churchill, W. (1994). *Indians are us? Culture and genocide in Native North America* ("Let's spread the 'fun' around," pp. 65–72). Monroe, ME: Common Courage Press.

"Maybe Now You Know How Native Americans Feel"
Reprinted with permission from the National Conference for Community and Justice, Washington, D.C.

Making Room for Education
Excerpts from a statement issued by the U.S. Commission on Civil Rights on April 16, 2001. Retrieved January 5, 2002, from http://www.usccr.gov/nwsrel/2001/041601st.htm

Battle Rages Over a 5-Letter Four-Letter Word

Schmitt, E. (1996, September 4). Battle rages over a 5-letter four-letter word. *New York Times,*
    p. A16.

New Prosperity Brings New Conflict to Indian Country

Egan, T. (1998, March 8). New prosperity brings new conflict to Indian country. *New York Times,*
    pp. 1, 24.

Never Sell Your Parents' Bones

Page 419 of Young Joseph. (1879). An Indian's views of Indian affairs. *North American
    Review, 128,* 412–433.

VIII. Heterosexism

Reynolds, P. (1989, February 26). Judge creates uproar in Texas. *Boston Globe,* p. 15.

Biblical Statements on Homosexuality

Leviticus: Page 158 of *The New English Bible: The Old Testament.* (1970). Oxford, England: Oxford
    University Press.

I Corinthians: Page 286 of *The New English Bible: The New Testament* (2nd ed.). (1971). New York:
    Oxford University Press.

A Biblical Statement on Cross-Dressing

Page 263 of *The New English Bible: The Old Testament.* (1970). Oxford, England: Oxford
    University Press.

Do You Believe It?

Lumpkin: San Francisco rights aide agrees with Bible: Stone homosexuals. (1993, August 22). *New
    York Times,* p. 28.

Moore: Alabama Supreme Court, Ex parte H.H., No. 1002045 (February 15, 2002). Sack, K.
    (2002, February 20). Judge's ouster sought after antigay remarks. *New York Times,* p. A15.

Moral Trespassing

Excerpt from a letter to a gay alumnus: Christian university bars visits by its gay alumni.
    (1998, October 25). *New York Times,* p. 40.

Amendment approved by the Presbyterian Church's General Assembly: Niebuhr, G. (2000).
    Presbyterians would ban same-sex links. *New York Times,* p. 17.

Rule adopted in 1996: Niebuhr, G. (1998). Methodists act against homosexual unions. *New
    York Times,* p. A10.

Robert Black: Page A19 of Berke, R. (1998, June 30). Flurry of anti-gay remarks has G.O.P.
    fearing backlash. *New York Times,* pp. A1, A19.

Biblical Verse: Is It a Reason or an Excuse?

Price, D. (1993, August 24). Biblical verse: Is it a reason or an excuse? *San Francisco Examiner,*
    p. B-7.

A Monster in Human Shape

Pages 11 and 22–24 of Katz, J. (1976). *Gay American history: Lesbians and gay men in the U.S.A.*
    New York: Thomas Y. Crowell Company.

Violence Toward Homosexuals

Franklin, K., & Herek, G. M. (1999). Violence toward homosexuals. In L. Kurtz (Ed.),
    Encyclopedia of violence, peace, and conflict (pp. 139–151). San Diego, CA: Academic Press.

Arrested Development

Pages 419–420 of Freud, E. L. (Ed.). (1961). *Letters of Sigmund Freud, 1873–1939* (T. Stern & J.
    Stern, Trans.). London: Hogarth Press.

Diagnostic Category 302.0: Homosexuality

302 Sexual deviations: Page 44 of American Psychiatric Association. (1968). *Diagnostic and Statistical Manual of Mental Disorders* (2nd ed.). Washington, DC: American Psychiatric Association. [*Note:* In December 1973 and in subsequent editions of the DSM, the American Psychiatric Association eliminated homosexuality as a mental disorder.]

302 Sexual Deviations and Disorders: Page 585 of Puckitt, C. D. (1994). *The educational annotation of ICD-9–CM* (4th ed.). [International Classification of Diseases, 9th revision]. Reno, NV: Channel Publishing, Ltd.

The AIDS Epidemic: Don't Ask, Don't Tell

Human Rights Campaign. (2001). *HIV/AIDS & HRC: Two Decades of Fighting for Life.* Washington, DC: Author.

U.S. Supreme Court Decisions

William Rehnquist: Pages 199 and 203 of Murdoch, J., & Price, D. (2001). *Courting justice: Gay men and lesbians v. the Supreme Court.* New York: Basic Books.

Warren Burger: Pages 149–150 of Michael J. Bowers v. Michael Hardwick, and John and Mary Doe. (1998). *United States Supreme Court Reports: October Term, 1985* (Lawyer's ed., 2nd series, vol. 92, pp. 140–165). Rochester, NY: Lawyers Co-operative Publishing Co.

American Public Opinion on Homosexuality: Yes on Equal Rights, Divided on Legality

Poll data from the Roper Center for Public Opinion. Retrieved January 1, 2002, from Lexis-Nexis Academic Universe [http://web.lexis-nexis.com/universe/].

Is Homosexuality a Sin?

Fram, A. (1998, June 16). Lott calls homosexuality a 'sin.' Associated Press.

Is Homosexuality a Disease?

"It is a pathology": Page 16 of People for the American Way. (1999, December). *Pat Robertson on . . .* (white paper report, 34 pp.). Washington, DC: PFAW.

"Acceptance of homosexuality": Can politics cause hate? (1998, October 26). *Time,* p. 32.

Is Homosexuality Unnatural?

Seelye, K. Q. (1995, July 5). Helms puts the brakes to a bill financing AIDS treatment. *New York Times,* p. A12.

Is Homosexuality a Biological Error?

Pages 59–60 of McDowell, J. (2000). Preacher, teacher, nag: Dr. Laura speaks her mind. *Time,* pp. 59–60.

We're Standing for the Truth That Homosexuals Can Change

We're standing for the truth that homosexuals can change [advertisement]. (1998, July 14). *Washington Post,* p. A2.

Sexual Orientation vs. Sexual Preference

Page 973 of Committee on Lesbian and Gay Concerns. (1991). Avoiding heterosexual bias in language. *American Psychologist, 46,* 973–974.

Is Homophobia Associated with Homosexual Arousal?

Adams, H. E., Wright, L. W., Jr., & Lohr, B. A. (1996). Is homophobia associated with homosexual arousal? *Journal of Abnormal Psychology, 105,* 440–445.

Some Gender Differences In . . .

Same-Sex Behavior (Females): Pages 114 and 475 of Kinsey, A. C., Pomeroy, W. B., Martin, C. E., & Gebhard, P. H. (1953). *Sexual behavior in the human female.* Philadelphia, PA: W. B. Saunders Company.

Same-Sex Behavior (Males): Pages 168 and 623 of Kinsey, A. C., Pomeroy, W. B., & Martin, C. E. (1948). *Sexual behavior in the human male.* Philadelphia, PA: W. B. Saunders Company.

Attitudes: Page 33 of Moore, D. W. (1993, April). Public polarized on gay issue. *The Gallup Poll Monthly,* pp. 30–34.

Antigay Violence: Page 19 of National Coalition of Anti-Violence Programs. (2001). *Anti-lesbian, gay, transgender and bisexual violence in 2000: A report of the National Coalition of Anti-Violence Programs* (2001 preliminary ed.). New York: Author. [*Notes:* The National Coalition of Anti-Violence Programs is a network of U.S. anti-violence organizations that monitor antigay hate crimes. Of the perpetrators whose gender was recorded, 15% were female and 85% were male in the year 2000.]

Club Faggots Not Seals!

Anti-homosexual T-shirts prompt suspension of Syracuse fraternity. (1991, June 26). *New York Times,* p. B4.

The Inescapable Conclusion

Adapted with permission from pages 169–170 of Blumstein, P. W., & Schwartz, P. (1993). Bisexuality: Some social-psychological issues. In L. Garnets & D. Kimmel (Eds.), *Psychological perspectives on lesbian and gay male experiences* (pp. 168–183). New York: Columbia University Press.

A One-Drop Rule for Sexual Orientation?

Page 469 of Kinsey, A. C., Pomeroy, W. B., Martin, C. E., & Gebhard, P. H. (1953). *Sexual behavior in the human female.* Philadelphia, PA: W. B. Saunders Company.

As Unique as Fingerprints

Adapted with permission from DeAngelis, T. (2001, April). Our erotic personalities are as unique as our fingerprints. *Monitor on Psychology,* p. 35.

Transgender Identities: Like Stars in the Sky

Baird, V. (2001). *The no-nonsense guide to sexual diversity* (pp. 112–128). London: Verso.

Females Who Test "Male"

Adapted with permission from Lehrman, S. (1999, April 5). Sex police. Retrieved January 12, 2002, from http://www.salon.com/health/ feature/1999/04/05/sex_police/

The Problem with Categories

Adapted with permission from page 26 of Beeman, W. O. (1999, Fall). Laws preventing same-sex marriage are factually flawed. *Transgender Tapestry,* pp. 26–27.

Suit Over Estate Claims a Widow Is Not a Woman

Wilgoren, J. (2002, January 13). Suit over estate claims a widow is not a woman. *New York Times,* p. 18.

Heterosexism Doesn't Just Hurt Sexual Minorities

Adapted with permission from pages 8–13 of Blumenfeld, W. J. (Ed.). (1992). *Homophobia: How we all pay the price.* Boston: Beacon Press.

IX. Making Connections

Page 54 of Dreifus, C. (1993, November 28). The Dalai Lama. *New York Times Magazine,* pp. 52–55.

A Single Garment of Destiny

Pages 69–70 of King, M. L., Jr. (1967). *The trumpet of conscience.* New York: Harper & Row.

Putting Oneself in Chains

Page 688 of Foner, P. S. (Ed.). (1999). *Frederick Douglass: Selected speeches and writings*. Chicago, IL: Lawrence Hill Books.

No Hierarchy of Oppression

Lorde, A. (1983). There is no hierarchy of oppressions. *Interracial Books for Children Bulletin, 14*(3&4), p. 9.

Beyond Equality: A Latina Perspective

Adapted with permission from pages 4, 8, 11, and 246 of Martínez, E. (1998). *De colores means all of us: Latina views for a multi-colored century*. Cambridge, MA: South End Press.

Peace is Every Step: The Path of Mindfulness in Everyday Life

Nhat Hanh, T. (1991). *Peace is every step: The path of mindfulness in everyday life* (Editor's Introduction and pp. 95–134). New York: Bantam Books.

Quiet Rhythms

Copyright © 2002, Scott Plous.

Your 50th Cousin

Pages 345, 357, and 380 of Murchie, G. (1978). *The seven mysteries of life: An exploration in science and philosophy*. Boston, MA: Houghton Mifflin.

Prejudice as a Generalized Attitude

Pages 68–69 of Allport, G. W. (1954). *The nature of prejudice*. Reading, MA: Addison-Wesley.

Antigay Prejudice in Nazi Germany

Page 57 of Kersten, F. (1994). *The Kersten memoirs: 1940–1945*. (C. Fitzgibbon & J. Oliver, Trans.). New York: Howard Fertig.

The Bars of Prejudice

Page 544 of Mandela, N. (1994). *Long walk to freedom: The autobiography of Nelson Mandela*. Boston, MA: Little, Brown and Company.

Environmental Justice for All

Adapted with permission from Bullard, R. D. (1994). Environmental justice for all. In R. D. Bullard (Ed.), *Unequal protection: Environmental justice and communities of color* (pp. 3–22). San Francisco: Sierra Club Books. Wright, B. H., Bryant, P., & Bullard, R. D. (1994). Coping with poisons in Cancer Alley. In R. D. Bullard (Ed.), *Unequal protection: Environmental justice and communities of color* (pp. 110–129). San Francisco: Sierra Club Books.

The Web of Life

Page 71 of Seed, J., Macy, J., Fleming, P., & Naess, A. (1988). *Thinking like a mountain: Towards a council of all beings*. Philadelphia, PA: New Society Publishers.

X. Reducing Prejudice

Eiseley, L. (1978). *The star thrower*. New York: Times Books.

What Individuals Can Do for Social Justice

Page 472 of Stowe, H. B. (1852/1981). *Uncle Tom's cabin*. New York: New American Library.

Going North

Page 98 of Nhat Hanh, T. (1987). *Being peace*. Berkeley, CA: Parallax Press.

Reducing the Expression of Racial Prejudice

Blanchard, F. A., Lilly, T., & Vaughn, L. A. (1991). Reducing the expression of racial prejudice. *Psychological Science, 2*, 101–105.

The Part of You That Chooses

Page 72 of Lewis, C. S. (1952). *Mere Christianity*. New York: Macmillan. [*Note:* This quote comes from *Christian Behavior*, a 1943 book that was revised and reissued in 1952 in a larger collection entitled *Mere Christianity*.]

Long-Range Experimental Modification of Values, Attitudes, and Behavior

Rokeach, M. (1971). Long-range experimental modification of values, attitudes, and behavior. *American Psychologist, 26,* 453–459.

The Role of Empathy in Improving Intergroup Relations

Stephan, W. G., & Finlay, K. (1999). The role of empathy in improving intergroup relations. *Journal of Social Issues, 55,* 729–743.

A Home Inventory

Kivel, P. (2002). *Uprooting racism: How White people can work for racial justice* (rev. ed.). Gabriela Island, Canada: New Society Publishers. [*Note:* See pages 220–221 of Kivel, P. (1995). *Uprooting racism: How White people can work for racial justice.* Philadelphia, PA: New Society Publishers.]

The Challenge of Aversive Racism: Combating Pro-White Bias

Gaertner, S. L., Dovidio, J. F., Banker, B. S., Rust, M. C., Nier, J. A., Mottola, G. R., & Ward, C. M. (1997). Does White racism necessarily mean antiblackness? Aversive racism and prowhiteness. In M. Fine, L. Weis, L. C. Powell, & L. M. Wong (Eds.), *Off white: Readings on race, power, and society.* New York: Routledge.

Martin Luther King Explains Nonviolent Resistance

King, M. L., Jr. (1967). Martin Luther King explains nonviolent resistance. In W. L. Katz (Ed.), *Eyewitness: The negro in American history.* New York: Pitman Publishing Corporation.

Together Action

Page 126 of Sahn, S. (1982). *Only don't know.* San Francisco: Four Seasons Foundation.

Like a Blowtorch on Steel

Page 33 of Spira, H. (1996). *Strategies for activists: From the campaign files of Henry Spira.* New York: Animal Rights International.

$1 for Every Minute of Hate

Adapted with permission from Dahir, M. (2001, August 14). Keith Orr sparked a national trend by turning a Fred Phelps protest into a gay fund-raiser. *The Advocate,* p. 52.

No Such Thing as Means and Ends

Page 47 of Griswold del Castillo, R., & Garcia, R. A. (1995). *César Chávez: A triumph of spirit.* Norman, OK: University of Oklahoma Press.

In Closing . . .

Pages 613–614 of Hamer, F. L. (1972). It's in your hands. In G. Lerner (Ed.), *Black women in white America: A documentary history* (pp. 609–614). New York: Vintage Books.

Appendix: Animals as an Outgroup

Pages 246–247 of Kerasote, T. (1993). *Bloodties: Nature, culture, and the hunt.* New York: Random House.

Is There Such a Thing as Prejudice Toward Animals?

Adapted and updated from: Plous, S. (1993). Psychological mechanisms in the human use of animals. *Journal of Social Issues, 49,* 11–52.

A Sampler of Dissonance-Reducing Statements in Support of Harming Animals

Animal Industry Foundation. (1989). Modern farming is humane. In J. Rohr (Ed.), *Animal rights: Opposing viewpoints* (pp. 106–112). San Diego, CA: Greenhaven Press.

Anthony, H. E. (1957, August 17). But it's instinctive. *Saturday Review*, pp. 9–10, 40.

Aquinas, T. (1273/1969). *Summa Theologiae* (vol. 29). New York: Blackfriars/McGraw-Hill.

Archery World. (1989). Hunting helps animal conservation. In J. Rohr (Ed.), *Animal rights: Opposing viewpoints* (pp. 158–165). San Diego, CA: Greenhaven Press.

Ardrey, R. (1976). *The hunting hypothesis: A personal conclusion concerning the evolutionary nature of man.* New York: Atheneum.

Babcock, M. C. (1987, June). Poultry men are now practicing animal welfare at the highest scientific level in history. *Poultry Tribune*, p. 27.

Bakan, D. (1968). *Disease, pain and sacrifice: Toward a psychology of suffering.* Chicago: University of Chicago Press.

Barahal, H. S. (1946). The cruel vegetarian. *Psychiatric Quarterly* (Supplement), *20*, 3–13.

British observer praises U.S. boars, says sows are the worst. (1978, March). *National Hog Farmer*, p. 27.

Budiansky, S. (1989, March 20). The ancient contract. *U.S. News & World Report*, pp. 75–79.

Byrnes, J. (1976, September). Raising pigs by the calendar at Maplewood Farm. *Hog Farm Management*, pp. 30–32, 36.

Curtis, S. E. (1987a). Animal well-being and animal care. *Veterinary Clinics of North America: Food Animal Practice, 3*, 369–382.

Curtis, S. E. (1987b). The case for intensive farming of food animals. In M. W. Fox & L. D. Mickley (Eds.), *Advances in animal welfare science 1986/87.* Boston: Martinus Nijhoff Publishers.

Descartes, R. (1646–1649/1989). Animals are machines. In T. Regan & P. Singer (Eds.), *Animal rights and human obligations* (2nd ed., pp. 13–19). Englewood Cliffs, NJ: Prentice Hall.

Dodds, W. J. (1983). Discussion following Parts I and II. *Annals of the New York Academy of Sciences, 406*, 62–67.

Eaton, R. L. (1987, January/February). Hunting and the great mystery of nature. *Utne Reader*, pp. 42–49.

Fitz-Barnard, L. (1921). *Fighting sports.* London: Odhams Press.

Francis, D. (1960). Hunting and the horse. In D. James & W. Stephens (Eds.), *In praise of hunting: A symposium* (pp. 89–127). London: Hollis & Carter.

Frey, R. G. (1979). Rights, interests, desires and beliefs. *American Philosophical Quarterly, 16*, 233–239.

Fur Information and Fashion Council. (undated). *Furs naturally.* New York: FIFC.

Geary, S. M. (1989). Fur trapping is justified. In J. Rohr (Ed.), *Animal rights: Opposing viewpoints* (pp. 173–176). San Diego, CA: Greenhaven Press.

Harrison, P. (1989). Theodicy and animal pain. *Philosophy, 64*, 79–92.

Hearne, V. (2000). *Adam's task: Calling animals by name.* New York: Akadine Press.

Hendrickson, D. (1989, April 16). A tasty bit of controversy. *Milwaukee Journal Magazine*, pp. 10–22.

Hochswender, W. (1989, March 14). As image of furs suffers, so do revenues. *New York Times*, pp. 1, 18.

Jacobs, F. S. (1984). A perspective on animal rights and domestic animals. *Journal of the American Veterinary Medical Association, 184*, 1344–1345.

James, D., & Stephens, W. (Eds.). (1960). *In praise of hunting: A symposium.* London: Hollis & Carter.

Johnson, D. (1990, February 12). An unlikely battle in snow country: Aspen to vote on banning fur sales. *New York Times*, p. A14.

Kasindorf, J. (1990, January 15). The fur flies: The cold war over animal rights. *New York*, pp. 26–33.

Kennedy, H. R. C. (1962, January 30). Layers under stress. *Farmer and Stockbreeder,* p. 39.

Leo, J. (1979, November 5). How to beat the beef against meat. *Time,* p. 112.

Levin, M. E. (1977, July/August). Animal rights evaluated. *The Humanist,* pp. 12, 14–15.

Martin, M. (1976, Fall). A critique of moral vegetarianism. *Reason Papers, 3,* 13–43.

Miller, R. M. (1983, January). Animal welfare—yes! Human laws—sure! Animal rights—no! *California Veterinarian,* pp. 21, 98–99.

Moffat, A. S. (1991). Three li'l pigs and the hunt for blood substitutes. *Science, 253,* 32–34.

Muller, H. (1981, October). Animal welfare: A problem that won't go away. *Poultry Tribune,* p. 22A.

Newman, J. H. (1900). *Sermons preached on various occasions.* New York: Longmans, Green, and Co.

Paget, R. (1960). Introduction: Cruelty in sport. In D. James & W. Stephens (Eds.), *In praise of hunting: A symposium* (pp. 1–7). London: Hollis & Carter.

Pridgen, T. (1938). *Courage: The story of modern cockfighting.* Boston: Little, Brown.

Reiger, G. (1977, June). The king and us. *Field and Stream,* pp. 20, 24.

Robinson, W. L. (1987). The case for hunting. In M. W. Fox & L. D. Mickley (Eds.), *Advances in animal welfare science 1986/87.* Boston: Martinus Nijhoff Publishers.

Rodale, R. (1980, December). Good words for meat. *Prevention,* pp. 20–25.

Satchell, M. (1987, January 12). Refuge hunting: Perverse use or logical harvest? *U.S. News & World Report,* p. 26.

Simmonds, R. C. (1986, March). Should animals be used in research and education? *The New Physician,* pp. 34–36, 51.

Smick, E. B. (1973). Animals. In C. F. H. Henry (Ed.), *Baker's dictionary of Christian ethics.* Grand Rapids, MI: Baker Book House.

Smothers, R. (1990, May 1). High-stepping horses: Persistent issue of pain. *New York Times,* p. A8.

Swan, K. G. and Swan, R. C. (1984). Man's best friend or man? *The Physiologist, 27,* 347–350.

Tudge, C. (1973, October). Farmers in loco parentis. *New Scientist,* pp. 179–181.

Van Gelder, R. G. (1972). *Animals and man: Past, present, future.* New York: Foundation for Environmental Education.

White, R. J. (1971). Antivivisection: The reluctant Hydra. *American Scholar, 40,* pp. 503–512.

White, R. J. (1988, March). The facts about animal research. *Reader's Digest,* pp. 127–132.

Our Moral Schizophrenia About Animals

Adapted with permission from pages 4–5 of Francione, G. L. (2000). *Introduction to animal rights: Your child or the dog?* Philadelphia, PA: Temple University Press.

Gaps in the Mind

Dawkins, R. (1993). Gaps in the mind. In P. Cavalieri & P. Singer (Eds.), *The Great Ape Project: Equality beyond humanity* (pp. 80–87). New York: St. Martin's Press.

Moral Progress

Page 91 of Wynne-Tyson, J. (1985). *The extended circle: A dictionary of humane thought.* Fontwell, England: Centaur Press.

Unheard Voices: Institutionalized Prejudice Toward Animals in the U.S. Meat Industry

Pages 13–47 and 61–95 of Eisnitz, G. (1997). *Slaughterhouse: The shocking story of greed, neglect, and inhumane treatment inside the U.S. meat industry.* Amherst, NY: Prometheus Books.

Other Nations

Page 25 of Beston, H. (1956). *The outermost house: A year of life on the great beach of Cape Cod.* New York: Viking Press.

Credits

The following individuals and organizations contributed material to this collection, often at a reduced fee and in some cases with no fee whatsoever (donors who waived all fees are indicated with an asterisk in the list below). All contributors are gratefully acknowledged, for without their generosity this anthology would not have been possible.

With the exception of minor changes in formatting (e.g., conversion of footnotes to endnotes, renumbering of tables and figures), an effort has been made to preserve the original style of all readings. Consequently, some articles follow British rather than American spelling, some capitalize racial groups whereas others do not, and some use American Psychological Association format instead of other publication formats. This decision reflects a belief that faithfulness to the original material is more important than uniformity across readings.

SECTION IV

SECTION V

SECTION VI

SECTION VII

SECTION VIII

SECTION IX

p. 425, From an interview with the Dalai Lama by Claudia Dreifus as appeared in *The New York Times Magazine,* November 28, 1993. Copyright © 1993 by Claudia Dreifus. Reprinted by permission of Ellen Levine Literary Agency, Inc.

*p. 429, From *Interracial Books for Children Bulletin* by Audre Lorde, 1983. Reprinted by permission of the Charlotte Sheedy Literary Agency.

p. 431, From *Peace is Every Step* by Thich Nhat Hahn, copyright © 1991 by Thich Nhat Hahn. Used by permission of Bantam Books, a division of Random House, Inc.

p. 444, From *The Nature of Prejudice* by Gordon W. Allport. Copyright © 1979, 1958, 1954. Reprinted by permission of Perseus Books Publishers, a member of Perseus Books, L.L.C.

*p. 448, From *Unequal Protection: Environmental Justice and Communities of Color* by Robert D. Bullard. Reprinted by permission of the author.

SECTION X

p. 467, From "Reducing the Expression of Racial Prejudice" by Fletcher A. Blanchard, Teri Lilly, and Leigh Ann Vaughn, *Psychological Science,* Vol. 2, 1991. Reprinted by permission of Blackwell Publishers.

p. 474, From "Long-Range Experimental Modification of Values, Attitudes, and Behavior" by Milton Rokeach, *American Psychologist,* Vol. 26, 1971, pp. 453-459. Copyright © 1971 by the American Psychological Association. Reprinted with permission.

*p. 481, From "The Role of Empathy in Improving Intergroup Relations" by Walter G. Stephan and Krystina Finlay, *Journal of Social Issues,* Vol. 55, 1999. Reprinted by permission of Blackwell Publishing as publisher.

p. 491, Copyright 1997 from "Does White Racism Necessarily Mean Antiblackness? Aversive Racism and Prowhiteness" by Samuel L. Gaertner from *Off White; Readings on Race, Power, and Society* by Michelle Fine. Reproduced by permission

of Routledge, Inc., part of The Taylor & Francis Group.

p. 500, From "Martin Luther King Explains Nonviolent Resistance" by Martin Luther King, Jr. Reprinted by arrangement with the Estate of Martin Luther King Jr, c/o Writers House as agent for the proprietor. Copyright Martin Luther King 1963, copyright renewed 1991 Coretta Scott King.

*p. 504, Excerpted from *The Advocate,* August 14, 2001. Copyright 2001 by Mubarak Dahir. All rights reserved. Used with permission.

p. 506, Fannie Lou Hamer, May 7, 1971, in a speech delivered before the NAACP Legal Defense Fund Institute. Reprinted by permission.

APPENDIX

*p. 509, Adapted and updated from "Psychological mechanisms in the human use of animals" by Scott Plous as appeared in *Journal of Social Issues,* 49, 11-52, 1993. Reprinted by permission of Blackwell Science Ltd.

p. 517, Copyright © 1978 by Dick Gackenbach from the book *The Pig Who Saw Everything* published by Seabury Press. Reprinted by permission of McIntosh and Otis, Inc.

p. 517, Illustration from *Old MacDonald* by Amy Schwartz. Published by Scholastic Press, a division of Scholastic Inc. Copyright © 1999 by Amy Schwartz. Reprinted by permission.

*p. 517, Photographs by J.A. Keller reprinted with permission of Jim Mason.

p. 520, Laboratory Supply Co., Inc. ad as appeared in Laboratory Animal Science, December 1980.

p. 537, From "Gaps in the Mind" by Richard Dawkins. Reprinted with permission from *The Great Ape Project* edited by Paola Cavalieri and Peter Singer, Fourth Estate, London, 1993.

p. 543, From *Slaughterhouse* by Gail A. Eisnitz, pp. 13-47, 61-95 (Amherst, NY: Prometheus Books), copyright 1997. Reprinted by permission of the publisher.

Name Index

Subject Index